PHILIPPINE DUCHESNE

Portrait by the Austrian Artist Buvard.

Recevez, ma chère mère, ma vénérée mère les
expressions d'un cœur qui sent ce qu'il vous doit, j'ai
toujours la mort devant moi et elle ne sera pas si douce
que si j'avais toujours été au plus bas lieu dans
la Sainte   Je suis à vos pieds   Votre plus indigne
                                                              fille
St Ferdinand   26 avril 1840   Philippine Duchesne
                                                              r.s.c.

Louise Callan, R.S.C.J.

PHILIPPINE DUCHESNE

Frontier Missionary of the Sacred Heart
1769—1852

ABRIDGED EDITION

With an Introduction by
JOSEPH E. CARDINAL RITTER
Archbishop of St. Louis

THE NEWMAN PRESS · WESTMINSTER, MARYLAND
1965

Nihil obstat :

WILLIAM M. DRUMM, J.C.D.
Chancellor

Imprimatur :

JOSEPH E. CARDINAL RITTER
Archbishop of St. Louis

December 10, 1954

The nihil obstat and imprimatur are official declarations that a book or pamphlet is free from doctrinal or moral error. No implication is given that those who have granted the nihil obstat and imprimatur agree with the opinions expressed. In conformity with the Decree of Pope Urban VIII, the author unreservedly submits all statements herein to the judgments of the Holy See and the decisions of the Sacred Congregation of Rites.

dedicated

through the hands of St. John Francis Regis
to the Sacred Heart of Jesus

author's Note

THIS book is in no sense a new life of Blessed Philippine Duchesne. It is merely an abridged version of the definitive biography published in 1957 by The Newman Press. As that volume has been out of print since 1959, and as there have been continual demands for copies, it seemed advisable to make available a shorter life, patterned closely on the original biography but stripped of much of the primary source material incorporated in that life and of all the trappings of scholarship which now seem nonessential. For anyone interested in the sources from which the facts and documents included here are drawn, reference can easily be made to a copy of the 1957 edition.

I am again in debt to Mother Marion Bascom, R.S.C.J., for her gracious help. Mother Margaret Maxey, R.S.C.J., has also given precious time to an accurate reading of the manuscript in order to check it for slips that might otherwise have gone unnoticed. To Janet Braun, Maryville College, '63, I owe sincere thanks for typing almost the entire manuscript.

Picture credits must again be given to Mother Marie Kernaghan, R.S.C.J., Mr. Ryne Stiegemeier of St. Charles, Mo., and my niece, Mrs. Cecil Rogan Allen of Nashville, Tenn., who supplied the excellent picture of old Grenoble in the late eighteenth century and that of St. Charles in about 1850. I owe the Jacket design to Miss Barbara Wall.

LOUISE CALLAN, R.S.C.J.

MARYVILLE COLLEGE OF THE SACRED HEART
ST. LOUIS, MISSOURI
September 8, 1963

introduction

IN THE FACE of the complexities of modern life, of the material-
ism and secularism that seem to engulf modern society, and especially in view of the world's forgetfulness of God, everyone
today needs to be enlightened and encouraged and inspired to
persevere in the gigantic struggle for salvation. The servants of
God who have trod the rough road before us provide just that
enlightment, inspiration, and encouragement.

In this study of the life of Blessed Philippine Duchesne, the
gifted author has accurately and painstakingly traced the earthly
career of an illustrious and saintly woman. More than that, however, she has penned a warm and inspiring story of the life, the
labors, the struggle for holiness of a humble servant of God. From
its pages, the very heart of Blessed Philippine speaks to the modern
man and woman; her soul pours out its treasures for their enrich-
ment; her labors eloquently beckon to them to follow.

Philippine Duchesne was a pioneer apostle on American soil,
and like a true apostle, her soul was literally on fire with an unquenchable zeal for souls and love for God. Her vigorous apostolic
life was nourished by interior recollection and prayer that became
almost habitual. Truly she was a "valiant woman" spoken of by
the inspired writer, one whose name is held in benediction.

May this work of one of her devoted daughters, now appearing
in an abridged form, open the way for her influence to enter more
readily into a world that needs her inspiration.

JOSEPH E. CARDINAL RITTER
Archbishop of Saint Louis

November 27, 1964

contents

PROLOGUE | *Of the Frontier*

prologue

PHILIPPINE DUCHESNE WAS OF THE FRONTIER in practically every aspect of her life. The rugged and beautiful province of her native Dauphiny was a frontier of old France which developed a vigorous genius for opposition and resistance, for initiative and independence. The men of Dauphiny, like all frontiersmen, were good at war and at trade, and many of them were expert in the law. Philippine's family belonged to that middle class of society which, during the closing decades of the eighteenth century, was making its influence felt all over France by hard work, increasing wealth, and a remarkable measure of wisdom. On her mother's side the Perier name was prominent in industrial circles before the revolution swept the country in 1789, while her father, Pierre-François Duchesne, was to win distinction in both the provincial and the national life of France, becoming a political figure whom even Napoleon himself feared and against whom he used his dictatorial veto.

Philippine's home training was wholesome and without luxury. The growing girl mastered practical skills that stood her in good stead in later years—churning, baking, dipping candles, trimming wicks, making and mending clothes. She learned to nurse the sick and to care for little children. She was intense in her natural affections, yet sacrificed these with a spontaneity that was at times interpreted as selfishness. She sought religious life in an eighteenth-century cloister, from which revolution drove her. She knew then what it meant to risk her life in order to bring help to those who were in physical or spiritual need.

She became a pioneer member of an order in which a new type of religious life was tried out with remarkable success. As her patron saint she chose that "mountain man" beyond compare, John Francis Regis, missionary of the Society of Jesus. Long years of

3

positive training stamped her with habits and loyalties that would endure through life, no matter how the grind of circumstances might wear down her strength. Her lifework brought her at middle age to the very fringe of migration on the American frontier for nearly thirty-five years of strenuous labor. Hers was the task of clearing the land, breaking the ground, preparing the soil, and garnering the first meager yield. The cion she planted was sprung from Old World roots. In the new environment it developed hardy and true to the parent stock, as one with it as the branch is one with the vine, yet bearing fruit whose flavor was unmistakably American.

She had little creative imagination or practical foresight, yet a vision lured her westward, always unfolding before her mind and heart vast opportunities for spreading the Kingdom of Christ along the American frontier and beyond it. She knew the isolation of remote regions, the primitive conditions of a one-room cabin with a loft overhead. She learned to live at peace with disappointment, yet eagerly to press forward, to extend a helping hand without discrimination to neighbors in need, especially to missionary priests whose exhausting labors she longed to share. Like many another pioneer woman, she was a strong, lonely soul, intimate with few in America, and those few usually much younger than herself— young women who spoke her language, to whom she revealed the beauty of the Master's face, the love of his Sacred Heart. This kind of intimacy was characteristic of her, for she was possessed of the spirit of youth even in the last decades of a long life of self-oblation. Never hardened by contact with an untamed environment, she was venturesome enough at three-score-and-ten to gamble with the uncertainties of the Indian frontier to win souls for Christ.

She shared life on both sides of that frontier, settling first in what she called almost desperately "the remotest village of the United States," pioneering in the Mississippi Valley among Creoles and Americans, and crossing the line to work among the Potawatomi. She journeyed over roads that had once been Indian traces or buffalo trails. She traveled in primitive fashion, on foot or on horseback, in springless carriage or two-wheeled cart, by pirogue or raft or steamboat. She knew the mighty Mississippi and the turbulent Missouri, knew their fog and fever, their treacherous current and unpredictable course, their seasons of freeze and flood. She experienced the changing fortunes of pioneer life, now heartwarming, now heart-breaking, its times of soaring hope alternating with spells of drab depression, for which only heroic faith and love could muster enough grim determination to carry on.

Her name has been associated through more than a century with strength, endurance, austerity, with burning zeal for souls and patience under trial and failure, with a certain severity of manner and outlook, and complete detachment from the things people generally cling to so tenaciously. Yet in this apostle of the Sacred Heart there were sweetness and sympathy, as well as strength; and hand in hand with endurance went a sensitiveness that made it all the more heroic. Her austerity was not born of any natural relish for suffering, nor was her patience the flowering of innate self-control. Hers was a vigorous personality, an intensely affectionate nature not ashamed to give expression to its inmost sentiments, a will fired with ambition to do big things and motivated from her 'teens by the single, dominating urge of love for the Sacred Heart. Her devotion to our Lady was as strong and tender as her own character, while her childlike trust in Divine Providence, her reliance on God, her Father, sustained her courage and hope, no matter what difficulties she faced in her mission on the frontier.

She kept through life her gracious Old World charm, a gentle and reserved manner, a dignity that impressed mere acquaintances as somewhat aloof and out of touch with American ways of life. To a great extent her inability to express herself in English accounted for this impression. Let the conversation flow in French, and then the intensity and vivacity with which she spoke revealed her in a truer light. Her culture and refinement, as well as her education, which was of a rather high type for her day, made her respected and admired by the people who were privileged to know her, and she was loved with loyal affection by the young American and Creole girls who gathered around her in schoolroom or cloister and by the nuns who made up her religious family. The institutions she founded were all *firsts* on the religious and educational frontier of the Middle-West, and the name of Rose Philippine Duchesne heads the list of pioneer women of Missouri commemorated in bronze in St. Louis. She broke a trail that has led thousands of souls to Christ and has broadened into a highway of culture in the United States, Canada, and Latin America.

She had become, early in life, a settler on the spiritual frontier to which prayer draws the soul, that borderland of the supernatural which lies far beyond the ken and reach of mediocrity, but which was the constant dwelling-place of *Quah-kah-ka-num-ad*, the "Woman-Who-Prays-Always." That was the name the Potawatomi Indians gave her. That is the way they say it today. They were keenly observant of the white people who came amongst them. They singled her out from the rest. To the "good old lady," as they sometimes titled her with grateful affection, they brought the best of what they had—fresh meat, tender corn, or a newly-laid egg. And with intent gaze they watched her, hour on hour, as she knelt in prayer in the log church at Sugar Creek, where at long last in 1841 she reached the haven for which she had embarked on the *Rebecca* in 1818. She was old and broken in health. She was too weak to bear the hardships of the Indian frontier—almost too weak to throw the yarn over her knitting needle, yet feeling a need for that little natural activity, as she expressed it. But there was no faltering in her courage, no flagging in her prayer. That was her apostolate now. The ecstasy of night adoration, so frequent in her early years, may have passed long since, but the flame of love for the Sacred Heart burned with ever increasing ardor in her heart. In the August heat, in the December blizzard, "from the rising of the sun to the going down thereof," she was to be found almost continually in her little corner of the church, or lying exhausted on a hard pallet in the cabin-convent, rapt in communion with the God of her heart and the Heart of her God—*Quah-kah-ka-num-ad, Woman-Who-Prays-Always.*

PART ONE | *Preparation*

one

A Girl's Will
to Serve God

I. 1769—1788

THE ROTTEN FABRIC of French political and social life was beginning to sag and tear and fall to pieces as the eighteenth century passed into its seventh decade. The ugly rent that had long divided Parisian from provincial life grew wider every year. Paris still imposed its will on many of the less resolute towns, but there were sections of the country where outmoded views were no longer current in discussion, where the warp and woof of life were not spun from servility to local conventions or to privilege in court or army or church. That intangible yet very real political force called "public opinion" was operating in all grades of French society, but with especially marked effect among the bourgeoisie. Taste, fashions, aspirations, all were changing as the century progressed. The hardworking middle-class folk were coming into easy circumstances, improving their condition in many ways: better housing, better furnishings, better food and clothes, and better education; yet they were always economical in expenditure. There were few costly pleasures or amusements, but religious and family feasts were celebrated in a lively fashion. If strict economy prevailed in everyday life, even among the wealthy, this was offset by gaiety, kindliness of heart, and that careful attention to little things in which the French excel. Undoubtedly the great social event in

France during the eighteenth century was the rise of these very people, the bourgeoisie, whose power was to be revealed astonishingly in 1789.

In the provinces, where many a town was beginning to grow in importance, there were interesting middle-class people, not tailored to the Parisian pattern, but very much themselves—alert, intelligent, home-loving, and well-bred. The Duchesnes and Periers belonged to this class. Their native Dauphiny was, and is, a province so diversified in natural beauty that it is difficult to say of any one area, "Here we have the real Dauphiny." The people of this old frontier province were possessed of characteristics that identified them in the minds of their countrymen of the eighteenth century, characteristics which remain today wherever the true *Dauphinois* is to be found: love of independence, readiness for a struggle—whether military or civic or domestic—courage combined with a certain rashness which led frequently to adventure, if not to romance, and an attitude of caution which Stendhal has embodied in a telling phrase, *la peur d'être dupe,* a native dread of being "taken in." They were good talkers, these people of Dauphiny, but not loquacious. Their taste for political and philosophical discussions was well developed, though the lively and impertinent manner in which they spoke so lightly at times of the most serious things often surprised the outsider who failed to grasp the depth of thought hidden under the cloak of gaiety. They were practical in their way of life, tenacious of their rights, proud of the moral integrity which gave them self-respect, and conscious of the influence which won for many of them a place of honor in the history of France. There are Duchesnes and Periers on the list. Tradition has a proverb to the point: *Gens du Dauphiné sont fins, fidèles, et fiers.*

There is a brisk and sunny atmosphere along the valley of the swift Isère that lends an indefinable charm to the lovely countryside. Ascending the river from its meeting with the Rhone, one passes the town of Romans and the wharf of Saint-Marcellin and reaches the old provincial capital, Grenoble, built on both sides of the stream. The city has perhaps the most impressive situation of any in France. Its background in the *massif de la Chartreuse* is unique, and the range of snow-clad Alps rising abruptly to north and east forms a picturesque screen that shelters it as a natural windbreak. It is a pleasant place, with bracing air and unrivaled scenic beauty, still glorying in its frontier history.

In the last quarter of the eighteenth century it was a small town, with narrow streets and massive old buildings so crowded within the ramparts that these protecting walls seemed to squeeze and stifle the twenty-five thousand people they were meant to guard. Though there were some attractive dwelling-places, on the whole, gray facades and grated windows lined the crooked lanes that were paved with small cobble-stones. Less crooked and more dignified than other streets was *Grande Rue*, which ran between the city's two most vital public squares, *Place Saint-André* and *Place Grenette*. At Place Saint-André all was usually serious and dignified exteriorly, a bit pompous, perhaps, for it was flanked by several imposing buildings—the town hall, the fine old Church of Saint-André, which gave the square its name, and the *Palais de Justice* or courthouse, a veritable legal beehive. At the other end of Grande Rue, lay Place Grenette—the town's ancient market square, lively, bustling, surrounded with shops and cafés. A noisy town pump, a litter of refuse, and groups of talkative town and country folk constantly breaking up and constantly renewed made Grenette more typical of provincial France than Place Saint-André.

The city itself, with its vivid and turbulent past, had been a focal point in the development of France, for as the capital of an important province it was the scene of almost every great event in the history of Dauphiny, from the Roman conquest to the movement of 1788 when, leading the way, it was the first among the cities of France to formulate the program of the Revolution. And there were Duchesnes and Periers taking an active part in that formulation.

The Periers are an interesting family, native to Dauphiny. On the old feudal estate of Chatelard one hamlet grew up in a particularly rocky area, hence its name, from Low Latin, *Pererium* (rocky) or Perier, and the name of its principal tenants. From this stock came Jacques Perier, who was living there at the close of the seventeenth century with his wife and their large family. The son who bore his father's name arrived in Grenoble about 1720 and went into business with a relative whose shop and home were in a large rented building in Rue Portetraine, later called Grande Rue. This Jacques Perier had ability and education and was successful from the start, not only as a merchant but as a citizen, respected for high principles and manly conduct. He was welcomed into the social life of the upper bourgeoisie and in 1741 married Marie-Elizabeth Dupuy, daughter of a city consul of Grenoble. Jacques took his bride to the big house in Grande Rue, which he had purchased. After the fashion of the day the ground floor was used as a place of business, the basement served as a ware-house, and the upper stories became the home of the Perier family. A covered passage from the street into a courtyard offered privacy and access to the home by a side door. It was very much like the other homes in the neighborhood, large and uncomfortable, per-haps, but it housed a family highly respected in the city and joy-ously satisfied with life.

For five successive years the household was increased each May by a new baby: Claude (1742), Jean (1743), who died in infancy, Jean-Antoine (1744), Hélène-Elizabeth (1745), and Jacques-Augustin (1746). Then, as if to make up for a break in the se-quence, twin girls came to complete the family circle on June 4, 1748. These were Marie-Elizabeth and Rose-Euphrosine.

It was a hard-working, fun-loving, ambitious, well-to-do family. Jacques Perier took into business with him his nephew François, a clever, enterprising young man, who became keenly interested in textile manufacturing and drew his uncle into that field of business. To distinguish his own branch from other branches of the family, François later added to his name that of an estate he purchased at Saint-Ismier, and so came to be known as François Perier-Lagrange. His wife was "Tante Lagrange" to the children of three generations in the family.

Jacques Perier's income and civic importance seem to have increased as rapidly as his family, while his reputation for honesty in business and fidelity to his Catholic faith won for him a prestige of which his children were justly proud. The home at Number 4, Grande Rue, was well managed; the children were well educated. The girls were trained in the arts and skills that made home life attractive and bound the family into an intimate and loyal group. There was friction at times among the boys, for Claude, though gay and personable, was given to brusque self-assertion, and Jean-Antoine hid his sensitive nature behind a casual reserve, while Augustin was jealous and moody and apt to be rash in word and action. The girls were an attractive trio to whom tradition attrib-utes charm of manner as well as beauty and all the "elegant ac-complishments" that graced young womanhood in those formal days.

Hélène had reached her nineteenth birthday when her father gave her in marriage to Esprit-Alexandre Gueymar, a lawyer from Die in southwest Dauphiny, who had taken his place in the courts of Grenoble in 1757, when Hélène was only twelve years old. Later on Gueymar became a judge of high standing and vice-president of the court of appeals. He was, moreover, raised to noble rank as Gueymar de Salière.

In the municipal library of Grenoble there is a curious manuscript dated June 16, 1764, containing some verses "in praise of the Misses Perier, twin sisters and daughters of a rich and honorable merchant in Grenoble." The admirer who wrote the lines ascribes to the twins "identical charms: beautiful eyes, small feet, white teeth—in a word they are equally beautiful. Indeed they are so very attractive, it is hard to know which one a sincere admirer should choose. In this predicament and at a loss to decide which is the lovelier, the truest good fortune for a man would be to marry them both." Here in the badinage of an eighteenth-century wag, no doubt, we see the Perier twins come to life and grow more interesting. They had just passed their sixteenth birthday, and the fortune that would make up their dowries was certainly a considerable attraction in itself. Suitors were numerous enough to be exciting—doctors, lawyers, merchants, and the handsomely uniformed military officers who brought much romance into the social life of Grenoble. Among all these it was Pierre Jordan, a merchant from Lyons, who won the hand of Marie-Elizabeth. They were married in October, 1765, and though they were to live in Lyons, their children spent much of their young lives at the home of their grandparents in Grenoble.

That very year, 1765, Jean-Antoine Perier came home from the University of Orange with his degree in civil and canon law. His friend, Pierre-François Duchesne, who had been admitted to the parliamentary bar of Grenoble just the year before, now became a frequent caller at the Perier home. Soon another trousseau was under way, and on October 1, 1766, Jacques Perier's third daughter, Rose-Euphrosine, became Madame Duchesne, with a dowry, like that of her twin, of one hundred thousand francs. Her father also provided an apartment for the young couple on the third floor of the family home, where they began married life in a calm and comfort that gave little hint of the storms that were ahead.

The Duchesne family had lived for generations in Dauphiny—first in the northwestern part of the province and later at Romans on the Isère to the southwest of Grenoble. There they built up a reputation as textile manufacturers and carried on a large export business, finding wide sale for their goods both in France and in her colonies. As this trade was lucrative, the Duchesnes, like the Periers, had money. But there were other assets on which both families relied with greater confidence—religious faith, personal integrity, and strength of character.

Antoine Duchesne, head of the family in the mid-eighteenth century, married Marie-Louise Enfantin in 1737. Six of their twelve children grew to maturity, four daughters and two sons. Three of the girls became religious in the Visitation Monastery at Romans. The older boy inherited his father's business ability and carried on the mercantile tradition of the family. The younger one devoted his remarkable talents to law. This was Pierre-François Duchesne, who was to distinguish himself in Grenoble along legal, political, and social lines. His marriage to Rose-Euphrosine Perier gave him as life companion a woman of poise and distinction, who managed her home and family with a firm hand and an affectionate heart. She was, moreover, so true to Christian faith and principle that she deserved to mother a great saint.

The first of her seven daughters was born in 1767. Marie-Adelaide was a frail child on whom Madame Duchesne lavished care during the little girl's short life. In the spring of that same year Claude Perier married Marie-Charlotte Pascal and moved into an apartment adjoining the Duchesnes. The sisters-in-law became close friends, and for twenty years they shared joys and sorrows and personal interests in an intimacy that gave strength and courage to both. Life was gay and interesting at Number 4, Grande Rue, and its momentum was increased almost every year by the "great event" of a new arrival in the family. Marie-Charlotte Perier was a woman of quiet wisdom and devoted love, who entered so heartily into her husband's commercial concerns that she became as keen a business woman as he could desire, yet family life was dearer to them than their unique economic partnership. Of their twelve children ten grew to maturity. Their first baby was a boy, named Jacques for his delighted grandfather, but the year of his birth, 1768, was also that of his death: the first sorrow had come.

A second daughter was born to the Duchesnes on August 29, 1769, and placed under the protection of Rose of Lima, first saint of the Americas. Her maternal grandmother held her at the baptismal font and her uncle Jean-Antoine Perier acted as godfather. There in the Church of St. Louis of France on September 8 an apostolic patron was given her with the name Rose Philippine.

Philip the Apostle . . . Rose of the Americas . . . St. Louis of France . . . September 8 . . . 1769: the combination was prophetic rather than coincidental. Through the long lifespan that stretched before this child, she would repeat to countless souls St.

Philip's "Come and see," and experience joys akin to his when he heard that unexpected confidence from strangers, "Sir, we wish to see Jesus." And in that very September of 1769 a woodsman from Virginia, Daniel Boone, was edging westward to hunt in a new wilderness and spy out lands in the great meadow of Kaintuck; and a French-Canadian hunter, Louis Blanchette, was at work on his new frontier cabin some twenty-five miles northwest of the trading-post young Auguste Chouteau had set up just five years before on the Mississippi and called *St. Louis de France*. Blanchette was staking a claim on the west bank of the Missouri where sturdy bluffs would give a future village the unromantic name of *Les Petites Côtes* or *Little Hills*, which Spanish officials would change to *San Carlos* and Americans would speak of as *St. Charles*.

Philippine was just a few months old when in April, 1770, the Perier household rejoiced in the birth of a baby girl, christened Elizabeth-Josephine. These two children were to grow up together almost as twin sisters. Soon there were enough little Duchesnes and Periers to make things lively for many a year. (Even in a double household, twenty babies in twenty years is something of a record.) Amelie Duchesne and Marine Perier were born in 1771, but the baby Marine died in infancy. In Lyons that same year the Jordans' first boy was born—Camille, who was to make a name for himself in the political and literary history of France, and a place for himself in the heart of his cousin Philippine. Euphrosine Duchesne was born in 1772, and in 1773 the Periers were delighted with the arrival of another son, called Augustin for his moody and impetuous uncle. Three more boys had been added to the Perier roster by 1777, when Pierre-François Duchesne became godfather to little Casimir-Pierre Perier, who would one day dominate the political life of France. The Duchesnes had lost their fifth girl, Agathe-Justine, some months before Casimir's birth.

The children of this big double family were greatly loved by their parents and grandparents, but never spoiled. The Duchesne in Philippine came to the fore early, revealing itself in a thousand wiles and wails of wilfulness and self-assertion, of stubbornness and independence, which called for more than ordinary handling on the part of her mother. Firmly but gently the child was trained to obedience and self-control, to courtesy and consideration for others. She had in her natural make-up strength and generosity, and a depth of affection that for all its seeming reserve was easily stirred to unselfish service. It was not a simple process to temper the iron in that character, but her mother found that this child responded quickly to motives of piety and grasped with more than ordinary intelligence the fundamental religious training that was given the children at home.

Philippine would grow up to be beautiful, her parents thought. That pleased Pierre-François Duchesne. The child's eyes were deep and luminous, her features well-proportioned, her forehead high, her mouth firm, if a trifle large, her smile direct and winning. As she grew older, and learned the secret of bringing sunshine into the lives of others, her smile was an index of the sincerity with which she offered her services and accepted comradeship. But small-pox disfigured her face while she was still quite young, a rather common misfortune in those days in France. The scars softened and even disappeared to a great extent in later life, but Philippine suffered keenly from the comments of thoughtless grown-ups who contrasted her with her pretty cousins. Yet there was no petty jealousy in her, though she could be very stiff and uncompromising.

Philippine was still a child when her uncle Claude Perier purchased from the Duke of Villeroy one of the most magnificent estates in Dauphiny, the chateau and park of Vizille, some ten or twelve miles south of Grenoble on the Romanche, a mountain tributary of the Drac River. In the early seventeenth century this famous old castle had been the feudal stronghold of the notorious Constable of Lesdiguières, and by a strange reversal of destinies it was to become the cradle of the revolution that would deal the final blow to feudalism in France. Claude Perier converted large sections of the building and its dependencies into a textile factory, reserving spacious apartments overlooking the park for a residence, though he and his family continued to live most of the time in Grenoble.

Grenoble was an exciting town to live in and grow up in, especially if one lived on the main thoroughfare and had many relatives in the magistracy and city council. Parliamentary opposition to royal authority amounted at times to a bold struggle for independence in Grenoble. Little local revolutions frequently upset the quiet tenor of provincial life. Edicts from Paris levying new taxes met with such sharp resistance in the 1760's that the next decade brought sterner measures. On November 7, 1771, the last of the local *parlements* of France—that of Dauphiny—was suppressed by command of the King. That was a day to remember and to rehearse for many a year.

Another was May 2, 1775, which saw the re-establishment of the *parlement*. When the edict was registered and the ancient courts functioned again, the whole town celebrated the local victory. The grand illumination that night made a fairyland of public buildings and private homes. Laughter and dancing and horseplay gave evidence of the people's joy and satisfaction. Philippine and her sister Marie-Adelaide and Josephine Perier were old enough to watch the scene in Place Saint-André from the safe distance of a third-story balcony. But they did not understand how much the re-establishment of the courts meant to the several lawyers in the family, nor could they follow the conversation of their elders about Grandfather Perier's withdrawing from the post of city consul and being succeeded by his son Claude.

Uncle Claude was a great favorite with Philippine. Though a man of shrewd business acumen, he was the best of company at home. He had a gay, humorous manner with the children, and his stories were far better than any found in books. It mattered little to them that he was a royal counselor, charged with the salt tax in Grenoble; that he was the leading business man in town and drove, perhaps, the sharpest bargains. He was their personal banker, and they often had more spending money than other children in the neighborhood. Philippine used her money as she pleased—she gave it to beggars or to the poor whom she visited with her mother. No use arguing with her about it. "That's what I choose to do with it," she would say in a tone which the family came to recognize as final. She had a mind and a will of her own, but more—she had a heart that went out in sympathy to all who were in need, and she was not slow to answer affection with proofs of love.

It was but natural that these children would draw together in groups according to age and taste, that intimacies would form and affections deepen as the years passed. Philippine and Josephine became inseparable friends. When they were old enough to begin formal lessons, they were placed under the tutelage of "Mademoiselle Sophie," later Madame Luc, a capable governess for whom the girls had great affection. The Perier boys were studying under a tutor. Among them, Augustin was best loved by Philippine and Josephine. He was younger than they, but he and Camille Jordan, who was nearer their age, became their playmates and intimate friends.

Dolls had no appeal for Philippine. She loved living things and enjoyed reading about real people. Her literary taste may seem a bit austere, but she probably had no opportunity to enjoy lighter books. Lives of the saints (preferably martyrs terribly done to death) gripped her imagination and roused in her a desire to imitate their heroism. She and Augustin spent long hours together, poring over these fascinating true stories and dreaming of similar exploits in some far-off land and time. Tales of antiquity also attracted her. At the age of nine she chose to entertain sick little Marie-Adelaide with selections from a volume of Roman history. This, however, was a very normal choice. Grenoble has antiquity, and childhood, alive to past and present, could bring Hannibal and his elephants on the scenes, or Caesar with his Roman legions, or the Emperor Gratian, for whom the village of Cularo was renamed *Gratianopolis*, which in time was softened to Grenoble. Rollin's *Ancient History* was on a shelf in her father's library—long-winded and dull, perhaps, but full of heroes and heroics. Grande Rue was the oldest street in town, following the route of a Roman road that once ran through it. Traces of those far-off days were to be seen in near-by courtyards, an inscription here, a tower there, a terrace built on the very ramparts constructed by the Romans. Grande Rue was a place where history came alive from the past and where it would be made in the not-too-distant future.

The year 1778 was crowded with new experiences for Philippine. The death of her sister Marie-Adelaide brought real sorrow into her life for the first time. Soon she became aware of her position in the big family: she was the eldest of the children, and that was a maturing responsibility. There was much sickness and suffering in Grenoble that year as a result of the "Flood of Saint Crispin," which occurred on the night of October 26–27 and was one of the worst inundations the town ever experienced. The poor who lived along the river banks were homeless for days, while fetid slime covered floors and furniture in homes and merchandise in warehouses. The Duchesnes and Periers were active in helping the flood victims. While their fathers and uncles worked with the townsfolk in carts and boats to bring them aid, Philippine and Josephine helped their mothers prepare food and clothing for distribution. When the water subsided, a wretched condition prevailed along the water front: mud and ooze in houses, streets, and aqueducts; disease rife among the people, thieves at work, shortage of food in spite of the efforts made to supply the needs of those in want. It was a season Philippine would not forget, an experience she would meet again on the banks of rivers whose names were as yet unknown to her, but never in after-years would she see generosity comparable to that of her own family toward the poor.

Philippine did not enjoy romping, boisterous games, but she loved the steep climb up Mount Rachais, the rambles along the

Isère from the Porte de la Graille to the confluence of the Drac
River, the happy give-and-take in the courtyards or the schoolroom, the sunny afternoons spent at Cousin François' home at Saint-
Ismier or picking daisies in the meadow beyond the Church of
Saint-André. Delightful holidays were spent at Vizille. Philippine
loved the quiet of the woods and countryside, where she roamed
about with Josephine, or played in the beautiful park, or lay in the
shade of a spreading tree and watched the white clouds piling up
on the horizon to the east. She was fond of wandering off by herself, but this love of solitude was not an indication of morose in-
troversion. She was a healthy, strong-minded child, serious for her
age, who enjoyed being alone at times with her own thoughts and
with God, who was already making known his claims upon her
love and her life. There was, however, no isolating herself from the
family. Her mother kept her busy with little household duties that
developed in her a sense of responsibility which was to mark her
in later years, but the light-hearted gaiety of childhood was not
stifled by restraint.

In spite of the wealth which might have brought luxury to the
home, Madame Duchesne reared her children in great simplicity.
The cold of an Alpine morning was no excuse for lying snugly
in bed. The presence of servants did not dispense the older girls
from looking after the younger children. Lessons from books were
followed by needlework or visits to the sick poor or a turn in the
pantry or kitchen, though the mysteries of cooking always seemed
to baffle Philippine. There was seldom an idle moment in the
Duchesne-Perier home, though there were leisure hours for conversation, discussion, and repetition of precious traditions inherited
through generations. Family dinners were part of life in Dauphiny,
and Philippine kept even in old age the happiest memories of these
gatherings in the home of her maternal grandparents. At times
Pierre-François Duchesne aired some of his increasingly rational-
istic views. Then his wife's eyes grew troubled and imploring as
she noted the impression made by such talk.

Philippine was still too young to realize that her father had
drifted with the current of "liberal thought" away from Catholicism as a way of life. He had long since followed that strange
fashion of the day that confused faith with understanding and so
rejected what it could not comprehend; that lost its hold on the
supernatural in searching after the purely natural; that relegated
religion to the underestimated level of children and women, especially nuns—and nuns had been numerous among the Duchesnes.

The Visitation Monastery at Romans had drawn several members of its community from that family during the eighteenth century. Two of Monsieur Duchesne's sisters were now active and competent religious, and Philippine sometimes visited these cloistered aunts—Sister Françoise-Melanie, who was so fond of her irreligious brother, and Sister Claire-Euphrosine, who had entered the convent in 1766 and taken the name of her new sister-in-law.

There was a monastery of the Visitation at Grenoble which claimed the distinction of having been founded by St. Francis de Sales and St. Jane de Chantal at the request of the citizens of the town. It was built on the left bank of the Isère, halfway up the side of Mount Rachais. Philippine and Josephine frequently climbed the steep winding street that led up to it. At a sort of alley-way between high walls they would turn and mount a few low platform-steps toward an arched entrance surmounted by an inscription: *St. Francis de Sales chose this place for the foundation of the fourth monastery of his Order of the Visitation of Holy Mary. The first stone was laid in his presence on October 16, 1619.* High up the mountainside, remote from the town, cut off from worldly contacts and backed by the snow-capped Alps, this fourth monastery of the order commanded a magnificent view of the valley below, where the sweeping torrent of the Isère had cut its bed in fantastic curves. It came to be known as *Sainte-Marie-d'en-Haut,* an almost untranslatable expression. It was "St. Mary's on the Heights," or "St. Mary's High-up-there," or "St. Mary's Up-high," or "High-up," to distinguish it from the Church of *Sainte-Marie-d'en Bas,* in the town below. To Philippine it was alway *Sainte Marie.* She was well acquainted with the place when she and Josephine were placed there as boarding pupils in 1781 to be prepared for their first Holy Communion.

It was not easy for their mothers to give them up that year. Much had been happening of late in the double household. There was the arrival of two baby girls, one in each family, in 1779. In the following year Claude Perier purchased the house on the corner of Grande Rue and Place Saint-André, next door to Number 4. There was a doorway in the wall separating the courtyards of the two houses and this gave private access from one house to the other, so family news and chatter passed easily back and forth, and the voices of the children echoed gaily as they played together. The Duchesnes now had the two upper floors in Jacques Perier's home, while the old grandfather still lived downstairs with his sons, Jean Antoine and Augustin.

On February 27, 1781, the long awaited son was born to Pierre-François and Rose Perier Duchesne. He was christened Antoine-Louis-Hippolyte, carrying in a fourth generation a name familiar in the Duchesne family. In August a sixth son was added to the Perier family. So the older girls were really needed at home. But they were eager for boarding school and for the great spiritual event to which they looked forward with an ardor more mature than their years.

Mother Anne Félicité de Murinais was then Superior of the community at Sainte Marie. Philippine became deeply attached to Sister Eugenie Latier de Bayanne, who was to influence her, not only during her brief years of formal education, but also in the training school of religious life. Faith had already struck deep roots in the girl's pure soul and prepared her for the religious instruction she was now to receive. Her piety was based on doctrine rather than on sentiment, and her devotion became more and more the aspiration of a soul that wills to give itself to God and so lifts itself up to him in simple, direct prayer of faith, expressive of both reverent fear and ardent love. To offend God was Philippine's greatest dread; to love him was her deepest joy and surest means of avoiding all offense.

There was a certain austerity in the training given at Sainte Marie. Character formation was the objective, and its motivation was drawn from faith and the tradition of womanly worth and dignity so carefully guarded in Dauphiny. Another and a far more powerful element entered into this motivation. Just a century before, devotion to the Sacred Heart had been confided by Christ himself, in private revelation, to the humble Visitandine nun, Saint Margaret Mary Alacoque, and through her to the Order of the Visitation and the Society of Jesus. At Sainte Marie the devotion held a prominent place in the spiritual life of the community, and throughout the church and cloister symbols of the Sacred Heart were to be seen on all sides. Soon "the Heart that has so loved men" became the center of Philippine's life and love, giving her courage to take herself in hand and determine to correct the asperities of her character.

Strength and weakness were blended in this girl just entering her teens. She was accustomed to leadership in a group of boys and girls who loved her and relied on her, no matter which way the wind of their childish fortunes might blow. They turned to her instinctively and she enjoyed this compliment. There was an imperiousness in her manner at times that got results in the home circle, but boded ill for the future if left unchecked. She had a will of her own, and what she willed she set herself to obtain or carry out, with high disdain for obstacles. Her impetuous impulses sometimes sent her headlong into trouble or involved her in difficulties that tried her patience almost beyond endurance. She could be petulant and uneven in manner, but never petty or selfish toward her school companions; and they loved her for her adventurous spirit and sincere friendliness.

That Philippine retained many of these defects in after-years is evident from letters of advice written by one who undertook her training in a very different school. "Strive to acquire gentleness, a more pleasant manner, evenness of disposition which produces patience" is a telling sentence. Defects and faults were to bring many a humiliation to Philippine, but her honesty in facing the problem of a difficult character and the earnestness with which she tried to conquer her stubborn pride and sensitive reserve were evidences of the grace that was at work in her soul.

The idea of devoting her life to God did not come to her for the first time at Sainte Marie. Even as a little girl she had been thrilled by stories of heroic mission life in distant lands. From time to time missionaries appeared in Grenoble. They spoke in the churches, were welcomed in the homes of the townsfolk, gathered alms for the furtherance of their work. Among them were former Jesuits who had labored in the colonies of France and had been expelled from their missions even before the general suppression of the Society of Jesus in 1773. One of these, Father Jean-Baptiste Aubert, lived in Grenoble when Philippine was growing up. He had been in Louisiana and the Illinois Country as a missionary to both the French settlers and the Indians. He told of places with the strangest names—Kaskaskia, where he had signed the parish register as late as 1764, and Cahokia, just across the river from the site staked off that very year for a trading post to be called *St. Louis de France*, and Michigamea with its mission of St. Francis Xavier long since abandoned. Weird Indian names rolled smoothly from his tongue, but his eyes were wistful as he spoke of the work left undone among the forest folk of America and the heroism of the Jesuits who had given their blood in martyrdom in the great valley of the Mississippi. His stories of the wilderness held Philippine enthralled. An unquenchable desire to devote her life to missionary work was enkindled in her soul, and an ever deepening determination to do great things for God that would carry her in middle life to the farthest edge of Western civilization. She has left a sketchy paragraph about this earliest inspiration to follow Christ:

> My first enthusiasm for missionary life was roused by the tales of a good Jesuit Father who had been on the missions in Louisiana and who told us stories about the Indians. I was just eight or ten years old, but already I considered it a great privilege to be a missionary. I envied their labors without being frightened by the dangers to which they were exposed, for I was at this time reading stories of the martyrs, in which I was keenly interested. The same good Jesuit was extraordinary confessor at the convent in which I became a pupil. I went to confession to him several times, and I loved his simple, informal manner of speaking, a manner he had used with the savages. From that time the words *Propagation of the Faith* and *Foreign Missions* and the names of priests destined for them and of religious in far-away lands made my heart thrill.

So Philippine cherished her desire and fostered it by prayer and acts of self-sacrifice and self-control. She seems not to have talked about it to her sisters or even to her mother. Josephine Perier had all her confidence and she kept the secret, especially from Uncle Pierre, who would have had little patience with such pious dreams. Duchesne was a practical man who had no sympathy with those who would give all and apparently get nothing in return.

School life was simple and happy at Sainte-Marie-d'en-Haut. The curriculum included both the practical arts of living and subjects whose content required some studying and a good deal of writing. Along with religion there were arithmetic, history, geography, and the reading of selected classics of French literature, with plenty of needlework and the exercise of a variety of feminine skills. The small number of pupils—not more than twenty—made it possible for them to receive a good deal of individual attention. Philippine was serious and earnest about her studies and made steady progress, laying a good foundation for the more advanced work she would do under a tutor later on.

Reminiscing half a century later, she wrote to Josephine Perier:

> I find delight in recalling the simple pleasures of our childhood; our modesty in dress, the good times we had at the convent, eating salad with our fingers, the two of us with a single plate between us and sitting together on the same seat beside the fire—all of which moved dear Sister Colombe to tears. She used to say: "How these two children love each other!"

Sainte Marie was, in her own words to Josephine, "the home

of our childhood . . . the cradle of our faith and of the intimacy that has united us." They received their first Holy Communion on the feast of Pentecost, May 19, 1782. With whole-hearted generosity Philippine responded to the call of grace in her soul and offered herself to God. She knew he wanted her to belong entirely to him. She was a Duchesne, and the Duchesnes did nothing by halves, but she was also a Perier, whom family ties held fast in a web of intimate love. Religious life became the goal of her ambitions. Daily she prayed for light to know God's will in her regard and grace to accomplish all he expected of her. Confidently she placed her vocation under our Lady's protection, reciting the *Memorare* many times a day for guidance and strength. There were conflicts in her soul at times. Her love for her family seemed to gain an even greater hold on her. Then, too, the apostolic life of the missionary attracted her, while the prayer-life of the Visitation cloister grew more appealing, more personally satisfying, as she watched and imitated the nuns by whom she was being educated.

It was not long, however, before the Duchesnes were discussing with the Periers what Philippine's schoolmates related about her. Inquiries at Sainte Marie were answered truthfully: Philippine was thinking seriously of a religious vocation. Her parents were displeased at this, to put it mildly. Madame Duchesne was a very affectionate mother; she thought Philippine too young to give the matter serious consideration, and she dreaded the sacrifices such a vocation entailed. While a formal prohibition would never have come from her, she had not yet the courage to put Christ's claim on her daughter before her own. But Pierre-François Duchesne acted with swift decision, withdrawing Philippine from Sainte Marie and from the influence of the nuns after she had spent just two years there. Both he and his wife expected a scene, with their daughter playing the lead. To their surprise she yielded with an obedience that was disarming and took up home life once more. The flame of her desire had not been quenched by her mother's affectionate outbursts or her father's vigorous wrath. She had simply covered the fire, until it seemed safe to let it leap up again.

At home some changes had taken place during the past two years. Her grandfather Perier had died in the summer of 1782. His fortune had been settled according to his will, Claude as eldest son receiving two-thirds, the other two sons one-sixth each. Jean-Antoine, Philippine's godfather, accepted the arrangement quite amicably and in 1783 left Grenoble for Paris, where he practiced law and remained unmarried. Augustin had from boyhood resented his position as youngest son in the family. He had recently married Marie-Charlotte Carrier and soon he too left Grenoble. He was not as keen a business man as were his father and his eldest brother and he lost most of his inheritance in ill-advised speculation.

So Philippine found her own family in possession of the entire household space of the old Perier home. She entered once more into comradeship with her sisters and grew more intimate with Josephine Perier. She gave much time to the little children of the family in order to relieve her mother and Tante Perier. Camille Jordan was living with them now, and he and the Perier boys were being tutored by a scholarly priest, Abbé Raillane, who kept them hard at work during school hours. He was a thin little man, very prim and neat, with sharp eyes and heavy eyebrows which gave him a severe appearance and helped him maintain strict discipline. He loved poetry and history and communicated this taste to his pupils. He was austere and very priestly, and his way of life made a deep impression on his pupils and on Philippine, who now came under his tutelage with her cousins. Latin, history, French literature, along with Dante, St. Augustine, and the Psalms, were a part of the curriculum, and the abbé could not complain of the quality of his pupils. Yet love of books and study was not native to Dauphiny, and there was among its people far more cleverness than love of learning. If Philippine Duchesne was not studious by nature, she had trained herself to the steady pursuit of learning and she made good use of the opportunities offered her. When problems in arithmetic proved too difficult, she turned for help to her younger cousins. Then Casimir Perier and Camille Jordan enjoyed a momentary superiority over the girl they loved and admired so wholeheartedly.

The historian, Alphonse Vernet, describes old Grenoble as a very gay place, and it is not difficult to picture Philippine watching with amusement the torch-light parades, the street illuminations, the fountains of wine flowing in the Place Saint-André, the masked revelers on their way to the theatre for the Mardi Gras ball. She certainly attended balls and met the officers who were stationed at the garrison, and the young lawyers who were trying out their legal wit in the *Palais de Justice*, and many another young *bourgeois gentilhomme* wearing the scarlet coat with steel buttons and the three-cornered hat that was the fashion of the day. It was, on the whole, a full life, and she took part in it without argument. There were soirées, concerts, and dancing parties, all of which she thoroughly enjoyed.

It was an age of graceful feminine styles and gay materials. Philippine wore full skirts and panniers, broad hats, fine gloves, and light stockings. Her manner was simple and gracious, dignified without stiffness. She liked to dance, though her sisters teased her about the seriousness with which she practiced the difficult steps. Her sister Euphrosine wrote later on, "When she took me into her confidence, she assured me that even in the midst of these amusements she was thinking with joy of the time when she would be a nun, but in the meantime she applied herself quite willingly to her dancing lessons."

Philippine also studied music and drawing. Her musical talent was nil, her artistic ability mediocre, but she would put this to practical use in later years. She had a flair for writing which Abbé Raillane encouraged her to cultivate. Her style was quick, natural, unadorned, with the strength and directness that were native to her character. She could write with precision and care for the niceties of language, but more frequently her sentences seemed to flow spontaneously from her quill with a sort of rough energy that sought only to record the outpourings of her soul. This ability for self-expression became an asset in later years when she needed an outlet and there was no one to whom she could talk confidentially. She was a good talker and loved to speak of spiritual and intellectual things, but she was never talkative and she learned early in life the value of silence as an aid to prayer.

While entering graciously into her parents' plans for her education at home and taking part in the social life of Grenoble, Philippine held inflexibly to a line of conduct that called for strength of will and courage of conviction. Her private devotional practices were never neglected for pleasure. Morning meditation had a place in every day. She braved the wide-eyed critics who with Jansenistic prejudice looked askance at her fortnightly confession and Holy Communion. Her love for the Blessed Sacrament increased through these years, as devotion to the Sacred Heart took fuller possession of her soul. The spirit of reparation inspired by this devotion was developing in her, and she gave herself to voluntary penance with a generosity unsuspected by her family. A little silver cross that had been given to her as an ornamental pendant became an effective instrument of penance when heated and pressed against her bare breast.

She sought out personal discomforts as well as fatiguing work about the house and relieved her mother of many household cares. Her small brother, whom all the family called "Duchesne," was just old enough to need watching, as he romped about with the youngest Perier boys. She listened with interest to her father and Uncle Claude as they talked of business and political affairs, of the needs of the General Hospital, of which Perier had become administrative director, or the development of the public library in which her father was interested. But she avoided all discussion of her vocation, dreading the clashes with her father which the mere mention of it brought on, and wishing to spare her mother pain. This attitude was interpreted by them as a sign that Philippine had accepted their views and was willing to have her future planned for her in the conventional manner of the day.

Pierre-François Duchesne had many plans. He had become prominent in Grenoble as a consistorial advocate in the *parlement*. He was director of the public library, which he helped to found and organize. In 1785 he was elected president of the local bar association, an office he held by re-election several times. He was irascible and self-assertive and often made himself unpleasant company, but his forthright manner and personal integrity commanded respect. He was an enthusiastic supporter of the new political and social ideas that were permeating all France in the last decade of the Old Regime, and he took an active part in spreading them in Grenoble. To the grief of his family he had by this time gone completely Voltairian, and his activities in radical clubs and Masonic groups brought anguish to Philippine and her mother.

The year 1786 was eventful in the family. There had been from time to time news from Uncle Augustin. In the spring of the previous year he had got into the service of the newly reorganized Company of the Indies which had an exclusive monopoly of trade in practically all countries beyond the Cape of Good Hope. This offered a wide expansion to the Perier business and Claude co-operated willingly. Augustin had been to India in the interests of the company and was back in Grenoble in the spring of 1786. On April 11 another baby girl was added to the Duchesne family and named Augustine-Melanie, with Uncle Augustin as her godfather. Success had come at last and Augustin Perier was director of the Company of the Indies, with his home at Lorient, the great port of shipment, handling millions of dollars worth of merchandise yearly and building a fortune which he hoped would match that of his brother Claude. Augustin was very busy and was growing very rich, yet he was restless and dissatisfied still.

Not so Pierre-François Duchesne, who was busy with plans for his several marriageable daughters. He and Claude Perier were in a position to judge the most suitable prospects, after deciding on dowry terms. Joseph Constans de Mauduit, Chevalier du Plessis, was an officer of the Royal Marine Infantry then stationed in Grenoble. He came of old Breton stock and had a promising future. In October, 1786, Amelie Duchesne became his bride. It was a satisfactory match, for Amelie—just entering her sixteenth year—was very attractive, but also very difficult to handle; and it was hoped that her alliance with de Mauduit would mature her character and soften its already hardening lines. The ceremony was a social event in Grenoble, and the marriage register of the Church of St. Louis bore the signature of thirty-nine witnesses, among them the bride's older sister, Philippine.

Within a year there was question of other weddings in the family, for Jean-Joseph Jouve, a young merchant of Lyons, was asking for the hand of Euphrosine Duchesne, while the Periers were discussing the prospect of Josephine's marriage to Jacques-Fortunat de Savoye-Rollin, advocate-general of the *parlement* of Grenoble since 1780. He was fourteen years older than Josephine, but that proved no obstacle to their happiness.

And what about Philippine? Her parents would have preferred to marry off their daughters in the more conventional order. The eldest was now eighteen, so her father brought up the matter tactfully, with a suitable young man in the offing. Whoever he was, Philippine had no case against his suitability. Her arguments were positive: *she* wished to be a nun. She had heard the call of Christ; she had pledged to *him* the full measure of her love and service; she felt she had a right to consecrate herself to God as many another Duchesne girl had done.

The pattern of life now changed for Philippine as she took her stand and held her ground. No more pretty clothes would she indulge in, except the really indispensable; no more parties, concerts, dances for her; in fact, no more social life than was strictly necessary, "and every time she was urged to do differently she showed the same fixed resolve." But there was much more prayer now and a rule of life that she followed as faithfully as if she were back at Sainte Marie. The Duchesne in her was in the ascendancy, but it was to Tante Perier that she gave her confidence after Josephine had become Madame de Savoye-Rollin in January, 1788. Madame Perier understood the girl as no one else in the household did. She sympathized with her suffering and encouraged her resolution. Together they discussed the situation and agreed on the wisdom of waiting a little while. Soon they noted a gradual breakdown in the opposition, ascribable perhaps to Pierre-François Duchesne's satisfaction with his other daughters, but also to his stubborn but very intense affection for Philippine. Watching her alone now with the older Perier boys, or teaching the group not yet in their teens, or caring for the least ones, especially the baby sister Melanie, it seemed as if he could not part with her. Yet he knew he could not keep her much longer.

One day in the spring of 1788 Philippine slipped through the inner door of the courtyard and made her way about the vast six-story home of the Periers until she found her aunt. She wanted help. She felt she must consult Mother de Murinais about her admission into the Visitation cloister and she begged Tante Perier to go with her to Sainte Marie. Though she was eighteen and a half years old, convention required a chaperone through the streets of the town. Besides, her aunt was such good company and such substantial support that Philippine had come to rely upon her in all circumstances. They went up the steep winding street, passed through the archway, lifted the knocker, and were quickly admitted to the monastery parlor. The interview with Mother de Murinais was informal. She had talked frequently with the girl about religious life. Philippine was eager, but restrained. Quite suddenly she announced a decision: she was at Sainte Marie; she was sure of God's will for her; she would remain now with the Visitandines if Mother de Murinais would accept her as a postulant. Tante Perier was not prepared for this. She pleaded with her niece, gently reproached her, argued for a return home. But Philippine had answered an inspiration of divine grace by an unshakable resolution which Mother de Murinais sanctioned.

Madame Perier returned alone to the double house in Grande Rue to break the news to the Duchesnes. Her sister-in-law, upset by this unexpected turn of events, was greatly distressed, but too reasonable to lay blame where it did not belong. Supernatural views were dominant in Madame Duchesne, but even the deepest faith does not steel a mother's heart against poignant grief. There was still a slight hope that Philippine might yield to entreaties and return home, if only she could be made to realize how greatly she was needed, how deeply she was loved.

Madame Duchesne had recovered her poise and self-control to some extent when, a few days later, she went with her husband and little Melanie to call at Sainte Marie. The interview was stormy and the resulting pain felt as keenly by the unyielding daughter as by the pleading parents. True, Philippine was now in possession of what she had desired for several years, but her self-control hid a terrific conflict in her soul. Hers was a heart that loved intensely, that gripped its love tenaciously. Her family was a part of her very self. To break the external ties that bound her to them, to leave forever the dear old double home and the precious people it housed, called for detachment that only abundant supernatural graces could supply. But Philippine was in love with Christ and sure of his divine support, no matter what the trial of her faith might be. How often she had whispered in prayer, "*Introibo*—I will go unto the altar of God!" Now grace gave strength to her resolution. The Duchesnes went down Mount Rachais without her, not knowing that as they made the descent from Sainte Marie, Philippine was kneeling before the Blessed Sacrament, offering them all as her most costly sacrifice to God and thanking him, in spite of the tears that ran unheeded down her cheeks, for the victory she had won in this battle of hearts and wills. Renewing her consecration to Christ through the intercession of St. Jane de Chantal, she left the chapel and went about her simple duties with peace in her soul, though pain still racked her heart.

2. 1788—1792

TURBULENT OLD GRENOBLE was seething with political disturbance when Philippine Duchesne entered as a postulant at Sainte Marie. The first phase of her religious life was spent in times when events were in the making whose repercussions have been felt ever since. The civic-minded Periers and Duchesnes were actively involved in the movement which set the opening scene of the French Revolution. The *parlement* of Dauphiny was the first to protest against the royal edicts of May, 1788, in which Louis XVI announced the remodeling of the judicature throughout the country and the proroguing of all provincial *parlements* until the formation of new courts. A copy of the royal decrees was sent by courier to the Count of Clermont-Tonnerre, then Governor of Dauphiny, with special instructions regarding the suppression of offices and the reorganization of the judiciary.

When the Governor ordered the decrees registered, the magistrates of Grenoble protested. The General Council of the city then drew up a memorial expressing to the King the grievances of the people and representing the disastrous effects that might result from the enforcement of the decrees. The royal reply came swiftly in the form of a *lettre de câchet* forbidding the City Council to assemble to discuss the edicts and warning the council members against attending meetings of a similar nature under penalty of severe punishment. The letter closed with a phrase characteristic of absolutism: "for such is our will in this matter." The will of the people, however, was at variance with that of the King, and opposition was strengthened by the determined efforts of men like Pierre-François Duchesne and his colleagues.

The situation was not improved when the *parlement* of Dauphiny threatened to withdraw the province from its allegiance to the Crown if the royal edicts were put into effect. The procurator-general summed up the situation when he wrote to Paris: "Consternation is general in the face of the complete annihilation of our privileges, which are one of the conditions essential to the union of Dauphiny with the Crown. Justice has ceased in the city, and the people refuse to pay the taxes." The Count of Clermont-Tonnerre was under no illusions as to the danger, for he realized that people of all social ranks were now thoroughly aroused. Military measures seemed necessary and troops were called out, two companies encamping on Place Saint-André, in front of the *Palais de Justice.* Excitement must have run high in the Duchesne-Perier homes as the small boys watched the grenadiers drilling in the streets and the sentinels on guard day and night. One can picture members of the family going up to Sainte Marie to describe the situation to Philippine.

The precautions taken by the Governor were the prelude to a more drastic measure decreeing the arrest and exile of the magistrates of Grenoble. This act brought down on Clermont-Tonnerre the full wrath of the populace and ushered in what has been called "the first battle of the French Revolution." Excitement and tension mounted to a high pitch, and on the morning of June 7 the town presented an ominous scene: men and women milling around angrily in the streets, gates barricaded, church bells tolling. By noon the Governor found himself facing an angry mob demanding the convocation of the *parlement* of Dauphiny. The royal troops had been ordered to protect the Governor. In the rush on the palace fighting began. Soldiers fired. Then the populace let loose with paving stones and roofing tiles. A score of people were wounded, but the mob had won a victory on that "day of tiles," and the foremost citizens of Grenoble had supported them. Clermont-Tonnerre recalled the magistrates, who came in dignified procession to the *Palais de Justice* and used their influence to calm the populace.

A week later the Notables of Grenoble, in consultation with members of the Clergy and the Third Estate, decided to assemble the ancient Provincial Estates of Dauphiny, which had been suppressed in the days of Richelieu. Acting on their own authority, they agreed that the representation of the Third Estate should equal that of the other two groups and that all should deliberate and vote in common. This was indeed an innovation. The date set for the meeting was July 21. The place, Grenoble.

At the Court of Versailles all this was treated as rebellion, which it certainly was. Now the mild Clermont-Tonnerre was superseded by the more energetic Marshal de Vaux. With 20,000 soldiers at his disposal he was expected to restore the old order immediately. But he had scarcely reached Grenoble when he wrote laconically to Versailles, "It is too late." There seemed but one course open to him, that of granting permission for a meeting of the Provincial Estates on condition that it should not be held in Grenoble.

In the cloister at Sainte Marie the nuns were kept informed about the current of events that had begun to swirl and eddy through Dauphiny. Visitors to the parlor grille gave details of happenings that were creating disturbance, and the Duchesnes often called on Philippine to relate to her the incidents in which the family was most concerned. Anxiety about her father was keen when she learned that it was he who had called that extraordinary meeting of the Grenoble lawyers, in which they passed the resolution to plead no case in the courts until the unjust edicts had been withdrawn. On the "day of tiles" he had been in the delegation that went to the home of the first president of *parlement* to accompany him and the other magistrates to the *Palais de Justice*. On June 14 he had taken part in the meeting at the Town Hall, and even now he was preparing a *Memoire* in the form of a *Remonstrance to the King*, embodying a protest against existing conditions and a statement of the reforms, financial and political, for which there was crying need throughout France. Duchesne intended to present this at the meeting projected for July 21, which Philippine soon learned was to be held at Vizille.

Her Uncle Claude had placed his magnificent chateau at the disposal of the deputies of Dauphiny, and the offer had been accepted. Through the mild summer night and early dawn the four hundred and sixty-three delegates made their way on foot, on horseback, in carts and carriages, along the country roads, paying little heed to the troops sent to intimidate them. Perier had spared neither trouble nor expense in preparing for the assembly. The vast indoor tennis court and *salle d'armes* of the old warrior-chateau were arranged to house the meeting that opened that Monday morning with the Count de Morges presiding and Jean-Joseph Mounier acting as secretary. After the formality of seating the deputies came the choice of a *Remonstrance to the King*, which occupied several hours. Dinner followed, and some relaxation in the gardens of Vizille; then the men reassembled for deliberations which continued until long after mid-night. By three o'clock in the morning of July 22 the final report had been signed, and all unknowingly this assembly had, with remarkably dispassionate wisdom, formulated the program of a mighty revolution. Before the adjournment the Count de Morges expressed to "the honorable Claude Perier, lord of the marquisate of Vizille" the sincere appreciation of the entire body for his generous hospitality.

Throughout the province of Dauphiny order seemed to have been restored, and the sessions of the assembly held in the autumn and winter at Romans carried forward its work in a less dramatic setting, but with determined independence. Pierre-François Duchesne did not attend the session of the Estates of Dauphiny that opened at Romans on September 10, 1788. On that day he was at Sainte Marie, witnessing the ceremony in which Philippine received the black habit and white veil and coif of a Visitandine novice. That her father was present at the ceremony and signed the convent register proved once more to Philippine how dear she was to him.

With characteristic fervor she entered upon the period of training that would prepare her for religious life and the vows by which she hoped to bind herself to Christ. Writing thirty years later, she gave a few details about her novitiate days:

> When I entered religious life at the age of eighteen and a half years, a desire to share in the apostolate made me choose the Visitation, where children were educated, in preference to Carmel, which I loved very much. My community was animated by the spirit of the Jesuits, from whose Constitutions they boasted their own had been drawn. The library was enriched with nearly all the works of Jesuit authors, because at the time of the suppression of the Society of Jesus three of its members found a refuge in our chaplain's house, and when they died they left their library to the convent. During two whole years of my novitiate I read

only Rodriguez, without ever tiring of it; and when we assembled after Vespers I used to relate to my Sisters the lives of nearly all the saints of the Company of Jesus. That of St. Francis Xavier appealed most strongly to me. . . . I loved his touching appeals to the European schools to send him missionaries. How often have I not said to him since then, in my impatience, "Great Saint, why do you not call me? I would respond at once." He is the saint of my heart.

He was, indeed, a great favorite with her always, but a rival patron came upon the scenes out of the same Company of Jesus, that mighty mountain-man of Vivarais, whose name she would carry halfway round the world and stamp on the first permanent Jesuit mission of mid-western America, as well as on her own first foundation there. If with Xavier she longed to share the apostolate of the foreign missions, with John Francis Regis she dreamed of devoting her life to the poor. Her devotion to him began in a conversation with one of the Visitation nuns who had chosen him as her patron. A relic of the great "social crusader" was honored at Sainte Marie, and Philippine often prayed before it for the grace to follow his example in an apostolate far more obscure than that of Xavier.

Novitiate life is seldom eventful or romantic. There is an apparently monotonous routine to be followed, a fixed order of day, spiritual duties, homely tasks, penitential practices, a whole new life to be learned, a life under rule and regulated to the least details. Wearing the holy habit, the novice must gradually be clothed in the spirit of Christ, growing in recollection as she concentrates her efforts lovingly on silence and prayer. The novelty of the life wears off quickly enough. The vitalizing spirit seems at times to die down to a mere flicker, and only a stout heart and a fixed resolve can weather the storms that may break over the soul of the novice. Philippine Duchesne was no exception to the rule, yet she seems to have been blessed with so lively a spirit of faith, such intense love of God and charity toward her Sisters, that the usual noviceship difficulties troubled her only slightly. She could write long afterwards: "The day I entered at Sainte-Marie-d'en-Haut I took the resolution never to fail on a single point of rule, and indeed I do not recall ever infringing a single one." For a character so independent, so impetuous, and so mature, this unswerving fidelity must have been the result of heroic self-conquest. The continuous austerity of a completely regulated life rapidly developed in her that sensitiveness to grace which marks all sanctity.

The Visitation novitiate offered her countless opportunities for unselfish service in the little duties assigned to her and in the chance to help others by doing their work or replacing them in the various employments about the monastery. Her days, filled with activity motivated by love, were physically very tiring, yet fatigue seemed to drop from her easily when toward evening she went to the Mistress of Novices, Sister Eugenie de Bayanne, to beg permission for an extra hour of prayer before retiring. Those who lived with her at Sainte Marie always knew when she had obtained the permission, so radiant was her smile, so light her step, as she passed down the corridor to her favorite place in the choir before the tabernacle. There she found rest in prayer. Sometimes, forgetful of all but the divine Presence on the altar, she spent a great part of the night, even the whole of it, in silent adoration, kneeling motionless, truly lost in God. The spirit of St. Margaret Mary was already taking hold of her, and she was being prepared for an apostolate that would carry the knowledge and love of the Sacred Heart to mission lands she had dreamed of as a child.

The picture of those lands was being etched more realistically on her mind than she was aware by the reading of a seventeenth century biography—a book she pored over time and again. The *Life of the Venerable Mother Marie of the Incarnation* exercised a profound influence on her prayer life and missionary aspirations. The holy Ursuline's zeal thrilled her and inspired her with increasing ardor for the salvation of souls still groping in the shadows of paganism. The missions of Canada became the goal of Philippine's ambition even as she prepared for a life in the Visitation cloister. In spirit she traveled to that far corner of the world in search of souls redeemed by Christ. She loved to use the prayers of Mother Marie as she knelt before the tabernacle, and those prayers contained the very essence of true devotion to the Sacred Heart.

Philippine had entered an order whose spirit and traditions were well defined. St. Francis de Sales had emphasized that "it is a spirit of profound humility toward God and of great gentleness with our neighbor." Its contemplative life is modeled on Nazareth. No outward severity marks it, but complete inward self-renunciation is pivotal in the institute. Sweetness in strength, loving intentness in prayer, simple, unconditional self-surrender to God and his representatives, were instilled into it by the founder at the very beginning of its development.

Although Philippine was well acquainted with the community at Sainte Marie and quickly at home there, she still had much to learn about little observances of common life, the practices of humility and penance, the words and phrases that formed a sort of family vocabulary intelligible only to its members. In joyous recreations, in hours of silent labor, in the quiet of prayer, in simplicity, kindliness, and fidelity to the little virtues which make great saints, she tasted the sweetness and experienced the charm of the fervent hidden life of the Visitation. She studied the crest of the order, bearing a heart crowned with thorns and surmounted by a cross, and came to realize how truly prophetic had been its choice by St. Francis de Sales. Devotion to the Sacred Heart was a precious heritage of the Visitandines from their founder, who called them "Daughters of the Sacred Heart of Jesus."

The training given in the novitiate at Sainte Marie adhered faithfully to the Visitandine tradition, to which had been added the teaching of St. Margaret Mary. Love and fidelity to the Sacred Heart had been the burden of her divinely inspired message, from which followed reparation and self-sacrifice. In the fervor of her offering Philippine would naturally have gone to extremes in the matter of corporeal austerities, had not the Visitation Rule and spirit checked her and shown her how prayer and recollection, charity and self-renunciation were to supply for the severities of Carmel. But moderation was to be a life-long problem for her. She found, however, an outlet for her love of God in humility and prayer. To one of her disposition it was not easy to kneel humbly when asking permissions, acknowledging mistakes, receiving corrections, but the custom was accepted gladly for the sake of the inner meaning and motive that gave it spiritual value. Self-accusation may have cost her even more, but she made it a lifelong habit, along with silence under rebuke, and the inevitable revelation of personal faults and weaknesses. All this combined to develop in her a deepening sense of her unworthiness of such a high vocation and her need of grace and direction. Under the guidance of Sister Eugenie she sought to acquire the habit of continual awareness of the presence of God, which St. Francis de Sales enjoins in his Constitutions; and it was evident from her fervor and recollection that her actions were animated by the realization of that divine presence. Prayer became her greatest joy, and from it sprang its inseparable complement, generosity in service and sacrifice.

So the happy novice was preparing to pronounce her vows of profession when the votes of the community in Chapter would admit her to that honor. It is customary at the Visitation for profession to take place a year and a day after the reception of the

religious habit, unless for some reason the time of training is prolonged. Philippine's longing for this event increased with her
realization of the dignity of a spouse of Jesus Christ. In spirit she
advanced to the choir grille for the ceremony and rehearsed in her
heart the words of the sacred promises. The community of Sainte
Marie voted her acceptance in September, 1789, but Philippine
Duchesne was to know a long agony of hope and disappointment
and uncertainty before she was privileged to enter fully into the
sanctuary of religious life.

The winter of 1788–1789 had been a time of great suffering
in Dauphiny, as in nearly all France. Meager harvests caused a
shortage of food. The weather was severe. Deaths from cold and
starvation were numerous, in spite of generous alms from all who
had money or supplies to give. Food riots occurred in the spring,
and Grenoble was saved from more serious disturbances only
through the generosity of Claude Perier. There followed a kind of
panic that spread through France as summer came on.

It was a momentous summer. Excitement stirred Grenoble as
news was received of the meeting of the Estates General in Paris,
the division of opinion and delegation, the storming of the Bastille,
fighting in the capital, brigands loose throughout the country.
Such news was reported in the parlor at Sainte Marie. A reorganization of the local militia by the governor of the province seemed
wise but ominous, and wealthy families began to leave the city,
seeking refuge in country residences or secluded villages. This hurt
trade, and a breakdown in economic life threatened.

The September of 1789 should have brought Philippine the joy
of making her religious profession at Sainte Marie, but to her father
this step seemed sheerest folly. He was too clear-headed not to
realize that the revolution now under way threatened not only the
monarchy but also the Church, with its clergy and religious orders.
The confiscation and sale of ecclesiastical property had already
begun. The suppression of religious orders would certainly follow.
So Pierre-François Duchesne forbade his daughter to make her
vows. He was willing for her to remain at Sainte Marie for the
moment, but she must promise to make no religious vows before
the age of twenty-five. This was a crushing blow to the novice,
"the severest trial God could have sent me," she admitted later on.
But a wise old priest to whom she confided her suffering counseled
her: "Adore God, my child. He has his secret designs in what he
allows to happen today. Later on you will understand."

News that the suppression of religious orders was already being discussed in the National Assembly strengthened Monsieur Duchesne in his decision regarding Philippine. On February 13, 1790, a decree was passed secularizing the old monastic orders. Nuns were allowed to remain in their convents, those engaged in education and charity being especially favored. The religious women of France, remarks Lavisse, resisted both the decrees of the National Assembly and the urgent appeals of the patriots. Very few left their cloisters in the early days of the revolution, for neither attacks nor persuasion had any effect on them. Fear undermined the courage of very few; the vast majority resisted until they were actually forced to leave their convents in 1792.

To the disappointment which Philippine experienced and the insecurity that now threatened the community at Sainte Marie there was added anxiety about her father. He had continued his political activities, though the revolution was making too great headway to suit him, and he had only contempt for the theatricals staged publicly in the name of liberty. He had represented the town of Gap in the assembly at Romans in November, 1788. When the Estates General had been convoked in 1789, a report on the happenings in Grenoble during the preceding year had been presented to the assembly. The leading lawyers of the city considered it a very garbled account, so they drew up a vehement protest. Duchesne was a signer of the document. Early in February, 1790, Philippine learned that her father had been elected to membership in the municipal council, an honor and office she knew he had hitherto refused. As councilman he was riding the crest of a great wave of popularity, but there was trouble ahead and he seemed to sense the danger. For some months he had been searching for a country home to which he might transfer his family. Now he settled on a place in southwest Dauphiny near the village of Grâne. After a last visit to Sainte Marie, Madame Duchesne moved there with Adelaide, Melanie, and young Duchesne.

Two months after his election to the municipal council, Monsieur Duchesne was requested to compose the formula for an oath which the newly federated National Guard would take in public ceremony. The formulation of this oath was his undoing, for into it he wrote the words: "Supreme power belongs to the King." The document became public property. A hue and cry was raised by revolutionary sympathizers and personal opponents of Duchesne, who accused him of attempting covertly to induce his fellow-citizens to swear away their own safety, or craftily to stifle their nascent liberty and re-establish the old abuses. Duchesne revised the oath to read: "Supreme power is vested in the King," and the men of Dauphiny were satisfied with the text but not with its author, who now withdrew from public life to the home at Grâne.

The shock of revolutionary changes was being felt in Grenoble that same year. Churches were still open; religious services were still allowed; but by mid-July the Civil Constitution of the Clergy had been completed and soon the priesthood of France would undergo an ordeal that had had no counterpart in the past. There was general uneasiness among the people and anxiety in the hearts of all who had regard for the religious welfare of the country. In October, Camille Teisseire, a man of sterling faith and principles, was appointed to the municipal council, to which Claude Perier also belonged. It was hoped at Sainte Marie that their influence might ward off the danger that was creeping nearer every day.

So far the religious institutions in Grenoble had been spared, but rumor had it that this state of affairs could not last. Gossip grew. Discussions were endless. The City Council had addressed a memorial to the National Assembly in Paris for the preservation of the *Grande Chartreuse*, the religious serving in hospitals, the two monasteries of the Visitation, and that of the Ursulines. Prayer grew more intense at Sainte Marie when it was learned that all the religious in the city not mentioned in the memorial had been dispersed. Dispersed! The very suggestion of such a course was heartbreaking, but the fact remained that the Visitandine nuns of Grenoble might share the fate of many another community. Philippine's aunts, Sisters Françoise-Melanie and Claire-Euphrosine, had already been forced to leave their monastery at Romans and find refuge at home.

In May, 1792, Philippine learned that the great cross that had stood for generations in the Place Saint-André had been torn down and the square itself renamed *Place de la Constitution*, while Grande Rue had become *Rue de la Regénération*. All this was a symbol of what lay ahead. In July a cryptic warning flashed from Paris to the remotest villages of France: "The Fatherland is in danger." The Legislative Assembly made way for the Convention, which deposed the King and sent the royal family to the Temple, but not before it had completed the temporary destruction of religious life throughout the country by two decrees. The first of these, dated August 4, 1792, suppressed all the religious orders of women which had up to that time been spared. Their crime was that of "making common cause with the refractory priests." The second, on August 18, abolished all congregations of men and women that had continued in existence since 1790 for work in schools and hospitals.

Throughout the length and breadth of France the tempo of revolution was being speeded up. War and insurrection were heading the country toward the Terror. There was no hope of saving Sainte Marie. In September, 1792, Philippine Duchesne was obliged to lay aside her religious habit and leave the cloister-home where she had spent four and a half years. That was a short period, as religious training goes, yet during that time of grace she had laid hold of the supernatural ideas and ideals that were, in great part, to give impulse to the rest of her life. The heartache of the departure echoed in the cry that escaped her lips and pen: "Dear Sion, shall I never see thee again?" One ray of hope beckoned to her and she pleaded to be allowed to go to Italy, where Mother Eugenie de Bayanne was now Superior of a monastery. When her father refused this request, Philippine went down Mount Rachais to the Perier home. It was a descent she would repeat many a time in the years that lay ahead.

A sincere and hearty welcome greeted her, and the whole family vied in efforts to make her feel at home once more. They sympathized with the trial she had undergone, and their understanding made it easier for her to accept the new life. While she was with them, her days were very full. She renewed her friendship with Augustin, now in business with his father. He was showing marked ability for both banking and commerce, but he loved books of another sort, too, and talked with lively interest of those he was reading. Philippine read to Scipion, whose weak eye-sight was always such a handicap to him. She listened to Casimir's stories about boarding-school life at the Oratorian college in Lyons, now closed. Casimir was a handsome lad. The family thought he looked like Philippine. She helped the younger boys with their lessons and played with the little ones. On Sundays, at least, she could attend Mass, if not in a church, then in the drawing-room of Dr. Gagnon's house just down the street, where Grande Rue met Place Grenette.

She spent many hours with Josephine in her beautiful apartments and shared the works of charity that were already gaining for Madame de Savoye-Rollin the title by which all Grenoble knew her for half a century—"*la Bienfaisance en poste*," which might be translated as "kindliness personified." There were many members of the family with whom she had not kept in touch and of whom

Josephine could give her news. Before the political storm broke over France, Uncle Augustin, living at Lorient, had brought the Company of the Indies to full prosperity and had become a very wealthy man, but financial success had not given him contentment. In 1789 he had gone headlong into the Revolution. That year he had been elected commandant of the National Guard at Lorient and each succeeding year he had been re-elected. But Augustin Perier had enemies.

And Camille Jordan? He had been in favor of the Revolution at first, but Camille could not keep faith with a movement that broke faith with God. He was just twenty-two, but his adventurous spirit, his courage and influence had already given him remarkable power with the conservative element in Lyons. Euphrosine saw him frequently when he came to discuss affairs with her husband, Jean-Joseph Jouve, who held the same political views and whose mercantile interests were suffering greatly as a result of the economic dislocation throughout the country.

There was comparative quiet in Grenoble just now, but Philippine heard her Uncle Claude and Camille Teisseire, now a frequent visitor at the home, talking seriously with the older Perier boys and planning security for the town, economy in expenditures, and safety for the family. She missed her father's positive, often vehement, assertions of opinion and her mother's gentle restraining influence on him. She longed to be at Grâne for Christmas, though Tante Perier pleaded with her to stay with them. Soon there was a safe opportunity to travel, and she was off.

The road was not new to her, nor would Grâne be new. She loved the roomy chateau and the pleasant gardens and woods. The family had often gone there for the summer when she was a child, and two little Duchesne girls were buried there. From Grenoble, Philippine could go down the familiar road to Vizille, then on southwest to Die, in the new department of the Drôme. From there the road followed the river to Crest, where a change was made from the regular stagecoach to a smaller vehicle that crossed the Drôme River by ferry or bridge and brought her safely to Grâne, a village that had grown up beside a little stream bearing the familiar name Grenette. In her childhood the approach to Crest was always signaled by the one who first sighted the great old feudal keep that stands on a rock high above the town. The castle had been destroyed, but the huge keep remained intact and was used as a prison. Silhouetted against the horizon, it was no longer a symbol of feudal domination to the close-mouthed, reticent countryfolk of the neighborhood, but to children it was the setting for endless stories of fancy and adventure.

In this section of old Dauphiny low spurs of the mountains replaced the towering Alps, and wide pasture lands spread their grasses to feed large flocks of sheep. Vineyards and orchards covered the hillsides and plains along the Drôme and its small tributaries. Philippine had known it always in summertime. Now the mountains wore a thick winter covering of white. The fruit and nut trees were gaunt and bare. The piercing wind cut sharply at her as she sprang out of the carriage at the entrance of the chateau and ran to the door that was opened wide to her. She had come home, though all unwillingly, and she realized the strength of the love that welcomed her. But she had not come home to stay. Neither earthly affection nor human upheaval could shake the resolve of her total commitment to Christ.

two

Through Years
of Uncertainty

I. 1793—1801

PHILIPPINE FOUND AT GRANE not only her parents and the younger children of the family, but also her sister Amelie with her two little boys, who had sought shelter and safety in the country while her husband, Captain de Mauduit, was serving the fatherland with his regiment, the 58th Infantry. They were joined almost immediately by a cousin, Julie Tranchand, a Visitandine from the monastery at Romans. Philippine and Julie at once devised a way of life for themselves patterned as closely as possible on that of the cloisters they had left. Following the monastic order of the day, they rose early, made their morning meditation, recited Office, said the prayers and kept the fasts prescribed, and observed the Rule as far as they could. When members of the household found this manner of life too austere, Philippine accepted the criticism without irritation, but also without relaxing her efforts to live up to her vocation in altered circumstances. Her critics were, in fact, forced to admit that no selfish motive inspired her life of piety, nor did she allow her hours of prayer to interfere with any duty she owed the family. She helped irritable Amelie with her children, gave time and affection unstintingly to little Melanie, and did all in her power to relieve her mother of household cares. Cousins, friends, servants, all grew more attached to her than ever

43

because of her unfailing thoughtfulness and kindness. She came to know her father better and to realize the price he had paid in leaving Grenoble at a time like this.

Philippine has left few details about her life during this period. The following paragraphs, however, from her *Story of Sainte Marie*, written in 1805 are revealing:

> The decree which obliged all religious women [in France] to return to secular life obliged me to go back to my family. My heart was never attached to this sort of life and it was a land of exile for me, a foreign land, and Sion, my true country, remained the goal of my desires and of my costliest endeavors. The dwelling for which I longed was the sanctuary of religious life. Although I was very lovingly inclined toward the cloister in which I had received my vocation—and never for an instant did I feel a repugnance toward it—still, from the time of our dispersal several orders in different countries attracted my thoughts and became the object of my prayers, that I might know the will of God in my regard. Several times I changed my mind about the place and the order, but never did I lose sight of my high ambition. I lived two years in a town of the Drôme which was in the vicinity of the tomb of St. Francis Regis. . . . Nearly everyone who was given to piety made a visit to his tomb and some went every year. I went there in spirit frequently, but my family objected to the trip of twelve or fourteen leagues [perhaps thirty or forty miles] and I had to defer that pleasure.

There is far more of Philippine's character in these paragraphs than of her activities. The "two years in a town of the Drôme" must have been the years from 1795 to 1797. She gives only one hint regarding the worst period of the Revolution, which she spent at Grâne. During the first months of 1793 fugitive priests sometimes found their way to the Duchesne home. They ministered to the spiritual needs of the household, and there was the rare, tense joy of Holy Mass. This state of affairs was a sore trial to Philippine, who felt a great need for guidance. God answered her prayer for help by bringing into her home a man of marked holiness and learning. Her father was planning to build a small textile factory, most probably in connection with the Perier industry. One day a stranger called on him to ask for employment as superintendent of the construction. The man was intelligent and reliable and before long was acting as overseer both of the estate and of the business enterprise, to the relief and satisfaction of Monsieur Duchesne.

The new overseer was a reserved man who kept in the background as much as possible, avoiding notice and seldom appearing when visitors came to the house. At the end of a few weeks he identified himself as the Abbé Poidebard, who had barely escaped the guillotine and for whom search was still hot. He resided with the Duchesnes through the greater part of the next two years, becoming tutor, friend, and confidant in the family. By day he was a conscientious, hard-working manager of affairs. In the evening he frequently gave religious instruction to the younger members of the household or held spiritual conferences with Philippine and Julie Tranchand. Before dawn he might offer the Holy Sacrifice of the Mass in a secluded room and give Holy Communion to those who were allowed to attend this secret service. That they did so at the risk of their lives made all the more precious the tryst they kept with Christ. The active part played by Pierre-François Duchesne in the early stages of the Revolution and his continued interest in all that happened in Grenoble seem to have shielded his family home from suspicion. His willingness to harbor a fugitive priest during the worst period of the upheaval points up his love for his family and his respect for their convictions.

At Grâne the Duchesnes were not cut off from contact with the members of the family who were living in Grenoble and Lyons. From time to time news came by letter or visitor or in a sheaf of printed pages bearing the marks of eager use by those who had already handled them. Toward the close of January came the shocking news of the execution of the king. Grenoble remained fairly quiet for two more months. The municipal council was composed of men of moderate views who hoped to save the city from excesses. There was want and misery, unemployment and the disorders that usually accompany it. Children ran undisciplined in the streets since the closing of schools and orphanages, and many lived like little animals, escaping the vigilance of the police and exulting in an unsavory freedom. Relief agencies were at work, and the need for charitable helpers was urgent.

Spring had come to Grenoble when the "people's representatives" began their activities. The town was too moderate to suit the revolutionary government. Now domiciliary visits became the order of the day. Priest-baiting was their special game. Non-juring priests who were caught were thrown into prison. A decree for the arrest of citizens "notoriously suspect" of lack of patriotism brought about the arrest of many of the leading townsfolk. Sainte Marie became a prison in April, 1793, when the proscription lists were said to include hundreds of names.

When news of all this reached Grâne, along with snatches of information about the work Josephine de Savoye-Rollin was doing for the poor, Philippine could no longer endure the inaction of her sheltered life. With fine disregard for danger she set off for Grenoble to share in an apostolate of charity whose hazards must at times have satisfied her most venturesome inclinations. There were many homes open to her in Grenoble, but she determined to involve none of the family in her enterprises. She lived with a trusted companion in a section of the town where she would have the greatest freedom of action, though there is nothing to indicate that she refused altogether the hospitality of the Perier home or the joy of companionship with the Savoye-Rollins. The prominence of her uncle and the position of Savoye-Rollin afforded her a measure of safety.

Organization was needed. Philippine formed an association known as the Ladies of Mercy, whose primary purpose was to bring material and spiritual help to the priests who had stood courageously on the side of the Church and who were now either imprisoned at Sainte Marie or in disguise and hiding. This was a work of mercy after her own heart, but a second aspect of the work also appealed strongly to her. Public religious worship had ceased in Grenoble, but not sickness and death. At the risk of her life Philippine guided priests to those who needed their ministrations. She cared for the sick and dying and prepared the dead for burial. Sometimes a priest was among the pall-bearers on whose charity she called, for there was often as much safety in public risk as in private hiding.

At times Philippine went about her work with a heavy heart. It was hard to react against grief and anxiety about her loved ones. There was that terrible day in 1793 when she learned of the tragedy that had befallen Uncle Augustin and his family. He had failed to obtain re-election that year as commandant of the National Guard at Lorient. A violent reaction had set in against him. He was arrested as a suspect and hurried off to Paris for trial, but he did not reach the capital. On the way Augustin Perier was murdered at an inn. His wife and daughter were in Paris when they learned of his death. They set out at once by stagecoach for Lorient, but they were ambushed and murdered on the road by Breton insurgents.

France was now at war with her neighbors, and Grenoble was once more a very important post of defense on the frontier. Detachments of troops arrived to strengthen the garrison; the local militia was increased; and a "regiment of hope" enlisted lads from eight to eighteen years of age. Even the youngest Perier boys were drilling on the square in front of the Town Hall. Then came the news of the insurrection in Lyons against the terrorism of the Convention. Philippine knew that Camille Jordan was a leading spirit in the movement, that Jean-Joseph Jouve was an active sympathizer. Euphrosine was in Lyons with her husband and children.

The siege of Lyons lasted seven weeks. When the city surrendered in October, the Jouves escaped with their lives, but with little else. Philippine notes that Jouve "distinguished himself" during the siege. "In order to save life and fortune, he was obliged to take refuge with his family in the mountainous district after the surrender of the city. . . . Here he experienced great suffering and poverty in his efforts to bring up a growing family." Camille Jordan also escaped, but he was obliged to go into exile until the fall of Robespierre.

And now it was another member of the family on whom the revolutionary government bore down severely. Captain Constans de Mauduit was dismissed from the French army in October, 1793. His noble Breton blood and name had made him suspect, but his connection with the Duchesnes and Periers saved him from forced emigration. He now joined his wife and family at Grâne, but Philippine remained in Grenoble.

She had to be more on her guard as she went about her dangerous activities. She must remember to address her friends as *Citoyen* or *Citoyenne*, for the old courtesies of Monsieur, Madame, and Mademoiselle were banned in the new order of things. Churches were now deserted—even by the Constitutional clergy. The great bells of Saint-André were silent; the Cathedral of Notre Dame had been desecrated. With the streets renamed, she often found it difficult to give directions to those who helped in her charities or to find the poor who were recommended to her care. There were dire poverty and distress in the city in the winter of 1793–1794. Food shortage brought on riots; troops were called out to maintain order. Claude Perier subscribed 24,000 *livres* to pay the troops, and Camille Teisseire, procurator of the commune, was sent to Paris to solicit aid. His efforts failed completely, but soon he was back in Grenoble, making more successful appeals for help for the prisoners who were being crowded, without pity or provision, into Sainte Marie and other places of confinement.

The terror had come late to Grenoble and its form was rather mild. But at the beginning of June, 1794, the priest-hunt was renewed, and the city saw the guillotine at work in Place Grenette on June 26. The two priests executed that day were the only victims condemned to death. A great number of people, however, died in the prisons, where an epidemic of typhoid fever raged through the summer months and the work of charity reached highest heroism. Philippine gave herself to the care of the prison victims with courage and competence. Though her association of mercy had been disbanded by the radical authorities, she was undaunted in her apostolate.

The record of her activities during this period is meager, but the known facts are characteristic. She visited clergy and lay folk imprisoned in filthy dungeons, knew the hiding places of proscribed priests, and often risked her life to bring them to the bedside of the sick whom she was tending. Her sister Euphrosine related that on her round of visits to the sick one morning, Philippine came upon a poor woman who was obviously very near death. Realizing that it would be too great a risk to bring a priest to that section of the city, she had the woman lifted on to a litter and carried to her own lodgings. There she put her in the bed which she herself shared with her companion, made her comfortable, and brought a priest to minister to her. When her companion came home that evening, she was somewhat taken aback at what she found there, but she was equal to the situation and could not help smiling at it. Philippine made no explanations, but begged her to watch with her through the night. Together they prayed by the woman, who was already in her agony and who died in the arms of *Citoyenne* Duchesne. "As a matter of fact," her sister continues, "nights like this were very frequent for Philippine, whether she spent them at the bedside of the sick or assisted at the Holy Sacrifice, which could be celebrated only furtively, under cover of darkness."

Her relatives were in continual anxiety about her and frequently tried to check her perilous zeal by dwelling on the consequences that might so easily result from the risks she was taking. To these representations and to their pleadings that she return to live with some of her family she always gave the same answer: "Let me alone. It is my happiness and glory to serve my divine Savior in the person of the unfortunate and the poor." She was not, however, lacking in affection or interest where her family was concerned, and one event gave her much pleasure in the midst of the turmoil and terror. On July 31, 1794, Claude Perier gave his daughter Marine in marriage to Camille Teisseire. Camille was thirty years of age, a rich wine-merchant with a spacious home near Place Grenette; Marine was in her sixteenth year and "one of the prettiest women in the town," so Stendhal thought. Philippine had had no more loyal helper in the town than Camille Teisseire, and she always considered him a close personal friend.

The wedding had scarcely been announced when couriers rode into Grenoble with news of Robespierre's downfall. The city's reaction was true to form in Dauphiny where the people had been disgusted with the extremes of terror, persecution, public crime, and godless life. At once the Ladies of Mercy were allowed to reorganize. A movement to ameliorate the condition of the prisoners gave them free scope for their charity. It was fortunate that municipal authorities with moderate ideas and a sense of justice had been retained, for the period of readjustment was critical. As the year 1795 opened, Dauphiny, if not the whole of France, was at peace.

Philippine was now free to return to Grâne. She had, most probably, visited her family at least once or twice during the past year and a half, for she wrote that she was there "during the stormiest days of the revolution." She found her mother in very poor health and her father active again in political life. Since her sister Amelie was expecting her third child, Adelaide was managing the household for her mother, though she was rather bored with life in the country, especially since Cousin Marine's wedding. Duchesne was now sent away to school, and Philippine devoted herself to nine-year-old Melanie's education. In February, 1795, the law of freedom of worship was proclaimed; but since church assemblies were still forbidden, the church at Grâne was without liturgical services.

There is no record of this period in Philippine's life. We know, however, that in the spring of 1797 Madame Duchesne's illness grew steadily worse. Her twin, Camille Jordan's mother, had died the previous December, worn out at the age of forty-eight by the terrible strain of the Revolution, but comforted by the knowledge that her sons were strongly Catholic in faith. The death of Marie-Elizabeth, the "Lise" of her childhood, seemed to drain from Madame Duchesne her last resistance. There were others who might have cared for her with constant attention, but from no one else would she have received the loving devotedness that Philippine lavished upon her. Madame Jouve wrote later on: "That daughter, who had formerly left her to follow God's call, was her most faithful nurse during her entire illness. Day and night she was at her bedside, caring for both body and soul; nor did she leave her until she had drawn her last breath."

The absence of their father at this time was an added grief for the Duchesne sisters. Since his re-entrance into political life, he had first been named syndic at Crest, then chosen by the electors of the department of the Drôme as a member of the Council of Five Hundred in 1797. He had gone to Paris that spring with no premonition of the sorrow the summer would bring. Madame Duchesne would not allow the family to send for him, for she felt he was at his post of duty. She tried, however, to write him a farewell letter, but she could not finish it. After telling him of her condition and of having sent for her absent children, she gave a last expression to her love for him:

> Death would have been too sweet if I had had the satisfaction of having you, my best friend, with me in my last moments. I die in sweet peace, leaving to my children the best of fathers, and to you affectionate and respectful children who will do all in their power to make up to you for my loss. The only anxiety I carry to the grave, my loving companion, is . . .

Pierre-François Duchesne knew well what his beloved wife had left unsaid. Death came for her on June 30, 1797, and she was buried near the children she had lost in the early years of her motherhood. Euphrosine and Duchesne had not reached Grâne in time to kneel at her bedside; Amelie and Adelaide were elsewhere in the chateau when she died. It was Philippine who held her mother in her arms, and Melanie who knelt beside the death bed.

In the property settlement after the death of Madame Duchesne, Philippine turned over to Amelie her own share in the estate at Grâne and gave to her other sisters and brother her portion of the property situated in Grenoble and elsewhere, in return for a yearly income which they agreed to pay her during her lifetime. This arrangement was made at her own suggestion, since it would free her from the care of real estate or commercial interests and would allow her to live independently wherever she chose and devote herself to works of charity.

The first of these charitable enterprises was no drain on her income, but a severe test of her virtue and a somewhat humiliating failure. At her father's suggestion she went to Romans to live for a time with her grandmother Duchesne. The old lady was not alone. The elder of her Visitandine daughters was still living with her, and there were tenants and servants on the place. Philippine seems, however, to have been concerned about her, feeling that some members of the family neglected her selfishly, exaggerating certain eccentricities that made companionship with her unpleasant. Philippine was to learn the truth, and quickly. Grandmother Duchesne was a character. Through a long life she had given free rein to a temper now ungovernable because seldom governed in the past. From morning till night she stormed at all who ventured near her, not excepting her elderly daughter or the faithful house-maid, Rose, who cared for her with docility and self-control inspired more by compassion than by fear. Philippine was in admiration of Rose. She herself was soon exhausted and was cogitating how she might withdraw from Romans without giving further offense, when Grandmother Duchesne dismissed her in words so clear and pointed as to free her from all hesitation about leaving. Meditating on these experiences, she wrote to Amelie with charming frankness:

> I am still at Romans. It is not as easy to leave as I had thought it would be. I have let slip several opportunities, not wishing to leave Grandmother alone, and now I have no means of getting away. Julie is already rather surprised at my delay and seems put out with me for postponing my visit, but I have no wings on which to fly to her. Grandmother has expressed herself in no uncertain terms regarding my departure—it will make her quite happy. I had a pretty lively scene with her as a result of some representations I tried to make to her. I did not succeed in calming her wrath against either her tenants or her house-servants. From the conversation I gained only my own dismissal, and that in very pointed language.
>
> In seeing the changes which the years have wrought in our grandmothers, I cannot but make a few sad reflections. Their blood flows in our veins, and already we feel in ourselves flashes of their fiery impatience. Let us try to control ourselves now in the first stages of this defect, which increases with age and may become incorrigible. Let us try not to be exacting with others, but rather to pass over in silence those thousand little annoyances which tend to embitter us. For we know that no one is perfect in this life and we must put up with the defects of others.

While Philippine may have felt in herself a tendency toward the defects that made her grandmother so unbearable, she had seen similar faults displayed by Amelie and knew that the household at Grâne was often shaken by her outbursts of temper. The forthrightness with which she speaks of their common failings is indicative not only of the intimacy existing between them, but also of the fearlessness with which Philippine was accustomed to express her thoughts and the assurance she had that her remarks would be taken in good part. She also knew that her return to Grâne would give the family great pleasure; nevertheless she did not return. Instead, she set off for Saint-Marcellin, where Julie Tranchand was eagerly awaiting her. During the past few years the town had been the hiding place of many a confessor of the faith and future martyr. The Church of St. Marcellin was still closed, but now and then a priest appeared in disguise and made his presence known to the faithful by a trusted underground. Then, too, the chateau of Murinais was in this vicinity, and Mother Anne-Félicité, Philippine's former Superior at Sainte Marie, was living there.

But Saint-Marcellin held an even greater attraction for Philippine. The town had had its monastery of the Visitation before the Revolution, and a group of fervent nuns had gathered there as early as 1795, still holding fast to their ideals and hopes, in spite of the price such fidelity entailed. At their head was Mother Claire-Euphrosine Duchesne. She had known a quarter-century of religious life at Romans before the Revolution drove her and her older sister from their cloister back to the family home, where Grandmother Duchesne made things so lively for all who came under her roof. Visitation annals speak of Mother Claire-Euphrosine as a woman of deep faith, selfless generosity, superb courage, and keen sense of humor. During the years spent at home (1791–1795) she carried on a remarkable apostolate, but living in relative security did not satisfy her. With her niece, Julie Tranchand, and another Visitandine, she moved to Saint-Marcellin. Taking up residence in what had been a boarding school, they carried on common life according to their Rule as far as possible. A few more companions joined them. The young girls who were their pupils often saw the priests who found refuge in the house, but no indiscretion or disloyalty ever betrayed their hiding place. Domiciliary visits were frequent, but no arrests were made, thanks to the presence of mind, the affable manner, and the gay disposition of Mother Claire-Euphrosine. There were times when her family accused her of rashness, selfishness, lack of consideration for others, but she refused to compromise; and she was upheld in her resolution by Monseigneur d'Aviau, Archbishop of Vienne, who more than once found shelter at Saint-Marcellin.

This was the group Philippine now joined temporarily. There is no record of how long she was with them or why she was not content to remain. Two facts are known: she was not satisfied, and she made a spiritual retreat at Saint-Marcellin. During those days of solitude and prayer she came to a decision: she would return to Grenoble and devote herself to an apostolate of charity among the poor of the city and the victims of persecution who were still in prison or in hiding. She hoped, moreover, to see religious life re-established in her own beloved monastery. The Visitandine stamp was imprinted deep in her soul, and Sainte Marie was the monastic home to which she was whole-heartedly attached. Writing of this period some twenty years later she said:

> The time of trial, but not of indecision, seemed an eternity to me, and if, reflecting on its length, I wondered at times whether God meant me to remain in the world, he saw to it at once that some passage of the gospel referring to detachment from one's family came to my attention and revived my courage. The separation from my father, who went to Paris, and the death of my mother, which occurred shortly after that, set me at liberty to leave home and return to Grenoble in order to associate myself with some women who wished to live under a religious rule. One of the Jesuits whom I had known was still living. As soon as he learned of my decision, he wrote to me, saying that *I had taken a step for which God would reward me.*

The encouragement of this Jesuit was evidently a strong moral support for Philippine at a time when she needed it badly. She seems to have been misunderstood by both the religious at Saint-Marcellin and her family. When she informed the family of the decision she had reached, they made things unpleasant for her. Madame de Mauduit seems to have leveled at her the severest reproaches, with an insinuation of selfishness and weakness that cut to the quick. Amelie's pen could be as sharp as her tongue, and Philippine's reply is self-revealing. Addressing the letter to *Citoyenne* Mauduit at Crest, as Grâne was off the postal route, she wrote from a very full heart:

> You know already, my beloved Sister, that I have reached Grenoble, and you surely understand the motive of my trip. Certainly I would never have had the courage to undertake it for a few days of pleasure here. Do not suggest deception on my part toward you, my dearest friend. If on leaving the home where you are residing I did not state my ultimate intentions, then subject to a thousand uncertainties and to the duty I might have felt obliged to shoulder at Romans, I really had no fixed plan at the time. I simply left to Providence the care of lighting my path and showing

me the divine will. It was easier, too, when leaving sisters whom I love so tenderly, not to consider the possibility of a long absence.

The reception I got from Grandmother and the dismissal she gave me were the first incitement to put my project into action. Far from being angry at the reception she gave me, I regard it as a real favor, for it wards off the reproaches Father might have made me for refusing to carry out his wishes, since she herself refused to have me around.

My old desires were rekindled by the reflections that filled my mind during this period of leisure; and when I visited Saint-Marcellin, I really had no intention of remaining there. In the retreat I made there, I tried to strip myself of all over-eagerness in desires, of all attachment to my own views, of all merely human sentiments. But how could human sentiments have a part in a resolution that forced me to overcome those very sentiments and to lift myself above nature in order to correspond to a higher, stronger attraction? Stripped then of self, I sought to know the divine will, and I made up my mind. Few people understand what I am talking about, and few will refrain from blaming me. I excuse them because of their motives and beg them to act in the same way toward mine, if they cannot praise them.

My Father especially, having no religion to fall back upon, will always be prejudiced against me, and I shall carry to my grave the sorrow of having caused him pain. . . . I know that I possess no power either to console him or to bring him peace. But in uniting myself to Him who directs all events and consoles all hearts, I can do more for my Father than by seeking to please him by my attentions and constant companionship. Often I have prayed to God that the pain of this separation may be felt by me alone, that I may endure its full force, and that in return I may win for my family happiness, cordial union, and constant peace. . . .

Formerly I looked forward without imprudence to a life of security in religion. Now all is changed; my plans are no longer the same, for it seems impossible to follow my desires, as there is no religious order in existence in France. But I want this letter to bear witness against me if ever selfish interest comes between us, and if I am not ready to make all the arrangements that are most advantageous to you. I have found a companion somewhat older than I and free like myself. She has a little revenue which, with some work added, suffices for her own support and that of a very good young woman who has been in her service for ten years and whom we shall continue to keep. We are just about to rent an apartment; and as we must make the first payment at once, I need some money. Will you have the kindness to send me about 300 francs, if you can do so without inconvenience to yourself? I intend writing to Father to ask permission to take from among the things he has in storage the furniture I need most. . . .

Plead my cause with Father and do so at once, I beg of you. Do not let him worry lest events should bring failure to our plans; they are so limited, there really is no risk. We shall not undertake anything dangerous, but only some good works. We shall live in obscurity—that is our wish—so do not talk to anyone about me or what I am doing. Prudence requires this.

"Prudence requires this." Conditions in Grenoble were far from normal, and Philippine realized how careful she and her companion must be, if they were to carry out their plan, which must have been sketchy enough at first. The rehabilitation of Catholic life and worship was necessarily a very slow process, but it was Philippine's ambition to share actively in this restoration. Mission work at home, the re-establishment of monastic life, the education of children, social work among the neglected poor, all of these were the object of her desires and prayers as she went about the city on her errands of mercy, nursing the sick, sewing for the poor, begging help for priests still in hiding, bringing comfort and encouragement wherever she went.

Sometimes she was at Tante Perier's house, where there was much to talk about. Casimir was conscripted that year, 1798, and Augustin had married Louise de Berckheim. He had taken over the direction of his father's business affairs in Dauphiny when Claude went to Paris in 1795 and was making a success of the big textile factories. Sometimes Philippine was at Marine Teisseire's home, where there was a baby boy about a year old. Marine was interested in the wedding that was being planned at Grâne, where Adelaide Duchesne became the bride of Henri Lebrument of Bourg in 1798. Philippine may have attended the ceremony and seen her father there. He was, as always, a very busy man, having been chosen secretary of the Council of Five Hundred in March of that year. He could give her news of the Savoye-Rollins, who were living in Paris now, as Jacques had accepted a position under the Directory.

This did not mean, however, that the men of Dauphiny to whom Philippine was related were in accord with all the policies and actions of the government they were serving. Outspoken Camille Jordan, who had been sent by Lyons to the Council of Five Hundred in 1797, had stood up so courageously for religious liberty and freedom of worship as to acquire the nickname of "Church-bell Jordan" (*Jordan cloche*) and be listed for deportation in the September Revolution. So the road to exile reopened for him. He would return to France in 1800 and be interned temporarily in Grenoble, where Philippine would enjoy his friendship again. She had great affection for this sincere and courageous cousin, whose finely balanced character drew admiration even from his severest opponents.

In 1798 the henchmen of Bonaparte laid violent hands on Pope Pius VI. The venerable old man had seen a stormy pontificate and had upheld the Church's rights in the face of revolutionary despotism in France, but he was powerless against armed force. Hustled unceremoniously from place to place, the sick pontiff was borne in a litter across the Alps into Dauphiny. A jolting cart carried him to Vizille, where a twenty-four-hour halt was allowed at the Perier chateau. Grenoble was reached early in July, and soon the invalid began the final lap of his earthly journey to Valence on the Rhone, where he died on August 29, 1799. That was Philippine's thirtieth birthday, and also Napoleon Bonaparte's.

While the resurgence of France under the Directory gave partial satisfaction to those who had the best interests of the country at heart, the growing power of Bonaparte was viewed with concern by those who read aright the signs of the times. Among these was Pierre-François Duchesne. With a fearlessness that scorned consequences he took his stand, and in November, 1799, distinguished himself by his opposition to the *coup d'état* by which the Corsican militarist overthrew the Directory. On that *journée de dupe*, at least one man from Dauphiny was not taken in, nor did he lose his seat in the Council of Five Hundred. So outstanding was Duchesne's legal ability that he was appointed to membership in the Tribunate after the Constitution of the Year VIII was inaugurated.

Philippine, meanwhile, had begun to realize that she must center her energies on one project rather than scatter them on a dozen enterprises. The thing she longed for most was the reestablishment of religious life at Sainte Marie, and the vision of the old monastery as once more a house of prayer and cordial community life now became her dominant inspiration. The story of her efforts to accomplish this restoration and the final outcome of her striving is contained in the longest autobiographical record she has left us, a record compiled in 1805 at the suggestion of obedience.

In the spring of 1800 she risked another trip to Romans and, while there, decided to make the pilgrimage to the tomb of St.

Francis Regis at La Louvesc. Travel was safe enough now, though its discomforts made it a penitential undertaking. The route took Philippine first to Valence, then across the Rhone and west to La Louvesc. As she had made no inquiries before setting out as to conditions at the shrine, her disappointment on arriving there was great. She writes:

> I was accompanied by one of my grandmother's servants who was very devoted to this saint. The pilgrimage was on the feast of the Holy Cross, May 3, 1800. . . . I did not go to La Louvesc in search of sensible consolation and I did not experience any, though I had expected to. Everything about the place had an air of desolation, resulting from the devastation of the Church. Mass could not be offered in the sanctuary, as one altar was smashed to pieces; several figures of angels which had supported [the statue or relic of] the saint were broken; and one could have gathered up handfuls of dust on his altar. The Mass was offered in a miserable barn and I could not receive Communion on account of the crowd; but I had this happiness after the crowd had withdrawn.

Philippine touches but briefly on the spiritual experience of that day of pilgrimage, yet it must have been filled with prayer and meditation on the heroic life of John Francis Regis—his missionary zeal, his apostolate among the poor of all categories in whom he saw only souls for whom Jesus Christ had died.

> I left the shrine [Philippine continues] completely gripped by a desire to devote myself to the instruction of the poor in imitation of St. Francis Regis. Arriving again in Grenoble, where good schools for little girls were not lacking, I took charge of a few little boys who were entirely neglected and were living like animals. I dwell with pleasure on them for they were a real trial to my patience. . . . I got them to pray that God would enlighten me as to my vocation, and indeed the hour of his mercy was drawing near. On Pentecost Sunday, 1801, I went for a walk up to Sainte Marie, where I had lived for two years as a pupil and four and a half years in the trials of the novitiate. I was with some former Carmelites and I talked of almost nothing but my love for that house and my desire to return there. I grew so enthusiastic in the conversation that I seemed already to see the place peopled with Visitation nuns, and the Carmelites installed in what had been formerly the chaplain's house.

Philippine had with her that afternoon her sister Melanie, then fifteen years old, and her niece, Amelie de Mauduit, just six. The two girls were playing together on the terrace when suddenly

small Amelie cried out, "Yes, I am coming here to school someday
and I shall make my first Communion here." To Tante Philippine the child's words were a prophecy and she in turn prayed
aloud, "My God, You have put these words on the lips of this
child. Make them come true."

2. 1801—1804

THAT FEAST OF PENTECOST, 1801, was a day of decision.
Philippine determined to get possession of Sainte Marie and turned
confidently to prayer. Her *Story of Sainte Marie* needs little an-
notation and much of it is transcribed here because of its wealth of
detail and character revelation. She writes:

> The feast of St. Francis Regis was drawing near and I felt an in-
> crease of confidence in him. Both before and after the feast I made
> novenas in his honor to know the will of God in my regard. It
> occurred to me one day that my return to Sainte Marie would be
> quite possible if it were reconverted into a religious institution, and
> I felt inspired to make a vow in honor of St. Regis in order to ob-
> tain that grace. I asked the permission of my confessor and worded
> my promise this way: "If within a year I am back at Sainte Marie
> in a manner conformable to my desires, I will: 1) send someone to
> La Louvesc to have a novena of Masses offered at the tomb of St.
> Regis, and also a novena of prayers; 2) receive Communion on the
> feast of St. Francis Regis every year and fast on the eve in his
> honor; and if I cannot do this, I will ask someone else to do so;
> 3) arrange in the convent an oratory in honor of St. Regis; 4)
> instruct twelve poor people in religion or have someone else do
> this."
>
> With my intentions placed in such good hands I felt new cour-
> age and I began to take action. I consulted, or had others consult,
> the administrators of the diocese as to the proper course to take in
> order to get possession of Sainte Marie. They all thought it very
> desirable to do so, but they did not agree as to the wisdom of try-
> ing just then nor on the means that would succeed best. One of the
> vicars general was Father Brochier, a man of wide experience and
> animated by the spirit of God. I set great store by his approbation,
> foreseeing even then that many people would blame our enterprise
> and that it was wise to have the support of highly respected
> authorities. I was not at that time acquainted with Father Brochier,
> so I asked my confessor to consult him for me.
>
> As he [Father Brochier] was not in favor of my purchasing the

monastery, and as it was, after all, my own project, I wrote to him, hoping to influence his decision. I told him in detail my motives and my hopes and all that the vivacity of my desires put into my mind. My letter was long; so was his answer. It began with the words, *Digitus Dei est hic,* "The finger of God is here;" but he insisted that it was not wise to purchase the place yet, that the money could be better employed in other ways, and that to all appearances *that house would be given back to us some day,* but that we should try to get possession of it by some other means. I held to buying it, and I ended by going to see Father Brochier myself in order to obtain his consent, but he held firmly to his opinion and advice.

It was not enough to act with the consent and advice of my ecclesiastical superiors. I could not overlook the former Superior of the house on which I was building my hope for a re-establishment [of religious life], so I went to the country place where she was living, in order to find out her intentions. She seemed quite pleased with the prospect of returning to her convent. I went a second time, and she wrote a letter in concert with the former confessor of Sainte Marie to Monsieur [Joseph] du Bouchage, who was then holding the position of prefect of Grenoble, to ask his help in this enterprise. I carried the letter myself and received his verbal answer to the effect that the time was not yet opportune for making such a request of the government and that we had better wait. This was also the opinion of Father Rey, one of the vicars general, who advised me to wait at least two months.

I waited longer than that, for my Father came home from Paris and asked me to spend the vacation with him, and I willingly did so. We went to Romans, and there I had the consolation of spending a few days in a convent of the Visitation which one of my aunts, a former religious of that monastery, had just rented in order to gather together her Sisters and establish a boarding school. We had conceived exactly the same idea at the very same time, but she had no need of contradictions, as I had, and in a short time her house was reorganized and the Rule was in full vigor.

The vacation at Romans lasted about two months. It must have been a joy for Philippine to recall it, though her condensed record taxes the patience of her readers, while it calls up one of the happiest pictures of her that imagination can construct. She and her father were intimate comrades again. As he listened to her confidences, he cautioned her against impetuosity, pointing to the mature experience that had enabled Sister Françoise-Melanie to accomplish so much for her monastery, and warning her that his income was not large enough to allow him to give her much help.

Philippine, however, was not asking him for material aid, but for his approval of the plan she had conceived.

She always knew when she had pressed her point sufficiently. Then they would talk of her loved Uncle Claude, whose death had occurred so suddenly in Paris the previous winter. Philippine was eager for news of young Duchesne, who had become a congenial companion to his father and was following him in politics as well as the law. She asked many questions about Josephine and Augustin and the younger Perier brothers who were making a name for themselves in banking circles—a remarkably gifted set of men, these *Perier Frères*, as Paris was coming to know them. There were chats, too, about her sisters. Melanie was living with Amelie at Grâne, but she liked to get away to Lyons or Grenoble frequently. Euphrosine and Adelaide had growing families and very moderate means with which to care for their children. These children would need to be educated, and this brought the conversation back to Philippine's plan. The re-establishment of Sainte Marie would help take care of the education of her nieces. In the end she won her father's approval by arguments and promises and prayers. Now indeed she was free to return to her cloistered life. Recalling the joy of that victory, she wrote:

> No sooner was I back in Grenoble than Madame de Rollin, my cousin and most loyal friend, begged her husband to petition the prefect to let us have Sainte Marie, and he promised to rent it to us on favorable terms, though at a rather high price. We had to address a petition to him, which I expected to have signed by the Superior of the house and the religious who would contribute to the establishment. Divine Providence allowed it to happen that the authorities were slow in drawing up that petition; and when at last they brought it to me, it was worded in the singular.
>
> The anxiety which the delay had caused me, the need of secrecy to avoid a raise in the price, the distance of Mother de Murinais [from Grenoble], the complaints of some of her religious who had got wind of my visit to Monsieur du Bouchage, all were reasons which determined me to sign the petition myself in order to take advantage of the kind efforts of the people who were actively interested in our project.
>
> The building was made over to me on December 10 [1801]. The prefect seemed to enjoy my happiness. I was to pay 800 francs in rent yearly and to be responsible for the repairs, which were rather extensive. My first impulse on leaving the prefecture was to go and thank God for his goodness at the bedside of a poor sick man

whom I visited almost every day and in whose room I had invoked St. Francis Regis, both for him and for my own intentions. . . .

From there I went to the house of Madame Faucherand [former Visitandine of Sainte Marie] who had shown the most enthusiasm about a reunion; but the agitation that was apparent in her whole person made me foresee her lack of perseverance. From her house I wrote to Mother de Murinais, offering to send a carriage for her and never dreaming that she would make the least delay [in taking possession of the house]. She sent me an answer, stating that she could not leave her present home without consulting her nephew, who was supporting her. I called again that same day on all the vicars general [in Grenoble], and they congratulated me and said I had certainly been inspired in my action.

Then I went home and began to pack my things and dispose of what I would not need. I remained indoors in order to avoid meeting the people who were displeased with me. All the former religious of the house were. They said I was rash in going to live in a building that was falling in ruins and from which I might be expelled again. They accused me of acting without consulting anyone and of sacrificing all to my own selfishness. "Has she the means on which to support the religious who have lost all their revenues? We do not want to starve to death. We have made a vow of poverty, but not of begging our living. We will not return to our convent until we can be sure of the same security as we had before." All these remarks were made with ill-temper and repeated in the same spirit, so I considered it useless to make any advances toward these women, as they were angered by the least suggestion of a return [to Sainte Marie]. It was enough for my peace of conscience that the door was now open to them and that both the ecclesiastical and the religious superiors had been consulted.

Father Rivet, whom I knew but slightly then, came to congratulate me, inspired by his zeal for the glory of God. His visit gave me great joy, for he knew about the signing of the concordat and encouraged me with the thought that I was not too far ahead of time in this work.

On December 14 I returned to the house of the Lord. It would have been a consolation to have done so the previous day, anniversary of the death of St. Chantal, but I could not manage it. All the lads of my catechism class carried my bundles with remarkable alacrity in spite of the rain that poured all day. Not one of them stole a thing. I thought my only companion would be a poor girl of twelve whom I had instructed in religion, for Madame Faucherand had written me that she had had a slight hemorrhage and thought it only charity to wait until Easter in order to give her Sisters time to make up their minds. I replied that I was not going to put off for a single hour my return to that holy place for which I longed so earnestly, and that it was time to show the world that it had lied in daring to say that we had been kept in the cloister as victims of force and that we were glad to be back in secular life.

Then I hastened to leave my apartment. Late in the evening, in a storm of wind and rain, I reached Sainte Marie in the wake of my baggage, which the care-taker had put in safety. I was not as badly drenched as my poor little boys. Water streamed from their clothes, but every face beamed with pleasure, an indication, I took it, of our Lord's approval. Madame Faucherand, realizing that I was determined to carry out my plan, had got up courage and reached the house some hours sooner than I. In spite of my happiness at having a companion, I was a bit put out, for I had to sleep in the room with her to quiet her fears. My dearest wish had been to spend the night in the august sanctuary where for so many years the Name of the Lord had not been hallowed. I wanted to have the whole night for prayer, enjoying God's favors and giving him my humble thanks.

The building was without lock and key, but I was not afraid, for I realized that as God had been my guide, so he would be my protector until I had had time to assure us of safety. I got to work on this at once, and my days were spent either with the workmen doing repairs, or cooking meals for the community of two, or sweeping parts of the house that had not been cleaned for nearly ten years, or shoveling out snow and mopping up water, or trying to repair the window-panes—the most thankless task of all, for the paste froze immediately I put it on and would not stick and gave me plenty of occasions to exercise my patience. With the exception of this one task, all the labor in the house was pleasure for me. I experienced all the consolations that St. Teresa had when sweeping her monastery. Never had the keenest worldly pleasure given me such satisfaction. We went for our spiritual duties to the church, where three windows and a door were missing. The cold was intense, but we did not feel it and neither one of us took cold.

At the end of two weeks we finally had the first Mass offered in the church. The outer door was still closed. As no priest could come for Mass on Christmas day, we went to assist at midnight Mass in the city, accompanied by a young girl who had been with us only for a few days and a workman who had formerly been a brother at the *Grande Chartreuse* and who was always a kind friend of the house. We had made habits for ourselves, and they were blessed before Mass. We took them afterwards as a present from the Infant Jesus, and I had mine on two days later when we had a visit from Monseigneur Spina, Archbishop of Corinth, and

Monseigneur Caselli, both of whom are cardinals today [1805]. They had finished their work on the concordat. . . .

Realizing by this time that if I was going to get companions at all they would have to come from different orders or be seculars contemplating religious life, I came to the conclusion that there should be a Rule we might propose to new-comers. The Visitandine Rule of Sainte Marie could not be observed strictly just then, but many parts of it could be put into practice. I gave a copy to Father Brochier, begging him to indicate the articles of the Rule that should be observed and those that might be modified for the present. He consented to do this and composed a Rule very wisely planned, which kept the interior spirit of Sainte Marie: seclusion, detachment, obedience, all things in common, but was outwardly less strict. He wished a superior to be elected for a year as soon as there were four in the group; then a superior elected for three years, according to the Rule, as soon as there were twelve of us and we could be more sure in our choice. . . .

This Rule, from which I had hoped such great things, produced the worst effect. The religious criticized it loudly, especially the article on all things being held in common, which they found simply impossible. They had no scruple about retaining the ownership of their belongings, yet they raised an outcry about the overthrow of the Rule because the order of day was not exactly as it had been formerly and the election was slightly different. "Our former Superior is alive," they said, "why speak of electing another?" They did not consider the fact that there was no question of a superior for the religious who were still dispersed, but only for those who would come to the convent, which must have a head. Another article of the Rule answered all their objections, as it expressly stated that as soon as circumstances allowed, all the proposed changes would give way to strict observance of the former Rule. . . .

The majority [of the former Visitandines] did not come to celebrate the feast of St. Francis de Sales with us at Sainte Marie, but went instead to a private oratory, and after Mass assembled *to protest against what they called the measures taken by Madame Duchesne.* They then acquainted some of the vicars-general with that protest. I was in complete ignorance of what was going on and I enjoyed the greatest consolation on that feast of St. Francis de Sales [January 29]. Several priests of high standing came to offer the Mass for us with the joyous enthusiasm that holy souls experience at the sight of a work begun that may bring glory to God. The public entrance of the Church was still closed, but the people came in crowds by the interior of the monastery, and our church was the first in Grenoble in which Catholic worship reappeared in all its splendor after the revolution.

Some days later I learned that I was considered an intruder. I said this jokingly to my companion [Madame Faucherand], who had been joined by a young girl and an out-sister. Her mind was somewhat unbalanced and in former days she had had some mental lapses. . . . One morning, feeling ill, she told me she needed a change of environment; she left the house and did not return to live with me again. I felt this keenly, and all the more because it presaged further departures. . . . I went through some very bitter hours in view of all this, though I still counted a little on Mother de Murinais. She had told everyone that I had done nothing in the matter of recovering possession of the house without her consent and that she intended to keep her word and return to the monastery. Many people even told her that it was a point of honor for her to do so, especially since her letter to Monsieur du Bouchage [the prefect of Grenoble] was generally known. The former confessor of the house was of that opinion. He was her director, and I chose him, too, thinking that since the house was to be re-established, this was a point of rule for me. . . . There were certain people who feared to have Mother de Murinais return to Sainte Marie. They . . . urged me to write to her not to come. . . . I firmly refused to write such a letter, considering it contrary to the good of the institution and to general edification. It would, moreover, confirm the suspicions of those who said I wanted to dominate everything.

The gossip and criticism current in Grenoble through the winter of 1801–1802 were not the least part of the trial that Philippine was enduring. In a letter to her sister Euphrosine, written on February 14, 1802, she revealed her own reaction quite frankly, along with her affectionate interest in the Jouve family:

How relieved I am, my dear Sister, to learn that your children are recovering. Two days ago I had a letter from Melanie which left me little hope for the life of your Euphrosine. I have been thinking of you constantly and was about to write you a letter of sympathy when yours arrived, telling me that God has heard your tears and prayers and spared your daughter. . . .

You are very kind to take an interest in the difficulties inseparable from an undertaking such as ours. What I feel most keenly is the opposition of some persons from whom I had expected gratitude. I have gotten myself talked about, both favorably and unfavorably; but as I did not act through worldly motives, I am not upset by blame nor elated by praise. I want that to come from God alone and from the indescribable joy of finding myself once more in his House. As to the repairs needed, they are very extensive. But Providence, always so generous to us, has inspired some zealous people to contribute funds; and if we succeed, I know many others who will help us. My confidence increases when I reflect on the charity already shown me. . . . At present there are just four of us; but at Easter I expect Mother de Murinais and several religious who have reserved their rooms. We are making good use of our garden and hope to profit by what we raise. The church is charming, but Mass is still celebrated behind closed doors. We had six Masses on the feast of St. Francis de Sales and two sermons, one given by Father Brochier, who is greatly interested in our work and a counselor in both spiritual and temporal affairs. *Adieu,* my dear and loving friend.

Philippine had relied more on the presence of Mother de Murinais at Sainte Marie than on any other human factor. At one time this religious had been an excellent superior, firm and motherly, valiant in trial and persecution. She had kept in touch with many members of her dispersed community and had encouraged the project of rehabilitation. But she was past eighty years of age now, sickly, infirm, dependent in many ways on those around her and easily swayed by those who showed her personal attentions. Her arrival at Sainte Marie marked a short-lived triumph for Philippine, as she herself relates:

Finally Mother de Murinais decided to come during Passion Week, with a young nun who laid down the condition that she should have no employment but the care of the superior's health. She also brought with her two lay-sisters, one of whom was about eighty years of age, as was also Mother de Murinais. I had been joined a few days before by a new companion, an Ursuline nun, who was really only a boarder. The young girl had left at once.

At this time Father Rivet gave a retreat in our church. It was very well attended, though the public entrance was still closed. We made bold to open it on Holy Thursday, and it has remained open ever since, as has also that of the hospital, which was opened even before ours. It was a great joy for me to lead into our choir, in the presence of so many people, the venerable Mother for whom I had waited so long. It was a triumph. I had reasoned that her arrival would produce a very good effect on outsiders, would please my family, who really suffered because of my solitary position and the heavy [financial] burden of the house, and would edify the public who were gossiping about the indifference of religious who did not take advantage of the cloister opened to them. I hoped, too, that a boarding school would be established. I limited my hopes to that when Mother arrived.

Certainly things were better than before, but they in no way came up to my expectations of a religious institution. We had only Office in choir and meditation; there was no silence, no religious practices, . . . no cloister, no uniformity of dress, nothing. There was not even question of introducing these gradually. They all said they were just making a trial of it, for they had not made up their minds to persevere even in so easy a manner of life. . . . In the depths of my heart I experienced much bitter anguish, realizing what all this augured for the near future. But while all this was in no way satisfactory, I was more distressed by the illness of the superior, which seemed to justify the predictions that a change of residence at her age would be fatal, and indeed they were already blaming me for her death. She recovered. I thought God intended to spare me, but he was really preparing me for a still greater affliction. . . . Afterwards I told the confessor that I had wept bitterly when I realized with what intentions they had come, and that there was no hope that the government of the house would be firm enough to enforce the mildest rule, verging really on disorder. He shook his head and replied *that I had not wept enough, that I had but begun to weep, and that I must realize that it was enough for me to propose a thing to have it rejected, but that I must arm myself with courage.*

The spring and summer of 1802 brought to Philippine Duchesne some of the deepest anguish her soul was to experience. All she had hoped for, prayed for, worked for—all seemed utterly wasted. The fervent love that burned in her heart and urged her to a life of strict observance, penance, reparation, prayer, made the situation all the more unbearable. The inspiration she had interpreted as coming directly from the Heart of Christ seemed to mock her by the failure with which she was surrounded. Had she again misunderstood the designs of his Heart in her regard?

An agony of doubt and desolation pressed upon her at times as she went about her duties, silent, recollected, uncomplaining, where all about her murmured against the hardships inevitable in such an enterprise. And her very fervor, acting as a reproach to others, brought severe reprimands and sharp criticisms upon her. Had the situation been kept a community affair, there might have been some chance of its improving, but this was not the case. All Grenoble seems to have known what was happening at Sainte Marie.

It was also discussing the conduct of Pierre-François Duchesne that spring and summer. The republican element in Dauphiny admired him greatly for his political courage and acumen. He had escaped the purge of the Tribunate in 1801, but matters moved swiftly to a climax in the following year. In both the Council of Five Hundred and the Tribunate he steered a middle course on principle, now fighting a bill for the return of the *émigrés,* now upholding the right of former nobles to hold public office. He made a sensation on April 27, 1802, by attacking a projected law relative to public education, though he knew the First Consul himself had had a hand in its formulation, and by accusing the government of trying to keep the poorer classes in ignorance. Two weeks later, on May 10, Napoleon proposed himself as consul for life. The Assembly resigned in a body. Three members of the legislative body, whose names are unrecorded, voted "no." In the Tribunate only Lazare Carnot and Pierre-François Duchesne dared to voice their opposition to the dictator. This vote marked the close of Duchesne's political career at the age of sixty years.

Resigning office almost immediately, he returned with his son to Grâne. The younger Duchesne was in perfect agreement with the stand his father had taken, though he realized that for them both it meant the sacrifice of careers which would have accorded with their tastes and for which they were excellently fitted. Later on, after his father's death, young Duchesne would again appear in political life. Even under the Empire the electoral college of the department of the Drôme honored Pierre-François Duchesne by choosing him for the Senate, but the Emperor Napoleon vetoed the choice on personal grounds and Duchesne remained for several years at Grâne.

When he reached there in the summer of 1802, the news he received about Philippine must have caused him anxiety, for he had grown sympathetic with her holy ambitions and had given her some financial aid, as the Periers and Savoye-Rollins were doing. Her description of life at Sainte Marie during these months continues:

> The household was composed of a superior who, in order to attract subjects, accepted all types of character, or rather yielded in turn to each of several religious who were doing each as she pleased, and to some young girls who were boarding pupils. When the superior first came, I asked her what employment she assigned to me. She replied that I was to remain in charge of the repair work being done on the building, the sacristy, the portry, and of one pupil. . . . I realized that wills were unstable. Often there was such coldness toward me, I foresaw the break-up of the community. I did not want to have the least thing with which to reproach myself for having contributed to this, but everything

tended that way. . . . A few days later I learned that they were planning to leave, but did not want me to know it. One of the Sisters who was loyal to me came to tell me what she had learned. I hastened to throw myself at the feet of Mother de Murinais in an effort to keep her, but . . . she held firmly to her resolution. . . . On the feast of St. de Chantal I probed the depths of my soul to determine whether some passion, some selfish interest, some resentment kept me from taking the steps necessary to prevent the scandal of a rupture in the community. It seemed to me I could say I would in all sincerity submit myself entirely even to the person who had made me suffer the most, if only she willed to enforce the strict observance of the Rule, and I begged St. de Chantal to be judge between me and her daughters. That thought occupied me all during the High Mass, and I offered myself to God, being willing even to leave Sainte Marie if I was the obstacle to the good that could be accomplished there. But I knew that if I left the cloister, not a single person would remain, and so I resigned myself to being practically alone again.

That very day I learned secretly that they were leaving me in just four days, on August 26. And at just this very moment of bitterness God sent me a great consolation. Father Rivet, who knew how matters stood in the house, suggested the possibility of some of the Dilette [from Rome] coming to Sainte Marie. At the first mention I was strongly attracted to that recently founded order; and had it not been for my agreement with the government and my desire to prove to the world, in the very face of the collapse of our efforts, that the yoke of Jesus Christ was my happiness in spite of so much trouble, I would have asked to be allowed to go to Rome at once.

On August 25, the feast of St. Louis of France, Mother de Murinais sent for me to tell me they were leaving the next morning. She was quite calm and spoke kindly to me. I have since thought that God took from her all regret in order that I might act more freely in a greater enterprise. I replied to Mother by tears rather than by words, and I expressed the hope of seeing her return, but she offered me not the least encouragement on that score, saying that she was too old for such undertakings and that they called for youth and courage like mine.

On August 27 I found myself left with a select few—an Ursuline nun, Sister Giraud, then a boarding student, who had come to the school on the feast of St. Aloysius Gonzaga [June 21, 1802], a fact to which I called her attention that very day as an exceedingly good sign, and one lay-sister, a former novitiate companion of mine, who got her sister to come and help her with the work, and six or eight pupils. I was crushed. I was a subject of scandal.

Gossip had it that I had driven away the religious, that I would not yield in anything, that no one could bear to live with me, that Fathers Brochier and Rivet with their high-flown ideas were the only ones who took my part. The latter came to see me on that day of greatest affliction and pointed out to me that on just such a day St. Teresa had begun her reform and that all the city had risen up against her. He also wrote at once to Father Roger to inform him that the house was now free, if he could only induce Father Varin to send some religious. But that grace had to be merited by a long delay. Meanwhile God consoled me very much by the coming of Madame Rivet [Father Rivet's sister Marie]. After making a retreat with us she decided to join our group and came on the feast of All Saints. Just before Christmas we were joined by Mademoiselle Balastron.

As there were now four of us (the Ursuline still wanted to remain free), we begged Father Brochier and Rivet to form us into a little society, as there was no prospect that the ladies whom we were awaiting would come soon. Father Rivet had offered to take charge of the direction of the house. Then Father Brochier was named our ecclesiastical superior by the bishop. He made some changes in his first Rule, gave us temporarily the name of *Daughters of the Propagation of the Faith*, and on March 3, 1803, received our simple vows of chastity and obedience at the moment of Communion, after having preached a very touching exhortation. After Mass, Madame Rivet was named superior and I had the tremendous consolation of seeing at last in that holy house a form of religious life and the practices customary in communities. We had not given up the recitation of Office even when we were only two. Our boarding school increased to sixteen or eighteen and we spent several months in that uniform and peaceful life.

Our peace was disturbed at times by the fear that the house would be taken for a seminary. . . . Kind relatives who had secured the good will of the prefect toward us also parried the blows and even succeeded in saving me from paying a single sou of rent for the house. Although we were quite happy together, we always aspired to join a larger religious society in which we could do more for God. So when Father Rivet was going to Bellay to make a retreat, we begged him to plead with Father Varin to admit us into the order of the *Ladies of the Faith* and to send us one of those religious as superior. Father Varin instructed Father Roger to come to Grenoble to examine the people and the place, and he gave us hope of a speedy accomplishment of our desires.

Soon the Holy Spirit made Father Varin understand *that he is opposed to delay*, and that a decision in our regard must be given, since the humble St. Francis Regis, who had become our protector, deserved that for love of him the Fathers of the Faith should not despise what was worth very little. After that inspiration Father Varin sent us word that he was coming to celebrate the feast of St. Ignatius with us. He and Father Roger arrived on the eve [July 30, 1804]. After Mass next morning they went through the whole house. I took my place directly behind Father Varin so I could hear all he might say and note any least sign he might give of satisfaction or disapproval. But there is no knowing the thoughts of these people who are so completely self-controlled, and I, who am not of this type, began to be not a little irritated.

When he came to the chapel of the Sacred Heart of Jesus, he exclaimed, "Ah, here we see what makes religious life at the Visitation appeal so sweetly to souls." That was not what I wanted at all. Father Roger gave me no more satisfaction than Father Varin did. When I asked him why they had made this trip [to Grenoble], he said, "We came to see Father Rivet." I thought to myself that for men so completely detached from all earthly things this was yielding a good deal to friendship. That evening at Benediction the Holy Spirit inspired Father Varin with a decision completely in our favor, but he kept that to himself. When Father Roger, however, suggested that I should note the fact that we had celebrated the feast of St. Ignatius together, his superior added that he was considering that augury. . . .

Well, the morrow dawned. Madame Rivet and I went again to see the two priests after Mass. Father Varin spoke to me again of *Holy Indifference and of the slowness* with which the works of God are accomplished. I think I answered him that, on the contrary, Holy Scripture represents him as *racing with giant strides,* and I followed this up with the statement that had St. Francis Xavier acted with such deliberation before undertaking good works he would never have accomplished them nor done so much in so short a time. The Father laughed at my vehemence and agreed that I was right and that he must send Madame Barat to found a convent for us as soon as possible. This consoling promise lifted at last from my heart that heavy mountain of uncertainty that had weighed me down for so long. That was a day of joyous happiness. In the afternoon I had a private interview with Father Varin which was very helpful, and on the following day, before leaving, he assured us that we could depend on his promises. He urged us to pray for the health of our future Mother, and we did so frequently with all our hearts.

During the weeks that followed this visit the soul of Philippine Duchesne was disturbed by conflicting emotions. The upsurge of joyous hope gave way to impatience at delay and fear of disappointment, and she gave vent to her feelings in letters to **Father** Varin. From Lyons he wrote on August 15 to reassure her:

> I do not need to repeat to you that I shall use all interest and zeal in co-operating with the plans of Divine Providence for your house. *I would sooner forget my right hand than the project about which we came to an agreement.* . . . I shall hasten matters, in as much as they depend on me; help me by your prayers in the delicate business I have on hand. I count also on the prayers of Madame Rivet and your other companions. Every day I offer you and them in the Holy Sacrifice of the Mass.

Soon he was writing from Amiens:

> Madame Barat will leave here early in October to fulfil the promise I made you. She will take two of her young companions with her. They will be accompanied by a priest who, I assure you, is worthy of all your confidence. It is a great sacrifice for me to let him leave me, but I shall be repaid by the services he will render to your house, and I shall do my best to see for myself how things are going just as soon as possible.

There were further delays which Philippine could not understand and which she could scarcely bear. "That was one of the most painful periods Madame Rivet and I ever endured," she commented. Early in November, however, she could record:

> At last there was an end to the trial. A letter from Father Varin, written on October 25, gave us courage again: . . .
> "Madame, I wrote to you a few days ago, and my letter—since it left still some uncertainty at least about the departure of those whom you so greatly desire—my letter, I say, could not have given you full satisfaction. *I do so love to give you some consolation that I am not waiting for your answer before telling you something positive.*
> "Every day I feel urged to fulfill your hopes. I see by Madame Barat's last letter that she too shares these sentiments of mine. . . . Your perseverance and that of your companions in the project of reunion which we decided upon is a sign to me that the dear Lord will bless its execution. I shall leave on Monday for Amiens, and I hope in a very short time to announce to you the day on which your friends will set out for Grenoble. Remember, I did not deceive you when I assured you that I took your interests as much to heart as if they were my own and that your religious family will be as dear to me as my own. . . ."

Recalling the joy and gratitude that letter brought her Philippine continued:

> From the time I was twelve years and some months old, when God gave me the grace of a religious vocation, I believe I never let pass a single day without praying to him to enlighten me about it and make me faithful to it. From the beginning I put it under the protection of the Blessed Virgin, and the Memorare was my favorite and continual prayer to her. The many favors I received through the intercession of St. Francis Regis had inclined me to pray more directly to him. But during my retreat I read how the Carmelites of St. Denis, at a time when their monastery was about to be closed, were saved by the entrance of Madame Louise into their community as a result of a novena to the Blessed Virgin, in whose loving protection they had the utmost confidence. It seemed to me that I had in a way neglected this dear Mother of Mercy, so I begged her pardon, addressing her as mediatrix of all graces, and I begged her to obtain for us an end to our painful uncertainty. I asked Madame Rivet to have the entire household make a novena of fasts, Communion, and prayers in honor of our Lady. This was done, and before the close of the novena we received the assurance of at last being admitted into the Society [of the Sacred Heart] and of undisputed ownership of our monastery. . . . This last piece of news was not really true . . . and at any other time knowledge of this fact would have crushed me, but Father Varin's letter had brought such joy to my soul that I really felt the weight of my happiness needed some counter-balance. And I had in the depths of my heart the hope that the house was assured to us by the will of Heaven.

The autumn of 1804 had brought Philippine another joy, a further proof of the love and confidence of her family, when her sister, Madame Jouve, entrusted to her the education of her eight-year-old daughter Euphrosine. The child was delicate and precocious. Her adjustment to strict discipline and formal school life was difficult, but in time she developed into one of Sainte Marie's outstanding pupils. She was one of the little group of pupils whom her Aunt Philippine mentions when describing those who welcomed Mother Barat to the old monastery in December, 1804:

> The community was at this time composed of four persons whom I have already named [Madame Rivet, Emilie Giraud, Marie Balastron, and Philippine herself], along with Mademoiselle Second, . . . two widows who resided with us, an Ursuline religious on the same footing, that is, following exteriorly the same spiritual exercises as we but not bound to dependence or to our Rule as far as personal

conduct was concerned; there were also twenty boarding pupils and five girls helping with domestic work. . . . Besides our individual employments, all helped in the boarding school except Mademoiselle Second and the Ursuline, who conducted the free school for the poor of Jesus Christ. For more than two years Father Rivet had helped us with the boarding school; he said Mass for us daily and his zeal was untiring. He increased the solemnity of our liturgical feasts by inviting many priests to take part in them and to preach, and twice the Bishop [Msgr. Claude Simon] honored us with his presence. . . .

three

Under the Guidance
of a Saint

I. 1804—1805

THE RELIGIOUS ORDER to which Philippine Duchesne and
her companions had asked admission was only four years old when
its foundress arrived at Sainte Marie to organize her second community. She had been guided in her work by Father Joseph Varin,
who had inherited from the saintly Léonor de Tournély a legacy
of inspiration and obligation which he held as a sacred trust.
Tournély had gathered about him a group of priests bearing at
first the name of *Fathers of the Sacred Heart,* then the safer title
of *Fathers of the Faith,* and ambitioning the resurgence of the
Society of Jesus. Before his death in 1797, he had confided to his
followers a vivid inspiration received in prayer—the founding of a
congregation of women consecrated to the Sacred Heart of Jesus
to help in the regeneration of France by a contemplative life, to
which the activities of teaching and directing retreats would be
added.

From a mustard-seed beginning in Paris in 1800—four members,
only two of them persevering in the venture—the association had
increased encouragingly at Amiens, where the first convent was
opened in 1801. By the autumn of 1803, Father Varin was writing
to the frail and timid superior, who was known as Madame Barat:
"It will soon be absolutely necessary to open a second house, for

74

there are other postulants who are, or seem to be, fitted for you, and where shall we put them?" When Father Roger visited Sainte Marie in the spring of 1804, he was completely noncommittal on the subject of merging the two communities.

On returning to Lyons, however, he made so favorable a report to his superior that, in July, Father Varin decided to visit the old monastery and see things for himself. While rejoicing in the outcome of that visit, Philippine Duchesne little suspected the impression she had made, but within a week Father Varin was writing to Madame Barat: "On this trip I have made a fine acquisition for you, but it seems to require your presence. Can you cut yourself in four?" Six days later he added:

> There is no need, my dear Sister, to cut yourself in four, but only in two. I can hear you exclaiming, "My God, how can I? It is already so difficult to carry on this little establishment. And if the whole does so badly, what will a half do?" . . . O soul of little faith, why do you doubt? Our Lord will see to it that each half will equal the whole. Only have confidence.

There was much to be done at Amiens before Madame Barat could undertake the trip to Grenoble, and she pleaded for delay. Faithful to his promise, however, Father Varin continued to urge the acceptance of Sainte Marie, writing from Paris on October 6:

> Pray and get others to pray. Bolster up your own courage with lively confidence, and in holy abandonment hurl yourself headlong into the arms of our Lord Jesus Christ. I wrote to Mademoiselle Duchesne today. Her letter gave me much pleasure. Oh, I am sadly mistaken if she is not a great and generous soul. . . . When you know her, you will say, "Now there is one, indeed."

A few days later Father Varin was at Amiens. He found the little community quite at home in the Convent of the Oratory, to which they had transferred the previous September. He knew the place well, for the Fathers of the Faith had but recently vacated it. Assembling the household, he put before them his plans for the new establishment. There was hesitation on the part of the nuns. They argued their poverty and lack of personnel for such an undertaking.

"You could certainly spare two or three," the priest insisted. "You, for example," and he looked straight at Madame Barat, "and this novice," he indicated Rosalie Debrosse, "and you should take Sister Maillard along." He knew what a treasure she was. Ignoring the astonishment shown on every face, he continued earnestly:

"You will find some companions there—especially one. If she were alone and at the remotest corner of the world, you should go after her." Then he spoke with such enthusiastic admiration of Philippine Duchesne, with such supernatural conviction as to the designs of Almighty God in her regard, that all fear and hesitation vanished and the plan was courageously accepted. It was decided that Madame Baudemont would fill the post of superior during Madame Barat's absence, which would begin after the ceremony of first vows on November 21.

In the meanwhile the tempo of life had quickened considerably at Sainte Marie. There were preparations to be made, further repairs to be completed, school duties to be carried on, letters to be written, negotiations with the government to be pressed, hopes and fears and anxieties to be entrusted to the Sacred Heart. At recreation they rehearsed what they knew of Madame Barat: she was a peasant from a small place in Burgundy, the province just north of Dauphiny. Her priest-brother, Louis, several years older than she, had given her an education far above the ordinary level for girls in those days. He was one of the Fathers of the Faith, but he had been a professor at the seminary of Sens and had narrowly escaped the guillotine during the Terror. Madame Barat's name was Madeleine Louise Sophie—she had signed just "Sophie Barat" at the end of her letter to Madame Rivet. She had completed her studies under her brother's guidance in Paris after the Revolution— her mother had not wanted this, but Louis had his way—and she was planning to become a Carmelite when Father Varin met her. Her appearance was not very impressive, for she was slight and shy and plainly dressed; but he had recognized in her the person needed to carry out the inspiration of Léonor de Tournély and to found an order of religious women completely devoted to the Sacred Heart of Jesus and having the glory of this Divine Heart as their sole purpose in life.

It was always hard to get further than that point in the story: love for Jesus Christ, complete consecration to him through love, no other motive but love for him, no other purpose but the glory of his Sacred Heart. . . . It was well that prayer and silence always followed these recreations. Such thoughts and aspirations carried these ardent women out of themselves with joy. Even talkative Marie Balastron and lively Emilie Giraud fell silent and drew deep breaths and longed more intensely for the day when Madame Barat would come.

Winter had set in and fires were blazing in a few wide chimney-places at Sainte Marie when the courier from Lyons rode up the steep street and turned in at the monastery with the letter from Amiens dated November 2 and addressed to Madame Rivet. It was the first greeting from Madame Barat, and reading it, the five women who awaited her felt that they knew her and belonged to her. They counted the days till November 21—then she would start on her journey. How long would it take her to reach Grenoble?

The fourth birthday of the Society of the Sacred Heart was celebrated at Amiens with mixed emotions. Catherine de Charbonnel, Marie du Terrail, and Rosalie Debrosse pronounced their first vows with joyous fervor in the presence of Father Varin and Madame Barat. The day brought an extra amount of work, for the final preparations had to be made for the departure next morning. Even short trips were not very common in France in those days, and it was something of a journey to go by public coach from Amiens in Picardy to Grenoble, six hundred miles away.

The party made it in four stages: to Paris first, where business kept them two days; then to Joigny, where they spent a week at the home in which Sophie Barat had been born and raised. The attic room, the vineyards on the hillside, the church of St. Thibaut in which she had been baptized, all were of interest to her companions. There were many relatives and friends to greet, and Sophie could have long talks with her parents and her sister, Madame Dusaussoy. There was a stop-over in Lyons, with letters from Father Varin, one dwelling on the central figure in the group at Sainte Marie.

> Have really lively faith [he wrote], faith that will pierce the heavens, that will open to you the Heart of our Lord and reveal to you what an abyss of goodness and mercy it is. That realization will fill you with wonder, and courage, and confidence. Then you will be that valiant woman who is so difficult to find. *Mulierem fortem quis inveniet? Procul. . . .* Who will find a valiant woman. . . . Afar off? . . . You will not need to go further than Grenoble to find her.

Madame Barat had already found her when he wrote another eulogy of that valiant woman whom so many women had failed to appreciate, but whom holy priests and prelates of the Church recognized at her true worth in the midst of many an apparent failure: "I have not misled you by the way I have praised your future companion. I tell you again: *there* is a soul worthy to serve our Lord. Here in Paris I have met many people who have known her. All esteem her highly and no one speaks of her except with great admiration."

The diligence from Lyons usually rumbled into Grenoble in the middle of the morning. The town, with its drab, slate-colored buildings grouped together in varied and curious heights and shapes, its labyrinth of narrow streets and squares and bridges over the swift Isère that divided it, was of interest to Madame Barat, who was seeing it for the first time. She was a woman on whom details were seldom lost. "There, *en haut,*" a fellow passenger in the coach may have indicated, "is Sainte Marie," and the young superior would have got her first glimpse of the old monastery and church, a gaunt and forbidding pile. She felt very young. Just the day before she had passed her twenty-fifth birthday, and it was with the greatest self-diffidence that she was undertaking to mother this new group. She had, according to her own account, never seen a cloistered monastery until she rode into Grenoble that thirteenth day of December, 1804.

As the stagecoach ascended the narrow street leading up to and beyond Sainte Marie, she was astonished at the grandeur of the setting, the snow-covered Alps, and the view of the city and valley below. It was just eleven o'clock when she and her companions turned into the narrow passage between high walls that led up a terraced slope to the doorway opening into a deep vestibule. They entered a dimly lighted corridor that seemed more chilly and damp than the street outside. Suddenly a slender figure in black came swiftly toward them, and before Mother Barat realized what was happening, Philippine Duchesne was prostrate before her, kissing her feet and repeating the psalmist's words: "How lovely on the mountain are the feet of those who bring the gospel of peace!"

"I let her do it through pure stupefaction," Mother Barat used to say, as she told of their first meeting. "I was utterly dumbfounded at the sight of such faith and humility, and I did not know what to say or do."

There are few scenes more touching in the lives of the saints than that of the frail little woman in her plain traveling bonnet and shawl, a satchel in one hand, a bundle or two under her arms, gazing down in wide-eyed amazement at the prostrate figure before her. It all happened so quickly that Philippine was on her feet again, giving a more conventional welcome to Father Roger and Abbé Coidy, to Rosalie Debrosse and Marguerite Maillard, before her companions reached the entrance door. It was all very simple and informal. Father Roger installed Mother Barat as superior and settled details with Abbé Coidy, who was to act as chaplain and confessor. There had been question of a retreat for the community before Christmas, but Mother Barat considered it wiser to postpone it for awhile, so that the members of the little family might learn to know one another and a cordial union of minds and hearts might be established from the very beginning. So Father Roger went back to Lyons, leaving Mother Barat to guide the foundation as best she could. He had no fear as to how she would accomplish her task.

Philippine and Madame Rivet were at home with her at once, and Marie Balastron was quickly won. Cecile Second was still somewhat ill at ease in her monastic surroundings, while Emilie Giraud avoided her new superior, allowing groundless fears to keep her at a distance for some time. The wisdom, tact, and maturity with which Mother Barat handled them all gave proof of the sanctity she brought to her work. She studied her new daughters as she came in contact with them in the cloister, at recreation, at household tasks or school duties, and as she knelt with them in the choir. She made them the subject of her prayer, holding each close to the Heart of Christ and begging for the grace that would enable her to develop in them the spirit and virtues that must characterize all who would be true members of her little society: prayer and interior life, generosity and cordial charity, along with boundless zeal in the service of the Sacred Heart. It was a sublime vocation, and she knew the heights to which Father Varin expected her to lead Philippine Duchesne.

The day after Mother Barat's arrival, Philippine wrote to her sister, Madame Jouve, a hasty, happy note in which she said:

> What a joy it was to recognize your writing on one of the letters handed to me a few days ago. This was proof that you had recovered. . . . Euphrosine is not writing to you today, as the schedule in the school is somewhat upset by the arrival of the three religious who have come to us from Amiens. Father Roger accompanied them from Lyons. It looks as if we have been most fortunate in getting them here. One of them is to be our superior. She has won all hearts by her cordial manner. . . .

The formal opening of the novitiate was deferred until Mother Barat had initiated the little group into some of the ways and customs already established in the new society. The season of Advent

gave her an opportunity to stress silence, recollection, and detachment. At the age of thirty-five, Philippine found herself once more
a "beginner" in a spiritual school whose lessons were based on the
same fundamental teachings as those she had first learned in the
Visitation cloister. The *Journal of Sainte Marie* shows how the
little community received these lessons from their new Mother:

> As the feast of Christmas drew near, the contemplation of Jesus in
> his manger-bed naturally occupied our thoughts. . . . Our Mother
> put him before us in all his attractive loveliness. At recreation she
> placed on her table a little figure of this Divine Savior in order to
> teach us to center our love on him as she did. She suggested the
> practice of offering to him whatever we were most attached to. . . .
> Jesus received these first sacrifices through the hands of our
> superior and in her presence in order that, giving her our complete
> confidence, we might be more pleasing in the sight of him who is
> the perfect model of religious dependence and detachment.

The poverty and suffering of the Christ Child were reproduced
at Sainte Marie in many ways. The stable at Bethlehem was
scarcely more open to wind and weather than were some parts of
the old monastery, in spite of all that had been done to make it
more habitable. The snow drifted in freely where doors and windows were still lacking. The cold was intense and there was no
means of heating many parts of the building. In the community
room an open fire-place gave a cheery glow as the nuns sat together
at spiritual reading or at recreation, and small charcoal braziers
were sometimes lighted in their sleeping quarters or hot bricks
placed in the beds to insure warmth enough for sleep.

To Philippine all this seemed as nothing. She had become accustomed to it, and her fairly robust health was not affected then
by such privations. In fact, she scarcely adverted to them at all.
But to Mother Barat and the others in the community they were
a source of suffering that supplied them many hours of corporal
penance. Yet all was accepted with joy and generous love.

The novitiate was formally opened on the last day of 1804. By
that time Mother Barat had become well enough acquainted with
her new community to begin the spiritual training which was the
chief purpose of her coming to Sainte Marie. While the work of
the two small schools had to be carried on—there were seventeen
boarding pupils and twenty in the free school—this was not allowed
to absorb more time than necessary, and the daily schedule was so
arranged as to give time for the instructions and conferences by
which Mother Barat was to initiate her novices into the way of life

and prayer already characteristic of the order. Before she began her work at Grenoble, Father Varin had written to her: "To gain souls for God or to train them for him, one must have, not a little, ordinary soul, but one as great, as vast, as the ocean." As a New Year's greeting in 1805 he wrote: "No compliments, but some wishes: that you may work and suffer for Jesus Christ, and never withhold from him a single instant of your life; that you may die in his love and reign eternally with him."

The difficulties confronting Mother Barat in the first weeks of that year arose from several causes. She was having her first experience of founding a convent by adapting an old one to the new mode of religious life which seemed better suited to the times. She was also dealing with women of widely different ages, education, and spiritual training. Emilie Giraud and Marie Balastron were just past twenty-one, Jeanne-Cecile Second was not much older, while Marie Rivet and Philippine Duchesne were mature in age and experience. The younger members of the group had had little formal schooling and not much religious instruction, while the two older novices were already leading deep interior lives based on solid religious formation. Yet all had to be initiated into the ways and methods accepted in the new society, and a fresh start made for each new postulant.

In the matter of prayer the Ignatian methods of meditation and examen had been adopted. These differed somewhat from the forms prescribed in the Benedictine order, to which Marie Rivet had belonged, and in the school of St. Francis de Sales. While superficial critics have judged them formal, even mechanical, the intelligent application of the directions given by St. Ignatius leads to the development, in each individual soul, of a personal manner of prayer that allows the fullest flowering of the spiritual life in response to the attractions of grace. And it was to prayer that Mother Barat directed her novices before all else. Faithful to Father Varin's teaching, she felt that a transformation could be effected only in the measure in which love of the Sacred Heart grew in the hearts of her daughters. To enkindle that love more ardently and to inspire them to feed its flame by prayer and sacrifice was her constant aim. The generosity with which they responded to her suggestions made her grateful to God and careful to guard against imprudence.

Many things had to be changed at Sainte Marie—traditional ways of acting, customs belonging to Visitandine life—and this called for tactful handling on the part of the young superior. Old ties had to be broken, but in the breaking there should be no shock or irritation, no impression of substituting a better way, but only a more suitable method for the purpose and work in hand. Mother Barat took as a guiding principle a sentence written to her by Father Varin shortly after her arrival at Sainte Marie: "Firmness when it is needed, harshness never, kindness and charity everywhere and always."

Keenly sensitive herself, she realized how costly for Philippine Duchesne would be the changes now being planned for the old monastery. The cloister choir was to become an open chapel; the grilles would disappear; the time-honored pronoun *our*, so expressive of dependent communal poverty, would drop from the community vocabulary; and many little formalities would disappear from daily life. "Should these sacrifices be imposed gradually or at once?" asked the young foundress. From Father Varin she received this wise advice: "Where a reform is undertaken, patience is needed more than ardor, prudence more than zeal. You must begin gently and so gain hearts. The rest will come in time and in detail, without protest or disturbance."

On January 11 Father Roger opened the novices' retreat, giving the meditations and conferences in a little oratory above the sacristy, where the Blessed Sacrament was reserved. The house still bore all the exterior marks of a cloistered monastery, but he was acquainted with the remodeling that was planned to bring it into conformity with the type of life and work envisioned for members of the Society of the Sacred Heart. To achieve this purpose, he explained, the religious would present outwardly to the world far less poverty and austerity than had been the custom in monastic orders before the Revolution, but within the privacy of the cloister there would be the same severely simple furnishings, communal use of possessions, ascetic silence, and joyous obedience in the least details of life. Every day he dwelt on the necessity of self-renunciation and the stripping off of every personal attachment. The generosity with which his retreatants responded to grace proved their will to belong unreservedly to the Sacred Heart of Jesus.

The routine of novitiate life began again, and Mother Barat had the joy of seeing her novices advance steadily along the path of religious perfection. Frequently she was obliged to check their ardor. This was particularly true in the case of Philippine. Her age and former position in the community seemed to inspire in her only a claim to the most menial tasks, the most inconvenient lodgings and assignments, the most hidden and continual mortification, the most supernatural obedience.

While Mother Barat was training her novices in prayer and in the spirit of the Society, she was also initiating them into the work of education as she understood it. In the boarding school she acted as mistress general, teaching the children and developing in them that ardent devotion to the Sacred Heart that stamped every soul that submitted to her influence. The school was increasing; the community was ideally happy; and all seemed well. But there were people in Grenoble who were bent on disturbing the peace of Sainte Marie. Curiosity asked questions; rumor answered them; and stories spread. Old gossip was revived; old sufferings were renewed. Writing an account of these months in the *Journal of Sainte Marie*, Philippine gave vent to her feelings in regard to the unpleasant occurrences that were causing anxiety:

> People simply cannot leave this convent in peace. . . . They have repeated all the old accusations against the former inmates of Sainte Marie. Disgraceful jealousy and irreligion have dared to attack the stainless virtue of the courageous women who have given up the peace and happiness they were enjoying to take the risk of founding a new institution, having in view only the glory of God and the accomplishment of his will. . . . They have had the baseness to call them "penitents," to question their orthodoxy. They pretend to see mystery in a life completely hidden in God with Christ Jesus, and they imply that this life deserves reproach. Without going so far as this, many other people have taken the liberty to criticize the firmness with which useless visiting has been checked and only young postulants capable of taking the training have been accepted. . . . For myself, when I see our Mother acting always under the guidance of God, when I compare the sweetness and unction of her words with the sharp language of those who attack her, I have no difficulty in distinguishing between virtue and passion, and I laugh at the agitation which may check God's work for a time, but will never destroy it.

In these telling lines one can sense the workings of grace in the soul of Philippine Duchesne. There is, moreover, a depth of affection for Mother Barat that points quite clearly to the bond of intimate friendship that was drawing together these two gifted women. From the first they had understood each other. In spite of difference in age and experience, the younger had become quite simply the mother and the guide, and the older, with a docility almost foreign to her natural character, had become a spiritual child again, eager to form her religious life on the pattern of sanctity that the saintly Madeleine Sophie had drawn from the Heart of Christ. There are vigor and vivacity, loyalty and indignation in the brief account and comment, and a sense of security, for Philippine can now laugh at criticism, ridicule, and calumny, having learned to trust completely in the Sacred Heart. And she had need of such trust when, early in Lent, Mother Barat was obliged to make a trip to Lyons. Philippine had expected to accompany her, and in a letter to Madame Jouve, in whose home they would have received such warm hospitality, she wrote quite simply of her disappointment and of the supernatural motives that brought joy into her sacrifice.

Mother Barat had hoped to meet Father Varin in Lyons, in order to consult him and interview some candidates he had proposed for admission to the novitiate, then to return with all speed to Grenoble. But her stay was prolonged, and it was by letter that she continued to direct her novices. Some of those she wrote to Philippine at this time have been preserved.

As character may be judged quite as much by the informal letters one receives as by those one writes, Mother Barat's letters to Philippine are precious as a sketch of her "eldest daughter," limned all unwittingly by the saint. One realizes, on reading them, that she herself has come under the sweet influence of Philippine's Visitandine training, for she has adopted the *Vive Jésus et sa Croix* always associated with that religious family. Then, too, she has found in Philippine's spirituality an element already personal to her and so a close bond between their souls—a relish for the *Canticle of Canticles* not found in souls that walk the lower paths of prayer. With Philippine she can climb to the "cleft in the rock" and enter in; to her she can speak, heart to heart, of the Beloved, the Spouse who makes his voice heard and draws the soul irresistibly to union with himself. But she speaks with a practical direction, a personal suggestion, revealing the close contact of friendship already existing between them, the depth of the Mother's holiness, and the height of the ideals she was proposing to her mature novice. Buoyant, virile, she can make a quick transition and let the gaiety of her humor shine through the sprightly teasing she offers to this first close soul-companion she found in her little Society. Happily there is no need for analysis or comment on the short excerpts from the letters given here; unhappily none of Philippine's, written in 1805, are extant.

Vive Jésus!   Lyons, March 27, 1805

I wanted to be the first to write, my dear daughter, but I received your little note, which gave me a pleasure I had no scruple in dwelling upon for a minute. You see I do not blame you for the consolation you experienced Sunday evening, provided you were disposed to give it up willingly if your vexatious Mother had sent you to bed. I hope you did not forget me before God, for just then I had little time for prayer. If I had not been away, I should have spent those three hours with you at the feet of our beloved Savior. I hope to have that joy on Holy Thursday night, if I am back by that time. . . .

Continue to keep yourself well in hand and to grow constantly in the love of Jesus Christ. May that love consume all in you that does not belong to him. Your divine Spouse asks for your heart, undivided and without reserve. He says to you continually: *Surge, amica mea, et veni;* and the words that precede those in the Canticle of Canticles: *Tempus putationis advenit, flora apparuit in terra nostra, vox turturis audita est; propera, amica mea, et veni.* But whither must the beloved hasten? To Thabor? No; to the caves in the rock, into solitude—a solitude dreaded by nature and the senses—complete self-renunciation, absolute detachment. . . . You realize, of course, that I am not referring to any new sacrifices you should make. You might think so and wear yourself out with uneasiness. . . . For you the "cleft in the rock" is this: to acquire the spirit of humility and meekness, the spirit of prayer. Set to work in confidence and peace.

What Philippine answered to this letter may be inferred to some extent from the following lines, written in quick response by Mother Barat on April 5:

I received your letter, my dear daughter, and you must realize how much pleasure it gave me. You know too well the loving interest I take in you not to have understood what a satisfaction I would find in this account of your dispositions and the resolutions you have taken. Realizing your own weakness, however, you fear you will fail to keep them and you beg me to promise to continue to help you to the end and not to weary of your slow progress. You know me very superficially if you need such a promise to count on. Our Lord, who gave you to us, has set no limits to this charge but that of death. Until then, if I can help you I shall do so with all my heart. I do not belong to myself but to you. Read that sentence again, if you like, and never come back on the matter. . . .

Fours days later the saint wrote again:

I have just a few moments to tell you, my dear daughter, that I received the package, the money, and your letter. I am so grateful for all your kindness. Our Lord, for whom you have done all this, will reward you. You are the only one to whom I gave permission to spend the entire night before the Blessed Sacrament. You gave me to understand that our Lord would not be pleased if it were otherwise. But in turn I must tell you he will not be pleased with you if you sacrifice too much sleep. . . . I am sure that vigil will not pass without your renewing your resolutions, above all that of embracing the Cross. I would have you accept the crosses that are in store for you and that Jesus will send you as soon as you have made that act of generosity, for you realize that the Cross is the greatest of treasures! A large portion of it is reserved for you, but be courageous and ready to accept it willingly, without asking for it. You will have crosses that come from yourself, but there will be others that may seem more painful. You are going to tell me I make sad predictions—yes, sad for nature but precious for grace. I wish, however, to furnish you with subject-matter for prayer during that happy night of yours. . . . Pray for me during that night. My heart will be closely united with yours and my mind will travel there many times.

A few days after Easter, Mother Barat wrote to announce her return to Grenoble the following week with a companion, and a very happy group of nuns and novices welcomed her back to Sainte Marie. They had been in good hands during her absence, for early in March Mother Geneviève Deshayes, one of the foundress's first companions at Amiens, had come to take temporary charge of the house, bringing with her a postulant, Virginie Piongaud. She had had some experience in the classroom and came with a generous spirit to share the training and the labor at Sainte Marie. Mother Barat brought with her a postulant from Lyons, Henriette Girard. She had already passed her fortieth birthday and had been somewhat prejudiced against the Society by misinformation regarding the trials she would have to undergo in the novitiate. The gay, happy atmosphere in which she found herself, the cordial family spirit, combined with lively discussions about the cross, its necessity, its advantages, its sweetness, all puzzled Henriette until Mother Deshayes gave her the simple answer: "Our cross is realizing that we do not love God as much as we should and as much as we wish to; it is seeing that others do not love One who is so lovable; it is being unable to make him known and loved by all mankind." That was the spirit Mother Barat had inspired in her daughters.

Once more they came under the charm of her strong and gentle personality, as she tried to satisfy their desire to know all that was tellable about the stay in Lyons. News about a projected foundation at Belley, about the work of Father Varin, and above all, and over and over again, the account of the audience with the Holy Father. Pope Pius VII was returning to Rome after the coronation of Napoleon, and his journey had been turned into a sort of triumph by the Catholics of France. Privileged to assist at his Mass, Mother Barat had knelt, tremulous with reverent joy, as the frail, saintly Pontiff gave her Communion. In the audience that followed she could appreciate his heart full of loving kindness, his mind free from bitterness and guile. Illumined by the light of the Holy Spirit, he gave close attention to this little woman kneeling so simply before him and telling him of an enterprise she had set on foot with a certain Father Joseph Varin, whom he knew, to glorify the Sacred Heart of Jesus by a new religious order that would have this one and only purpose. Its members now counted about twenty-five, and there were just two convents founded so far, but with the blessing of the Vicar of Jesus Christ they would prosper and expand, and by the holiness of their lives and the thoroughness of their teaching they would contribute in some small measure to the Catholic renaissance in France.

With the encouragement and blessing of Pius VII Mother Barat took up the training of the novices again. Living in her company, they came to realize that humility and truth are synonymous, and that simple disregard for self achieves liberty of spirit. She gave the impression of being constantly in the presence of God and of looking on herself merely as an instrument in his hands. This was a lesson she seemed always to be teaching: let yourself be used by him for the glory of the Sacred Heart; this will lead to perfect confidence in his unfailing guidance.

The *Journal of Sainte Marie*, which Philippine kept up to date, shows that Mother Barat was frequently helped in her work by the Fathers of the Faith who came to Grenoble on mission work. During the summer of 1805 the jubilee was preached there by Fathers Gloriot and Lambert with remarkable results. When Philippine noted that they had "changed the face of a guilty city and brought the word of God home to hearts that had been estranged from him for thirty, even fifty, years," she was not exaggerating their success. Their visits to Sainte Marie always meant a conference or instruction for the novices. These men were deeply interested in the new order, which they considered, in a way, a part of their own religious family.

An interesting entry in the *Journal* records the first visit of Father Louis Barat. Philippine had heard much about him and was eager to make his acquaintance, but at first she was ill at ease with him. His austere virtue and scholarly conversation combined to repel her and inspire a kind of fear she could scarcely explain. Quite simply she admitted this, along with the change that soon took place as a result of his kindly interest in all that concerned the community over which his little sister Sophie presided as superior. In his instructions to the novices over a five-day period he dwelt in detail on union and conformity with the Heart of Christ as the very essence of their vocation. This was the spiritual element in which Philippine delighted. But when Father Barat took for the subject of a conference apostolic zeal, there stirred once more in her soul the inspiration, the driving ambition to become a missionary, to help establish the Kingdom of Christ in foreign lands, to carry the knowledge and love of the Sacred Heart to the uttermost ends of the earth. Reading again the life of Mother Marie of the Incarnation, she set her heart on Canada. Before the tabernacle she pleaded in the words of the great contemplative missionary:

> O Eternal Father, I come to you through the Heart of Jesus, my way, my truth, my life. Through this Divine Heart I adore you for those who do not adore you, I love you for those who do not love you, I acknowledge you for those who in wilful blindness and contempt refuse this recognition of your goodness. By this Divine Heart I desire to make satisfaction for the neglect of all mankind. In spirit I go through the world in search of every soul redeemed by the Precious Blood of Jesus, in order to make reparation for all through his Sacred Heart. I embrace them all in order to present them to you, O Eternal Father, and through him, and by him I ask for their conversion.

To Father Barat she now confided her great desire, and from that time forward he encouraged her hopes and seconded her efforts, though he directed her thoughts toward lands less favored with missionaries than Canada.

When Father Varin came to Sainte Marie in August, he was delighted with the spirit and virtue he found there. A joyous mood and a glad generosity were traits he considered essential at the Sacred Heart, and these were in evidence, especially when the religious and novices gathered around him and Mother Barat for the evening recreation. No pious platitudes were passed around with darning cotton or skeins of wool, no efforts at edification for the sake of the visitor amongst them, but there was that most charming element in the cloistered community life of the order, spirited and spiritual conversation. He was struck, too, by the dignity and recollection of these women whose life bore so markedly the stamp of austerity, but without a trace of rigidity.

Among the novices he noted particularly Philippine Duchesne, when a smile lit up her fine strong features, when a humorous notion danced in those eyes whose glance could be so penetrating, when the warmth of her words revealed the sincerity of her heart, when the rapt attention of her whole being betrayed the intensity of her prayer, or a quick response to a summons showed how steadfastly her will was set on God. The years of trial had in no way quenched her spontaneity, but the months of training had brought out her finest qualities, and Father Varin knew again that he had judged her correctly: *this was a great soul.*

Before going off to mission work again, he discussed with Mother Barat the possibility of allowing the novices to make their vows before the close of the year. This raised the problem of a rule and constitutions for the order. For months she had been urging him to put into writing a statement of what he considered essential for the guidance of the society they had established. Up to this time they had followed the Summary of the Constitutions of the Society of Jesus, along with its Common Rules and Rules of Modesty, but they were convinced that the Jesuit Rule would require much adaptation to make it acceptable for an order of women. It was agreed that the time had not come for the formulation of a complete religious code. The life must be lived over a longer period of trial and error, perhaps another decade, before accumulated experience would justify decisive legislation. But it was necessary to have at least a general plan of the institute to present to the Bishop of Grenoble before the novices at Sainte Marie could be admitted to religious vows. Father Varin would give the matter serious thought as he went about his work in Lyons, in Paris, in Amiens, and he would return to Grenoble within three months.

Meanwhile the school work and the spiritual training went on side by side. Interest in the children was an apostolate Philippine loved, and she watched with guarded care the progress of her nieces, Amelie de Mauduit and Euphrosine Jouve. In the late autumn Madame Jouve came from Lyons for a short visit. After her return home Philippine wrote in her warmly affectionate fashion on November 17:

> The joy of seeing you frequently for a few days makes me feel all the more keenly the sacrifice of living almost always at a distance from you. Although you warned me that you might not be able to write immediately on reaching home, I shall feel a little anxious until you announce your safe arrival. On reaching Lyons you will have learned that Adelaide is again a mother. Her husband has just informed me of the birth of their fifth daughter. He accepts the fact with resignation. Your own daughter is such a joy to me. She brightens up my heaviest occupations. . . . Being separated from you, I look with more pleasure than ever at your picture reflected in your child, and I love her all the more.

Philippine wrote this letter while in retreat. Fathers Varin and Roger had arrived on November 11 to prepare seven of the novices for their complete self-donation to the Sacred Heart. The community and several postulants also followed the exercises of the retreat as well as they could while carrying on the school work. They were aided by Mother Henriette Grosier, who had come from Amiens some weeks before and would go on to Belley in December to found the third convent of the order. While the two priests worked also on an abridged plan of the institute, Mother Barat called on Philippine for help in composing a memorial that would serve as an introduction to the document. The purpose, the spirit, the means, the manner of life, the general rules —all that is essential to the Society of the Sacred Heart was contained in the first plan. Only the title was omitted through precaution. Mother Barat called her daughters *les Dames de l'Instruction Chrétienne* until it was safe to adopt publicly the name they cherished and aspired to bear, *Religious of the Sacred Heart of Jesus.*

Bishop Claude Simon approved verbally the document submitted to him and gave permission for the ceremony of vows at Sainte Marie, after naming Father Gaspard Rey ecclesiastical superior of the convent. On November 21, 1805, a very simple ritual was carried out when Philippine Duchesne, Marie Rivet, Marie Balastron, Jeanne-Cecile Second, Emilie Giraud, Virginie Piongaud, and Henriette Girard made their first vows. Father Rey presided, and in the sanctuary were Fathers Rivet and Rombaud, Varin and Roger. Taking as his text the words of Moses to the Israelites, "This day shall be celebrated amongst you," Father Varin preached in a vein far more prophetic than he knew.

On the following Sunday he announced that Mother Barat would leave for Amiens before the end of the week. This was not a surprise to Philippine and the older nuns, but it was a sacrifice calling for generosity from them all. Friday morning found them gathered at the entrance door to say *Au revoir*—for Mother Barat had promised to return in a few months. From the cloister they watched her and Mother Maillard climb into the coach, settle themselves with their bundles and satchels and the little basket of provisions, then wave gaily to them as they stood grouped around their new superior, Mother Genevieve Deshayes.

2. 1806—1812

LESS THAN A WEEK LATER Philippine broke the seal on a letter from Paris dated December 10, 1805:

Just a word, my dear daughter, about a draft I am sending you. It is payable in 30 days. If you can get your cousin [Perier] to cash it, you would render a great service to Madame de Luiset, who has promised to pay the workmen [at Belley] on the first of the year and has not a sou. See that she gets the money as soon as possible. Your brother gave it to me. Madame de Rollin has just left the city. I would have been so happy to see her. M. Jouve paid me a visit in Lyons. He was not satisfied with giving me some money; he came a second time with all possible kindness to offer me his services on the trip to Paris, if I needed him. I assure you I was deeply touched by such thoughtful kindness, and the family of my dear Philippine, which was already so dear to me, has become more so every day. . . .

I shall be expecting to receive a little note from you soon, assuring me that you continue to enjoy peace of soul, and that you are growing in union with our Lord, that union which I desire so ardently for you. Safeguard your peace of soul and sacrifice all else for it. In possessing it you possess all, for it conditions the soul for the reign of our beloved Jesus. Grow, then, in his love and you will have peace. Daily I beg this grace for you from our Lord. Do the same for your friend, who is all yours in life and *in aeternum*.

Sophie Barat

Philippine would stand in need of this peace of soul in the coming years. The Christmastide was a period of joy in the possession of that holy security which religious profession brings to a soul determined on the entire gift of self to God. It was a busy time in both school and community, and more than ever Mother Duchesne claimed the heaviest share of the work. She knelt in adoration before the tabernacle as the Old Year slipped quietly into the past and the New Year took its place in the mysterious rhythm of time. She had more to offer to the Sacred Heart now than ever before—more love and gratitude, more submission and sacrifice, more prayer and high resolve, more joy and much more work. It was her way to bring everything to the feet of Christ, to lay before him her duties and responsibilities, her problems and anxieties, and then to lose herself in more selfless prayer. Now, as the year 1806 opened, she accepted from him anew the multiple offices and employments that had been entrusted to her: assistant and secretary to Mother Deshayes, mistress general of the boarding school, procuratrix, instructor of the higher classes, infirmarian of both the community and the children. True, there were at first only thirty pupils, but Sainte Marie was also a novitiate, where comings and goings were numerous.

In the life of Philippine Duchesne there is no single decade of years more important for her spiritual development than that which followed her first vows in the Society of the Sacred Heart. Nor is there a period in which her natural temperament and character are more clearly revealed. As a woman approaching forty, she undertook a life crowded with activities and responsibilities which left little time, according to her reckoning, for prayer. Yet prayer was the very breath of her soul. The expansion of the boarding school was a matter of importance, for education in this type of school was the principal external means by which the Society hoped to contribute to the glory of the Sacred Heart. The office of mistress general brought Mother Duchesne into contact with the parents and friends of the children attending the school and gave her the supervision of the educational work both in the classroom and in the cloister, for young nuns and novices alike were engaged in teaching, and some of them had scant preparation for this. To give them more time for study, she also took charge of one of the dormitories and much of the children's mending. It was indeed a crowded life.

As she prepared her points for meditation on the afternoon of January 5, the meaning of the morrow's feast came home to her with that vividness of insight which was a characteristic of her spiritual life. She herself said she found it difficult to reason in prayer, to follow out a prolonged train of thought and draw conclusions that would move the will. Instead, by an intuitive movement of the soul she reached the heart of the mystery proposed for consideration and rested at once in prayer. That was her way, though the "resting" might mean spiritual activity embracing every soul in the world, or wrestling under the burden of personal faults and desires, under the urgency of grace or the trial of aridity and darkness that at times overwhelmed her. The sweetness of prayer was often lacking to her; the will to pray was a constant gift of God.

On the feast of the Epiphany Dom Augustin de Lestrange paid a visit to Sainte Marie. He was on a begging tour through Europe, seeking funds and recruits for the rebuilding of Trappist life in France. He talked of his own work and of the mission in America where in 1802 twenty-five Trappists under Dom Urban Guillet had made a settlement near Conewago in Pennsylvania. Letters from Dom Urban had given details about the migration of the Trappists to Kentucky, where settlers were numerous and land plentiful and cheap, but missionaries were lacking for work among the pioneers and Indians. In spite of the grueling hardships on the frontier, Dom Urban wanted to take his monks farther west into the lands that lay along the fringe of American settlement where vast opportunities were offered the missionaries for spreading the Kingdom of Christ.

The abbot's words were deeply moving, and Philippine felt that this visit was meant for her personally. Like the radiance of the star that led the Eastern wise men, his conversation lighted up her soul, recalling the enthusiasm of her childhood, when Father Aubert had told his tales of Louisiana and the Illinois Country. An overpowering desire to share in this tremendous apostolate gripped her soul with the strength of an inspiration coming from the Heart of Christ. Under the impression of this vivid call of grace she continued her daily meditation on the mystery of the Epiphany during the octave of the feast, and on January 10, as she wrote later on, she resolved to offer herself for the foreign missions, "to teach the pagans of China or any other distant land." For nearly two weeks this whole-hearted offering of herself to God was the subject of her prayer, but she kept it to herself until she heard the outcome of a decisive meeting then being held at the convent in Amiens.

The touchstone of interior life is detachment. For Mother Barat the departure from Sainte Marie in December, 1805, meant the facing of an ordeal that would result, for her, in lifeling self-sacrifice, the total gift of self to God and to the work she had inaugurated for the glory of the Sacred Heart. The plan of the institute presented to the Bishop of Grenoble called for "an entire detachment from the world and from self" and a formal organization of government under a superior general holding office for life. Up to this time superiors had been appointed by Father Varin, his choice falling in December, 1802, on Sophie Barat, then just twenty-three years old.

During the year Mother Barat had spent at Sainte Marie, Madame Baudemont had governed the convent at Amiens. Exteriorly all had gone well, but to the foundress, returning in December, 1805, it was evident that a change had taken place. The spirit was no longer the same. She was received with marks of respect and deference, but there was lacking the warmth of cordiality and ease of companionship which from the beginning she knew must characterize community life in the Society of the Sacred Heart. Father Varin was worried, too, sensing the influence of a priest whom he had reason to mistrust, the Abbé de Saint-Estève, confessor at the Amiens convent for the past two years and close friend of Madame Baudemont.

The guidance of the Holy Spirit in the events of this period is unmistakable. The plan of the institute approved by Bishop Simon was now to be submitted to the religious at Amiens, as it had been at Sainte Marie in a general council composed of the professed nuns in the community. Fathers Varin and Roger presided at the council early in January, 1806. Two decisions were reached: first, to add one article to the plan, namely, that the title of the Sacred Heart of Jesus would be assumed openly by the little Society as soon as prudence might permit; and second, to hold the election of a superior general on January 18, feast of the Chair of St. Peter, every professed member of the order having a vote. The nuns at Grenoble and Belley were advised at once to send their sealed ballots to Father Varin who, with Father Roger, presided at the election. The Abbé de Saint-Estève acted as witness to the casting and counting of the votes. By a majority of *one* Mother Barat was chosen for the office in which, more than in any other, "an entire detachment from the world and from self" would be required.

Two days after the election, Mother Barat resumed her correspondence with Philippine. The dignity of her position was no barrier to their friendship, and the Mother General's letters are the only extant record of the workings of grace in the soul of her great religious daughter. On January 20 the saint wrote to Philippine:

For several days I have been reproaching myself for my want of alacrity in answering your letters. Of course, we must be eager only for God, I know, but you might easily cite an authority to prove that we may be eager about things for God's sake, especially where charity is concerned. . . . I cannot understand how you dare to cry for the wretched milk [of novitiate days] which has been taken from you. At your age, to seek such insipid food! Why, that is childish. . . . God forbid that you should have further need for a milk diet! That belongs to the past, both for you and for your Mother. When she returns to Sainte Marie the present she intends giving her eldest daughter is the bouquet of which the Beloved speaks, *fasciculus myrrhae* [a bundle of myrrh]. . . . You can complete the quotation, especially that beautiful word that thrills you with joy: *Sedi.* My dear daughter, to attain to this *Sedi,* milk is not sufficient nourishment. . . .

I had to interrupt this letter for several days. Much has happened to your Mother in this short interval. I have still to resign myself to it, and I can scarcely fix my attention on anything else. Pray for me and let's say no more about it. . . . Continue to grow in the love of our beloved Jesus, and do not deprive yourself so often of the happiness of receiving him in Holy Communion. I meant to tell you that I was displeased with you when you made this avowal to me. . . .

Philippine now opened her heart to her spiritual mother. She knew that her missionary aspirations would be understood, but she never dreamed that her letter would, in turn, open to her the inmost secrets of a saint. Mother Barat's reply, dated February 3, 1806, is the beginning of a new phase in Philippine's spiritual life.

Your letter gave me great joy, my dear daughter, touching, as it did, a very tender chord in my heart. I felt that my prayers had been heard. Yes, I have been asking for this ever since our Lord entrusted you to my care, and I have often prayed for it ardently because I was convinced that he desired of you this devotedness, this complete sacrifice. But I had another motive that I can tell you now. This is just for yourself—it is one of my secrets. Even before I knew our little Society, the desire to carry the knowledge of God to the heathen was in the depths of my heart. . . . Once I spoke of it to a holy soul who was inspired by a similar idea and from whom I hoped to receive encouragement. But what an answer I got: "No, you are destined for France; you will never leave it. That is your battlefield." . . .

And now, my dear daughter, I seem to see you kneeling at the feet of our Lord and of your unworthy Mother, asking whether you are called to this work. You are awaiting the *yes* that you have sought and that seems so long in coming. Give me time; I cannot answer yet. But I say, instead: Hope on, foster these desires and sentiments, try to grow more worthy of the signal favor you long for. . . . How happy I should be if our Lord, who has so many reasons for refusing my services, were to accept yours. . . .

Pray much during Lent, and do no more penance than I have given you permission for. You also must begin to make your sacrifices. You are not to spend the nights in the chapel at Shrovetide. I am converted and I can no longer allow you all these devotions. I assure you I have a hard time making my conversion sincere, but if you only knew how I have been lectured on the score. I simply had to give in. . . .

Philippine's letter in response to this is the first one preserved for us by Mother Barat. The manuscript is undated, but it must have been written in March, 1806:

I have been longing to express to you my joy and gratitude to the divine Source of all good ever since I received your letter. So you allow me to foster this dearest wish! You do not deprive me of the hope that my desires will one day be fulfilled! In desire and in prayer I may visit the countries where someday I shall serve our Lord and have him alone for my riches. What a spur to the work of self-reform is the fear of being unworthy of my high destiny! With what respect and deep emotion I shall hear from the lips of my loving Mother those thrilling words: "I send you . . . among wolves." Oh, if only you could add, "as a lamb"! With what transports of joy I would take your venerated hand and place it on my head, that you might bless me, saying: *May you be blessed by him in whose honor you will be consumed!*

I often fancy myself at the decisive moment and oftener still in places where I hope one day to be. But would you believe this if you did not really know me? The more eagerly I look forward to the work ahead, the more conscious I am of my present cowardice. It is years since I spent such a weary Lent. I am not merely natural, I am wholly immortified, wholly self-centered. . . .

I am your very unworthy
Ph.D.

Dieu Seul!

In reply Mother Barat wrote on March 28:

. . . Do you really wish me someday to give you that blessing: *May you be blessed by him in whose honor you will be consumed?* How ambitious you are! Yet quite lawfully so. But if you lay claim to that grace, if you really wish God to bestow it upon you, with what fervor you must serve him now, and with what generosity you should offer him at every moment the sacrifice he expects from a soul to whom he has been so lavish in his gifts and for whom he prepares such great graces! Yes, you must become a little lamb; otherwise could we venture to say, "in whose honor?" Would any other victim be acceptable to our Lord? No, my dearest daughter, he wants a lamb. Try to train one for him—begin at once. Desires would be a waste of time if they were spent only on a future perfection. You must concentrate your strength on the present; that is, you must be careful to follow all the inspirations our Lord gives you and be attentive to that interior voice that reproaches you so often for your infidelities. . . . Does our Lord not frequently ask you to practice humility and meekness—in a word, to become a lamb? . . . This letter will, no doubt, reach you too late; if not, I give permission for night adoration. You may spend the night as you requested.

The coveted permission to spend the night of Holy Thursday in prayer reached Sainte Marie that very day. With her dearest devotion sanctioned once more, Philippine went directly after supper to her favorite place before the tabernacle. That night of prayer was one of purest joy. For twelve hours she knelt motionless, the incense of her adoration mingling with the myrrh of her sacrifice. It was a night of faith and hope and love, her entire being lifted up to God and surrendered to his grace through intense, living faith, boundless, assured confidence, ardent, generous love. It was the night of a contemplative at work on her great apostolate of saving souls for Christ. Impetuous and whole-hearted, courageous and daring, Philippine gave herself to prayer in her own way: her prayer was her very self in action under the inspiration of the Holy Spirit.

Her account of it, written with simple candor to Mother Barat, reveals the activity of a soul immersed in God, carried out of herself by the intensity of love and the yearning to spend herself to the utmost in spreading the Kingdom of Christ:

What happiness your letter gave me and how much good it did my soul! For three weeks my heart had been as hard as a rock, but when I read your words it melted like wax before a fire. My eyes were no longer dry, and my heart experienced a sweet joy that I seemed to taste all night, for your letter came before the night-watch of Holy Thursday.

O blessed night! For a second time I believed my prayer had been granted. I am convinced of it, my dear Mother, because of the pure joy I feel and the firm confidence I have. Oh, if only I might go before the year is out! I have almost persuaded myself that I shall. All night long I was in the New World, and I traveled in good company. First of all I reverently gathered up all the Precious Blood from the Garden, the Praetorium, and Calvary. Then I took possession of our Lord in the Blessed Sacrament. Holding him close to my heart, I went forth to scatter my treasure everywhere, without fear that it would be exhausted. St. Francis Xavier helped me to make this priceless seed bear fruit, and from his place before the throne of God he prayed that new lands might be opened to the light of truth. St. Francis Regis himself acted as our guide, with many other saints eager for the glory of God. All went well, and no sorrow, not even holy sorrow, could find place in my heart, for it seemed to me that the merits of Jesus were about to be applied in a wholly new manner.

The twelve hours of the night passed rapidly and without fatigue, though I knelt the whole time, and in the afternoon I had felt I could not hold out for one hour. I had all my sacrifices to offer: a Mother—and what a Mother!—Sisters, relatives, my mountain! And then I found myself alone with Jesus—alone, or surrounded by dark, uncouth children—and I was happier in the midst of my little court than any worldly prince. Dear Mother, when you say to me, *Behold I send you,* I shall answer quickly, *I will go.* It is well that I must wait a while for the pleasure of talking to you about all this. There would be too much natural satisfaction in such an outlet. And besides, I would not like to have nuns knocking every instant at the door and wishing to speak to their Mother. I should want her all to myself.

I have tried to be sorrowful for the remainder of Good Friday, but I cannot rouse that sentiment within me—my hope has risen so high. Kneeling respectfully at your feet I am

Your humble and obedient daughter,

Phil D.

Good Friday morning [April 4, 1806]

Easter came and went, and Mother Barat was detained at Amiens. It was May before she made her second trip to Grenoble. During the weeks that followed her arrival Philippine learned that the Fathers of the Faith had come under the suspicion of the French government and persecution threatened. Father Varin had, through precaution, resigned the authority he had held in the little Society up to this time, but he would continue to be Mother Barat's principal adviser. He had proposed a foundation at Bordeaux, the port of embarkation most frequented by missionaries on their way to foreign lands. A second foundation under consideration was at Poitiers. These would require the presence of the Superior General, and Sainte Marie would again be called upon to make the sacrifice of her. And who would accompany her? Philippine might hope to be chosen, though she was given no encouragement on that score.

To prepare for the work ahead of her, Mother Barat decided to make a retreat, but she had not got beyond the foundation exercises when a letter from Father Varin informed her that the project at Bordeaux had proved abortive and that her presence at Poitiers was needed at once. The will of God was evident, and on July 10 she left Grenoble, having chosen as traveling companion Mother Henriette Girard. There was wistful longing in Philippine's eyes as she watched them climb into the coach for Lyons. The Mother General knew all that was in the heart of her "eldest daughter," and the generosity with which she would renew her sacrifice in the chapel after the good-byes.

Of the correspondence between them during the years that followed, only the letters of St. Madeleine Sophie have survived, but they are an illuminating record of the spiritual life of Philippine Duchesne from 1806 to 1812. Thoughtful reading of them throws interesting light on her character. It is evident that much of the spiritual training received as a Visitandine novice had stood her in good stead through the years of the Revolution and its aftermath. Her attraction for prayer and interior life had not only been maintained, but had increased during the difficult period from 1792 to 1804. Under Mother Barat's guidance it had become the dominant trait of her spiritual life. At times her prayer reached a height far above the level to which souls can ordinarily lift themselves with the aid of grace. Her determination to give herself to God in the work of saving souls had never wavered. The motive of love for the Sacred Heart burned ever more brightly in her soul, and she was dauntless in her efforts of kindle this love in others.

Yet there is no escaping the conclusion that Philippine had climbed the path of contemplation before acquiring those habits of virtue which are needed to steady the soul on the lower walks of daily life and apostolic activity. Impatient, irritable, highly sensitive, she had now to face and recognize some of the acute spiritual losses sustained during her years outside the cloister. The gentleness, sweetness, humility which form so distinctive a part of the Visitandine spirit had suffered partial eclipse in her soul. The struggle against circumstances that were personally so trying, opposition that used every means to divert her from her purpose, and persecution that roused her combative daring and self-assertion, all this had tended to develop the irascible side of her character.

Recalling the influences that had been at work through the decade before she met St. Madeleine Sophie and the single year they had spent together at Sainte Marie, one may read in the excerpts that follow a graphic revelation of Philippine's struggle during this period. They bring into relief the faults and defects which she must constantly have regretted, repaired, and resolved against, and they point the way to the acquisition of those sterling virtues which were later on so much a part of her as to appear quite naturally hers. She would never grow placid and imperturbable, but the surge of native impulses would be calmed to serenity through prayer and self-control. More than this, the letters show a saint unafraid to express the tender affection she felt for the friend she was guiding to sanctity.

St. Madeleine Sophie had placed the material management of the convent, as well as the educational activities, in Mother Duchesne's hands. Repairs were still in progress throughout the old monastery. The nuns had not yet dared to adopt a mode of dress that would identify them publicly. Religious life in France had still a very tenuous hold on existence, and Mother Barat thought it best to retain semi-secular costume: a plain black dress with ample skirt, close-fitting bodice, and soft white fichu, over which was worn a triangular shawl of the dress material, held by a pin at the breast. The head-dress was a white cap or bonnet such as women of France had long been accustomed to wear both inside the house and out-of-doors, with the hair parted and drawn back softly from the forehead.

Mother Barat had been gone from Grenoble almost a month when Philippine received a letter from her, dated from Poitiers on August 1, 1806:

> In the three weeks since I left you the Lord has given us many proofs of his goodness and his love. . . . Have you not said more than once since then: "Yes, Lord, you really had to deprive me of this friend whom I love in all truth for you, but who is, I admit, a human support. I must lean on you alone. Be, then, my one and only friend. I want no other since you are so good as to choose me and even to seek so persistently the love of my poor heart." . . . I open my heart to you, my very dear Philippine, but what I write is just for you. I have so great a desire that you should love our Jesus, that I disregard myself; I only long to enkindle in your soul the confidence and love I myself should have for him, in order that you may love him for me. . . .
>
> I realize, my dear Philippine, that for the moment our Lord

seems to leave you to yourself, and this makes virtue more difficult to practice. You are without the sensible consolation that ordinarily accompanies a big sacrifice generously made, and you are forced to say with the spouse in the Canticle, "A bundle of myrrh is my Beloved to me." Oh, may you be able to add the rest of the verse, and with similar generosity. Yes, even if your Beloved offers himself to you only on the cross, you should press him to your heart with more eagerness than if he showed himself to you in the radiance of Thabor. . . . I tell you, my dear daughter, when I reflect on the magnificent graces our Lord has bestowed on you from early childhood, I have the firmest confidence that with your responsive and grateful heart you will love him after the manner of great souls. . . .

Shortly after her arrival in Poitiers, Mother Barat made a trip to Bordeaux to meet a group of young women who desired to enter the Society. On August 30 she wrote to Philippine from the seaport:

Some days ago I went to the wharf to see some of my companions off to Poitiers. As they were crossing the Garonne, I remained on the wharf watching them or rather looking at the vessels riding at anchor in the harbor—a great number from all parts of the world. Losing sight and thought of my Bordeaux sisters, I was suddenly back on your mountain. Then it seemed to me that you and I were here on the wharf together, ready to embark on one of these ships for the land of your dreams. How I wished that you were sharing with me the sight of this beautiful port and all the thoughts it aroused in your Mother. . . .

Our Lord wishes to entrust his work to souls who prove their love for him by earnest fidelity in acquiring the virtues of the saints. Now humility, meekness, charity, patience, these are the virtues which must characterize the apostles of this new Christendom [won by missionaries]. They must be filled with the spirit of our loving Savior. Concentrate your efforts on acquiring this, and above all, while cherishing your desires, make acts of conformity to the will of God. Tell him you are willing to sacrifice this joy if such is his good pleasure and if he wants only your generous offers of service. Then pray for those who are already working in the foreign mission fields.

Mother Barat remained at Poitiers to establish a novitiate and train the candidates who were sent to her by Father Varin and other Fathers of the Faith. Her letters to Mother Duchesne were not numerous at this time, but they were carefully treasured, read, and reread, and sometimes wept over before the tabernacle at

Sainte-Marie. The continual sufferings to which they allude form one of the most painful trials a strong soul must endure in its ascent to God. The saint wrote on November 10:

> Every day I have to put off writing to you I regret it more keenly. The thought that I might be able to lessen your interior sufferings by a little advice urges me to write today. Believe me, I count it a real sacrifice not to be able to do so frequently. The details you gave me in your letter grieved me, both on your account and on account of those who share your anxieties. . . .
>
> The sufferings which try you so severely are the result of the many promises you have made to your divine Spouse. You should consider this a privilege, but there are times when one has need of support and encouragement. The trial which your divine Master is now putting you through is one that calls for some help, and he will not refuse you what you need; but he requires of you more lively faith, more purity of intention, more simplicity and detachment from self. This will, I trust, be the fruit of your retreat and renovation of vows. . . .

Dom Augustin de Lestrange paid a second visit to Sainte Marie on the feast of All Saints that year. This time he could tell of Trappist monks who had gone to re-enforce the American mission, among them Father Joseph-Marie Dunand. Neither the abbot nor Mother Duchesne could foresee that at a future date Father Dunand would be supervising the building of the first permanent convent of the Sacred Heart in the New World. Father Louis Barat came frequently to Sainte Marie. His stern asceticism appealed strongly to Philippine, but the encouragement he gave to her desires for mortification and prayer was often at variance with the views of his sister. When Mother Barat yielded to his representations in such matters, she never failed to let Philippine know it. Writing to her in February, 1807, on the subject of Lent, the saint advised prudence and a positive program:

> Take care of your health and do not weaken yourself by fasting. . . . Endeavor to acquire the virtues so necessary for drawing hearts to Christ: meekness, humility, affability, evenness of manner, which is the fruit of patience, and above all that love of Jesus which I so desire to see in you. Oh, my dear Philippine, when will you be able to say and to experience the meaning of these sublime words of the great Apostle: I live, no, not I, but Christ lives in me? Try each day to die to self in order that Jesus Christ may live more fully in you. Meditate frequently on these words of the *Imitation*: My son, the more you renounce self, the more you shall

find me. . . . Again I recommend very specially to you a kind and gentle manner toward others, and I beg you to use it also in dealing with yourself. Be patient with yourself. Do not get downhearted about your faults, even if you commit a hundred a day. Draw from them, instead, an increase of humility and confidence.

During the Paschal season Mother Barat wrote:

The thorns that irritate you so often simply prove that you have not that holy detachment you need; there is still too much self-will in what you wish to do for God. . . . Remember, my dear daughter, our Lord calls you to carry his Cross. Have you forgotten these words he has so often whispered in the depths of your heart: *"You must become a victim, you must be immolated for love of Me"*? Have you forgotten the solemn promises you made to follow him wherever he might lead you? I must recall them to you, for you have so often confided to me the inmost sentiments of your heart. This is the bond uniting our souls. Because we both want to love and to suffer, Jesus brought us together, though we were so far apart, that we might love him alone and suffer for him alone. Now he has parted us, given us employments so uncongenial to our natural attractions, and ardent desires that we cannot fulfil. . . . Well, let us learn to wait, remembering that God's designs are accomplished slowly.

In the busy life at Sainte Marie her days were at times so crowded with duties and responsibilities, chores and charity, that Philippine often found herself at war with a repugnance that seemed beyond her strength to resist. One longing filled her soul—to have sufficient time for prayer in solitude. Happily she could pour out her heart to Mother Barat and be sure of understanding and sympathy, if not relief from her many distracting employments. When her pleading brought no change in conditions, she pressed her petition through Father Barat, hoping to obtain permission for greater freedom in the matter of night adoration. St. Madeleine Sophie replied:

I received your letter, my dear daughter, with one from my brother backing up your petition and counseling me to grant it if your health (about which he knows nothing) can stand these long night vigils for which you have such an attraction. Long ago I would have yielded to your pleading but for the well grounded fear of ruining your health. Oh, dear! I have so often experienced the need we have for prayer, the pressing need to beg the Heart of Jesus to be favorable to us, and it is at night, I think, when so few souls are mindful of him, that he listens most willingly to our prayers and grants the graces we ask. I should fulfil that office, for it is my duty to pray for you all . . . but who would allow me to do it?

It will be a great solace and joy for your Mother to know she has a substitute . . . who pays homage to the Heart of Jesus for her, for the Society, for the ungrateful world. Should it be necessary for my brother to plead with me for you? Does not Jesus himself from his Sacred Heart urge me even more strongly? . . . But your superior must get permission from Father Varin, . . . and knowing him as I do, I hardly believe he will give it. . . . If after some months of secret prayer with your divine Spouse you do not become more humble, more obedient, more patient, I shall withdraw the permission for night adoration. That will be the punishment for your infidelities. Oh, my dear Philippine, that will never happen, will it?

Philippine was quick to act on this permission, taking for granted Father Varin's acquiescence and not dreaming she would have to reckon with him in person very soon. The entry in the *Journal* describing his visit is full of charming candor, though one suspects it was written somewhat ruefully:

We had not counted on the favor of a visit from Father Varin, but he gave us that agreeable surprise on August 8. . . . He gave us the greatest joy by promising in a tone of voice that really seemed inspired, that our work of educating young girls would not be confined to this one country, but that, perhaps even soon, we would establish houses in the colonies. . . . The consolation which this visit brought us was somewhat lessened at its close when he forbade the continual night adoration that Mother Barat had allowed us to try, while awaiting his approval. . . . He based his refusal on such well founded reasons, particularly the fact that we were withdrawing ourselves from the uniformity which must exist among all our houses, that we could only praise his motives in asking us to make so great a sacrifice.

It was easier for Philippine to write these generous sentiments than to live up to them. One way still seemed open to her by which she might gain time for prayer, and that was freedom from responsibility: she would ask to be relieved of her several offices and to be allowed to hide herself in manual employments. Mother Barat's reaction to this petition was written on September 7:

You must hold on to your peace of soul by the practice of humility, meekness, obedience, and submission to your superior. Open your heart to her in all simplicity. Our Lord always blesses such straightforwardness. I am going to see to it that you have less to do by relieving you of the offices of mistress general and procuratrix, as you have been begging me to do for such a long time. Circumstances have made it impossible up to now. This is between us, however, until I can arrange with your superior.

The promised change did not occur immediately, and the transfer of Mother Emilie Giraud to Poitiers in the spring of 1808 was a blow to Philippine's hope of being called to live with Mother Barat. Her acceptance of this arrangement was not without struggle, and she wrote quite simply of it to the Mother General, who answered:

> You are disappointed because I did not bring you to our solitude at Poitiers. I assure you we have often to sacrifice personal tastes for the general good. I give you a proof of that in leaving you so far away. . . . Six months here would do you much good. Of course you would enjoy it too much, and for you life should never be a time of pleasure. Our Lord wishes you to be *betrothed in blood*. How fortunate you are in being called to follow him so closely! Try to appreciate this precious destiny.

Mother Barat left Poitiers in June, 1808, and went to Niort, some fifty miles away, where she founded a convent which she entrusted to the guidance of Mother Suzanne Geoffroy. Two other houses were founded from Amiens this same year, at Ghent and at Cuignières, making a total of six in the Society. In July Mother Barat traveled to Amiens with Mother Thérèse Maillucheau, but conditions there under Mother Baudemont and the Abbé de Saint-Estève made it impossible for the foundress to remain without bringing about a conflict of authorities, and she preferred to withdraw to Grenoble.

Before the middle of November, Mother Barat decided to return to Amiens, leaving Mother Thérèse at Sainte Marie. Soon her correspondence with Mother Duchesne was resumed. The letters now are shorter on the whole, but not less vigorous, affectionate, and illuminating as regards the spiritual life of Philippine. On December 5, 1808, Mother Barat wrote from Amiens:

> Your letter filled me with joy, my dear daughter. I could not desire a greater consolation than that of learning that your heart-suffering is over and that you are at peace. I have thanked our Lord, who gave this solace to the keen pain of our separation. I admit that it would still be very hard if I had learned that you were a prey to continued sufferings and anxieties, for my happi-

ness is, in a way, bound up with yours. . . . Now as to the past—leave it entirely to the mercy of God. Repair it by great fidelity to the present moment and a complete abandonment of the future into his hands. . . .

I cannot help missing the friend whom I left with you, but I am happy in my sacrifice, knowing how you will benefit by her presence. . . . I do not forget your missionary desires. In the course of this month I shall see someone [Father Varin] and discuss matters with him, but it cannot be decided yet. You well know you could not leave me just at this time.

In the history of the Society of the Sacred Heart, the name of Thérèse Maillucheau is linked inseparably with those of Madeleine Sophie Barat and Philippine Duchesne. She was born, like Sophie, in 1779, and christened Elizabeth. When Father Enfantin first met her in Bordeaux, she was a well educated young woman who loved poetry, was musical, and played the harp well. She had faced the dangers of the Revolution with intrepidity and had been in the vanguard when the first lull in the storm allowed the rehabilitation of the parish church of St. Andrew in Cubzac, where the Maillucheau family had a summer home and took refuge during the days of peril.

In the solitude of Cubzac the girl gave herself to prayer and the study of St. Teresa. The call to religious life was accompanied by graces of interior recollection and prayer that became almost habitual. After assisting at a series of sermons preached by Father Enfantin, Elizabeth placed herself under his direction and became the leading spirit in a group of young women who were determined to give themselves to God in a life of prayer and good works. Among these were the postulants whom Mother Barat admitted to the novitiate at Poitiers in 1806.

Under the guidance of St. Madeleine Sophie, Elizabeth's spiritual progress was constant and rapid. Through devotion she took the name of Thérèse and concentrated her efforts on the development of an intense and loving interior life. The austerity of the novitiate offered no difficulty to her. She had rather to be held in check by obedience, lest her generous fervor ruin her frail health. She brought a joyous note to the recreations, with her sweet voice, her merry laugh, her sense of humor that enjoyed nothing better than a joke on herself. And there were plenty of these, for at best Thérèse was not highly endowed with practical judgment. Early in 1807 she was allowed to make her vows.

When Mother Barat decided to return to Amiens in the sum-

mer of 1808, she chose Thérèse as her traveling companion with
the intention of soon carrying out her promise to relieve Mother
Duchesne of part of her work by entrusting to Mother Maillucheau
the office of mistress general, as well as that of mistress of novices.
She had foreseen, moreover, the bond of friendship that would
unite these two contemplative souls, and she hoped that the advice
and example of Thérèse would be a powerful influence in the
spiritual development of Philippine. She was not disappointed.

The Society of the Sacred Heart was still in its infancy when
Mother Thérèse took charge of the novices at Sainte Marie. As the
majority of the community had had only a year, some even less, of
regular novitiate training, they gladly profited by the permission
to assist at the conferences for the novices and to give their confidence to her in order to receive her advice and direction. The
foundress realized that the influence of Mother Thérèse was
already at work when she wrote to Philippine from Amiens in
February, 1809:

> I have had two letters from you, my dear daughter, which I
> loved reading because in them you promise that once and for all
> you are resolved to love our Lord and to correct your faults of
> character in order to please him and draw souls to him. We have a
> double purpose in our efforts: our own perfection and the salva-
> tion of souls. We must be saints. If you only realized how ardently
> I desire this for you, I believe you would make the necessary ef-
> forts. But if you grasped how much more our Lord desires it—then
> you would indeed be faithful to his call. . . . I hope that the help
> our Lord now provides for you through personal contact with a
> soul he loves so tenderly will break down your long resistance and
> enable you to rival her in virtue.

The winter of 1808–1809 was very severe in Dauphiny, and
there was much illness at Sainte Marie. Postulants came and left;
the children were difficult to handle; and life on the whole was
very austere. There were dark days, spiritually, for Philippine,
but Mother Barat's encouragement never failed her:

> I always read your letters with pleasure [she wrote in March]. If
> I do not find in them all that I desire, my heart clings to its hope.
> . . . Grasp this fact clearly: our Lord, in his goodness, wishes you
> to become a great saint. He brought you into this little Society just
> to give you the means of doing so. . . . Oh, you can do all things
> now, if only you are faithful. Success depends on your willing it.
> Do not fear, I shall never lose patience with you. . . . I know
> you cannot correct yourself suddenly. How could you become

meek, stripped of all attachment to your own judgment, etc., when the contrary faults have been rooted in your character for so long? . . . But at least the virtues will have taken root, the soil will have been cultivated, and you will have only to keep up the habits now formed.

The letters St. Madeleine Sophie wrote to Philippine during the next few months show to what extent Mother Maillucheau's direction influenced her. The saint's joy in the improvement she noted herself or learned from others mingles with the encouragement she offers and the spurs to greater perfection which she never fails to apply. All was not plain sailing at Sainte Marie; anxieties, heart-suffering, near-discouragement were still Philippine's portion at times, and she was forever straining toward the missionary goal:

> You seem to reproach me for not telling you about the departure of that group of missionaries whom you wish to imitate [wrote Mother Barat in July, 1810]. I knew nothing about them. The ones about whom I had information certainly were not suitable companions for you, and I could not let you set out on such a venture. . . . Only keep your soul in peace, if that is possible, and desire the will of God in this as in all things else.

Mother Thérèse's sojourn at Sainte Marie lasted just fourteen months. Soon after her departure for Ghent, Mother Barat returned to Grenoble, and for a year Mother Duchesne had the joy and grace of her strengthening direction. The old intimacy was renewed; the old affection deepened; and the Mother General had the satisfaction of seeing how sincerely Philippine had profited by the care lavished upon her soul. In mid-November, 1810, Mother Barat was obliged to set out once more on her round of visitations, hoping by this means to insure union and uniformity among the convents under her care. Traveling almost the whole of this year, she continued to encourage Philippine in her upward striving for self-conquest and union with God. The tone and substance of the letters remain constant, and one feels the saint's contentment in her spiritual daughter, though there are still faults calling for reproof, and there is no hint that perfection had been attained along any line. From Poitiers she sent her this all-embracing little program in November, 1811:

> Your letter is short, but it tells me much, accustomed as I am to read the thoughts and vexations of your heart. I answer: Courage and patience. Let God have his way. He will lead his servants to the goal of their desires. If we only will his holy will, I believe I

can assure you he will do our will. Let us abandon ourselves to his good pleasure and lean securely on him. I shall see you soon. I say soon, for the four months ahead will pass quickly.

They were long hard months for Philippine, for Sainte Marie was severely tried by sickness and sorrow. Mother Barat reached Grenoble again in May, 1812, and spent more than a year there. She had much to confide to Mother Duchesne, much to discuss with her. The Society was again involved in a situation that threatened disaster. The foundress had need of solitude for prayer and patient waiting. She knew that in five of her convents the true spirit of the Sacred Heart was in full vigor, but Amiens, the first house she had founded, was infected with a poison whose only antidote might be the cutting off of members who were still very dear to her. In this year of trial she came to know more intimately than ever the loyal heart of Philippine Duchesne.

four

The Outward Apostolate

I. 1806—1812

THERE HAVE BEEN FEW PERIODS in the history of France less favorable to the development of new religious orders than that of the Napoleonic empire, and there were few ecclesiastics more continuously shadowed by the French imperial police during that period than Father Joseph Varin. Even as early as 1801, all correspondence between him and the other Fathers of the Faith was censored, and Father Varin had the unenviable honor of occupying a good deal of the First Consul's, and later the Emperor's, attention. When Napoleon wrote in October, 1804, "My main purpose is to hinder the re-establishment of the Jesuits in France. . . . I want nothing that resembles an organized religious group," he was referring directly to orders of men, but there was little desire in his imperial heart for the resurgence of religious life among the women of France. Yet on January 26, 1805, he restored the monastery of Sainte-Marie-d'en-Haut to Mother Duchesne for the religious group with which she had associated herself, and he did the same in countless other cases.

Through the next two years prudence required Mother Barat and her nuns to have as little external connection with the Fathers of the Faith as possible. The guarded tone of her letters gives proof of this, as well as the expression *nos amis* (our friends), referring to their priest helpers. So cautiously did the foundress conduct her affairs that in the spring of 1807, when a petition was presented for the imperial authorization of the Society throughout France and its colonies under the title of "Ladies of Christian Instruction," Napoleon signed it on March 10 at Osterode in Prussia.

The news of this authorization brought Mother Duchesne not only joy in the prospect of an increased and stable apostolate for the Society, but also personal relief from a situation which she had found trying. Although Mother Deshayes had been superior within the community at Sainte-Marie, conditions in Grenoble were such that it seemed advisable to keep Mother Duchesne at the head of the school as mistress general and procuratrix, and to have her assume the responsibility of administration whenever there were official contacts with outsiders, especially with the local civil authorities. This arrangement was approved by the Bishop of Grenoble, and it was taken for granted in the community, as all understood the social and political influence of the Duchesnes and Periers in the city, and the need there was for prudence.

Mother Duchesne had more than once begged Mother Barat to relieve her from a position that brought her into frequent contact with seculars and was a source of personal annoyance and distraction in her life of prayer. In November, 1806, Mother Barat answered: "It is my intention that you continue to sign [all official papers] until my return, and this on our Friend's advice." Philippine submitted for a while, but with the announcement of Napoleon's favor, she returned to the subject with some insistence, and the foundress gave the assurance that on at least one point her plea would be granted:

> Have patience just a little longer [she wrote in May, 1807] and then your name will not appear again. Just as soon as the local authorities receive copies of our Decree [from the Emperor], the name of the superior will be given and Mother Deshayes will take her place as such. But mind you, you are to continue as mistress general until further orders.

While positions of authority were repugnant to her, Mother Duchesne realized the opportunity which the office of mistress general afforded her for spreading among the children the knowledge and love of the Sacred Heart and for training them to true Christian living. It was her duty to direct the work of the boarding school in what concerned the studies and in all the activities that made up the life of the school. The enrollment was gradually increasing as the reputation of the school was built up, and the children spent eleven out of the twelve months of the year at the convent. Although the Society of the Sacred Heart had as yet only the barest outlines of a rule for its members, a rule for the boarding-schools had been drawn up, and Mother Duchesne found herself faced with the problem of enforcing it in opposition to the wishes of many parents. The formal schooling of the *ancien régime* had disappeared with the revolution of 1789, and it was not easy to establish strict discipline among the children of the new generation, especially in Dauphiny. St. Madeleine Sophie was convinced of its necessity, however, and thought it "to the greater glory of God if the children went out as little as possible." Yet she advised: "Prudence must be your guide in this matter, and there are some children for whom exceptions must be made. But let this be rare and hold to the general rule: once each trimester."

The scholastic year was divided into three terms, with reviews and examinations held regularly each trimester, with prizes given informally in mid-winter and in late spring, but quite formally at the close of the year, when the Bishop presided at the assembly known as the "distribution of prizes." The responsibilities attached to the office of mistress general were often the theme of Mother Barat's letters to Philippine. There was, the foundress knew, no better training-ground than this for the soul she was guiding to sanctity, and the ideal she set before her was always illumined by love. Writing in February, 1807, she says:

> There is no better way of proving your love for our Divine Master than by taking care of the children for whom he has shed all his Blood. Strive earnestly to acquire the virtues that are so necessary for you if you are to win their hearts: gentleness, affability, evenness of temper which insures patience with them, and the love of Jesus which I desire for you more than all else. Oh, my dear Philippine, how I wish you were on fire with this love!

As we have seen, Mother Duchesne was relieved of the position of mistress general when Mother Maillucheau came to Sainte Marie in the autumn of 1808, but in less than two years the management of the school was again in her hands. In the school Mother Duchesne was loved with sincere devotion by the children. They would have died for her, they said, but they also helped her die to self at times by their mischievous conduct. From the pen of Louise de Vidaud, who later became a religious in the order, we have a charming and lively picture, somewhat abbreviated here, of Philippine Duchesne in her apostolate among the children of Sainte Marie:

> Among the sweetest memories of childhood, I treasure the lasting impression made upon me by the strong, pure virtue of that Holy Mother, so humble, so fervent, so generous in her devotedness. . . . She taught the higher classes, the upper section of Christian Doctrine, and geography. She presided at meals in the children's refectory and sometimes ate with them [as was then customary]. We could never understand how she did it all, but we found out that her working hours stretched far into the night, and sometimes she was so weary, she napped a little while presiding at our study period. She must certainly have possessed a robust constitution to have endured the fatigues of such a life. But that was not all. When it was decided to separate the younger and more troublesome children from the older ones, in order to insure discipline in the school, Mother Duchesne took almost entire charge of the younger group, acting as a true mother to them. . . . Of course their studies were not neglected, but in those days education had a more spacious meaning than it has today and there was time for all sorts of things besides the formal class instruction she gave us. When we were so fortunate as to have her as mistress of the higher classes, we found her manner of teaching very clear and interesting, but woe to the girl who was inattentive to her explanations. . . .
>
> Our dear Mother Duchesne took a keen interest in all we did, even our sewing and our recreations. Frequently she spoke about her ardent missionary desires. One day, while we were playing blind-man's-buff, one of us caught her and guessed at once who it was. Now she was "it"—but how could we blindfold her, we asked. Quite simply she took off her bonnet [the little house cap worn then by the nuns] and let us bind the handkerchief over her eyes. We were tremendously impressed by her gray hair, her direct simplicity, and her complete confidence in us, her troublesome set. We were impressed still more when at the end of the game she gaily adjusted her bonnet, then turned toward us with radiant enthusiasm and said, "Now, children, which of you wants to go with me to America to convert the Illinois? Let anyone who is willing make a pact and give me her hand as a pledge." Every child in the group held out her hand, and indeed many of us would have followed her to the end of the world. But only one amongst us [Lucille Mathevon] could ever keep that rather hasty promise, though many religious vocations germinated there and saw a happy development. . . .
>
> If a child was sick, Mother Duchesne became her nurse. How

often we met her, wearing an apron and carrying a pot of tea to the dormitory or the infirmary. She put so much heart into her care of us, yet it was marked also with an austere simplicity. A little unsweetened tea, a day in bed on a meager diet, easily cured our colds. Who would have dared to complain, knowing the pattern of her religious life?

But it was not only in the development of our minds and the care of our bodies that she showed her motherly interest in us. Our souls were far more precious to her. Her corrections were often severe and often met with stubborn ill-humor on our part, but when we finally came around, she pointed out our faults and mistakes in such a kindly way that we gave in and made reparation, especially to God, by a sincere act of contrition. I recall with lively gratitude the gentle, persuasive manner in which she reached down, as it were, into the depths of our souls to root out evil tendencies and plant a little good in their place.

She taught us to offer all our actions to God, suggesting that we learn to use the prayers composed by Mother Marie of the Incarnation, and by this means she gradually led us to devotion to the Sacred Heart. Her words had all the more influence with us because they were accompanied by such great virtue. An angel in adoration in the church would not have impressed us more, so reverent and recollected was she at prayer. Kneeling on the floor, upright and without support, hands clasped, she remained motionless for hours. One felt the presence of God in her. Besides the holy hours of prayer at night, which were the ordinary thing with her, each year she spent the entire night of Holy Thursday to Good Friday rapt in adoration before the Blessed Sacrament. Aloysia Rambaud, who often noticed her in the chapel as late as ten o'clock in the evening, and found her in the same place next morning, cut tiny bits of paper one Thursday night and dropped them on the skirt of Mother Duchesne's dress before retiring. "If she moves," the little imp remarked covertly, "the papers will tell me so." Hurrying to the chapel early Friday morning to gather evidence, she found the good Mother in the same posture, the papers undisturbed, so the whole night had been spent motionless. It is easy to understand why we considered her a saint!

And that impression engendered another—a sincere and respectful affection. But how could we ever show her how we loved her? It was difficult because she was so humble. When her feast-day came, however, we tried to put into words our gratitude, but she in turn tried to hinder our every effort. . . . Yet the more she tried to hide herself, the more she revealed to us the extent of her virtue and the rare qualities of her character. We knew the reserved and austere manner she assumed was only a disguise, for her character was tender and sympathetic, her heart sensitive and affectionate, and we counted on her love.

During these years at Sainte Marie, Mother Duchesne was in constant contact with her family. Several of her nieces were in the boarding school. Her sisters came occasionally to visit her—Amelie from Grâne, Euphrosine from Lyons, Adelaide from Bourg. Melanie and Duchesne were with their father at Grâne for some years after 1802; then the men returned to Grenoble and lived at Number 5, Grande Rue, where family gatherings brought together old aunts Gueymar and Lagrange, the Periers and Teisseires, and often the Jordans from Lyons and the Savoye-Rollins on their way to or from Paris. Philippine kept in touch with them all, for she knew that all had need of spiritual help. God had blessed many of them with material wealth, but the treasure of faith had been lost by nearly all the men in the family.

In her letters to her sister, Madame Jouve, her personal interest in all that concerned the family is revealed. She is frank and affectionate, not hesitating to express the sentiments that welled up from her heart. The presence of her nieces in the school at Sainte Marie was a joy and a responsibility. She studied them, trained them, wrote of them in her forthright manner. Health, diet, clothing, progress in classwork and piety, and character formation were reported on with discernment and sincerity, and the personalities of some of them were deftly portrayed. At times the duplication of names must have caused some confusion even within the family circle, for there were Amelie de Mauduit, Amelie de Mauduit II, who married Henri Bergasse, Amelie Jouve, and Amelie Teisseire; and the mention of "Camille" might have raised a similar problem.

Mother Duchesne followed a somewhat formal style in writing to and about members of her family, using *Madame* and *Monsieur* in preference to their baptismal names. Her fondness for the colloquial *amie* (friend) as a term of endearment to her sisters must be understood in its significance. Many of the excerpts given here contain nothing of real importance in the life-story of Philippine Duchesne. Their value lies in the fact that they allow her to speak for herself, and this clear self-portrait is far more valuable than any second-hand sketch of her could be. The letters cited in this chapter were all written to her sister Euphrosine, Madame Jouve, and addressed now to the Jouve home in Lyons, now to the country place at Grâne, where the Jouves spent a part of each year.

In the autumn of 1806 Philippine was doing what nuns seem to do in every generation and in all parts of the world—she was sending letters and parcels "by opportunity." This became a life-long habit with her, and she enjoyed the inward thrill of saving postage, though the carrying costs may sometimes have inconvenienced the friendly "opportunity."

> Madame de Vaulserre's maid is going to enter with us [she wrote], but first she wants to go to Lyons to see her son . . . so I am taking advantage of this opportunity to send you some of your daughter's drawings and her first geographical map, with which I am quite pleased. She does give promise. Tell me what you think of her work, and also of her résumé of the *Iliad*. . . . You complain about the brevity of my letters, but I really feel I cannot reform on that point, as I have so few free moments. I can tell you in a line that I am daily more and more content with the good fortune that has come to me, and my companions are also. I am very well, and the time just flies by.

For several years Philippine had been watching the development of a religious vocation in her sister Melanie. She had hoped to see her enter the novitiate at Sainte Marie, but she was called to the Visitation and at the age of twenty-one entered the monastery at Romans, where her aunts and a cousin were members of the community. Philippine wrote very briefly about it to Euphrosine: "Melanie's departure is a great sacrifice for me, but she has so much joy in being at Romans that her own sacrifice is greatly lessened. I received a letter from her yesterday. She was simply carried out of herself with happiness." Melanie received the habit of the Visitation on May 24, 1807, with the name of Sister Marie-Xavier.

Meanwhile Madame Jouve was begging to have Euphrosine come home for a few weeks. A minor conflict ensued between duty and affection, and loving Tante Philippine was happy over its outcome when she wrote on April 9:

> To satisfy your desires, my dear Sister, we are allowing Euphrosine to go home for 10 days, or two weeks at most. I do not like the arrangement, for she is the first pupil for whom this exemption from the rule has been made, and others will take advantage of this fact or will complain. However costly it is for parents, I cannot change the rule nor find fault with it, realizing as I do that the children are quite noticeably more contented and studious when their heads are not full of outings and trips. Last year's trip was certainly detrimental to your daughter. . . .

After giving you this little sermon, it is only fair to tell you that I am so glad you and Euphrosine will have this happy time together and that I really helped to secure it by pointing out how sad you would be at a refusal. . . . Euphrosine is taking home with her a chronology to study. She should also read over the history of the emperors in order to keep up with her class. You will find in her satchel two heads she has sketched, two geography maps, and her most recent exercise in church history. . . . I love you tenderly.

Philippine

Little Amelie Jouve was about ten years old when she joined her sister at Sainte Marie in the autumn of 1807. Four of her cousins were also in the school—Amelie de Mauduit, Caroline and Henriette Lebrument, and Amelie Teisseire. Tante Philippine was kept busy trying to satisfy their families with news about all these children and at times excused herself for her brief letters by a reference to her own crowded days and nights.

Believe me, my dear Sister [she wrote in November, 1807], it is as hard for me to have to write briefly as it is for you to receive letters that give you insufficient details about your daughters. But forgive me because of my many occupations. I am responsible, in part at least, for 38 children. I have to order meals for sixty people. There are days when I should have quite enough to do if only I answered the door and went over the children's mail, yet I must also teach my classes and secure time for my prayer and other spiritual duties. I only wish Euphrosine could supply for what I leave undone. . . . She has a brief, concise way of expressing herself, very laconic, that shows little feeling, though she is intensely affectionate. But she will never excel in self-expression. . . . Amelie has become very negligent about her little personal affairs, but she promises much as to piety and good conduct, and also as to study.

In the letters of the next few years there is an interesting character study of Euphrosine and Amelie Jouve as their devoted aunt saw them. Both were to become members of the Society of the Sacred Heart, the younger entering on a long religious career as the older was finishing her short life of suffering and sanctity. On May 2, 1808, Philippine wrote to her sister, her "Bonne Amie," as she called her:

I put off sending Amelie's letter until today so as not to overweight the letters you will receive from Euphrosine and from Mother Deshayes, with the report cards. A second reason was that

Euphrosine had an attack of fever the very day she wrote, and I wanted to know how it would develop before telling you about it, for we have had some cases of scarlet fever. Fortunately Euphrosine's illness lasted only a day. She had energy enough to learn and act a part in a little play given on my feast [St. Philip's day, May 1]. She and her sister did very well. The latter is now quite hoarse from singing too much. The prize Euphrosine received and her first *accessit* to the ribbon of merit have gone to her head and she has again assumed her haughty and imperious manner. . . . I embrace you and your little baby [Constance]. Give my affectionate respects to Father.

Soon she was writing again to her "chère amie":

Euphrosine is well aware of her own merits. But at least she is improving; her manner is calmer; she is more affable and pious. If this continues, she will be allowed to make her First Communion on the feast of the Assumption of the Blessed Virgin. As to the trip you want her to take, that is quite impossible. We are refusing that permission to all who ask it. She can be godmother to the baby by proxy. . . . On his recent visit your husband was very generous about offering me some money, but as we shall need to purchase many things during the year at Lyons, it would be more convenient, if it suits you, to be able to draw on you for the money there.

August came and went, and there was no ceremony of First Communion at Sainte Marie. To Madame Jouve's inquiries Philippine replied:

I see you are impatient to know when the children's First Communion will take place. It has been retarded for them all. . . . Euphrosine is preparing for it rather coldly; still I think she will merit this privilege. Her character simply lacks the effusive tenderness of more demonstrative souls. She will serve God generously, but she will not enjoy much sensible fervor. The stiffness that marks all her conduct gives her a proud and disdainful air. She has real need of all the help grace can give her for working on her character. . . . Amelie is very good, except for a little stubbornness when corrected for her faults.

Euphrosine made her First Communion with seven of her companions on November 13, 1808. St. Madeleine Sophie was there at the time and took special interest in this gifted, difficult girl who would one day be the perfect religious of the Sacred Heart, the one of whom the foundress said, "Such was my dream for all of them." From the day of her first meeting with Jesus in the Blessed Sacrament, Euphrosine began her steady climb toward sanctity. In a fragment of a letter written on Christmas Eve, 1808, Philippine noted the fact:

> Euphrosine is improving steadily in character and piety, but not much in politeness and thoughtfulness. In this matter she still consults her own inclinations, with little regard for respect and duty. She is always first in studies and is very skilful at needlework, though she gives little time to this on account of class work. . . . Amelie will have skilful fingers, too, but she is less gifted than Euhprosine. I am busier than ever just now and so I am forced to cut this short and tell you very briefly but with all possible tenderness that I am always devotedly yours,
>
> Philippine

While life at Sainte Marie seemed to be moving at a normal pace, all France was seething under the impact of the military campaigns by which Napoleon was striving to increase and consolidate his imperial position. Grenoble on the French frontier was often astir. War in Italy, revolt in the Tyrol, troop movements through Dauphiny, and the threat of Austrian invasion, all disturbed the peace of the old fortress town. From time to time Philippine got news of the members of her family who had thrown in their lot with Napoleon or had been drawn into his army. Prominent among these were Josephine Perier's husband, Jacques-Fortunat de Savoye-Rollin, whose services were rewarded by a baronate in 1809, and Camille Perier, a financial genius, who had held the post of auditor in the Council of State. Even closer to her heart was her young nephew, Amédée de Mauduit, who had left Saint-Cyr as a sub-lieutenant of infantry in 1808, taken part in the Spanish campaign, and been wounded at Ratisbonne. Later on he would see active service at Smolensk and Moscow and so distinguish himself as to gain his captaincy at the age of twenty-two.

News of another kind was now filtering into Grenoble. In May, 1809, the papal states were incorporated into the French empire, and early on a morning in July Pope Pius VII and Cardinal Pacca were arrested. Though weak and ill, the Pontiff had still the moral courage to defy the brute force of the emperor's soldiers. Five years of exile and suffering lay ahead, but through it all the saintly bearing of the august prisoner awakened religious fervor as well as sincere sympathy among the people of France. Packed off hurriedly to the French frontier, he reached Grenoble in a pitiable condition. In the *Journal of Sainte Marie* Mother Duchesne wrote an account of his stay in the prefecture of the town, two passages of which are quoted here:

> The most thrilling event of this whole year was the stay of the Pope in Grenoble, and it procured many blessings for our house. Pius VII has occupied the Chair of St. Peter in very difficult times. He was arrested in Rome during the night by order of Napoleon, Emperor of France, not being given time to take anything with him nor liberty to choose a companion on his journey. By the goodness of Divine Providence and without a direct order from the Emperor, the captain in charge brought him to Grenoble by an almost uninterrupted journey and without seeing even Cardinal Pacca, who was a prisoner with him, but kept entirely separated from him. He arrived at four o'clock on the afternoon of July 21, 1809. As he was lodged in the prefecture directly opposite our windows, but on the opposite bank of the Isère, we could see his carriage arriving, escorted by soldiers. His very meager suite followed in miserable vehicles. . . . We saw the Cardinal kept at a distance from him and conducted to a different lodging place. Next morning we had the joy of lending a missal and cruets for the Pope's Mass.

Through the favor of the captain in charge, Mother Deshayes was allowed a brief audience with the Holy Father and the children of Sainte Marie were also invited to meet him. This was an exciting occasion for them. Dressed in white, bare-headed, with their black veils on their shoulders ready to be donned for the audience, the sixty girls waved goodbye to Mother Duchesne and filed down to the prefecture, accompanied by Mother Deshayes. When they had assembled in the room assigned to them, the Pope came in. With gentle kindliness he laid his hand on the head of each child and gave her his ring to kiss. Then he blessed them all, after telling them what a pleasure it was for him to see "such well-behaved children." Mother Duchesne's account continues:

> The other members of the household who could not go to the prefecture received the Holy Father's blessing each evening at the windows, for he gave it to the immense crowd that tried to see him when he took his walk between 6 and 7 o'clock. . . . In spite of our distance from the prefecture and the slope of our mountain, we could see him clearly; and we noticed that he looked attentively at our house and seemed to bless it very particularly. . . . On August 1, feast of St. Peter in Chains, the Pope was obliged to leave at 3 o'clock in the morning with only a few moments' notice. In the bustle of this hurried departure he retained his perfect out-

ward calm, spoke kindly to all, and praised the welcome given him in Grenoble.

The Pope was to be held as a captive for a time at Savona. Going by Valence and Avignon, the little cortege reached there on August 15. That day Philippine wrote to her sister:

I received your letter, *ma bonne Amie,* and put off writing until after Adelaïde's departure, also awaiting a good opportunity for sending a letter. You can just imagine what a pleasure it was to see this sister of mine after more than two years of separation from her. And how I enjoyed seeing her happiness in being with her children whom she loves so much! She came on Friday night and stayed here with her two little girls; she spent Tuesday and Wednesday at Vizille, then left us on Thursday after dinner. . . . Camille was also kind enough to come to see me yesterday and give me news of you. . . .

We are very grateful to you for your solicitude about us, but we are remaining quite calm, just living from day to day. We are children of Divine Providence. God has given an increase to the works of this house without visible means. If he destroys it, he is the Master; so we live in security.

Answering her sister's greeting for the New Year, Philippine wrote in January, 1810:

Being powerless to give you all I wish for you, I beg God to bless you and your children very particularly, so that the seeds we are sowing in their hearts may bear fruit in his good time and so give you much consolation. This will be your reward for all the care you have lavished, and are still lavishing, on them. Euphrosine is too strong a character ever to waver in her principles. She does not possess great personal charm, but that is so dangerous, I do not desire it for her. If she is faithful to duty, that is the main thing. With fewer personal attractions she will have more peace. You simply have to be content with what contents God. He did not make all the good people lovable, but he loves them just the same, and he does not change them. This is just a word of warning, lest you expect a great many courtesies and attentions from your daughter. She simply is not observant. One has to suggest things to her. . . . Still I prefer Euphrosine, stiff and positive in character, to Amelie, who is often too soft and lazy and who does not work to develop her character, dreading to make the least effort. Euphrosine is meant for great things. Amelie will merely ornament a household, and not without shadows here and there, for she is rather temperamental.

While her judgment about Euphrosine was correct, Mother Duchesne was quite mistaken with regard to Amelie. There was fine stuff in the child, and happily her aunt would see its development. The older girl was finishing her formal schooling that year and leaving Sainte Marie to take her place in the home where she was greatly needed just then. "I hope she will be a big help to you," wrote Philippine, "and relieve you of part of your work. . . . Amelie will suffer because of her departure. Her character is gentler than that of her older sister, but I doubt that she would be as helpful to you; she is indolent and not very generous about overcoming this defect."

In the spring of 1811 Euphrosine fell dangerously ill, and Philippine wrote to Madame Jouve:

> Your letter, my dear one, has brought grief to me and to all who know dear Euphrosine, especially Mother Deshayes. She has begun a novena with the entire household for this sick child whom we all love. I rely on prayer for her cure. She will be more fervent than ever after her illness, and you will be doubly indebted for her to the Giver of all gifts. He is making you realize just now that he has only loaned you your children and that they really belong to him. I beg him to strengthen you in this hard trial.

For several years Mother Duchesne had watched eagerly for some sign of a vocation in this favorite niece of hers. Euphrosine had kept her counsel and had given no direct hint as to the working of divine grace in her soul, but her secret had been divined by her devoted aunt, as appears in her next letter to her sister:

> How intimately I share your anxieties regarding dear Euphrosine, and how I desire to ease your sufferings! At least I try to do so by praying to God with all the fervor that the sincerest love and interest can inspire. Mother Thérèse shares this interest and presses me for news of your daughter. . . .
> When you were so near to losing her, did you not think of offering her to God, even in this world, since human means were powerless to save her for you? Euphrosine has never given me her secret confidence, but I have reason to suspect that she has some idea of the cloister. . . . Without letting her realize, you can find out whether my ideas are correct and sound out her courage in this matter. Who knows but what some interior struggle may be the cause of this illness. Amelie is good, but not very pious. I am as eager as you to see her obtain her great desire [of making her First Communion]. The ceremony has been postponed a few days.

Euphrosine's recovery was slow, but before the close of 1811 she was again in normal health. Her mother's reaction to the suggestion of a religious vocation was decidedly unfavorable and Philippine wisely dropped the matter for the moment. Characteristic of the letters she wrote to her family is her silence regarding her own life within the cloister. There is never any emphasis on the personal. There is no hint at the difficulties that gave battle daily in her soul, no selfish enumeration of the fatiguing activities that filled her days and nights, no mention of the continual round of charities she performed. She wrote with a simple disregard for self and a liberty of spirit that sprang from a sense of being an instrument in God's hands.

Buoyant, virile, conscious of her responsibility towards the children she taught and the family she loved, Philippine wrote as she was learning to live, with singleness of purpose and little thought of herself. She was learning her lessons the hard way, but that was of the pattern of her life. St. Madeleine Sophie had still to urge her to "join recollection, gentleness, humility, and obedience" to her Lenten fast in 1812. When Philippine found herself groping her way once more through a fog of interior trials and personal difficulties and crying out for help, the Mother General answered, "Courage and confidence. This difficult period will pass, I assure you." Some weeks later the saint suggested affectionately: "If you want to put off your retreat until I reach Sainte Marie, I should be very glad. If, however, your soul is more disposed to solitude during Lent and you can secure the time, then make it. We shall have much work to do when I arrive."

2. 1812—1817

DURING THE OPENING MONTHS OF 1812 Sainte Marie was severely tried by illness. The cold was intense, and the old building was damp and drafty. Nuns and children alike suffered from heavy colds, rheumatism, pneumonia, tuberculosis. Entries in the *Journal* show the number whom Mother Duchesne cared for that winter when from January to May the infirmaries were always occupied. As Mother Deshayes was often ill, the responsibility for the entire household fell to Philippine. "Courage and confidence," she repeated, as she read Mother Barat's letter over and over again.

"This difficult period will pass, I assure you." And it did pass with the arrival of the Mother General in May for a stay of sixteen months at Sainte Marie.

"We shall have much work to do when I arrive," she had written, and Philippine had wondered what that sentence meant. She knew that the Society was faced with serious problems, but she became aware of the gravity of the situation only when Mother Barat confided to her the tangled details and asked her help.

The Society was still without rules and constitutions of its own. Mother Barat had worked on these with Mother Duchesne on former visits to Grenoble and with Fathers Varin and Barat at Amiens recently, striving to combine in them the apostolic ardor of Ignatius with the contemplative spirit of Teresa. But the Abbé de Saint-Estève had presented a fantastic compilation of his own, drawn from divergent sources. Copies of this weird document had been sent by Mother Baudemont to the several houses of the Society, and the Mother General, journeying from one to another, watched the reaction when it was read to the professed nuns.

In the community at Sainte Marie there was surprise, disappointment, repugnance. Where was that precious thing they all desired—that spirit of ardent love, adoration, consecration, and total sacrifice that flowed from devotion to the Sacred Heart? Above all, where was devotion to the Sacred Heart? St. Madeleine Sophie assured them that this was but a tentative draft and begged them to trust a little longer and pray much more. With Mother Duchesne she discussed the matter more freely and explained the reasons for delay. The Abbé de Saint-Estève was both dangerous and determined. He had already caused such trouble to Mother Julie Billiart and the Congregation of Notre Dame as to force that order to leave Amiens for Namur in Belgium, in order to escape his domination. Mother Barat hoped to save her religious family from a similar fate by retiring into obscurity. Father Varin approved this course, but advised her to continue her work on the rules and constitutions while at Grenoble. This was the work the foundress had hinted at to Philippine.

An unexpected turn of events occurred after Mother Barat reached Sainte Marie. The Abbé de Saint-Estève was arrested in Amiens and carried off to prison in Paris. He had run foul of episcopal authority, and the imperial police were glad to put one more priest in confinement. But all this only strengthened Mother Baudemont's resolution to force his rule on the Society or to withdraw the order from Mother Barat's jurisdiction. To keep the Society intact and to preserve in full vigor the true spirit of the Sacred Heart was the object of all the prayers and efforts of the foundress during the sixteen months she spent at Sainte Marie. And it was to Mother Duchesne she turned for help in this trying situation.

Her presence was a tremendous joy to Philippine. Things that could never be put into writing were so easily expressed in conversation, talked over, laughed over—for the tragedies of daily life are often comedies in retrospect. The project of the foreign mission was often broached by Philippine, but the answer was always the same, "Not yet," and the reasons against it were numerous. One was Philippine's health. Mother Barat had cause to worry at times about that. Seeing her going about her multiple duties, tall, straight, resilient even under the pressure of the heaviest work, few in the community suspected that physical suffering was becoming a companion with whom she would travel through many years of her life. Yet rheumatism was at work in her strong active body, affecting her hands particularly, as she admitted to Madame Jouve by way of excuse: "It is a long time since I wrote to you, as I have had a very painful condition in the fingers of my right hand." And Mother Barat lamented later on: "Our Philippine is unable to write."

In December Mother Josephine Bigeu was called to Grenoble to take charge of the novitiate, which the Mother General herself had been directing for some months, as illness had now incapacitated Mother Deshayes. Among the postulants who entered in 1813 were Lucille Mathevon, a former pupil of Sainte Marie, and Hélène Dutour, a young woman from Savoy. These are names to remember, for they are linked inseparably with Philippine Duchesne's. As novices they learned to know her well, to see her as St. Madeleine Sophie described her at this very time to Mother Giraud:

> We have had the blessing of the cross, too. Several of the children ill, eight, I believe, in the infirmary now. Your dear Mother Duchesne spends her days and nights there, teaches her classes, manages the house without constraint and almost without being over-burdened. What a valiant woman! . . . No, she will not leave the mountain—we just could not get along without her. If anyone is transferred, it will be Mother Deshayes.

Philippine's continued residence at Sainte Marie was a comfort to her father. He had returned to Grenoble with Duchesne soon after Melanie's entrance at the Visitation in Romans and taken up residence at the Perier home. As president again of the local barristers' association, he became once more a familiar figure at the Palais de Justice, on Grande Rue, and in Place Grenette. But age was beginning to tell on him, though his white hair and careful gait added dignity to his appearance. He was still the forceful, outspoken legal expert, but he had mellowed so noticeably that Philippine could recognize the stirring of faith that had lain dormant in his soul for half a century. From the windows of his rooms he could look across the river and see Sainte Marie perched high up on the mountain side. Sometimes he climbed the steep ascent to visit his daughter and give her news of the scattered family. In the summer of 1813 Philippine told Madame Jouve:

> Yesterday I had the pleasant surprise of a visit from Father. I found him looking as young as ever, but I noticed that his legs are getting stiff and it is difficult for him to go down the stairs. Still I just cannot believe that he is growing old. His kindness makes me wish he would never die, but unhappily there is no earthly joy untroubled by the thought of death.

In September Mother Barat left Sainte Marie with Mother Deshayes for the chateau of Chevroz, near Besançon, where Father Varin was awaiting them at the home of his sister. The time had come for the final drafting of the constitutions and rules over which they had prayed and labored intermittently for nearly ten years. For many weeks founder and foundress worked steadily in the solitude of that lovely country place, while news of military disaster echoed through France and defeat at Leipzig opened the way to invasion by Napoleon's enemies.

Philippine had no news from the Mother General through the autumn months. She bore the responsibility, but not the name, of superior at Sainte Marie and prepared as best she could for any emergency that might arise as a consequence of invasion. Grenoble was exposed to attack and poorly prepared to resist. Austrians, Bavarians, and troops from Italy were reported massing on the frontier. And in the midst of this anxiety there came a great personal joy. Young Euphrosine Jouve confided to Tante Philippine her desire to enter the novitiate at Sainte Marie and begged her help in overcoming the objections of her parents. Praying for guidance and self-restraint, Philippine began a spiritual campaign that would cover the next twelve months. On October 29, 1813, she wrote to Madame Jouve:

For a long time, my beloved Sister, I have suspected the secret yearnings of your eldest daughter, though she tried to keep them well hidden from me. And this was the subject of a suggestion I made to you when she was so ill—a suggestion which, I was told, caused you much pain. Yet what I merely guessed then is a reality today. Euphrosine wishes to leave you, not for a human husband and an earthly home, but to give herself to God, who has given her everything she has. Only recently did she confide to me her desire. Knowing her love for Mother Deshayes, I told her that dear Mother is no longer superior of this house. That fact, however, did not alter her desire to enter here. She has but one obstacle to overcome—her love for you and the pain she feels in trying to speak to you of this matter.

I have promised to do so for her, knowing, of course, that I speak to a loving mother, but still more to a Christian mother who is accustomed to the most heroic acts of resignation. I am not going to preach to you. I prefer to let grace plead—that grace which is active in the generous hearts of both mother and child. . . . Forgive my straightforwardness if it wounds you. Accustomed as I am to see God as the only end of all things, I did not think it would offend you to suggest him as the one end for which your beloved daughter was created. I must stop hurriedly and embrace you tenderly.

Madame Jouve was wounded, and the mention of Euphrosine's vocation called forth the unexpected threat of withdrawing Amelie from school. Philippine parried this with some hard facts about the young girl when she answered her mother's letter:

If you withdraw Amelie in the spring, I fear she will not be much help to you because her character makes her often sullen, peevish, and intractable. Her piety is undeveloped, and it is very difficult to influence her as she does not give anyone an opening and sets a standard for herself that is very comfortable. One cannot reproach her for not studying; she has great facility in that line, but she does her work carelessly, as you can see by her writing and spelling, though she could do much better. She would like to neglect everything for reading, which is an easy occupation. I was obliged to put a limit on that. . . . This letter will take the place of a report.

Meanwhile at Sainte Marie a change had taken place. The work at Chevroz had been completed, and St. Madeleine Sophie, on her way to Amiens, wrote to tell Mother Duchesne that Mother Bigeu would replace Mother Deshayes as superior. Philippine was authorized to install her in her new office and accompany her when she went to call on Father Rey, who was still acting as ecclesiastical superior of the convent. Following the instructions she received, Mother Duchesne assembled the community on November 21, and after the customary prayer to the Holy Spirit she read a letter from Mother Barat making the appointment. In a simple ceremony each member of the community, following Mother Duchesne's lead, knelt and kissed the hand of Mother Bigeu in token of respect and submission, then the recreation went on joyously.

As the year 1814 opened, Philippine was still pleading with Madame Jouve to give Euphrosine a chance to try out her vocation under Mother Bigeu's direction. Within a few weeks she was able to discuss the matter with her sister personally. Their father's health had been causing anxiety. Early in February Madame de Mauduit came from Grâne and Madame Jouve from Lyons to care for him. Philippine, too, was allowed to visit him and help with the nursing, as the rule of cloister had not yet been made binding in the Society. It is not difficult to divine what was in her heart as she ministered to him, knelt beside him, prayed for him, and won him back to God.

Pierre-François Duchesne lingered through the month of March—that last month of Napoleon's empire. Madame Jouve was obliged to return home, lest she be caught in Grenoble by invading troops. All France was in turmoil, with Napoleon fighting a coalition now sure of victory, with the English in Bordeaux by March 12, and the Austrians, victorious in Italy, pushing through Switzerland into old Dauphiny. The courageous defense of the town was broken down before the close of the month, and the enemy moved forward to enter Grenoble on April 12. The empire had already collapsed in defeat at the battle of Paris, which was begun the very day Pierre-François Duchesne was buried. A loyal, upright figure had passed from the scene, leaving a void in many hearts, but greatest in the heart of his eldest daughter.

A relative calm was soon restored in Grenoble. The municipal council drew up a declaration of allegiance to the Bourbon Louis XVIII, and among its signers was Augustin Perier. His presence had been a support for Philippine and her sisters through these weeks of personal sorrow and civic upheaval, and she had hoped that both Augustin and her brother might be influenced by a realization of the grace given to Pierre-François Duchesne. Her father's conversion was a triumph of faith and trust and prayer made powerful by the complete sacrifice of self, but Philippine wrote with quiet restraint to Madame Jouve on April 18:

I do not want to keep you waiting longer for news, so I shall write. Our brother leaves next week for Paris. He will give you all the details you desire. Amelie was detained here by God's snow and by the troops that barricaded the other route, so she left only to-day. She and I were at Father's side when he died. His agony was long and painful; for several days he did not speak, his body no longer functioned, yet his soul was at times a prey to fears. He had received Extreme Unction in good time and had a second and a third absolution with the plenary indulgence. The funeral was very simple in view of conditions here and the prohibition against ringing of bells that day. It was March 29. I trust he is with God.

Now that all is quiet again, I repeat my request that you send Constance to us. I think M. Durand, who is certainly coming to see his daughter, would be glad to bring her. He is a very nice gentleman. No one expressed more sincere sympathy to me than he at the time of Father's death. If you are generous enough to let Euphrosine come with Constance, you will have the merit of mothers who willingly offer their children to God. But I leave this to God's grace.

The casual mention of "M. Durand" is interesting. His daughter Caroline was a pupil at Sainte Marie at this time, and her older sister Coralie had been at school there with Euphrosine Jouve and Louise de Vidaud. Now Hippolyte Duchesne was paying Coralie much attention and M. Durand seemed to consider the young lawyer a suitable match for her, in spite of his lack of practical religious faith.

The summer of 1814 was critical for France, for the Church, and for the Society of the Sacred Heart. The fall of Napoleon had put an end to both the captivity of the Pope and the dispersion of the Fathers of the Faith. Father Varin went quickly into action, visiting the convents he had helped to found. He was eagerly awaiting what he knew must happen soon after the Holy Father reached Rome. Two months passed. Then on August 7 Pope Pius VII promulgated the bull *Sollicitudo Omnium Ecclesiarum*, re-establishing the Society of Jesus throughout the Church and the world. The venerable Pierre Joseph Picot de Clorivière was named superior of the order in France. For forty years he had kept intact the Jesuit tradition. Now within two months he admitted nearly seventy novices into the Society of Jesus. The greater number of these were former Fathers of the Faith, including Fathers Varin, Roger, Barat, and many others who had befriended Mother Barat and her companions.

The re-establishment of the Jesuits had far-reaching consequences for them. Up to this time they had lived under an adaptation of the rule of St. Ignatius. Their spiritual life had been built
on Ignatian principles. They were to experience continued guidance from the friends who had entered the Ignatian company and
to enjoy the spiritual direction of a countless number of fervent
Jesuits who became their staunch supporters. There was not one
among them who admired the Society of Jesus more than Mother
Duchesne, and her admiration would only increase when she saw
them at work on the American frontier. But foreign missions
seemed a very remote possibility in the autumn of 1814. Conditions within the little order were still strained. Through the influence of Saint-Estève the convent at Ghent withdrew from the
general government. Some of the religious stationed there set up
an independent institution, while the majority returned to Amiens.
Following this distressing episode Mother Barat was critically ill,
but the five loyal convents carried on their work with courage
and fidelity. At Sainte Marie all went on as usual in peace and
charity and plenty of hard work.

There was some social excitement in Grenoble that autumn of
1814. Plans for Coralie Durand's marriage to young Duchesne had
taken shape. Relatives from far and near gathered at the Perier and
Teisseire homes and came, singly or in groups, to call on Philippine and give her the details of the event. When she learned that
Jean-Joseph Jouve was coming from Lyons, she made bold to
suggest that he should bring Euphrosine and little Constance with
him, and he did so. Philippine appreciated the sacrifice her sister
had made, and when the latter expressed her great unhappiness
about her daughter's entrance at Sainte Marie, she tried to console
her with all the love and sympathy her heart felt and her pen could
express. But it took time and God's strong healing grace to restore
peace and happiness in the Jouve family.

Euphrosine entered the novitiate on Christmas Day, 1814, with
Louise Rambaud, Octavie Berthold, and Josephine Meneyrond.
Louise, be it recalled, was the child who had strewn bits of paper
on Mother Duchesne's skirt to secure evidence of her night-long
prayer. Octavie and Josephine would both come to the American
mission, but in very different roles. Together the four received the
religious habit, still merely a mitigated secular dress, on Easter
Sunday, 1815, Euphrosine changing her name to Aloysia out of
devotion to the young Jesuit saint, Aloysius Gonzaga. Soon the

new novices began to help in the boarding school, as was the custom then.

There was sharp anxiety at Sainte Marie that spring when Napoleon returned to France with his heroics and showmanship. Landing in Provence, he took the Alpine route that brought him through Vizille and into Grenoble in triumph. The people of Dauphiny had, to a great extent, been taken in by fair words and the promise of a resurgence of liberty. The road to Paris lay open; by mid-April not a Bourbon could be found in France.

Turmoil again, and the call to arms! Mid-June saw the French troops cross the Belgian frontier. The Hundred Days were drawing to a close at Waterloo. By June 18 all was over, and Napoleon was back in Paris three days later. In the Representative Assembly there, it was a deputy from Isère, one Antoine-Louis-Hippolyte Duchesne, who made the formal proposal that the Emperor be asked to abdicate. Strange turning of the tables this! But peace was not yet won. The Austrians, coming in from Switzerland, were threatening Grenoble early in July. After a courageous attempt at defense the city capitulated on July 9. Although the terms imposed by the enemy were harsh, this second occupation of Dauphiny by the Allies was of short duration. Before the winter snows blocked the roads again, the foreign troops had been withdrawn. But the returning Bourbons did not bring real peace to France. The Church, however, could now enjoy a measure of freedom, and this meant activity among the many groups that were working to restore Christian life and worship to the country and establish the schools that were so sadly needed.

The constitutions and rules of the Society of the Sacred Heart, drawn up at Chevroz, had not yet been adopted. Now the collapse of Saint-Estève's scheme to control the order gave the foundress an opportunity to convoke the Second General Council to meet in Paris in November, 1815. Two professed religious from each of the five convents were invited to form the deliberative group. Mothers Bigeu and Duchesne traveled from Grenoble in late October by way of Lyons. At last Philippine was to visit her sister's home for a day or two. She set out on short notice, as nuns so frequently do. Madame Jouve was at Grâne with the younger children, but she came home as quickly as the diligence would carry her. Meanwhile Josephine de Savoye-Rollin was welcoming Philippine with warm affection, and there was too little time for all they had to tell each other. The nuns were soon on their way to Paris. From there Philippine sent her sister a delightful letter on

November 2, full of love and gratitude, comments on persons and things, and a few after-thoughts, as was her way in letters:

> Through your care, my dear Sister, and that of my kind brother I made the trip without inconvenience. . . . Here I am in Paris, I am sorry to say. With what difficulty the love of solitude adjusts itself to the noise and bustle of a great city! The soul finds itself under a kind of tyranny. Try to rejoice with Euphrosine in the happiness she is experiencing. The joys of the spirit are as far above other pleasures as heaven is above earth. You did more for her in giving your consent to her reception of the habit than if you had made her a queen.
>
> I was worn out by my first ventures into the world during my short stay at your home. But I was so happy to know your charming family, and it was a great pleasure for me to see you. I do not know when that will happen again, but I do not want to give you so much trouble. It pained me when I realized how much inconvenience I had caused you. I think I left a little combination knife and corkscrew at your house. Do save it for me. . . .
>
> A thousand affectionate messages to your kind husband and the children. The lunch you provided was sufficient for the entire trip to Paris, and your warm shawl gave the cold no chance to reach me. I did not take it off the whole way. May I keep it until the return journey? Without it I should certainly have suffered.

"The return journey?" For Philippine Duchesne there would be no return to Lyons, and Grenoble, and her loved Sainte Marie. Her life was to be a forward course until she reached the Indian frontier in mid-western America.

In Paris Philippine, seeing St. Madeleine Sophie for the first time in two years, marked the effect of trial and strain and illness on her, and marveled at her energy and gaiety. She also met old friends among the council members—Emilie Giraud and Henriette Girard, Mothers Grosier and Deshayes. Mother Geoffroy was there, and others whose names were as familiar to Philippine as hers was to them—Mothers Desmarquest, de Charbonnel, and Eugenie de Gramont. Her intense love for the Society made it a joy for her to share the friendship and labor of these women who were, like herself, the foundation stones of the order.

The council opened on the feast of All Saints, with Mass in the chapel of the Jesuit house in the Rue des Postes and a sermon on devotion to the Sacred Heart by Father de Clorivière. The meetings were held at the convent of St. Thomas of Villanova, where the religious had found hospitality. Mother Barat presided.

Father Varin proposed, one by one, the statutes drawn up at Chevroz. The members of the council considered, discussed, and at length adopted all unanimously. The result of these conferences gave the order a rule that breathes the spirit of Christ's own Heart, a way of life by which successive generations of Religious of the Sacred Heart have lived for nearly a century and a half.

The all-pervading thought and purpose is stated in the opening sentence of that rule: "This little Society is wholly consecrated to the glory of the Sacred Heart of Jesus and to the propagation of its worship." The means of personal perfection proposed to the members are union and conformity with this Divine Heart by prayer and the imitation of its virtues. The work of education and all other zealous activities must be fed from the deep springs of interior life. Action and contemplation must be so mingled that the one is but the external manifestation of the other, the work being enriched and glorified by the prayer which directs the simplest and most ordinary actions to the glory of the Sacred Heart. By the *Constitutions* the authority of the Superior General was established once and for always; the name and spirit of the Sacred Heart came to reign throughout "this little Society," as Mother Barat ever called it.

With the adoption of the new rules and regulations, the obligations of religious poverty had to be examined by each member of the council before the formal renewal of vows closing the assembly. With the exception of Mother Eugenie de Gramont, the only one of the group who had any wealth to contribute to the order was Mother Duchesne, as the others all came from families completely impoverished by the French Revolution. For the sake of the Society she resolved to sacrifice the satisfaction of giving further financial help to her family. On December 14 she wrote to Madame Jouve:

> As I am about to renew my vows and hope to do so with more peace and security under a stable constitution, I want to arrange my temporal affairs in such a manner as to preclude all anxiety of conscience. It would have been a great satisfaction for me, in breaking completely with the world, to have left my sisters in easier circumstances. But Divine Providence, which does all things well, has willed to detach you from worldly goods that are of little real value, and allowed that I, who have few personal needs, should not be at liberty to strip myself entirely of my possessions because of those who are associated with me. I have only been able to arrange matters in such a way that if nothing unforeseen happens to

the Society, Constance and Josephine can complete their education at Sainte Marie during my lifetime.

Wishing to give my godson [Henri Jouve] a little mark of affection, I am going to ask my brother to send you a note for a thousand francs from me. He will address it to your husband without knowing its purpose, and you will be careful to keep this secret from him and also from Henri. It is best that way; then no one will talk about it. . . . I received the bill of exchange which your husband sent me and cashed it. I beg you to tell him so and thank him again for all his kindness. . . . What detains us here at present, and may continue to do so, is the foundation of a convent of the Sacred Heart in Paris. It cannot be made just now, but we must secure a house, and that has not been done yet. In any case, do not write to me again before hearing from me. If I do not see you before New Year's Day, find here my greetings and good wishes for the coming year.

On the day after this letter was written, elections were held within the council. The votes gave Mother Barat three Assistants General: Mothers Bigeu, de Charbonnel, and Grosier. The office of Secretary General fell to Mother Duchesne. The decision to found a convent in Paris as a residence for the Superior General and a central novitiate sent the nuns on a hunt for property. A suitable house was found at Number 40, Rue des Postes. It was small, but had some attractive features and could be enlarged. The work of preparing and organizing the new convent was entrusted to Mother Duchesne.

The council closed on Saturday, December 16, with Mass in the chapel of the Franciscan Sisters in Rue de Grenville. At the Communion, the eleven religious of the Sacred Heart went to the altar-rail, each carrying a lighted candle, and renewed their vows aloud before receiving the Sacred Host. Mother Duchesne called this little ceremony "the rebirth of the Society." Soon the other council members left for the houses from which they had come, and Mother Barat went to Amiens before the close of January. Mother Duchesne was left in Paris with plans and a little money and just two helpers.

Mother Bigeu returned to Grenoble to install Mother Maillucheau as superior at Sainte Marie. She carried with her a letter for the community from Philippine, written on January 8 and headed with the initials *SS.C.J. et M:*

As I am not going to see you again, my very dear Sisters [she wrote], I pause at the beginning of my letter to think seriously of the meaning of these words which henceforth ought to be placed at the beginning of all our letters: *Sacratissimi Cordis Jesu et Mariae.* All we do is for the Divine Heart, and it is in the Heart of Jesus that we bring all to a close. So we cannot withdraw from the Heart of Jesus, either in beginning or in ending our actions; and even if we are entirely separated from each other, we declare that we shall always be united closely in this lovable center of all our affections, the Divine Heart of Jesus.

I am so grateful for all your New Year's wishes, and if I put off answering your letters until the departure of Mother Bigeu, I did not fail to say how much I appreciate them, for I spoke of them to God in prayer the very moment I received them, and in his presence I formed special wishes for your perfection. I rejoice in the thought that God will be glorified in that house which is so dear to me and in which I have often taken too keen a personal interest. But God watches over it better than I can. You know this very well, and so you must live in peace under the sheltering care of Divine Providence. . . . It is really not my fault that our absence has been prolonged, for I am very tired of my worldly life. All the beauties of St. Sulpice are of less value to me than the quiet of our own chapels. I long for the day when we can secure a little corner for lodgings in our own little convent and I shall see no more of the Streets of Paris.

Mother Duchesne and her two companions continued to live at the convent of St. Thomas. Each morning after prayer, Mass, and breakfast, they went to Number 40, Rue des Postes, to spend the day in heavy manual labor. As usual, Mother Duchesne took the hardest work on herself, scrubbing and polishing floors, cleaning walls and windows, and occasionally inserting a missing pane of glass. While directing the workmen who were remodeling the house, she frequently picked up a trowel to speed a mason's job, or a brush to finish up some painting or whitewashing. She was a tireless worker, yet a considerate superior, careful to safeguard both the physical and the spiritual life of her companions. At recreation in the evening she often entertained them with stories of Sainte Marie, as they sewed on caps and veils and habits fashioned after the new pattern adopted at the council. When she admitted that she was "always there in spirit," she gave the measure of the sacrifice she had made when asked to remain in Paris.

Sundays gave time for more prayer, some rest, and the accomplishment of the many little things they had put aside during the week. There were also visits to the well known churches of Paris, and Mother Duchesne became acquainted with a great many places of pilgrimage before the cloister regulations were enforced. Easter Sunday fell on April 7 in 1816. Philippine seems to have expected visitors that day. Duchesne and his wife were in Paris, as were also Camille Jordan and three of the Perier men—Augustin, Scipion, and Casimir—who made frequent trips between the capital and Grenoble. With this in mind she used her leisure on Holy Saturday to give Madame Jouve some information about things of special interest to her:

> With the hope of having a chance to send you a letter, dearest Sister, I am hastening to write it today. Euphrosine's tendency to brevity makes her overlook the fact that you love us too much not to want details about us. I am going to give you some: we now bear the name of religious of the Sacred Heart. Our costume is a thin veil over a plain bonnet fastened under the chin. The novices wear white veils; the others wear black. The habit is of black material, cut à la vièrge [high-waisted with full skirt]; we wear a silver cross and a gold ring. The work of the institute is the education of young girls and also of poor children; we also offer seculars the opportunity of making closed eight-day retreats.
>
> The general novitiate is to be in Paris. Candidates have from three to six months' trial in the different convents at which they apply; then they go to Paris for two years of novitiate. After that they make vows for five years and are employed in the different convents of the Society. At the end of five years, if they persevere, they make perpetual vows. There is no fixed dowry: that depends on the means of each one. The ample resources of some make up for the penury of others. You know that I have provided for Euphrosine, and it would have been a joy for me to have done more, but we are without income, and our houses are at greater expense than other religious institutions because of the retreats, so all my income is used up.

On April 15—it was a Monday morning—the three religious of the Sacred Heart moved into the habitable rooms of the new convent. Gradually the entire house was furnished and made ready for the community that was soon to assemble there. As Madame Jouve had written during May, asking for some further information and giving news that delighted Philippine, the latter answered on June 1, and for the first time the name of "Monseigneur Du Bourg" flowed from her quill. She knew his visit to Lyons had aroused enthusiasm and his appeals had met with generous response. Many priests had volunteered for the distant mission in Louisiana, and some large donations in money and church equipment had been made. A movement had been set on foot, moreover, that would result in the formation of the Society for the Propagation of the Faith, one of the most remarkable charities ever organized. Philippine was eager to know more about Bishop Du Bourg, but she wrote with circumspection:

> You gave me much pleasure in writing about Monseigneur Du Bourg. I also heard a great eulogy of him from Augustin. We hoped he would come to Paris, but trouble arising in his diocese has, perhaps, delayed his trip. I am told, however, that the government of the United States wishes to reach an understanding with the Pope, and that the faith is making great progress in that part of the world. At Georgetown there is a fine Jesuit college and a monastery of the Visitation, no doubt the first in the New World. Monseigneur de Neale [sic] is the Catholic bishop of that place. . . .
>
> Our house here is still in foundation. The community will gather here on July 21st; I hope that will be the day of our installation and the solemn blessing of the chapel, which is not yet completed. We are in a quiet quarter of the city, surrounded by gardens, near a supply of fresh water, in the most elevated part of Paris, near St. Etienne du Mont, formerly St. Genevieve. At her tomb and in the other places of devotion I have not failed to pray for you, your husband, and all your children, especially for Henri, my dear godchild, and your three daughters, who are also mine by the affection and interest I bear them.

The new convent was occupied by the foundress with a small community in July. Mother Duchesne remained in Paris as her secretary and assistant; Mother Bigeu became mistress of novices, and Mother Eugenie de Gramont took up the work of mistress general in the boarding school which was soon to be organized. Among the novices whom St. Madeleine Sophie called to Paris to form the nucleus of a general novitiate, there were two with marked attraction for the foreign missions—Octavie Berthold and Eugenie Audé. When Mother Duchesne presided at their recreations, she often told the novices stories she had heard from visiting priests, for missionaries came frequently to the *Sacré-Coeur* in Paris, asking for hospitality and aid. Her position as assistant gave Mother Duchesne the pleasure of welcoming them, offering them refreshment, and pleading their cause with the Mother General, whose fund of alms was kept replenished by generous gifts from charitable friends.

Philippine's heart beat high with eagerness as she listened to stories of work and trial and suffering and success in pagan lands.

She was encouraged in her desire by Father Barat. Living in Bordeaux, he frequently met missionaries on their way to and from America and other foreign lands. He had talked with Bishop Du Bourg sometime during 1816 and had assured him that Mother Duchesne was just the person to work in his diocese. The type of work was vague enough in Father Barat's mind; the type of religious order to which she belonged was not investigated by the bishop at the time, as its reputation was already well established in France. Father Barat had written to his sister and to Philippine about the bishop of *La Louisiane* and the mission field in his diocese, and Philippine had reason for excitement when she received a letter from him in mid-November, telling her of an interview he had had with Bishop Du Bourg:

> On the eve of his departure for Provence [he wrote], I had a long conference with the bishop, during which we talked seriously about the Louisiana mission and you. Your superiors have recognized the supernatural character of your vocation, and Monseigneur wants you to help with the work in his vast diocese. You desire it sincerely and steadfastly, so the matter is arranged. There remains only to decide on the time of your departure and the means of accomplishing the project.

It seemed as simple as that to Louis Barat. Having no authority in the matter, he counted on his influence as the Mother General's brother and even began to direct proceedings with a bit of dry humor:

> Now [he continued] you will need three generous religious to accompany you. But they must be great souls, and among women great souls are very rare. That thought may discourage you, but you have sighed so long a time for your savages and with such constancy, it is probable that God will make an exception in your case and not require you to be a wholly great soul.

This letter sent Philippine into a transport of joy, hope, and prayer: the way was really opening before her. Eleven years had passed since she had first revealed to Mother Barat her inspiration to sacrifice all for the sake of souls in some distant corner of the world. During those years she had done invaluable service for the Society. She had proved her worth, her loyalty, her fidelity to trust. She was one of the group to whom St. Madeleine Sophie gave her confidence in matters of gravest import to the order. And the influence of the saint had been at work in her soul, softening the rugged energy of her character, curbing the vehement impulses that shook her whole being, guiding, restraining, helping her to co-operate with divine grace and so become a fit instrument for whatever work God had in store for her. To her pleading to be off on the enterprise beyond the seas Mother Barat always answered: "Wait and pray. Later, perhaps, we may think of it. It is out of the question now."

> So matters stood [Mother Barat related in after years], when on January 14, 1817, Monseigneur Du Bourg, bishop of Louisiana, arrived and had the kindness to call on me. Mother Duchesne knew of the visit, for she was acting as portress just when he arrived. When she came to tell me he was there, she implored me not to let such an opportunity slip. God's hour had come, she assured me, and I had only to say the word. I did not let her see that I shared her conviction, but only answered that if the bishop brought up the subject, I might discuss it, but that I should want a year or eighteen months to prepare.
>
> On the following day the bishop offered Mass in our chapel and I sat and talked with him while he took his breakfast. He told me he wanted to establish religious orders in his vast diocese and was eager to have the religious of the Sacred Heart there. As he urged me to consent to this, I said to myself, "Things are certainly looking well for Mother Duchesne." To him I replied that if the plan were feasible, I should have some one quite ready for the work. Then I told him about Mother Duchesne and her vocation. Monseigneur Du Bourg was delighted and asked to meet this future member of his diocese. When she came in, she threw herself on her knees for his blessing. It is easy to imagine her joy, and the rapturous way she showed it, and the gratitude she poured out in prayer to her divine Master.

Monseigneur Du Bourg continued his European tour in search of missionaries and financial aid for his diocese. In May he was in Paris again. To his dismay he now learned that opposition was being raised by people who had a right to advise the Mother General. Although Father Varin had allowed Philippine to make a vow to devote herself, under obedience, to the foreign missions, he was very much averse to her leaving Mother Barat at a time when she seemed so necessary in the Paris convent. Father Perreau, who was acting ecclesiastical superior of the order in the name of Cardinal Tallyrand-Perigord, considered that the interests of the Society required Mother Duchesne nearer home. Yielding to the opinion of her chief advisers, the Mother General had decided to postpone the departure of her missionaries.

On May 16 the bishop came to pay a last call at the *Sacré-*

Coeur. He was a keenly sensitive man who knew how to use to advantage both the gifts and the defects of his temperament: that Friday afternoon he was sad, disappointed, displeased. He had set his heart on the project; and as he walked slowly toward the outer door with Mother Barat, he made little effort to conceal the chagrin which opposition always aroused in him. Suddenly from a doorway Mother Duchesne appeared. She knew what was happening and could no longer restrain her pent-up ardor and anxiety. Now she was kneeling with clasped hands on the threshold the bishop was about to cross and pleading with the Mother General: "Your consent, Mother! Give your consent." A moment of silent prayer in three dedicated hearts, then St. Madeleine Sophie spoke with all the deep affection she felt for this, her "eldest daughter."

"Yes, my dear Philippine, I consent, and I shall begin at once to look for companions for you."

Father Barat learned of the decision from Bishop Du Bourg, who arrived in Bordeaux in the middle of June to take ship for America. Four months later the bishop wrote to Mother Duchesne from Baltimore, giving her a guarded warning that the trans-Atlantic voyage offered many difficulties, but adding that every day women and children, as well as men, crossed the ocean to travel to the Mississippi Valley for the sake of temporal advantages. "And shall we not do the same," he added, "with much greater zeal for the glory of our good Master and for the salvation of souls that have been redeemed by his Blood?"

One missionary companion Mother Duchesne had hoped for was her niece, Aloysia Jouve. Not, perhaps, in the pioneer group, but after she had completed the training required in the Society before final vows. But Aloysia's health was by this time quite seriously impaired. What at first was an apparently insignificant sore on her foot had carried a vicious infection into the blood stream, and there was no curing the disease. The best doctors in Dauphiny were called in on the case. Then Madame Jouve begged to be allowed to bring her daughter home for treatment. Aloysia was opposed to the plan and Mother Duchesne tried to dissuade her sister from pushing the request, but soon she was writing for the Mother General a letter containing the desired permission. The young nun spent some weeks at home, but there was no improvement in her health. The suggestion of a trip to Paris gave Philippine the hope of seeing her once more, but that was beyond the invalid's strength. Aloysia returned to Sainte Marie to face a pro-

tracted agony with courage and love, while her aunt made preparations for the venture to America.

She began the study of English with strong resolve. Happily
she could not foresee how completely that language would elude
her. She began to draw in as much money as possible from the
several investments she had made through her cousins, the *Perier
Frères*, and from property which she still held in common with
her sister Amelie. The Paris convent was in need of funds, and she
felt bound to aid it, knowing that in turn she would be aided in
her mission. The sum of 10,000 francs was agreed upon as a fair
settlement for Philippine's share in the family estate at Grâne, and
her sister made the payment in 1817.

Although Philippine was determined to hide from her brother
and sisters her hopes and plans regarding the American mission, she
had already given her confidence on this subject to her loved
cousin, the Baroness de Savoye-Rollin. Josephine always went to
see her when she was in Paris, and the two women talked with the
same affectionate understanding as when they were girls together
at Sainte Marie. While Philippine aspired to the difficult life of a
foreign missionary, Josephine found an outlet for her zeal in
generosity toward the poor. With her, charity was not so much a
kindly habit as an innate quality of soul. In the several cities where
her husband had been prefect during the Napoleonic decade she
had a brilliant reputation for wit, gentleness, and charity. In the
evenings she did the honors at the prefecture after having worked
all day to make the poor happy and in some degree less uncomfortable. She possessed great wealth, but never lived in luxury;
and she honored her wealth by the use she made of it.

On her forty-eighth birthday Philippine sat down to write to
Josephine. She was already trying to cultivate a characteristic that
seems essential to missionaries—the begging habit. It was always
difficult for her to practice, and she was never very successful at it,
though she wrote with ease to Josephine that twenty-ninth day of
August, 1817:

> I am taking advantage of an opportunity to write to you. I am also
> very much interested in writing to you, and I am not ashamed to
> use the word "interested" because the matter is not personal, but
> regards the service of God and our fellowmen. Since you left
> [Paris], my desires for the American mission have not diminished,
> and God seems to be listening to my prayers. I saw the bishop of
> Louisiana on the eve of his departure. He must be in America now.

Our Mother General promised him six of our nuns for next spring, and I am one of them. So we must prepare what is needed for a sacristy. Furthermore, the vicar general [of Bishop Du Bourg], who is remaining at Bordeaux as agent for the mission, writes to our Mother General, begging her to procure material, muslin, linen, galloon, all that can be used to make vestments and all that can impress the savages in the pomp of liturgical ceremonies. You are so sympathetic toward physical miseries, I know you will be even more interested in the conversion of souls, since their eternity depends on this. . . .

You have learned through my cousin [Augustin Perier] that we have drawn a part of the money you had deposited, and you know why we did so. . . . Remember me, please, to Monsieur de Rollin, to my aunt [Tante Perier], and to all my cousins, especially Madame Teisseire.   I am, in the Heart of Jesus,

Your devoted cousin,

Philippine

This is the first of Philippine's letters that Josephine saved. For years they wrote to each other—not very frequently, it is true, but often enough to make the extant letters one of the surest and most illuminating sources from which to study the character of Mother Duchesne.

five

"To St. Louis in the Illinois Country"

I. February—May, 1818

JOSEPHINE WAS IN PARIS just when Philippine needed her most. She was at home in the capital; she had entree and influence; and she was at the service of her cousin. The maturity of their friendship and the sympathetic understanding with which each shared the other's interests, joys, reverses, drew them closer than ever in the face of a separation they knew would in all probability be lifelong.

There were many other members of the big double family in Paris that winter, as a wedding was scheduled for January. Marine Teisseire's eldest daughter, Amelie, was betrothed to Louis Bergasse, a merchant from Marseille. Since the marriage ceremony was to take place in Paris, Philippine had the opportunity of seeing many dearly loved relatives. A wealthy, well dressed, well mannered group gathered at times in the parlor of the convent in the Rue des Postes to visit her and talk, not about her and her plans for the future mission, but about the wedding and, still more, about Casimir Perier and the stir he was making in the capital.

For fifteen years he had been prominent in financial circles. As director of *Perier Frères*, he had worked with his brother Scipion, the administrator of the firm, in a remarkable combination, and their banking house had attained European renown. Now they were among the top bankers of Paris, the younger brother being more active because he was in better health. In 1815, Casimir had published the first of the pamphlets with which he made his debut in political life. He was a recognized genius at finance, and no matter how severe his criticisms of the government might be—it was the policy of obtaining secret foreign loans to pay the heavy penalties imposed by the Allies in the peace treaty of 1815 he denounced—his patriotism and loyalty could never be questioned. The dignity of his character and the uprightness of his life eliminated all suspicion of personal selfishness in his fight against the methods used by the minister of finance.

In the September elections of 1817 he was voted a seat for Paris in the Chamber of Deputies. At the royal seance opening the session in November he was the youngest member of the Chamber, having reached his fortieth birthday on October 12, between election and seating. For the rest of his life he was to be in public office. All Paris was talking about Casimir Perier after his first speech on December 13, 1817, for that speech, with its brief, incisive style, its perfect phrasing and dynamic delivery, placed him among the finest orators of his day, and gave him a claim to the position he held for a dozen years as a leader of the opposition in the Chamber of Deputies.

Philippine loved this handsome cousin, who had groaned as a lad over her lack of talent for arithmetic, and she was proud of the high principles he was defending. And there was his sister, Marine Teisseire, mother of the bride-to-be, prettier than ever and always doing thoughtful things for cousin Philippine. Augustin and his family were in Paris, too. The Periers shared the mission secret before Mother Duchesne wrote it to her sisters, though the date of departure was actually set before she had the courage to tell anyone but Josephine that she was leaving France.

Preparations for the voyage were, however, under way. News of the Superior General's promise to Bishop Du Bourg had traveled to Amiens, Poitiers, Grenoble, Niort, and Quimper. In all the convents contributions for the mission were being collected and packed for shipment. Many nuns who shared Mother Duchesne's aspirations offered for the venture to America, but Mother Barat was slow in announcing her choice. The Paris convent had been through a serious epidemic in the autumn of 1817. "For three months we had much illness in the house," wrote the annalist, "and we lost several religious and children. Mother Duchesne was on duty day and night, sometimes spending entire nights by the bedside of the sick, never giving a thought to herself."

The New Year dawned—1818—and ran its course quietly enough for nearly three weeks. Then a letter from Father Bertrand Martial, vicar general of Bishop Du Bourg, announced that he was sailing for America in mid-February and expected to take with him the Religious of the Sacred Heart destined for St. Louis. This advance in the schedule delighted Mother Duchesne, though it complicated life for her family. An eye-witness of those last days in Paris gives an affectionate account of what took place:

> Mother Duchesne would have forgotten all that concerned the temporal side of the preparations, had not our Mother General strictly charged her with the whole affair. She set to work vigorously, and God certainly blessed her efforts. What an influx of merchants, tradesmen, workmen of different types! People coming and going, all wanting to see Mother Duchesne! And how joyous she was in the midst of it all! It was a calm, thoughtful, deep joy, that forgot nothing but self. She packed the trunks, cases, satchels, without the least anxiety or trouble. Everything ran smoothly; everything was ready on time. Seeing her joy, we could not be sad at her going; and I fancied to myself the emotion she would experience on setting foot in that land she has longed for so ardently and embracing the first little Indian girl.
>
> The passports gave most anxiety, for it was feared they would not be obtained in time. But a relative of Mother Duchesne took the matter in hand, battled with the difficulties, and brought the papers a few hours before the party left us. All was arranged with so much speed and success that even those most opposed to the enterprise as an extraordinary adventure just at this time, recognized the finger of God in all and his plans for making the adorable Heart of Jesus known in the New World by means of our little Society.

Josephine's part in the battle to secure the necessary papers was crucial. Acting now as chaperone to the nuns, now as their diplomatic agent, she had a busy time during those last two weeks her best friend was in Paris. The menfolk, too, were busy with notes and bills of exchange amounting to nearly 20,000 francs— their own money or Philippine's—to finance the missionary venture of this middle-aged cousin whom they loved so sincerely. On Sunday, February 1, she found time and courage to write to her sisters. The letters to Melanie and Adelaide are missing. To Amelie de Mauduit she wrote:

For a long time a very strong and definite attraction has drawn me to the teaching of the infidels. I even thought of going to China, but that is not practicable, as women cannot appear in public there. God has listened to my prayers and has let me find nearer home and at less financial cost the happiness for which I prayed. In Paris I met the Bishop of Louisiana, and it is in his diocese that I shall work to instruct the savages and found a house of the Society. The departure was at first set for May, but other missionaries are going this month on a vessel that is well known and has a good captain, so it has been decided that we shall go with them. I leave Paris next Sunday. Only five of us will sail this time, but in September others will embark. . . . I hope you will write and give me news of yourself.

Believe me, my beloved Sister, I shall always be closely united to you. You and your daughters, your husband and your son will be continually in my prayers. Tell Amelie to recall the days of her first fervor and never forget the *one thing necessary. Adieu,* my dearest Sister. Have a Mass offered in honor of St. Regis.

To the Jouve family she made the same announcement and added affectionately:

So, unless untoward circumstances arise, I shall leave France this month. But in doing so, I carry with me my memories and my affection for my dear sisters and their children. You will pray for me, as I shall for you. At the moment when I am leaving all to work for the salvation of souls, I pray most earnestly that you will cling to the *one thing necessary.* Say this above all to Henri and to my Amelie, to whom I shall not have time to write. One does not make a change like this, and so hastily, without having much to do. I am, and I shall always be, closely united to you in the Sacred Heart of Jesus.

And now it was time to write a farewell to Sainte Marie. The letter to the community there is both an act of reparation for the past as it appeared in her eyes and an expression of humble gratitude for the grace that was at hand. In it appears that tone of self-deprecation which is so difficult for most people to understand, but which was the sincere expression of Philippine's opinion of herself, and that opinion was according to her Rule. Her days of self-sufficiency were over; her natural independence was giving place gradually to complete reliance on God, and humility was becoming a settled habit. To her "very dear Mothers and Sisters" she wrote:

When I look into my own soul, I cannot find any reason for expecting you to remember me. I know full well that I deserve to be forgotten, and I really ought to desire this very thing. For if you remember me, you must inevitably recall all the faults I committed—faults that were prejudicial to an institution for which I would willingly give my life, faults I repent of most sincerely. But when I think about the charity which is the bond of union in our holy Society, I am not surprised at your thoughtfulness, and I beg you to add this kindness—pardon for all my past faults and prayers that I may avoid such conduct in the future. You must be as merciful to me as God himself is.

Ordinarily he gives one outstanding grace to a soul, and this becomes the source of many others. In my case that signal grace was my return to Sainte Marie and membership in the blessed Society of the Sacred Heart. This was far beyond anything I had hoped for. And still—in spite of the fact that I have profited so poorly by all the instructions and the examples of solid and sublime virtue I have received—still God in his goodness is opening to me a new career that calls forth all my gratitude and overwhelms me with confusion when I think of it. . . . I hope you will not cease praying to the Blessed Virgin and St. Regis for this great enterprise. I have poured out many tears and prayers for America at the shrine of our Lady where St. Francis de Sales was freed from his temptation. That statue is now at the convent of St. Thomas, where I lived for several months. I believe I gained much grace at that shrine and at Montmartre. I beg you again to pray very specially to them for us. We should be on fire with zeal. . . .

It was harder to write to her beloved niece, and the note enclosed to her in the letter to Sainte Marie tells by its rather incoherent style the strain under which it was written:

I am leaving Paris, my dear Aloysia, and soon I shall be leaving France. We shall meet in heaven at least, I hope, if we never have that consolation again here on earth. Offer your sufferings for us and we shall pray for you. . . . I hear that you are ill again. Let your sufferings be your prayers for me and for my poor charges. I shall offer for you the eloquent prayers of the poor. Envy my happiness and relish your own. God wishes us to be separated on this earth and reunited in his Heart. Affectionate messages to Mothers, Sisters, and children at Sainte Marie. I have announced my departure to my sisters and my brother.

The six months' journey to St. Louis began on Sunday, February 8.

On the eve of the departure [wrote an eye-witness] our Mother General assembled us all and gave Mother Duchesne her obedience as superior of the mission band. She dreaded this office and believed she would never be able to bear it. She certainly had not foreseen, when begging for the foundation, that she would be placed at its head. She submitted to the burden, however, realizing, no doubt, that it would offer her more opportunities for suffering. Our Mother General recommended, above all, union among themselves and inviolable attachment to the Society in France as the surest safeguards in their efforts to glorify God. And she told them to send us news of themselves as frequently as possible.

Next morning Father Perreau offered the Holy Sacrifice of the Mass, at which Eugenie Audé made her vows. Then the Blessed Sacrament was exposed for adoration all day, for this was a great day in the history of the Society. There were many visitors that morning, among them Fathers Varin, Druilhet, and Roger. The Periers were there—Augustin, Josephine, Marine—and Camille Jordan, all adding to the provisions already prepared for the trip. Hippolyte and Coralie Duchesne may also have been there, for they had been in Paris for the wedding, and Duchesne had contributed a generous sum toward the expense of the journey. Subdued excitement and the sound of many footsteps were audible as novices hurried through the halls, carrying baggage. Joy and heart-suffering struggled in Philippine's soul.

The missionary group was summoned to lunch. It was a hasty meal, for in the midst of it Mother Bigeu came in to say the carriage was waiting. Philippine rose from the table immediately for her final good-bye to Mother Barat and the community. Then she went quickly to the parlor for a last word with the family she loved so dearly. The nuns had gathered near the outer door, and one of them noted briefly afterwards:

> The moment of separation was very painful for us all. As for Mother Duchesne, she did not shed a tear, though we know how deeply she felt it all, for she is naturally so affectionate. Seeing Mother Octavie crying as she said good-bye, . . . Mother Duchesne took her gently by the arm and led her out of the house. The carriage was waiting and there was no time to lose.

In the emotional crisis of the departure Mother Duchesne's response was one of fine controlled maturity. She would admit later on how costly the sacrifice had been, but at the moment she gave no outward sign. Happily she could not see the length of the way that stretched ahead nor the circumstances in which she would be called upon to sustain that generosity. Her gift for sustained effort was one of the splendid natural endowments of her character.

A crowd of curious onlookers gathered around the stagecoach before the nuns climbed in with their satchels and packages. The trunks and packing-cases had gone ahead in a wagon. With a smile and a last wave of her hand to friends who had come to see them off, with *bon voyage* outside answered by *adieu* from within, Philippine took her place in the coach with her companions. The reins were lifted over the horses, the whip cracked sharply in the chill air, the crowd shouted a noisy send-off, and the coach headed south on the road to Orleans. The nuns prayed silently. An army officer, soon bored with the journey, sang lustily to while away the time. Evremond Harissart, a seminarian bound for the American missions, intoned psalms and hymns to drown the words of the drinking songs he feared might shock the nuns. He was a tall, spare, ascetic-looking young man, grave in manner, deliberate and earnest in speech. Sister Lamarre would have liked to join him as he sang, for she had a very good voice and enjoyed using it.

Mothers Berthold and Audé had dried their tears even before they boarded the coach and were alive to the changing scenes through which they were passing. Like Mother Duchesne they had been born and reared in mountain lands. Octavie Berthold was from Geneva. A well educated Swiss convert, her beauty might have attracted attention, but her reserved manner and religious bearing impressed all who saw her. Eugenie Audé's home was at Moutiers in Savoy, some fifty miles northeast of Grenoble. She had lived in Italy, had been presented at the court of Napoleon, then under the impulse of grace had chosen the cloistered life at Sainte Marie.

A new world was already opening up to Philippine and her companions. This was for them a new part of France, a section in sharp contrast with their Alpine country, and they were interested in every feature of the countryside and towns along the way: Orleans, with its memories of Jeanne d'Arc; Tours, with its tower of Charlemagne and the ruins of St. Martin's ancient church and the River Loire that Philippine found so beautiful, but the town was especially appealing to her as the birthplace of Marie Guyart, who as Mother Marie of the Incarnation had set out from here on her journey to Canada in 1639. A halt at Blois gave an opportunity to send letters back to Paris, and every morning there was Holy Communion in a different place. At Poitiers the travelers were at home again for just two hours, and Philippine saw for the first and only time the old monastery of the Feuillants that Mother Thérèse had so often described to her. Here, too, she met Sister Marguerite

Manteau, fifth member of the missionary band. Then on to Angoulême, and into Bordeaux, the fine old seaport on the Garonne, with its beautiful thirteenth-century Cathedral of St. Andrew looking out over wharves and ships and commerce from the four corners of the world.

Father Barat was on hand to greet them, with Father Boyer, vicar general of Archbishop d'Aviau, who drove with them to the convent of Notre Dame, where Madame Vincent, the superior, welcomed them and gave them hospitality until the embarkation. They had expected to board the vessel immediately, but in this matter the weather had its way, and the waiting seemed very long. The first few days were filled with the business of material preparations that were necessary in the days of ocean travel by sailing vessels. The arrival of mail from Paris and Grenoble helped to keep up the morale of the nuns at a time when there was danger of spiritual depression after the excitement of the departure and the novelty of the trip had worn off. Letters from Lyons and Grâne tore at Philippine's heartstrings, adding a measure of suffering she had tried to ward off.

Before leaving Paris, Mother Duchesne had given Father Perreau a lengthy *Memoire* in the form of a letter addressed to Mother Barat. In it she had tried to outline the history of her missionary vocation, the encouragement she had received at various times from her spiritual directors and from the Mother General herself, and the signs by which Divine Providence had marked the way for her toward this goal. One of her consolations in Bordeaux was a letter from Father Perreau.

> I am happy to be able to tell you that the document I handed to your dear Mother Barat was gladly received by her. As for myself, the more I reflect on it, the more I see that God has called you to this mission. In order to stamp your holy enterprise with the symbol characteristic of all that is done solely for his glory, he has allowed it to go through trials of many kinds. . . . Continue with the same perseverance and the same abandonment to God's will the work you have begun so nobly. He will always be with you to uphold you. I dare to say more: you should count on our Lord's very special protection, for with the apostles you can say in all truth: Lord, we have left all things and followed you; what shall we receive? The reward he will give you for this great act of renunciation is his own Divine Heart for your refuge, his Spirit to guide you, and some drops from his own chalice of bitter-

ness to purify, to detach you from self, and to teach you to rely on him alone.

Mother Barat's first letter gave Philippine further assurance, bringing sunshine into her soul at a time when she had great need of it:

> It is not without emotion, dear Mother, that I write you this first letter since you were given the task of leading a little group so far away from us. It was very hard to part with you! When the anticipation of it cost me so much, what must the reality have been! Our Lord did sweeten it wonderfully by the thought that you would be happy in doing his most holy will in the midst of labors and privations. Your example strengthened me, and I could not help envying your lot. . . . Pray for me; you owe me this for the tender love I bear you, which distance will only increase.
>
> I did not need your letter to be convinced that your high vocation is from God. The persistency of your desires, the ease with which the plan, apparently so beset with difficulties, was carried out when God's time had come, the way everything concurred to bring about the departure that cost us so much, the strength God gave you to overcome obstacles, all proves to me that in spite of the arguments of human prudence our Lord has called you to found a convent of the Sacred Heart in *la Louisiane*.
>
> Now, my dear daughter, enter more and more fully into the designs of our loving Lord. Try to grow each day more worthy of his work by laying a deeper foundation of humility in your soul, for out of this will spring gentleness and forbearance with the souls entrusted to you. I am happy about your love for them, and I know you will do all in your power to lessen the sacrifice they have made. . . . Take care of your health. The hard penance of the position of superior, which you have always dreaded so much, must replace all other penances. . . . Everyone here sends most affectionate greetings. We are praying for you. Pray for me. . . .

In the first letter she wrote to her family from Bordeaux on February 15, the influence of Father Perreau's encouragement is apparent, for Philippine repeated the quotation he had used. In it, too, she shows once more the kind of work she expected to do on reaching America.

> In this hour when I am giving up everything almost as if I were going to die, since it is practically certain I shall never see you again, nor my many Mothers and Sisters in religion, my relatives and friends, I believe I have a right to ask great things of God, with

the same confidence as St. Peter when he said to Jesus Christ: We have left all for you; what shall be our reward?

Oh, the reward I ask of him is the great, the ineffable consolation of learning that you are all fervent in loving him. . . . Across the enormous distance that will soon separate us, my heart will always be seeking you and praying for your happiness. If I can contribute to this by obtaining prayers for you from the interesting children who will become the flock of Jesus Christ, I shall not neglect a means that is so strongly according to my heart. When I see myself in the midst of a crowd of simple, innocent souls, I shall say: Pray for the children I left in France, for every dear memory of them adds value to my sacrifice. Pray, too, for your very first benefactors. They did not know you, yet they prayed for your conversion and helped procure it by the gifts they contributed for you. . . .

That same day she wrote more intimately to Mother Thérèse:

I was deeply moved by the tenderness of your recent letters, as I am moved also by the mercy of God in my regard. I am impatient to board the vessel that will carry me to the goal of my desires. I may set sail any day now—and I may also have to wait. It all depends on the weather. I leave in France so many people I hold dear and shall always cling to by the strongest bonds of love. These bonds will tighten continually when I think of all I owe to the Society. I am going to have the joy of helping to extend it in the New World and to see devotion to the Sacred Heart flourish there. You would like to share this joy—but God makes use of you right where you are. As I am good for nothing here, he is giving me a chance to do something useful elsewhere, like the nuns who are changed from one house to another frequently in the hope of finding them useful somewhere. Pray that I may not always be unfaithful. My companions are very courageous and people envy them. . . .

Monsieur Morange has been so thoughtful as to supply us with wine for the sea voyage. I owe this to you. After waiting several days I had the pleasure of greeting Madame Morange and Mademoiselle Emiline. They are wonderfully kind. I have never had a more cordial welcome. Eliza could not come, but she sent me a charming letter. They are going to supply us with preserves and apples—they say apples are the best fruit to quench thirst. In so much kindness and cordiality I recognize the heart of my Mother Thérèse. I shall see them again.

As the sailing was delayed rather indefinitely, the nuns made a retreat. This was quite to Philippine's liking, but she could not look back to it with consolation. It was made at a difficult time and under such trying circumstances that even the spiritual direction of Father Barat did not call forth much enthusiasm. There was time for letter writing, and Philippine used it to advantage. She had already given details about their five-day trip and safe arrival in Bordeaux when she wrote to Mother Barat on February 18:

> How grateful we are for all the proofs we have had of your maternal love for us and for Mother Bigeu's remembrance for each one! I delivered her letter to Father Barat. We see him almost every day. He hears our confession on alternate days, but he is not giving us any sermons. He says he is exhausted every night because he has so much work to do. . . .
>
> I have been to the home of Madame Fournier, Bishop Du Bourg's sister. She had rented a lodging for us and also got us a servant and a person to attend to our meals—all near the *Réunion*, where she really wanted to take us. I declined her arrangements because of the retreat. She has reserved our sleeping quarters on shipboard and is now talking about *comforts*, that is, things to take with us for the sake of the body—mostly food. As to the wine, Monsieur Morange has kindly taken care of that. . . .
>
> It would be impossible to show more cordiality and charity than Madame Vincent has shown us. And the same is true of her Sisters. They are very edifying. But all this kindness surrounding us is not you or my Sisters; and although God sustains my courage and even the intensity of my desires, still, when I arrived here, my soul was in a state of anguish, hard and dark. Going into the Church of St. Andrew, I dwelt insistently on the words: *O bona Crux, diu desiderata, et iam concupiscenti animo praeparata!*
>
> My companions, too, have had their moments of weakness. I realize this and tried to be of help to them, knowing full well my own wretchedness. All this only makes it seem more astonishing that God in his goodness should have made choice of us. Your brother gives a good push forward on the pathway of perfection to souls who lag behind. . . .

That same day Philippine wrote to Josephine and her sister. The old address in Rue St. Honoré escaped her mind, and she sent the letter to Madame Bergasse:

> It would have been a great satisfaction for me to have written to you as soon as we reached Bordeaux, to try to express my undying love for you and all the gratitude I feel. How much these sentiments have increased during the past weeks, if increase was possible, seeing all the trouble you went to for me, all the important services you rendered, all your tender solicitude. When my

thoughts revert to what I am leaving in France—all that is dear to me—I put them aside, being intimately convinced that, as I have desired only one thing: to answer God's call and abandon myself to his Providence, so the voyage and the trials ahead will never be as great as the help I may confidently expect from him.

So far our journey has been pleasant. As the vessel is not yet ready to sail we are making a retreat for a few days. I have gone out only to call on the Archbishop and the sister of my future bishop. She has made this ocean voyage six times, so she knows exactly all that we need. As she is very zealous about her brother's mission, she has arranged about the making up of our berths and is directing our embarkation, conjointly with her brother.

I learned from them that the *piastre* is now very high, being the medium of exchange most used in the India trade. So they will draw only a small sum for us and convert our notes into bills of exchange on Baltimore and New Orleans. They assure me that navigation on the Mississippi becomes easier every day. There are always about a dozen steamboats traveling up and down, and they are almost as large and convenient as a sea-going vessel. They have informed the Ursulines in New Orleans of our coming, and we shall lodge with them or with relatives of our bishop. . . .

Remember me very specially to all my loved relatives. . . . The vessel leaves Bordeaux Tuesday to go to Pauillac, but I do not know what day we shall go aboard. It cannot be long now. Respectful greetings from all my companions. As I cannot recall Madame de Rollin's address, I beg Madame Bergasse to pardon the liberty I have taken.

March came in with the westerly winds still blowing a fierce gale from the sea and keeping the *Rebecca* at her mooring in the Garonne, but a change in the weather was predicted, and the *Rebecca* nosed away from the city wharf and sailed downstream to Pauillac on the west shore, where the passengers would embark.

But there was a further delay, which gave Philippine time for another letter to Josephine containing a paragraph of details straight from her sensitive heart:

The vicar-general with whom we are traveling is not very happy about this arrangement; we add so much to his responsibility. That will help toward my perfection, for I suffer when I see I am causing trouble. No one but you, my dear Cousin, has the art of taking the weight out of gratitude and leaving only the sweetness. . . . Everything seems to promise us a pleasant voyage. A multitude of prayers are rising to heaven for us; even the holy Archbishop of Bordeaux has offered Mass for us. So I leave in peace about all things. If the enterprise ends in misfortune, God will have allowed the efforts for a better purpose than the one we envisaged as his will. May he be blessed in all that happens. A thousand affectionate messages to the Teisseires and the Periers and all my dear relatives. Farewell, dear Cousin. This carries the sincere and tender expression of my eternal devotedness to you.

In a postscript to this letter of March 5, Philippine adds: "We did not sail today; a contrary wind detained us." Five weeks had passed since the nuns had left Paris, and only on March 14—a Saturday, they noted—did they go from Bordeaux to Pauillac. Sister Lamarre's account of the stay there is a charming bit of narrative, introducing her lively personality which blended courage and ability with the intense affection of a keenly sensitive nature. She had taught in the free school at Cuignières and in the orphanage at St. Pezenne nearby, and had shown there the virtue and power of adaptability that made her a valuable member in any community. She was active and independent by nature, a bit headstrong at times, and inclined to chafe under restraint. Her letter, dated from Royan at the mouth of the Garonne on March 16, is addressed to Mother Prevost, superior of the house at Amiens, where Sister Lamarre had been living when called to join the mission band.

As you see, we are not yet dead. One needs great patience and resignation, however, to go through all that the Heart of Jesus has willed for us and allowed to happen. We thought we were on the point of sailing when I wrote you last, but bad weather made its appearance again and detained us longer in Bordeaux. . . . Fair weather seemed to reappear on Monday of Passion Week, along with a favorable wind. The captain notified us that we must be on board at ten in the morning, and we obeyed. . . .

Kind Father Barat gave us his blessing before we went down to the wharf, where we were to take a small boat carrying the passengers to the ocean vessel, which was at Pauillac, some twenty miles from Bordeaux. During that short navigation the weather changed. After spending a night on the *Rebecca*, we were obliged to land again by means of a little boat that seemed about to be submerged at any moment. There was reason enough for fear. The wind was terrific, but God was good to us, and what confidence I ought to have in him. . . . We had expected to find lodgings near the pastor's house, and what was not our surprise on learning that we would have to separate into three groups. We have with us a lady from Bordeaux who is none too wealthy and who was glad to share the charity offered us, and of course it fell to my lot to be named with her. So here I am with her. I leave the rest to your imagination. . . .

I meant to tell you about the first night on the vessel. When the time came to retire, I did not know just how to manage in the narrow berths. Of course there was a good deal of laughter among us, but I finally managed with patience and some pain. My berth was the top one. When at last I got into it I found I had very little covering, but I could not get out and down again. When I tried to turn over I bumped first against one thing, then against another. I got settled, but there was no sleep, and there was not room even to raise my head. But it is all for the love of the Heart of Jesus that we endure this and much else . . . the more the better, and God be praised for all. And now fair weather has come. The captain has just sent for us, saying we embark at 7 in the morning, Holy Thursday. God grant we reach America alive.

The *Rebecca* was piloted through the last channel, and on Holy Saturday put out to sea. For a whole week she tossed in rough weather on the Bay of Biscay, and her passengers experienced the desperate helplessness of sea-sickness. Then things improved and they were able to take some interest in life again, to note the progress of the boat: March 30 they reached the latitude of Lisbon, nearly identical with that of St. Louis; April 2 they rounded the Azores. Then came the long stretch of unbroken ocean, when there were pleasant days on deck and they could think more coherently, pray more peacefully, listen more attentively to Father Martial's little spiritual talks and to the English lessons they all found so difficult. They chatted with subdued gaiety—Father Martial was very firm about its being subdued—each telling of her vocation and the houses of the Society she had known. Three of them had known and loved Sainte Marie, and Mother Duchesne had much to tell them about its history and her own experiences there and in Paris.

Sometimes she sat a little apart from them and meditated on the contents of a creased sheet which she guarded carefully from the wind and ocean spray. Her companions recognized the handwriting and knew it was the document the Mother General had given to her when she named her superior of the mission. It was the supreme mark of trust on the part of St. Madeleine Sophie toward her "eldest daughter," bestowing on her the exceptional authority which alone would enable her to carry on the Society's work in America, "clothing her," as the document stated, with powers which normally only the Mother General herself could exercise.

The admission, retention, and dismissal of subjects, temporary changes in the religious costume, the disposal of funds, the acquisition of property, the foundation of convents, nomination to offices in the community, changes of employment, dispensation from cloister during the day for the sake of teaching in free schools and for hearing Mass on Sundays and feast days in the absence of a chaplain—such were the powers delegated to her who was to bear the responsibility of a mission undertaken, as the letter of obedience stated, entirely for the honor and glory of the Sacred Hearts of Jesus and Mary.

On this trans-Atlantic crossing the *Rebecca* encountered as many tribulations as a caravel of fiction might have to its credit in a fantastic tale of the sea: terrific storms that threatened to drive the vessel on rocky islands, torrential rains and violent headwinds, excessive heat and calms that kept the helpless boat drifting idly in the doldrums, an encounter with a pirate ship from Buenos Aires, manned with one hundred and twenty sailors and armed with eleven cannon. "They forced us to stop," noted Mother Duchesne, "but on being informed that this was an American vessel, they allowed it to pass unmolested." The stench of the hold came up sickeningly when wine casks burst and food was rotting; the water was contaminated and the ship-biscuits were moulding. Superstition was stirring among the sailors: who could interpret the double sign of a partial eclipse of the moon, followed shortly by a comet that was visible for several nights? And then a fire on the deck, with Sister Catherine giving the alarm and the passengers extinguishing the blaze.

But the voyage was not all of that pattern. There were stretches of beautiful weather, when a good stiff wind filled the sails. There was Holy Mass at four or four-thirty in the morning whenever Father Martial was well enough, and Communion for the nuns, followed by a long thanksgiving before the ship's bell sounded for breakfast. Often in the late afternoon the nuns stood together in the bow of the boat, their full skirts rippling out in the breeze, their thin veils waving in the fading twilight. Then the captain called for "the hymn," and the sweet strains of the *Ave Maris Stella* floated over the waters. As her nuns sang, Mother Duchesne's intent gaze studied the sky, the waters, and the western horizon. The long weeks of the voyage, the stench, the nausea, the still tender memories of separation from loved ones, laughter, news about people and things that were part of her life—all seemed to drop away as she stood there, looking westward toward the sunset and her promised land.

When the evenings lengthened and were fair, they remained on deck "as late as nine o'clock," Father Martial sitting quietly near them as they talked of France and the friends they had left so willingly, yet so reluctantly, or of the events that had broken the monotony of the day: a ship sighted and signaled to—"bound for Granada," they learned through the *porte-voix*; a porpoise caught —"so big it took several men to haul it in, and when served at table it tasted like beef, but the fat was like pork"; latitude reckonings and islands coming in sight, and "the trail of light behind the vessel when it made good speed." That phosphorescence was a phenomenon they gazed at with astonishment and delight.

While the nuns suffered a good deal from their crowded and stuffy sleeping quarters, they had no complaint to make about the meals served on the *Rebecca*. Mother Duchesne said only that the food was nourishing and abundant, though she found cabbage soup disgusting when she was seasick. Mother Audé, however, praised the menu, remarking that:

> Dinner was usually an affair of six or seven courses—soup, fresh roasted chicken, ham, vegetables, fish or eggs, dessert, dried fruits, liqueur. At breakfast there was omelet, herring, anchovy, ham, sausage, fruit, tea or *café-au-lait* three times a week, preserves. Once a week a sheep or a pig was slaughtered, so there was very little dried meat served. Fresh fish was caught frequently, and there was plenty of excellent wine.
>
> The captain was very nice to us. . . . The sailors of the crew were as meek as lambs, working quietly and without any objectionable language. The second-in-command was a very intelligent man, silent and reserved, whom the sailors obeyed without a word of objection to orders. As for the passengers, they were all bound for New Orleans to rejoin their families. They were polite and friendly on the whole. One lady stayed close to us during the whole voyage.

A little feast was celebrated privately on Ascension evening. It fell on April 30, and the nuns surprised Mother Duchesne by offering their good wishes for her feast on the following day, May 1, St. Philip the Apostle. She took it all quite simply and embraced each of her daughters with that tender affection they knew so well, though they saw it frequently masked with gravity under the burden of responsibility. That day they began the devotions for the month of May and the novena in honor of the Holy Spirit. At sundown on Pentecost, May 10, the watch in the crow's nest thought he sighted land. But a terrific storm struck them toward evening, and the captain decided to lie to for the night. On the twelfth they passed Great Inagua. Two days later they were sailing in superb weather through the channel between Cuba and the Bahama Bank.

Nearing Havana on May 16 the ship was becalmed, and Mother Duchesne took out her writing materials, knowing there would soon be an opportunity to send a letter back to France, the letter she yearned most to speed across the Atlantic. As she sharpened a quill, her mind went back through the last twelve months, and she smiled as memory pictures flashed clear-cut to her mind. For a moment quiet peace enveloped her as she wrote to Mother Barat:

> A year ago today at this very hour we received the visit of the bishop of Louisiana, and you gave your consent regarding our mission to the New World. Happy as I was then, I did not dream that the anniversary of that day would find us so near the holy goal of our journey, for what are 180 leagues as compared with the 2,200 we have traversed in fair weather and foul, since we sailed from Royan! An officer who was detained by some irregularity in his passport boarded our vessel by a small boat last night and told us there were reports of trouble in Paris and Bordeaux. The very thought that you may be suffering, along with so many people who are dear to us, is the severest trial I have had so far, for if we had been lost at sea, only a single branch of the tree would have perished, a branch that so far has produced no fruit, but if the trunk of the tree was endangered! . . .
>
> We are nearing the end of our journey in fairly good health. As it is summer, we are able to sail the whole length of the coast of Cuba, a passage not usually chosen because of the currents, but shortening the trip by 400 leagues. . . . For fifty-two days we saw only sea and sky. It was May 11 before we actually caught sight of land in the distance. . . .
>
> The ocean holds such terrors at times that I was more than once on the verge of writing to beg you not to send another person out here until you received assurance that all is well with us and that such a sacrifice would be of real worth. I should keenly regret missing the opportunity of our nuns traveling with Monsieur Velay and the Ursulines in September, but even at best you can scarcely hope to hear before October that we have reached St. Louis or know our needs with any measure of certainty. It may even be later than that. So if you are able to send us the help, I shall not count on their coming before next spring, and I earnestly

entreat you to send only persons of solid virtue. . . . I owe you the truth, and I shall not hide from you either the perils of the sea or my own cowardice.

A storm at sea is really a terrifying sight. The roaring of the deep mingled with the crash of the tempest would drown both thunder and the booming of cannon. Add to this ear-splitting din the rolling of the vessel in the midst of great waves. The shouting of the sailors as they encourage themselves at their work has a tragic, a lugubrious effect. But their silence is even more dismal, and still worse is the sight of the captain pacing the deck in deep thought. A vessel tossed violently in an angry sea gives one some idea of the confusion of Judgment Day. The sky and the stars seem to disappear suddenly behind mountains of water. The sea, nearly black during the storm, gapes wide, revealing its bottomless depths, then suddenly closes.

The waves sweep over the deck and are hurled out to sea with a new rolling of the boat. Twice during the night the high waves burst open the portholes and flooded our berths. The bending masts, the sails furled or torn, the steering wheel abandoned, lest the boat be too strained—all this is very terrifying unless one sees God in the storm.

The odor that permeates the whole ship is another trial, the confinement, the stench from the hold that is so nauseating and that can be avoided only by going on deck for fresh air—and one cannot always go there, especially in bad weather or when the sun is very hot. At night men sleep there; in the morning they are getting up. Besides, we cannot leave our little holes too early because people dress in the common room.

But if I have realized regretfully that many of our nuns could not endure the terrors of the sea, I have lamented still more over the great number who could not survive the stifling atmosphere of the cabins, the hard, narrow berths, the continual noise. In addition to the handling of the rigging and cordage, which often goes on at night, there is loud talking as if it were daytime. Eating and drinking go on in the common room, where two of us sleep and which adjoins the cabin occupied by the other three.

Seasickness is a wretched malady, affecting both stomach and head. One is utterly good for nothing: connected thought is impossible. One can scarcely drag from one's dull heart the least little prayer of love. I could only repeat the "*Ita, Pater,*" and "My God, I have left all things for you." . . . Eugenie and Marguerite were either more courageous or in better condition for the trip, for they have suffered less from this illness. For two or three days we were all so ill, we could not help each other at all, and the steward had to take care of us. Either he or the captain's boy served us tea or broth through the opened curtains. As for Father Martial, we did not see him at all those days, for he was very ill. . . .

The *Rebecca* had been two months at sea when this letter was written, and ten more days were ahead of her before she reached the mouth of the Mississippi. Mother Duchesne and Sister Marguerite bunked in an alcove of the ship's lounge—the "common room"—for seventy days. It was Philippine's way to take the less desirable place and to keep close to her the Sister who was finding it so difficult to adjust herself to change. Already Marguerite was showing more nervousness and inadaptability than had been expected. Anxious and restless, she found calm security only in Mother Duchesne's company. Of the whole group, however, Father Martial had formed a very high opinion, for he wrote to the Superior General shortly after landing in New Orleans:

> I leave to good Mother Duchesne the telling of the tale of our voyage; you will get from her a very correct account. I reserve to myself the right to tell you what is in my heart with regard to the interior life of your religious. I shall begin by reproaching Monseigneur Du Bourg and you for having humiliated me for seventy days by putting under my guidance women whose virtue surpasses my power of expression. You will both have to answer to God for having chosen for them a director whose capacity and virtue were in no way proportioned to the souls confided to him. You can rejoice, however, in having furnished me with means for a renewal of interior spirit by the example I witnessed daily, for I feel obliged to tell you that not one of your Sisters was ever guilty of the least shortcoming. The passengers, the whole crew, all were in admiration. I had only to moderate their zeal—and this for my own sake: the contrast between my easy-going ways and their constantly increasing fervor would have been too noticeable.

The value of this tribute is enhanced in the case of Mother Duchesne by the fact that for her the whole voyage was a period of spiritual desolation. With remarkable fortitude she showed unvaryingly for nearly three months the same joyous courage, the same thoughtful consideration for others, the same uncomplaining acceptance of circumstances and events that tried her soul at times almost beyond endurance. Yet she admitted, once the trip was over, that throughout it all she had known only darkness and disgust that were unrelieved by sentiments of hope or love. Physical

debility was in part at least a cause of this: she had left Paris fa-
tigued to the point of exhaustion. The responsibility laid upon her
by Mother Barat had added to the depression. The retreat at Bordeaux had left her in spiritual dusk that deepened into a night of
darkness. As yet the vision was far off. She sought relief in prayer,
remembering Xavier's terrible description of the desolation that
drove him to write, "I cannot go on"; yet he persevered. So she
fought resolutely, concealing the struggle as far as possible, with
that heroism which is the only antidote to this spiritual malady.
If Father Martial knew about her suffering, he made no allusion to
it in his letter to the Mother General.

The *Rebecca's* passage through the Gulf of Mexico was fairly
smooth, and the nuns used this opportunity to write letters announcing their safe arrival, in the hope that these might catch a
vessel leaving port soon after they docked in New Orleans.
Mothers Berthold and Audé had kept a diary of the voyage, as had
Mother Duchesne. Their account of the landing in America is more
detailed than hers and better than any second-hand description
could ever be, though repetition has made it something of a classic
in the literature of the Society of the Sacred Heart:

May 25. We have reached the point where the waters of the
Mississippi mingle with those of the sea, forming a distinctly different color. Today the pilot from New Orleans boarded our
vessel to guide it through the difficult channel. The customs officer also came on board to talk with the captain. We entrusted to
him letters we had written to St. Louis, to Madame Vincent at
Bordeaux, and to the Mother House and our families.

From this point on we were directed entirely by soundings,
which diminished as we advanced up the river. Once the vessel
touched bottom. Passing Balize, we saw huge rocks in the channel
which only a skillful pilot could have avoided. The view is becoming more and more interesting. Dense shrubbery lines both
sides of the river, and at night fire-flies twinkle here and there,
much brighter than our glow-worms of France. We saw several
crocodiles at a distance. The sailors caught a small one measuring
about an arm's length. It looks like a lizard, black skin mottled with
yellow, scaly and rough. . . .

Every day things grow more interesting. There are plantations
with big houses, Negroes large and small on the banks of the river,
herds of cattle, beautiful groves. We anchored so close to the bank
several times that some passengers got off for a stroll, bringing
back for our benefit anything curious they found. We have seen

the kind of straw from which they make hats, sycamore trees like those of France, other trees that produce enormous thorns, and still others from which hang huge masses of green hairy stuff which they say is used effectively for making mattresses both by the poor people in the country and by the townsfolk in New Orleans. As to the birds, the only one that sings well is the *mocker*, but there are cardinals, blackbeaks, and one they call the green pope, interesting because of his name and his plumage. . . .

May 29. The great Feast of the Sacred Heart of Jesus. Father Martial gave us a little sermon, and we renewed our vows at Holy Mass. All day we crept slowly up the river. The country along the banks is becoming ever more smiling and open. Wide fields of cotton and corn under cultivation bespeak the industry of the inhabitants. While we were gazing at these new sights, came a message that a carriage awaited Father Martial on the river-bank to take him and us to the city, for we were still some twenty miles downstream. Actually there were two carriages and it was about seven o'clock. By eight our satchels were packed and we were being let down into a small boat by means of the famous armchair which we had eyed so often with fear and envy during the crossing. . . .

It was with the deepest emotion that we set foot on this soil which is for us, in the eyes of faith and the designs of God, the Promised Land. Mother Duchesne's heart could not contain its sentiments of gratitude. In spite of the marshy ground she knelt and kissed the very soil. Her eyes were wet with tears, tears of joy, the kind Father Varin desired for us. "No one is looking," she whispered to us. "You kiss it, too." If only you could have seen her face! It was radiant with joy that only the Heart of Jesus could inspire in a soul filled with his grace and bent on glorifying his Sacred Heart.

It was a glorious night. The stars that studded the deep blue heavens were mirrored in the silvery waters of the stream. Fireflies sparkled in the low bushes. . . . At a plantation we bought some fresh bread, which we had not tasted for seventy days. Father Martial had sent a letter to the Ursuline religious announcing our arrival. Two priests who were at the convent when the letter was opened did not wait to hear it through, but went off immediately to engage the carriages, which came for us with a cordial invitation from the Ursulines to hasten the pleasure they anticipated in welcoming us. It was about two-thirty in the morning when we reached New Orleans, so we went to the priests' house to await the dawn. As the *Angelus* was ringing, we reached the Ursuline convent. The religious received us with a charity of which every moment has given us new proofs.. . . .

2. June—August, 1818

THE GRACIOUS WELCOME extended to them by the Ursuline nuns made the travelers from France feel at home immediately.
Their very first day in New Orleans was filled with experiences
they would record and long remember: the joy of Mass and Holy
Communion in the convent chapel after eleven weeks out of
cloister; the visit of Mr. Du Bourg, the bishop's brother, and the
French consul; Mother Duchesne's first sight of Indians—two of
them begging near the convent grille—"sad-faced but vigorous,"
she thought, and she gave them an alms; a brisk tour of inspection
through the convent and its adjacent buildings; news about the
house that was being prepared for them in St. Louis—false report,
they learned later on—but no news from Bishop Du Bourg. That
was rather disconcerting, but this was only the first day. The nuns
were fascinated by all the works they saw conducted so efficiently
by the Ursulines, and they began to write glowing letters to France.
As the weeks passed, however, and still no word came from the
bishop, anxiety clouded the eager eyes of Philippine Duchesne.
She was, moreover, very sick, though at first she tried to conceal
this fact, hoping she could be her own physician.

She became acquainted with the Ursuline community so
quickly that on May 30, her first day in their convent, she was
writing about them to Mother Bigeu:

> Here I am in New Orleans since two o'clock this morning. . . . I
> am very eager to receive the blessing of the Holy Father. He him-
> self wrote to the superior of this house while she was still at Mont-
> pellier. She had written to him, without the knowledge of her con-
> fessor or her bishop, to get a decision about coming out here. The
> answer was prompt and favorable, and Monseigneur Fournier told
> her it was a unique case for a pope to answer an individual's letter
> without first consulting with her bishop.
>
> In this hospitable community there are several Creole nuns, one
> of them the daughter of a very early settler in the city. Two came
> from Pont-Saint-Esprit thirty-two years ago, and I had the fun of
> repeating to them all I remembered from the account of their trip.
> Their third companion is dead. Eight of the community came
> from Montpellier with their superior eight years ago by way of
> Philadelphia and Baltimore. . . . For undertakings like ours it is

important to choose silent, mortified people with good judgment. Americans are not soft in their ways, nor do they seek delicacies. They admire culture as much as the French do, but they do not like the French. . . .

The Ursuline convent is the haven of religion in this city. Besides the five of us, the nuns are now housing six ecclesiastics. Ordinarily they board and lodge two priests, who live here and have no source of income. In this country there are no revenues set aside for ecclesiastics.

To her brother and sisters she sent a brave, chatty letter on June 2, yet the next day a cry of anguish welled up from Philippine's heart to Aloysia Jouve, enclosed in a letter to Mother Thérèse:

I have entrusted myself and all my dear ones to the Sacred Hearts of Jesus and Mary, but I do not know what you are doing or where you are—in his Hands always, I hope, and disposed to do his will. I submit beforehand to all He arranges, and still I feel that I cling to you. Even in sleep I seem to hear you calling me, urging me, saying I shall be too late. I seemed to run; but just as I thought I had reached you, I awakened to realize that I am many hundreds of leagues from you. I renewed my sacrifice. . . .

There was a very disturbing side to life in New Orleans; and as Mother Duchesne became aware of it, she was puzzled, grieved, disillusioned to some extent. It was not long before she learned why Bishop Du Bourg had chosen to travel by way of Baltimore and to establish his residence in St. Louis. When he had first come to New Orleans as Apostolic Administrator in 1812, he had been dismayed by the conditions prevailing in the city: the laxity of morals, the lack of religious practice, the neglect of religious instruction—a very sickening state. Still worse, he found himself opposed by Père Antoine de Sedella, a Capuchin monk of enigmatic character and baleful influence, and his backers, the trustees of the cathedral. Though somewhat timid in handling the situation, Father Du Bourg had suspended Père Antoine, as he had authority to do, and laid an interdict on the Cathedral of St. Louis of France. But he had fled to St. James Cabahanoce, to escape the mob violence aroused by this exercise of authority.

He had regained prestige, however, by his conduct after the British attack on New Orleans in January, 1815. He had carried out the ceremonies of thanksgiving for victory with imposing dignity and delivered an eloquent address, for he was a masterful speaker. But in September of that same year he had gone to Rome to lay before the pope the difficulties under which he was trying to administer the diocese, leaving Father Louis Sibourd as vicar general to manage as best he could. Even after his consecration as Bishop of Louisiana and the Floridas, Monseigneur Du Bourg did not return to face the situation in New Orleans, but obtained from the Sacred Congregation *de Propaganda Fide* permission to establish his see temporarily at St. Louis in Upper Louisiana. Such a step did not gain popularity for him in New Orleans.

Father Sibourd was acting as chaplain at the Ursuline convent on Chartres Street when Father Martial, Evremond Harissart, and the Religious of the Sacred Heart arrived. Even as vicar general he could not officiate in the cathedral nor claim the least pittance of a revenue on which to support himself. His efforts to carry on under such trying circumstances had proved his patience, loyalty, and devotion to the Church, but they had also undermined his health. Father Martial's arrival was a great relief to Father Sibourd, for he knew the tact and prudence of this priest, as well as his ability, and with Bishop Du Bourg's consent he persuaded him to remain in New Orleans.

Mother Duchesne learned all this and more from Mother St. Michel, the Ursuline superior, and the details were heart-sickening. She had had to admit, moreover, that she was ill, so ill, it turned out, that she had been put to bed soon after her arrival. The doctor recognized at once the disease so frequently contracted on shipboard in the days of sailing vessels. Mother Duchesne had scurvy. Her physical discomfort did not worry her, but to be a guest in such a busy convent and to need so much care caused her real embarrassment. In a letter to Father Barat, written on June 4, she mentions the doctor casually, for she had other things on her mind and heart. Happily her soul had at last shaken off the "desert dryness" of the long voyage, and hope and love were again in command as she initialed the letter paper *SS.C.J.et M.*, and wrote:

> Here we are, almost at the end of our journey, for four or five hundred leagues are very little when one has traveled thousands. And a trip on a gentle and beautiful river is a pleasure after one has seen the ocean and its storms. The Mississippi is not very formidable except at its mouth. It will soon be as heavily navigated as our rivers of France, so greatly is commerce progressing on its shores.
>
> The doctor who attends the convent where we are staying has pictured New Orleans to us, perhaps too optimistically, as becoming very soon the equal of Bordeaux, and St. Louis becoming like

New Orleans, and all Upper Louisiana transformed in a few years into another France, as far as climate, fertility, commerce, and civilization are concerned. The idea of so much progress in so little time has sent my thoughts flying after my heart. They have raced to the far northwest and across the South Sea to Korea or Japan to gain the martyr's palm. That is the way with ambition in this world—never satisfied. But I can assure you that would satisfy me. I aspire to nothing more than martyrdom. Before attaining this happiness, which may still be far away, I let myself form other wishes concerning our mission, and the most important for it and for us will certainly be to see some of your sons out here. If only you would work to bring this about!

How much there is pent up in my soul—expecting to find here only saints and meeting almost immediately a priest (not the one who has caused the schism, but another) who holds opinions bordering on heresy, who has no love for the august name which it is such an honor for us to bear, and who makes trouble for a convent which, after God, is the main support of religion in this city. . . .

The closer I approach it, the more clearly I realize how very difficult our work is going to be and how meager are our means for getting started. But God is in the work; his will was manifest; and far from feeling an increase of that dryness of heart which was such a trial for me at Bordeaux and on the ocean voyage, I feel my heart expand now with hope. I am the more blameworthy for not being more virtuous, since I have to recognize the fact that so many graces have been poured out on us. Help me by your prayers, and recommend me, I beg you, to the prayers of all your sons.

Mother Duchesne was spared a very severe case of scurvy, thanks to the competent nursing of the Ursuline infirmarian, Mother Gerard. The illness did not interrupt her letter writing, that happy gift by which she herself preserved for us the true Philippine Duchesne. A letter to Mother Eugenie de Gramont on the First Friday of June shows her in a bright mood, in spite of discomfort from fever, insects, heat, and some personal disappointments:

We have been received by the Ursuline religious with the greatest charity and kindness. . . . They have expressed the wish that we should spend the summer here with them, so as to give time for our house to be completed. They refrain from insisting only because of the illness that often occurs in the month of August here and affects nearly all newcomers. They say I shall be immune, as I have had a severe fever along with mosquito bites that set me on fire; they also think I had scurvy.

The mosquitoes are nothing in comparison with the creatures that appear by the millions at sunset, swarm on people's heads, even in their mouths. At night the only thing to do is fan oneself or stay under a mosquito bar. The heat is very moderate this year, and this is the more remarkable since there is no rain. Just at present there is no refreshing fruit to be had. The boarding pupils and the community have *café-au-lait* and butter every morning for breakfast, and so do even the Negro women in the kitchen. They also have milk at dinner and at goûter.

Mother Gerard has laughed a good deal every morning on seeing me take, not a little coffee without sugar, and that covertly, but a big cup of *café-au-lait* sugared to syrup. As I did not want to take any breakfast when we first arrived, the superior had the doctor order me to do so. He said it is absolutely necessary in this country, and it would be better to omit supper, so I obey his order. All my companions are well, except for mosquito bites. How much our poor Mother General would suffer from this! They say there are no mosquitoes in St. Louis. The milk there is also more wholesome and delicious, the fruit more abundant, especially the apples. But best of all, we shall find kindness more general, and more piety and innocence. They speak English rather than French, so we continue to study it.

On Sunday, June 7, she wrote at greater length to Mother Barat:

The longer I am away from you by God's will, the more keenly I long for news from you and from our Fathers, Mothers, and Sisters. Not knowing whether you received the letters we sent at the middle of May when we were near Cuba, or the one I sent Mother Bigeu from here by way of Georgetown, I shall repeat a little of what I said in those two letters. . . .

Perhaps we shall hear something from St. Louis before I finish this letter. The bishop has not written and that is not encouraging. Three days ago I met a rich man from the North, who told us there is a great demand for both a college for boys and a boarding school for girls. The college is to be located in St. Louis; our school is to be seventeen miles from there, at Florissant (or St. Ferdinand), a village situated in one of the loveliest and most fertile parts of the country. It seems there is no suitable house in good condition. The inhabitants build quickly but not solidly. . . .

Every day the Ursulines grow kinder to us here. They even want to keep us here, as they fear illness. These religious have had us purchase many things and want to pay for everything, saying, "We shall take care of that. We are so frequently given ten-dollar bills in alms." The superior told me today that her house will always be our stopping-place, and whenever more of our nuns come, they must choose a season of the year when they can stay here for a longer time. She has also offered to take care of any business for us or shipments for St. Louis. I hope that in time we may have many houses in this country. . . .

I have never met more manner and charm than these Creoles possess. On the plantations the education of the girls may be somewhat neglected, but among the Americans in the cities much care is expended on it. I saw a little ten-year-old girl today whose schooling will be completed when she is twelve. To keep her busy at her books they are teaching her Latin. Her brother, now twelve years old, speaks French and English, writes these and also Latin, and is studying Greek. He is going to St. Louis with Father Martial. . . .

The religious who come to join us out here should have very light clothing for the tropical part of the ocean voyage and the river trip, with long-sleeved linen undergarments. They ought to bring along boullion tablets or a bottle of powdered consommé—it can be purchased for three francs in Bordeaux—to make broth with hot water when they are seasick; and a small kettle that can be heated with a lamp and so supply hot water for the broth; also some peppermint lozenges, sweet wine, lemons, and vinegar. One gets so thirsty. I laughed at all the provisions they made us take when we set sail, but nothing was superfluous. . . .

They say we may have to remain here a good while longer, so Father Martial has gone to the country for two weeks. I am giving an order at Lyons for our charitable benefactresses, the Ursulines. Their kindness really overwhelms me. They expect a priest and three more nuns to sail from France in September. If you could have them bring as a gift to this convent a very pretty embroidered flounce for an alb, I should be most grateful. They have none here. They have lavished a hundred times its value on us, and with a delicacy I cannot express in words. Here is the end of this sheet of paper. Another vessel is sailing in three weeks. . . .

Not a word about her illness, a single remark about the strange silence on the part of the bishop which was causing her such anxiety, paragraphs of praise for the Ursulines, information picked up from John Mullanphy or the nuns—she filled the large sheets with thoughts of everyone except herself. She regained her strength as the weeks passed. She discussed with her companions this unexpected situation—they had been so sure the bishop would send them some directive regarding their trip up the river to St. Louis. Now the news that the convent of the Sacred Heart was not to be located in St. Louis drew earnest pleading from many people that they remain in New Orleans. Responsibility for the decision lay with Mother Duchesne, and there seemed to be but one answer—to go on to St. Louis. Her letter of June 12 to St. Madeleine Sophie is more personal in tone than many others:

> This is my fourth letter to you. I have repeated things in them all and have even contradicted myself several times, for I wrote as things happened and quoted different opinions. And more than this, the heart suffers from sacrifices whose value is known only to faith and love. But even in distress love cries out bravely, "My God, gladly have I offered thee all things."
>
> I experienced this sentiment quite definitely when the doctor declared with a sinister air that I had scurvy. The questions he asked showed how astonished he was that the physician who visited our vessed at the mouth of the river had not noticed it. Other people asked me why I ever left France. . . . I was not worried, but I was very serious when I thought that God had no further work for me; that Eugenie could steer the boat, which would only gain by the change; that, more fortunate than Moses, I had entered the Promised Land and had brought here a colony destined to struggle for the glory of the Sacred Heart. . . . I assure you death held every attraction for me, since I have every reason to fear I may spoil the work of our foundation; but God has shown me only his divine attractions. . . .
>
> I do not know how to describe the touching kindness shown me by the superior during this illness. It is quite inexpressible. We are the object of her continual attention and also those of her community. After having cared for us in our distressing illness, she now wants to help defray the expense of our river trip, calling the 500 francs she offers us a "widow's mite." I scrupled to accept it, fearing she thought us worse off than we are. So I was perfectly frank with her and told her about the 10,000 francs sent by way of Philadelphia. At the same time I expressed the fear that, when we reach St. Louis, we shall find that this sum has been spent. She shared my fears on this score and advised me to write to the bishop. She approved of what I wrote and asked me not to mention the 10,000 francs to the members of her community, in order not to lessen their sympathetic interest in our affairs, for they decide everything in Chapter here. We shall certainly never be the losers in dealing with these religious, so I beg you to pay Monsieur Jouve in Lyons the amount necessary to cover an order they have sent him through me. They like Octavie and Eugenie very much, and they want to keep us here in the city. They promise us all success, assuring us of their help with a disinterestedness that is admirable. However, while they wish to help on our work, they see as we do

that it is more for the glory of God that we go on to St. Louis in the Illinois Country. . . .

We are finding English very difficult. Even Octavie, who succeeds best among us, is not yet able to converse with the children's parents. In St. Louis they will be chiefly Americans, and these will not be satisfied with mediocrity. They can go a long way intellectually, and nothing in Europe is beyond their ability. The Creoles, who are in the majority in New Orleans, are softer, lighter, and more pleasure-loving. They marry at twelve or fifteen and consider sixteen too late. One of them, after taking music for a month, was able to compose. They are like those trees that grow quickly and die early. Their appearance is charming in every detail. . . .

We have been told that the trip up the river is not dangerous and that the captain, who has already been informed about our passage, is a very trustworthy man. The steamboats operate under very strict regulations. The men's quarters are entirely separate from the women's, so during the entire trip we shall be able to have neither Mass and Communion nor confession. We do not know yet when we shall leave. Not a word from the bishop. Travelers tell us we are much wanted in St. Louis, that we shall lack nothing, and that all success will be ours. We need an English-speaking postulant. One who wanted to join us here is too delicate. . . .

You will see from the letters of my companions that they are suffering. Fortunately they are kept very busy by the Ursuline nuns. All are longing for a letter from you. This long silence is not your fault but that of the vessels—they are all delayed this year. While we offer to God this privation of news from you or advice and directions, we find some consolation in telling you how we long to hear from you. Pray and have others pray for us. I kneel in spirit at your feet.

This letter and others had been sealed and packeted, and samples of Indian handicraft carefully wrapped for the voyage to France, when the *Rebecca*, true to form, it would seem, was again delayed. The *Gustave* had been in port nearly three weeks when at last its mail bags were released and letters were brought to the convent for Mother Duchesne and her companions. After carrying them to the chapel, they sat down together to read or to listen, to laugh or to cry with joy, to talk things over once more and by so doing to strengthen their determination to carry out the original plan of their journey.

The letter Mother Duchesne received from St. Madeleine

Sophie in New Orleans is missing from the collection she treasured and guarded so carefully to the end of her life. But her own letter of June 24, 1818, is preserved:

> God, who loves to console his own, has permitted a delay in the departure of the *Rebecca*, in order to allow us time to receive and answer your letters, along with those of Mother Bigeu and your brother. They came on the *Gustave*, but had not been released. We have not gotten the picture of the Sacred Heart yet, but M. Fournier says it was taken on board by the captain. I shall not repeat what I wrote in my last letter. We carried yours to the foot of the altar before reading it—we wanted to thank God for this great joy. You can understand the sentiments of our hearts. The superior of the Ursulines brought the mail herself and asked quite graciously that we give you her regards and say she would love to know you. She is really a great-souled religious. . . . I am every day more fully convinced that I have no ability whatsoever for guiding souls. But God is doing the work for himself, and my Sisters are happy. They will tell you so. . . .

For nearly three more weeks the five Religious of the Sacred Heart remained in New Orleans. Though they were within the cloister most of the time, they became acquainted with many features of the old colonial town. In the convent garden or on the galleries overlooking it, they heard the cry of the vendors mingling with thin strains of street music, the shouts of teamsters and the peculiar drawl of Negro voices, the quick staccato of Creole women calling to neighbors, the banter of boys playing on the banquettes, and a hundred other sounds combining to make a din that contrasted sharply with the noises of Paris or the silence of Sainte Marie. The garden air was heavy with the scent of flowers— a lovely place in which to walk and pray or to sit and write in the early morning or late afternoon, though one would need to keep a fan at hand to ward off the mosquitoes.

Sometimes Mother Duchesne and a companion went on business to shops or offices, passing attractive houses in Spanish or French style, with their paved courtyards, wide grilled gateways, and shops fronting on the streets. Flowering vines and oleanders growing against the brick and plaster walls added color and fragrance, though they encountered less pleasant odors at times as they walked along the banquettes and made their way down the Street of the Levee. There on the waterfront a babel of voices greeted them, and Philippine was more convinced than ever that the gift of tongues was a requisite for the missionary in the Mississippi

Valley. Often, as she rested at night on her moss-filled mattress while the breeze from Lake Pontchartrain stirred the protecting mosquito bar above her, she listened to the street sounds die away. Then she would realize how tired she was—not from any bodily exertion, but from her effort to conquer physical weakness and from anxiety. She could not kneel through the night hours in the Ursuline chapel, but she could pray in the quiet sanctuary of her own soul, laying down the burden of her responsibility in simple faith and trust.

These were difficult weeks for Mother Duchesne because of the increased pressure brought to bear on her by the Ursulines and other friends who wished to keep the Religious of the Sacred Heart in New Orleans permanently. Zeal and charity motivated the urgent appeals and arguments, and the reasoning was always plausible enough. Then, too, Bishop Du Bourg's silence was so hard to explain and to accept. Mother Duchesne turned more than ever to prayer, spending long hours each day before the Blessed Sacrament, begging for divine assistance and guidance, for courage to cling to the original plan, and making fervent acts of faith in the grace of obedience. She discussed the matter again and again with her companions, and they agreed with her that they should go to St. Louis on the first available steamboat.

The *Franklin* was booked to leave on Sunday, July 12. The nuns began to pack their valises and to make the rounds of the Ursuline convent, saying good-bye to each member of the community, to the children they had learned to know, and to the Negro women who had served them so cheerfully and so well. Many friends came to call on them, insisting that this was just *au revoir*. Mother Duchesne's last letter from New Orleans was begun on July 9 and written at several sittings during the next two days. It is a crowded epistle, very characteristic of its writer, summarizing conversations, abounding in faith and humility, in ardor and gratitude, in fear of self and childlike dependence on the fatherly protection of Divine Providence.

> This is the fifth letter I have written you since we reached here, and I realize with sorrow that it may be a long time before I receive any answer. The letters that came on the *Gustave* were pretty old. Our picture of the Sacred Heart is held in the customs office because Madame Fournier fastened under the wrapping paper a little packet for the bishop unstamped. We hope to get the picture by Sunday, the day set for our departure from New Orleans. It was to have been tomorrow, and our boxes and baggage are al-

ready on board the steamboat for St. Louis. We did not unpack anything, as we used only what we had in our valises. The Ursulines had our clothes laundered every week, and we have bought cotton dresses of light material for the trip up the river.

Father Martial has been very kind to us and has continued to direct us fervently in the confessional. I have skipped him, however, three or four times and taken advantage of the presence of an Italian priest, who is much like Father Perreau. He is a man of deep piety who loves the Society of Jesus. His soul is great and noble, like the family to which he belongs. He has taken a very kind interest in us.

After a repetition of many of the difficulties confronting her, she continues:

But why should I worry about the future? When the time comes for action, Divine Providence is always on our side and on that of the missions. For the last one hundred years no boat carrying missionaries has been wrecked, though so many accidents occur. . . . The Ursulines say a foundation here is indispensable, as it would be the center of all the houses we may one day have in America, and that this is a suitable place for our novitiate, as the city is large and cosmopolitan. They think, too, that we should have a house here for those whose health is too delicate to stand the cold in St. Louis. Those who cannot bear the heat here could go up there. Finally, they have impressed on us how glad they would be to have us and all the religious who will join us later on. But they stress the fact that later on there may be no opening for us.

I saw the wisdom of the inducements held out to us, but I answered consistently that it is God's will for us to go on to St. Louis. . . . We know the will of God. But I am so impressed by their arguments that I beg you to make a foundation here next spring. . . . I am so glad to have come out here, I shall willingly make sacrifices in order to procure foundations. I think I should be ready for anything, even to face again the terrors of the sea or to cross uninhabited wilderness.

The *Franklin* pulled away from the landing and headed upstream as scheduled on July 12, with just fourteen passengers on board, but with a heavy lading in the hold. It was a new boat in its second season, and Captain Reed was flattered by the lively interest of the French nuns in everything he showed them. The machinery occupied almost the entire length of the first deck, leaving only a small space in the rear for "deck passengers." The domain of the cabin passengers was the second deck, where the ladies' parlor was well to the rear for the sake of safety in case of a boiler explosion.

The pilot house and officers' quarters were on the top, or "hurricane," deck.

It was all novel and interesting, but it was a very expensive trip, costing perhaps five hundred dollars for the five nuns. When Mother Duchesne had tried to offer Mother St. Michel and her community a little gift in return for their cordial hospitality, the Ursulines would not hear of such a thing. Instead, they pressed on their departing guests another three hundred dollars to help defray the expense of the river trip. And through the decades that followed, their charity continued with a generosity that is beyond all counting.

The nuns had been assured that the river trip was not at all dangerous. But the fact that it took the *Franklin* forty days of navigation to reach St. Louis shows that perils abounded, for the Mississippi was so notoriously dangerous that travel at night was rarely attempted in the early decades of steamboating. Shallows and sand bars, planters and sawyers were practically everywhere and difficult to avoid. A snag could rip such a rent in the wooden hull that the boat would sink in a few minutes. In the summer and autumn when the river was low, shifting sand bars changed the channel continually and built up hidden traps on which boats ran aground and listed perilously, if not disastrously. Spring floods, carrying great loads of debris from upstream, occasioned troubles of another kind.

There were man-made dangers, too, on the river trip. Mechanical inefficiencies abounded, for the steamboat was still in a trial-and-error stage. Faulty boilers sometimes burst under high pressure of steam. Wood used for fuel threw off showers of sparks that often set fire to the highly combustible boats. Crude sanitary conditions added danger to discomfort, for the steamboats became carriers of the dreaded epidemics that ravaged cities and towns along the river for nearly a century. Mother Duchesne would experience the rougher side of river travel in the years to come, but both the *Franklin* and the Mississippi were on their good behavior during the summer of 1818.

From the time the boat was loosed from its moorings and headed out into the stream, the nuns were engrossed in the beauty of this new phase of their new world. Three of them had known the grandeur of Alpine country, the placid beauty of its high valleys, the clear current of its swift rivers that raced between narrow banks and were bridged by a span or two of arching. Here was a mighty expanse of mud-yellow water, so wide that its fearful swiftness was almost unperceived, yet holding unpredictable destruction in its treacherous current. Gulls soared or sailed overhead or skimmed the surface of the water. On either side, beyond the lavish tangle of rushes and sedges, stretched flat land without so much as a hill to break the monotonous vista to the horizon. As the *Franklin* moved up the great waterway, the nuns noticed how the dense growth on the shoreline was first a mingling of palm and willow and cane, then changed to brakes of cypress, live-oak, and cottonwood. Here and there along the continually winding stream appeared wide plantations of corn and cane and flooded rice fields. Cattle grazed in the moist green meadows, but the grass, Mother Duchesne noted, was *not* so tall as to hide the animals from view. Now and then on the lower stretches of the river, substantial plantation houses could be seen, gleaming white or creamy yellow in the sunshine, with stately avenues of trees leading from the river landing to the pillared gallery, with sugar houses and slave quarters, stables and carriage houses scattered at no great distance from the big house.

In the swampy bayous, once a part of the river's channel, alligators floundered or swam or crawled about, and pelicans fished with awkward dignity. Tall, moss-draped cypress trees rose from swampy land sunk in brown ooze and formed an impenetrable forest wall. Sometimes the *Franklin* plowed along in their deep shade and the passengers found relief from the mid-summer sun. Herons rose from the tangled thickets, startled by the splash of the paddle wheel that left a choppy white wake on the water. Swarms of mosquitoes attacked the passengers, and their stings were like sparks of fire, Mother Audé thought.

As the steamboat took its zigzag course up the highway of the valley, it stopped now on one shore, now on the other, to take on passengers or freight or fuel wood. At the Donaldsonville landing Father Benedict Richard came aboard with two seminarians, Evremond Harissart, whom the nuns knew quite well, and Michael Portier. Heading upstream again, Captain Reed pointed out the entrance to Bayou Lafourche, a steady, langorous stream that had broken away from the river long ago and taken an independent course through rich lands that attracted early plantation settlement.

When the river was lashed by summer storms, the angry waters were dark under the gray sky, but the *Franklin* rode them sturdily, and the nuns were unafraid, for they had weathered ocean storms far worse than those that struck the river in 1818. Fair weather meant oppressive heat, but sundown brought relief and the soft, still night, when a million stars hung low in the rich, dark sky above, or the golden moon rode behind the giant trees or shone in splendor on the rippling water, hiding its murkiness under a lustrous sheen. Then a mockingbird, perched high, would pour forth its sweet melody and all else was still, save the swish of disturbed waters. In their diary the nuns kept an almost day-by-day account of incidents and accidents. Nineteen hours aground on a sand bank was worth noting, also a sudden halt and reversal of the boat, when a great drift of tree trunks and other water-logged debris barred the channel where the river had torn away a vast stretch of its eastern shore.

The high, green bluffs of Natchez came into view on July 17, and the *Franklin* drew in to the landing. During the day some drunken Indians on horseback rode down to the river bank, the men bedecked in native finery of skins and bright-hued feathers, the women wearing red calico and shining ornaments. The sight of them attracted and repelled Mother Duchesne, and she was relieved when they rode off, swaying and sagging on their mounts. In the sunset at Natchez the river was tawny gold, reflecting the glory of the horizon beyond the flat green of the western shore. As she gazed across the water at the crimson sky, Philippine did not suspect the agonies she would endure on that shore one day, nor the charity with which she would be received into one of the many beautiful homes that had already been built in and around Natchez.

The river was gradually narrowing as it led into the heart of the wilderness. The landscape was changing to gently rolling country, but it was not a gentle country they were heading toward. Here and there appeared a pioneer's clearing, a log cabin, a patch of cultivated ground. Further on, tilled fields, small orchards, and fenced pasture lands marked the outskirts of settlements and the industry of the pioneers. Early in August the *Franklin* passed the Arkansas border, and Missouri lay on the left bank. Mother Duchesne noted the course of the boat in her *Journal:* "We met with many accidents," she wrote, "because of snags and sand bars, but we saw other steamboats treated much worse than ours."

On August 19 the boat stopped at Ste. Genevieve and the pastor, Father Henri Pratte, came to see the religious. Mother Duchesne was so impressed by this young priest and all he told her about the town and its people, that when she found herself in what seemed to be a situation impossible of acceptance in St. Louis, her thoughts turned eagerly to Father Pratte and his parish, but she was not allowed to found her first convent in that fervent Catholic community.

The long river trip was drawing to a close. As the limestone cliffs grew higher along the west shore the travelers strained to catch a glimpse of the spreading group of houses that was the town. From the river, St. Louis presented a charming sight—white buildings high on the bluffs against a backdrop of green. With more than half a century of quiet annals to record, it was still just a frontier trading post, but its unique geographical position as the center of the fur trade and western commerce gave it promise of a splendid future. Pierre Laclede Liguest had chosen well when he marked the site in the winter of 1763 at a spot where an abrupt wall of limestone rose from the river bank. On the level, well drained tract of land fronting the bluffs a plan was laid out for the village which Laclede himself declared would someday become "one of the most beautiful cities in America."

The growth of the village was slow. Small groups of settlers came from the Illinois Country just across the river, which had fallen into English hands, and from Lower Louisiana, Canada, and France. The place was distinctively French. Fur trade, traffic in assorted merchandise, and agriculture in common fields made up the bulk of the livelihood among the inhabitants. They were honest, hospitable folk on the whole; they were happy and not too hard-working. They loved their traditional way of life, and in spite of the cession of the region to Spain and the infiltration of Spanish and American settlers, the village remained decidedly French in manners and customs, language and law until 1804, when the western flow of American population began to stream across the Mississippi. By 1818 the population of the area of which St. Louis was the chief town totaled more than sixty-five thousand and raised a national crisis when Missouri asked admission to the Union as a state in which slavery was allowed by law. All this the nuns had learned when the *Franklin* anchored for the night a mile below the foot of the Market Street landing on the evening of August 21.

They were expected by Bishop Du Bourg, and he had made arrangements for their coming. General Bernard Pratte and his wife gave hospitality to these first nuns who ever crossed a threshold in St. Louis. Their home stood at the corner of Main and Market Streets, a French colonial structure of the best frontier type, built of upright posts set on a stone foundation, two stories high, with a gallery extending around the four sides. There was the usual detached kitchen to the rear, and a roomy garden and orchard were neatly fenced in. Bernard Pratte and his wife had lived there since 1797. For twenty years the lower floor was used as a general store, where dry goods, groceries, liquors, hardware, and sundries were sold, the common medium of exchange being furs, which were usually stored in the small warehouse that stood on the southeast corner of the property facing the river. In 1817 General Pratte remodeled the home and added a two-story brick building, which fronted on Main Street, as did the home, and housed the general store on the first floor.

So Mother Duchesne and her companions were welcomed to the newly renovated home, and there they remained for three weeks in the midst of kindness and consideration that rivaled even the charity of the Ursulines. The Prattes were a happy French Catholic family, presided over by a charming Creole mother, who had been Emilie Labbadie, and including two sons and five daughters. They were related to "almost everybody in town," as their maternal grandmother was Pelagie Chouteau, sister of the co-founder of St. Louis, and intermarriage had been frequent among the best Creole group in the town.

Neither the sultry August heat nor the fatigue of travel and first acquaintance with so many people deterred Mother Duchesne from writing to her Superior General on the night of August 22 to give an account of much that had happened on the trip up the river and much that she had learned during her first day in St. Louis:

> We are now nearly 3000 leagues from you, but the farther I go, the closer I try to keep to you by my desire to act according to your intentions and to carry out your instructions. But at such a distance I can at times only groan inwardly as events happen and situations arise and I am unable to ask your advice. Here we are at our third halting-place since we left Paris. Bordeaux and New Orleans were unpleasant only because they retarded the joy we were anticipating. We had our hearts set on St. Louis, and it turns out to be another camping place. We are lodged in a comfortable home, where we are getting acquainted with the children who will be the first pupils in our boarding school. In a week we shall leave for St. Charles, where we are to begin our work in a rented house. Monseigneur is going to accompany us there and remain a few days to help us get settled.
>
> He is very kind to us. He heard our confessions today and says he regrets that he cannot keep us in St. Louis, but there is not a single room for rent in the town. He puts before us the great advantages St. Charles possesses. He thinks it will become one of

the most important cities of North America, as it is situated on the Missouri River, along which the population is growing daily and which is about to give its name to a new state of the Union. No day passes without the arrival of four or five families with their belongings, who come to settle in a country which is making astonishing progress. If they carry out the project of opening a canal which will give a water route from the Mississippi and the Ohio to New York, then letters from France will come that way more quickly than by New Orleans.

We left there on the steamboat *Franklin,* July 12, and arrived here only today, August 22—that is, the steamboat did. But last night when we stopped just a mile below the town, I disembarked with Octavie, and the captain escorted us to the Bishop's residence. He greeted us graciously and brought us to the home in which he had so kindly procured lodgings for us. He is going to give us as chaplain Father Richard, who knows your brother, Father Barat, and who was for a time with the Jesuits, they say. The bishop says he will visit us often at St. Charles, which can be reached from here in a morning's drive. Although Ste. Genevieve is a little further away from St. Louis, I asked him to send us there instead. . . .

This section of the country is becoming more and more English in language, and it will become Protestant in religion if the Catholics are not given more help, for it is being settled by people from cities on the eastern coast, among them Swiss, Germans, and others. Monseigneur says there can be no question of a foundation in New Orleans at present. . . . As to Ste. Genevieve, he says it is gradually being ruined, as the Mississippi is slowly eating away its land and it is losing its commerce without hope of regaining it. But the land along the Missouri is steadily developing into a rich country. . . . Our *Journal* will tell you other things. I beg you not to worry about us. You expected us to have something to suffer, and the example of our holy bishop, who might have had a brilliant career in Paris and who chose poverty, labor, and suffering instead, is an inspiration to us. . . .

During the next three weeks Mother Duchesne became fairly well acquainted with St. Louis, a town of four long streets, with farms beginning just beyond and extending over the hills and out on to the prairie. In the freshness of the early morning the nuns went each day to assist at Mass in the old church that was falling into ruins. No wonder the Bishop was so insistent about the construction of a cathedral! After the first day or two, they noticed a young girl waiting each morning at the street corner near the church—a slight figure in a cotton dress and sunbonnet. Her large blue eyes were fixed on the nuns with a devouring gaze, but she kept aloof as she followed them into the church and knelt where she could watch them. When Mother Duchesne inquired who she might be, Mrs. Pratte recognized at once a protege of hers, Mary Ann Summers. She was just about twelve years of age, but she was doing a woman's work, keeping house for her family—a sickly mother and an older brother who worked on the waterfront. When Mrs. Pratte sent for Mary Ann one day, the girl was at first speechless with joy and could only hold out shyly the apples she had brought as a gift for the nuns. Mother Duchesne put her at her ease very quickly and they talked together for a little while, for Mary Ann spoke French as well as English. She had just one desire—to go with the nuns wherever they might open their convent. But that was out of the question now; her sick mother needed her care.

The nuns went on foot through the town with General Pratte, inspecting first one place, then another. Mother Duchesne drove to Florissant with the Bishop to look at a house. It was a delightful drive through one of Missouri's most beautiful stretches of country —virgin country almost uninhabited—but the house proved to be as unsuitable as the locality itself. There were lengthy discussions— in French, to Mother Duchesne's great relief—regarding the prospects of a convent at Ste. Genevieve, but St. Charles had been decided on, long before the nuns reached St. Louis, and after their arrival the bishop gave no serious consideration to any alternative. He listened to the arguments, suggestions, and generous offers of General Pratte, who doubted the wisdom of placing the nuns in an outlying district and was willing to put at their disposal a house in St. Louis. He admitted the need for an educational institution in the town and the desire which many prominent Catholics had expressed with regard to the Religious of the Sacred Heart. Yet he held to his first decision, and Mother Duchesne knew that soon she would have to say good-bye to St. Louis with its pleasant homes and gardens behind high picket fences of rough saplings, its narrow streets bustling with activity, its river-front crowded with boats of many kinds and shapes, and the wagons lined up on the Illinois shore and waiting to be ferried across to the "promised land." On her birthday she wrote several letters to France. Thinking of her sisters and their families, of Josephine and her brothers, she gave them a few details about her new world:

The river trip from New Orleans to St. Louis took 40 days and was pleasant. In a few more days we shall set out for St. Charles on the Missouri, where we shall reside for the present. This section of the country is going to be organized into a state, which will enter the Confederation of the United States, of which it is now only a territory. St. Louis will be the capital, and its population is increasing every day. They are building on all sides, yet it is impossible to find lodgings. Rents are higher here than in Paris and so is the price of food. Luxury is a strange thing. It has penetrated even into the midst of some savage tribes that are partly civilized. Since the coming of Monseigneur, religion has begun to take some hold, and it has been established in Kentucky by the zeal of Monseigneur Flaget, who is the bishop there. Before he came, the people really had no religion. He has had several churches built. The only churches I have seen here are made of wood.

The presence of the nuns at church on Sunday, August 30, caused more than a little stir. Visitors had been calling on them frequently—pretty, intelligent Creole women who compared quite favorably with those whom they had met in New Orleans. They carried themselves with easy grace, were light-hearted and impulsive and just a trifle curious. Their conversation, spiced with gay repartee, reminded Philippine of happy gatherings she had known in distant Grenoble, but their French, though quite correct, was spoken with a somewhat languid drawl and often interspersed with expressions borrowed from Spanish or English, which she did not always understand. But their esteem for culture and their desire to give their children opportunities for education she did understand, along with their regret that the bishop intended relegating the nuns to a village beyond the Missouri. Monseigneur Du Bourg's decision regarding their place of residence had aroused opposition, as his decisions so frequently did during his years in St. Louis, and many of the prominent Catholic men of the town had offered suggestions on the subject. They were serious and sincere; they had daughters to be educated. A group met after Mass that Sunday morning to discuss tuition fees as well as ways and means of helping Mother Duchesne. After reaching an agreement on several points, they decided to call on the Bishop the next day.

General Pratte was the most active friend the religious had, and Mother Duchesne seems to have relied on his influence with Bishop Du Bourg, even though the prelate gave her no grounds for hoping he might yield to representations or entreaties. On Monday she gave St. Madeleine Sophie an account of what had been happening and what had been suggested:

It is a real suffering to have no news from you and to be so cut off by distance from the means of hearing from you when I am in such need of guidance. . . . I have so many things to tell you that expressions of sentiment must give way to business and details about our trip. My letters are disgustingly dry, and still I ought to write more concisely in order to give you more information. . . . Bishop Du Bourg's episcopal palace resembles a little barn in France, and his church is a wooden structure that is falling into ruins. He is having another built at the expense of the Catholics in St. Louis, who feel that they are already overtaxed. He was not able to rent a house for us anywhere except in St. Charles, a village twelve leagues from here. . . . I refused to open our school at Florissant. The country is beautiful, but very sparsely settled, and we should be obliged to build there. St. Louis seems out of the question, for it has grown so quickly in the last two years that a piece of land now sells for five times what it did before.

The brother of the parish priest at Ste. Genevieve, Mr. Bernard Pratte, in whose home we are living while we go about house-hunting, is so eager to keep us in St. Louis that he simply refused to hire a vehicle to take us to St. Charles. He was willing to buy a house here, such as would cost 36,000 francs to build, and then rent it to us. I visited the house. It is very well situated and quite new, but it would need changes which we could make only if we owned it. . . . I proposed to buy it from Mr. Pratte, and I do not think my proposal was rash, for at least 7,000 francs must be left from what you sent the Bishop for us.

Mr. Pratte may also offer us some aid. He is gong to entrust to us his five daughters in succession. He deserves already the title I have given him of "temporal father." He owns a well-equipped store where prices are moderate, and he has promised us credit as long as we need it. His wife is the most highly esteemed person in the city. Her five little girls, though dreadfully spoiled, have taken such a fancy to us that they want to come to our school, wherever it may be. When we go out, they are distressed lest we should not return. In season and out of season Celeste torments her parents at least four or five times a day to send her to school sooner than they planned. These five interesting children have the happiest dispositions and such charming voices. They seem to be related to almost everyone in St. Louis. A great number of their cousins, delightfully well-mannered, have come to see us and want to be our pupils. . . . We cannot hope for large institutions at first in this country. During the next few years we must be satisfied with houses on the same footing as Cuignières. . . . Monseigneur says English is as necessary here as bread, and that at fifty years of age one cannot learn it. That is something to consider.

Philippine was interrupted in her writing. General Pratte wished to talk to her again, as there was still some possibility, he thought, of overcoming the Bishop's opposition to the pleas of many Catholic families. Later she continued her letter:

> Mr. Pratte just called me for a little conference. He is working hard to get us a house and a number of pupils with whom to begin our work. The parents themselves have fixed the tuition at 225 dollars, that is 1125 francs, including laundry. If I do not hear the outcome of their efforts before the *Franklin* leaves for New Orleans, I shall write to you by way of one of the eastern seaports, and perhaps that second letter will reach you before this one.
>
> The bishop's kindness does not prevent him from being very firm. He knows me already and tells me the truth. Eugenie and Octavie please both him and the children's parents.
>
> There is a Madame de Perdroville here with her two very attractive and talented daughters. She wants to open a boarding school. Although Mr. Pratte is in some way connected with her husband, he prefers to entrust his two eldest daughters to us right away.
>
> That will be an inducement to others. He just returned home, having been at the bishop's house with several other fathers of families. He refused Florissant positively, saying a house there large enough to lodge twenty-five children would cost, not 40,000, but 80,000 francs. As things stand now, we shall certainly be obliged to go to St. Charles. . . .

For another week the religious enjoyed the hospitality of the Pratte household. Mrs. Pratte continued to "overwhelm them with kindness," as Mother Duchesne recorded in her *Journal*. She and the General, however, had lost the campaign for residence in St. Louis, so the nuns sadly packed their valises again. And again Philippine said her *Credo* in the midst of doubts. She could go forward courageously, knowing in Whom she believed. The children were heart-broken at losing the nuns and spread the unhappy news among their cousins and friends. This brought more visitors, but they were always welcome. Emilie and Therese Pratte had obtained their father's solemn promise that they would be the first pupils of the boarding school, once Mother Duchesne and her companions were settled in their new home. The General reluctantly ordered a charette for the baggage, a carriage for the nuns, and saddle horses for the bishop and Father Richard, to be ready early on Monday morning, September 7.

The *if's* of history furnish fascinating material for speculation. *If* General Pratte had had his way, the American life-story of Philippine Duchesne might have been quite different in many respects from the tale of struggle with poverty, anxiety, hardship, isolation, and suffering that stamped her thirty-four years on the frontier.

PART TWO | *Oblation*

First Year
at St. Charles

1818—1819

"BUT YOU DID NOT EXPECT TO LIVE IN ST. LOUIS, did you?" The bishop's question stirred again in her memory, rousing the tumult of emotions Philippine had been struggling for days to control. The carriage, with its clerical outriders, was moving up the Market Street hill toward the old fort. The charette lumbered heavily behind. Philippine prayed. The little procession crossed the "common fields" to the prairie beyond. They were now on the "King's Highway," a worn dirt road, rutted with the traffic of rough carts, and the carriage offered little comfort to its occupants.

Yes, she *had* expected to live in St. Louis. Mother Barat had expected it, too. The Bishop had promised the Mother General exactly that when she yielded to his plea for missionaries. Philippine had expected to begin her work among Indians, not among the children of Creoles and Americans, whether rich or poor. She had had no thought of opening schools for them when she talked so eagerly with the bishop in Paris—how long ago? It seemed much more than fifteen months. The bishop had stressed the need of missionaries to bring the light of the Gospel to the savage natives of America. She had built her dreams around *les sauvages*. In New Orleans she had begun to suspect the type of work Monseigneur

Du Bourg really intended her to inaugurate. Still she had clung to the hope of fulfilling her ambition and the vow she and her companions had made before leaving Paris. She had not allowed herself to dwell at length on her disappointment while in St. Louis. Now as they headed toward St. Charles, the truth was borne in on her with almost sickening realization.

As she prayed, she recalled some other words the bishop said he had written in the letter that had not reached her in New Orleans. He had written on June 24. How had that letter gone astray? "You say you have come seeking the Cross. Well, you have taken exactly the right road to find it." She had indeed taken the *King's Highway*, and now it was leading west-northwest through stretches of rolling country and meadow land, broken here and there by little streams and groves of oak and walnut, hickory and sycamore, and wild fruit trees. The persimmon trees bore their hard, bitter fruit that only sharp frost in late autumn would mellow to sweet succulence. Dense thickets of wild berry bushes sometimes lined the roadside that was bright with tall blue sage and sunflowers, goldenrod and rose and blue asters in rank profusion, and clumps of scarlet sumac blending with yellowing cottonwood trees. The road was dusty; the day was uncomfortably warm; yet autumn's mark was already on the countryside.

There were some signs of human habitation along the road: here a log cabin near a field of withered cornstalks drying for fodder, with orange pumpkins and striped squash scattered on the ground; there a cleared plot where a woodsman was lopping off branches from newly felled trees and preparing them for a house-raising. A thin wisp of smoke at a little distance indicated the camping place where a pioneer mother was bravely making a home in a shelter of boughs. These were American settlers. What had the bishop said about English? "As necessary as bread out here. . . . No one could learn that language at the age of fifty." Philippine had begun her fiftieth year just a few days ago. But Divine Providence might aid her in that as well as in other matters. The road led uphill for a last time, and the bishop explained that they were nearing the bluffs along the south side of the Missouri River. These stood far back from the stream, leaving wide bottom lands that made good farms, but were exposed to damaging floods. St. Charles had a well protected site, resembling St. Louis in several ways. The bishop always stressed these advantages.

It had been a long drive, but now they were descending the gently sloping approach to the river. Looking across to the opposite shore, where the bluffs rose sharply one above another, the bishop pointed out an opening in the trees that gave a glimpse of a house with smoke rising from a chimney. But Philippine had caught sight of a band of Indians near the ferry landing, and they absorbed her interest. They were from the Upper Missouri and had come down to see General William Clark, then Governor of the territory, "The Redhead" whom they respected and trusted. Trade and friendship were their purpose; and when they caught sight of the nuns, they expressed reverence and friendliness by gestures of courtesy they had learned from the white man.

Lafreniere Chauvin was in charge of a ferry at St. Charles. He advertised good crafts, experienced watermen, and a crossing made with safety and dispatch. It took some time, however, to unload the charette. Since the vehicles were returning that same day to St. Louis, they were not taken across, but the seven passengers, the saddle horses, and the baggage gave the ferrymen plenty of work. On the opposite bank another cart was procured and loaded with the trunks and cases and the precious picture of the Sacred Heart. The bishop entrusted the horses to a man on the waterfront, and the little party went on foot to the house up on the hillside.

St. Charles began as a trade center for white men and Indians on the north bank of the Missouri, some twenty miles from its confluence with the Mississippi, at a spot where the river's almost due north-south course gave the trail along its shore a fairly straight direction. The first streets of the village lay parallel to the stream, but the steep bluffs rising in a first and second gradient taxed the endurance of those who made the ascent and offered a dangerous downward trail to riders or drivers of heavy carts. Blanchette Chasseur, a French Canadian, had been shrewd in his choice of the site in 1769, so the town and Philippine were the same age. For some twenty years or more he acted as civil and military governor of *Les Petites Côtes*, as he called it. The first huts and houses were built well back from the river's edge where the bluffs dropped down on the north to a sheltered cove. A belt of good timber crested the bluffs, and the prairie land gave open fields for farms and pastures.

When the English colonies on the Atlantic coast were declaring their independence, Blanchette the Hunter was directing the construction of a log church for the village, and the missionaries were beginning to visit there, finding hospitality in the founder's log house and served by his Pawnee Indian wife. The Franch name of *Les Petites Côtes* (Village of the Little Hills) had given place to the Spanish *San Carlos del Misouri* when Blanchette died in 1793, but French customs and language prevailed for many a year. Each villager had his lot of land in the town, a share in the "common fields" to cultivate, and a right to cut wood and to pasture on the "common." Indian dangers may have been an influence in all this, for there were Osages on the Missouri near the mouth of the Kansas River, and Sioux on the Mississippi above the Des Moines, and Kickapoos in the neighborhood of San Carlos, where in the earliest decades of its existence the bulk of the population was made up of Indians and Canadians.

Another French Canadian who left his mark on the town was François Duquette. Coming into Upper Louisiana as a young man, he lived for a time at Ste. Genevieve, then moved to St. Charles, where he obtained a grant of land at a short distance south of the village. There he built a frontier home, roomy and substantial enough to be called a "mansion" in those days. It was constructed in true French pioneer fashion, of upright white oak posts, with slant roof of pegged shingles and a five-foot gallery around the house. Duquette married Marie Louise Beauvais of Ste. Genevieve and brought her to this new home while the Revolution was in full swing in France. The Duquette house became a religious center for the Catholics at St. Charles, for priests were seldom able to visit the town. Devotions were held there on Sundays and during Lent, with François Duquette reading the prayers and passages from the Gospels. He was a merchant, trading peltries and merchandise, not always successfully, but he and his wife lived comfortably and were highly respected in the town.

In 1816 François Duquette died. His widow then opened her home to boarders, and in September of that same year the Reverend Timothy Flint and his family came to occupy half of this "peaceful and pleasant residence," which stood "between the first and second bluffs, a little distance from the village, in a situation delightfully sheltered by fruit trees and shrubbery." This was the home to which Bishop Du Bourg led the Religious of the Sacred Heart. Madame Duquette received the party kindly and turned over to Mother Duchesne the seven-room house with its furniture, reserving for herself temporarily the use of one small room, but she did not occupy it after the nuns arrived. Mother Lucille Mathevon, who lived there later on, gave the dimensions of the seven rooms: the large central room extended twenty-eight feet across the front of the house and was almost square; the six little rooms, three on each side of the big room, were about eight feet by five, with three doors and two windows each. So one could enter the house by either the front door or the back door of the central room, or one could come in from the gallery by any one of the small rooms, and these also had communicating doors in all contiguous walls, and windows looking out on the gallery. There was a loft over the central room which could be reached by a ladder against one wall. Two chimneys gave fireplaces in the central room and in one of the small rooms on each side of the house.

In her *Journal* Mother Duchesne described the installation at St. Charles:

> Madame Duquette welcomed us kindly on September 7. The next day, September 8, we arranged an altar hastily and the bishop said the first Mass for us. While he paid a visit to Portage des Sioux, we prepared a little chapel in the house. . . . The bishop said Mass there on September 11 and left us the Blessed Sacrament, our greatest Treasure. He took his departure on the 12th, after naming Father Richard pastor here. The latter will lodge near us, will say one Mass on Sundays in our chapel and also on week days.

The nuns had been very busy while the bishop was installing Father John Acquaroni as pastor at Portage des Sioux. Unpacking the furnishings they had gathered in Paris nearly a year before, they found them all in good condition and placed them where they would show to best advantage. Mother Duchesne was pleased with the effect and noted an important detail in her *Journal:*

> We placed in the chapel a picture of St. Regis before which prayers for the American mission had so often been said. He has been chosen as special patron of the house in accordance with a promise made in Paris, with our Mother General's permission, on condition that he obtain this favor for us. We also promised to erect a shrine in his honor and celebrate his feast as the patronal feast of the house. Monseigneur Du Bourg has agreed to this.

Describing the new convent, Mother Duchesne wrote of the "tiny chapel" and compared the size of the central room to that of the parlor of the Paris convent. This was a schoolroom by day, a recreation and study room after school hours, and a dormitory at night. When a few boarding pupils arrived in October, they slept on mattresses in this room, as did Mothers Duchesne, Berthold, and Audé, and Sister Lamarre, while Sister Manteau put down her pallet on the kitchen floor.

Mother Duchesne's first letter from the little frontier convent was written to Mother Barat on September 12 and sent to St. Louis for mailing by the Bishop himself. It is a brave, loyal letter, without a suggestion of the intense personal disappointment that was weighing her down. The bishop is the central figure. His views, his activities, his remarks are recounted, and his troubles hinted at sympathetically. Some of the problems and needs of the nuns are touched upon, and some of their hopes, though the sense of the impending failure of their mission at St. Charles is already felt. The bishop had evidently tried to encourage them by the suggestion of some property at Florissant, but he had no intention of giving them the large tract he owned there. Certainly Philippine must have made a tremendous effort to restrain the outpouring of her heart and soul to the saint, who always understood her and who would read much between the guarded lines written on September 12, 1818:

> Having made the rounds, either in spirit or in person, of St. Louis, Ste. Geneviève, Florissant, and St. Charles, we are now settling down in the last place, which seems to put us as far away from you as is possible in America, because of the many halts and detours one must make in order to get here. Monseigneur Du Bourg, who looks very far into the future, considers this place quite important, as it is the largest village on the Missouri, about 20 miles from its junction with the Mississippi. American settlers from the eastern states are constantly pouring into this section of the country—restless people, who hope St. Charles will become a great commercial link between the United States and China, for the Upper Missouri rises not far from another river that pours its waters into the Pacific Ocean at a place where the crossing to Asia takes just two weeks. Hence everything is very scarce and very expensive here. We cannot get a workman even for ten francs a day. We are renting a house, but it is too small; and the rent is exorbitant. . . . If we do not succeed in St. Charles, we shall be able to count on a large tract of land at Florissant. As for St. Louis, there is not the slightest chance of our going there. The bishop has troubles enough in that quarter. On the trip to St. Charles he was extremely friendly, riding close to our carriage, seeing us safely on and off the ferry boat, and bringing us to this house, where he has visited us several times. He leaves St. Charles today, and I do not know when we shall see him again. . . .
>
> Monseigneur is appointing to the Missouri mission some of the priests who are coming here from Rome. The Holy Father takes a great interest in this part of the country. It is no longer called Upper Louisiana, but the Territory of Missouri, and soon it will be a state of the Union.

The men who ferried us across and those who brought our baggage up to the house in a cart would not accept a penny, saying that we represented our Lord Jesus Christ. The bishop wants us to accept Protestant children, though many of these people say that girls educated by nuns never want to leave them. He inspires us by his example and says that we are the mustard seed and that great good will come of all this labor. He is quite pleased with our sacristy equipment and still more so with Eugenie and Octavie. . . .

On September 14, Mother Duchesne opened at St. Charles the first free school for girls west of the Mississippi. The children whom Father Richard had gathered throughout the village came to learn the elements of the Christian religion, along with an introduction to reading, writing and counting. In them Philippine saw a living counterpart of one class of children for whose instruction St. Madeleine Sophie had provided in her Rule, and soon that section of the Rule was being admirably applied. They were impetuous, undisciplined children, a rather motley group, to whom Mother Duchesne devoted herself whole-heartedly, delighting to find that many of them spoke French. Gradually they responded to the efforts of the nuns, and an atmosphere of affectionate respect was created, which made the schoolroom a homelike place where devotion to the Sacred Heart could develop. Soon there was a separate class of day pupils who could pay a nominal tuition fee. This was a small group of girls—Creoles, half-breeds, mulattoes—whose program of studies was quite as elementary as that of the free school. When the weather was pleasant, they had class on the gallery with one of the nuns, while Mother Duchesne and the others taught in the central room. The house looked out across the rolling waters of the Missouri to the meadowlands beyond. There were small boats on the river frequently, and these were at times far more interesting to the girls than were catechism and the alphabet and the mysteries of arithmetic. One period of the day brought all the children together for prayers and the singing of hymns. This assembly was held in the big central room with the chapel door open.

On Saturday, October 3, the boarding school opened, when General Pratte redeemed his promise to Émilie and Therese and brought them, with their cousin, Pelagie Chouteau, to St. Charles. The girls were delighted to be with the nuns again, no matter what inconveniences they had to put up with. Pelagie's affection for Mother Duchesne had begun in St. Louis, and it went on increasing until her death in 1823. This happy trio of cousins came under the special care of Mother Octavie, though all five nuns helped at times with all the children under their care.

General Pratte also brought with him on that first Saturday of October mail from France—letters from the Mother General, Fathers Barat and Perreau, and copies of letters from Cardinals Litta and Fontana which had accompanied the blessings of Pope Pius VII for the American mission. The letters were six months old, but that did not lessen their value. One can fancy General Pratte and the girls left to entertain themselves while the nuns ran hurriedly through the three packets of mail and then came to tell the General about the Holy Father's blessing. Mother Duchesne read again and again the lines written by Mother Barat on April 21: "You see, our Holy Father the Pope has approved your mission; it was, then, God's will and that is why all circumstances converged so remarkably to make it succeed. . . . How happy we shall be to learn that you have reached the end of your journey safely."

A few days later Philippine began a long letter in answer to this, first giving free rein to the joy that filled her heart, then describing sketchily both the work the little pioneer community was engaged in and the living conditions in which they were trying to carry on:

> After we had languished with desire for news from our dear Society, three packets of mail arrived at the same time, two addressed by Father Barat and one by Mother Girard. No doubt they came on different boats as far as New Orleans, but the same steamboat brought them to St. Louis, where they were again delayed. We received all this dear news from France last Saturday, when our three boarding pupils arrived. So our Lady, on this day dedicated to her, added to the many graces we owe her that of the foundation of our first American boarding school and the arrival of the letters from Rome. We are invoking her under the title of Our Lady of Prompt Succor, as we promised the kind Ursulines we should do. We shed happy tears on learning that the Sovereign Pontiff has added his approbation and blessing to the many signs that our mission is God's will. Tomorrow we shall chant the *Te Deum* and have a Mass of Thanksgiving offered.
>
> By now you have learned that Divine Providence has brought us to the remotest village in the United States. It is situated on the Missouri, which is frequented only by those trading with the Indians who live not very far away from here, but I have not seen any little Indian girls since we came here, only a *half-breed* who is promised to us as a domestic or postulant, according to her apti-

tudes. Against this race there is not the same prejudice as there is against *Negroes* and *mulattoes*. Monseigneur Du Bourg has said positively that we may not admit them to either of our schools, and he has appointed one day a week for the instruction of the colored people; otherwise, he says, we should not hold the white children in school. . . .

In our free school we now have twenty-two children, and in proportion to the population this equals a school of one hundred in France. These children have never heard of our Lord, of his birth or his death, nor of hell, and they listen open-mouthed to our instructions. I have to say to them continually, "Yes, this is really true." All except two are learning the alphabet. Among the children who pay a little fee there is the same ignorance. When we complain to the Bishop that we have no savages, he replies: "Indeed you have, and your work among these children will be wider and more lasting because of the influence of the rich over the poor." We have to combat worldliness as well as ignorance. Some of the boarding pupils have more dresses than underclothes or handkerchiefs; they have embroidered dresses of gaily colored silk, with lace trimmings and fancy sleeves of net or lace. The day pupils who pay tuition dress on Sundays like our boarding pupils in Paris. They scorn black shoes and must have pink or blue, yellow or green ones, and the rest to match, but they do not use handkerchiefs. We have had to require them to do so at school.

Winter came on, and the religious at St. Charles were exposed to new hardships. First there was a bread shortage, with not even corn meal for sale in the village. As the Missouri was blocked by floating ice, no supplies could be obtained from St. Louis. But there were quantities of apples stored in the cellar under the front of the house, or still on the trees in the orchard, for Divine Providence had sent a fine crop that matured quite late that year. A more serious shortage occurred when the Duquette well went dry; the little springs nearby were muddied by animals or icebound, and no regular supply of water could be obtained from the river. But worst of all physical hardships was the cold. There was no "central heating" in the Duquette mansion. There may have been four open fire-places, certainly not more than that, but at times fuel was lacking for these. With little money to buy food, the nuns were often hungry, and this added to their sensitiveness to the cold. Mother Duchesne felt her strength diminishing to such an extent that she believed death was at hand. Hunger blurred the brain of this usually clear-headed woman. She sat dazed before the tabernacle in the tiny chapel. The cold was beginning to send little knife-blades of pain through her joints as rheumatism again set in. She tried to conceal her suffering from her companions in order to deprive herself still further for their sake, and she found courage for this in prayer and in reading again and again the letters of Mother Barat which she had saved through the past twelve years.

Bishop Du Bourg spent a few days at St. Charles in November, offering the Holy Sacrifice of the Mass in the convent chapel on November 21, when the nuns renewed their vows in union with the Society in France. Although he had in his possession more than 7,000 francs belonging to them, he gave them no financial assistance, and Mother Duchesne was left to her own resources for the support of the community and schools. Whatever she may have thought of the bishop's attitude, she made no comment on it in her letters. His name does not even appear in the long account she wrote to Mother Barat and asked him to post in St. Louis, along with a letter to the nuns and children in France. The serious tone of her letter, however, is indicative of the anxieties that weighed upon her mind and heart:

> Living in this remote corner of the world, cut off by the Mississippi and the Missouri rivers, I do not know whether you have received a single one of the letters we have written, but I have had the inexpressible consolation of receiving several from you, Mother Bigeu, and Father Barat, written before you had news from us, but your kind brother knew that the *Rebecca* had arrived at New Orleans. . . . This is the tenth letter I have written you. I shall not repeat what I said in any of the others. . . . What interests you most is our present condition: it is what we should have desired, thorny and difficult, but it is made easier by the unction of grace and alleviated by an all-kind Providence whose help is never withdrawn and whose protection is felt at every moment. . . .
>
> Among all the things we shall need and those I have already asked for, the essentials are such as may keep us alive, as here on the earth the soul depends on the body. . . . We look on potatoes and cabbage as you in France regard rare delicacies. There is no market. The gift of a pound of butter and a dozen eggs is like a fortune received. In spite of our desire to fast, we have had to avail ourselves of permission to eat meat on all Saturdays of the year. During the hunting season, which we are in now, we can procure venison and ducks, but in the spring and summer one can get only salted fish and meat. Many of the cows are almost dry. . . . If we have to buy milk, it costs twelve cents a bottle, and fifteen cents in winter. And with all the salt diet we lack water. The well in our garden is dry and it costs twelve cents every time

we send someone to the Missouri to get us two little buckets of water.

We are learning by experience what faith teaches—that those who are lost have only themselves to blame. The Indians have respect for the priests; why, then, do they not go to them for instruction with the same eagerness they show in begging for whisky on which to get drunk, though they realize the fury it brings on them when they drink it? We sweetly dream of instructing docile and innocent savages, whereas the women as well as the men are afflicted with indolence and drunkenness. Jesuits are needed to make men of them before we attempt to make them Christians. So far we have dealt only with half-breeds—born of one Indian and one white parent; there are many such in the vicinity of St. Charles.

I am persuaded, however, that God had his designs in bringing us here. Already pictures of the Sacred Heart adorn several churches, for I have revived my old talent for painting and making paper flowers, and we have made decorations for several tabernacles. At St. Charles no one knew when to answer *Amen* at church. Now our day pupils sing at Benediction, and they have learned some of Father Barat's hymns, particularly one to the Sacred Heart. They are eager to learn and they learn easily. . . . I am already hard pressed to provide for our household on what comes in from the tuition of three boarding pupils, for the cost of living is exorbitant. We must live from day to day and stint even drinking water. But there is consolation in this poverty and daily dependence on the help of Providence, which is quite evident. My strength is diminishing in both body and soul. This humbles me before God and warns me that death may be near. I see with pleasure that the other nuns are liked better than I am; I really only help them. Octavie is in charge of the boarders; Eugenie helps her with the day pupils; and God blesses their work.

As we are making many friends with our painting and paper flowers, we shall need a great deal of carmine and rose coloring, needles, pins, thread. We are trying to cook without pot-hangers, pots, kitchen stove, a spit for meat, a warmer, etc. . . .

Many of the letters Mother Duchesne sent to France are filled with information and stories she had picked up in conversation with the chaplain, the missionary priests who called at the convent when passing through the village, especially Father John Acquaroni and Father Marie-Joseph Dunand, and with local visitors who came to bring a small gift or pass the time of day with her and lingered a bit curiously, perhaps, to talk to the nuns who always stayed at home and whom the school children spoke of so affectionately. Philippine was by instinct friendly, as those who spoke her language readily understood, and to this friendliness the community and children often owed their meal of venison or wild turkey, the butter that made dry corn bread more palatable, or the homemade wild grape wine and cherry bounce that cured their colds and added cheer to their meager meals.

On December 15 Mother Duchesne noted in her *Journal:* "Today we received a postulant, Mary Mullen, who speaks English. Monseigneur sent her to us. He realized, as we do, our need of an English teacher. Fortunately all our children speak French, so Mother Octavie can handle their classes, helped by Mother Eugenie. . . . Letters have come directly from Grenoble, where our Mother General and Mother Bigeu are just now." Mother Barat had been in Grenoble during the previous summer, and for Philippine time suddenly folded back and she was in spirit at Sainte Marie. As she read, a change came over her features—they softened, glowed, and her deep eyes grew wistful with remembrance:

> Ever since I came to your dear mountain [wrote Mother Barat], my mind and heart have been filled with sweet and heart-breaking thoughts and memories of the past, which struggle for the upper hand in my soul. Once more I seem to see you receiving me for the first time, turning over to me this house, this religious family. I recall what pleasure I used to experience when I came back after my journeys and found you here in this peaceful solitude. How keenly I suffered this time when not only you were not here to greet me, but also I knew you were so far away from me! Of course, faith comes to my aid; and when I forget my pain, I realize your good fortune. . . .
>
> I suppose you are having your dose of trials and hardships. I am so anxious to know how you stood the trip, whether you have reached St. Louis, how your health is, and how your companions are. I must be patient. Not a line from you since Easter. It is such a long time. My love to your dear daughters. You know how we all pray for you. Do the same for us, and receive the assurance of my tender and inviolable attachment in C. J. M.

It was only on August 21, the day Philippine reached St. Louis, that Mother Barat received letters from New Orleans announcing the safe arrival of the nuns. Now in mid-December there was an opportunity to send letters to St. Louis with the friends who had brought Miss Mullen out to the convent, and Mother Duchesne availed herself of it. Only the letter to Mother Thérèse Maillucheau is extant. It was written after a long, hard day, when the other occupants of the little house were asleep. Gusts of cold wind coming in through chinks in the wall threatened the tenuous life of the candle-flame as Philippine gripped her quill with aching fingers and wrote:

All the news from France fills us with joy and lightens the pain of separation. Thank you for Aloysia's journal and, above all, for the details about the two new foundations. God is good in thus bringing about the growth of this little Society. You see, Upper Louisiana will not be your rival; *we* were suited only to a land still in a half-civilized state. I do not know how to describe the place in which we live. Its population is made up of a mixture of American emigrants from the East, French and Canadian Creoles, German, Irish and Flemish settlers, along with half-breeds who seem to inherit the worst faults of both Indian and white parents. As for real Indians, we never see them because the Americans from the East are pushing them out and making war with them. They are withdrawing further away. We would need Jesuits to bring them to us, as they brought them to Mother Marie of the Incarnation. We would attract them more quickly with liquor than with sermons. They will give anything they have in exchange for that. But in conscience no one should give it to them, seeing what a state it puts them in and how dangerous it makes them. . . .

We have had the privilege of doing without bread and water. I had expected the former privation, but I never dreamed that on the banks of the Missouri we should lack water with such an abundant flow of it in sight. We may not go down to the river, and no one is willing to go there for us. Sister Marguerite came back today from the two springs nearby, carrying her buckets, one only half full of water and the other filled with ice. The Missouri is almost frozen over, and it is so cold that the water freezes beside the fire, as does the laundered linen hung there to dry. Neither doors nor windows close tight, and no one here knows how to make a foot-warmer; besides, it would cost at least 25 or 30 francs. A little stove cost us 250 francs. We have logs, but they are too large, and there is no one to chop them for us and no saw with which we might cut them ourselves. Laziness is the vice of this region; it belongs to the way of life. People work only when obliged to do so, and pride keeps many from working for wages. For food we have corn, pork, and potatoes, but no eggs, butter, oil, fruit, vegetables. . . . I do not see how we shall survive Lent with only fish cooked without either butter or oil, and not an egg to be had till spring. But we are willing and glad to be in want. Not a single thing we brought from France or New Orleans has proved useless. I scarcely know what I am writing. It is late at night, but tomorrow will be too late to write. I cannot reply to all the dear letters I received. Please make up for me. *Au revoir* in C. J.,

Philippine

The Christmas season brought little relaxation from regular work, as only the great liturgical feasts were school holidays then, in both France and America. The girls who had already made their First Communion were invited to spend Christmas Eve at the convent with the boarding pupils. They arrived with their blankets or buffalo robes, each prepared to make her own shake-down for the night in the school room. After supper they gathered around the log fire that lighted the rough, low-ceilinged room with its bright glow, and enjoyed a story hour. The wonders of the Christ Child's first coming to earth held their minds and hearts in rapt attention, then gay Noëls were sung, and Mother Duchesne told them of Christmases in France and of the children she had known and loved at Sainte Marie. While the nuns prayed or completed preparations, the children slept for a couple of hours. At the sound of the bell all assembled in the chapel or its adjoining rooms for midnight Mass. The Christ Child was reborn on the altar and in the hearts of the twenty nuns and children, who welcomed him with love and gratitude. Then silence enveloped the little convent, and the children slept until the nuns called them to breakfast. The Christmas dinner was a festive affair, thanks to the kind Prattes, for Emilie was twelve years old that day, and her family had sent bountiful provisions for the celebration.

Bishop Du Bourg's greeting reached St. Charles on December 28. He wrote "with paternal affection" and added some flourishes about his desire "to see his diocese covered with convents of the Sacred Heart." With the punctilious courtesy of the cultured French, Mother Duchesne returned New Year's greetings from the community and children, and followed this up with a letter setting before him the major problems and anxieties that beset her and a plan by which she hoped to work more effectively in the diocese. Four months in St. Charles had demonstrated beyond doubt the unsuitability of the place at that time for a boarding school. But Mother Duchesne loved the children of the free school. She realized how great was their need of schooling and how well they were responding to the training now being given. She loved this remote village on the Missouri and knew it was the river that had proved the greatest obstacle to the development of the boarding school, her only source of revenue. The Bishop had offered only one alternative to St. Charles, and that was Florissant. She had visited Florissant and had refused to consider a foundation there. What was she to do? Had she been able to consult the Mother General and take a stand with the support of her advice and directives, she might have been able to bring the Bishop to a more reasonable and practical decision. But she had no more chance of doing so now than she had had in the previous August.

The idea of dividing the community into two groups had come to her even then. She felt that, given the conditions in which they found themselves and for which they were so unprepared, she and her companions might accomplish more by such a division. Now that they had made friends in St. Charles and were offered some definite help by the people of the village, the idea of division recurred to her more strongly, and she wrote of this and much else to Bishop Du Bourg. His reply is dated January 29, 1819:

> I heartily approve the plan of dividing the community and leaving only a free school at St. Charles under Mother Eugenie, Sister Marguerite, and Miss Mullen. The boarding school will be far better situated at Florissant. There the property is assured you. I will give you the greater part of the money needed for the construction; day-labor is cheap in that locality. To oversee the work you will have the Prior, a man more experienced and more active than any in St. Charles. Material is abundant and not too expensive; firewood will cost you almost nothing; and you cannot fail to draw a large number of pupils for the boarding school, which is a more important work than you seem to realize, for it is from the education of the upper levels of society that reform must come, and they are just as ignorant as the lower classes. This seems the time to consolidate your establishment. For my part, I am quite decided on this point. If you are determined to follow my advice (I give no orders in this matter), then we must get to work and lose no more time. . . .

The generosity with which Bishop Du Bourg volunteered to provide the greater part of the money needed for the construction of the new convent must have surprised Mother Duchesne, who was well acquainted with the financial difficulties he was facing in St. Louis. Evidently she did not rely much on this promise. Had not the bishop promised Mother Barat that the Religious of the Sacred Heart would found their first American convent in St. Louis? She wondered what Mother Barat had thought when she heard of the foundation at St. Charles. How long would it be before she heard from her again?

Early in February came a packet of mail containing a letter from Father Martial, along with the letter Bishop Du Bourg had written on June 24, 1818, and sent to New Orleans. Then on the fourteenth of the month letters from France arrived—but none from the Mother General. Father Perreau's long letter of spiritual direction was in answer to the one she had written to him eight months before. Alluding to the desire for martyrdom she had then expressed to him, he replied:

> It would be very consoling for a soul that really loves God to finish off this mortal life by such a sacrifice. But always bear in mind the fact that you are not worthy of so glorious a death, and so live with the firm resolution to give yourself unreservedly to your divine Spouse and always to make generously the sacrifice of all he may ask of you.

With renewed courage Philippine wrote to her Superior General on February 15:

> The experience of a winter here, and that a very mild one, has made us realize that at present we would only vegetate in this place, without accomplishing even the little good we might do elsewhere. But it is hard to abandon so many interesting children, several of whom desire to belong to the Sacred Heart of Jesus, and it seemed to me advisable to arrange temporarily to leave Mother Eugenie here with Sister Marguerite to help her. She would be able to run the day school for a while with the help of some young people. . . .
> You see, my dear Mother, that though we are forced to give up the boarding school here, it is heart-breaking to leave no help at all for these children, who could be nicely trained. In four months many have learned to read, to write, to know the whole of the little catechism, a number of hymns, and the prayers at Benediction. They do all the singing now, and formerly the priest could not get a single person to say *Amen*. I hope you will approve what Monseigneur desires so earnestly. . . .
> As to cloister, in the whole country for 500 leagues around us there is not a single wall around property. They put up wooden fences that keep out animals better than human beings. Our cloister consists in staying at home, but people come in as often as they please. They make openings for themselves anywhere. We shall have to be in our own house in order to regularize our life. In this house it is impossible. . . . If our Sisters in France imagine us surrounded by savages, they are quite mistaken. I have seen only a few old ones who made their First Communion at fifty or sixty

years of age, when temptations to passions had passed. But to compensate for our disappointment we have new employments: we dig in the garden, carry out the manure, water the cow, clean out her little stable—the only one in this place, for all the animals wander at large. And we do all this with as much joy as we would have if we were teaching Indians, for God wills it this way, and our poverty, along with the false pride of the settlers, prevents us from getting servants. . . . The letters of Mother Marie of the Incarnation can give you some idea of our country, which has been settled only within the last forty years by Canadians, so the first settlers all speak French.

The weather has been very clear, on the whole, since we came here, but they tell me there are often furious wind storms and loud thunder. We have had a few slight earthquakes. As the country is not well organized and it is easy to get away by stealth, it is also easy to set fires deliberately. . . . People sometimes set fire to the woods and to the wide prairies where the tall grass is very dry. One night the Americans in St. Charles had to keep watch lest the fire spread into the village, for it spreads like a whirlwind. In the autumn we saw fires on all sides and in the woods opposite us on the other side of the Missouri. . . .

On February 20 Mothers Duchesne and Berthold drove to Florissant to meet the bishop there and inspect the property he offered as a gift to the Society. It was not a part of the farm he had purchased, but a separate plot in the village, intended originally as a church site, and for this purpose the bishop was retaining a portion of it. He showed the nuns plans that had been drawn for the convent and for a church to be erected contiguous to it, but he was very vague about ways and means to finance the construction of these buildings.

Fear of expense in the matter of building gave Mother Duchesne long hours of anxiety. She had known trials of this kind before—at Sainte Marie and in Paris, but she had had money at her disposal in those days and had also been able to enlist the aid of her relatives. Letters had come recently from her sister Euphrosine and from Josephine de Savoye-Rollin. It had been months since she had written to them. Now she did so. To the Jouves she barely hinted at the anxieties confronting her, though she did mention the rheumatism in her hands that made writing very difficult. To Josephine she expressed herself more freely, repeating many details she had already written to France, details she knew would appeal to her *très chère Cousine,* and asking help in her usual straightforward manner.

Having reached the end of our journey, I counted securely on your tender friendship following me here. It is as precious to me now as when I tasted all its sweetness in the days when every circumstance drew us together in our childhood, and I shall never forget my first, my most intimate friend.

We are perfectly happy here, for we have found the cross which we looked for; but since the truest crosses are those we do not choose ourselves, God has prepared for us many trials we did not expect. We thought we would find innocence and ignorance combined, and we meet with children whose fathers are given to drunkenness and laziness, and whose mothers are consumed with a love for fancy clothes and dancing, and quite indifferent as to whether their children ever learn any more than they themselves know. But the children are attracted irresistibly to us. Some beg to come to school; some even cry in order to get leave to do so. We cannot teach them to sew, for they have no material at all. A hank of cotton for knitting costs five francs; thimbles, thread, needles are very expensive. So even if we had room enough to house them from all danger, we could not furnish them with occupation. Here where everyone is so poor, each one makes her own chemise, her dress, even her shoes, and one must speak of these articles of clothing in the singular, so poverty-stricken are these people.

We are paying nearly 2,000 francs for the only house that could be found for us. As this section of the country is newly settled, houses have not been built. The expenses of the trip were simply enormous, and we have on hand just 5,000 francs with which to build a little house that will cost 15,000, without a basement, every-thing being so costly, especially the hire of laborers. The bishop is giving us the ground for a new house and garden at Florissant, with a small cabin to use for a free school. Minds are very favor-ably inclined toward us in St. Louis, and we shall be nearer there when we leave St. Charles.

Since you ask me to confide in you and tell you my troubles, these are the anxieties that weigh upon me, but do not discourage me. For since the general attitude toward us in St. Louis is be-coming more favorable, we shall have enough pupils to enable us to pay back what we borrow. See if you can procure a loan for us. I shall pay it back as soon as possible. I gave Mother Barat the address of a banker in Philadelphia who has an agent in St. Charles. This agent has done us a thousand services, and the quickest and safest way to send us money would be through him.

I am so grateful for the detailed news you gave me of your family and mine. Give affectionate messages to all, especially Tante Perier, your husband, Augustin and Madame Perier, my brother and his wife. When I was leaving Paris I sent my brother my life-certificate so he could collect my entire annuity for 1817. Now I am having another sent for 1818. I do not know whether they will be accepted. I shall know in a year from now. Ask my brother if he got the two certificates and assure him at the same time of my tender affection. You know how sincerely I love you, my dear Cousin. Everything here at St. Charles recalls your generosity. Our chapel, above all, is decorated entirely by you. All yours in our Lord Jesus Christ. . . .

Lent came, and with it some help that gave the nuns courage and hope. Divine Providence was "very wonderful" in their regard, Mother Duchesne recorded gratefully, but she had added anxieties. The bishop, who was very fond of talking, had given Sister Lamarre to understand that he wanted her to help inaugurate a free school in St. Louis. She was zealous, earnest, capable, but she was talkative and gave the impression of wanting to act independently at a time when Mother Duchesne was expending prayer and energy on the solution of the problem of their future home and work, which, as superior, she felt she must handle in concert with the bishop and in conformity with the Society's usual manner of acting. Mother Eugenie Audé was also causing her some anxiety. Tense and high-strung, Eugenie was sometimes upset emotionally. The idea of being in charge of a little school at St. Charles after Mother Duchesne moved to Florissant created fears which were difficult to control. In a large community this condition might have passed unnoticed, but in so small a group it was disturbing. Moreover, Mary Mullen had grown dissatisfied and was asking to return to St. Louis. Her departure relieved Mother Duchesne of one anxiety. Soon her place was taken by a more reliable girl, Mary Ann Summers of St. Louis. She was too young to become a postulant at once, and at first she chafed under confinement and discipline, but she became a reliable and helpful member of the household, finding in Philippine Duchesne a second mother and loving the life of prayer and work and family joys. She had been through sorrow in the past months; she was an orphan now, befriended chiefly by Mrs. Pratte, the first of many orphans to whom Mother Duchesne gave a home.

The slight friction perceptible in the community that spring was aggravated by the bishop's criticism of some points of the Rule which he considered incompatible with pioneer conditions, particularly cloister and the distinction between choir and coad-jutrix nuns, though this distinction has held a place in communal religious life almost from its very inception. Mother Duchesne mentions the matter almost casually in a letter of March 15 to Father Barat. After comparing the customs of the Ursulines in New Orleans with those of the Society of the Sacred Heart in regard to distinction within the religious community, Mother Duchesne drops the matter and turns to more personal affairs:

> During the winter I thought I had lost my health, but it is quite restored and I have no pain at all now. But I shall have much to expiate, for in that improvement in my condition the measure of consolation outweighs the suffering. What a joy it was to hear again that the Holy Father approved of our voyage! Realizing from this fact that it was the will of God takes away the cruel anguish caused by the thought that under the pretext of following an inspiration I was merely doing my own will. . . . So now my prayer is just an outpouring of gratitude for the assurance of that most completely desired will of God, which will seem all the more desirable in all that is ahead. Then the Society of the Sacred Heart and its members will spread the reign of Jesus Christ in these new lands. . . .
>
> The dear Lord is trying us in another way. Our first boarding pupil, a ribbon of merit, is ill. She is the eldest daughter of the lady who gave us such a kind welcome in St. Louis. If she dies, it will be a severe blow to us, humanly speaking. But God is all-powerful.

Emilie Pratte's illness was so serious that Mother Duchesne sent for her mother. Mrs. Pratte arrived with the family nurse, a competent Negro woman who cared for all the little Prattes and who loved "Miss Emilie" as her own child. Madame Duquette's room was used as the school infirmary, and Mrs. Pratte was lodged there with her sick daughter. There was great excitement in the little house one evening when the nurse made too hot a blaze in the stove in the infirmary and the chimney, a stone and wood structure, caught fire. Nuns and children were badly frightened, "having no man to help them and almost no water." But the blaze was extinguished and no serious damage resulted. Emilie soon recovered and life returned to its normal routine. This trial united the little community by a closer bond of love, for all had shared the anxiety and prayed with increased fervor, and there is no more efficacious means of union than shared responsibility and prayer. All was going fairly well now, and Mary Ann Summers was proving a far more willing helper than Miss Mullen had been.

Holy Week was approaching, and Father Richard had expressed his intention of performing the liturgical services in the convent chapel, as the villagers seldom came to Mass except on Sundays and other days of obligation. Mother Duchesne's joy in this "favor of Divine Providence" was intense, and she was looking forward to Holy Thursday and a night of prayer like those she had spent at Sainte Marie, though her frontier vigils of adoration had been as prolonged as her strength would permit. Mother Audé and the children prepared the repository, decorating it with fresh white muslin and artificial flowers. It was pretty, they thought, and very devotional.

After Mass on Holy Thursday the little convent was more silent and prayerful than usual, as the day pupils had no classes and the boarding pupils followed the example of the nuns. Toward evening, while three of the nuns were playing in the chapel, a gust of wind through a chink in the wall blew a corner of the cotton drapery across a candle flame. In an instant the altar was ablaze. The religious pulled away whatever furnishings they could reach as the flames licked upward along the wall. Cries of alarm brought Mother Duchesne to the scene. Mary Ann and the other girls ran for buckets, dipped them into the rain barrel, which had been filled providentially by an April downpour, and passed them up the ladder to Mother Duchesne who had climbed to the attic ahead of all the others. Balanced against an upright post, she threw the water on the dry beams and up to the shingled roof to prevent the spread of the fire. How she succeeded in doing this was a matter of astonishment to all. By prayer and self-control and intelligent direction the little group extinguished the flames and saved the house, and not a person in the village saw the fire or came to their assistance.

Through the spring and summer Mother Duchesne and her nuns worked steadily with the children, trying to give them all the training they could crowd into the few months that remained. May and June were celebrated with the same devotional practices in the convent on the Missouri as in those on the Seine and the Isère, and the feasts of St. Francis Regis and of the Sacred Heart were days the children would remember for many a year.

There was plenty of food now for nuns and children, as the garden yielded an ample supply of vegetables and the fruit trees bore an abundant crop. The long, hot summer days were relieved now and then by hours of relaxation, when the children played under the spreading trees or waded in the creek that flowed through the south meadow or gathered fruit for their goûter in the orchard. On July 22 they celebrated in honor of the Mother General in far-off France, nuns and children enjoying a gay holiday. But Philippine was heart-sick with disappointment when she wrote to Mother Barat a week later:

> The dear Lord has favored us with a share of his cross. The greatest and undoubtedly the hardest to bear is the lack of success in our work here. If a saint had been in charge, all would have gone well. That thought makes the burden of my office all the heavier. Every day I see more clearly that I do not possess the qualities necessary in a superior.
>
> The new house at Florissant is progressing. They say we can move into it by December 1. . . . I am trusting in Divine Providence with regard to the debt that house has brought on us and the transfer to Florissant. One day recently I was down to almost nothing. The paper money I had on hand all proved worthless at the same time, but that is the only kind of money people pay us. God will be our refuge. I am more and more convinced that he wants us here, and it consoles me greatly to know that the other four nuns feel as I, even the one whose perseverance seemed somewhat doubtful. If at times we feel the thorns that press upon us from all sides, still we know we are your daughters, we have Fathers, Mothers, Sisters, and children all praying for us, and so our courage cannot fail.
>
> There is little hope of our working among the Indians. In the days of Marie of the Incarnation the Jesuits went everywhere among them, gathered the children together, appeased the parents, interpreted their diverse languages and skillfully reduced them to writing in the dictionaries and books they composed. This kind of work is far beyond the ability of a few isolated missionaries, as we who are on the spot well realize. But my desire to devote myself to these poor souls has not diminished, if only God opens the way for me. . . .

August was a very busy time. The First Communion ceremony was set for the fifteenth of the month, and this meant material and spiritual preparations before the retreat, which Father Richard gave the children. Then the "closing exercises" were planned and practiced, for the bishop had promised to come for this event. Packing, too, was under way, but Philippine found time to write to Mother Barat on August 28:

> It is a real suffering when we count the months and realize that we have had no word from France since January, and even then I had only five or six lines from you on a letter from Mother Girard. . . . I did not write any letters from April to July, as I had no way of sending them. . . .

I allow myself the pleasure of reading again and again the letters I have received from you and others in France. They console and encourage me. I do not say they bind me more closely to you all; the ties between us could hardly be drawn tighter. That is why it gave me such joy to hear Monseigneur say one day in commenting on us: *Ah, c'est bien de la race.* However, dear Mother, I am beginning to realize that there will be differences because of national character and climate. The summer heat has been as prostrating here as it was in New Orleans last year. It is impossible to sleep with the windows closed at night. The children will not endure even their curtains closed in a dormitory. Out here they draw the beds in front of open windows and doors and fireplaces, and no one pays any attention to drafts. . . .

Knowledge of English is bringing Mother Octavie forward. The Americans are quite proud of her. Their national pride seems to make them scorn those who do not speak their language, so English is a real necessity. I simply despair of ever speaking it. Eugenie hesitates, too, but she has enough to do with the French-speaking children. She is venerated by them. From all this you will realize that God has not bestowed on us the gift of tongues. Perhaps he wants his missionary nuns to sanctify themselves on failure. That is what I conclude when I see young priests preaching fluently in English at the end of a few months. . . .

On Sunday, August 29, Philippine found time for a last letter from St. Charles. Her heart was full of memories of August 29 in former years—in Grenoble, at Vizille, at Grâne, at Sainte Marie— and of those who had always made it such a joyous day for her by their constant love and devoted friendship. And so she wrote to Josephine. She had had no news from her in more than six months, but she had learned the way of the mail on the frontier and she was schooling herself to accept this circumstance, which she found so trying. Her interest in the dear ones she had left in France was as keen as ever, her love as tender and grateful as she wrote:

A year ago today I was writing to you from St. Louis just after our arrival there. Since then our situation, though always precarious, has presented few variations. We have had very few boarding pupils, as both St. Charles and the section of the country north of the Missouri are too poor to send any. Then, too, the river separates us from St. Louis and is subject to terrible floods, storms, and ice, so the mothers have considered all this an insurmountable obstacle to putting their children in school here.

A house is being built for us at Florissant, which is nearer St. Louis. We shall pay for it little by little and we shall leave St.

Charles next month with keen regret. This place is better populated than Florissant; the day pupils are so well disposed; and the site of the town is much more desirable. It will be an important place some day, for trade on the Missouri with the Indians or the new American settlements on the Upper Missouri is growing every day. To aid and encourage this, the government is putting troops and cannon on the steamboats, which were not seen hitherto on the Missouri. Someone told me recently about a steamboat that went from New York to New Orleans with steam and paddle-wheels in ten days. At New Orleans it discarded its sails and came up the Mississippi just as other steamboats do. It was the first trial of such a voyage. With regard to boats on the Missouri, we saw the first four that ever attempted the navigation of that stream.

I am fifty years old today, my dear friend. That age makes me realize my unfitness for the venture I have undertaken, but it does not lessen the tender affection that has bound me to you, to Augustin, and to Camille for so many, many years. You were my dearest friends in all the world; and though I left the world, my love for you has survived a sacrifice that was akin to death. Thank you so much for your tender interest in my work. Your letter touched the deepest chords of my heart. My companions are greatly loved here and do much good. They want to be remembered to you. You heard about our accident by fire on Holy Thursday, when we had all your gifts displayed in our chapel. Your generosity made it possible for us to see other gifts from your hand used as decorations on Easter Sunday. Many other things in this sanctuary remind me of Josephine and her tender and solicitous love.

Our greatest problem has been to get a house. Monseigneur, the bishop, is having one built, but at our expense. Where shall we find 30,000 francs, when we have only 5,000? I shall know the actual cost of the house only when we are in it. I dread it, yet I trust it all to Divine Providence. I grasped at a means offered me in a proposition you made in the letter you enclosed with one from Father Dumolard. I explained to you our situation and asked a little loan to help us; but if this is not possible, rest assured it will not lessen my gratitude to you, my remembrance of you in prayer before God, and my eternal friendship. Affectionate regards to my aunt and her family. . . .

Bishop Du Bourg arrived at St. Charles with Fathers Martial and De La Croix on August 30. Presiding at the distribution of prizes next day, he congratulated Miss Odile DeLassus on winning highest honors and complimented the children on their good manners as well as on their recitations and singing. He was sincere in his praise and expressed great satisfaction at all that had been accomplished in the classes. Then he spoke with regret of the necessity that forced the nuns to leave St. Charles. The evening before, he had told the community that the convent at Florissant, which not even Mother Duchesne had seen yet, was not ready for occupancy and that, since their lease on the Duquette house expired on September 6, the best arrangement he could suggest was for them to use the log cabin on his farm a mile from Florissant. True, Father De La Croix was living there at present—and was also listening to this conversation—but he could move elsewhere for a few weeks. No one asked where "elsewhere" might be, and no more was said on the subject. The bishop's optimism was equaled only by his vivid imagination, which always by-passed the difficulties involved in the arrangements he proposed. He rode off on horseback next morning, the priests following with two gentlemen in the carriage that had conveyed them from St. Louis, and the nuns were left to face an unhappy task.

It was easier to close the school than it was to dismiss the children. They wanted to spend at least part of the First Friday of September at the convent. On the eve they came to rehearse the hymns they had sung at the First Communion ceremony in August. On Friday morning all who had made their First Communion then or earlier in the year came for Mass and breakfast. "Father Richard was as deeply moved as we were," noted Mother Duchesne, and after a very touching little sermon "he went off without taking his breakfast."

So the first long, laborious year in the frontier mission field came to a close. In Mother Duchesne's eyes it was a failure, and failure, whether real or apparent, was one of the severest trials that could come to her. She belonged to a family that had been eminently successful and to a religious order whose steady growth and development were remarkable. She had been put in charge of an apostolic enterprise which seemed to offer high hopes of success and which now had every appearance of failure. In spite of the very evident material factors that had conditioned the failure, she felt that its primary cause had been herself. She was not blind to patent facts nor to the almost hopeless circumstances in which she had worked for twelve months, but she was blind to the courageous leadership, the unswerving loyalty, the selfless devotion with which she had carried on that work. The struggle had been constant, even heroic, yet she was so alive to a sense of her own incapacity that she simply could not see things in any other light. This very conviction of incapacity was a forward movement in the contempla-

seven

Building
on the Frontier

I. 1819—1821

THE TREK TO FLORISSANT was true to frontier pattern, and no one could describe it better than Philippine did. She seemed to enjoy her own narrative, for she wrote it with the quiet humor and directness that characterize so many of the little accounts she sent back to France. The migration began on September 3, when baggage and furniture were taken in carts down the steep road that led to the river and loaded on two small rafts, which were poled downstream and landed on the south bank of the Missouri. Mother Audé, Sister Lamarre, and three of the pupils followed after a tearful good-bye from many of the children of St. Charles, who clung to the nuns and exhausted the patience of the waiting boatmen. At La Charbonniere they were met by Father Dunand, pastor of St. Ferdinand, and Father De La Croix. The former had brought carts that were loaned by the laborers working on the new convent; the latter, those belonging on the Bishop's farm. "They made seventeen trips from the river to the farmhouse," noted Mother Duchesne. "This does not mean that we have great possessions, however, for a one-horse cart can carry only three people, or baggage in proportion."

This expedition was followed by a second, when Mother Octavie left with two of the older girls in an open carriage sent by the father of one of them. I intended to bring up the rear that afternoon with the cows, the calves, the chickens, and Sister Marguerite. But our cows revolted when they found themselves tied and obliged to walk in the sun, so we had to wait until early the next morning, when the rest of our belongings was packed into three carts, along with cabbages to appease the cows. These animals started off on the rampage, but soon they were mastered by their ropes and by fatigue, and they decided to follow with their calves. I perched on top of a cart, dividing my attention between the care of my relics and that of the chickens. After driving about ten miles, we crossed the Missouri just opposite Florissant on a raft. When we landed, Marguerite lined up the chickens with motherly tenderness and gave them food and water. I did the same for the cows with my cabbages. Then Father De La Croix appeared on horseback to show us the way. As we had let the cows loose, he had to gallop after them every time they tried to run into the woods. By evening we reached the little farmhouse.

Describing this new residence Mother Duchesne wrote:

It is composed of a single room, which will serve as the children's dormitory, refectory, parlor, and classroom. Above is a loft under a roof that is pierced by many holes. This will be our living quarters night and day. We shall stop up the holes as best we can and use the loft also as kitchen, refectory, and storeroom.

The farmhouse was a log cabin of American type, measuring about eighteen feet square and having two windows with solid wooden shutters and a single entrance fitted with a door of thick planks that was fastened with a wooden latch on a leather thong. A stone fireplace at one end accommodated enormous logs. Soon a great fire was roaring up the chimney, giving light and warmth to the room, for the erratic Missouri weather staged freak changes that September, with freezing temperature following close on the burning heat of the moving days. "We are in a situation that calls for continual self-renunciation," wrote Mother Duchesne, "at times pestered by visitors, without a corner to which we can withdraw for prayer; now overcome by heat in such crowded quarters, and now racked by the cold and wind that come in on all sides."

Another circumstance that distressed her was the illness of Father De La Croix, who had been named chaplain to the convent. In order to give the nuns and children a home, he had vacated the log cabin and taken shelter in a dilapidated corn crib, "as open as a bird cage," commented Mother Duchesne. Exposed to wind and cold, he contracted a fever and for several days was quite sick.

> We could not even pass a chair into the place through the hole that serves as door and window. When the bishop was informed of his condition, he ordered a two-room house to be built—one room for the priest and the other for a chapel. Some old timber was at hand, a few workmen were put on the job, and within a week Father De La Croix had a roof over his head, and the Blessed Sacrament reposed in the little chapel, and we were settled in the way we most desired, for "he who has Jesus has all."

To the surprise of the nuns, the school began to increase immediately. First came Mathilde Hamilton, at whose home near Ste. Genevieve many of the young French and Italian priests who came as missionaries to Missouri spent several months in order to learn English. On October 19 three more pupils arrived—Virginia Labbadie, a cousin of the Prattes, and the Rolette sisters, Émilie and Betsie. They were gentle, womanly girls, and like their companions they were drawn to Mother Duchesne because there was about her such a complete lack of affectation, such simplicity of speech and manner, such unobtrusive tact and sincere friendliness. On their coming to the cabin-convent, she commented: "People are so accustomed to poor lodgings in this country that even the wealthiest families do not mind sending us their daughters." She was happy to welcome these new pupils, but they increased her anxiety at a time when she had her hands full.

> All the tenants on the farm contracted fever and as they could not help themselves, Sister Marguerite cooked their meals. Mother Eugenie had to milk six cows morning and night—two of ours and four belonging to the farm. This did not last long, but another trial followed, for Mother Octavie and two of the children caught the fever. As there is only one room for all the children and one for us, we feared everyone in the household would catch the disease; but Divine Providence was watching over us, and today, September 28, all are well.

The defying challenge offered by the one-room cabin with a loft called forth the finest virtues in Mother Duchesne and stimulated like virtues in her religious. There was plenty of room for discouragement at times, but there was always at hand that dauntless combination of faith and hope and trust, all glowing with love. Although the community and school were lodged so inconveniently, Philippine noted appreciatively several advantages that compensated for their discomforts:

> We have an abundance of fruit and vegetables; we have salted down a little heifer; we get bread and corn meal from Florissant on credit for six months. The wood that was used in making the bricks will furnish us with fuel for the early winter months. Many of our fifty chickens will lay eggs all winter. And there are the frequent visits of the bishop and missionary priests, the assurance of the presence of Father De La Croix and of the pastor, who is using every cent he has to pay our workmen. All this makes us realize that it would be very ungrateful and very wrong for us ever to fail in trust toward Divine Providence in either spiritual or temporal affairs.

Besides her account of the transfer to Florissant and the first weeks in the log cabin, two letters written by Mother Duchesne in September, 1819, are extant. Six months had passed since her last letter to Father Barat, though she had received many marks of kindness from him during that time. Without apology for her silence she wrote by candlelight in a corner of the cabin loft while the household slept on the night of September 17:

> You certainly give us proof that we are still your daughters, for your solicitude for us does not diminish, but rather increases. Your letters to Mothers Octavie and Eugenie did them the greatest good and strengthened them in the path of perfection along which they are determined to walk. Far from being frightened by difficulties, they are never happier than when they have something to suffer. . . . The money shortage is being felt sharply in the United States also. A large number of banks have stopped payment and this means total loss for all who hold their notes—which is the kind of money in use in the country. It is very rare to find a few dollars or other coins among the paper notes we receive. I know that because of the money shortage Monseigneur wanted to stop the work on our house, but it is going on and we shall be in it within a month, even if they do not plaster it until the spring.
>
> I was really sorry the details of our straitened circumstances caused you and our Fathers and Mothers in France any anxiety about us. That was a temporary situation, and I assure you such experiences bring very real delight, and one must be on guard against taking pride in them. Divine Providence does not keep us waiting long, and in spite of the uneasiness caused by moving into our new house with a debt of perhaps 20,000 francs (they have not yet stated the exact sum), I have not the slightest doubt that we shall find a way to pay it in a short time, since we were able to

live at St. Charles with so few pupils and still not incur the least
debt. . . .

Among the many holy priests I have met, I do not find one who
helps me. It seems as if my soul were quite alone—but I have too
little feeling to be distressed about it. I do not know what condition my soul is in. I am unfaithful and I do not worry; I am haughty
and impatient and I taste only the sweetness of Jesus; I rarely
humble myself, yet the strongest conviction I experience is that of
God's goodness to me. Father Richard did not handle me gently,
and I am grateful to him for that. Yet with him, as with our
Bishop, respect does not call forth that confidence which puts the
soul at ease. My own is, as it were, passive, without movement
except toward the soul of Jesus, toward Mary and St. Regis.

Please distribute the letters we are sending. . . . It is night-time
and I am nodding with sleep, but I must thank you on the part of
Monseigneur for Sister Nativité's work, which he took even before
he knew it was for him. We cannot hide anything from him. He
sees through everything, exterior and interior, spiritual and temporal. . . .

Ten days later she opened her heart to Mother Barat, laying
before her some of the problems that were weighing heavily on
her. The spectre of debt was creeping up to haunt her for many
a day and in circumstances that tried her severely. But the picture
she sketched was never entirely dark, for her buoyant spirit and
unfailing trust in God lifted her above the workaday worries that
lay like snares in her path. Recommending her letter to St. Anthony, as was her custom, she wrote on September 27:

It grieved me to learn that you have been anxious about us, but it
was very sweet to be told: "I should like to have a letter from you
every month." I had not received that loving invitation when I
omitted writing from April until July. . . . I received your April
letter before that of March. The latter told me all the gifts you
planned to send us; the former announced the shipment of these
things. . . . What we need most of all just now is money. Monseigneur's purse is drained for his seminary at the Barrens and his
college in St. Louis, not to mention the cathedral. Our building
overwhelms him with embarrassment, so it is very urgent for us
to pay our debt. . . .

I do not yet know the total cost of the building. At one moment
Monseigneur was for stopping the work on it for lack of funds,
but the pastor at Florissant took upon himself the business of urging on the work and even adding another story, giving the brick-
maker a piece of land in payment and spending his last cent on the

house. He shows extraordinary eagerness to have us in his parish. . . .

I was the more deeply touched by your gift of the *piano* when I realized that you had purchased it with money you needed. Oh, my dear Mother, believe me, we suffer only when we learn that you are suffering. . . . Neither Eugenie nor I can understand English yet, and even Octavie, with all her facility and assurance and constant study, cannot understand some Americans nor make herself understood by them. A miracle is worked in favor of the priests, I think. . . .

Early in October Bishop Du Bourg paid the nuns a visit in company with Father Felix De Andreis, superior of the Lazarist Missions in Missouri. The bishop was pleasant and friendly, praised the children's singing, even asking for a repetition of the hymns sung at his Mass, and gave the community a deed to the plot of ground on which the convent was being constructed. "Then he required Mother Duchesne to write a letter to Mr. Mullanphy, asking the loan of $2000, as there is no money on hand for the completion of our building," Mother Duchesne recorded in her *Journal*. Next day she sat down to write Mother Barat, yet strangely enough she made no mention of borrowing money from John Mullanphy. Instead she betrayed the emotional strain of the day before by giving free rein first to a reminiscent mood, then to a little day-dreaming about St. Charles.

Early in November she sketched in a few lines in her *Journal* the life of the nuns on the Bishop's farm:

Our days are filled with work for the children and our spiritual duties, along with chores to which we were formerly unaccustomed. As we have no servant, we have frequently to gather wood in the forest. In this country people would look with scorn on the little fires we made in Paris. Here, when we have a visitor, we burn up our whole provision of fuel in a single day; then we have to bring in more wood. We gather corn, apples, vegetables in the garden. When the children go for a walk, they often bring back wild fruits and farm provisions, but we sometimes lack meat and often have only corn meal for making bread; and even this is expensive.

Bishop Du Bourg was at Florissant again for the feast of the Presentation, November 21, presiding at the renovation of vows, preaching, and giving Benediction of the Blessed Sacrament. By this time Mother Duchesne was so well acquainted with him, she could interpret with fair accuracy the look in his expressive eyes—now puzzled and uncertain, now hardened into resolution, and again genial and laughing. She knew the set of his sensitive mouth, the lines of his fine forehead and weak chin. It was a handsome face in which obstinacy rather than strength seemed to dominate. The Bishop's magnificent physical build gave him an imposing appearance, while his exquisite courtesy made him a charming guest.

All was pleasant enough that day until he again broached the subject of changes he wished to make in the Society's rule of life. "We would not consent to these," Mother Duchesne noted laconically in her *Journal;* and the bishop must have admired her courageous loyalty. At least he took no offense, for he proceeded to arrange for a retreat to be given at the cabin-convent during a missionary trip Father De La Croix was planning. Up the Missouri River was the Indian country where white men were penetrating for fur trading, trapping, and hunting. No priest had as yet gone into those woods and prairies to carry the Gospel to the savages. There were settlers living in villages on the lower reaches of the river beyond St. Charles, and among them, too, the missionary hoped to sow the seeds of a rich harvest.

In a letter to Mother Barat written about this time Bishop Du Bourg expressed his admiration for "the rare virtues and remarkable gifts of the religious whom you have sent me. I cannot tell you how excellent an impression they have made in this part of the world. Mother Duchesne is a saint." Meanwhile she herself touched indirectly on his visit in a letter to Mother Barat which is a sort of running comment on life at Florissant:

> The last letters we had from France were written in April. . . . We had hoped to be in our new home by the beginning of November, but we will be fortunate if we move in by January 1. In the meantime we live on the bishop's farm. He has given us the legal title to the land on which our house is being built. . . . Recently we borrowed 10,000 francs from rich Mr. Mullanphy in order to get the building finished. . . .
>
> Our consolation in this wilderness is that our boarding pupils are much better off here than at St. Charles. Several show signs of vocation, but we must be very prudent in this matter because of their wealth and the opposition of their families. The daily regulations here are the same as at Grenoble. The uniform is magenta, trimmed in black velvet, without flowers or tulle or lace. One very irksome thing here is the scandal the Americans, especially the Protestants, take at the least game or outing on Sunday. I spoke to the bishop about this and he said we must respect the opinion of the people here. He experienced the same thing at the college in Baltimore. . . .

If any of our religious come to join us, I wish they would bring some pairs of sabots as models. These are greatly needed here, where one goes around daily through water rounding up the animals, with no servant to help, and where the kitchens are built at a distance from the house for fear of fire. Prairie fires and forest fires have done great damage this year. We have seen them at close range.

So much about material things, dear Reverend Mother, but my heart is with you and with the Societies of Jesus and of the Sacred Heart. When I meditate on the fact that I belong to our Society, my soul expands with joy, tears of gratitude flow, and I see only happiness in privations. Could God do more for me? Only one greater favor could he bestow—the privilege of martyrdom. But on my side, how much more I could do! What sorrow I feel at having corresponded so poorly with grace!

Father De Andreis arrived for the retreat on December 5, and for a week held his audience of five nuns and a few of the older pupils under the spell of his fervent preaching and personal sanctity. The carriage that came to take him back to St. Louis brought Mother Duchesne a letter from Mother Barat dated July 9 and containing some reflections that Philippine noted in her *Journal:* "Our Mother General regrets that our first convent was not built either in New Orleans or in St. Louis. She insists that we establish a mother house and novitiate, from which small missions might be founded later on. But for the present she considers it very unwise for us to divide our group."

The transfer from the bishop's "chateau" in the woods to the new convent in the village has been described in detail by Mother Duchesne in charming letters:

We moved from the bishop's farm in very cold weather when the pastor of Florissant informed me that "the holy land was ready and could be entered before Christmas." I set off the next day with a young American girl, who acts as our interpreter with the workmen. As we reached the village I heard the bell for Mass, so we went first to the church. The pastor announced that this was the feast of St. Thomas the Apostle. It gave me a thrill of joy to think that we were taking possession of our new home on such a day, and I begged this saint, along with St. Francis Xavier and St. Regis, to obtain for us the grace that all our labor might be for the glory of the Sacred Hearts of Jesus and Mary.

The two-mile tramp through the snow and the two days of labor to clear the building of debris and prepare it for the community and children are in her estimation negligible details. Of importance, however, is the fact that

> on December 23 Mother Octavie with one of the Sisters and six of the older girls trudged through the snow to join me. They were wrapped up in blankets and had stockings over their shoes to prevent them from slipping on the ice. A wagon hauling our baggage and furniture followed them. I rode back to the farm in it to make up the last bundles and pack the chapel furnishings. That afternoon another wagon took the remaining children, escorted by Father De La Croix on horseback. On the 24th we sent Marguerite in a little wagon with our boxes and bundles. Later Mother Eugenie and I set out on foot, hoping to conduct our last cow across the fields in a friendly fashion. We had never been able to lead her with a rope, and she had no calf to attract her this time. I filled my apron with corn in order to coax her to follow me. But she preferred her liberty and ran headlong through the bushes and trees along our path. As we tried to keep up with her we floundered and fell several times in the snow, tore our veils and habits on the brambles, and at last gave up and let her go back to the farm, while we pursued our way to Florissant. The snow was falling more heavily now and we had only pig tracks to guide us. We were such a sight to behold, we actually frightened a herd of these half-wild animals. I was carrying our money and papers in my pockets, but the string broke and everything, including my watch, fell into the snow. We had a very hard time recovering our possessions and carrying them, for our hands were numb with cold and could not take hold of anything. So we were very late in reaching Florissant because we had lost our way. But we had to hurry with the work of preparing the chapel. Owing to the severe cold, the room intended for it had not been plastered. We removed the lumber that had been piled there and hung sheets as a curtain behind the altar which we set up. After supper we decorated it during the hour of *veillée*, then went to confession. At midnight Father De La Croix offered the Holy Sacrifice of the Mass.

In her *Journal* Mother Duchesne recorded other details: the nuns recited Matins promptly at eleven o'clock that Christmas Eve; the midnight Mass followed by a second one, and both were attended by the "pious Irish workmen" who had built the house. There was a third Mass on Christmas morning, with joyous Christmas hymns, as at the other two, and in the afternoon Vespers followed by Benediction—both "solemn," though it is difficult to understand in what the "solemnity" consisted. The Bishop came next day to bless the new convent, and the children in their bright uniforms sang "some couplets expressing gratitude to him." Father Dunand was also present, so two verses were addressed to him. General Pratte attended this little reception and next morning directed traffic in the village, for a stream of carriages brought visitors, some coming through curiosity, others, like the Pratte family, to attend the bishop's Mass, at which Therese Pratte and Mary Ann Summers received their First Holy Communion. The year 1819 closed with the customary Benediction of reparation and gratitude, and the New Year opened with festive wishes expressed first to Mother Duchesne by both nuns and children, then to Father Dunand and Father De La Croix.

The boarding school increased with the arrival of the Leduc, Chenier, and Cabanne girls on January 6, and with them on this day of gifts came some handsome ones from the bishop—oil paintings of the Sacred Heart, St. Francis of Assisi, St. Agatha, Benedict Joseph Labre, and one representing the death of St. Francis Regis. Now a little shrine could be set up temporarily in fulfilment of the promise made to honor him on the American frontier.

On Friday, March 17, a heavily loaded wagon lumbered out from St. Louis, bearing the long-awaited cases that had been shipped from France the previous spring. Their contents delighted the nuns and children alike: silver-plated candlesticks and crucifix for the altar, material for vestments, clothing, an assortment of writing paper for letters and classroom use and of colored paper for the manufacture of the highly prized flowers, books, seeds, and last and largest, the piano—to delight (and, at times, nearly to madden) all who dwelt in the convent. On the following day another cart unloaded several cases of provisions sent from New Orleans by the charitable Ursulines.

These were busy days for Mother Duchesne, but not so busy as to prevent her from writing letters to France when an opportunity for sending them presented itself. On March 19, Bishop Du Bourg ordained two young Italian priests, and each expressed the desire to say his first Mass at the Convent of the Sacred Heart. That very afternoon Father Angelo Inglesi was welcomed cordially. This was the man styled by the bishop "my most beloved son . . . whom Divine Providence has placed at my side . . . a new Timothy," than whom he thought "no one to be more acceptable" as his successor. As the young Roman stood at the altar, no one suspected the truth about him; and when he announced his immediate departure for Europe as the Bishop's personal representative, Mother Duchesne hastened to write letters to France. That

Inglesi delivered them is something in his favor. With joy and gratitude Philippine wrote to Mother Barat to tell of the arrival of the gifts, but she had to admit they had cost 400 francs for shipment up the river, besides 900 francs in customs duty. "The thousand franc note you sent paid the duty," she added, "but the remaining money had been spent for us, so we are obligated to the father of one of our children for the freight charges. He is willing to wait for his money."

Meanwhile there had been much activity around the convent, for a real frontier house-raising was under way. Logs for the parish schoolhouse had been cut and trimmed under Father Dunand's direction, and on March 21 twenty-six men of the vicinity assembled to erect the building in a day and to enjoy a hearty dinner, prepared by the grateful nuns and served more bountifully by the addition of raisins, preserves, and other delicacies drawn from the provisions sent by the Ursulines. The feast of the Annunciation brought the second young Italian priest to Florissant to say his first Mass. Father Philip Borgna, C.M., proved to be a steadfast friend of the order and a zealous helper both in Missouri and in Louisiana.

In St. Louis and the settlements nearby there was excitement that twenty-fifth of March when a handbill went into circulation—a kind of frontier "EXTRA"—announcing the "happy intelligence" that the Missouri State bill had passed the Congress in Washington "without restrictions"; this meant that Missouri was now numbered among the nation's slave states. The news had been brought by a traveler who carried in his satchel a copy of the *National Intelligencer* of March 4. So the paper was three weeks old when it reached St. Louis, but its contents were news and called forth demonstrations in town and country. Mother Duchesne did not allude to it in her letters for several weeks, for she was preoccupied with matters more directly connected with the church and convent at Florissant.

Holy Week was at hand with its liturgical ceremonies and devotional exercises. Through the night of Holy Thursday, Philippine knelt in adoration at the repository. There was deep peace in her soul, but intense pleading in her prayer. On Good Friday *Tenebrae*, and the *Tre Ore*, and the solemn Way of the Cross, and on Holy Saturday the long morning liturgy—all were carried out in simple solemnity. One reads the record with astonishment. A retreat during Easter week prepared a group of children for Confirmation on April 6. The bishop seemed preoccupied. He spent much time in conference with Father De La Croix. The Father Prior was invited at times to join them, and he was sad at heart as he confided to Mother Duchesne the subject under discussion.

On April 22 this was made public when Father De La Croix was named pastor of St. Ferdinand. Father Dunand, who had taken up his residence there in 1814 and had been the lone missionary in the entire area until the coming of Du Bourg, was now obliged to move from the rectory in which he had been living and build a little house for himself in the neighborhood. The situation that developed was very unpleasant. The trustees of the parish were devoted to the Father Prior and resented the bishop's action as unfair to him. The parishioners sided with their old friend and the choir, "both men and women," refused to sing in the church when the new pastor made his solemn entrance.

Mother Duchesne was now caught between the upper and the nether millstones. Gratitude to Father Dunand turned her sympathy to him, for he had certainly proved himself a generous and devoted friend. She still owed him at least one thousand francs, and now he was in poverty, without parish or fixed missions, after years of unselfish zeal for the salvation of Catholics on the Missouri frontier. On the other hand, loyalty to authority was a sacred duty. The bishop was acting within his rights with regard to the pastorate of St. Ferdinand, though his action seemed untimely and inconsiderate. Mother Duchesne dreaded the consequences to all concerned and seems to have realized how far-reaching these consequences would be. In the minds of the parishioners who loved Father Dunand and the Catholics of St. Louis who already disliked Monseigneur Du Bourg, the Religious of the Sacred Heart were linked inseparably with the bishop, whose unpopularity increased alarmingly through the coming years.

As Mother Duchesne was under the impression that the Trappist was leaving soon for France, she wrote letters early in May which she expected him to carry back to the homeland. Her note to St. Madeleine Sophie was unusually brief, but a postscript practically doubled its length:

> We have received many invaluable services from Reverend Marie-Joseph Dunand, religious of La Trappe. He is the one who directed the building of our convent; he urged forward the work; he sweated for it and advanced money to help us. We still owe him one thousand francs, which he paid out to purchase many useful things we needed. We promised payment in France to his

Father Abbot de Lestrange or to himself, if he decided to return there. I beg you to draw on the money still owed us by the convent at Niort. . . . This is a sacred debt.

P.S. I thought this letter would be enclosed in Reverend Father Dunand's but he sent it back to me along with his own, for me to send myself. I add just a few lines to repeat my affectionate and respectful sentiments and to beg you to send us two more nuns who are essential here, one to be superior, the other to take charge of the kitchen. . . . If the dear Lord should inspire you and enable you to send a larger group of nuns, it would fulfill all our hopes and be so very helpful.

To Father Barat, Philippine expressed more fully her anxieties and her sentiments in regard to Father Dunand, to whom she and her community were so deeply indebted:

Sometime during this year you may see a priest from this section of the country. He is a religious of La Trappe, and it is chiefly on his account that I am writing this letter, for we owe him a thousand francs, for which he will accept payment in France. This is a great help to us as we are always short of money here. If by any chance you have a thousand francs to spend on us, I beg you to hold it in order to pay this sacred debt, in case there is not enough left in our fund to meet the payment. I hardly dare hope there will be any money left, so it might happen that this good priest would not be paid without your aid. All that comes to us through Mr. Du Bourg in New Orleans is used to pay Monseigneur what we owe him, and he still expects the 15,000 francs he asked our Mother General for. I have harbored no such an illusion.

The Father to whom we owe this money is the one who directed the building of our house. It was really watered by his sweat and it witnessed his care of us. We would not be living in it now if he had not procured a loan which only he could obtain. How much opposition there is to active zeal! After laboring fifteen years on this mission and a great part of that time alone, he must give way before the accusations and complaints that are made against him and see his place in this parish given to someone else, the pretext being his desire to return to his convent. We went through a difficult time on his account. We owe so much to this Father, and yet another type of spiritual director was more suitable to us. Each side was trying to gain our support, and we could not take sides either against gratitude or against the welfare of our house. We could only let those in authority act and on our side commend the whole affair to God. It would have been very despicable of us to say a word that might influence the departure of a priest who had made every sacrifice to have us in his parish.

We now have 20 boarding pupils, the majority of them docile. We are trying to get our property enclosed, but have not succeeded yet, for in this part of the country the fences are made like ladders. We are not rich enough to afford a board fence such as the Ursulines in New Orleans have. As for stone, there is none.

Repeat to our Mother our plea for religious. Three American postulants have just left, having neither vocation nor aptitudes. Vocations will be rare out here. For the welfare of us all we should have a good superior and a good cook. Among the nuns here no one has both the health and the ability for the latter employment. I think Monseigneur's good judgment will make him approve of a change of superior. There is no one in the community who is not suffering. I will never gain the confidence of either the community or outsiders, but everyone trusts my two companions, and they use this confidence to do good. . . . I am the least useful in the community, but I am happy to share the hard work. I wish I were put in just that kind of employment; then I would be content. It is heart-breaking, after such ardent desires, to see our success hindered or slowed up and to realize that I am the obstacle. Happy, too, would I be if, having no support from anyone on earth near me, I were deprived even of those consolations that really are too sweet for a life that is dying in Jesus Christ. That is what I desire, though I am not preparing myself for it by my fervor. . . .

May brought a trio of new pupils, Maria and Adeline Boilvin and Elisa Bosseron, all of whom would in later years enter religious life. Maria would be obliged to withdraw on account of poor health. Elisa would die at an early age, and Adeline would become an outstanding religious of the Sacred Heart, one of those who came to know most intimately the mind and heart of Philippine Duchesne. Another pupil, Emilie St. Cyr, the aunt of the Boilvin girls and only a little older than they, had been at the Sacred Heart since the first year at St. Charles. From her pen comes a word picture that shows Mother Duchesne among the children as a religious educator:

In my childhood I always looked on Mother Duchesne as a perfect model of all virtues. It was my good fortune to have our holy Mother Duchesne as class mistress during more than two years. Never once did I see her lacking in poise and self-control; never did I notice in her the least movement of impatience in dealing with the group of children who were so difficult to handle. She showed the same gentle kindliness toward all. More than once I called the attention of my schoolmates to the heavenly radiance that shone on her countenance. One might have mistaken it for sunshine, but the light was softer than that. Then we would say, "Mother Duchesne has just come from the chapel. She has had an ecstasy," and we were sure she had had a vision of our Blessed Lord. We certainly had a saint for a teacher. Even the most troublesome girls venerated her. She never brought the class period to a close without some little word about God, but she never talked at length or let us lose a moment of time. During my religious life I have always considered Mother Duchesne as a perfect religious, a superior quite impartial and so mortified there is no one with whom I could compare her. She was completely dead to nature and self and faithful to the very least points of the Rule.

An outstanding event occurred during this period when Mother Duchesne welcomed Mary Ann Layton, the first American postulant to persevere in religious life at the Sacred Heart. She was a nineteen-year-old girl from Perry County, Missouri, whose land-rich father, Bernard Layton, had donated more than fifty acres on which the county seat, Perryville, was laid out. In the southeastern part of the county, along the Brazeau Bottom and the Saline and St. Cosme streams, lay the open prairie called "The Barrens," where descendants of Maryland-Kentucky families had settled—Mannings, Moores, Haydens, Fenwicks, Laytons. They were a Catholic group who treasured their religious heritage and handed on to their children the knowledge, love, and reverence with which their own lives were enriched and their worship guided.

Mary Layton had been born in Kentucky on July 2, 1802. Her mother died when she was a little girl, and Mary became the idol of her devoted father and brothers. The child was spoiled and not well educated. Yet she had more than book learning or domestic training, and from her earliest years her great desire was to love and serve God by belonging to him alone. Her father had placed her in a special manner under the protection of the Blessed Virgin, and Mary entrusted to her spiritual Mother, under the title of "Mary Immaculate," her desire to belong to God. It was Father Henri Pratte who first told her of the arrival of the Religious of the Sacred Heart in Missouri, and the Lazarists at St. Mary's Seminary who guided her to Florissant. She came from the Barrens with Father Rosati, who was joined on the way by Fathers Borgna and Deys. From these visitors Mother Duchesne gathered the information she retailed to Mother Barat on August 29, the third birthday she celebrated in America:

I have picked up some interesting information that may call forth some prayers in return. An event that gave me the greatest amount of pleasure recently was the deputation that reached St. Louis from the Osage Indians, a savage tribe. The chief came to ask Bishop Du Bourg to pay a visit to his people. The bishop is going there next month with some Missouri River traders who have promised to help him in every way so that he may be treated with respect among these peoples, something like the way the Portuguese merchants helped St. Francis Xavier. . . .

To her beloved Cousin Josephine she sent a letter on that fifty-first birthday:

It is a long time since I wrote to you, but I know you often read the letters I write to other members of the family, so you always have the most recent news from me. That satisfies your loving heart that is so faithful to your old friend. Sometimes people say old hearts grow hard or lose their tender sentiments. But by experience I can declare that quite the contrary is true. The names of Josephine, Augustin, and Camille will always call forth the purest, tenderest sentiments of friendship and gratitude from my heart. Now that the dear ones whose faces these names recall are no longer the direct instruments of Divine Providence in my regard, God uses other means to show me his loving kindness. . . .

This year Missouri has become one of the federated states of the Republic. St. Louis is to be the capital for six years. The father of our very first pupils [General Pratte] is the most influential man in the town and is very devoted to us. At present the laws of the state are being drawn up. The most disputed point and the one that has caused the greatest conflict concerns the admission of slavery. It seems that all those who now own slaves will be allowed to keep them and that the children of their slaves will belong to them, but there can be no more African slave trade. We do not want slaves and we have no money to buy them, yet we scarcely know how to get along without them, especially as we are cloistered and do not go about. No one wants to hire out as a domestic servant; all want to be on the same social level. Up to now we have given a home to some young girls who are orphans and who have been placed with us legally until they are twenty years old. . . . Believe in my undying affection.

The second scholastic year had scarcely begun when Mother Duchesne fell dangerously ill. Bishop Du Bourg came several times to see her, bringing Dr. Todsen with him from St. Louis, but Philippine preferred the village doctor, who handled the case skilfully and *gratis*. For two months she was confined to her room, for she had been obliged to accept a room during her illness, at least, though she clung to the little cubbyhole under the stairway that led to the second story. In her eyes that *petit trou* had several advantages—poverty, inconvenience, discomfort, but best of all, nearness to the chapel. She chafed under the regime of convalescence, especially since it rendered her incapable of helping care for Mother Octavie when she met with an accident. On October 30 she gave Mother Barat an account of what had been happening at Florissant during the autumn and revealed the working of grace in her own soul:

> Never have I been in greater need of a letter from you and never have I had to wait so long for one. At last here is the packet entrusted to M. de Menou, and we are consoled by your letters and those of dear Father Varin and our Sisters, and also by the hope that some religious are coming to join us. My preceding letters, which must have caused you anxiety about the health of Mother Octavie and Eugenie, made you realize our need of recruits and this one will give you still further proofs of it. After these generous souls had been delivered from their bleedings and blisterings, I too had an illness that has lasted two months, including the convalescence. I received Holy Viaticum and was never so near to meeting my God. After having burned with desire to be with him, at the moment when I could hope for it I felt only the emptiness of my life, the severity of God's judgments, and the hardness of my own heart.
>
> The disease was erysipelas. It covered my whole body and was accompanied by a fever that became malignant after the sores on my body disappeared. As I was delirious, Monseigneur brought his own doctor to treat me. He put me through three blisterings and gave me two mustard plasters. After that treatment I was no longer delirious, nor have I taken any more mercury, a drug widely used in American medicine. I felt many ill effects from it—sore mouth, salivation, continual weakness in my limbs, and my head so unbalanced that for a long time I labored under the illusion that I was two people; if one of them died, I said, there was always the other one left, and I tried to find her. Before I stop writing about myself, I want to show you once more how wonderful Divine Providence really is. A young American doctor treated me with the tenderness of a son for his mother, saying he saw in me a resemblance to his own mother. One morning he came as many as four times, and he charged nothing at all.
>
> Scarcely had I began to regain some strength when Mother Octavie, shod in her beautiful new black velvet shoes that had just come from France and had very slick soles, slipped and fell and broke a bone in her leg; now she will be in bed thirty or forty days. This is

just the seventh day, and yesterday she was delirious with fever. She is better today, but she is already tired of lying in bed.

This whole diocese, and we in particular, have suffered a great loss in the death of Father De Andreis, provincial of the Lazarists and first vicar-general. He was a man of great holiness, remarkable gifts for the ministry, and prodigious learning. . . . Father Richard, our first chaplain, is replacing him as a saint and as vicar-general. Father Rosati is now superior of the Lazarists. He sent us a postulant and has suggested another, but how very difficult it is to explain religious life to people who speak a different language and know nothing at all about it and are accustomed to entirely different ways in food and clothing! . . .

I know you will make an effort to help your poor mission that stretches out its arms, but cannot reach across the distance to you. As for me, do with me just as you wish. All desire but that of doing God's holy will is extinguished in me, and my illness has rooted me still deeper in indifference. Monseigneur has ordered me to take care of myself and I am doing so quite simply. Today I am writing my first letter. I have eaten four meals and I remained in bed until seven o'clock this morning.

Mary Layton had adjusted herself to convent life with surprising courage and proved so fervent in her quiet, friendly way that Mother Audé, to whom her training had been entrusted, was soon suggesting that she be clothed in the holy habit. Bishop Du Bourg gave his approval, but he was not present at this first reception of the religious habit by an American girl in the trans-Mississippi West. He was at the convent on November 18 to bid the nuns good-bye before leaving for New Orleans, where it was hoped he would be respectfully received. On November 22, Sister Mary Layton was clothed in the religious habit and began her long and fervent career of more than half a century in the Society of the Sacred Heart.

On February 19, 1821, Father De La Croix laid the cornerstone of the new church that was to stand beside the Florissant convent. The ceremony was very simple, but the joy it gave was very great, for a fervent hope had begun to be fulfilled—a church dedicated to the Sacred Heart of Jesus had begun to rise on the American frontier and its cornerstone had been presented by Philippine Duchesne herself. In deference to her wishes, moreover, her beloved St. Francis Regis had also been chosen as a secondary patron of the church—strikingly prophetic choice, and a special shrine in his honor was to be arranged in the convent chapel. On the eve of the ceremony her mind was filled with joyous hopes and anxious fears as she wrote to Mother Barat:

I have been deprived of news from you for a long time, as the ice on the Mississippi detained the steamboats downstream during the winter. Owing to a thaw, however, a boat has arrived, bringing us several packets of letters, some thirteen months old, the most recent written last August. More than a month ago I had one from our dear protector, Father Barat, written in September and sent by way of New York. He enclosed the triplicate of the note for $571, which I hastened to turn over to the man to whom we owed 10,000 francs. People say he had his eye on our house, holding the mortgage as he does and knowing the extreme difficulty with which people like ourselves get any money. I prefer to reject such an idea as dishonorable to him and contrary to the goodness of God, whose Providence toward us had been manifested in a thousand ways.

Tomorrow we shall have the laying of the cornerstone of the new church which the bishop is having erected contiguous to our convent. It will be named in honor of the Sacred Heart and will bear on the facade this inscription in English: *My Heart will abide here.* . . . The schoolhouse for day pupils had been completed at our expense and paid for; but when all was ready, not a child appeared. The roads were too bad and the weather too cold. We shall open it in the spring, and by that time I hope to have two novices prepared to teach the American children. . . .

I was delighted with the letter from the Irish novice. Her command of English will make her very useful here, but she should be given a true picture of our position—inconvenience in everything, especially our lodging, having no place even to put a sewing basket or writing pad, not a table for one's own use, food that is often disgusting, and very little variety in it, severe cold, prostrating heat, and practically no spring weather. *God alone and the desire of his glory*: nothing else matters.

After a forty days' prayer for this intention, three vocations were decided in the boarding school—young girls of sixteen to eighteen years—two Americans and a French Creole. The last named [Émilie St. Cyr] has her parent's consent. . . . Another [Eulalie Hamilton] has not obtained this yet. The third [Mary Ann Summers] is an orphan whose guardian does not object. She is sixteen years old, manages the kitchen with astonishing ease, is skilful along all lines, and might do well at studies, were it not better for her spiritual formation to keep her a little in obscurity. . . . She speaks and writes both languages well and reads so intelligently as to need no correction whatsoever. . . .

Another letter, written that same day to Josephine de Savoye-Rollin, reveals the thoughts of her heart and the bond of affection between these middle-aged friends:

> It is a very long time since I received a letter from you, but I know how much you have been concerned about me, and Mother Barat told me that you contributed 500 francs to a sum of money she was sending me. In this I recognize your loving heart and your zeal for good works. For even if ours is so insignificant and if we are unprofitable servants, still God, who sees the intention, will return you a hundredfold. And he wills me to add once more an expression of my gratitude for so much kindness and generosity on your part. . . .
>
> We are the grain of wheat dying in the earth; can we repine at such a destiny? But we are full of confidence and wholly animated with courage to persevere, hoping that someday our work will bear fruit. It matters little whether we taste of it in this life, provided only that we serve God's cause. He let it happen that when we arrived in St. Louis money was plentiful and the price of land and houses was excessively high. It seemed better for us to build here at Florissant. That was not my opinion, but I had to follow the opinion of others and borrow money to complete the building. And now the failure of the banks has caused the disappearance of the paper money which was practically the only currency here. We could buy lands and a house in St. Louis for nothing today, yet we must pay back the loan at a time when the money is worth ten times as much as when we borrowed it. These are the unexpected occurrences against which human prudence can offer no protection. But Divine Providence is with us, and we can count so trustfully on God, we shall stand firm at our post. So sincerely are we persuaded that God himself wants us here, not one of us regrets her position. . . .

The year 1821 was to be crowded with joys and sorrows, hopes and anxieties. March opened auspiciously with letters from France —always a great event for the community, and one from Bishop Du Bourg describing "the holy enthusiasm with which he had been received in Louisiana," and giving permission for the reception of the holy habit by the postulants. On March 7 Philippine sent one of her long, chatty letters to Father Barat. She wrote as she would have talked, with delightful vivacity, with sly humor in the midst of serious matters, with knowledge of the world around her and a spontaneous uplift of mind and heart that revealed the supernatural atmosphere of her life:

It was a great pleasure to learn from your most recent letter that you are still in Bordeaux and so can act as father to our little colony. No one except our reverend Mother has given us as much help or shown as much sympathy and kindness as you have. I am often so embarrassed by all the trouble expended on us, by all we have cost the Society, that I might regret our persistent efforts to come here if I were not thoroughly convinced that it is the will of God for us to be here. I quiet my anxieties also by the thought that the Sacred Heart, for whom alone we intended to work, helps us in every way and is our greatest reward. . . .

Shall I lament or rejoice over the departure of the Jesuit Fathers from Russia? If some of those from Siberia are looking for a mission field with the same type of work and the same climate during a good part of the year, they might come to our section of the globe. It takes souls of that quality to persevere out here; and if they went to a mission among the savages, they could even hope for martyrdom, either at the hands of the Indians themselves or with still more certainty at the hands of the lawless men who trade with them. . . .

I wrote to our Mother last month by way of New York. She gave me news, and so did you, of the agony my dear Aloysia is enduring. But when one is out here on the other side of the ocean, one can only hope to see one's loved ones again in heaven. It is there I picture them all, though I myself become more and more earthbound. I am by nature most fitted to be a servant. Something quite different is needed in one who guides souls. But God does his own work. My two young religious sisters advance steadily toward perfection and relish all the poverty and abjection from which they suffer so much, for ours is not a life of convenience. That should be the disposition of all who come to join us. They must accept suffering and have *God alone* as their support. . . . Our Mothers and Sisters here are fairly well and I am more vigorous than ever, but I have few teeth left. . . .

While Mother Duchesne was writing in such deprecating terms of herself, it is well to note what others had to say about her in their letters to France. In April of this year, 1821, Mother Berthold told St. Madeleine Sophie:

Charity binds us closer and closer to our Mother Superior. I obey her, but my love for her is so great, it may deprive me of the merit of obedience, for it sometimes makes my motive too natural. We are so happy under her care. Her three years are up, but, Reverend Mother, do not listen to her request to be relieved of office. What would we do without her? There are seven of us in her little family now. We love each other very much and our hearts are all one with hers. . . . Furthermore, she knows the country and the character of the people. Anyone else would be an apprentice, as it were, at all this.

The very next day Sister Catherine Lamarre was writing to Mother Prevost at Amiens: "Last fall we came very near losing our dear Mother Duchesne, but our Divine Master knows how necessary she is to us and so he restored her to health. What a terrible loss it would be if she were taken away! May the Sacred Heart be blessed a thousand times for having saved her for us."

In the reception ceremony on March 19, Emilie St. Cyr, just fifteen years old, received the habit of the choir religious, and Mary Ann Summers, aged sixteen, became a coadjutrix novice. To honor St. Joseph, Emilie took the name of Josephine, a practice Mother Duchesne had carried over from Visitation days and continued for a decade on the frontier. There was another pupil of the boarding school who watched this ceremony with deep soul-stirring. Eulalie Hamilton had heard the call of Christ and her generous heart had given a full, glad response, but as yet her mother had made no reply to the three letters she had written on the subject. The strain of waiting was beginning to tell on Eulalie, so Mother Duchesne took up her quill to request Father Rosati's mediation with the Hamiltons.

Spring had come to Florissant Valley when a heavy cart made its jolting way out from the Market Street landing in St. Louis to the convent, laden with substantial gifts from Philippine's faithful friends in New Orleans, the Ursulines. "Barrels of sugar, rice, codfish, raisins, and preserves," she noted with astonished gratitude. There were still four weeks of Lent ahead, so the codfish was welcome, though it would appear more often at community meals than on the pupils' menu. An early April entry in her *Journal* reveals once more how precious was every item of news she received from France. Each detail was used by her to strengthen the bond between the parent stock and the frail cion she had planted on the American frontier. Lovingly she summarized the news and wrote the names of the Mothers she had known in what may have seemed now a rather remote past, though she had left them just three years before:

April 3. We learned that the General Council of the Society has come to a close. Its most important decision was the transfer of the Convent of the Sacred Heart from Due des Postes to the Hotel Biron, Rue de Varennes, in the Faubourg of St. Germain, Paris. Mother de Charbonnel is the First Assistant General, Mother Bigeu, Second, and Mistress of Novices. The other Mothers of the Council are Mothers Grosier, de Gramont, Desmarquest, Geoffroy, Prevost, Deshayes.

There had been news of a more personal nature in letters from Grenoble. While Aloysia Jouve was nearing the end of her short and holy career, her sister Amelie and her cousin, Caroline Lebrument, became postulants at Ste. Marie. At the Visitation in Romans her old aunt, Sister Françoise-Melanie, had died, and Sister Claire Euphrosine, who was not so old, had been elected superior, while her own loved sister Melanie had been given the office of directress of the school. Of these dear relatives Philippine often spoke admiringly, praising their virtue and their work in contrast to her own.

Lent was always a time of intense fervor for Philippine. This year she encouraged her community to special efforts during the week preceding the feast of the Compassion of the Blessed Virgin for the intention of obtaining the consent of Mrs. George Hamilton for the entrance of not just one, but two, of her daughters into the novitiate. The affirmative answer came on the very day of the feast, and Philippine's soul was filled with joy and gratitude. That day she also learned with a sense of relief that John Mullanphy was leaving soon for France. This meant he would not dun her for at least some months, and it offered an opportunity to send letters safely and post-free, so she gave herself the pleasure of writing to her sisters and nieces, to Mother Thérèse Maillucheau and Mother Barat. These letters, remarkably varied in content, show us Philippine in turn as a loving sister, a devoted aunt, and intimate friend, and a true religious, bearing the responsibility that weighed so heavily on her and giving a faithful account of persons and things. The letter to Mother Barat is crowded with details, only a few of which are quoted here:

In three years I have had only one letter from Father Perreau and one from Father Varin. Tell them that although this silence pains me, it reminds me of the silence of the soul that is closely united to the Heart of Jesus. In this intimate converse no word is spoken—and it is there I remember them and express my gratitude to them. . . . Father Barat made no mention in his letter of nuns coming to join us. This grieves me, for we must have some nuns. You know the doctor who examined Mother Octavie said she has a bad heart condition that might carry her off suddenly. . . . Mother Eugenie grows more and more capable of administration. She has keenness of judgment and prudence that saves her from rashness in action. She has firmness and zeal, is pleasing in appearance and conversation, and she knows enough English now to direct American subjects and give them religious instruction. . . . Marguerite is always very good, though weak in health. Catherine has many employments and teaches a small group of day pupils. . . .

If Mr. Mullanphy brings you my letter in person, please welcome him in all simplicity, but keep the contents of my letter to yourself. You would never believe he is the richest man in this section of the country. He could buy up all St. Louis, and he is one of the shrewdest of bargainers. He is going to France to fetch his daughters and to see his son, who is in Paris. He is the man who loaned us the 10,000 francs at ten percent, and he has in hand your remittance of 3000 francs which was somewhat reduced in the exchange.

Yesterday I had a most agreeable piece of news: the best of our children, an American, has obtained her mother's consent to her taking the veil. She is already trained well enough to teach a class. Her older sister vacillates, but she has gifts that fit her remarkably for the Society. Father Rosati, superior of the Lazarists, will continue to urge her to follow her vocation.

The vacillation of Mathilde Hamilton called for action on the part of Father Dunand as well as Father Rosati. She was his godchild. He was sure of her vocation. He would fetch her himself from the home and family she loved so tenderly. Setting out for Fredonia in his *caleche* that was a familiar sight on the rough roads of Missouri, he returned in triumph ten days later with Mathilde beside him in the old buggy, just in time for the First Friday of May and the reception ceremony of Eulalie Hamilton, who took the devotional name of Regis. Father Dunand had been correct in his judgment of Mathilde Hamilton. Though she passed through stormy days as a novice, she became an excellent religious. The zealous Trappist had the satisfaction of seeing her clothed in the religious habit in June. Soon after this he left Florissant Valley to return to France and the silence of La Trappe, but the heart of Philippine Duchesne was not silent in his regard and her gratitude expressed itself in prayer and loyalty.

2. 1821—1823

BISHOP DU BOURG WAS IN ST. LOUIS in June and called at the Florissant convent on the seventh of the month. He came on serious business which Mother Duchesne summarized in her *Journal* and would repeat in many a letter before the year was out:

> He proposed to us a foundation at Opelousas in Louisiana, where Mrs. Smith, a rich widow, offers us a house, lands, furniture, and money for traveling expenses. We have accepted, and Monseigneur, who had already arranged for his niece to keep at her home the two religious who are said to be coming from France, thinks one of us should go down to Opelousas to await their arrival, as they will go directly there on reaching America.

In falling in so readily with the bishop's suggestions and advice, Mother Duchesne was acting within her delegated powers. Before writing of the matter to France, she discussed it many times with Mothers Berthold and Audé and prayed earnestly for light to know the will of God and the line of conduct that would bring the greatest glory to the Sacred Heart. Her counselors were in favor of accepting the offer, though they had no idea where Opelousas really was, and Mother Audé was particularly eager to share in the labors of the enterprise. The bishop came again to celebrate the feast of St. Francis Regis, and give the veil and holy habit to Mathilde Hamilton, who took the name of Xavier.

During the day the projected foundation was discussed again, and the religious were impressed more than ever by the many advantages stressed by the bishop. Remoteness and isolation, difficulties of transportation and communication, insecurity as to a resident chaplain, sparsity of population in the vicinity, all were passed over in silence. The prospect of recruits coming soon from France and the fact that in their own convent at Florissant there were now five excellent novices in training and several postulants asking admission seemed to point up the advisability of sending a small group of nuns to Louisiana in the near future. But the plans were as yet only tentative, and Mother Duchesne was busy with her four French-speaking novices, and happy to see that Sister Layton was beginning to understand when she spoke to her in French.

Meanwhile letters had come from France informing her of the death of her beloved Aloysia, along with a short sketch of her life and religious virtues. The knowledge that this favorite niece had fulfilled the Mother Foundress's dream of a perfect religious of the Society stirred in her new depths of joy and gratitude to the Sacred Heart. On June 30, Philippine put before the Superior General the proposal for the Louisiana foundation in a letter that seems to have been written with more care and deliberation than were usual with her. The projected establishment had been described to her in so rosy a light that she had set her heart on it and now endeavored to picture it to Mother Barat as she herself envisioned it. But there were other matters closer to her heart, and she began with them:

> The loss of Aloysia does not pain me except in so far as it makes me reflect on myself: that life so short, so well filled, makes me realize the uselessness of my own life and my abuse of so many graces, which leaves me still so imperfect and immortified. The more I think about them, the more they astonish me and make me tremble. Among them I prize most of all that of belonging to our beloved Society, and I brought Aloysia to it, also. May her merits repair my faults and obtain for me from God an opportunity to repair the past.
>
> The news of the choice made for us of three religious to help us overwhelmed us with joy. I conclude that Mother Lucille Mathevon is in charge of the group while traveling. A letter from Bishop Du Bourg tells us Father Dusaussoy [Mother Barat's nephew] is in New Orleans. Father Anduze praised him so highly that the bishop decided to keep him there as that city is in such need of priests. Monseigneur also has plans for our nuns which I am going to outline to you.
>
> Mrs. Charles Smith, a rich widow who lives sixty leagues from New Orleans in a place called Grand Coteau, has established a parish there and built a church; now she wishes to procure an educational institution for that section of Louisiana. She has given Monseigneur 400 arpents of land, partly woods, partly farmland where corn and cotton are raised. A house is being built there, larger than the one we have here. This lady offers to pay the expenses of several religious for a year, to give them a Negro family as servants, to furnish the house and pay all the expenses of the voyage from Paris. Monsiegneur dwelt at length on the advantages of such a foundation, which would procure for Lower Louisiana the good we have tried to do up here. The nuns would not be exposed to such cold winters nor to the epidemics that occur in New Orleans and oblige parents to withdraw their children from

school every summer or keep them at home. That section of Louisiana is rich and would furnish more pupils than this area does.

Monseigneur proposed that I should go down to talk things over with Mrs. Smith, but considering first the expense of a long trip, and second that Mothers Octavie and Eugenie could not go together and leave me without an interpreter, I thought that Mother Eugenie could do the most good because of her appearance, her virtue, her genial manner, and the ease with which she now speaks both English and French. I suggested to the bishop that she should take charge of the foundation, but be ready to return here if you should so order. . . .

We all agree on the need of a second foundation, first, because a house in Lower Louisiana is necessary to support the one in Upper Louisiana; second, because the milder climate agrees with some temperaments; third, because when the expenses of the trip are repaid, we in turn could pay off our most unpleasant debt. We shall never be able to do it without some outside help, as we still owe 13,000 francs. Fourth, because we now have five good novices, so there would be a sufficient number of us left here and we could accept the postulants who are asking to enter. It is not possible to do this if we receive the nuns from France, as several already sleep in the attic. That place is simply unbearable in winter, so every night they had to make up their beds in a classroom or in the refectory.

With two establishments we would not get involved in more debt, but rather liquidate the present obligations. Then too, we should be able to double the number of new religious, of pupils, and of poor children, and to spread devotion to the Sacred Heart of Jesus and set up new altars in his honor. These are very pressing motives. I realize that it is a very serious matter to change the destination of the religious you are sending us, but I believe this falls in with your intentions. So I have written to our nuns who are coming to follow the instructions left for them by Monseigneur. I have promised to send them Mother Eugenie, hoping she will send Mother Lucille to us. She will be very useful here because of her age, should anything happen to me. . . . Mother Eugenie will go courageously to her new destination when word comes that our nuns have arrived. God has fitted her for authority. . . .

July was a hot, busy time. There was work for all in the community, especially Mother Duchesne, whose active hours were devoted partly to the children and partly to the novices. They were her hope for the future, and from the very beginning she fostered strong virtues among them, that they might become humble, brave, self-sacrificing religious. She taught them to probe deep into the heart of the spiritual life, to free themselves from the subterfuges of self-love that blinds the soul to truth, to enter into the dispositions and sentiments of the Sacred Heart, and to find therein the model and motive for their entire religious life. Constraint had no place in her method, but self-renunciation was motivated so generously by love for the Sacred Heart that she had often to restrain the striving of these American girls who had determined to achieve independence by giving their wills to Christ and their lives to obedience.

She watched them prayerfully as they knelt at adoration, endeavoring "by the purity of their homage, the fervor of their love, and the fulness of their oblation to make reparation to him for the outrages he everywhere receives." She listened with restrained happiness as they pleaded to remain a while with her at night before the tabernacle. She was glad when she saw them follow Mother Octavie's humble reparation of the slightest faults, or Mother Eugenie's generous devotedness, when they were eager in their rivalry to help Sister Marguerite in the pantry or the parish school, and Sister Catherine in the linen room or the laundry. But there were times when she was overwhelmed by a sense of powerlessness in the face of the spiritual difficulties encountered by scrupulous little Emilie St. Cyr and passionate Mathilde Hamilton, whose natural temperament exposed her to temptations Philippine herself could scarcely understand. But the Holy Spirit was directing her work with these souls, and Divine Providence gave her prudent friends and advisers in Father De La Croix and the Vincentian priests on whom she relied for help.

The fairly even tenor of life at Florissant was interrupted on July 30 when Bishop DuBourg arrived, not to celebrate the feast of St. Ignatius, but to insist that Mother Audé should go down to Louisiana before the arrival of the religious who were expected from France. It was an unwise step and Philippine opposed it, but there was no resisting the bishop. When he announced, as he mounted his horse next day, that a steamboat was leaving St. Louis for New Orleans the following Sunday and he would reserve places on it for two religious, the reality of the venture was determined. There were four days in which to prepare for the departure. All that could be spared, and much that could not, was packed into boxes, satchels, and bags, and Mother Duchesne supplied one hundred dollars for the steamboat fare and the incidentals of the trip. Mother Audé and Sister Mary Layton left the convent

early on the morning of August 5 and three hours later boarded the
Rapide at the Market Street landing.

Within a week of their departure Mother Duchesne began to
be troubled by anxious fears in their regard. These were aroused
by news communicated to her by the bishop. On the feast of the
Assumption she opened her heart to Mother Barat on the subject,
then added details about the boarding school at Florissant, which
began its yearly vacation of two weeks that very day:

> From several different letters we understood that our dear Sisters
> had set out last March to join us. But a letter to Monseigneur from
> Bordeaux, dated May 1, does not mention any embarkation for this
> mission. This news causes us much anxiety and Monseigneur does
> not know what to think of it. He was all the more eager for their
> arrival as he was planning a second foundation at Opelousas, as I
> explained in detail in my letter of June 23. I fear that new house,
> for which I gave my approval, may cause you anxiety, but I shall
> repeat here the urgent reasons that influenced my decision.

After doing so at some length she continued:

> Mother Eugenie felt strongly attracted to this work, and I thought
> she was better fitted for it than I am, for she understands English
> and can express herself in that language. She is quite able to direct
> both the community and the external works; she is very skilful
> and can meet any situation that may arise in a house. Her health
> has been declining noticeably and she needs a warmer climate be-
> cause of her weak lungs. True, we have prostrating heat here in
> Missouri, but the weather changes suddenly to severe cold and it
> is difficult to take the necessary precautions. Last year we feared
> we might lose her, and her soul was more affected than her body.
> Her recovery was only temporary. A serious and persistent eye
> trouble developed, along with a cough and fever. All this made me
> fear a complete breakdown. God seemed to manifest his will in
> disposing her to undertake the direction of a house so willingly,
> though her humility must suffer under the burden. . . .
> No one has lost more than I by this departure. Mother Eugenie
> was my right arm. Monseigneur thinks very highly of her. He
> would have given her his whole house, had he been able to do so.
> He wrote to both the pastor of the place and the benefactress of
> the new house letters that were very complimentary to the Society
> and to Mother Eugenie. He told them he did not want them to
> meddle in any way in the direction and administration of the con-
> vent and said that such was our custom and that it was better that
> way. . . .
> We have at present 22 boarding pupils. I learned today of the

failure of the Bank of Missouri, the only bank whose notes were considered acceptable. I do not know how this will affect the school. The four novices we have here are very good, especially the Americans, and among them Sister Regis is an angel of candor, sweetness, and devotedness. She is the one best fitted to take Mother Eugenie's place in the work of the school and in the pantry, but like Mother Eugenie she eats too little and takes no care of herself. The novices are studying Rodriguez, the Catechism of Perseverance, and Sacred History. . . . When I first came to America I thought I had no further missionary ambition, but now I am devoured with interest in Peru. These desires, however, are more tranquil than those that made me importune you so impatiently in France. . . .

Classes reopened on September 1 with the reading of the School Rule and distribution of charges the day before. The novices had their share of classwork now, and Mother Octavie filled the post of mistress general. The tuition had been lowered to $140 a year, but there was little money coming in, though it was understood that the school bills were "payable in advance." Mother Duchesne made no reference to her straitened circumstances when she wrote an affectionate little letter to her sister Euphrosine on September 17:

I received your letter and that of my brother-in-law, which the customs officer must have taken from the box you were so good as to send me, but which I have not yet received. I am so grateful for the gifts you sent me. They will be so useful to us. I hope they will reach us by the first opportunity. Your letters came by mail. I already knew the consoling details about dear Aloysia and her sister and my dear godson. I call you a very fortunate mother, for the heart-suffering you felt at the separation from your children can never equal the sweet consolation of giving saints to religion and heavenly protectors to all your family. I wrote to our Mother General in Paris, asking her to keep the 150 francs due you from the religious in New Orleans. They sent the money to me.

I should like to write to you at greater length, but my eyes are giving me much trouble. As the ice cuts off the steamboat traffic at this time of the year, I am enclosing this little sheet in a letter going overland to New York. A thousand messages of love to my sisters. It is a great pleasure to have detailed news about them from you and Madame de Rollin. We have begun a second foundation in Lower Louisiana, where a lady donated a house and lands. It is 300 or 400 leagues from here, but that is like 30 leagues in France, for long trips are quite ordinary in this country. Regards to my brother-in-law. . . .

Philippine was right about travel habits in America, and she was often pleasantly surprised by visitors who found their way to Florissant. The Lazarist missionaries were particularly friendly toward the Religious of the Sacred Heart and often stopped for a visit and a meal, or at least some refreshment. Father De La Croix welcomed them cordially to his primitive quarters, and later on the sacristy of the new church was used as a lodging place by many an ill or weary priest.

> I admit that this is something of an expense [wrote Mother Duchesne in defense of her own generosity], causes some loss of time, and interferes with regularity in the community, but I believe it is justified. These poor priests, worn out by their labors, find a little rest and a change of air at Florissant, and there is no one to care for them but us. And besides, this is part of my vocation, as I told you one day before I left France. I said, "Even if I could do nothing but cook for the missionaries, I should be perfectly satisfied."

Bishop Du Bourg was at Florissant in September, 1821, with Father Rosati from St. Mary's Seminary. They chatted encouragingly with two new postulants who were finding religious life more difficult than they had expected, and Father Rosati expressed his desire to have the Religious of the Sacred Heart open a school at the Barrens. He even had some definite plans to submit. Father Acquaroni often stopped on his way to or from Portage des Sioux, where he was working among Indians, half-breeds, trappers, and traders—as motley a mixture of humanity as the frontier could breed. He was at the convent early in October, when the bishop held a little conference with him and several other priests. He spent a long afternoon in conversation with Mother Duchesne, telling her about his work, his needs, his hopes and plans; and when he left, she was aglow with new zeal, thrilled with renewed ambitions. At once she took out her letter pad to propose to the Mother General her latest missionary projects:

> Father Rosati is asking us to send a group of religious to his parish at the Barrens. The building would be erected by the parishioners—they have the material ready. They would contribute the flour needed by the community and would provide a chaplain and a doctor. But the foundation that would be most in accord with the original purpose of our mission is the one at Portage des Sioux, the most northern parish in the direction of the Great Lakes and Canada, which lies beyond them. And that parish stretches west-

ward with no boundary this side of Asia. A zealous priest stationed there [Father John Acquaroni] ministers to three parishes. He teaches a school, trains a choir, and runs a farm, and he is a true father to the poor, living just as they do. The town is the *rendez-vous* for all the Indian canoes that come down the Mississippi and for the boats of the traders who go into the wilderness in search of peltries. In their isolated posts, separated for whole years at a time from their wives, these traders often take to themselves for a time Indian women. They do not know how to provide for the children born of these illegitimate alliances. They leave them with their mothers, and so the children of Christian fathers are brought up like little animals. Many of these traders, however, are rich; and if they knew where to place the children, they would certainly have them educated. This is the good priest's project: he is going to build a house and provide a farm for an institution for orphans and half-breed children. He believes, and rightly, that since meat costs practically nothing in this section of the country, provisions of this kind could be salted down. The Indians in the neighborhood often kill deer now just to get the skins; and being completely improvident, they discard the meat or give it away for nothing.

This seems to me to be the most useful kind of an establishment we could found, and the easiest. It also resembles the work done by Marie of the Incarnation in Canada and is most closely conformed to the purpose that drew us to this country. I have no other desire than that of consecrating my life to this work, if God so wills. If Divine Providence enables us to pay our debts, we could this very year help to found such an establishment. Sister Marguerite would also be well suited to this work . . . which would be to her liking and not beyond her strength.

This letter, begun on October 8, was written at odd moments over a period of three or four days. Philippine had sat down to finish it on the twelfth, but she was interrupted by the sound of voices, then a knock at the front door. She opened it to welcome Father Acquaroni and a priest of whom she had heard much—the celebrated Father Gabriel Richard of Detroit. They stayed a long time talking of their great mutual interest—mission work, the salvation of souls, and the means to achieve their high designs. Philippine enjoyed that visit thoroughly, so she continued her letter to tell the Mother General about it and the urgent plea of Father Richard for a community of Religious of the Sacred Heart in Detroit. She even undertook to trace the routes by which she might journey through the wilderness to the region of the Great Lakes. As her knowledge of American geography was always a bit hazy, she certainly could not have mapped those routes, but her zeal for souls made her ready to undertake the trip if obedience sanctioned it. Meanwhile she would struggle on at Florissant in her great but obscure task of training new members for the Society.

And now an important event was at hand. Father De La Croix had chosen the date out of deference to the Religious of the Sacred Heart, who celebrate the feast of the Presentation of the Blessed Virgin with dual solemnity. From St. Louis on the eve came priests and altar-boys. Philippine tells the story in her *Journal:*

> *November 21.* First Mass in our chapel for Holy Communion and renovation of vows at 5:30. At 6 o'clock, Mass of Thanksgiving. At 7:30 a third Mass at which the Children of Mary received Holy Communion. Then a fourth Mass offered by Father Acquaroni. At 11 o'clock all the clergy went in procession from our parlor to the new Church, which Father De La Croix blessed without chant. High Mass was then sung in the church by Father Niel, pastor of St. Louis. Our children sang the Mass, accompanied on the piano by Father Deys. Father Anduze preached on the solemnity of the day, after reading the Bishop's decree abolishing trustees and ordering them to remit to the pastor the money on hand and the furnishings of the old church. . . .
>
> *November 29.* The solemn erection of the shrine dedicated to St. Francis Regis. It had been impossible to fulfil our vow sooner. The altar stands in our choir at the left near the balustrade where the religious receive Holy Communion.

Above the altar hung the picture of St. Francis Regis which Bishop Du Bourg had presented to Mother Duchesne. In company with the holy missionary of Vivarais, she kept her night-vigils before the tabernacle, sometimes allowing novices to share this privilege, but more often alone with the Divine Lover of souls, to whom she yearned to draw all hearts.

Christmas came, bringing midnight Mass in the convent chapel and exposition of the Blessed Sacrament immediately following and through the whole day, and the two parish Masses and sermons in French and English, Vespers and Benediction. Philippine was in her element on days like this, and she strove to impress on her novices a true sense of worship. With her, adoration was acknowledgment of her own nothingness in the face of God's All. It was reverence and awe in the face of his infinite holiness. It was tender filial love that was prepared to go all lengths in generosity to make return to the Father whose Providence never failed her. The inspired beauty of liturgical worship, with its exterior graces and its interior spirit, appealed to her quite as strongly as did the intimate communing of the soul with God in silent night-watches before the tabernacle, or the devotional closing of the Old Year with its *Te Deum* of gratitude and *Miserere* of reparation. Each year her soul expanded in strong, sweet praise of God's abundant gifts, then sank low in self-humiliation as she realized her radical incapacity as a creature to attain to the supernatural perfection to which she aspired or to accomplish the work entrusted to her. But faith in the grace of obedience was her support as she endeavored to develop in her novices an ever deepening appreciation of, and fidelity to, their vocation as spouses and victims of the Heart of Jesus.

On February 2 a new work was inaugurated at Florissant when Mother Duchesne accepted as "orphans" two little motherless girls. The work was placed under the protection of the Blessed Virgin, "with the hope of soon being able to give a home to a greater number of children." In March Father Henri Pratte came from Ste. Genevieve with another postulant, Judith Labruyère, and a letter from Bishop Du Bourg told of the arrival in New Orleans of Mothers Lucille Mathevon and Xavier Murphy. In her eagerness for news from France, Philippine was just a trifle hard on Lucille when she wrote to Father Barat on April 1:

> The bishop sent Mother Xavier to Opelousas and will bring Mother Lucille here himself. She also wrote to me, but her letter told me all about her trip and not a word about our Fathers and our Mothers in France. From this I conclude that she is not accustomed to writing many letters, as she had not the intuition to choose what would be the most interesting news to put in a letter. No doubt she is bringing me some mail. She did not mention the fact, and this really annoyed me. The Decrees of the General Council, the Summary of the Constitutions, etc., etc., which we were awaiting with so much eagerness—all, she writes, are in Mother Xavier's trunk and have gone to Opelousas. Madame Josephine Meneyrond also arrived in New Orleans on Christmas Eve. That news greatly astonished me—and also Mother Eugenie, with whom she is already lodged. . . .

There were many times when Mother Duchesne found great consolation in the work that was being accomplished at Florissant. On Easter Monday, 1822, nine children received baptism. A week later Mother Mathevon arrived under the escort of General Pratte, and Philippine could note with satisfaction: "She gave us all the news about our dear Society and informed us that through the kindness of our Mother General our debt to Mr. Mullanphy has been paid. He went to see her in Paris." In the early hours of April 16 she was writing to thank for this help and to give details of the success with which God was blessing the apostolate on the frontier:

> We had planned to have several of our pupils baptized on Holy Saturday, but we put it off until Easter Monday in order that the parents might be present at the ceremony. We decorated the baptismal font and the children wore white dresses. I stood as godmother for the step-daughter of General Clark, a very prominent man in St. Louis. . . . Mother Octavie and I also stood for two of the orphans to whom we give a home. . . . Besides these children, there were five others, four of them pupils of the parish school, and a little boy who had not even a pair of stockings for the ceremony. We furnished clothing and a feast for these poor children in order to impress more deeply on their untrained minds this day of grace. . . .
>
> I cry for joy at times when I realize that in one way or another more than one hundred people are learning to love Jesus through our efforts here. I do not know how to thank God for this. Mother Eugenie will have greater success than ours, once her house is firmly established. She is very glad she undertook that work alone. God blesses quite visibly all she does, even at times seeming to work miracles for her. But I miss her so much. . . .

When Father De La Croix undertook a missionary trip to the Osage Indians that spring, there was stirred in the soul of Philippine a kind of holy envy. There were, moreover, other opportunities beckoning to her, and she put her thoughts on paper, begging Mother Barat to allow a few of the religious to reopen the school at St. Charles. After a lengthy defense of this proposal, she added:

> You were worried, Reverend Mother, by the suggestion of the new foundation at Grand Coteau. But just think, that is the only means by which we could support ourselves. By it we can now receive more postulants and be able to feed and lodge them. You will see that within a year Mother Eugenie will be as far advanced as we are after four years. It will be the same at St. Charles. All we need is the spirit of sacrifice. If a mission is established by priests among the Osage Indians, they will also want two nuns to teach the children, but *there* complete death to nature! It would be flying in the face of all prudence, but I would be very glad to devote myself to the work if you approve of it later on. . . .

Back from Louisiana early in July, Bishop Du Bourg paid a visit to Florissant at once and stirred the household to activity resembling that of the previous summer by the news he brought from Grand Coteau. The annual retreat of the pupils had been scheduled for the week preceding the feast of St. Vincent de Paul, but Mother Duchesne could give little time to the retreatants, for she was busy packing boxes and satchels and guiding little Emilie St. Cyr through the spiritual exercises in preparation for her first vows. What a day was that of July 19! Crowded with religious ceremonies, last minute instructions and advice to Mother Octavie, who was being left in charge of the convent as Mother Assistant, and at least one letter. This was posted by Mother Duchesne herself before boarding the steamboat in St. Louis on the afternoon of July 20 and told the reason for this hurried trip south:

> Monseigneur reached here a few days ago. He informed me that Madame Josephine Meneyrond has returned to France, that a coadjutrix novice from New Orleans has left Grand Coteau, that Sister Layton has made her first vows, Miss Carmelite Landry has received the habit, and Mother Xavier Murphy has made her final vows and is having some difficulty getting accustomed to things, and last of all, that Mother Eugenie is in urgent need of help. All this, along with complete silence on her part—which is most unusual for her and so causes me to suspect carelessneess on the part of someone who was entrusted with her letters—all this has determined me to accompany the two young religious whom I was sending to her. One is a choir nun who made her first vows today in view of the long trip ahead of her and because of her courage in obtaining her parents' consent to the departure. The second is a coadjutrix novice who will take charge of the kitchen, which Mother Eugenie is still managing herself. As Mother Lucille is ready to handle any emergency, her presence here makes this trip possible. Monseigneur hastened my decision in order that we might travel on the same steamboat with four priests, and I can return on this boat before the winter freeze sets in. Monseigneur distributed the prizes at Opelousas and says the children are making astonishing progress there. Some people in St. Louis say the standard of our boarding school has gone down since Mother Eugenie left. That is not true. . . . Monseigneur will take us at daybreak in the carriage that brought him here. . . .

When Philippine set out on this mission of charity, she little dreamed of the adventurous journey that lay ahead. Nor could she realize how fascinating an account her letters would make.

When she is her own biographer, the pages come alive with her vigorous personality, and the story glows with her own animation. She had already visited Grand Coteau and was on her way to New Orleans to board a northbound steamboat when she wrote to Mother Barat from a dingy inn at Plaquemine, Louisiana, on September 8:

> Before I left St. Louis, I wrote to you by way of New York to tell you I was going to Opelousas. . . . I wanted to make this trip when we first found out that Mother Eugenie had been ill. Then I put the idea out of my mind, once I knew our Sisters from France had arrived. . . . But when Monseigneur returned from Louisiana, I realized again that I should make the trip and bring some help to that convent, for there was no priest in the neighborhood and the enemies of the pastor had forced him to leave. Monseigneur had withdrawn the convent chaplain in so imperative a fashion that the priest would lose his faculties for administering the sacraments if he remained a day beyond the time appointed for his departure. . . . Mother Xavier Murphy was ill at ease in her new home; Mother Girard was even more so; and help was needed. Two young novices with much good will can be of service with the work, and one of them can teach. The house will now be able to get along if they do not accept more than 30 pupils, and I believe they will never have more than that.
>
> We left St. Louis on July 20 by steamboat. A former pupil of ours [Therese Pratte], who is devoted to Mother Eugenie, had obtained permission from her parents to go with us at their expense. So there were four of us traveling together. There were also three priests on board but they were no help whatsoever. . . .
>
> On July 22 we stopped at Ste. Genevieve. There we had Mass and the joy of offering our Communion in union with all our Sisters for our very dear Mother General. From then until the 28th we could only offer to God the great discomfort of the intense heat of this season, the proximity of the boilers, and the other arrangements on the steamboat. We were all covered with prickly heat and mosquito bites. In the evening we had recreation on the deck and passed the time singing hymns, led by Father Desmoulins, one of the priests, who has so fine a voice it gave him quite a reputation at St. Sulpice. He left us at Baton Rouge on the left bank of the Mississippi, where he was named pastor.
>
> On Sunday, July 28, we hoped to reach Natchez in time for Mass, but the priest had already reached the elevation, and as he does not keep the Reserve in the tabernacle when he is absent, we were deprived of Holy Communion. We went to the home of the pastor, Father Mano [Constantine Maenhaut], a young Flemish

priest whose health is greatly undermined, more, I think, from heart-suffering than from physical toil. Very few Catholics live at Natchez; the little wooden church stands humbly among beautiful Protestant temples. There are five different sects in the place. Such a crowd was going into a Protestant church, we followed along, but were informed of our mistake, so we turned away with sad hearts and went to witness the solitude that surrounded the Catholic church.

Father Mano told us he sincerely regretted having allowed Mother Eugenie to leave Natchez. He thinks a foundation would have been better located in that fairly prosperous town on the great river where there is continual traffic, than in a little hole like Opelousas, where we can never reach more than a very restricted circle. But we were just badly informed and God allowed it to happen in order to recompense the faith of Mrs. Smith and to save the souls of the children in those parts. . . .

On July 29 we left the river boat and waited at an inn at Plaquemine for a chance to board the bayou steamboat, which was undergoing repairs. We spent seven days there at 20 francs a day, besides 60 francs for transportation three leagues to where the steamboat was. . . . We had hoped to reach the landing in it, but the receding waters had left the place so mirey, the oxen could not be driven into it. So the boatmen decided to transfer us and our baggage to a small boat that cost us 50 francs to travel four leagues on another little bayou which, they said would bring us to dry land. As the captain considered this a good plan, I thought it best to do what these men who knew the country advised, so we got into the canoe. The men at the oars were soon pretty tired, and from the second little bayou we passed into a third.

You can form some idea of the place we were in if you recall the descriptions of the waters surrounding Tartarus. The water was black and evil-smelling. As far as the eye could see, it flowed through the most dismal forests which stand in water all but one or two months of the year. The trees have only a little dark foliage high up near their tops, and this is almost hidden under the long gray beards that hang from every branch of these old trees. (This hanging moss is a parasitic plant; when dried and beaten, it becomes a kind of fiber from which the countryfolk make mattresses.) The further we advanced, the denser the forest became; but there was no dry land in sight, not even a sign of it. The day wore on. We had only a little bread to feed the eight people in the boat. I said to the guide, "I think you have lost your way. Would it not be more prudent to turn back and find a place where there is dry land, no matter where?" He replied that that was impossible, and his embarrassed manner convinced me that we were lost in the

Grenoble in the late 18th century

Pierre-François Duchesne

Amelie Duchesne de Mauduit

The Chateau
at Grâne,
the Duchesne's
country home

Courtyard of the monastery of Sainte-Marie-d'en-Haut, Grenoble, France

General and Mrs. Bernard Pratte, Senior

Ursuline convent, New Orleans, where Mother Duchesne and companions
were given hospitality on reaching America in 1818.

Claude Perier

Charlotte Pascal Perier

Casimir Perier

The Chateau of Vizille, the Perier country home

Place St. André, Grenoble, France

Palais de Justice

Statue of Bayard
Home of Claude Perier

Bishops Rosati and Du Bourg

Architect's Drawing of the City House, St. Louis, 1828

St. Charles *circa* 1850—Jesuit Church and Convent in center of picture

Convent built at Florissant in 1819 by Mother Duchesne.

Stairway in Florissant convent showing door opening on closet used as sleeping room by Mother Duchesne.

St. Charles in 1860, showing: 1. Central portion of convent built in 1835   2. Chapel of Our Lady, in which Mother Duchesne's body was interred in 1855   3. Jesuit Church of St. Charles Borromeo, first used in 1828   4. Parish school taught by the Religious of the Sacred Heart.

Tomb of Philippine Duchesne

Unfinished memorial church of Blessed Philippine Duchesne, St. Charles Missouri

swamp. Just then we heard shouting. "Listen," he said, "they are calling from the bank to tell us they are waiting for us." I answered, "But notice, the shouts are coming from a very different direction."

At that same moment we saw coming rapidly from behind us a canoe filled with Indians, Negroes, and whites, mostly naked except for loin cloths, the most frightful looking men, yelling and whistling as they are represented when rushing to an assured victory. Our boatmen grew pale and not one of them would have been able to put up any resistance. My three young companions were terrified, though they never dreamed of dangers as great as I was picturing to myself. I told them to pray earnestly to God and place themselves under the protection of the Blessed Virgin, and I immediately promised a novena of Masses in return for our safety. The canoe was already upon us. The savages stared at us as if petrified, then passed by, after having stopped some time close beside us. They eyed our water bottles, which they thought were filled with the liquor they are so crazy about. They seemed to have nothing to eat with them, yet they left us without asking for anything. I thought they had passed us by just to go ahead and wait for us at a place where they could attack us more easily, so I gave myself up to prayer, recommending my soul to God in preparation for death, but to my companions I only suggested prayer and patience. As the boatmen were exhausted with rowing, I feared my complaints might annoy them.

At last, just when I was positive we were lost in the swamp, dry land suddenly appeared, and we saw a cart drawn by four oxen waiting for us. It was like a resurrection—I really was *not* ready to die. I shall never forget the names of those animals: *Flambeau, Rousseau, Gaillard, Tout-Blanc*—the words rang through the woods every minute, for the driver had to urge them on continually over the muddy ground. We spent the night at an inn, where a few days before all this the travelers staying there had been robbed. But we were quite safe. At two o'clock in the morning we set out again in a cart and at nine o'clock reached the convent of the Sacred Heart.

Mother Duchesne gives not the slightest hint of the good she accomplished at Grand Coteau by her fervor, her sympathetic love and interest, her self-forgetfulness, nor of the reaction of the community to her visit, but Mother Eugenie Audé described to Mother Barat the emotional welcome this surprise visit called forth from her, and Mother Xavier Murphy wrote to the Mother General on August 27:

And now, my dear Mother, your prediction has come true. On

the 7th of this month I had the sweet consolation of embracing our
dear Mother Duchesne. You can easily understand my joy that
day. . . . I had such need to pour out my heart to someone in
whom I had confidence. Yet in that state of soul I knew that there
was no sacrifice I would not make for the greater glory of God,
no privation I would not endure in this dear land of my adoption.
Still the fear of offending God, of breaking the solemn promises
I had made before the altar alarmed me. But Mother Duchesne, to
whom I revealed my thoughts, quieted all my fears. She understood my French, and I have never spoken confidentially to
anyone with more ease and never experienced more peace and consolation than when she gave me her answers. She is a woman
entirely according to my heart.

Mother Duchesne had, as Mother Eugenie expressed it, "time
to examine the little house of Grand Coteau and judge for herself
how it is being conducted." She met the seventeen pupils of the
academy, among them Mary Ann Hardey, who, as Mother Aloysia,
would become illustrious in the Society's annals. She discussed
with Mother Audé the unhealthy physical condition of the nuns
and the means that might be taken to relieve some of them of their
too heavy load of work. She was puzzled by a certain aloofness in
Mother Audé's manner, though she did not know that the young
superior had during the past year made quite definite efforts to have
her convent withdrawn entirely from the supervision of Mother
Duchesne and placed under the Superior General in France. That
very request had caused St. Madeleine Sophie to emphasize to her
the fact that Mother Duchesne was, as it were, her Provincial—
though that title was not in use in the Society. "I have given her
full authority. . . . I have given her full powers. Have recourse
to her in all ordinary cases." There was, however, a strong bent
toward independence in Mother Audé and this would show itself
as the years went by.

Mother Duchesne spent her fifty-third birthday at Grand
Coteau. There was no Mass in the convent chapel that August 29,
but Mother Murphy noticed that she spent long hours that day
before the tabernacle. Only at the evening recreation did she tell
the little group that the day had special significance for her. On
September 2 she told them good-bye. "Judge of our feelings!"
wrote Mother Murphy, *"Dieu Seul! Dieu Seul!"*

The trip to New Orleans took almost a week. There Mother
Duchesne and Therese Pratte found hospitality for a few days at
the Ursuline convent. Several friends came to call, among them

Fathers Borgna and Ferrari, but Philippine found time to write a sheaf of letters. In one of them she commented: "I leave today by a steamboat that is going upstream. It is a long, expensive trip, but it was necessary; and Divine Providence is never wanting where necessity is concerned." *Today* was September 11; the steamboat was the *Hecla;* the trip would last *80 days.* After the harrowing experiences of the first six weeks, Mother Duchesne wrote her classic letter of October 30, 1822, "On board the steamboat *Cincinnati*":

It may astonish you that, having written to you at the beginning of September from New Orleans, as I was about to leave that city, I have not yet reached St. Louis. But God has punished me for some of my faults by leaving me to wander about the world for so long a time with no spiritual help whatsoever.

They had assured me that there was no danger of yellow fever in New Orleans this year. So I went with all assurance to ask hospitality with the religious of St. Ursula. But the pupil who was traveling with me was not feeling very well, and I developed a little fever on the eve of our departure. I realized that the nuns were frightened lest we should contract that dreaded disease which, they say, only attacks people who are not used to the climate. The doctor and the superior both thought it wise for us to leave at once in order to escape the disease. I wanted to do this myself, though I knew I was in no condition to undertake a trip of 300 to 400 leagues through the wilderness to St. Louis. How I do wish we had a house of the Sacred Heart in New Orleans!

They ordered a carriage for us and I went in horror to the steamboat. There my fever went up again, and on the second day of the trip, within 24 hours, we had three deaths on the boat: the captain, the first mate, and a passenger. A young man who had been sent from France by the hospital at Lyons was traveling with us. That same day he felt so ill, he got off the boat at a village where they tell me he died. Fortunately there was a priest in the place. Serious cases of fever continued on the steamboat and I was suffering in every way, seeing men die like animals, with no help either human or divine, without that tender sympathy that alleviates suffering, and hearing people singing gay songs beside the very bodies of the dead.

I thought it prudent to get off the boat at Natchez. . . . But on reaching there, we learned that we could not enter the town as we came from New Orleans and they feared we might bring yellow fever. So we got off the boat and remained on the sandy shore opposite the town while a passenger tried to find us lodging. We were refused at several houses, but finally a man took us in. He had lost his wife just three weeks before, and he gave us her bed, which still retained the odor of medicine and other marks of illness. The bedding had not been washed since her death. I was at the very crisis of the fever, but I held myself as straight as I could in order to hide the fact. I succeeded to some extent for four days, for they spoke only English and I remained hidden, as far as possible, treating myself. And God blessed my efforts, for since then the high fever has gradually worn off and for a week I have been quite well.

I wrote to the parish priest [Father Maenhaut] in order that I might see him and find a lodging where there were some women. He was ill at the time, but on the fifth day he came to see us and had us received into a very fine home on the same side of the river, where we had every physical care that could relieve and rest the body. The lady, a Mrs. Davis, is a Catholic of Spanish origin, who speaks English, Spanish, and French perfectly. She offered us just everything, even carriage and horseback rides. The pastor had promised that he would return to hear my confession, but I waited another week, for he did not have money for the trip across the river. I tried to get into the town to go to Mass on Sunday. The doctors had a conference on the subject, along with several other people, and the reply was negative. This contributed to my having another attack of fever. Never have I felt a greater need for Mass and the sacraments. This came from having seen death at such close range.

My fever was a good excuse for not appearing at dinner when several officials from Natchez were present. They had been told that there was a nun in the house—a superior, what's more—and they wanted to see what kind of an animal that was. They kept on asking my traveling companion if I would not appear at least after dinner, and how was I dressed. One in particular, who spoke French, said it would give him much pleasure to talk with me. All this was repeated to me that evening by the mistress of the house. I told her I was delighted to have had an excuse to remain in my room.

Two days later the pastor came with charity to hear my confession, but that is the only spiritual help I had had since leaving New Orleans: neither Mass nor Communion nor any other confession and that with a trip of 10 or 12 more days ahead of us if the navigation was smooth. In all it will be 60 days of the most rigorous fast I have ever made, perhaps in all my life, even including the time of the Revolution. Still in the midst of these hard privations I always see the Arm of Divine Providence stretched out to us. We came upon the steamboat *Hecla* which we had left at Natchez. It could no longer navigate; its boilers had burst; the steam had killed two men and burned several others badly, and thirteen men had died of the fever on board. . . .

P.S. [undated]

I intended to finish this letter when I reached St. Ferdinand, but the slowness of our trip makes me want to close it now, so that if by good luck I can find an opportunity of mailing it before my arrival there, it will be ready. I made my retreat on the steamboat. Everyone on board spoke English, and those who understood French did not speak it at all. So I took advantage of being alone with God, for after such a long absence I foresaw it would be difficult to get my retreat in after I reach Florissant. . . .

Part II of this adventurous story appears in the letter Philippine wrote the day after reaching home. Exhausted though she was— for she had been obliged to rest in St. Louis for two days with the Pratte family before driving out to Florissant—she was eager to undertake new works of zeal. Her insatiable love for the Sacred Heart of Jesus and her desire to bring into his kingdom the neglected children of the frontier whom she had seen at close range in her travels urged her to plead with Mother Barat the cause of ventures for which she had no human means of accomplishment:

My last letter to you was written on board the *Cincinnati*. I had already sealed it when that steamboat ran aground on a sandbank in mid-stream about 100 leagues below St. Louis near New Madrid. I wanted to finish the trip by the overland route, and that would have been quite possible. But in this land age must bow to youth. The young girl with whom I was traveling did not want to go that way. People sided with her and built up imaginary fears in her mind. They tried to deceive me; and as I would not in conscience leave her to travel alone nor make the difficult trip myself without a companion, I remained there doing nothing until Divine Providence inspired a French lady in New Madrid [Mrs. Lafond] to invite us to her home. We went there in a canoe and stayed five days until the water rose in the river and lifted the steamboat off the sandbank. Then we returned to the boat by canoe with two young ladies who were going to St. Louis to make their First Communion. . . .

On this trip I have seen so much ignorance in the many little villages that have sprung up in the last four years along the neck of the river, that I am more than ever convinced of the great need there is for teachers who could be placed gradually in the larger towns where there are priests—towns like New Madrid, where there are sixty or eighty Catholic families. . . . I wish you would approve of our training some of the girls in the parish school for this work. . . .

I found everyone well when I reached here, but nearly all the community had been ill, several dangerously, also some of the children and three priests—these latter all at the same time in the sacristy, which was turned into an infirmary for them. The chaplain came home from the Osage Indian missions in an almost dying condition. Florissant never had so much sickness before, and the same is true throughout the United States.

Mother Octavie governed the house very well during my absence. They tell me Bishop Du Bourg has announced that he is going to live at the rectory in Florissant and take his meals in one of the sacristy rooms, so as not to bring distractions into our convent. On my trip I missed 120 Masses, counting just one a day, 80 communions, about 20 confessions, and practically all the Benedictions of the Blessed Sacrament for four months. But I believe all these sacrifices are not without value; perhaps several foundations may come from them.

eight

Stability in
Suffering and Joy

I. 1823—1825

DURING THE WEEKS THAT FOLLOWED her return
from Louisiana, Philippine learned much that distressed her. Mother
Octavie's management of the household had been less satisfactory
than appeared at first sight. Lacking firmness, she had let the children get out of hand. Mother Duchesne found it hard to reprove
her, but that was her duty. She was troubled, too, by the worldly
ways reported of former pupils of the Sacred Heart and made a
subject of gossip in St. Louis. The town was just then agog with
scandal over the conduct of a group of prominent Catholics who
were taking advantage of the Bishop's absence to foment discon-
tent and carry out a scheme that did them little credit, yet only
a handful of the faithful were upholding the bishop's cause. There
was danger that the nuns at Florissant might be involved in the
unhappy affair if they were asked to shelter the luckless prelate.
All this and much else was weighing on Philippine's heart as the
New Year dawned, and she wrote to Mother Barat on January 4,
1823, beginning with an outpouring of affectionate memories, then
telling of the distressing conditions in St. Louis, and adding by
way of a report on the convent at Florissant:

> On the account sheet which I am enclosing . . . the amount spent
> on food is in no way proportioned to the other expenses because

259

we receive so much help in this matter from our garden, which yielded a hundred bushels of potatoes and many other things, and from the milk of our eight fine cows and the eggs of our sixty chickens. The repairs include the replastering of some rooms along with some wainscotting, and the building of a long plank fence instead of a wall. We do not owe Monseigneur any money now, but we do owe 2500 francs to a gentleman who cleared us of debt. Such is our financial standing at the close of five years, whereas Mother Eugenie at the close of one year gave us more than 4000 francs. From this you may judge of the real necessity there is for our having a convent in New Orleans to help support our work. Here, far from receiving help from anyone, our first duty is to aid the priests, and perhaps Monseigneur himself.

Mother Lucille is excellent, except that she is inclined to run up bills too quickly. Mother Octavie is always amiable and everyone loves her. Sisters Catherine and Marguerite have grown stout, but they are active and helpful. The five novices have good will and are taking the training. I hold very much to study and I have put Mother Lucille back to it; for if she is ever superior, she will need it. . . . My last letter went off on a steamboat that got ice-bound on the river. This one will go by post to New Orleans. I am addressing it to kind Father Richard. He was stricken with yellow fever, but has recovered, as has also one of the vicars general [Father Philip Borgna], but another one [Father Andrew Ferrari] died of it, and this is a great loss.

Some days later Philippine sat reading the *Missouri Republican* for January 9. Scanning the Post Office Notice inserted by Wilson P. Hunt, postmaster in St. Louis, she saw her own name listed among the 247 persons notified that letters were waiting to be called for. Four letters on hand in St. Louis! At once the convent factotum, Martin Lepere, was dispatched for them. Though they required no immediate answer, Philippine had much on her mind and heart that could be expressed only to Mother Barat, and she was happy to have an excuse for a second letter within the month. Her reference to Monseigneur Du Bourg as "our Seer" (*notre Voyant*) seems slightly ironical, but it is impossible to know the exact connotation with which she used the term on January 16, 1823:

I received two letters from you at the same time. There is universal joy when we hear from you, for then we feel nearer to our Mother and to the dear religious family, and that is a very pleasant feeling, even if it is an illusion. Your first letter went to Opelousas before coming here. Perhaps it was enclosed in a packet of mail.

The people in New Orleans always prefer to send things to Eugenie rather than to me, so completely has she won the esteem and affection of all who have the good of the Society at heart. . . .

I do not know where we shall get the 6000 francs we owe in France. We are in neither Peru nor Mexico nor in the rich islands, but rather close to Canada which, far from enriching France, cost her dearly and was the land in which her missionaries suffered most. Here we can hope to gain only souls—and a very small number of them. Only our desire to support our work and have more children in the school urges me to plead for [a convent in] New Orleans. I still hope the letter I wrote from Opelousas about New Orleans may change your decision, since we are not asking any help for the foundation, and it really is necessary to make a change at Opelousas. Those two heads do not fit into the same bonnet. There is no talk of this new foundation just now, for we have said we must first have your consent. Our *Seer* is away just now. I think he went to Baltimore to straighten out a misunderstanding with his colleagues or to ask the Jesuits to help with missions to the savages. I feel that nothing of this kind can be done without them.

After some complicated explanations about money matters, she continues:

I am really chagrined and humiliated to think you lost that note for a thousand francs. It happened as a result of the naïveté of our Sisters. They had not been in New Orleans fifteen minutes when they gave a scrupulous account of all the money they had to the person interested. That person [Bishop Du Bourg] wrote to me the same day, pointing out to me the *beauty* of our position, and saying that in consequence he was going to dispose of the 1000 franc note on Bordeaux. The same thing happened to the 1500 francs Mother Eugenie sent me, in spite of my cleverness in hiding the money. We owed him that, however, so it was a matter of justice to pay him. . . .

The single entry in Mother Duchesne's *Journal* for February, 1823, is made up of jottings that paint a sad picture:

The withdrawal and complaints of two postulants who had no vocation; the worldliness of our pupils who have left school and their forgetfulness of us; the indocility of the present pupils; calumnies circulated about us. All this makes us feel the weight of the cross. And to it must be added our poverty and an illness that has attacked nearly all the religious and a number of the children.

There is, however, a note of hope in the entry: "We have

learned that Father Rosati, superior of the Lazarists, has been named Coadjutor to Monseigneur Du Bourg. He has asked us to make a novena for his intention without telling us what it is."

The news regarding Father Rosati's nomination was not accurate. True, he had received apostolic letters from Rome in November, 1822, informing him that the territories of Mississippi and Alabama had been erected into a vicariate apostolic and that he had been oppointed Vicar Apostolic of the region with the title of Bishop of Tenegra *in partibus infidelium*. These letters, bearing the date of August 13, 1822, had been brought to America by Archbishop Marechal upon his return to Baltimore from Rome. Believing that circumstances justified a petition on his part to be spared the episcopal dignity, Father Rosati returned the apostolic brief to Rome. He did not know at the time that Bishop Du Bourg, on learning of the appointment in Baltimore, had written a strong protest to Rome and had recommended Rosati as his coadjutor with special jurisdiction in the upper portion of the vast diocese of Louisiana and the Floridas. The misinformation circulated in and around St. Louis regarding Father Rosati's appointment reached Florissant at about the same time as the letter he wrote to Mother Duchesne begging prayers.

Father Philip Borgna, who had been stationed in New Orleans since his ordination and had suffered from an attack of yellow fever in September, 1822, passed through St. Louis on his way to Europe in March, 1823, and spent some days at Florissant. This gave Philippine a safe opportunity to send letters across the Atlantic. To Mother Barat she gave news of the novices, who were a grave responsibility to her, and of the hardships they faced so courageously:

> The priest who will deliver this letter is one of our most fervent Lazarist missionaries. His superior is sending him to Rome on business connected with the mission to which he is completely devoted. For two years he has braved the danger of death during epidemics in New Orleans. He expects to return there in a year. If we make a foundation there, it would be very safe for two of our religious to travel with him. He acts as our devoted commissioner in that city and buys all provisions for Mother Eugenie.
>
> I shall write no Jeremiad in this letter, for on Sunday during the novena to St. Xavier [March 4–12] I had the consolation of seeing the veil given to Sister Elizabeth Huber, a pupil of our parish school. She is sixteen years old, an active worker, and seems very firm in her vocation. A still greater joy was ours on the feast of

St. Joseph, when Sisters Xavier and Regis Hamilton and Mary Ann Summers made their first vows. These are the élite among our novices. Regis thought she would not live through the day, so great was her joy; and she repeated this so often I began to fear she might be right. That would have been a terrible loss for us. There is in that soul no obstacle to grace. She does all the good she can. Her capacity for study is mediocre, but she is not yet 18 years old, though she is quite tall, so she may develop further intellectually. Her sister has great talents along all lines except those of household duties—these will be Regis's part. Xavier will have to work harder for perfection, but she has real courage and devotedness. All three have the advantage of speaking and writing the two languages.

I was hard pressed to clothe our novices in new habits for their vows. An old soutane left by the Trappist Father made a choir cloak for one. Sister Mary Ann's shawl and veil were made from a black crepon dress left by a pupil, and Sister Xavier's habit was entirely new except for an old cape which she wore in honor of her Spouse, the Poor Man, by choice. There are advantages in the life of hardship and privation here. I must admit I fear for those who have had a life of ease and convenience. Here we must be ready for anything; one of us milks the cows, not in a stable but often in mud ankle deep, in rain, in snow; another makes the fire in the kitchen; another heats the bake-oven; at almost any time they have to cross the swampy yard that cannot be drained properly. Clothing and rooms suffer from these inconveniences—no sabots or galoshes, as these are unknown here.

On the feast of the Finding of the Holy Cross, May 3, the community and the children of the boarding and day schools gathered in the meadow and went in procession to the little grove beyond to assist at the erection of a devotional cross that faced the convent and stood out against the background of trees. It was the first outdoor shrine Mother Duchesne planned for Florissant. Bishop Du Bourg saw and approved when he came on May 8 for First Communion and confirmation. He had just returned from the East by way of Kentucky and had much to tell, though little time for telling. Mother Duchesne noted briefly in her *Journal*, then wrote it all on May 20, 1823, to the Mother General, along with comments on persons and things that reveal more about her than do the bits of information she delighted in recounting:

It is a long time since I had any news from you, and this is a great privation for my heart. None of your last letters told me you had received those in which I told you about my trip to Lower Louisiana, during which I reminded you about the project of a foundation in New Orleans. Your replies to my former suggestions in regard to this indicate rather plainly that you are not in favor of it. Monseigneur Du Bourg, who was among the first to speak of this establishment, no longer shows any interest in it. Unquestionably he considers us too few in numbers to attempt such an enterprise without help from you, and he knows you have no one to send just now. . . .

Monseigneur spent hardly any time in St. Louis, came on the feast of the Ascension to give confirmation in our church and First Communion to 14 children, boarders and day pupils, left the next day, and that was the extent of his visit. He made far fewer inquiries than usual about what concerns the convent. People say he is no longer our bishop, and as a matter of fact he signs himself *Bishop of New Orleans* now, and not *Bishop of Louisiana*, as formerly. It is rumored that our new bishop is a Sulpician—others say Father Rosati, a Roman priest and a member of the Lazarist order. I believe that neither of them will be more than coadjutor to Monseigneur Du Bourg. His hurried departure for the South [on May 11] is causing the departure of several priests. . . . Our own pastor is thinking of going south, for he says the Jesuits will serve us adequately.

If you do not yet know what took place at Georgetown between Monseigneur and the Jesuits, that last sentence may surprise you. Bishop Du Bourg did not give us all the details about that fine and inestimable acquisition for this part of the world, where the desire for the greater glory of God should be one's only riches and support. A priest told me that the Jesuit superiors were considering the closing of the novitiate [in Maryland] because there were too many foreigners in it. Among them seven young Flemings, full of ardor, zeal, and devotedness, raised a great hue and cry, protesting that they had been brought to America, that they would not leave the house unless they were placed in another novitiate of the Society of Jesus. Thereupon the superior decided to send them to Missouri, along with the master of novices and his assistant, some lay-brothers, and some Negro slaves. They are coming, I am told, in complete dependence on Divine Providence, but they are perfectly happy about it.

According to an agreement made between them and Monseigneur, the latter is giving them his Florissant farm, for which he paid 20,000 francs, and the horses and cattle on it. As the house is too small for the 12 or 15 people who are coming, he told us that some of them will live temporarily in the rectory. Unfortunately the roof and ceiling have not been finished, and we haven't a penny to help with this work. The pastor was having the house completed slowly, as he too is entirely dependent on Providence. There will be no furniture except what we try to give them, and we do not want to be outdone by these good Fathers in trust in Divine Providence. Monseigneur has assigned to them the Missouri country to visit, with St. Charles and two other villages. This is a great deal of work for two priests, as none of the novices have been ordained. . . .

As for us, we have only 18 boarding pupils now, and several of these are gratis; others are slow to pay; besides, we have six orphans and seven novices or aspirants who did not even furnish their own clothes. I should like to send home the pupils who do not pay, but several of them might lose their faith, and we should prefer to deprive ourselves of everything rather than have that happen. An establishment in New Orleans would have supported this house, but God does not will it, *Fiat;* for the money-shortage, *Fiat;* for the illness, *Fiat.* I have been afraid that Mother Octavie has contracted consumption. She has had several abscesses in her mouth; these have healed, but one of them came through on the outside of her neck. She suffers with the greatest sweetness; her perfect fidelity makes me fear that she is very near her eternal recompense, and her loss would be a severe blow to our convent just now when we are in such a depression. I scarcely think we shall ever get out of it. I even expect to lose other children soon—money is so scarce. . . . Our parish school is also small. You could not find more careless, inept, and unappreciative children. But God be praised in all. All our privations, all our humiliations would not have been too high a price to pay for the happiness of witnessing the success of our Fathers [the Jesuits] and their heroic virtue. This happiness is so great, I dare not count on it yet, and I dread lest once more someone has built for us a beautiful castle in Spain.

It was not, however, a "beautiful castle in Spain," but a great reality—the Jesuits were at that very moment nearing Shauneetown on the Ohio on a double "broadhorn" raft, and a new chapter was about to open in the life of Philippine Duchesne—a chapter in which joy and pain were strangely intermingled. For five years she had hoped and prayed, yearned and anticipated, pleaded and almost insisted in prayer. If only Divine Providence might send Jesuits to the American frontier! On June 2, 1823—it was a Monday afternoon—Father Charles Felix Van Quickenborne, S. J., arrived at Florissant with Brother Henry Reiselman and Brother Peter de Meyer and three couples of Negro slaves. On Thursday, eve of the feast of the Sacred Heart, came Father Peter Joseph Timmermans and seven novices. The liturgical feast was celebrated solemnly, but there is no least note of exaltation in the *Journal* entries, nor any allusion to the circumstances of their journey to Missouri.

Their arrival meant change, and on June 14 there was grief in many hearts as the nuns and children bade farewell to Father De La Croix, the friend and guide of the past four years. He was going south to join Bishop Du Bourg in Louisiana, hoping that the milder climate might restore his shattered health. Mother Duchesne's reverent affection and gratitude toward him came out in her letters to him through the years that followed. He had been so cordial and sympathetic, so ready to accommodate himself to the circumstances and needs of the convent, so eager to help and so grateful for help—all this she would miss, and she seemed already to sense the fact that Father Van Quickenborne, "an excellent religious . . . of too vehement a temper," would be less cordial in his dealing with the nuns.

As Father De La Croix had urged her to send recruits to Opelousas with him aboard the *Dolphin*, the convent was again the scene of a hurried departure, this time for Sisters Marguerite Manteau and Mary Ann Summers. Another of her first companions to America was being sacrificed for the good of the Louisiana mission, another of her best young nuns—and the only one skilled in the preparation of meals. But they were going under very safe escort, and Mother Duchesne was happy on that score.

By this time Mother Duchesne was acquainted with the entire Jesuit community, though it took her many a day to master the spelling and pronunciation of their names. They were Fathers Charles Felix Van Quickenborne, Superior, Master of Novices, and pastor of St. Ferdinand, and Peter Joseph Timmermans, Assistant Master of Novices, seven young Belgian novices—Felix Verreydt, Francis de Maillet, Judocus Van Assche, Peter John Verhaegen, John Baptist Smedts, John Anthony Elet, and Peter De Smet, and three coadjutor Brothers, Henry Reiselman, Charles Strathan, and Peter De Meyer. She came to know the three couples of Negro slaves, too—Tom and Polly, Moses and Nancy, Isaac and Succy. There was no language barrier to be broken down, for the Jesuits all spoke French and soon all mastered English. But from the outset there was a cool, deliberate aloofness on the part of the Reverend Father Superior and his religious sons that baffled Philippine. She was friendly, eager to help and be helped. She had expected a return of friendship like that to which she had been accustomed in France, where the Jesuits were *nos Pères* ("our Fathers") to the Religious of the Sacred Heart.

For five years she had yearned for spiritual direction of the Ignatian kind, and on June 26 she noted in her *Journal* that the community and novices had gone to confession and placed themselves under the direction of the Jesuit superior. But this was quite contrary to the taste and conscience of Father Van Quickenborne. There had been no mention of the spiritual care of the nuns at Florissant in the agreement drawn up between Bishop Du Bourg and Father Charles Neale, superior of the Maryland Jesuits. There is nothing to indicate that Father Van Quickenborne had even been informed of their presence in his new parish before he reached St. Louis. Had he known it, he would certainly have asked some directive in their regard before setting out for Missouri. As it was, soon after his arrival in Florissant he was writing to his superior in Maryland to know whether he, being a Jesuit, could take charge of the *Dames du Sacré Coeur,* hear their confessions, and attend to them as his immediate predecessor was accustomed to do. The answer was that the matter would be laid before the Father General in Rome and his answer relayed in time to Father Van Quickenborne, but *ad interim* he was authorized to attend to the "*nuns du Sacré Coeur,*" provided Bishop Du Bourg gave him the requisite powers to do so. It was autumn, however, before this answer reached Florissant.

In mid-July Mother Duchesne received news that caused her anxiety. The *Dolphin* had run aground on its downstream trip. The passengers had been transferred to another steamboat, with some additional expense, and Father De La Croix hoped that he and his party would reach their destination safely. They did on July 1, but Mother Duchesne was unaware of this when she wrote on July 18 to Mother Barat in a very serious vein:

> My last letter of June 10 must have given you real consolation, for in it I told you of the arrival we had so longed for—the arrival of our Fathers [the Jesuits]. But you must not think things are the same here as in France. Their interest in us is not the same at all, and already four times within this present month—they have told me they would have nothing to do with us if the highest authority did not impose it on them. . . . This condition still exists, and I depend on Divine Providence not to leave us without spiritual food. This would be all the harder to bear since no one would sympathize with us, thinking that we preferred the Jesuits to all other priests, and that three of those who could have stayed here and helped us need not have gone to Lower Louisiana.
>
> The plague of penury is felt down there as well as up here. Even

before I was informed of this with certainty, I realized how few
religious there are at Opelousas, how many more pupils they have
to care for than we, and how delicate Mother Xavier Murphy's
health is. So I considered it necessary to give them some help. Not
being able to go myself, I sent Sister Marguerite, the oldest among
us, with Sister Mary Ann Summers, an aspirant. . . . The departure of these dear Sisters leaves a great hole in our ranks, and
this is enlarged by the departure of Marguerite Tison, coadjutrix
novice, who had been with us about ten months, but has given us
continual doubts about her vocation. Her place has been filled by a
French-speaking postulant of 21 years who is gifted for studies
and seems very well disposed for religious life. Her name is Therese
Detchemendy.

In spite of our poverty I had to call a doctor from St. Louis to
treat Mother Octavie, who had such a repulsive ulcer close to her
mouth. It is much better now. . . . The other religious are fairly
well. All find consolation in the direction of the Father who is
both rector and master of novices. He is a Baltazar Alvarez, a real
Rodriguez. . . . We have had the honor of being severely criticized, and in order to undermine our work still further, report has
it that we are leaving here. There are people who wish we would.
We must devote ourselves more and more to the poor and to our
own perfection, happy to work among thorns and to be aided by
living models, imitators of him whom we propose to imitate. What
joy I have had cutting out and making up clothes such as I had
seen on our Holy Protectors! Here they are wearing the regular
Jesuit costume. . . .

When Father Van Quickenborne wrote to his Maryland superior a week later, "We *all* go in full Jesuitical dress at all times and
in all places," he might have added, "thanks to the industry, inge-
nuity, and self-sacrifice of the *Dames du Sacré Coeur*" who were
such a thorn in his side. To no one did this full Jesuitical dress give
greater satisfaction than to Mother Duchesne, and in her *Journal*
she recorded on July 31: "Feast of St. Ignatius, celebrated solemnly
in the church. On this day the Jesuits, all wearing their religious
costume, sang both Mass and Vespers. Father Neil preached and
the *Te Deum* was chanted after Benediction." Kneeling close to
the shrine of her beloved Jesuit patron, Philippine listened to the
deep tones of the men's voices, her tired eyes sightless with tears of
joy, her whole being surrendered to God in an elan of praise and
gratitude. What if her nuns no longer had their enveloping choir
cloaks to wear at liturgical services, or decent habits and under-
skirts to don on Sundays and feast days! What if the Father Supe-

rior was stern and gruff, strict and even severe! What if he spurned the extras she tried to supply for his novices' meals! He had been grateful for the clothing that she and her community had tailored for them, and she had a Jesuit director for herself, her nuns, and her novices—a privilege and a security for which she would never cease to thank God.

A new school year opened on September 1, after ten days of vacation. There were just eleven girls enrolled in the boarding school. In a long letter to Mother Barat that month Philippine touched on many topics but made only a passing mention of the school at Florissant. By reading thoughtfully both the lines and between the lines, one comes to realize more clearly what sort of person she was. Her character was of an extremely positive type— clear-headed, strong-willed, warm-hearted. Part of the charm of her personality lay in the fact that it was colorful, vivacious, enterprising, and often varied with unexpected slants and changing moods. Faith, courage, self-forgetfulness, and humor undiminished by her austerity—these were ingredients that made her life beautiful against the drab background of the frontier. As her constancy would have done honor to the martyrs, so too would her acceptance of the obscure and ordinary sufferings that purified her soul. And no one understood her better than the friend in France to whom she wrote on September 25, 1823:

> I do not know what delays your letters, or whether you have forgotten us. Never before have we been so long a time without news from you. The last letter from you was more than a year old when I received it, and that was six months ago. The most recent news we have had came from kind Father Barat. He must have had great consolation in learning that his Jesuit brethren are carrying on the missionary work he wanted to do in this sterile region. They alone could regenerate it, and to do so one must have a love of sacrifice, unwavering zeal, and sympathy to share the troubles of one's neighbors, all in the highest degree. We see all that in the angels on earth whom God has established here as our guardians. The more we see of the Father Rector, the more we appreciate his direction and recognize in him the spirit of his Father, St. Ignatius. I have found a Father Master. I no longer do as I please, but he is not yet satisfied with my efforts. He insists on deeper interior life, greater detail in the account one gives of one's soul—and you know I never have much to say! He gave a retreat of three days on the occasion of a prise d'habit [Therese Detchemendy's] and First Communion, which occurred on the 14th, feast of the Holy Name of Mary and of the Holy Cross. If it could only have been longer!

He has the power to persuade and move hearts. Seeing your daughters in such good hands, I am now quite tranquil as to their spiritual direction.

This Father would be quite capable of converting a kingdom, but up to this time he has accomplished very little. The whole country is going down hill. They [the Jesuits] are putting up a building on the Bishop's farm. I did my best to induce them to build nearer the church, but there was no getting them to do so. They do not want to be near us. I was deeply grieved at this, realizing fully that in spite of their courage we should often be without Mass in winter. They have their own chapel on the farm and our church is terribly deserted. The settlers in the neighborhood rarely come to it, and we have only eleven children. Of these just two are assured for the whole year, as their tuition was paid in advance. The others may be withdrawn any day.

So you see we are entirely in the care of Divine Providence, and it is very sweet to remain there in peace. We have never lacked what is absolutely necessary; we even have a little more money than formerly when we had more pupils. This gives me security for the future. Sometimes we have even been able to help the Fathers, who are much poorer than we. They are *suffering*, and how I wish some of the magnificence of France might be turned a little to their profit. Help will be slow in coming to them out here. One rich man has refused them a loan. They have cultivated some fields with great difficulty, and a freeze during this month of September has killed all their hopes of harvesting the most necessary crops. Here again one must adore God's Providence, and abandon oneself entirely to it. . . .

Monseigneur [Du Bourg], who sees everything through rose-colored glasses, has given the Fathers reason for concern. They were expecting more than they have received. And while I was talking to him about our loss of pupils, he told me he had an offer to make me of an establishment that would help us very much. It is at a place some 30 leagues above New Orleans on the river, which would make communication very easy. The people of the parish will build the convent. But he asks for *six choir nuns* from France, religious of tried *virtue* and *discretion*. . . . I replied that I did not think you would accept that foundation, that you had warned us not to expect any subjects or money in the near future, and that Mother Octavie's ill health has taken from me all idea of dividing this community. . . .

This establishment at *La Fourche*—the name of the place—would replace the one projected for New Orleans, where there would be little success for a long time, as commerce is in stagnation there and several epidemics have laid low that section of the country where God is so forgotten. We certainly could give a few subjects to Mother Xavier. Her bishop in Ireland considered her quite fitted to be a superior, and Mother Eugenie thinks she is capable of governing a house. Eugenie is the only one to whom I have expressed my thoughts. It would be time enough to speak of it to Monseigneur after we have your answer, which I beg you to hasten to send. . . .

Philippine was learning the doctrine of the cross from within her own heart. While suffering much from the criticism of people who should have appreciated her work, she felt more keenly the trials in which her sympathetic heart gave her a share. One of the severest was the frequent serious illness and the continual physical suffering of Mother Berthold. Another was anxiety with regard to the new project at La Fourche. The Bishop seemed to have set his heart on it and might persuade Mother Audé to undertake it without sufficient approval from France. There was also her interest in the Jesuits, whose poverty she longed to alleviate. As winter came on and cold winds whipped around the little brick convent, she knew that the suffering of those who were living in the Bishop's "chateau" was increasing and her own slender resources were diminishing. Her inability to help them was in itself a heavy cross.

Before the close of the year Philippine received a letter from her sister Amelie which roused her to the realization that many months had passed since she last wrote to members of her family. Money was scarce and postal rates were high, so she economized in ways that were particularly costly to her. She had made the perfect surrender of her dearest earthly ties, yet the love of this woman of strong and deep affections seemed to grow more tender and intimate with detachment. This is evident in the letter to Amelie de Mauduit on December 28, 1823. It was a brave letter in which she tried to depict favorably her drab frontier surroundings:

Perhaps your heart longs to know just where we live in the New World. On a map you would find the place on the right bank of the Mississippi, between the mouth of the Missouri and that of the Arkansas River. Each of these streams is more than 500 leagues long. We are further upstream than where the Ohio flows into the Mississippi on the left side. If your map is detailed, New Madrid and Ste. Genevieve may be marked; we are further north than these towns—they are really only villages. . . .

My health is very good and would allow me to do much more work, but I must be satisfied with what God gives me to do. I would not choose rest just because I fear pain, but it would be very sweet to have it before I die, for the natural element often insinuates itself into the holiest enterprises and makes us lose the merit of them. . . .

The village in which we live is five leagues from St. Louis, the principal town in the new state of Missouri, and about the same distance from St. Charles, our first place of residence, which has been for some time the capital of the State. . . . Our convent is built of brick and joins the newly erected parish church, which is also of brick. Monseigneur gave the land for the church and made us a gift of the property we own, consisting of a big meadow, a small woodland along a creek, and a garden with a courtyard and a pasture for our animals. We have about 100 chickens, 7 cows, 1 horse. We do not have to buy feed for the animals—we just open the gate and let them out; in the evening they all return to exactly the same gate without shepherd or shepherdess. I forgot to mention our five lambs and sheep and some very handsome geese. In good weather all the livestock graze in the common fields and woods, and in winter these animals have no shelter except a shed covered with thatch.

Philippine's first letter of 1824 gave details that are as so many strokes of an artist's pencil sketching the cartoon for a picture of frontier life. Describing the retreat she had made under Father Van Quickenborne's direction, she mingled humor and realism:

Those eight days were really a time of spiritual abundance. The devil was jealous, however, so he arranged for the delivery of nine large hogs that we had bought. They arrived on the second day of the retreat. As somebody had to take up the disgusting work of caring for them for two days, I was the willing victim. I took the work as a punishment for my lack of recollection. The following days were peaceful, and that happy retreat closed on the feast of the Immaculate Conception. We had five exercises daily and a conference. All were full of the most solid doctrine and were very devotional.

Realizing that the number of our pupils is bound to diminish still further, we are trying to make for ourselves all we possibly can. We make our soap, candles for both the house and church, altar-breads, our butter, woolen yarn, and cotton and linen thread. We sowed some cotton this year, but had no success with it, as the seeds were not suited to this climate. We hope to succeed better another year and to purchase a loom for weaving cotton and woolen cloth. We know how to dye in several colors—black, grey, and yellow. There is no expense in this as we obtain the dye from native wood or plants. We are going to plant some indigo to obtain a blue coloring matter which is easy to use. Salted pork, milk, vegetables from our garden make up our food supply. But I have written enough about the animal side of life. I beg you, pray to the Sacred Heart of Jesus for us, that he may assure us of one day possessing eternal life. There we hope to see you again someday.

In her first decade in America, Mother Duchesne suffered practically every hardship the frontier had to offer, except the threat of Indian massacre—poor lodging, shortages of food, drinking water, fuel, and money, forest fires and blazing chimneys, the vagaries of the Missouri climate, cramped living quarters and the privation of all privacy, and the crude manners of children reared in rough surroundings and without the slightest training in courtesy. The thing that seems to have astonished her most about the parish school children was their apparent ingratitude toward the nuns who tried to teach them. But these same children came at times with the best gifts they could offer—wild berries, nuts, honey, fresh eggs, even a side of bacon or a block of home-made soap, and Mother Duchesne poured out on them all the treasures of her mind and heart, longing to draw them to knowledge and love of Christ.

Another frontier hardship was the loneliness of remote places and a foreign tongue. But she had friends in and about Florissant, and her letters to Father De La Croix are filled with little news items about the parish of St. Ferdinand and the people who had been so deeply attached to him during his pastorate there. The drudgery of farm and household work wore down her strength, but she did not complain of this. Only the slowness of mail from France seemed to tax her patience.

This often kept her for months in ignorance of the sorrows that came to her family. The death of Josephine Perier's husband occurred in July, 1823, when the Baron de Savoye-Rollin was sixty-eight years old. Through more than twenty years he had been a loyal and generous friend of Philippine, and in his will he remembered her with a legacy. News of his death and of the legacy had come to her in a letter from Mother Barat, which reached Florissant just a week before the one in which Josephine herself told Philippine of her widowhood. Answering immediately, Philippine wrote on February 16, 1824:

I have just received your letter of last summer, and I have shared all your sufferings. My tears have mingled with yours, and this sympathy is shared by all those who, like myself, have benefited by your generosity. How often I have spoken to my companions about your goodness to us! And it is always very sweet for me to tell them about my first and dearest friend, of all she has done for me—and this is very apparent at our religious ceremonies—and of the life-companion who made her days so happy and who, because he shared her loving interest in me, was the first to help in opening my way to happiness.

My sentiments of gratitude have never diminished toward that happy couple who have been so blessed by God. You may judge, then, my beloved friend, how as I spoke to my Sisters of the blow that has struck you they shared your suffering and offered their most fervent prayers in union with you. But I have sorrowed most. And that last mark of kindness toward me on the part of your husband was certainly calculated to touch the tenderest chord in my heart. I offer for him in return the Masses, the Communions, the little we do in the line of good works, and I trust that God has already heard these many prayers offered for his intention to speed his entrance into a blessed eternity. Our Mother General wrote to me about you and about the legacy you turned over to her for us. She realizes its value as much as we do. . . .

The dear Lord has prepared much suffering for me, too, since the days when we opened our convent here with such a promise of success. The scarcity of money has caused the withdrawal of the majority of our boarding pupils—only 10 remain. This same circumstance, in conjunction with the persecution of the bishop in this corrupt town [St. Louis], has forced him to withdraw 400 leagues from us to New Orleans. But the hardest of all has been the fact that practically all the pupils who have left us and who seemed so fervent and thoroughly good, have fallen back into their former neglect of religion, as a result of their natural levity and the influence of pleasure and bad example. I still hope that their faith is not dead and that age, reverses, and other trials from the hand of God will someday bring them to repentance—that is my only hope for them. But we have also the opportunity of offering to those whom God will call to his service a haven in which to practice virtue far from the contagion of the world. This will be our most enduring work here, and it has already drawn a shower of blessings on us and on those who have joined us. Up to now there have been twelve religious trained here and at Opelousas. We have had other foundations proposed to us, but prudence warns us not to undertake them until we receive more nuns and more money from France. These cannot be sent just now. . . .

The progress of the Church in Missouri was a matter of vital concern to Mother Duchesne. The consecration of Bishop Rosati, which took place on March 25, 1824, at Donaldsonville, Louisiana, put an end to a peculiar situation that had arisen in the diocese. For more than a year he had been a bishop-elect, but only in December, 1823, had he received the papal brief appointing him coadjutor to Monseigneur Du Bourg. By rescript obtained from the Prefect of Propaganda the new bishop was not compelled to sever his connection with the Congregation of the Mission, but continued to reside as superior at St. Mary's Seminary.

After an informal visitation in parts of Louisiana, Bishop Rosati boarded the *Dolphin* and arrived in St. Louis on May 19. Two days later he was at Florissant. Uppermost in his mind and heart was the problem of missions among the Indians. As it was not possible to send missionaries into the Indian Country before the Jesuit scholastics had completed their training, Father Van Quickenborne had taken up Bishop Du Bourg's suggestion and opened, at Florissant, St. Regis Seminary for Indian boys. On May 11, two little Sauks, aged six and eight years, were received into the school. Three Iowa lads followed in June. Mother Duchesne was keenly interested in the new school and eager to help with its support. That her generosity towards the Jesuits had been reported to the Mother General is evident from a sentence or two in her next letter, but she did not dwell on the matter when she wrote to Mother Barat on June 10:

> Since my last letter, I have had the joy of receiving two letters from you in the same packet with letters from Mothers de Gramont and de Coriolis. All this news, which we had awaited so impatiently, was welcomed with the greatest eagerness. I beg you to thank Mother de Gramont very specially. In our poor little convent we experience month after month a succession of trials that always furnish the subject matter for our letters, so our respect, our attachment, and our loyalty are expressed in and to the Heart of Jesus, our Divine Master. I admit frankly that I am as much concerned about the Jesuit foundation as about our own convent, and even more. And I sincerely regret that I can do no more for them than the fly on the coach-wheel did to speed up the coach. They are severely tried, but they are not discouraged. The fine old spirit of zeal, courage, and poverty lives again fully in them.
>
> Alas, the poor Rector has no priest of the Society of Jesus to help him now, and he has far more than he can do. His companion, Father Joseph Timmermans, died suddenly a week ago as a result of exhaustion following on missionary labors during the Eastertide. . . . The Father Rector is in very poor health. Now he has four parishes on his hands, along with several remote missions, the

direction of the studies [of the scholastics], the buildings which
will not be completed before September because of lack of
funds, recurrent illness among the Brothers, Negroes, and Indians.
The first two savages are dangerously ill just now with whooping-
cough, which has carried off more than a hundred children in St.
Louis and causes severe suffering. I avow to you that when I see
how calm he [Father Van Quickenborne] is in the midst of the
many anxieties and occupations which pull him this way and that,
I cannot but conclude that his soul is stabilized in those high
regions of peace which are reached by way of complete self-renunciation and union with God. On Sundays he says two Masses,
preaches three times, presides at the catechism lessons, and hears
confessions at all intervals between services. To live in the neighborhood with saints has such an attraction for me that I delight in
our poor country place more than I would in the most brilliant
establishment in town. . . .

The letters Mother Duchesne sent to France can often be
understood only with reference to the ones she received from the
Superior General, and these were frequently more than a year
old when they reached Florissant, whether they crossed the ocean
by post or in the dispatch case of a French consul or the satchel
of a missionary or the pocket of an American gentleman bringing
his daughters home from school in France. In August, 1823, St.
Madeleine Sophie wrote affectionately:

I still cherish the hope of seeing you before I die. Now keep that
little overture to yourself; for if it is impracticable, there is no use
rousing similar hopes in others. I also want to whisper something
else in your ear, but it must be a secret. . . . We are thinking
seriously of petitioning for the Holy Father's approbation of our
order. Ask special prayers in your two convents, but keep the intention to yourself—or perhaps you could tell Eugenie, but bind her to
secrecy. Pray and ask prayers for me, your Mother. Believe me, I
often pray for you. Who, better than I, understands your many
anxieties and privations? I have so many of my own to offer to
God. What miseries there are in poor human nature? What patience and forbearance are required in those who direct souls! You
will find these virtues in the Heart of Jesus, my dear Philippine.
That Heart was opened for us; let us go to it and draw from it the
strength and courage of which we stand in need. In that Heart,
dear daughter, I remain very lovingly united to you.

Mother Duchesne responded affectionately, reassuringly, but
with all honesty:

We have just celebrated the feast of St. Mary Magdalen, recalling such dear memories. We tried to rejoice in spirit with all our Sisters who are gathered around you, trusting to the Heart of Jesus our love and our good wishes. Mass, Holy Communion, and a little extra recreation was all circumstances permitted by way of celebration, but we do not want any community in the Society to surpass us in heartfelt affection and devotion to our loved Mother.

I am afraid that news about the Catholic institutions in the United States may make you uneasy about us. But I beg you not to worry. We wanted the cross and not honor, poverty and not ease, the will of God and not our own. So even if the work is hampered, we can always gather from this circumstance the precious advantage of being in a situation that can unite us closely to Jesus Christ, our Divine Spouse. All those among us who wear the black veil are in these dispositions—Mothers Octavie and Lucille, Sisters Xavier, Regis, Catherine, and Ignace [Judith Labruyère], who made her first vows on the feast of the Sacred Heart. As for the novices, two are firm in their vocation; the third, a young Spaniard, wavers a good deal. If she leaves, that will make the third to do so in a year. Of all my trials that is the most painful, for I am to blame for this lack of perseverance, as it can be attributed to a lack of care and good example on my part.

I am eagerly awaiting the happy day that will set the seal of papal approbation on our Constitutions. . . . Since the death of Father Timmermans we are often without Mass, though the Father Rector goes far beyond his strength in his efforts for us. If he succumbs—and his health is not good—we shall really feel the weight of the cross. He no longer speaks hopefully of other priests coming to help him. It would be very desirable if preparations for the missions to the savages could at least get underway. The five Indian boys the Fathers have give them a great deal of trouble now. They do not like to wear clothes; they want to sleep nude; they do not want to work, they are very greedy. One day when they felt they had not been given enough meat for dinner they charged up to the scholastics' quarters, demonstrating that the skin on their stomachs was not stretched tight.

I do not know when we shall be able to take the Indian girls. We are all eager to do so, but this has been a year of disasters. The Missouri has flooded to a great width and carried off the farmhouses and cattle of many settlers and ruined the crops. There will be almost no grain or vegetables, and we shall soon have only three or four pupils. The main thing just now is to support our little community. . . . In this section of the country there are so many reverses of fortune, so much instability in enterprises, so little support to rely on, one would almost need the visible finger of Divine Providence pointing the way before one would change one's residence. Here at Florissant we are no longer afraid of starving to death, and that is something. If God takes from us the means of doing good, we must accept his will. Sometimes I think God upset all our original plans and our first school in order to build up gradually the important work of training the savages. One really must merit a share in that work by humiliations and other sufferings. Do not worry about us. Not a single one of us is discouraged. I am the most dissatisfied because I have reason to think I have turned God's blessing from our labors. You are the only one who can remedy this, Reverend Mother.

In the late summer of 1824, Mother Duchesne received from her superior general a letter suggesting that the convent at Florissant be closed, since it could scarcely be supported on the tuition of half a dozen pupils, and that Mother Duchesne and her companions go to Louisiana to staff the second establishment which both Bishop Du Bourg and his coadjutor had urged her to accept. In her reply one feels the soul of Philippine Duchesne at grips with circumstances that threatened to destroy the frail cion she had nurtured for five years in the Valley of Florissant, which in her case had so belied its name:

> I realize that I am not capable of advancing the Society's work in this country. I am the more convinced of this because the Father Rector has so often told me to ask you to send a new superior. I told him I had often begged you to do so, adding that you had not promised us anyone as you were pressed for religious to staff the new foundations in Europe; but I suggested that if my Sisters made the request, you might pay more attention to it, as the need would then be more evident. He did not like that suggestion at all, so I am left with the sorrow of thinking that I am not fulfilling my duties, that souls suffer in consequence, yet I have no hope that in the near future I shall be put in my proper place. I beg you to weigh before God the interests and needs of this part of your religious family, which is all the dearer to you because it is so insignificant and so suffering.
>
> Do not listen, I beg you, to Mother Eugenie's proposal to transfer me to Lower Louisiana in case of a new foundation there. I carry in my heart a great fear of spoiling things wherever I shall be, and this because of words I think I heard in the depths of my soul: "You are destined to please Me, not so much by success as by bearing failure." This may have been an illusion or a figment of a too lively imagination; still I cannot rid myself of this thought, and

so I dread undertaking anything, lest I should hinder its success. If I had only to follow the dictates of obedience and carry out the work planned by others, I should not have all this interior distress, but the condition in which we are living at present strengthens me all the more in this conviction. Since the bishop was obliged to withdraw from here, we have been completely forgotten; or if we are remembered at all, it is with contempt or a kind of pity that results from indifference. The children who have left our boarding school follow the broad road of pleasure, and we have almost no influence with those who attend the parish school.

The sufferings of the Jesuit Fathers are also ours. I hope they will succeed, but the difficulties, privations, ingratitude they are experiencing, all weigh heavily on my heart. It would be too great a joy for me to be able to contribute munificently to the important work they have begun. Divine Providence has arranged matters, however, by a secret means I cannot explain to myself, so that I have been able to lend or give them a little now and then. For although we have only seven boarding pupils, we still support three orphans, pay for the upkeep of the church, etc. And of our seven pupils, two pay nothing at all. The number may be further reduced, though I lowered the tuition to $100, or 500 francs, a year. There is simply no money in the country. All that is in circulation here comes from either France or Spain. And as pleasure comes before all else, there is not much left to pay for a good education. There may still be a few people who desire to assure this to their daughters, so we are keeping the large convent for that purpose, and we are going to try to organize in what was formerly the parish school building a boarding school more in conformity with the general poverty of the country, charging 180 or 190 French francs, but this is to be paid, not in money—that cannot be found in the country—but in corn, potatoes, lard, beef, and butter. This would furnish food for the girls, and they would take turns helping in the kitchen, milking the cows, doing the laundry, and cultivating the kitchen garden. They would also learn to spin and weave cloth for the convent and for the little Indian girls whom I hope we shall soon have—a very few at first, and we shall have to beg help to support them. . . .

One of my anxieties is the fact that it is so inconvenient for the Jesuits to care for our spiritual needs. The distance of their farm from the church causes them much trouble. The Father says Mass on alternate week days here, the other days at the farm, but on Sundays he is obliged to come at an early hour to hear confessions, and all his community have to come also—in the heat of the summer, in the downpouring rain, in the most severe winter weather. The creeks in floodtime are difficult and dangerous to cross and frequently quite impassable. They really ought to own our house, which is contiguous to the church. But if we give it to them, we have to begin all over again somewhere—and I am too lazy for such an effort. In St. Louis success would be uncertain and housing expensive. Here our cows cost us almost nothing, for they graze in the common meadows and return by themselves at milking time. Firewood is less expensive here than in St. Louis. I know of no one who would contribute enough to counterbalance such a sacrifice, and what would we do for spiritual help in St. Louis?

We are in complete obscurity here, but it is very sweet to lean for support on Divine Providence, awaiting each day what we need for soul and body. On the other hand, who knows but there may come a letter from the higher Jesuit Superiors forbidding the Fathers here to continue with our spiritual direction. I have had reason to fear this several times, but there is no way in which I can parry the blow, so I just live in complete abandonment. Even if there were several priests in the community, they would not want to reside near the convent, and given the farm as their residence, the inconvenience of the cross-country trip is serious. Our house stands between two creeks which are so swollen this year that our gardens and yard have been washed away several times. Coming to the church or returning home, the Father has had to let his horse swim across, and he has at times crossed on a floating log. One day we saw the horse come trotting up without saddle or rider. We looked at one another in terror, fearing the Father had been drowned. But after a while he arrived, wet from head to foot. His horse had thrown him. The young man who found the saddle said in an insolent tone, "What will you give me if I return it to you?" Such is the courtesy, the helpfulness, and the gratitude of his parishioners. . . .

While describing with simple accuracy the anxieties and external hardships that made up such a large part of life at Florissant, Mother Duchesne gives no hint of the extent to which she carried on personal mortification. Since, as time went on, things grew not easier but harder, she might have been expected to accept these God-sent circumstances as penance enough. But that was not Philippine's way with God. Possessed of great vitality of mind and body, she gave herself to the duty and privilege of serving Him with astonishing energy. She rose early to secure time for prayer before she gave the morning call to the community. Then she made her way to the sacristy to prepare for Holy Mass. The eve of a feast usually found her in the chapel or church late at night, decorating the altar and shrines. In her work as sacristan she ex-

perienced contact with the admirable qualities as well as the rough
idiosyncrasies of Father Van Quickenborne. There were clashes
between them at times; and when she held her ground, she knew
she was likely to suffer for her courage. Where principle was involved, she would not compromise, and on occasions she felt it
her duty to appeal to Bishop Rosati.

Mother Duchesne's day was long and arduous. Often keeping
the roughest manual work in the house for herself, she gave the
novices a rare example of loving God "not in words, but in deeds."
They reverenced her already as a saint, yet they were not shy
or ill at ease with her. The lesson of self-sacrifice which made up
the fabric of her day impressed itself indelibly on their souls. Her
position as superior would certainly have entitled her to a room
for her own use, but it also gave her the privilege of claiming for
this purpose the cubby-hole under the stairway leading from the
hall to the second story—a place of stifling heat in the summer,
of bitter cold in winter. In this as in so much else, she imposed on
herself privations and austerities which she would not have tolerated for her Sisters. When she gathered up the fragments of food
that remained after the children's meals, she kept them for her own
use at table; but when the children brought in nuts and fruits after
their rambles in the woods, she saw to it that the nuns had a share
in these.

As Mother Duchesne was the first in the household to rise in
the morning, she was the last to retire at night. After making the
rounds to assure herself that lights and fires had been extinguished
in the house and its dependencies, and windows and doors fastened
securely, she often sat down in the little parlor to write letters—
a relaxation from the tensions of the day and an outlet for a heart
that needed comradeship, to bring her *Journal* up to date, or to
balance the convent account book. This done, she would make
her way noiselessly to the chapel for a last hour of prayer—an
hour of soul-surrender to God. Before the tabernacle her awareness of the Divine Presence was almost tangible. Recollected in
her union with the Sacred Heart of Jesus, she made him more than
ever the term of all her endeavor, the inspiration and reality of her
life. In prayer she came to judge as he judges, to desire only what
he willed, to hand herself over without reserve to the Providence
of God. It was a complete and wholehearted surrender of self, yet
there was frequent need of renewal when particular circumstances
and renunciations called for a deeper plunge into the Sacred Heart.

Sometimes her absorption in prayer kept her kneeling upright for hours. Sometimes, wearied with work and anxiety, she fell asleep and woke only at dawn. "One night as she passed before the picture of St. Regis, she lifted a lantern to get a better view of her beloved patron and stopped to pray. Her eyes, heavy with sleep, closed, and she lost consciousness. Firm and erect she stood there until one of her religious, coming to look for her, found her asleep on her feet." She laughed off the incident, but Mother Mathevon tried after that to keep a discreet surveillance on her superior's nocturnal devotions. Her own fatigue, however, made the task hopeless.

The strain of life at Florissant was often relaxed by Philippine's delightful stories of Ste. Marie or Paris or St. Charles, or of her childhood and her family, by her sly humor within the community circle, by holidays and little "celebrations." Sometimes she took the novices for a ramble across the meadow and through the woods for relaxation and nature study, in which she found real delight. They came to know just what to expect when Mother Duchesne drew out her watch and examined it attentively, suggested a little rest on logs or stumps or boulders or in the tempting swings dropped by the wild grapevines, then took from her capacious pockets some *rafraichissement* in the form of apples or nuts or raisin cakes or a little chocolate.

Her gay spirit enlivened recreations and encouraged all to contribute to the conversation that added interest and amusement to community gatherings. She was constructive in her approach to character training, endeavoring to plant virtue rather than uproot faults; and she showed endless patience with difficult characters. Respecting the personality of each, she made no attempt to force souls into a common mould. She was too deeply imbued with the Society's spirit to adopt such a method.

She could give a severe reprimand when necessary, along with a suitable penance as a means of reparation, but she was never coldly unjust or partial. She knew she could ask more of some than of others, but all were conscious of her maternal love for them—a love so supernatural that it was always counted on and always the same. Very sensitive herself, she had great sympathy with those who suffered from depression or discouragement, and she offered no mere conventional compassion. She knew what it meant to be self-willed and headstrong, to shudder under humiliation, to cringe under pain, to lose all sense of proportion in the very intensity of one's fervor. So she was prepared to deal with her nuns and her novices in a cheerful, practical way, ready to listen, resolute and self-possessed, ready to joke a little and let things drop.

Her greatest consolation in this work of training souls lay in the tremendous confidence she placed in Father Van Quickenborne. The change in his attitude toward the *Dames du Sacré Coeur*, whose presence at Florissant he had at first resented, is described by Philippine, along with other things, in her letter to Mother Barat on November 24, 1824:

> Your letter expresses the acute suffering of your heart over the condition of Mother Octavie last year at this time. But ever since we had the idea of asking you to write to Prince Hohenloe, her condition has improved and she is practically well now. I cannot call it a miracle for medication was continued; but if it is one, I am inclined to attribute it to the Father Rector. He asked to see the troublesome sore and little by little he cured it. God made use of the medicine he used. It was mercury, used internally and externally over a long period of time. There remains only a scar at one side of the mouth, but the Father Rector uses it as a matter for humiliations; he asks her to let him see it, then he says "Oh, how ugly it is!" He has worked earnestly on that soul and with success, leading her in the way of renunciation, detachment, and humility.
>
> We are all very fortunate in having such direction. I much prefer poverty in the shadow of the Jesuits to the comforts of life under any other influence. For quite a while I feared this good fortune would not last, either because of their poverty or because of the rules of the Society of Jesus. But the Father Rector told me recently that the Father General has given the necessary permission. The Rector no longer keeps aloof from us and has gone so far as to say he might someday build us a little house at St. Charles, with a street between the Jesuit residence and ours. As soon as there are two priests in this group, I think one of them will reside there, as there is no priest north of the Missouri yet, and crossing the river was so dangerous this year, the Father Rector realizes the necessity. He was highly pleased with the choice of Monseigneur Rosati as our coadjutor bishop. He will be titular bishop very soon. Between them [Van Quickenborne and Rosati] confidence and esteem are mutual. The good bishop speaks earnestly of his love for the Society of Jesus. He solemnly baptized a little savage for whom Mr. Mullanphy and one of his daughters were sponsors. He gave minor orders to several of the young scholastics and has conferred the sacrament of confirmation.
>
> Since the bishop's departure for the Barrens, where he resides, the Father Rector gave a retreat to his sons, and then one to his daughters, as he has called our nuns several times. Last year we

were only *Mesdames!* This change of title delighted our Sisters, who had a perfect retreat. He spoke six times a day, for the four meditations, the consideration, and introduction. The points of meditation given in the evening were repeated in the morning. The good Father also gave his time generously to each one individually, though he and a companion were also making their retreat. I was in charge of the pupils, and Sister Catherine had the care of the orphans. She has had to walk a chalk line recently under Father Van Quickenborne's spiritual direction. . . . We have only five boarding pupils. One of them owes a year's tuition and board, and there is no hope of collecting a cent. Another is the youngest Miss Mullanphy [Octavie], who was placed here to prepare for her First Communion, after the Father Rector requested it. Monseigneur Du Bourg does not write to us any more. You know, I am sure, that he does not want a convent of the Sacred Heart in New Orleans. . . .

The Father Rector told me recently he had not money enough to buy a single hog, and pork makes up half of life out here. He has no altar for the chapel at the farm. A few days ago I received a worn-out piece of heavy cotton material with this note pinned to it: *Please mend this for me. It is our antependium for the altar. Miserere nostri.* Something more suitable that had come to us from our dear France replaced that ragged thing at once. Everything that has ever been sent to us has been useful and precious. We appreciate Father Barat's interest in us. I have often wanted to write to him recently, but I do not want to be importunate. The Father Rector here has his spirit and his method. This paints the most perfect picture of him, according to our heart. I cannot conceive how Mother Eugenie could advise our abandoning this house. Though it is poorer, I find it much happier here. The *essential spirit* can be preserved here always under the influence of this good spiritual direction. . . .

2. 1825—1826

ON NEW YEAR'S EVE a letter from Mother Audé informed Mother Duchesne that with the sanction of the Mother General she had accepted the offer of a foundation at St. Michael's, Louisiana, on the Mississippi River. Father De La Croix, the pastor there, had been working zealously to bring this about and had collected $4000 to finance the building of a convent. The negotiations had been carried on by Mother Audé and Philippine's reaction was generous and impersonal. As the school at Florissant was now practically empty, it seemed only reasonable to encourage a new beginning that offered every promise of success. But Mother Duchesne's heart was in Missouri, and she showed more enthusiasm for projects there than for those in the deep South when she wrote to Mother Barat on February 28, 1825:

> There is disillusionment in store for anyone who comes to this country in search of success, honor, pleasure. But those who desire only the good pleasure of God abide in peace even in the midst of failure, for God has not told us he requires us to be successful. All your daughters whom God has chosen for this mission are contented with their lot. . . . In my last letter I wrote you about the establishment of St. Michael's. They have already raised 75,000 francs in voluntary contributions. Mother Eugenie, who has accepted the offer, will have given you all the details. I think that house at St. Michael's will do much good in Louisiana and will support the one here in Missouri, where there are only three boarding pupils now. I expect Mother Eugenie this very month. She is coming to get some of the religious in our community. She cannot take anyone from Opelousas, and her departure will leave an enormous place to be filled there. It seems to me that Mother Xavier Murphy, who was well trained in France and who has gained the confidence of the people, is the person best fitted to replace her.
>
> Banking entirely on confidence in God, the Father Superior of the Jesuits has bought the house we formerly lived in at St. Charles. He wants to erect a church near it and has promised the people there that we will open a school. I am very much in favor of doing so, as we have so little to do here. St. Charles has a larger population, and the canal planned by the Government and already completed between New York and the Great Lakes is going to establish communication between the two oceans by way of the Missouri River. That will attract more settlers to its banks, and that is the region assigned to the Jesuits by Monseigneur Du Bourg. . . .

The arrangements for the foundation at St. Michael's were going forward swiftly—too swiftly for Mother Duchesne, who wrote in evident alarm to the Mother General on March 8, 1825:

> I have just received a letter from Monseigneur Du Bourg telling me of the arrival of Fathers Borgna and Dusaussoy. He adds that they have brought many letters for us from you. They will send them to me when they come up to the Seminary [at the Barrens]. . . . Monseigneur writes that you told Father Borgna I should go

to St. Michael's, and so he wrote that to Mother Eugenie. I do so wish he would go more slowly, for I think I should wait for a direct and positive letter from you before making so extraordinary and so unexpected a change. Quite a while ago you named Mother Eugenie for the foundation in New Orleans. Since that cannot be made because Monseigneur does not want it, St. Michael's takes its place. Mother Eugenie is well known in all that part of the diocese. She will build up a good reputation for the house and she is quite capable of sustaining it by her zeal, her prudence, and her talent for handling children. I have already written you all my thoughts on that score, especially in my last letter of February 28. Here, more than in France, the old and the ugly are held in low repute. I grow more unsightly every day. Gray hair, no teeth, horribly roughened hands, all make me in no way suitable to cut a figure in that fastidious section of the country. They are all right here in the village where, indeed, they call me quite affectionately *"poor devil."*

Philippine certainly quoted this good-humoredly. God had planted in her soul a personal contempt for the world and the things it esteems, yet she knew they could be used effectively for furthering the interests of the Sacred Heart. Eugenie Audé's talents and abilities were frequently the theme of her praise, and she was sincere in urging the Mother General to entrust to her the enterprise at St. Michael's. There was a further reason, and Philippine continued:

If I should dwell on the spiritual side there would be still greater disadvantage in sending me. So I really think Eugenie is the only one suited to be superior at St. Michael's. Mother Xavier Murphy is the one for Opelousas, where she is known and loved. As to this community, I realize full well that I should be in the last place. But the Reverend Father, with whom I discussed the matter, said that, if such a change were made, this house would soon be closed. True, it is miserably poor, but for that very reason it is dear to me, and it was never before so favored, as far as spiritual help is concerned. The Reverend Father now takes a great interest in it, and in time we will develop the work for Indian girls, which we so desire. I have even been told by him that if Mother Octavie or another religious whom he named was at the head, neither he nor any of his brethren would take any more interest in the house.

I am simply telling you what I think I should. When one vegetates in this country, one must be satisfied with one's lot. Except for food, we are not in want of anything, not even clothing. We can get some help from the South. And if, as our Rule says, the poor should be preferred to the rich, we have no reason to envy

Opelousas. We care for as many souls as they, and we shall always have more novices. You know Mother Eugenie has trained only one novice so far, and here ten have persevered. This number will increase when the new type of spiritual direction has overcome the old prejudices. . . .

Mother Audé came up to St. Louis on the steamboat *General Brown* and arrived at Florissant on March 21. "She brought us $160 from various friends in France and America and a supply of provisions from the kind Ursulines," Philippine noted in her *Journal*. "She informed us of the prosperous condition of her convent [at Grand Coteau], where there were 27 boarding pupils, and also told us the collection for St. Michael's has amounted to $7000 in free gifts." There was no temporal prosperity at Florissant for her to boast of, but there were spiritual riches such as Eugenie had not enjoyed since her departure in 1821: Palm Sunday, with the blessing of the palms and the liturgical procession, the Passion chanted at Mass by the rich voices of the young Jesuits; *Tenebrae* chanted by Jesuits and nuns in church and choir alternately as dusk fell in the valley on Wednesday, Thursday, and Friday of Holy Week; adoration on Holy Thursday kept up by the Jesuits during the day and by the nuns at night. On Easter Sunday morning Matins and Lauds were recited at half past five, followed by meditation and an early Mass with a First Communion ceremony for children of the parish, who spent the day at the convent, regaled at both breakfast and dinner on the supplies received from the Ursulines.

But there was an unexpected and triumphant joy for Philippine when, in the late afternoon of April 6, Father Van Quickenborne arrived at the convent and presented to her two little "savages" as the first pupils of the "Female Indian Seminary" she had dreamed of opening. Housed in a little building by themselves and cared for by Mother O'Connor, these little Indian girls became Philippine's delight and a shining jewel in the crown of Mother O'Connor.

On April 17, the little church at Florissant witnessed the first solemn profession ceremony of a Religious of the Sacred Heart in America when Mathilde Hamilton made her final vows, receiving the gold ring of perpetual espousals and the silver cross of full membership in the Society. With her Mary Ann O'Connor pronounced her first vows as a strengthening preparation for the labor she would expend and the mortification she would practice in caring for the Indian children. Mother Duchesne wrote of all this in a happy vein to Mother Barat on April 23:

> Mother Eugenie reached here on March 21 and will leave again about the first of May with young Mother Xavier Hamilton, who will be a great help to her in making the new foundation. As I have begged you for a long time to shorten her five years of aspirant-ship, and also as I received from you her profession cross, I thought I was sufficiently authorized to allow her to make her final vows on Good Shepherd Sunday. The Father Superior presided at the ceremony and preached a fine sermon. The other Hamilton sister, for whom you also sent a profession cross, is not yet twenty-one years of age, but she begs you to allow her, as soon as she reaches that age, the same happy privilege as her sister, who is our first American professed member and the first choir nun chosen to help in a foundation. With her will also go Sister Ignace [Labruyère], an excellent coadjutrix aspirant, and Sister Aloysia (Timon), an American coadjutrix novice. These are the three Mother Eugenie has chosen, and they are all we can possibly give, for we now have three groups of boarding pupils—those who pay 900 francs, those who pay 179 francs, and the Indian girls who have begun to come at last. We put them under the care of an Irish religious who made her first vows on Good Shepherd Sunday. She speaks English, is about 40 years of age, and is a person of solid virtue, so she is the best qualified among us for this work, which occupies part of her time during the day and keeps her separated from us at night in the Indian school house. The little savages call her *Mamma*, and they all dance around her wherever she takes them, whether to the cows or the chickens or the garden. We let them spend their time in these active occupations, for they cannot endure a sedentary life. . . .

During the weeks immediately following the departure of Mother Audé and her companions, Mother Duchesne was particularly concerned about the Indian school. She was eager to do her share of begging and more eager to see aid given to the Jesuits. When friction arose between Father Van Quickenborne and Bishop Du Bourg she was caught in a conflict of loyalties that was unpleasant for her; but when she found herself involved in a misunderstanding with Father Van Quickenborne himself, she paid bitterly for her zeal. On June 8 she wrote to Mother Barat in part:

> If Father Niel, pastor in St. Louis, comes to you to beg financial help, will you please state the purpose of what you give him—whether for the Jesuits or for ourselves, since we are carrying on

work for the Indians. They now have ten boys, and we have six girls. The government has appropriated a sum of money for the civilization of the Indians. As the Secretary of War is in charge of this, I am writing to him to ask support for four teachers and money to help erect a school building which will cost at least three thousand francs. The policy of the government is to give aid and encouragement only to associations which have means to found institutions. So even if he gives us something, it will be but a fraction of our expense. But we must rely on Divine Providence and not do less for God than the Protestants, who have schools for the Indians in many sections of the state. . . .

Philippine's letter to the Secretary of War drew upon her head the wrath of the Jesuit Superior. Of course the letter was never put into the mail as she later recounted, but in early June of 1825 they were both sick; both were weary and overworked; both were strong-willed and hot-headed; and both were zealous and holy religious. His changing judgments on her as a superior must have been particularly hard to bear, perhaps even baffling, for she relied on his spiritual discernment. Had she been less frank and confiding, she certainly would have escaped some hard blows. Perhaps the severest humiliation she ever received occurred as a consequence of a lively argument they carried on in the sacristy one summer day. There was question of some minor change in the arrangement of the sanctuary. Tradition says it was all about a little piece of carpet on which she wished him to stand, and the chronicle runs as follows:

Both held to their views on the subject with that tenacity which is sometimes to be observed in the saints when there is a question of what is for the greater glory of God. Father Van Quickenborne went so far as to threaten to have the altar removed, as he said he had given it to the church. "In that case," replied Mother Duchesne, "I shall take the tabernacle, which belongs to me." An altar without a tabernacle, or a tabernacle without an altar—either condition would have been embarrassing—so very embarrassing that the matter rested there. But the feast of the Sacred Heart was at hand. On the eve Mother Duchesne presented herself for confession, but instead of absolution which she had come seeking, she heard this terrifying sentence: "Tomorrow you will not renew your vows," and the shutter closed, putting an end to her pleading. Next day the poor superior, in order to avoid comments, could only feign illness and remain in bed instead of leading the community to the altar rail for the renovation of vows. When she was sure they were all in the chapel and no one would see her, she crept noiselessly across the hall and prostrated herself behind the chapel door, weeping silently. When Mass was ended, she went back to her cubbyhole, to spend a day of agony and shame. And only after a week of suffering was she accorded the absolution she had sought.

This is the story that must be kept in mind as one reads Philippine's letter of July 3, 1825. The original is not extant; the existing copy is mutilated, but the missing portion may be supplied from the authentic source quoted above. The *Journal* entries for this period make no allusion to personal suffering on the part of Mother Duchesne, though they do mention Father Van Quickenborne's illness on, and immediately after, the feast of the Sacred Heart, and Mother Duchesne's recovery on the feast of St. Francis Regis. The letter cited below is stamped with the affectionate interest, earnest sympathy, and ardent zeal that always marked her attitude toward the Jesuits:

> Tomorrow we celebrate the feast of *Independence* in this country. There will be rejoicing among all social classes and in all regions, for the Catholics do not forget that this day gave them freedom of worship. Up to that date (1776), at least so I am told, anyone could kill a Catholic with impunity in Virginia. As for myself, I shall anticipate July 22 and celebrate in my heart now and always the treasured and inspiring *dependence* that binds me to you. Yes, I shall bless God for it to my dying day, and we shall be united in spirit to all the good wishes addressed to you on the feast of St. Magdalen.
>
> In my recent letters I told you my health was failing. I did not know myself, I was so changed. On the eve of the feast of St. Regis I was very weak, but I did not ask for anything or pray for a cure. Then on the day of the feast I found myself in my former state of good health. And in order that I might recognize with certainty the hand that had touched me, everything just then should have contributed to sap my strength; very great heart-suffering, troubled future, disturbed conscience, ill success, difficulties as superior, long and anxious waiting for news from our Sisters who left on the feast of the Ascension, prostrating heat. It only remains for me to make better use of the time ahead. Still, as this is uncertain, I beg you to let me know your wishes with regard to the government of this convent in the future. The work for the Indians is at last under way; since it is so dear to your heart, I trust you will decide to send here a person with a good *head* and one young enough to learn English.
>
> I presume that the feast of the Sacred Heart was celebrated with

pomp in the Paris convent this year. It was a very different matter here. I could not even have communion on this, our most solemn feast, and in consequence I could not renew my vows in public. I could do so only in the depths of my heart. . . . Low Mass, no sermon; none the following Sunday when the feast was celebrated in the church, which is dedicated to the Sacred Heart. When the choir was still singing the Kyrie they saw that the priest had finished reading the Epistle. He felt indisposed, so the rest of the Mass was in silence. . . . One priest cannot serve four parishes, two communities, and the sick people living at great distances from here. His life is in continual danger. Lately, while crossing a river on horseback, he was thrown from his horse, but he held on to the reins until his feet touched the river bank. On his way back the water was even higher, and though he was on horseback he was drenched from the shoulders down from the splashing of the horse as it galloped eagerly to get home. . . .

I intended writing to the Secretary of War to obtain help for the Indian girls. But the Father Superior, who is acquainted with the government's intention of putting the boys and girls together here as in other *seminaries* of this kind, told me that I should be cutting his throat if I did so. That was enough to stop me. He wrote instead and stressed the advantage of separate education for the two sexes. I have small hope of success. The Presbyterians watch keenly for any advantage, and they will make an outcry against the novelty of the plan.

Through the weeks that followed the writing of this letter Mother Duchesne had frequently to record in her *Journal* "No Mass," for illness prevented Father Van Quickenborne from making the trip from the Jesuit farm to the church. When Bishop Rosati became aware of this condition of affairs, he sent Father Leo De Neckere to officiate at St. Ferdinand and give the Rector an opportunity to recuperate. But this arrangement displeased the irascible Rector. Yet Mother Duchesne judged him leniently. No one knew him better than she did. For two years now she had stood almost daily at the sacristy window in the early morning and watched for his figure to appear. At times dust-covered, perspiring, and weary almost before the day had begun, at other times drenched with rain or chilled to the bone with snow and sleet, the priest would be seen tramping across the fields, his black cassock flapping as he walked. Or he might come on horseback, his voluminous cloak held tight under his knees and billowing out around him like a balloon. She learned to interpret his moods— gruff and taciturn, or cordial and interested. She had suffered

keenly under his sharp criticism, his brutal frankness, his unexpected rebuffs, and she had grasped hopefully at the judgments he
expressed as to her incompetence, repeating them to her Superior
General in the belief that they might bring about her release from
the office of superior. In every letter addressed to her from the
Mother House in France she looked for that news, but instead,
there came in September letters written many months before in
which St. Madeleine Sophie spoke her mind and heart as only the
saint could do. In the letter of January 10, Philippine read:

> Now a word regarding your request to be relieved of the office
> of superior. If you will just reflect a little, you will realize that this
> is impossible, for I have no one to put in your place, and if you
> make a third foundation, how can you hope to be relieved of su-
> periority? Besides, my dear daughter, would someone else do
> better than you? I think not. She might, perhaps, have more virtue,
> but certainly less experience and less self-diffidence. In a spirit of
> zeal for the work confided to you and for the salvation of souls,
> can you not make greater efforts to acquire the virtues you lack?
> When you have such powerful motives for advancing in perfec-
> tion, what can hold you back? Alas, I have little right to preach to
> you. I need this lesson far more than you do, my dear Philippine.
> How much reason I have to reproach myself! Still I must con-
> tinue to carry the burden, and it grows heavier every day. Then
> let us both put our trust in the Heart of Jesus. He will uphold our
> weakness, repair our foolish mistakes, and bring good out of them.
> If he has always acted in this way toward your Mother, who is so
> unfaithful, so blameworthy, what will he not do for you?

And in a letter written three months later the saint told her
self-diffident daughter:

> Now, my dear daughter, you are going to have three convents in
> America. You realize that two of these are entrusted to young
> superiors who will need guidance. The enormous distance that
> separates them from us makes it impossible for me to assume their
> guidance without serious ill-consequences. You have experienced
> the fact that long delays in correspondence bring about many
> abuses. So it is only fitting that the eldest of those to whom I have
> confided the American mission should be in charge of the whole
> of it. Now to you, my dear Philippine, I entrust the direction of
> these three establishments. Though we have not adopted the term
> *provincial* in the Society, you must function as a provincial in
> Louisiana. You will begin to groan again at that new responsibility,
> but God will help you bear it. And, moreover, since you are living
> close to our Fathers, they will give you advice, and indeed it is

from that source that there flows the fresh stream that waters our poor labors.

There followed the welcome information that the loan of 6000 francs, borrowed by Mother Barat in 1822 to satisfy Mr. John Mullanphy, had been paid off by Madame de Granville. Gifts from her brother, from Josephine, and from other benefactors in France had been a substantial aid to Philippine in the past year. Mother Barat added another piece of information that was of vital interest to her American families:

> Our affairs in Rome have met with delay. The main work is done, but several articles in our Constitutions present difficulties, especially the matter of cloister. We insist, however, that we shall not have *grilles*. Now I ask you, where would you be [in America] if you were fettered by that impediment? Keep on praying, for the matter is so important.

On September 14 Philippine answered, first revealing anxieties that were disturbing her peace of mind, then with greater emotional intensity accepting the Mother General's decision that was so repugnant to her. Years before she had offered herself wholly to God, and he had taken her at her word. Perhaps this accounts for that sense of disgust with self that appears so frequently in her letters.

> This Feast of the Cross [she wrote] recalls a day when our little girls at Grenoble acted out a little play for you on the love of the cross. You yourself had asked them to, and we enjoyed it as a recreation. Experience teaches that always and everywhere the drama of crosses may be renewed. Personal crosses are light in comparison with those that are a drawback to our work. And I see so many of this kind, they actually hinder me from desiring death. That desire is a delightful sentiment when one is prepared and when work will not suffer by our loss. While I do not love life, I do love the houses we have founded, and I realize that the least important person—if she is sincerely devoted to a house—is a support necessary to uphold it. . . . The religious most essential to the good of this house is Sister Regis Hamilton. She has to take on all the heaviest and most unpleasant employments, one after another, because she is so solidly virtuous and courageous. But she is greatly needed for the classes, being the only one having a good English pronunciation—a thing so highly prized here that nothing else is considered comparable to it. What I tell you is true of the other houses and may prove to you, notwithstanding Monseigneur Du Bourg's opinion, that good coadjutrix Sisters, well trained and

courageous, humble and ready to supervise the kitchen, would be quite as useful to us as choir nuns and would give the latter a chance to devote their time to the classes. . . . The school here is rising from its ruins. For a while we had only four pupils; now we have eleven, and several others have applied. I do hope all will run so smoothly, there will be no cause for complaint. . . .

I am far from capable of holding the office you impose on me. I bow my head in submission, but I realize my incapacity. If I were at the source of light, near a Father Varin, or a Father Perreau, or a Father Barat—but here all thought is but confusion when I want to do good, poor blockhead I am—old, without talents, without lovable qualities, without virtue. Beg from these dear Fathers I have named an intention in their holy prayers for their Brothers and Sisters, for our white children and our Indians. God alone can see the outcome of our work, but there are terrible obstacles in the way of success. I desire to live only in order to sacrifice my life to the hardest labor. I realize that repose is not for this life. One must put one's body on the rack and one's heart in the wine-press. If I can be useful in the least little work for the glory of the Sacred Heart, I am willing to spend a long age here, without success, without friends, as my only means of imitating the Sacred Heart.

On October 27, Philippine recorded in her *Journal* the arrival of Father John Theodore de Theux and Brother John O'Connor, who had at last come to the aid of Father Van Quickenborne. This assured daily Mass again for the religious and the liturgical ceremonies that were so dear to Mother Duchesne's heart. There were other joys to record: in November the opening of the convent at St. Michael's by Mother Audé, with Mother Mathilde Hamilton as her assistant, Sisters Mullanphy, Labruyère, and Timon from Florissant and three choir novices from Grand Coteau, among them Aloysia Hardey; the installation of Mother Xavier Murphy as superior at Grand Coteau, with Mother Carmelite Landry as assistant and treasurer; and in December the entrance into the Florissant novitiate of Anna Shannon and Suzanne McKay, both former pupils of that convent. Of importance, too, was a letter from Bishop Rosati acquainting Philippine with another young Irish girl, Eleanor Gray, who would one day become a prominent member of the Society of the Sacred Heart.

Like a Christmas gift from Divine Providence came a packet of mail from France to Mother Duchesne, including a letter from Mother Barat answering her own letter of June 8. This exchange of correspondence within little more than six months was a vast improvement over the long delays they had experienced in the past, though it was by no means permanent. To Philippine's satisfaction the Mother General renewed her sanction of the projected reopening of a convent at St. Charles, but she made it clear that no help could be sent to America within a year or even eighteen months. The news that a general council of the Society would meet in 1826 inspired the unselfish missionary letter Philippine addressed to the holy foundress on December 27, 1825:

> I am delighted to know about the council that will meet in the spring. Next to getting us the three more religious we so desire, the most helpful suggestion for us would be to propose that a little annual fund might be assured us by a donation from each house, taken from the alms for the poor given by the children. This could be used to support one or two priests in the Missouri missions. A vast field is opening up here for their zeal, and many are eager to work in it. But a superior cannot send out his missionaries to face almost certain death from starvation or the diseases that result from it. The Father Rector suggested that I ask you for an annual fund drawn from our boarding schools or those of the Jesuits. Assured of this, he will take measures to extend the missions. So much good would come of it. . . . Mother Xavier Murphy thinks M[onseigneur] D[u Bourg] is planning to return to France. It is astonishing how this country discourages people. This only goes to show that an association of some kind is needed to support the missions. Poor America! When one thinks that between here and Canada and to the west as far as the Pacific Ocean there is not a single church, not one priest, it is just heart-breaking.

The New Year opened with the usual distribution of prizes for scholastic achievement, or good conduct, or encouragement, as the case might be, in each of the three little schools—Indian, parish, and boarding school. Then came the thrilling days when the first two Jesuit scholastics were ordained at the Barrens and returned for Mass at Florissant—John Baptist Smedts on January 29 and Peter John Verhaegen on March 11. It was like a personal triumph for Philippine. On the First Friday of March, moreover, Anna Shannon received the habit and white veil, and one month later Suzanne McKay's reception took place. Now Sisters Stanislaus and Aloysia, as they were called, began their formal novitiate training. They were earnest, fervent, and mature beyond their years, and their progress was a consolation to Mother Duchesne.

Father Van Quickenborne's project of a church at St. Charles seemed to be taking definite shape, so Philippine consulted Bishop

Rosati on the matter of a convent there. His gracious reply giving
"all the permissions necessary on my part" had not reached her
when she wrote to Mother Barat on February 18, 1826:

> I have twice acknowledged the receipt of the list of permissions
> you sent. You have divined all that could put us at our ease and
> make less of a trial the enormous distance that separates us from
> you. Only two points trouble me greatly. The first regards myself
> and is the responsibility to watch over three houses when I manage
> just one so wretchedly. My heart yearns more than ever for soli-
> tude, and I have neither silence nor solitude. I am growing old; my
> health is declining. I should weep in reparation for many years of
> my life, especially those of my religious life. I accept the work as
> penance, but it robs me of the spirit of prayer. If you only give
> heed to my request, I shall gladly obey anyone whom you may
> give us as superior.
>
> The foundation at St. Charles will not take place immediately,
> for the Reverend Father says he will not send a priest there until
> the stone church is built, and the stone is still in the quarry. I
> believe that if we follow the desire of the Pastor of St. Louis and
> open a school in that town, it will be the only means of supporting
> ourselves with security in this part of the country.
>
> The plan of going to St. Louis pleases me all the more since the
> suggestion came from you. I wish we could keep just a parish
> boarding school here, at 180 francs a year. The first-rate boarding
> school at 500 francs a year will need a suitable building in St. Louis
> and its location will depend on what we can find. Monseigneur
> Rosati is planning to bring the Jesuits to St. Louis. The Father
> Rector has not told me all, but he has suddenly decided to allow
> two of his young deacons to be ordained. One of them preaches
> well. I have no doubt but that the project will go through—an-
> other reason for desiring to found a house of our own in St.
> Louis. . . .

Projects were moving ahead rapidly and getting somewhat
complicated. Father Francis Niel was using his influence with
Mother Barat for the founding of a convent and school in St.
Louis. Bishop Rosati was urging the Jesuits to begin work in St.
Louis. Father Van Quickenborne had his heart set on a new church
and convent at St. Charles. Mother Duchesne had the bishop's
permission to cooperate in the work at St. Charles, and also the
Mother General's, and was being urged by her to consider the St.
Louis foundation as of prime importance. But she had neither
money nor nuns for a foundation anywhere. On March 1 she made
this entry in her *Journal:* "The Father Superior has purchased from

Madame Duquette the house and property where we lived in 1818. He is going to make all arrangements to build a stone church there."

This matter is not referred to again until after Monseigneur Du Bourg's last visit to Missouri. On April 26 he was given a little reception by the children of the boarding school at Florissant. On the thirteenth of the month he baptized six Indian children and confirmed sixty persons of the parish or neighboring missions. Then he made a trip to St. Charles with Father Van Quicken-borne, returned to St. Louis, and set out for Europe, "after making over to the Jesuit Fathers the Church of St. Ferdinand, reserving for us in perpetuity," noted Mother Duchesne, "half of the tribune, the first sacristy, and the opening of our chapel on to the church."

During the summer of 1826 it was becoming apparent that the schools for Indian children at Florissant were doomed to be short-lived. This was a poignant sorrow for Philippine, for the goal of her venture to America had seemed in sight. There was compensation, however, in the increased enrollment in the boarding school. Twenty-four pupils filled the little dormitory and crowded the two or three classrooms. Among them was Ellen Mullanphy Chambers, a grandchild of John Mullanphy—"*La petite Chambert,*" as Mother Duchesne called her. With the larger school came increased anxieties. A season of high water had set in, and once more the convent was isolated by the flooding streams that encircled it. There was illness among nuns and children, but worst of all was the condition of Mother Octavie. She had been stricken with fever early in April, and for nearly three months she was in a most pitiable condition, which Mother Duchesne's efficient nursing could not relieve. Another sorrow came from Grand Coteau with the shocking news of the death of Sister Mary Ann Summers, first Religious of the Sacred Heart to die in America, and scarcely out of her teens. But from St. Michael's there were glowing accounts of progress, prosperity, and multiple activities.

In contrast, there were times when the loneliness of life at Florissant weighed heavily on Philippine, when the way of the spirit was particularly rough, and she knew she must travel so much of that way alone. The sense of God's love was often lacking to her, and seldom did she find true and congenial companionship in America. There was no softness or sentimentality in her make-up, but a depth of affection that expressed itself lovingly, tenderly, as we know from the letters that traveled thousands of miles to loved ones of her own family or of the religious family

to which she belonged. Her yearning for news from home betrayed itself in a little note she sent to Josephine in August of this
year, after she had learned of the fire that had destroyed a huge
section of the chateau of Vizille, where Augustin Perier and his
family had their country home. She wrote sympathetically:

> Have I been remiss in the duty I owe you, dearest Cousin? Since
> your letter telling me the sad news of your widowhood I have
> had no news from you. Indirectly I learned of your moving from
> Paris to Grenoble, and of the unfortunate accident that caused a
> considerable loss to two of your brothers. I have shared deeply all
> these happenings, and not being able to express my sentiments to
> anyone but our Lord, I have talked to him very frequently about
> you all. I trust he has sent these trials only to raise your souls
> higher. We may not understand his will for us in time, but in eter-
> nity the veil will be withdrawn and we shall see that He acted
> only for our happiness. . . . Our three American houses are carry-
> ing on their works. The faith is making progress; the erection of
> new dioceses and of Catholic boarding schools will serve, I hope,
> to spread it more and more. We have more non-Catholics than
> Catholics in our little school, and the same is true in several convent
> schools recently established. Remember me to all our loved ones—
> they are all dear to me—and be assured of my deep affection for
> you. . . .

In the autumn of 1826, Mother Duchesne received from St.
Madeleine Sophie a somewhat disconcerting letter, urging her to
take steps at once to open a convent and school in St. Louis. Father
Francis Niel had called several times at the Mother House in Paris
and had painted so rosy a picture of prospects and advantages in the
town to which he had no intention of returning that the Mother
General wrote with enthusiasm:

> Yesterday [June 15, 1826], my dear Daughter, I saw Father Niel,
> the excellent pastor of St. Louis. He has returned from Rome, and
> I think we shall keep him for some months in France. He is con-
> sidering seriously the establishment of a convent in St. Louis, and
> after all the details he has given me of conditions there, I have not
> the slightest doubt that such a foundation is necessary. The motives
> and reasons I need not recount to you. You are on the spot and so
> you ought to know and understand them far better than I. If, then,
> my dear Daughter, after weighing the matter before God, you are
> inclined to make this foundation, here is what Father Niel proposes
> to me: buy a piece of land in St. Louis for ten or twelve thousand
> francs; on this you can build. The good pastor will find means, he

says, to aid you. You will have as a fund about 6000 francs which Mother Audé has drawn on me in New Orleans as a loan. I give you that for St. Louis, with about the same amount which our parting missionaries will bring you. I do not want this business undertaken before Father Niel's return. The property, however, must be secured as soon as possible, lest the desirable site be sold to others, or the price be raised. There are two places available, I understand—the one rather small, the other large. I prefer the latter, but before concluding the purchase you must inspect the property. . . .

Philippine was baffled by these instructions. She had not been looking for property in St. Louis. She seems to have had no idea on what land Father Niel was building the new institution as he talked to the Superior General. His begging tour in Europe had not been successful, and where else would he find means to aid her? The academy at St. Michael's had been opened but six months, and Mother Audé was not yet able to refund the 6000 francs. The arrival of religious from France, "the parting missionaries" referred to, was problematic; as a matter of fact, they reached St. Louis twelve months after this letter. From Louisiana Mother Duchesne was receiving news that weighed on her. The illness at St. Michael's was God's own gift of the cross, but the prospect of no chaplain at Grand Coteau called for a representation to Bishop Rosati, administrator of the diocese. She also informed him about the St. Louis project, which presented such difficulties to her.

Bishop Rosati acceded to Mother Duchesne's petition regarding Grand Coteau and answered that Father Rosti would remain there "*provisionally*, that is to say, until the time when I can replace him by another priest who speaks both languages." He also added: "An establishment of your Society in St. Louis will do much good here in every way. So I must second the views of your Superior General." Meanwhile Philippine had written to Mother Barat:

> The little house at St. Charles cost the Reverend Father 3,500 francs, for which I told him we would reimburse him if we reopen the convent there. But work on the church has stopped, and there may be a lawsuit with the contractor. And how can we go there without a priest? Father Van Quickenborne could easily station one there now. I do not know why he will not do so. Far from rejecting St. Louis, however, I am eager to go there because of the many children who can never attend boarding school and who would be day pupils. A Paris newspaper announcing the resignation of Monseigneur Du Bourg has reached us. That means a great

loss for this ungrateful diocese that made him suffer so severely. . . .

Perhaps the most significant event ever recorded in Philippine's *Journal* was the approbation of the Society of the Sacred Heart by Pope Leo XII on the feast of the Sacred Heart in 1826. The news, announced in a circular letter in July, reached Florissant on November 9, and Mother Duchesne gathered her community in solemn conference to read to them the message which the Foundress clothed in words well calculated to renew loving fidelity to the rules which now had become doubly sacred to them. Mother Duchesne wrote the good news immediately to Bishop Rosati and received an answer that was gracious and encouraging: "I am deeply grateful for the happiness that Providence has sent you, and for your kindness in letting me share your joy. A house of your Society in St. Louis will be completely in accord with my desires." Meanwhile she poured out her heart to Mother Barat at great length and in the buoyant style that always revealed an upsurge of joyous enthusiasm in her soul:

> Your letter of September 2, 1826, brought me the purest joy I can have here on earth, next to that which the soul experiences in its union with Jesus Christ in Holy Communion. We had the foreshadowing of the happy day of our approbation when Pope Pius VII favored us with his special blessing, and later when our present Holy Father so kindly sent us his blessing through one of our missionary priests. But what a joyous thing it is to have secured that approbation we had almost despaired of! How it obliges us to tend to perfection! And how ashamed it makes me, to realize what I am, after the many favors with which we have been overwhelmed! They have not even made me a worthy member of the blessed Society to which I have the happiness of belonging. . . .
>
> All my Sisters here have shared in the joy of the whole Society, but the Father Superior, more than anyone else, showed special interest. He repeated several times that no news could have given him more pleasure. He wanted to announce it himself to the community and then to the children. As the next day was Sunday, he had a solemn Mass of thanksgiving offered, with deacon and subdeacon, and he had each of his priests offer three Masses for the same intention and each of the brothers say the beads three times. He would have granted as many Communions as anyone might ask. So it is that in great events enthusiasm for the glory of God shines out in the saints. Since what I wrote you happened, there have been no more reproaches on his part, but he is not in favor of the establishment in St. Louis.

Strengthened by your authority, however, and that of Bishop Rosati, administrator of the diocese, I shall prepare the way. I am so eager for the arrival of the religious from France. Before going to work, they will need rest and time to get accustomed to the ways of the country. I think there is no reason to wait for Father Niel, if we can find a house. . . . I fear we shall get no help from the people of St. Louis, nor from Father Niel, for he will have trouble enough rowing his own boat. In your precious letter I found the letter from Madame de Rollin promising the gift of a thousand francs. I shall use it as you desire, trusting confidently that God will give success to the new foundation. . . .

Another laborious year was drawing to a close, and characteristically. On Christmas Day a scene in the convent parlor brought bitter grief to Philippine and must have made her regret the imprudent haste with which she and Father De La Croix had accepted the immature and sentimental piety of young girls newly in contact with religious teaching and devotional practices for genuine faith and doctrinal understanding. The *Journal* describes the shocking scene:

On this great feast day we had the sorrow of seeing and hearing one of our former pupils—one who had received baptism and First Communion in this house—blaspheme against our holy religion, and that right here in our own convent. Another of our pupils has denounced to their parents those of her companions who are inclined toward the Catholic faith, and the parents, being Protestants, have withdrawn their children. At the close of this year we have 23 boarding pupils, 10 Indian girls, and 12 day pupils in the parish school.

No hint of these unhappy incidents finds its way into her New Year's letter to Bishop Rosati. She writes, however, of a personal anxiety of conscience that would recur more than once in the years ahead, and that she would always submit to him with the utmost simplicity and confidence:

What troubles me greatly—and on this I need your advice—is my vow of poverty, by which I no longer retain the right either to receive, or own, or dispose of anything. I did not advert to this when, without warning, Bishop Du Bourg gave me the land where our house now stands and told me to make my will in favor of two of our religious. Later, when I explained the matter to him, he gave me the necessary dispensations. Now I shall have to do the same thing for the new foundation. Our Mother General, not wishing to remove my burden, wills rather that I should be charged in a way

with all the houses of our Society established in this country. I beg
you, Monseigneur, tell me what I can do in conscience in order to
secure the ownership of the property for our houses. I ask you to
excuse my bad handwriting and the lack of order in my letters.
You are a Father to me, and this gives me confidence.

With the Bishop's reassurance and further explanations, the
ghost of a scruple was laid for the present, and Philippine committed herself and her work once more entirely to the Sacred Heart.
She might know fear, hesitation, anxiety, yet her supernatural
conviction of faith in the reality of God's Providence never seems
to have wavered. Lacking all natural security, she went forward
all the more courageously, just because there appeared no human
help on which to rely. If he willed her to work in St. Louis, he
would furnish both the means and the grace for the enterprise.

nine

A City House
in St. Louis

I. 1827—1828

FLORISSANT VALLEY LAY BURIED IN SNOW as the New Year began. In the coldest hours before the dawn Mother Duchesne made her way through the icy chapel to find even the altar in the church covered with snow. Great drifts, as of fine white powder, were banked up in the sanctuary. The sacristy, too, was white with the snow that had sifted in around the doors and windows and through the long cracks in the poorly ceiled walls. There was work to be done even before meditation this morning; and after a prolonged adoration, offering, and acceptance, Philippine began to sweep out the dry snow, to wipe off the altar, communion railing, and sanctuary furniture, to sweep again, and then prepare for Mass. The best vases and candelabra were already on the altar—all reminders of her dear ones in France. What were they all doing this New Year's Day? Turning her thoughts from them, she wondered whether the pastor would be able to make his way across the two-mile stretch of snow-covered countryside.

Coming back into the church, she found Sister Shannon at work cleaning the floor and benches. The task was self-imposed—that was how novitiate training showed itself. Sister McKay was laying a fire in the nuns' chapel, and Mother Mathevon was wiping snowdrifts from the window sills. Then all were kneeling silently in prayer, offering to God the New Year with whatever it might hold for them. At six-thirty there was a stir in the room above, where the children were rising in the bitter cold and huddling before the fires Sister Catherine had kindled on the hearths at either end of the dormitory. Quickly and quietly they dressed under the eyes of Mother Hamilton, donning woolen stockings, soft shoes or moccasins, and pantalettes, knitted petticoats, hug-me-tights, flannel undershirts, and Sunday uniforms of heavy black serge. Even the slimmest among them grew rotund as successive layers of clothing were applied. The ice in their mugs and pitchers was left quite undisturbed. The strokes of the community bell gave the signal for the nuns to recite the morning Office. The children knelt for prayers, while downstairs the sound of shuffling feet and whispers told that the Indian girls had come in from their log house with Mother O'Connor. Then heavy stamping outside the sacristy announced that Father Van Quickenborne was there.

The church that morning was completely deserted of worshipers. The day was too cold for visitors, so Philippine had time to write to Josephine:

> It is quite a while, my very dear and much loved Cousin, since I received your letter of August 30, telling me of a new gift of 1000 francs. I am so filled with gratitude, I do not know how to express myself. I can only beg the ever kind and generous Heart of Jesus to pay the debt I owe you and to give you a hundredfold in return for all you do for us. . . . The work for the Indians is of very doubtful value. To carry it on successfully, the miracle of miracles is needed—that is, to change their very nature, which is corrupted from their earliest years. One would need to live in their midst. So far no women have risked this; and priests who have done so were not only unable to obtain support from them, but had to give them material assistance. Every year many Indians die in wretched poverty or as a result of drunkenness.
>
> The American government has followed the policy of buying up the Indian lands within the boundaries of the states in order to secure public peace. The Indians have been required to move into more distant territory. This is the last year the savages will be allowed to hunt in, or even to travel across, the state of Missouri. Having been herded together in restricted areas, they no longer have sufficient land for the hunt, and this makes them more and more miserable. Some efforts have been made to get the Indian children into schools, but the parents only allow them to remain for a short time, then come and reclaim them. The children are worse off then than before, because when they take up the old

licentious life, they act with more knowledge of right and wrong. Some Presbyterian missionaries, supported by a society in New York, took up residence near the Osage Indians, but they complained loudly about the conditions in which they had to live. They could not hold the Indian children in the school and had only half-breeds. It is rumored that they will give up the missions. . . .

I beg you to excuse my illegible writing, but we are having such severe cold just now, the ink freezes on the point of the quill, even here beside the fire. As you always take an interest in our Society, I shall give you some details; our two houses in Louisiana, one a day's journey from New Orleans, the other four or five days', are doing very well. The former in particular, though begun just a year ago, has more novices and pupils than we have. Many of the novices are excellent subjects, coming from the best Creole families. We have less success with the Americans on account of the quarter method of education in vogue here: three months to learn French, three months for music, three months for art, and then the education should be completed. Just recently four children left us, each having been here three months. Then, too, the Protestant parents fear their children may become Catholics. They all desire to do so, and the parents say they are free, but they always find some reason against the step.

Adieu, dear friend. Let us remain close friends in time, hoping that our union will be even closer in eternity in the Heart of Jesus.

There is no hint in this letter of the principal problem that was absorbing so much of Philippine's thought and prayer and activity at this time. She had been trying to enlist the co-operation of her acquaintances in St. Louis in the foundation of an academy in the town. The need was patent, but the means were lacking; and no one seemed willing to help her. She took the long, cold drive from Florissant more than once. She talked of the advantages a convent in town, *une Maison de Ville*—a City House—would have over the existing *Maison de Campagne*—the Country House—so far out in the country. It was all to no avail; no one was interested. In desperation she wrote to John Mullanphy. He knew about the efforts she had been making, but he had offered no help so far. She had discussed with Father Van Quickenborne the advisability of approaching the town's richest Catholic. The Jesuit Superior was not very encouraging; but since he had not forbidden it, she wrote.

On February 10 she went to St. Louis again, this time to talk matters over with Mr. Mullanphy himself. He had an offer to make, and she listened thoughtfully as he outlined the plan. Then she drove with him to see the property offered—twenty-four acres of high, rolling land and a two-story, twelve-room brick house just seven years old. That was a generous offer, but the conditions made her hesitate. If only Bishop Rosati were near; he had been away for many weeks on a winter trip to Kentucky. She could not give the immediate answer that Mr. Mullanphy desired; she must consult Father Van Quickenborne. He was vehement in his opposition, then modified his views. Father De Theux was in favor of accepting.

Philippine knelt before the tabernacle and reread the letter of February 7, 1818, in which St. Madeleine Sophie had given her authority to sell or acquire property in the name of the Society. She had acted before on that authority, and she had delegated that authority to Mother Audé in Louisiana. Now, after long hours of prayer, she acted again. On March 1 she wrote to tell the Mother General what she had done, and was doing, to carry out the wish the foundress had so often expressed for a City House in St. Louis.

> I have been pushing the matter of a foundation in St. Louis, feeling it a loss of both time and opportunity to wait for Father Niel's return, and many people say he is not coming back since he did not succeed in getting the financial aid he sought. After making many inquiries, I realized that we should need at least 30,000 francs on hand in order to procure a house in St. Louis as good as the one we have here, that we could not count on Father Niel for help, and that Mother Eugenie will not be able to pay us the money advanced to her for several years. I knew, moreover, that I could not count on the 6000 francs you spoke of in a preceding letter, since in the last one you mentioned only 1000 from Madame de Rollin. So I wrote to Mr. Mullanphy, asking him if he would not give us a house, as he owns a great many, and that on favorable conditions in view of our intention of opening a free school for the children of the poor. He answered by asking in turn how many orphans we would house on the following conditions: 1) that he would give us a brick house built about seven years ago, situated at a distance of a fifteen-minute walk from the Catholic church, with 24 arpents of land around it, not cultivated except for a vegetable garden, the house having 12 fairly large rooms, but not being as large as our convent here; 2) that he or his heirs would give each orphan at her entrance the sum of 50 francs for her bed, etc., and 25 francs yearly for clothing; and 3) that he would give 5000 francs cash for the initial expenses of the foundation. I replied that we would accept 15 or 20 orphans; he wanted 20, and they were to be presented by himself or his oldest daughters.

I went to inspect the house and found the site somewhat similar to that of Ste. Marie, though less attractive. It is high, solitary, and in a healthful location overlooking the Mississippi and the city, from which it is well removed. It seemed to me we should be going against our own best interests to refuse this offer. True, we are taking on a burden for which we shall be responsible, but think of a debt of 20 or 30 thousand francs, or the necessity of being confined to a village where we are shut in by six feet of water up to our door five or six times a year, and that quite suddenly and with such forces as to wash away the bridge leading to our house, to flatten all our fences, to destroy our entire garden, which has produced nothing these last two years, as the vegetables have rotted in the water. Besides that, there is the probability that if we do not take the lead [in opening a school], someone else may do so, and we shall be without any means of supporting ourselves. Are not these facts worth taking into consideration?

You counseled me to ask advice, and I did so. At first the Father Rector was opposed to the plan, then he thought better of it, though he was not enthusiastic. Perhaps he would have preferred St. Charles, but construction work on the church has been discontinued, and he does not want to station a priest there; and no secular priest will accept the parish as it lies within the area assigned to the Jesuit mission. I told him that you considered an establishment in St. Louis necessary, that you had told me to make plans for it, and that this should come before any other undertaking. The other Jesuit Father [De Theux] is wholly in favor of the St. Louis foundation. So I accepted, and things are getting under way, though the first contract that was drawn up has not yet been signed. Mr. Mullanphy is much interested in the repairs and is having them made at his expense, that is, with the money he promised to give. It was necessary to add a kitchen and a room above it for a hired man, also to repair the floors, etc. All will be ready by Easter, and we could open the institution then if the desired help comes from France. It was impossible for me to wait for an answer from you in this matter, as several parties were interested in the property—and how could I say when your answer would reach us, with the dangers and delays of sea travel? I am sorry you are not sending a good superior. . . . The people of St. Louis would certainly appreciate a religious who is American in both language and character. No other nation in the world admires itself as this one does. If for the moment I am disappointed in my hope, I cling to the thought that the religious who are coming are younger than I and may be able to learn the language and customs of the country.

I think it best for me to go to St. Louis for the foundation. The position might offer some dangers for others, as it is unwise to be too friendly at first with people, lest one make undesirable intimacies. Then, too, there are many well educated people in St. Louis, and some of our religious might not make a good impression. Relying on the protection of St. Joseph and St. Regis, I have the utmost confidence that our work both here and in St. Louis will succeed. Each convent will help the other, one in temporal, the other in spiritual matters. The nuns can go from one house to the other for their retreats or for a change of air, etc. One can make the trip back and forth in a day. It would have been very satisfying for me to know I was carrying out your intentions in all this, and I should then have acted with more assurance. But in a country so destitute of opportunities for the education of youth, should I have held back because of the orphans? We have the responsibility of training them, but we also have the good will of the most influential family in this part of the country. . . . The building in St. Louis will need to be enlarged, so we shall welcome the money promised for this foundation. We shall have a good number of day pupils, and if you agree to this, we shall use their tuition fees to support the orphans and their teachers. This work will be rather light in the beginning. . . .

Bishop Rosati returned to Missouri at the end of February, but not to St. Louis, and left for New Orleans without having learned of the contract between Mother Duchesne and Mr. Mullanphy. Hearing that he was at the Barrens, Philippine wrote on March 8 to inform him of the steps she had taken, to request a formal letter of episcopal approval, and to say that the opening of the new school was set for May 1. She closed her letter with a little heart-cry: "I have learned with sorrow that Mother Xavier Hamilton is very ill. I begged her to come back here if she could stand the trip. This climate agrees with her, for she was perfectly well when she was here. I wish at any cost to save her. . . ."

It was too late to save young Mathilde Hamilton. Her death had occurred at St. Michael's on March 1, when she was twenty-five. The Bishop learned this as he stepped from the steamboat in New Orleans, and he hastened to send the news to Mother Duchesne, his letter of March 11 crossing hers of March 8 somewhere on the river.

> On my arrival here [he wrote], I learned of the loss your community has sustained in the death of Mother Xavier Hamilton. We must resign ourselves to the dispositions of Providence. She was ripe for heaven. Her death was that of a saint. Nonetheless, I understand how much a sacrifice like this costs you. According to

what I have learned from Father De La Croix, Mother Eugenie has felt this death acutely, and so much the more since the number of religious is far below the needs of the boarding school at St. Michael's, which increases daily. At present there are ninety young ladies there. . . .

I understand the situation in which you find yourself just now; but if the establishment of a convent in St. Louis cannot be made without withdrawing religious from St. Michael's, then I would advise you to wait a little longer. It would be very unfortunate to ruin a house which is more promising than others and which at the moment, though still new, counts twice the number of boarders that are in the other houses. You must have regard to the health of the religious who, if overburdened with work, cannot long continue their apostolate. . . .

When Philippine's letter of March 8 reached the Bishop in New Orleans, he hastened to reassure her, fearing the misconstruction she might put on his last letter and the suffering she would experience as a result. The consideration shown by the young prelate must have been a balm to Philippine's troubled soul. While awaiting his reply, she had pushed her preparations ahead. On Easter Monday, April 6, Anna Shannon and Suzanne McKay made their first vows after a year in the novitiate. These were religious on whom the Society would rely for splendid, loyal service, Suzanne giving more than thirty years of active devotedness and Anna more than twice that long. Mother Shannon was, without a doubt, Mother Duchesne's most "illustrious" recruit for the Society. She lived with Mother Duchesne for many years and became one of the outstanding figures in the history of the order. From her comes precious information about the convent at Florissant and its Mother Superior when the foundation in St. Louis was about to be made:

The main building [wrote Mother Shannon], which was occupied by the community and boarding pupils, was equipped with all the furniture and appurtenances necessary for regularity and for carrying on the work of the house. There were, besides, three other buildings detached from the principal one. Of these, one (formerly used for the second-rate boarding school) was set apart for the use of the priests; another was occupied by the free school; and the third was the Indian girls' seminary. . . . These girls slept on the floor—some on pallets, others on buffalo skins they had brought with them. During the day the pallets and buffalo skins were rolled up and put away, for the same large room answered also for class purposes. The girls were intelligent and learned quickly; they were soon handy with the needle. . . . One of them became very ill and was the object of Mother Duchesne's care and solicitude for two months. . . . She suffered greatly, but was a very privileged soul . . . and her short but holy life was crowned by a happy death in the arms of Mother Duchesne.

The children of the boarding school were good and pious, and in manners and deportment compared favorably with any I have met since. . . . The majority of them understood French, and all were able to study it. Mother Duchesne understood English and could write it quite well, but she never trusted herself to speak it. She used to give the General Instruction herself, and her exhortations, supplemented by her holy example, sank deep into their hearts. . . . The families of these children were very generous; and whenever they came to visit them, they delighted to bring gifts of produce from their farms, or groceries received from New Orleans. If they received a quantity of French wines, for instance, a box or two was sure to arrive on their next visit to the convent. Such articles were carefully put aside to be served to the bishop and priests when they dined at the house.

We had several good cows on the place and plenty of milk. . . . The religious all helped with the cooking, Mother Duchesne being always first at the hardest work, though meals were not always improved by her share in getting them up, for her gifts did not lie in that direction. In the management of the farm work, however, she excelled.

The kitchen and dining room were housed in a separate log building behind the convent. The children had their meals first, then the religious. The diet was seldom "balanced," but it was wholesome and abundant, though Mother Shannon recalled being hungry almost all the time. Whatever was left from the service of the children was used, with additions, for the religious. Of course, reheated dishes are familiar items on convent menus, but hardly ever to the extent that occurred at Florissant in those days. No food was wasted, not even crusts of bread left by the children. These the Mother Superior gathered up for herself.

Mother Duchesne made the recreations very pleasant [continues Mother Shannon]. The dignity of her manner did not detract from her amiability, while her extensive and varied information, her ready command of French, and above all the love of God which seemed the very breath of her life, made her conversation not only entertaining and instructive, but also calculated to keep alive the fervor of us all. There was a singular earnestness and unction in everything she said that gave her a kind of power for drawing souls to God. The recreation after dinner was followed by Office,

which was always said with the greatest punctuality and exact-
ness. . . .

Mother Duchesne slept very little, for besides her prolonged
vigils before the Blessed Sacrament, she used also to sit up with
the sick whenever this was necessary; and when dressing in the
morning, the religious often found their shoes and clothing mended
and knew whose charitable hands had done the work. . . . She
also reserved for herself the night visit of the house and the morning call. . . .

Father Van Quickenborne was the superior of the Jesuits of
the mission. He greatly appreciated Mother Duchesne and lost no
opportunity of trying her by the sharpest mortifications. On one
occasion, when she presented herself to receive Holy Communion,
he gruffly refused her. Mother Duchesne stood up and returned to
her place with unaltered countenance. The community and the
people in the church had noticed the incident, otherwise it would
probably never have been known, for she did not mention it. Nor
did she ever speak of the frequent rebuffs she met with from the
same quarter.

Mother Shannon was impressed by two seemingly contradic-
tory facts—the occasional harshness of Father Van Quickenborne's
treatment of Mother Duchesne and his otherwise amicable relations with her and her community. "He was a real father to us,"
she wrote, "and we could always count on his help when we
needed it. He and Mother Duchesne were on the best of terms.
She and her daughters were used to his oddities and did not mind
them."

The influence of the Jesuit Rector on the training given the
novices of the Sacred Heart was evident in the introduction of
corporal penances after 1823. Mother Duchesne had been loath
to impose them, but by 1825 the novices were familiar with many
devices for self-inflicted penance, the common ones being the
discipline and the chain. They also kept the Church's fasts with
penitential severity. "After Mass on fast days those of the religious
who wished to do so took a cup of sweet-herb tea, sweetened with
a little molasses. Nothing else appeared on the table."

The clergy and laity, in fact everyone who knew her, esteemed
Mother Duchesne as a saint. She was gifted with an admirable spirit
of prayer [Mother Shannon continues] and often spent whole
nights on her knees before the Blessed Sacrament without any
support whatever; and when our Lord was exposed on the altar,
she spent long hours in his Presence in the same attitude. One Holy
Thursday night she kept me as the companion of her night-long

vigil, and she never changed her position, kneeling upright without any support, except to rise to go up to the Repository to trim or replace the lighted candles. At the end of five hours I was overcome by sleep and began to nod. . . . She noticed it and said to me: "Go to bed now. At four o'clock others will come, and I can remain alone until then." She was as alert and wide awake as if it were twelve o'clock in the day.

Mother Duchesne's soul seemed to be steeped in the fervent spirit of prayer and almost superhuman austerity of religious life in the early ages of the Church. . . . And from the very beginning she accustomed her daughters to make prayer the constant companion of their labors. While digging, hoeing, etc., we used to lighten our toil by frequent ejaculations and vocal prayers.

When I lived with Mother Duchesne, she was still strong and vigorous. She was rather tall and well proportioned, with a noble countenance and bearing and fine manners. She had blue eyes, and though slightly pitted by the smallpox, her complexion was fair and clear.

So an artist might picture her in the late afternoon of an April day in 1827, sitting in the community room at Florissant and speaking in her singularly earnest way to her little religious family, telling them the arrangements she had worked out with Mothers Octavie and Lucille. There would be more work for them all, as she was taking with her Mother O'Connor, Mary Knappe, an orphan, and Julie Coutremanche, a half-breed girl. The other orphans would follow later on. The trimester prizes would be distributed to the three schools on Sunday, April 29; a *congé* would follow on Monday, and Mother Duchesne and her companions would leave on May 1, in accordance with her promise to Mr. Mullanphy.

The last announcement called forth a subdued protest. May 1 was the feast of St. Philip the Apostle, and Mother Duchesne's feast, too. They would not hear of her leaving them on that day. As she knew they were sincere in this affectionate outburst, she yielded to their pleading. She would leave on May 2—and she would come out to see them as often as possible.

So they feasted her in the simple Sacred Heart fashion. They gathered, too, for a last evening recreation. She gave them her blessing when the bell rang and went for a last adoration in the chapel that looked into the church which at her suggestion had been dedicated to the Sacred Heart of Jesus. It was her last night under the roof with the Blessed Sacrament for many a week; but she could say now, as she had said so often before in the cause of Christ: "I am ready for anything."

May 2, 1827, fell on a Wednesday. The Mullanphy carriage was at the convent door. The Misses Mullanphy were calling for Mother Duchesne and her companions, whom they were honored to take to St. Louis. Baggage and some furniture had gone ahead in a cart. The good-byes were joyous in spite of tears, and the vehicle moved off. It was springtime in the valley, with a shimmer of green on the trees, a sunny warmth in the air, and the smell of newly-turned earth. Bob-whites whistled in the meadows and thrushes sang in the hedgerows. The drive was long, but pleasant enough. Once they reached the city they headed east, then south, taking the road to Carondelet and branching from it, once they crossed the Mill Creek, into the traces of wagon wheels that led as a road to the brick house which became that day the Convent of the Sacred Heart, St. Louis.

Nine years had passed since Philippine Duchesne had set sail from France with St. Louis as her intended destination—nine years since she had made her first acquaintance with the frontier trading post and its friendly, hospitable people. She had known them in less amiable moods at times since then. She had seen the village spread from a place of three streets paralleling the river to more than twice that number and double its population. Americans had been moving in steadily through these years, and English was now the language of the town, though one had best be bilingual to be really at home. Philippine had been in the town many times during the past nine years and was familiar with its dusty, or muddy, lanes, its noisy traffic, its dingy shops, its more pretentious stores, its abounding life. She was personally acquainted with its handsome, red-haired, young mayor, Dr. William Carr Lane, and had also known Missouri's first governor, Mr. Alexander McNair, whose untimely death had brought grief to many a heart.

The Indians on the streets were no curiosity to her now, but always objects of compassion and prayer. She had learned that they often encamped on Choteau's Pond, a pretty body of water that lay to the west of the property Mr. Mullanphy had given her and that was drained by the Mill Creek, "*le ruisseau de Monsieur Chouteau*," she called it. That creek was something of a problem to her just now, for she knew she would have to build bridges over it. That, in turn, meant that she had very real need of the services of Martin Lepere. She had known him for four years and had great confidence in him. Father Van Quickenborne had objected when she offered Martin the job in town, but she had held to the arrangement and the man was moving to St. Louis.

"The work will be rather light in the beginning," Philippine had written optimistically to Mother Barat, but it was drudgery from the start, for the house had stood vacant for some years and the workmen hired by Mr. Mullanphy had left a litter of debris in every room, besides the mud tracked in from the garden, where great mounds of loose earth were piled up from the excavating of the cellar. She and her companions were hard at work that first afternoon when Father Saulnier, the Cathedral pastor, arrived to offer his services and to promise that he and his assistant, Father Lutz, would do their best to see that the convent had Mass, at least on Sundays. It was a cheering promise, but one the good priest would find difficult to keep. In material matters, however, he was more helpful, for he sent the nuns a cow, to Mother Duchesne's satisfaction, and a quantity of useful furniture—the tables, school benches, and other equipment from the defunct St. Louis College, and bade them help themselves from his garden and orchard, though at the moment there was not much to be gathered.

On Sunday two other visitors called—Mr. Mullanphy and Mrs. Bernard Pratte. The latter had two more daughters to place under Mother Duchesne's care as soon as the school was inaugurated. On Tuesday, Father Van Quickenborne appeared on the scene. "He was quite pleased with the house and its location," noted Mother Duchesne in her *Journal*. He returned next day for Mass—and on that Wednesday, May 9, St. Joseph was solemnly chosen as patron of the new institution. On the following Sunday he arrived at noon, but she was fasting hopefully. The chapel had been prepared as well as possible, but there was no ciborium and so the Blessed Sacrament was not reserved. There could be no severer trial than this, Philippine thought, but there were worse days ahead.

She had the satisfaction, however, of showing the Father Rector a letter written by Bishop Rosati on March 23. This formal approbation gave her a tangible sense of security, but it left the problem of the chaplaincy unsolved, so she laid the difficulty before the bishop at once, along with a solution that had presented itself quite unexpectedly.

> I had hoped [she wrote on May 10] that one of the two priests in St. Louis would offer Mass here for us on Sundays, but Father Saulnier says he is already offering two Masses and Father Lutz goes to a mission station. . . . Meanwhile Father Richard is asking

to be our chaplain, having heard that a convent was to be opened in St. Louis. He asks only lodging and meals, which is very convenient for a new house that still has so many expenses to meet. Father Richard, morevoer, is a member of a religious community and very well suited to our needs.

Many visitors came to call on the nuns the following Sunday—a Sunday without Mass at the convent. "Old friends, former pupils, parents offering us their children," noted Mother Duchesne, "but we could not accept them at once. We are not ready." That evening she gave Mother Barat an account of her first ten days in St. Louis.

> The heading of this letter shows you that we are at last in the place you have long considered most suitable for a convent of the Sacred Heart. . . . I wrote you that the Father Superior did not like the contract with Mr. Mullanphy; and even after signing it with us, he urged us to get the approval of the bishop before having the contract notarized. Fortunately the bishop boarded the very steamboat that was carrying my letter to him, and it brought back his answer quickly. Along with his personal letter he enclosed a formal act of approval. . . .
>
> That enthusiastic approbation under the seal of the bishop and your frequently repeated wish give me the consolation of thinking that I am where God wills me to be, and that St. Joseph has greatly aided in this matter. So he is the special patron and protector of this house. The five thousand francs given by Mr. Mullanphy have alreay been used to pay for excavating a cellar and constructing a brick kitchen and a room above it that could serve as a convenient lodging for a priest, as it is well floored and ceiled and has outside shutters, etc.
>
> I promised to take possession on May 1. The approach of my feast and the distribution of prizes gave an opportunity to reorganize the classes and install a new teacher without delaying my departure from Florissant later than May 2. Not a room in this house was ready, so we did not have Mass until Sunday. To my surprise and joy the priest said the Mass of St. Joseph, as this was permitted in the *ordo* of the diocese. . . .

Mother Duchesne had not received an answer from the bishop with regard to Father Richard and the chaplaincy when she wrote to him again about another difficulty raised by Father Van Quickenborne, who seems to have been set at times on giving her trouble. Had he been officially named ecclesiastical Superior of the Religious of the Sacred Heart in Missouri, he could scarcely have exercised—

or attempted to exercise—more authority. This time the Reverend Father was objecting to Martin Lepere's moving to St. Louis to work for the nuns. "I am in real need of this man to attend to our affairs," she wrote on July 1. "He understands our rules and regulations and can direct the work for which a knowledge of the two languages is necessary." After some further defense of Lepere, whom Van Quickenborne considered lazy, she added: "As I could not get in touch with you quickly enough and as Mr. Martin was willing to make the change, I have not retreated from my position in spite of the Father's protest, and I shall carry the arrangement through, unless you counsel me to do otherwise."

By this time the bridges had been built, a well dug, the feast of the Sacred Heart celebrated with Mass and an outdoor procession of the Blessed Sacrament, a novice "with absolutely no training" added to the community, and the academy opened with a mere handful of pupils. Early in July, Father Van Quickenborne announced that he would come no more for Mass, nor would he send a substitute, as his priests were going to make their tertianship. "I have shed bitter tears over this decision," Philippine confessed to her Superior General. "There is a slender hope that the Father Provincial [Francis Dzierozynski] may decide otherwise; they expect him from Maryland this month." But he did not.

> Meanwhile we must live on privations. We have had no Exposition of the Blessed Sacrament either in the Octave of Corpus Christi or in that of the Sacred Heart; often we lose four communions a week. These are my fast days, for I just cannot take any breakfast while I am hoping that some stroke of Divine Providence may bring a priest to give us Communion. . . .
>
> We still need to build a fence of planks or upright posts. This will be expensive, and we need a stable and a servant's house. The latter is necessary because of our isolation from all other dwellings. This isolation, however, has its advantages—no one can ever look in on us. We are going to leave part of our twenty-four arpents in woodland, where we can gather wild grapes, which are often quite delicious, hazel nuts, strawberries, and blackberries in abundance. But we shall still have plenty of land enclosed for a garden, an apple orchard, a little woods for walks or playgrounds, where there is a very good spring that never goes dry, and fields for corn and potatoes, but these fields have never been cleared for tillage.
>
> I have been greatly aided by several ladies of the town. One of them put at my disposal both her vehicles and her servants for all the trips I might need to make to Florissant. . . . If our religious from France had got here we could have made the most of

the general interest our coming aroused, our two institutions would have been filled with pupils. But I begin to feel like a fabricator of tales when I speak of their arrival in the near future. I am particularly embarrassed in the presence of Mr. Mullanphy.

The strain of the first months in St. Louis was telling on Philippine; her nerves were on edge. When a letter from Bishop Rosati seemed to imply that the idea of Father Richard's coming to St. Louis had originated with her, she wrote in self-defense that she had had no intention whatsoever of attempting to withdraw the Ursulines' chaplain from them, but that he himself had written to tell her that he had given notice to the Ursulines that he was giving up the chaplaincy of their convent. The Bishop's reply was gentle and reassuring, and came to Philippine within a week:

> I am entirely convinced that you have not tried to take Father Richard away from the Ursulines. I also know that this holy man has for a long time wanted to leave Louisiana, where the heat is very hard on him. I should have had no problem in allowing him to go elsewhere, and certainly much less in seeing him go to your house, but it is absolutely impossible to replace him just now. Father Richard, as you have also seen by his letter, realizes this fact. That is why he did not venture to speak to me of it. Nevertheless, I shall write to France to have a priest sent who will be agreeable to the Ursulines. We must be patient while we wait for him and be reconciled to whatever is best.
>
> (P.S.) You know the Holy Father has decided my lot according to our own desires. Still I must retain the administration of the diocese of New Orleans for the present.

Philippine had now waited many months for the recruits she had expected from France to help her with the St. Louis foundation. The summer had been a long, hot succession of trials and disappointments, drudgery and privation. Her reaction to all this is evident from the tone of her next letter to Mother Barat. There is anguish in every line, but most keenly sensed in the closing paragraph. The Mother General did not approve whole-heartedly of the contract made with John Mullanphy. Two points of it were deemed unwise—first, the property was not donated outright, but merely leased to the Religious of the Sacred Heart, though the time-span was for 999 years; and second, the care of twenty orphans in perpetuity on so meager a support as five dollars a year for each was an almost preposterous condition. "That is a heavy burden," wrote the Mother General, "but God will aid you, I am sure." So Philippine wrote to her on August 18:

It grieves me very much to know that you do not approve of the contract with Mr. Mullanphy. At least your desires are partly accomplished. Bishop Rosati, who had been appointed definitely to St. Louis, told me he intends to reside here part of each year. That will assure us of more spiritual help. I have no hope that the Jesuits will come to St. Louis in the near future. . . .

On Sunday, September 9, the long-awaited religious from France arrived—Mothers Helene Dutour, a Savoyard, and Xavier Van Damme, a Fleming, with a postulant, Miss Marguerite Short, a recent convert of Bishop Fenwick of Cincinnati. They had traveled down the Ohio with Mothers Dorival and Piveteau, the former on her way to Grand Coteau, the latter to St. Michael's. That very afternoon Mother Duchesne took the newcomers to Florissant, returning next day with only Mother Dutour, as Mother Van Damme had insisted on remaining at the country house to make a little "spiritual review" under Jesuit direction. This was a bit disconcerting to Philippine, but she mentioned it only casually in a letter to the Mother General which she began on September 11:

On receiving new gifts from you, must I not feel my gratitude increasing? I want to express it as far as in me lies, and especially since our dear Sisters have arrived. The Blessed Virgin brought them safely to us. I had felt a bit discouraged when all our novenas to the Sacred Heart, to St. Regis, to St. Ignatius brought no results, and even those made for the feast of the Assumption and the Immaculate Heart were unavailing. Then on the morning of the feast of the Holy Name of Mary, when I was pouring out my heart to her, I heard these consoling words: My protection will never fail you. I put aside the thought as illusory, but after Mass I seemed to hear the same words again, and an hour later the beadle of the parish came in all haste to tell me that our religious had arrived at the rectory, and being there they would attend the Mass that would be offered at ten-thirty. So they got here just in time for dinner.

After Vespers I drove with them to Florissant, where the joy of seeing them was very great. On Monday the prizes were distributed by Father De Theux, who was accompanied by another priest. Father Van Quickenborne was away on a mission trip to the Osage Indians. Kind Father De Theux had taken part in our novenas and had offered Holy Mass that very day for the safe arrival of our religious. Mother Dutour and I returned to St. Louis that afternoon. Mother Van Damme wanted to remain a few days at St. Ferdinand in order to make a review. I made her promise to come back here, telling her that both her youth and her facility in speaking English would enable her to procure the glory of God here. . . .

Interrupted while writing, Philippine could find no opportunity to finish this letter in the days that followed. News of the approaching visit of Bishop Rosati stirred the little convent to full activity, for there was much to be done before all was in readiness for the blessing of the house. When nearly two weeks had passed and Mother Van Damme still remained at Florissant, Mother Duchesne wrote to Mother Berthold to come for a visit and bring with her the reluctant member of the St. Louis community. They drove in on September 24 and Mother Duchesne gave them a cordial welcome. She had understood from the beginning what was going on in the soul of Xavier Van Damme and she wrote sympathetically about her: "The very narrow quarters in which we live, the small number of religious forming the community, and our great poverty, all combined to astonish and discourage her a little, but her virtue seems to have conquered this trial. As to Mother Dutour, she was at home immediately."

On September 29, Bishop Rosati paid his first visit to the St. Louis convent. Mother Duchesne was happy to introduce to him the religious from France, to show him the copies of the brief of approbation and the new edition of the *Constitutions* which they had brought, and to tell him of financial help received from Josephine de Savoye-Rollin, Father Perreau, and the convent at Amiens. He returned three days later to offer the Holy Sacrifice of the Mass and bless the house, and on the following day he gave solemn baptism to Elizabeth Dodge in the convent chapel. He had arranged as best he could about the chaplaincy, appointing Father Lutz to the post temporarily. And now he had a new enterprise to suggest. Mother Duchesne must have been astonished at the proposal, but she listened attentively. The bishop was presenting them with a new opportunity for spreading the knowledge and love of the Sacred Heart, and Philippine could not turn a deaf ear to it, though wisdom lay in refusal. When he had driven away that afternoon, she took up her unfinished letter and wrote:

> Bishop Rosati called on us today and seemed quite satisfied with our location here, as he finds the place very pleasant. He laid before me a proposal that requires a prompt answer from you, for you have expressed the wish that we content ourselves with our four houses for the present, so I cannot accept a fifth without your approval. The Daughters of the Cross [Sisters of Loretto], who

have a good number of convents in Kentucky, opened a school at La Fourche, near St. Michael's in Louisiana. Father Bigeschi, a holy priest who has since returned to France and whom you may have met, built them a convent and gave them land, furniture, etc. But they are all English-speaking Americans, so they cannot go on with their work at La Fourche, where the language and customs are French. They find that they are unable to train their novices or teach the children, since only one among them can speak and teach a little French. Because of this situation they want to unite with us. Monseigneur Rosati and the priests in Louisiana are also in favor of this union. The bishop has explained to the Sisters our organization and mode of life. They agree to all, so only your approval is lacking. Will you refuse to help this well populated area, when all the convent needs is a religious superior?

I think Mother Carmelite Landry would do well there. She has been Mother Xavier Murphy's assistant; but since Mother Dorival arrived, she has not been so necessary at Grand Coteau. She seems just made for that convent at La Fourche. She is well known to the people there and is one of them. We would send these good Daughters of the Cross to our other houses where there is need for religious who can speak English, and in their place we could put some French-speaking nuns. In this way and without asking for more help from France, we could form a very desirable institution. Mother Eugenie could send there the children she cannot take at St. Michael's because of lack of room; she could also keep an eye on that convent and help it in many ways. Please, dear Mother, give me an immediate answer. I have asked Monseigneur Rosati for a delay of four months, hoping to receive your reply in that time, and I trust it will be favorable. I am asking it from our Lord through the intercession of Our Lady of Sorrows, the title under which the Blessed Virgin is especially honored at La Fourche. She has let me know that I shall always have her protection. . . .

The religious from France had brought with them supplies of many kinds for the American convents, but their baggage had gone astray en route from New York to St. Louis. Mother Duchesne considered this no reason for a delay in thanking for the articles she hoped soon to receive, so on the following Sunday she gave herself the pleasure of writing a letter to the Paris community. She knew that some unfavorable comments about the St. Louis house had already been sent to France, and she may have hoped to counteract the impression created by these criticisms. But she was too honest to do more than make light of the difficulties and inconveniences of which others complained. So she wrote as she would have loved to talk to the whole Society:

Our dear Mothers Dutour and Xavier Van Damme reached St. Louis on the feast of the Holy Name of Mary and have given us the news of you which we were awaiting very eagerly. They told us that nearly all our houses in France had contributed either to the cost of the trip or to the gifts sent to us. These, however, were shipped by another route and have not reached us yet. But whatever they are and to whatever convent they go, they call forth my sincere gratitude, and they are much appreciated on every score. We have never received anything from France that we could not make use of, and gifts coming from our own houses have a value all their own, being proofs of the holy and lasting bond that unites us in Jesus Christ. When we receive letters from you, or when anything comes from France, we no longer think of the vast ocean that separates us from you, and we fancy ourselves in France, witnessing your labors and your joys and learning at the school of your virtues. We even forget our own present situation—the crowded little buildings, the poverty of foundation days, the small number of religious in the community, the difficulties arising from different religions, different languages, different customs in the country, and the obstacles we encounter in trying to establish order in the community and the schools, that order which is so necessary, but to which we can at present only tend with all our hearts.

After reviewing the steps that led to the foundation of the convent in St. Louis, she added:

I was acting without the least promise of success. Mother Octavie was ill; Mother Eugenie refused to send anyone to help me; I had one leg so crippled with rheumatism, it threatened to incapacitate me. . . . I had to come to St. Louis with just one Irish aspirant. The house was not ready; there were no teachers for the classes; and we could have had a crowd of children at the moment, but now that we can take them they are going elsewhere. Our greatest trial is the uncertainty with regard to spiritual help. Beg our Lord to remove this privation by one of those strokes of his Providence that cost him nothing at all.

The gaiety that characterized New Year's Day in St. Louis seems to have found no echo in the woods beyond Chouteau's Creek. The motley bands of maskers roaming the streets on the eve and singing the *Guignolée* from house to house came nowhere near the convent property. Croquignoles and pralines find no mention in Philippine's *Journal*, and the New Year began the hard way, without Mass at the convent and with illness in the community. There had been no news from France since September, and the letters from Louisiana had added to Mother Duchesne's anxieties. On January 4, 1828, she wrote to the bishop, who was then in the South on a visitation tour:

> . . . . I have as yet received no answer from our Mother General regarding our reunion with the Sisters of the Cross. It seems that this was proposed to Mother Eugenie at St. Michael's even before you spoke of it to me, and it was discussed openly at Opelousas when she was there [in September]. Mother Eugenie is afraid that a foundation of ours so close to St. Michael's might hinder its progress. Mother Xavier, the superior at Opelousas, thinks that Mother Carmelite [Landry] is absolutely indispensable to her, while at the same time she admits that she would make an excellent superior for the proposed house. All these difficulties will disappear if our Mother General gives her approval, and I have urged her to do so.
>
> I am faced with fresh difficulties here. The Father Superior of the Jesuits, to whom we proposed a foundation at St. Charles, came to ask me if we were going to fulfil our obligations. I replied that we could not do so without a new permission from our Superior General; for after we made the foundation here, she told me that this was enough and that we should strengthen our four houses. He insisted on having *yes* or *no*, saying he must have an answer. I was unable to say *yes*, and I thought *no* would satisfy him, since he was asking something quite impossible at the moment. So I gave him *no* as an answer. He seemed satisfied; this made me feel sure he had other plans and wanted to get out of the situation if possible. But now, contrary to my expectations, he has become irate, saying he announced at St. Charles that there would be a convent and so the townspeople were ready for his plans. Our refusal, he said, was doing him a great deal of harm. My excuses did not mitigate his indignation. He is extremely put out with me and added that my high-handedness was causing great trouble in our convents.

On January 24 she wrote again to the bishop:

> . . . Mother Eugenie is against us in this matter [of the La Fourche convent] and has perhaps written to our Mother against it with greater eloquence than to me. She says 1) that this foundation will harm St. Michael's; 2) that she herself wants Mother Carmelite there; 3) that our Mother said to make no more foundations in Louisiana. Without contradicting her opinion . . . I I should like to answer: 1) that since an orphanage is desired, it would be better situated at La Fourche in a building already constructed than at St. Michael's where there is an already overwhelm-

ing amount of work and where we should need to build and so be in debt again; 2) that Mother Xavier, superior at Opelousas, can give up Mother Carmelite only in the extreme need of finding a superior . . . 3) Finally, our Mother did indeed advise us not to make any more foundations for a time. She was afraid we would ask her for money and subjects which she wanted to save for the foundation in the East, but which she is now postponing.

I am surprised at Mother Eugenie's displeasure—of which she says I am partly the cause. Our Mother General, in spite of my representations, has given me charge of all the houses in this country. Mother Eugenie refused to give any religious for this foundation and she has kept a Sister from here whom I need—but I left her there. Now her community numbers seventeen, and she wants to take a very necessary member from the Opelousas community, which numbers only five. Do you think this is fair? Because I told Mother Eugenie she was going beyond her power, she has taken offense. I cannot say that something wrong is right. And I have been telling her for a long while that, instead of getting herself into even greater debt by expansion, it would be easier to limit her enrollment to the number of children that can be actually cared for. . . .

But in Louisiana matters had taken very definite shape, and in ways of which Mother Duchesne was unaware as she wrestled at a distance with the problems that lay within her jurisdiction, yet not within her control. Both Bishop Rosati and Mother Audé had gone ahead on the La Fourche project without informing her of the steps they were taking. A letter from Mother Audé to the bishop reveals the astonishing fact that they had taken for granted the Superior General's approval, at least two months before it arrived. On December 27, 1827, Mother Audé wrote:

I have just received your Lordship's letter and I hasten to answer. If you think it wise for me to receive in this house the novices of the Sisters of the Cross who have an attraction for our kind of life and who desire to embrace it, they may come whenever they wish. We shall be happy to receive them and also disposed to love them sincerely in the Heart of Jesus. I fear, however, that they will miss the edifying example and holy direction of their good Mothers Xavier and Regina, which they will be far from finding in your humble servant. Have the goodness to warn them of this, Monseigneur, that they may be less surprised and disedified. . . .

As Mother Duchesne learned of the transfer of the novices only in mid-March, she must have wondered what conclusions the bishop had drawn when he received her January letters. His reply was, perhaps, more puzzling to her than Mother Audé's displeasure. After writing enthusiastically of his visit to Grand Coteau, he added a noncommittal paragraph:

> Regarding the matters on which you ask my advice, I think that with time and a little patience all can be straightened out to the satisfaction of everyone. I have always been of the opinion that the convent at Assumption [La Fourche] should be united to your Society, so I have not allowed it to be closed. That would be to act contrary to the desires of those who have borne the expenses of it and to betray the hopes of the public. Besides, it will never become a rival of the house of St. Michael's because it will have a different objective. I do not believe, however, that Mother Carmelite is suited to be its superior. Her virtues and prudence are well known, but we also know she has not sufficient education to inspire the confidence of the parents. A stranger would be better. I am of the opinion that you cannot take her from Grand Coteau without harming that house. That is what I have observed. As to the establishment at St. Charles, be patient. Time will furnish you the means for it; your postulants and novices will be formed; all will work out eventually.

Meanwhile things had been working out in St. Louis. A free school had been opened in March and installed in the room above the kitchen, which Martin Lepere had vacated. As the number of pupils increased, Sister Catherine Lamarre was transferred from Florissant to take charge of this important work. Mother Duchesne's confidence in St. Joseph was strengthened by the arrival of mail from France. In a letter written on November 29 of the preceding year, Mother Barat consented to the union of the La Fourche convent with the Society of the Sacred Heart and advised Mother Duchesne to make a trip to Louisiana, decide with Mother Audé on the details of admission, and let her carry them out. The Superior General insisted, however, that the Sisters must be received individually, placed in their proper rank, and given the regular novitiate training.

In another letter Mother Barat reviewed some complaints she had received about conditions in the convent in St. Louis and made suggestions for their improvement, adding encouraging words of praise for measures Mother Duchesne had taken and again advising her to go to Louisiana on a little visitation tour. "Your presence really is needed both at St. Michael's and at Opelousas," she wrote on December 13. Mother Duchesne was reluctant to make the trip south. She sensed, moreover, the imprudence of trying to regulate the work to be done at La Fourche on the model of schools for the bourgeoisie in France, as St. Madeleine Sophie had suggested. Her experience at Florissant had shown her that this arrangement would not work, yet she expressed herself with reserve when she wrote to Mother Barat on March 23, 1828:

> I learned through a letter from Mother Eugenie that Bishop Rosati has already sent her five novices of the Sisters of the Cross, two of whom she has sent home. The Sisters who have already made their vows must decide for themselves whether they desire to unite with us or return to their former community. . . . Mother Eugenie also told me she had your permission to accept orphans at St. Michael's. As she seems opposed to the union, I suggested that rather than overburden herself with orphans, it would be better to place them at the new establishment. She could help support them there. . . . That section is as yet rather poor, and the people cannot send their children to school at a distance. The necessity of crossing the Mississippi to get to St. Michael's is a very real obstacle to this and to visiting them, and it would be a great benefit for the country to have another of our institutions there. But it is repugnant to the American spirit to have two different class regimes in the same institution. . . . I do not agree with Bishop Rosati's opinion of Mother Carmelite. The fact that she is from La Fourche and a member of a highly respected family there would give her the chance to do much good. She has quite as much education as is needed for the position. . . .
>
> In my last letter I spoke to you of the necessity of building here in St. Louis and asked for the loan of 19,000 francs. With that we could build what we really need. But dreading debts quite as much as you do, we have cut down our plan rather than postpone the work. A brick building that will give us a dormitory with thirty beds, a chapel, and a sacristy with room for a priest will cost only 6000 francs. I can borrow that much at 10 per cent, which is equivalent to 6 per cent in France plus the exchange. So if you have not borrowed the money for us already, it could be postponed for a year or two. . . . We now have 12 boarders, 10 orphans, 10 day pupils who pay tuition, and 30 in the free school, besides a Sunday school for mulatto girls whom we instruct after the parish Mass. That makes 60 children to whom we have the happiness of making the Sacred Heart known. If the work far surpasses the material income, is it not all the greater gain in heaven? I am very happy about it.

The Father Superior, who has been appeased by the hope that we shall go back to St. Charles, offered the Mass and preached here on the feast of St. Joseph, and today when he was leaving for a month's trip to the Osages, he gave me the deed to the house at St. Charles. . . .

As to making a trip to Louisiana, 1) It is quite unnecessary. Mother Eugenie has the esteem and confidence of all the clergy in that section. 2) There is the expense. It would certainly cost 1000 francs for two of us. I need the money for our building. 3) Mother Octavie is sick again. If she grows worse, I shall be obliged to go out there for a while. People used to prefer her to me; but since I moved in here, they say I handled the children better than she does. In order to keep that boarding school going, I left Mother Regis Hamilton there, for she is the best trained religious we have for that work, and she could carry it on by herself if she were not so young and if there were not so many calls to the parlor.

Spring rains turned the walks and playgrounds into streams and pools of thick mud and washed down earth into the poorly ceiled basement chapel. Mother Duchesne and the orphan girls labored hard to clean parlors, halls, and classrooms, as well as the chapel, especially on Thursdays, which was the day pupils' weekly holiday. Rough manual work was never repugnant to Philippine, though she often felt the fatigue far more than she was willing to admit. At her work she was frequently absorbed in prayer and thought, planning, calculating, wondering how to grope her way out of the thicket of difficulties that seemed to encircle her. She always went about her tasks in forthright fashion, but her mood was very grave these days.

Sometimes, when the work was done, she sat for a while in the little sacristy, making or mending vestments. Taking refuge from anxieties in happy memories, she would let the past unroll before her inward gaze. The scenes she had so loved in childhood, the hopes that had come apparently to such paltry fruition, the affections that had played such a happy role in her life—these were precious and holy things to recall, fragrant with grace and love, consecrated by wholehearted sacrifice, inspiring an ever increasing spirit of gratitude toward God and rooting deeply in her soul the conviction of her utter insufficiency.

Such was her mood on a Thursday afternoon in April when she realized that Josephine's birthday was at hand. When had she last written to Josephine? She would write this very evening, April 10, 1828, and she did, beginning affectionately:

It is a long time, dearest Cousin, since I had news of you, and it is very pleasant for me to renew contacts with those to whom the bonds of kinship, friendship, and gratitude unite me. And I may add with more justice, the bond of religion. Your zeal for our holy faith has made you shower me with gifts and aid me in founding this convent in St. Louis. Though we lack sufficient space and the number of nuns needed for the work, we are now instructing more than seventy children as day pupils or as boarders. . . . The health of the religious who came to America with me has suffered a great deal. Mine has improved during the last year.

I am anxious about you, having had no recent news. When I recall how many in our family have been claimed by death since 1818, the year of our separation, I dread the fresh blows that each letter may bring. My dear one, we shall meet again. God did not unite us in friendship merely for the short period in this life. After this separation—you in one hemisphere, I in the other—we shall soon be reunited in an eternal union. How very beautiful and consoling our faith is! For the little work we do here on earth, it promises us in return all the joys of assured happiness. . . . How blessed we shall be if at the price of even great sacrifice we shall have made God known and loved by one more soul!

Visitors were not rare at the convent, though it was remote and somewhat inaccessible, but Mother Duchesne was sometimes surprised by those who came. That was certainly the case one April morning when she was called to the parlor to meet a stranger who presented her with a letter of introduction from Bishop Rosati. Opening it she read:

Sister Johanna Xavier Miles, former superior of the Convent of Assumption (La Fourche), will give you this letter. She wants, and has wanted for some time past, to be admitted into your Society. . . . I beg you to receive her with that kindness which is characteristic of your Society. She has no brilliant talents; her health is poor; but I think she will not be useless. I spoke to you in another letter about the Convent of Assumption; the plan that Mother Eugenie proposes for the superior to be placed there will, I hope, meet with no opposition on your part. I beg you to agree to it.

For the last two sentences of this letter Philippine was even less prepared than for the first. Yet she greeted the unexpected postulant with cordial charity. It was in moments like this that constant interior mortification gave control over feelings and exterior movements. Within a few hours Mother Xavier, as the postulant wished to be called, was on her way to Florissant in a carriage borrowed from either "kind Mrs. Pratte" or "dear Mrs. Chouteau." Next day Mother Duchesne wrote to the bishop, telling him of the postulant's arrival and entrance at Florissant, and adding:

> Mother Eugenie has said nothing to me about who is to be superior at La Fourche, and she cannot supply one. Mother Carmelite was recommended to our Mother General on the condition that you should approve of this choice. She is well able to manage a house, which ought not to be as large as St. Michael's. Otherwise it might be detrimental to the latter. . . . Here we are beginning to build our chapel.

For the moment things were running fairly smoothly inside the St. Louis convent. But outside it was springtime again, and down by the bridge that led from Fourth Street to the convent property there was a sheltered stretch of water in "Monsieur Chouteau's Creek" that had for many years been the favorite swimming hole south of the town. The swimmers could not be seen from the convent enclosure, but day pupils soon reported their presence to the nuns, not perhaps so much through maidenly modesty as through indignation at the taunts and teasing hurled at them by the boys who were splashing in the water near the bridge, or called from the bushes where their clothes were hanging. Such a nuisance could not be tolerated, of course. So Mother Duchesne addressed herself to no less a person than the city's mayor, the honorable William Carr Lane, sending him one of the very few letters she ever wrote in English:

> Sir,
> I have recourse to your authority for the redress of an abuse which I look upon as very much against the welfare of our establishment. You know, Sir, that our young ladies, day schollars [sic], in order to reach our house have to pass the creek that runs all around our house. The warm weather invites a number of men and boys to swimming in the creek, and every day our young ladies meet with that disagreeable sight, both coming [to] and leaving the house; and as I understand that some regulation of court forbids swimming in public places, I suppose that it is merely by some negligence of the sheriffs in discharge of their duty that it takes place.
> As you are, Sir, the father of an amiable family I need not say how much that rudeness is against the delicacy of sentiments we strive to endow our young ladies with, and I am convinced that you will be so good as to use your power to remove that obstacle.

I offer you beforehand my thanks and beg you to believe me with deep respect,

Sir,

Your most obed. servt.
Philippine Duchesne
Supr.

The response of Mayor Lane to this appeal is not extant. One can only hope that the sheriffs were called to order for their negligence and that the sensibilities of the young ladies were no longer confronted with "that disagreeable sight." As for Mother Duchesne, she had other matters confronting her. When she learned from Bishop Rosati that Mother Audé had proposed no less a person than Mother Hamilton as superior at La Fourche, she wrote to him: "It is impossible to accede to Mother Eugenie's desire to put Mother Regis there as superior. It would ruin her health and possibly upset her spiritually. The sudden death of her sister was a great shock and she has been seriously ill several times since then."

Mother Duchesne had a deep maternal love for Regis Hamilton. The strong bond uniting them was intimate and supernatural, a friendship of the most beautiful type. There was in the soul of Philippine Duchesne a natural need for affection and a tremendous power of love. She was conscious of this inward urge and knew there was no imperfection in it. And for that very reason the stream of her affection flowed warm and rich from her great loving heart, lifting, ennobling, sanctifying. She realized that God in creating friendship had made it very good, and she clung tenaciously to the family and friends she loved. It was particularly when loneliness and isolation pressed in upon her that she called across the ocean to loved ones in France in letters that gave little hint of the suffering from which they sprang. Such was a letter to her sisters on June 3, 1828:

> It is a long time since I heard from you . . . a long time, too, since I wrote to you, but that is a consequence of my vocation and the distance that separates us. I have learned of so many deaths in our family since I came to America, and deaths of members younger than we are, I do not know whether I can count among the living many of the friends of our childhood. You and I understood, when we said *adieu*, that it was for life. We have only to keep intact by our good works the sweet hope of being reunited forever in the next world. . . .

Does your love ask for news about a sister who always loves to get news? I have been in the episcopal city of St. Louis for a year. Our house here is still in its infancy, but it gives greater promise than the others because it is in a town that is becoming the central meeting place for all who are going into the Indian country and to the posts on the Mississippi and the Missouri for fur trade and the exploitation of the rich lead mines. I have not yet lost any of the companions who came with me from France, but we are living in four different convents. . . .

Our holy religion is making great progress in this country through the zeal of missionaries; and in spite of the return of Bishop Du Bourg and many priests to France, God has not left his vineyard without workers. The seminary established here has trained many good priests and promises many more. Pray often for this mission, but above all pray for me. I am growing old and I am not becoming holy. If you could arrange for a Mass for me at Notre Dame de Fourvière and one at La Louvesc, I should be very grateful. Please give my regards to your husbands, to your children, to the Lebrument family, to our relatives at the Visitation of Romans. I heard that Melanie is now at Valence.

The new chapel was used for the first time on the feast of the Sacred Heart, though it was not yet plastered. A few days later the bishop was in St. Louis, a very busy man. Mother Duchesne recounted some of his activities and some of her own to Mother Barat on July 3:

The Reverend Father Superior was highly pleased with your decision regarding St. Charles and asked me to thank you for it. Bishop Rosati is also delighted with your answer about La Fourche. I am very sorry Mother Carmelite cannot be named superior there. Having met Mother Dutour, Monseigneur asked for her to fill the post. I refused at first, but that evening she told me she could not put out of her mind the thought that she would go to La Fourche, and I realized that she would be happy to do so. Everyone is pleased with this choice, and as a phrase in Mother de Charbonnel's letter proves to me that you leave me completely free with regard to Mother Dutour, I decided I had the authority to make this appointment. I am obliged to take Mother Regis from St. Ferdinand, though she is such a help to Mother Octavie. But I simply must have her here in order to make the children love this convent. Many of them have found things repugnant for reasons which you know. . . .

The superior of the Daughters of the Cross at La Fourche came presumably to make her novitiate at Florissant, but she did not persevere. Bishop Rosati was quite displeased at this inconstancy.

He arrived in St. Louis on the eve of the feast of St. Aloysius Gonzaga. On the feast of St. John the Baptist I went with him to St. Ferdinand and next day to St. Charles to see the church and our future convent. . . . On July 1 he gave confirmation to some of our pupils and left us on July 2. . . .

This month of July always recalls your feast and the happy days when I used to offer you my good wishes in person. While I long to see you, Reverend Mother, I have never wavered in my missionary vocation, neither have the four companions who came with me. Our attraction for the missions is inseparably bound up with an incomparable love for the whole Society and its Mother General, whose lowliest daughter I am.

As the bishop had not yet assigned a chaplain for the convent in St. Louis, Mother Duchesne made another effort in that direction. To the joy of all concerned the choice fell on newly ordained Father Regis Loisel, first St. Louisan to enter the priesthood. His very name was music in the ears of Mother Duchesne. The appointment had not gone into effect, however, when she wrote to Mother Barat on July 24:

We spent your feast at the foot of the cross, without Mass, as there was only one priest in St. Louis, and he could not leave the parish without Mass just because it was your feast day. He came, however, to give us Holy Communion and Benediction. As we had all the day pupils of both schools here that day and as Mother Dutour was leaving the next day, we put off the extra recreation until today, Thursday. I considered seriously going with Mother Dutour, as Mother Xavier Murphy has been urging me to do. The people of Opelousas are pleading with her to transfer her establishment to their town. I consulted Monseigneur on the matter when it was first suggested, and he was against it. Being unable to ask his advice about taking the trip, I sent a letter to the Reverend Father Superior by a messenger who rode out to Florissant during the night. He replied that the trip seemed unnecessary. That set my mind at rest. . . . As Mother Dutour's departure leaves a great hole in our ranks, it would have been very difficult for me to go away.

The projected transfer of the convent at Grand Coteau to the town of Opelousas did not take place, but the merger at La Fourche was carried out. Mother Dutour's appointment as superior was confirmed in time by Mother Barat, but the bishop took this for granted at once and announced her coming to Sisters Regina Cloney and Rose Elder, promising that they would soon be sent to the novitiate at St. Michael's. This would have been in accord with the Superior General's instructions. As a matter of fact, these two religious donned the habit and white veil of the choir novices of the Sacred Heart, but remained at La Fourche, carrying on the work they had inaugurated in 1825 and becoming excellent religious of the Sacred Heart. Mother Duchesne, however, was left in ignorance of what was being done in Louisiana.

Mother Dutour took up her mission at La Fourche with more zeal than prudence, though she had held positions of trust in the Society before coming to the United States. St. Madeleine Sophie had expressed high regard for her and thought she would be very efficient on the American mission. She was a Savoyard, like Mother Audé, and Mother Duchesne may have expected this fact to create mutual understanding between them, but that was lacking. With only four in her community, Mother Dutour attempted to put the La Fourche school on a curricular footing with St. Michael's. Mother Audé, who, in spite of her ready acceptance of the Lorettine novices, was opposed to the merger, at once took a determined stand against it. She had had ample time to express opposition during the twelve months preceding Mother Dutour's arrival in Louisiana, yet only on August 25, 1828, when the latter had been less than one month at La Fourche, did she write to Mother Barat:

> Mother Duchesne writes that we should send to La Fourche the orphans we are housing here. But how can we do this to the poor children? They wait on themselves, are poorly clothed, have plain food, are trained to do all kinds of work and prepared to support themselves by manual work. How can they be placed with the boarding pupils at La Fourche, who are as fine ladies as our own pupils (*aussi grandes demoiselles que les nôtres*)? Would that not make a contrast harmful to some and humiliating to others? I await directives from you, Reverend Mother, to regulate my actions. Whatever you tell me to do, that I shall do. But I cannot resist the urge to tell you that you were poorly informed about that house at La Fourche. It seems to me that if you had known all, you would never have accepted it.
>
> You want to know, Reverend Mother, whether I ask advice of Mother Duchesne. I consult her, as I consult you, on all that concerns religious virtue, which she possesses after the manner of the saints. But in all other matters I prefer to have recourse to you. Your answers come as quickly as hers but with this difference—yours give me the assurance of acting in the Society's way and hers do not offer the same assurance. I am no further from you than from Mother Duchesne. . . . Then, dear Reverend Mother,

let me have direct recourse to you. Do not refuse this favor to your Eugenie. . . .

It is patent that by this time Mother Audé had practically withdrawn her convent from Mother Duchesne's authority, and the Mother "Provincial" was aware of the fact. Moreover, while St. Michael's continued to prosper, enrolling eighty pupils, besides the group of orphans referred to, Mother Audé seems to have been obsessed with the groundless fear that *her institution*—and the personal element is only too evident—would be endangered by the activities carried on at the little convent located across the mighty Mississippi and some thirty miles or more down Bayou La Fourche. Answering this letter Mother Barat wrote:

> I send you a letter for Mother Dutour; read it and send it to her. Mother Ducis received your August letter. . . . Write me the full details about La Fourche and tell me whether my last letter on the subject made sense. At such a distance I do not know what to say, nor whether what I say is wise. . . . Your own house seems to be making great strides. Your prosperity would frighten me, my daughter, if you did not refer all this success to the Heart of Jesus and ground yourself in deep humility. . . .

Through the autumn of 1828 Mother Duchesne was aware of the friction and rivalry developing in Louisiana. In September she welcomed two choir novices from St. Michael's, Maria L'Eveque and Eulalie Guillot, the former being one of six sisters who entered the Society, the latter one of the three La Fourche novices. They were scarcely the exchange Mother Duchesne had expected as replacing Mother Dutour, for they were both delicate young women for whom, it was hoped, the Missouri climate would be beneficial. Marie made her first vows in October; Eulalie continued her novitiate at Florissant. Mother Audé refused to send any further help to St. Louis.

One of Philippine's rare joys this autumn was the entrance into the novitiate of another of her Florissant pupils, Adeline Boilvin, a niece of Mother Emilie St. Cyr. Mother Duchesne had taken a special interest in this delicate and gifted motherless child, who had been raised by her Grandmother St. Cyr and had lost her father in a river accident in 1824. Adeline had proved worthy of the care and affection given her and had returned it with a personal devotion that grew stronger through the years, making her treasure the notes and letters written to her by her spiritual mother. She was preparing to receive the habit and white veil when she wrote to consult Mother Duchesne about a patronal name and received this reply:

> It will give me great pleasure to have you bear the name of a saint whose virtues, I hope, you will imitate. Choose among these: *Louise, Louisia,* or *Gonzague,* for Aloysia has already been taken. I hope Mother Octavie's illness does not interfere with the novitiate, but rather draws down many graces upon it. Your loving hearts will be happy to procure for her the sweetest satisfaction she could enjoy in the midst of her sufferings—that of seeing you work courageously to merit the title of spouse of the most perfect and most loving Heart of Jesus.
>
> You, more than anyone else there, can contribute to the fervor of the group. The yoke of the Lord which you have borne joyously since childhood has prepared you to practice the virtues of religious life and to walk manfully under the banner of the Sacred Heart of Jesus. On that banner one sees no other words but these: *patience, simplicity, recollection, obedience, regularity, silence, sacrifice.* May you deserve to have said of you what was said of the patron you have chosen, of Berchmans, and of many religious whom I have known—that you never, through your own fault, neglected the practice of the least point of observance. This is the happiness I wish for you. . . . Give a special message of affection to each of your companions.

Early in October Mother Duchesne was notified that the dedication of the new church at St. Charles was fixed for the twelfth of the month and that it was hoped that the reopening of the convent there would coincide with this event. She had understood the previous June that the old Duquette house would be repaired and made habitable before the nuns took up their residence again in it. She had chosen two religious on whose abnegation and fidelity she knew she could rely, no matter what difficulties had to be faced. She had worked with them at Florissant, knew the bright disposition, keen sense of humor, and quick intuition for the things of God that made them such congenial companions. Mother Mary Ann O'Connor was about ten years older than her superior, Mother Lucille Mathevon, whose merry laugh and sweet, clear voice made her a delightful community person.

Mother Duchesne reached St. Charles with them and Mother Berthold after an early morning drive from Florissant on October 10. The provisions they brought along were meager, and the conditions they encountered were appalling, even to women long

accustomed to frontier life. It called for courage even to enter
the old wooden house, and for stamina sustained by supernatural
love to clean it and make it habitable.

> Inner doors, as well as window frames and glass, were gone. In
> places the floor had rotted and fallen into the low basement, where
> pigs and sheep of the neighborhood had found shelter for the past
> years. The atmosphere was foul with musty dampness and decay.
> With the aid of an Indian woman who had come with the nuns
> from Florissant, they soon had the rooms in a presentable condi-
> tion. Village carpenters closed the gaping holes in the floor and
> roof, and laid in place the stones of the foundation which had been
> rooted out by animal intruders. The work accomplished was
> phenomenal, for by the afternoon of the second day the central
> room had been transformed into a temporary chapel. An altar was
> set up, and roughly constructed benches ran the length of the
> room on two sides. At six o'clock in the evening a small bell tinkled.
> Bishop Rosati and twelve priests filed in processionally, took their
> places, and chanted the Office for the Dedication of the Church
> "with all the dignity and piety that befit the liturgical service."
>   At dawn the following morning a series of nine Masses began
> in the little chapel on the altar stone prepared for the new church.
> The priests, long accustomed to pioneer life, accepted good-
> humoredly the breakfast served them in turn on top of an empty
> barrel. There was food in plenty, for the village folk had supplied
> roasted meats, corn bread, and many other provisions. Their gen-
> erosity won the heart of Mother Mathevon before she had been a
> day in their midst. At ten o'clock the dedication ceremony be-
> gan. . . . The Religious of the Sacred Heart assisted at it and shared
> the enthusiasm of the people, who flocked to the church the fol-
> lowing day when the Bishop confirmed sixty-six persons and
> preached in his simple and captivating style. Mothers Duchesne
> and Berthold remained another day, then returned to St. Louis.

Those strenuous days at St. Charles were followed by weeks
of anxiety that lengthened into months of distress as Mother Duchesne became aware that trouble was brewing in Louisiana. An
indignant protest from Mother Audé reached her at an unpro-
pitious moment, adding to the worries that were pressing upon her.
The convent purse was empty. Florissant was in need of financial
help. Mr. Mullanphy had asked her to give hospitality to the
Sisters of Charity from Emmitsburg, Maryland, and Philippine had
only the sacristy rooms in which to house them. That in itself was
embarrassing, for the superior, Mother Xavier Love, was quite
ill when they arrived. Keen distress, born of sympathy, had also

been weighing on Philippine for the past ten days since Bishop
Rosati had called on her for just a friendly visit and told her how
troubled he was about the heavy debts left on his shoulders by
Monseigneur Du Bourg and the priests who had returned to France,
and she had had absolutely nothing to offer him, except, perhaps,
a taste of good French wine from the "groceries" in which Mr.
Reilly paid his daughter Isabelle's tuition.

And why had Eugenie sent her protest to Mother Duchesne?
Its tone and contents may be judged from some lines from Philippine's letter to the Bishop on November 17:

> My reason for writing to you is a letter I received from Mother
> Eugenie, enclosing a copy of a newspaper clipping, which gives the
> prospectus of Mother Dutour's school. . . . Mother Eugenie com-
> plains that all the subjects we teach are offered there at a lower
> tuition, which will, she thinks, take pupils away from her house and
> perhaps prevent her from paying her debts. She adds that a group
> of people at La Fourche have sworn to make St. Michael's close in
> favor of La Fourche. I find, too, that Mother Dutour has com-
> pletely disregarded the conditions laid down for her foundation.
> She has done things that only the Mother General may do. . . . I
> warned her about all this, but my warning had no effect. I beg you,
> Monseigneur, insist that the conditions be held to and inform these
> good gentlemen of these conditions. . . . Forgive me, Monsei-
> gneur, for taking up your time with this business, but I feel that I
> am speaking to a father who encourages my fullest confidence.

Philippine's prayers were weighted with other intentions, too,
that autumn. Through letters from France and through the local
newspapers she had learned of the political disturbances rife again
in the homeland and of the religious persecution that accompanied
them. Mother Barat had written of "dreadful days" and "sad times"
and of the expulsion of the Jesuits as a part of the radical plan to
rob youth of Christian education. From Josephine de Savoye-
Rollin had come information about the active part the Perier men
were taking in the political life of France. Four of them were in the
Chamber of Deputies now, and they were all men who knew their
own minds: Casimir, always conservative, sat on the right; Augustin, center left; Camille, left; and Alexandre, extreme left. But this
difference in political opinion made no rupture in the close bond
among the Periers. There had been family sorrows that drew them
closer than ever, and Josephine had given the full details in a letter
that was more than five months old when it reached St. Louis.
Hastening to answer, Philippine wrote on November 25:

In your letter you gave me such a concise and interesting picture of the present state and circumstances of our large family. You forgot nothing of all that is dear to me and all I am bound to by ties of gratitude. Your heart guided your pen. Sensing the desires of my heart, you have written about all that touches me most poignantly. So I appeal to your heart to express my loving sympathy to Madame Augustin Perier and Madame Camille Teisseire in the sorrows that have come to them. Having known the children to whom they were so tenderly attached, I can appreciate their grief at losing them so soon. In such trials there is nothing to do but bow the head and adore the ways of Divine Providence, which are not our ways. But I am firmly convinced that God has cut short these splendid young lives only to reward the sooner those virtues which worldliness might have tarnished. . . .

Then she gave free rein to her pen, describing with evident satisfaction the ceremonies she had witnessed at St. Charles in October and the progress of the other convent schools in Louisiana and Missouri. "Here in St. Louis," she concluded, "we teach at least one hundred children, but most of them are in the free school. The money shortage has left us few pupils in the boarding school."

The seal on this letter was scarcely dry when word came that Mother Berthold was desperately ill again. Mother Duchesne felt she must again make the sacrifice of Regis Hamilton, who exchanged places with Mother Therese Detchemendy on November 29. The sorrow of the one was the joy of the other, and Therese appreciated the privilege of living once more with Mother Duchesne, for she lost no time in telling Mother Barat: "I am now in St. Louis with my dear Mother Duchesne. I cannot tell you how hard she works or how she deprives herself in order that we may have more. One can truly say she is like a victim continually immolating herself in the interest of our dear Society."

2. 1829—1830

IN HER NEW YEAR'S LETTER Philippine offered Bishop Rosati the greetings and prayers of the community of the Sacred Heart "who thanked the Lord for the progress they have made under your guidance." After giving him news of the convents in Missouri, she again stressed the Mother General's wish that La Fourche be kept on a level lower than that of St. Michael's, and begged him to use his influence with Mother Dutour, "who is extremely self-willed in her plans, and does not answer my letters at all, hoping to obtain all she desires directly from France." Two weeks later she told the bishop, "No news from La Fourche." And at this juncture the death of Père Antoine Sedella obliged Bishop Rosati to go to New Orleans, so he was absent from Missouri when Mother Duchesne received another letter from St. Madeleine Sophie advising her to go to Louisiana to see things for herself and to confer with Mothers Audé, Murphy, and Dutour as to the best means of securing uniformity in the American convents and an understanding among the superiors themselves. Mother Duchesne was still reluctant to undertake the mission and pleaded with the Mother General "to consent to whatever they will regulate among themselves."

There were, indeed, several obstacles to her leaving St. Louis just then—Mother Berthold's serious illness, her own rheumatic condition, aggravated by a fall, the expense of the trip, and the lack of a mature religious to fill her place during an absence of two or three months. She went to St. Charles, however, to discuss the matter with Mother Mathevon, accompanied by Sister Mary Layton, who became the third member of that community. Mother Mathevon's reaction to the visit was expressed in a letter to Mother Barat a week later:

> I had been here at St. Charles four months before I had the happiness of receiving your letter. What joy it brought to my heart! And I had another very delightful pleasure recently in the thirty-six hours that Mother Duchesne spent with us. That visit lifted our spirits and renewed our courage to endure the many hardships facing us. . . . We live in great peace and union here and in an entire dependence on our dear Mother Duchesne, to whom we write frequently. . . .

In Mother Duchesne's relations with Bishop Rosati there are many heart-warming incidents that show the prelate's understanding and sympathy. He had accepted a generous gesture with which she had refused a share, even a mere thousand francs, of the money provided for the missions of the diocese in 1828 by the Society for the Propagation of the Faith. "After all he had told me of his own needs," she explained to Mother Barat, "I had not the courage to accept the money. I prefer to suffer." But before his hurried departure for New Orleans in January, 1829, he instructed Mr. Mullanphy to give her a thousand francs as soon as the letter of exchange for the money was paid to him. Being now in actual want, Philippine applied to Mullanphy as soon as she was informed of the Bishop's kindness and obtained "$30 in advance," although the agent had not yet received the money from Europe.

Responsibility for the Louisiana convents was weighing heavily on her when she wrote to Bishop Rosati on April 5 to express her gratitude and to ask him to grant Mothers Audé and Murphy permission to come to St. Louis to confer with her. She had to admit that physical suffering was now her constant companion, but there was pain of another kind much harder to bear:

> Father Saulnier has been saying for some time that he wanted to talk to you about me, but he decided to tell me himself what he had to say. It concerns my manner of acting with my Sisters, which is too severe. Evidently they have been complaining to him about me, and this does not surprise me, but it is a fact that makes a meeting of the superiors all the more necessary, for Mother Octavie is very weak and she is suffering from several ailments. . . . Be assured, Monseigneur, that I shall be submissive to all that you may decide in regard to me and that I am well aware of my faults.

This letter crossed one from the bishop which must have pleased Mother Duchesne and at the same time increased her uncertainty as to what steps she should take, for the picture he drew of the La Fourche convent was, on the whole, quite favorable, and he urged the continuance of the work then being accomplished by Mother Dutour. After praising the simplicity, unworldliness, and economy he had noted at the convent on the bayou, he argued strongly in its favor and concluded with a paragraph of appreciation which contained a hint, at least, at one of the chief causes of disunion in the Society in Louisiana:

> I am of the opinion that you should see things for yourself, for it is just possible that seculars may perceive a kind of jealousy in the fears for the welfare of St. Michael's which are utterly unfounded, fears that these people should never have been allowed to hear expressed. It is the interest I take, first of all in the good of religion in general, and then in your own institute, which is so useful in our dioceses, that makes me speak this way. I have no prejudice and no preference. All your convents are equally dear to me, and it is a real joy for me to see them prosper and increase.

In spite of this assurance, Mother Duchesne retained many misgivings with regard to conditions at La Fourche. One thing, however, was clear—she must send help to Mother Dutour. The question was whom to send. She scanned her list of the Missouri communities. There were just three nuns at St. Charles; and no one could be spared from Florissant, where the superior was ill and where regularity was necessary on account of the novitiate. As she pondered in prayer, a great act of confidence in Divine Providence welled up in her soul and she made her decision. She would make the sacrifice of young Therese Detchemendy, who was proving quite capable in the classroom, and send her south with Mother Van Damme, who might find more happiness in Louisiana than she had in Missouri.

Nearly six months had passed since Philippine's last letter to the Mother General. Her letters to the bishop were always carried downstream by passengers on the steamboats and delivered for her without expense. Letters to her family had gone with travelers bound for Europe. There was reason for her silence toward the Mother and friend she loved so ardently: she simply had not enough money to pay the mailing cost on a letter to France, but she wrote on May 18:

> We have had the cross of poverty this year to such an extent as to prohibit us from writing to you, as we had not the money to spare for the postage and were not able to get some mail out of the post office for the same reason. The convents at St. Ferdinand and St. Louis have often been several days without a penny, and we have had to pretend that things were otherwise, so as not to lose credit at the stores. At last, however, Mother Eugenie wrote me to draw on her for the money which you were so good as to instruct her to give us. Then Monseigneur gave me 1000 francs from what was sent him by the Society for the Propagation of the Faith. So we were able to repay the 3500 francs we borrowed last year, along with the interest. That is a sharp thorn drawn from my foot, for we have such scanty resources—eight boarding pupils, twenty-seven people to feed, nineteen of them to support entirely, and 1250 francs to be paid to the hired man. The eighteen day pupils who pay tuition have kept us alive this winter. Day pupils also support St. Charles, where there is only one boarding pupil, along with several orphans who are cared for gratis. . . .
>
> We have sixty children in the free school, and within a year that school will have given us four postulants. So you see what the convent in St. Louis is accomplishing. We shall have many vocations from that group, which is so characteristically American, and very few from the boarding school. This, of course, will keep us in poverty, as we must provide everything for them, but several of

them will be gifted for studies. The convent at St. Ferdinand is
better suited than this one for the novices. Though always suffering, Mother Octavie trains them well. There they do not have the
distractions we have here.

Monseigneur Rosati is delighted with the house at La Fourche
and does not want us to limit the number of its pupils. The other
two convents are complaining a good deal that it is doing them
harm. I think Mother Dutour could be satisfied with thirty pupils.
She is a person who will push her requests until she gets her convent on an equal footing with the others. I cannot possibly leave
here to go on a visit to Louisiana. I have five classes, all the religious instruction, spiritual reading, Office, the prayers in common
to say, and what is more, the surveillance, which is very difficult.

Please consent to whatever regulations our three superiors in
Louisiana may decide upon. I am nothing but a worn-out stick,
fit to be cast aside right now. But I beg you not to agree to the
suppression of one of the houses in Missouri. St. Charles will be an
educational opportunity for the children of the vast spaces of the
western country. This convent is in the episcopal city, the most
important place in the state. St. Ferdinand is the novitiate and has
a boarding school with a lower tuition than we charge here.
Mother Octavie agrees with me in all this. . . .

This letter reached Mother Barat at about the same time as one
from Mother Audé containing the following crisp sentences:

Mother Duchesne wrote to me that she could not come down here.
She wanted me to go up there instead, but I cannot leave here now.
As she foresaw this might be the case, she invited Mothers Xavier,
Dutour, and me to meet and discuss the following points: 1)
whether the houses of St. Louis and St. Ferdinand should be
merged into one; 2) whether the number of establishments in
Louisiana and Missouri should be limited to six; 3) what dispensations in matters of rule are needed in this country. She gave
as her opinion, and that of Mothers Octavie and Lucille, a *No* for
the first two points. I have allowed myself only too often the
liberty of expressing my opinion on these same points in the several
letters I have written you recently. The third point can be handled
quickly enough right here. No dispensations are necessary, or if
one or two have to be requested, they are of small importance and
not absolutely necessary. . . .

It was a far cry from Paris and Lyons and Grenoble and Rome
to the frontiers of the United States in 1829. Although St. Michael's
and Grand Coteau were in a prosperous section of the country and
in the midst of a Catholic Creole population, there had often arisen

need for latitude in the application of the Society's rules and regulations. In Missouri circumstances had made that need more frequent. With only three religious at St. Charles and five at La Fourche it was impossible to expect exact observance in all details. For more than a decade of years Mother Duchesne had striven with all the energy of her loyal will to keep intact the spirit of the Society among the religious whom she had brought with her to America and to plant that spirit deep in the souls of the novices whom she accepted as members of the order, and she had succeeded magnificently, though the letter of the rule had sometimes to give way before the exigencies of circumstances. Love for the Society and its holy foundress were, with her, second only to love for the Sacred Heart, the Catholic faith, and the Church, and she transmitted that love to all her religious daughters with such steadfast conviction and ardor of spirit that the strength of the bond she created has never weakened nor the flame of love burned low.

The summer of 1829 was marked by few "events" to record in the *Journal* which Mother Duchesne kept so faithfully. Late in August she learned that the bishop was planning a trip east in September. A little letter to Madame Jouve, written the day he was leaving for the Council of Baltimore, may have traveled as far as the seaport in an episcopal pocket. The beautiful supernatural sentiments and tender sympathy of the first paragraph contrast pathetically with the weary note struck in the second, but it is a very characteristic bit of writing:

> God, who takes care of our family, sends us from time to time some consolations. I have enjoyed none more than the knowledge of the deeply religious sentiments in your soul and the graces you receive from the goodness of God and through the trials he sends you. I understand how great a sacrifice it is for you to give up Constance, how alone you are after raising so many children. But remember, they belong to God more than to you. You have offered them to him more than a thousand times in your heart, never dreaming that, when the moment of giving came, your heart would experience such suffering. But help yourself by the thought that even in this life your children enjoy more happiness in the service of God than they would in the most brilliant marriages. I have heard only recently of Constance's response to her vocation and of Henri's departure for Rome. I hope perseverance will crown their generous sacrifices.
>
> You want news of me. I consider myself still young because I do what I did in my younger days, but I often hear this comment, "My, but you are old!" I trust I shall not survive you, as I have

already survived two sisters who were younger than I, Adelaide and Melanie. Do not fail to remember me to my brother, to Madame de Mauduit, to your husband, to all your children who know me, and obtain for me all the prayers you possibly can. *Adieu*, my loved Sister. All yours in the Heart of Jesus.

For several months Mother Duchesne had been hoping and praying for recruits from France for the American houses. It was plain that Mother Berthold could no longer carry on the work at Florissant, and Mother Duchesne was finding it almost beyond her strength to fill the offices of superior, mistress general, treasurer, class mistress, and surveillante at the City House. The children were unruly, the parents exacting in their demands, the gossips were at their old tricks, and through it all she had before her the Superior General's instructions to go to Louisiana. Then came the long-expected travelers, Mothers Catherine Thiéfry, Fèlicité Lavy-Brun, and Julie Bazire.

The presence of these religious made possible a reorganization of classes and a reallotment of employments. Moreover, Mother Duchesne could plan her trip to Louisiana with a sense of security, for Mother Thiéfry was quite capable of directing the convent during her absence, though her English was as yet halting and uncertain. She was a fine looking woman, cordial in manner, attractive in conversation. She had been educated by Benedictine nuns and had entered the Society twelve years before coming to America. Much of her early religious life had been spent at Amiens, where in 1818 she had seen Sister Catherine Lamarre set out for Paris to join Mother Duchesne's first band of missionaries. Desiring to make to God what she considered the fullest sacrifice of herself, she asked to follow them, but only in 1829 was her request granted by St. Madeleine Sophie.

The scholastic year opened on September 30 with just seven boarding pupils, though day pupils were numerous in the academy, and the free school was crowded. The regulation was working smoothly when Mother Duchesne began her preparations for the trip to Louisiana. The *Missouri* was listed to sail for New Orleans on Thursday, November 5, but it was only on Saturday that the cables were loosed and the big steamboat nosed away from the levee and out into the murky stream. Seven years had passed since Mother Duchesne had traveled on the river, but the experience of that terrible trip in the autumn of 1822 was fresh in her memory. Now, however, the chill of the oncoming winter removed the danger of yellow fever, and progress in steamboat construction had made travel safer and more pleasant. Moreover, the presence of Father De La Croix on board relieved her of many little worries. He found her changed in appearance—thinner, older, with a slight halt in her walk that would increase to a limp as the dampness penetrated her stiffened joints. The expression in her fine blue eyes was often troubled and suffering, yet they could grow luminous again when a genial and friendly smile broke over her features.

She had aged considerably in the past three years, but this fact was less noticeable because of the more close-fitting frilled cap she wore now and the black bandeau that hid her pale gray hair. These modifications in the religious habit, adopted at the most recent General Council, were a great improvement, but the dampness of the river soon threatened the starch of her cap frill. So she and her companion, Mother Maria L'Eveque, for whom the doctors had advised a return to her native climate, sat in a sheltered corner on the deck or in the "ladies' parlor," talking, reading, knitting, praying. Sometimes Mother Duchesne drew from her pocket the letter from St. Madeleine Sophie that had sent her down the river at last on the mission she faced with such strong misgivings. Again and again she read the well-worn sheet which she had brought with her as a credential, though she realized that it gave her no increased authority:

> I see with anxiety [the Mother General had written in June] that union is somewhat compromised. The house at La Fourche is the cause of this—or the pretext. Believe me, dear Mother, it would be best for you to take a little trip to Louisiana; assemble Mothers Eugenie, Dutour, and Xavier at St. Michael's, and regulate affairs. I name you to preside at this little council. You can come to some definite agreements, as for example: 1) to make no more foundations for three or four years; 2) to decide on three first class academies and fix the other three on a lower level [about grammar school level]; 3) make regulations regarding uniformity in the matter of closing exercises, invitations to Prizes, etc. Then examine the decrees of the General Councils; decide which are not practicable in America and write this to me. At least let all the American houses do the same thing and let the dispensations or modifications be uniform in all our convents there. This little meeting should heal all breaches of charity and encourage each one to put the general interests of all before the particular interests of her own house.

At other times, as she sat writing, her quill raced across the paper and fixed there the thoughts that filled her mind and expressed themselves in the chatty style she had not used in many a month. But she did not write on Sundays. To her great astonishment Father De La Croix had asked her not to do so. As the *Missouri* dropped downstream, fatigue and weariness abated and Mother Duchesne was better able, physically, to cope with the situation she so dreaded. Her loyal will was one with the Mother General, whose instructions she desired to carry out. There was no flagging in her spirit of obedience, but she soon found herself unable to cope with the circumstances or fully to execute the orders she had received. Her authority was practically paralyzed by conditions too complicated by personalities to be easily resolved. Mother Audé was smooth and inflexible, determined to do as she thought best for her institution, regardless of general interests. Mother Dutour was unreasonable, changeable, yet set on her own will and judgment. Mother Murphy was generous and sympathetic, sincerely attached to Mother Duchesne, but she refused to yield where there was a question of what she considered her rights. No one has analyzed the situation better than Monseigneur Louis Baunard, first biographer of Philippine Duchesne:

At this time [he writes] and until 1839, all the convents of the Sacred Heart, in the New World as well as in the Old, were directly under the Superior General, who still found it possible to fulfil this task of government. *De Facto* and *de jure* local superiors had recourse to her as the one supreme authority, and a feeling of filial affection and veneration made all her daughters naturally desire to treat directly with so wise and holy a Mother. This was especially the case with Mother Audé, whose attachment to Mother Barat inclined her to repel anyone or anything that was an obstacle to her relations with this loved Mother.

"I consult dear Mother Duchesne on spiritual matters," she wrote, "for in these she excels." And she limited her consultations to just this. Mother Duchesne had no support for her authority when she advised or decided anything, save a vague mandate emanating from the personal desire of the Superior General, but having no foundation in the statutes of the Society, and no precedent in its history. Hence the repugnance she experienced toward the position of presidency at a local council arose as much from her wisdom as from her humility. As head of a conference where all was to be decided by plurality of votes, her authority rested mainly on her experience, enlightened but scarcely to be considered successful. . . . And she had good reason to fear that her manner of acting might be considered severe in comparison with that of Mother Audé, who obtained such attractive results at St. Michael's.

After a brief stay at the convent on the Mississippi, Mother Duchesne went to La Fourche for a friendly visit, then returned to St. Michael's, accompanied by Mother Dutour. This little trip gave her a clearer knowledge of the geography of the river and bayou parishes, involving, as it did, a short navigation west-north-west across the Mississippi by steamboat to Donaldsonville, and a change to a bayou boat or a wheeled vehicle to go some thirty miles south among the bayou plantations and settlements to Assumption de La Fourche, today called Plattenville. Moss-hung trees, thick reeds, and trailing vines lined the water's edge on either side, with clumps of palmettoes here and there. Small farmhouses of French type, built of cypress timber, with front galleries for shade and homey hospitality, stood back from the stream in groves of stately live-oaks. Here and there a mansion could be seen, like that of Colonel Pugh's, whose broad acres, lush with fertility, spread along the upper reaches of the bayou. It was not, on the whole, a rich district, nor was it as poor a place as Mother Duchesne had been led to believe. It was a section of French-speaking, home-loving people, still without affluence or aristocracy, still looking askance at the Americans who were making their way into the quiet bayou country where Acadians had pioneered as early as 1755. There were many Catholic girls here in need of education.

When Mother Xavier Murphy reached St. Michael's, the work of the council began. There were private conferences of the individual superiors with Mother Duchesne and some general discussions of problems facing the several houses, of abuses calling for correction, of dispensations or modifications to be granted uniformly to the American convents of the Sacred Heart, but only a few minor regulations were agreed upon for all and submitted to the Mother General. Although she represented the three Missouri houses, Mother Duchesne seems to have had but one vote in the council, and this placed her in a difficult, and at times a heartbreaking, position, for she was obliged to struggle for the very existence of her poor little institutions. In a letter to St. Madeleine Sophie, written while the council was in session, she touched on a variety of subjects and described conditions in the bayou convent, but made no mention of decisions arrived at in the conferences.

St. Michael's, December 11, 1829
Recommended to St. Anthony

My Very Reverend Mother,

This month of December always recalls the happy day of your arrival at Grenoble, December 13, 1804. Twenty-five years have passed since that day when I was admitted into the dear Society. In it my happiness has increased steadily with the progress made by the order, for what do we desire but the glory of Jesus! He has brought the Society through many trials, but those were to be expected when we contracted our noble alliance with Christ. Once when we were reading the chapter of the *Imitation* on the Royal Road of the Cross, I drew from it this aspiration: *Portavi et portabo* [I have carried it and I shall go on carrying it]. . . . I have nothing but my whole heart to offer you with my wishes for a Happy New Year. The year will have begun before my letter reaches you; still I shall be closely united with all my Sisters in France at the very moment when they offer you their greetings for the new Year, for hearts can be united across the greatest distances. . . .

That house of La Fourche—what an obstacle it is to our complete agreement, and how tenaciously Monseigneur Rosati holds to it! I am going to tell you, point by point, exactly what I see. Mother Eugenie has praised that house to me, and I have seen no sign of jealousy in her; but she does insist that it should be organized on a footing lower than St. Michael's, as the two institutions are so close together. She and Mother Xavier agree in saying that very few children go further than the third class in their academies, and that if La Fourche goes that far also and has a lower tuition fee, it will cut down their enrollments. St. Michael's, moreover, still has debts and needs to enlarge the building, as the community is too crowded for health and regularity. . . .

Mother Eugenie and I got an account from Mother Dutour in conference here. We could not budge her on these three points: 1) to continue teaching the third class; 2) to enlarge the building; 3) to train her novices at La Fourche. . . . Father Richard thinks it is unwise to displease the bishop and the priests and the people of La Fourche, one of whom gave the property for the education of children in that section. He also says we really cannot refuse the parents' request for a school there, as it is often difficult for them to cross the Mississippi to go to see their children at St. Michael's. I believe Mother Dutour is acting contrary to her own best interests. Still, in spite of the many problems connected with that house, we want to carry out your wishes and keep it going. . . . I shall return here from Grand Coteau, but that is a very difficult trip, so I shall post this letter now, anxious as I am for you to give the final decisions. I have been obliged to tell the superiors that I have no real authority, that I came as a Sister, an equal, that you wished us to consult together but reserved to yourself and your advisory council the decisions to be made.

During the conferences Mother Duchesne was ill at ease. "What influence can I have," she wrote, "in a house where all is admiration from within and from without, while in St. Louis I am in just the opposite position? I gave my opinion on every point discussed, but I was convinced that I should step aside without pressing my point in any way except in friendly fashion as a sister would act among her sisters."

The conferences lasted about two weeks. Mother Duchesne had intended to leave at their close with Mother Murphy for Grand Coteau, but death visited St. Michael's again, and they remained for the funeral of Sister Borgia Boudreau. Mothers Duchesne and Murphy had barely boarded the steamboat for Plaquemine when Mother Audé, who was dissatisfied with decisions that had been made relative to her convent, wrote in harsh and critical tones to Mother Barat on December 21:

> Our little meeting is over, Reverend Mother. Regarding this house it was decided, 1) that parents of the pupils will not be invited to the distribution of prizes at the close of the year; 2) that we shall not continue to send reports about the children's progress; 3) that we shall no longer display in the visitors' parlor the list of competition places. I agreed quite happily to the first point, as I had decided ahead of time to follow our Constitutions hereafter in that matter. The second, and still more the third, points distressed me to some extent, for I know the parents will not be pleased. They hold very much to the reports. When they see that several changes have been made at the same time—no more public examinations, no more lists in the parlor, no more reports—they will think the institution is going downhill, and that will be harmful to it. As a matter of fact, curtailment in these last two points will certainly not establish uniformity between our convents in Louisiana and those in Missouri. If you would only have the goodness to send as visitatrix one of our Mothers who is thoroughly imbued with your spirit, she could judge of the truth of what I am bold enough to state, and her visit would do the greatest amount of good in our little American mission. Without this step on your part it will gradually lose all resemblance with the Society in France. . . . With your permission, Reverend Mother, I shall continue to send the report

cards just as is done in France. . . . Will you have the goodness to
answer me at once on this matter? . . .

When one recalls that Mother Audé had known the Society
just four years in France, whereas Mother Duchesne had been a
member thirteen years before coming to America, one cannot but
wonder at the tone of superiority in which she writes, at the naïveté
of her haughty self-assurance, at the scorn implied in her severe
criticism. Yet Mother Duchesne had judged Eugenie with magna-
nimity, had praised her for her ability and her achievements, and
had justified her to the Superior General the day before this scath-
ing comment was written. She had admitted, however, that she felt
more at ease with the young Irish superior of Grand Coteau when
she wrote: "Mother Murphy is the one to whom I feel most personally attracted. We really could not help expressing our desire
to live together in St. Louis. But who could fill that Mother's place
at Opelousas?"

The trip to Grand Coteau with Mothers Murphy and L'Eveque
was a tiring expedition that kept them traveling on Christmas Day,
but Mother Duchesne enjoyed the affectionate solicitude of her
companions and the warm welcome that greeted her. She was
happy to gather the community around her in that friendly, maternal way that made her loved so loyally by those who appreciated
her high supernatural spirit and her lowly opinion of herself. Of
the ten nuns in the group she knew all but three—Mother Dorival,
Sister Cecile Boudreau, whose holy mother had just died, and
Adele Aguiard, a young Creole novice who would exchange her
white veil for a black one during this visit.

How lovingly she greeted her old companion of the *Rebecca*,
Sister Marguerite Manteau, and her first choir novice, Emilie St.
Cyr! And there was Mother Carmelite Landry, whom she had
known since 1822, and Eleanor Gray and Mary Frances Mullanphy, aspirants now. They all welcomed Mother Maria L'Eveque
with cordial love, and for three weeks enjoyed a happiness that was
enhanced by the very evident joy of their superior. The bond of
union between Mother Murphy and Mother Duchesne sprang not
only from supernatural charity but also from congeniality of
temperament. They were cultured, vivacious women, marked
characters who understood each other, seeing usually eye to eye
and looking always from the vantage ground of faith. There was
no pettiness in their make-up, no self-seeking in their apostolic
work, and the younger nun was eager to draw with joy from the

fountain of the older woman's spiritual depths. One day they walked together to the little cemetery where there was just one grave, and Mother Duchesne told the story of Mary Ann Summers and her vocation.

On January 16, 1830, Mother Duchesne left Grand Coteau. Back at St. Michael's four days later, she was writing to Mother Barat about her trip. The one thing that worried her at Grand Coteau was the presence of so many non-Catholic children in the school. She felt that religion had no part in the lives of many of these girls and she stressed this fact to the Mother General. Her sense of humor was not dulled by this anxiety, however, and she regaled Mother Barat with a description of her departure from Grand Coteau in the torrential rain of a sub-tropical storm, accompanied by a nervous Vincentian priest and a frightened Negro boy who acted as guide on horseback, clinging desperately to his mount and uttering low moans amidst lightning and thunder.

Philippine was eager to begin the homeward river trip, but steamboats going upstream were scarce at that season and she was obliged to wait for two weeks at St. Michael's. This gave her time for prayer and reading and resting. Among the twenty-two members of the community, eighteen had been strangers to her when she arrived in November. With seventy pupils in the academy the young religious and novices were kept busy. Only Sister Judith Labruyère came frequently to talk to her. She was preparing for her final vows and turned with love and confidence to the Mother who had initiated her into religious life. Judith was pale and noticeably thinner; a hacking cough interrupted her at times as she talked, but she made no complaint. There was joy in her soul and her desires soared up to an ideal of loving service that would make her worthy to wear the cross and ring of a professed Religious of the Sacred Heart.

Mother Duchesne had leisure for letters, too, and she wrote to Mother Barat:

> I do not know whether God has been pleased with my trip or not. Your will alone made it pleasant for me. My heart leans always to the side of the less fortunate, and that is Missouri. I am not made for a life of leisure, and I have not succeeded in bringing about the union you desired to have re-established. Bishop Rosati's letter has made you decide to leave La Fourche as it is. Father Richard also told me to tell you he believes that convent is really needed in that section of the country; he thinks it would give great offense to people if it were reduced to a lower scholastic level. There is a

kind of rivalry between the parishes on the two sides of the Mississippi, and Mother Dutour has already found more sources of outside help than the other houses have, for that section is religious-minded and offers many influential backers among the rich planters. . . . Will you please send directly to me a copy of the instructions you send Mother Dutour, so I may not suggest anything contrary to them, and if possible word the articles so definitely that we shall have done with objections. . . . I shall try to combine the two boarding schools in St. Louis, as you desire, and so bring together the religious who are teaching. I shall not repeat myself, as I have already sent you the details of this plan, but I beg you to consider it well before it is carried out. . . . Please accept, dear Mother, my apologies for the mistakes you will notice in my letters. Old age, which weighs on me, is my excuse.

While Mother Duchesne was in Louisiana, Mother Barat had received reports from St. Louis that praised Philippine herself, but represented her convent in a very unfavorable light. The young religious were described as "nearly all without much training yet, but this is not surprising when one considers Mother Duchesne's many occupations and the fact that she has been working almost single-handed here. She spends the greater part of her nights praying or writing, and the whole day in the boarding school." And again: "One must be satisfied with loving God and praying for the conversion of this wicked town of St. Louis. . . . This dear convent is worthy of Mother Duchesne, for it is poor, persecuted, and the happy dwelling-place of the Cross."

On February 2 Mother Duchesne had the joy of assisting at the religious profession of Sister Judith Labruyère, and on the seventh she boarded the *Oregon* for St. Louis. Again she was to experience the uncertainties of river transportation, but this time she considered the circumstances a happy arrangement of Divine Providence. At the mouth of the Ohio the *Oregon* ran aground and the passengers were obliged to disembark and continue the trip by ox-cart. This gave Mother Duchesne an opportunity to ask hospitality of the Sisters of Loretto at the Barrens and talk over with them the delicate matter of La Fourche. As it was from this community that Sister Joanna Miles and her companions had gone to Louisiana at Bishop Du Bourg's request, these religious felt keenly the unusual step taken by Bishop Rosati to bring the Sisters at La Fourche into the Society of the Sacred Heart. But their charity and religious spirit lifted them above personal resentment and made a deep impression on Mother Duchesne.

From the Loretto convent she went to St. Mary's Seminary to see Bishop Rosati, who had returned in January from his long trip to Canada after the Council of Baltimore. On reaching home he had found there the papal letters appointing Father Leo de Neckere to be Bishop of New Orleans. The bishop-elect was also there to greet him and would remain until May, when his consecration was scheduled to take place in his see city. Mother Duchesne was delighted with the good fortune that enabled her to discuss with these prelates the changes decided in the council for Missouri and the problems confronting the convent at La Fourche. The bishop-elect seemed to understand all that she put before him and promised to do all in his power to sustain the institution on the bayou and "to take on himself the office of ecclesiastical superior of the three convents of the Sacred Heart in Louisiana."

On leaving the seminary Mother Duchesne put into Bishop Rosati's hand a folded paper. She had driven away in the rough, two-wheeled cart when he opened it and found enclosed a note for $100. It is easy to imagine his emotion as he read the few lines she had written that February 22, 1830:

> Monseigneur, I realize that the $100 I have been able to save on my trip for the convent in St. Louis is more needed at the seminary, at least until you receive payment in March for your pupils from Louisiana. If it can be of use to your treasurer to pay the tradesmen, I shall be only too happy to relieve him of an anxiety with which I am only too well acquainted. . . .

The report sent by Mother Duchesne to the Superior General regarding the American convents contained many heartening facts. The statistics she compiled showed that the Religious of the Sacred Heart, after twelve years in the Mississippi Valley, had six institutions, in which more than 350 children were being educated. Of the sixty-four nuns carrying on the work, fourteen had come from France, fifty were Americans. There had been only three deaths in these twelve years, one at Grand Coteau and two at St. Michael's. The account of the meeting of the superiors was less satisfactory, as Philippine learned in the spring of 1830 from Mother Barat. Although "much good had been accomplished," and "the essential affairs" had been regulated, the Superior General felt that there was much more to be done. She approved of a new building at Grand Coteau and the remodeling and enlarging of the convent at La Fourche. She was also inclined to allow Mother Dutour to develop the scholastic level of her school as she thought best, but she added: "Without your consent, however, I shall not give this permission."

In St. Louis Mother Duchesne was faced with the task of carrying out the changes decided on by plurality of vote at St. Michael's, and she set to work immediately, though she doubted the wisdom of her action. The Florissant convent was to transfer its boarding pupils to St. Louis, retaining there only the free school and the novitiate, and depending for support on Divine Providence. This meant changes in personnel. Mothers Berthold and Hamilton accompanied the pupils to St. Louis, while Mother Thiéfry took charge of the Florissant convent as superior and mistress of novices, having Mother Shannon as her chief helper. While these arrangements were being carried out, another group of nuns prepared to go south. Mother Julie Bazire and Sister Tesserot were destined for La Fourche, Mother Lavy-Brun and Sister Lucille Roche for Grand Coteau.

Jottings in her *Journal* show Philippine faithfully recording all these moves, along with some events. There is an overtone of joy as she notes the early Mass offered on Holy Thursday by Monseigneur de Neckere, who hurried off to assist the bishop at the Cathedral; the celebration of Easter with Father Peter Walsh, S.J., at the altar; the presence of both the bishop and the bishop-elect on April 12, when Eulalie Guillot, Marguerite Short, and Josephine Miller made their first vows. Both the Reverend Father Superior, whose name she had not mentioned for quite a while, and the bishop-elect were at the convent on April 13, when five of the pupils of the academy received their First Holy Communion, "among them Miss Anne Stegar, a convert from Protestantism, about twenty years of age, who wishes to become a religious."

ten

Years Surcharged
with Suffering

I. 1830—1832

GENERAL WILLIAM HENRY ASHLEY, fur trader, explorer, politician, and officer of militia, paced the front gallery of his mansion on Third Street. The air was pleasant that Sunday afternoon in the spring of 1830, but the General gave little heed to its warmth or to the fresh beauty of the leafing trees and bushes in the garden. He was anxious about many things, especially his sick wife. It was not five years since he had married Eliza Christy, and she was fading like a flower under his very eyes. She had the best of care and all that wealth could provide, but she was feverish and restless, and also quite upset about Anne. Why had he kept Anne in St. Louis?

She was his sister Nancy's daughter and had come from Virginia for a visit. Her father was dead, and the General had thought to show his love by giving the girl some further education. The McNair children, who lived across the street, went to the convent school. They were younger than Anne, but she had joined them as a day scholar and had been greatly attracted to the nuns, especially to Mother Duchesne. When she began to talk of changing her religion, the General had gone to discuss the matter with this nun. He had found her broadminded and understanding, so he had not made objections; he had only insisted that the girl be well instructed

354

and not allowed to go impetuously into Catholicism. Many of his best friends and some of his keenest competitors were of that faith, and the Catholic bishop was the most highly respected man in St. Louis. Bishop Rosati had examined Anne and found her not only pious but also sincerely convinced in her faith, so the General had gone again to the convent for the Communion ceremony on April 13. But when his niece had declared her intention of joining the nunnery, he had refused his consent. Now he had let her go alone to visit the nuns, and he wondered what the outcome would be.

At the convent there was subdued excitement that Sunday afternoon when Anne Stegar jumped the fence to get in and then took refuge in the chapel near the shrine of the Blessed Virgin. In need of wise guidance, Mother Duchesne turned instinctively to the Jesuits, who counseled the utmost circumspection in the affair. But she could not send Anne from the convent. She had decided to let the girl remain, when quite suddenly the problem solved itself, and she could write on May 6:

> That evening the General, her uncle, sent his carriage for her. She told the Negro driver that it was useless for her uncle to send for her as she was not going to leave the convent. . . . We composed a letter to the family but were hesitating about sending it when, without any warning, her uncle sent to the convent all his niece's belongings—bed, clothing, etc. She hopes this means that he approves of her action.

Mother Duchesne had certainly been guided by the Holy Spirit in dealing with Anne Stegar. Even the death of her Aunt Eliza Ashley on June 1 did not shake her resolution, though she sympathized lovingly in the sorrow of her uncle. Her novitiate was tempestuous, but both Mother Duchesne and Bishop Rosati understood and trusted her, and they were justified in this confidence. On August 19 the bishop confirmed her.

Speaking privately with Mother Duchesne after the ceremony, he told her that he had information about a revolution in France. Just when it had occurred and what had happened he did not know. Philippine turned to prayer, then began a letter to Josephine:

> I wonder if you received my letter of thanks for the last help you were so kind as to send me. . . . Let me thank you again, and at the same time renew the expression of my deep gratitude to you and all the members of your family who in the past have helped me so much. . . . Your friendship has followed me to these distant

regions where one sees very few examples of attachment as generous and as lasting as yours. Now I am going to ask a new proof of
it: please write me the facts about the events that took place in
France toward the end of July. An extraordinary newspaper dispatch from New York has already informed us of some things.
The news was brought on a vessel from Liverpool, which had it
from France by way of London. Although the American nation
gained its independence with the help of France, the American
people do not love the French very much. I fear the news is not
reported truthfully, and you understand how earnestly I desire to
be correctly informed. . . .

There is no news to give you beyond what was in my last letter,
except that my health is better. I had a very sore leg, which was
considered serious enough to be taken care of. It got well in spite
of my neglect of it, and I am better. My greatest anxiety at present,
and the one which I trust entirely to Divine Providence, is the
matter of the donation of this house to us as an orphanage. . . .
Now that the town is growing so fast, this property has increased
greatly in value, and I have already been faced with very disagreeable accusations on the part of the donor, who can raise the most
unpleasant difficulties for us if he so desires. Being really helpless
in the matter, I can only trust in patience, hoping the more trac-
table heirs will find consolation in our establishment. . . .

The *Missouri Republican* brought information more quickly
than Josephine could send it. Under the heading "Revolution in
France," the issue of September 21, 1830, carried news of the de-
thronement of Charles X and the establishment of a provisional
government under the Duke of Orleans. The name of Casimir
Perier seemed to dance up and down the printed column: Minister
of the Interior—one of the wealthiest bankers in Paris—head of large
industrial plants—"although an ardent advocate for rational freedom, he has not the reputation of being a mere revolutionist"—
"his talent for government appears to have been generally acknowl-
edged, except by the late monarch and the party opposed to
doctrines Monsieur Perier entertains along with the Liberal
Deputies."

News of the succession of Louis Philippe was brought to
Philippine by Bishop Rosati some days later. The *Missouri Republican* of October 13 devoted much space to the events that had taken
place in the French Chamber of Deputies on August 6 and 7, and
Philippine read attentively the speeches of Monsieur Gerard and
General Lafayette. But it was the ceremonies of August 9 that
interested her most deeply, when "the Duke of Orleans, in the

presence of the Chambers and an immense crowd of spectators, took the oath to the Charter and was admitted to the sovereignty of France." It was Casimir Perier who had read the declaration of the Chamber of Deputies calling Philip of Orleans to the throne. As Philippine read the printed words, her heart echoed the cries of *Vive le Roi*, and with all her soul she prayed for the homeland that was so dear to her, for her family, and for the Society in France.

Through the autumn of 1830 her heart was heavy with anxiety about La Fourche. Unhappiness in that community worried her far more than temporal distress. When she consulted Bishop Rosati about the serious representations that had come to her in letters, he advised:

> Let Mother Therese Detchemendy remain at St. Michael's, Mother Dutour at Assumption, and persuade Mother Bazire to be patient. It is in circumstances such as these that we must practice the Christian and religious virtues. *It is necessary;* we are abliged to do so. Thus Mother Bazire must make this sacrifice. While waiting for your Superior General to send you a good subject from France, write to name her [Mother Bazire] superior. Her merit will not fail to win confidence. . . .

In suggesting Mother Julie Bazire for the office of superior at La Fourche, the bishop was making as serious a mistake as when he first chose Mother Dutour, but only time and experience would reveal this fact, and Bishop Rosati would never know it.

The winter of 1830–1831 brought much physical suffering to the people of Missouri. There was deep snow from December until the close of February. So severe was the cold that cattle died in large numbers from exposure, and a shortage of wood for fuel increased the suffering and brought on much illness. In the convent infirmaries Mother Duchesne nursed the sick day and night. Orphans, pupils, religious—all were the object of her efficient and motherly care.

At Florissant there was suffering, too, combined with penury, for the convent had no income whatsoever. Mother Duchesne did all she could to relieve privations there, but her resources were very meager. She was especially concerned about Anne Stegar, who had received the habit in the autumn and been sent to the novitiate for her training. Anne was showing much good will, but the severity of the winter and the consequent privations had tried her physically, while her difficulty in understanding Mother Thiéfry's newly acquired English put a strain on her spiritually.

In January Bishop Rosati advised that Anne be brought back to St. Louis and trained by Mother Duchesne herself. This advice was followed and Anne's happiness and perseverance were assured.

In April Mother Duchesne learned that the Superior General had relieved Mother Dutour of her duties at La Fourche and sent her to Grand Coteau. She had put the financial affairs of the convent in Mother Audé's hands and named Mother Bazire superior *pro tem*. Some days later Philippine told the bishop:

> Mother Dutour has written to me in a very religious manner. Mother Eugenie says that she showed great virtue in leaving La Fourche and that the departure did not cause a big stir. The debts are heavier than we had thought. Bishop De Neckere, however, is eager to keep the school open, and Mother Eugenie, who has already negotiated with several of the creditors, will do her utmost to carry out the bishop's desire. . . .

Life continued to present a succession of trials for Philippine that spring and summer. Early in May Mother Regis Hamilton was taken very ill. "Small-pox," the doctors said, and for three weeks Mother Duchesne nursed her day and night, convinced that the diagnosis was incorrect and that it was not necessary to close the school. It was a risk, but no ill effects followed, and the nuns were not deprived of the meager tuition fees that were their only means of support.

"What next?" Philippine may have wondered. The answer was not long in coming, for the *Journal* contains the following entry for June 3:

> There was a frightful storm during the night. Lightning struck a chimney and knocked it down. It fell through the roof and the ceiling of the room in which all the orphans were sleeping. Several of them were hurt, but not dangerously. We were obliged to get the roof repaired at once, even though the work had to be continued on Sunday, for the rain was pouring into the house. It took several days to complete the repairs, and we have put up a lightning rod.

As usual it was to Bishop Rosati she turned for help on the morning after the accident, asking him to send his own workmen to the convent and to give them directions, "as we know nothing about such work." Two days later she was asking him to arrange for a triduum of recollection for the nuns in preparation for the feast of the Sacred Heart. The bishop spent the feast day at the convent, pontificating at the High Mass and presiding at the singing of Vespers. He had news from France which he knew would interest her and call for her most fervent prayers. Since the accession of Louis Philippe, Casimir Perier had not only been President of the Chamber of Deputies, but had also sat in the Cabinet. On the fall of the Lafitte ministry he had been summoned to power as Prime Minister, taking the folio of the Interior on March 13, 1831. The French government was now in energetic and capable hands, and within a year civic order would be restored and national credit re-established. This strong, clear-sighted man could hold Paris in check by the force of his personality and quell revolts in the cities in which he had spent his boyhood—Lyons and Grenoble.

Through the long, hot summer the religious were at work in their classrooms, when they were not ill in the infirmary. While Philippine strained to complete vestments for the bishop by August twenty-fifth, feast of St. Louis of France, Mother Thiéfry was deeply concerned about her, knowing the long hours she also spent nursing the sick, so she wrote to Mother Barat on August 21:

> Do ask prayers, dear Mother, for our dear Mother Duchesne. We must beg God to take care of her for us; she certainly does not take care of herself. Just think of it—she has spent eleven successive nights at the bedside of one religious who was very ill, and she does not allow herself any respite from work. I cannot understand how she does it at her age. I think it is miraculous.

In the midst of the summer's trials came a letter from Mother Barat containing some cheering news. From Chambery, where she had found refuge during the revolution in Paris, she wrote:

> Thanks to your splendid cousin, Madame de Rollin, we are able to keep the convent of Sainte Marie for nine more years. At the end of that time I trust God will help us find a means of remaining there still longer. I am sending you some recruits. Mother de Coppens will go to Mother Audé's house; her health calls for a warm climate. . . . Mother Toysonnier goes to La Fourche; Mother de Kersaint is for your house, and the fourth will be for St. Charles.

On August 24 Mother de Coppens and de Kersaint reached St. Louis. Though destined for St. Michael's, Mother de Coppens had stopped at St. Louis instead of going south. From these religious Philippine learned much that had taken place in France in the past months. In fact, so avid was she for news that evening had come before she wrote a note to inform the bishop of the day's surprise.

Through the past year Mother Duchesne had never shaken off

the impression made on her by the contrast between the flourishing institutions in Louisiana and the cramped and poverty-ridden convents in Missouri. More than ever a distressing sense of failure oppressed her, for she knew Mother Barat had been disappointed not only with the outcome of the conferences at St. Michael's, but also with the small success achieved by the City House in St. Louis, on which she had built great hopes. With the coming of Mother de Kersaint, Philippine thought she saw a way out of the office of superior and on August 28 wrote to Mother Barat:

> Do name Mother de Kersaint superior. I shall keep so quiet in my corner as never to be in her way. I should add that I am ready to go anywhere you may send me, though I realize that wherever I go I may be in the way because of my age and my years as a professed religious. And, too, I can never deal easily with the parents of the children. The Americans do not understand me. The Creoles want good looks and attractive manners. The best thing for me to do is to disappear, either teaching a class or caring for the sick. I tell you this in all sincerity and shall act accordingly.

Such sincere insistence, repeated many times, could not fail to influence Mother Barat. She was inclined also to believe the letters written to her by some of the religious who had come to Missouri within the past five years. They said that in her humility and unworldliness Mother Duchesne had let the convent in St. Louis stagnate, had refused to furnish it in a suitable manner, had neglected to make it attractive enough to draw pupils. The critics felt, too, that she had alienated the best families by holding too rigidly to strict discipline in the matter of outings and holidays, that she insisted unswervingly on things being done as she had known them in the early days of the Society's existence and in the first schools it had conducted in France. She was not progressive enough, they thought, for the St. Louis that was emerging from frontier conditions and developing a sophisticated urban life. She was, moreover, too generous in her charity, especially toward the bishop and the priests who served the convent. The time had come, they urged, to yield to her own appeals and give the institution in St. Louis a chance to expand and develop along normal lines.

Mother Barat hesitated to take the step that was being represented as necessary. She knew the heart and soul of Philippine Duchesne, knew her love and loyalty toward the Society and toward herself, knew the motives that had impelled her to cling to old ways and rules and discipline. The principle of union, underlying all Philippine did in regulating the communities and schools under her direction, had maintained intact the bond between the Society in France and the little offshoot in the Mississippi Valley. That had been vital, and in that she had succeeded far better than anyone then living would ever realize. But the foundress came to a decision after mature thought and intense prayer and wrote quite simply to her old friend and companion, November 30, 1831:

> I sent you a letter quite recently, dear Philippine, answering one from you, but I had not then read all the mail that has since come from you, from your companions, and from the newly arrived religious. From the ensemble of details given me I cannot help being worried about the present condition of your house. For a long time I have been saddened by the small success attained in St. Louis and by the anguish this has caused you. I have tried to send you recruits for the community, such as Mother Thiéfry, and I hoped that you would be able to keep at least one of them to help you in St. Louis, and that the convent there might be established on a footing with St. Michael's or Opelousas. Friends had given me reason to hope for this. But after all I have read, it seems to me we shall never obtain this result unless we follow a course of action different from yours, dear Mother.
>
> I must then, for the sake of the general good, submit a plan to you. You will, of course, consult Bishop Rosati, to whose judgment I refer it for final decision, and I beg you to follow his advice. This is what I suggest: let Mother Thiéfry take your place in St. Louis and give her, as assistant, Mother de Kersaint, and perhaps Mother Regis as mistress general. Do your utmost to build a separate orphanage first of all, then little by little on a well constructed plan erect the other buildings necessary as the academy grows and additions can be undertaken prudently. You, dear Mother, may go either to Florissant or to St. Charles, whichever you think better.
>
> I realize, my dear daughter, that at your age and after all you have suffered, the foundation of an American academy, which calls for so much care and perfection along all lines, quite surpasses your strength. For several years all those who have been at the St. Louis convent have complained of the lack of order, the shabbiness, even the uncultivated condition of the property. Now God forbid that I should blame you, dear Mother. I know only too well all that you have done and suffered. But times change and we must change, too, and modify our views. I realize from experience that it is unwise to leave superiors for long years in the same house. Good government requires a change of superiors once in a while. . . .

That letter was still on the high seas when Mother Duchesne

learned of the death of her beloved Judith Labruyère at St. Michael's—"an excellent religious who rendered valuable service to the Society." Another letter told her that Mother Bazire was doing well at La Fourche and that Bishop de Neckere and Father Ladavière were making efforts to finance that convent, but this was uphill work.

The packet of mail received on January 31 contained Mother Barat's letter of the previous November. After reading it and praying about its contents, Mother Duchesne sent a note to Bishop Rosati asking him to come to the convent as soon as possible and providing a carriage, as usual, for his convenience. There is no record of their conversation during the interview, but the letters they both wrote on February 1 indicate the decision the bishop imposed on Mother Duchesne, who wrote at once to Mother Barat:

> I received your letter of November 30 in which you tell me your new plan for the convent in St. Louis. My natural tendency toward lowliness will make me find happiness in my position, provided I am not left with nothing to do. And even if you thought that necessary, I believe God would give me the grace to endure it. I am fully convinced that I do not possess the qualifications a superior should have. And for a long time one of my most fervent prayers has been to obtain what I felt should happen and what I hoped would raise the standard of religious observance and school work in this house and draw to it all hearts.

But she goes on to relate that when she consulted Bishop Rosati, as she had been instructed to do, he told her quite positively to remain at her post in St. Louis and make no change until she heard again from the Mother General. Meanwhile he would write to her himself. His letter to St. Madeleine Sophie testifies to the deep veneration as well as the personal esteem and affection he felt for Philippine Duchesne:

> Madame [he wrote in the formal fashion of the day], Mother Duchesne has informed me, according to your instructions, of your latest letter to her and of the changes you believe it proper and even necessary to make in regard to the government of your institutions in Missouri. After mature reflection on the plan you submitted to me, I have begged Mother Duchesne to suspend its execution until she heard from you again. I want you to think over what I am going to tell you.
>
> In the first place, I believe there is no one among your religious who can gain as much confidence as Mother Duchesne justly receives here. All who know her respect and venerate her because

of her virtues, which, joined to age and the experience she has acquired during her long sojourn in this country, make her esteemed by all. There are few persons whom I venerate more than this holy religious. She has the true spirit of her vocation and on many occasions, known only to me, has given most striking proofs of this. In the next place, I see by the complaints that have moved you to decide on the proposed changes that things have been misrepresented to you. I am well aware that no one wished to deceive you, but rather spoke from a lack of insight into the matter. If the boarding school is not larger, this is not the result of lack of space. The house can accommodate twenty-eight and has only eleven boarding pupils. The house is not elegant, as are your European convents, but it is suitable for this country. That is not the reason why parents do not send their children there. You have been told that the property has not been properly cultivated; one of your religious newly arrived from France told me the same thing. I replied that after she had been here a while and had made attempts like mine, she would realize that in America, where land is cheap and labor expensive, a religious community cannot obtain profits from its farm produce, for this must be sold at a very low price.

You have been told that she has not cultivated the friendship of the Founder [Mr. Mullanphy] sufficiently, but I can assure you that I do not know anything more Mother Duchesne or anyone else could have done in this respect. Besides, I know the Founder. Once he has done what he planned to do, he will do no more. So I think Mother Duchesne should not be blamed on this point.

With regard to the religious sent from France, whom Mother Duchesne has not kept here—this action was not prompted by the fact that she did not need them, but rather by her desire to work for the general good of all your convents. This generosity, which I admire and at the same time regret, led her to make sacrifices in order to satisfy the demands of the superiors of the Louisiana houses. These demands were such that had they always been heeded, the houses here would be empty. I speak from firsthand knowledge on this point. More than once she has had to make a change of house or climate to satisfy some of the religious or to prevent complaints. You yourself know that this is not rare in communities, where we feel the effects of human weakness unless we are well advanced on the way to perfection. Religious are also children of Adam, so this is not to be wondered at. On this point in particular Mother Duchesne has suffered very much. Instead of blaming her, we should pity her.

I am speaking very frankly, Madame, because I have at heart the happiness and prosperity of your houses in my diocese. I believe that the contemplated change will in no way contribute to this end. No religious whom you may designate to fill the position now held by Mother Duchesne could really replace her. I greatly fear this excessive desire to enlarge the house, to make it appear more like the French convents, and to put the houses here on the same footing with them. You have had an example of that policy at La Fourche. Very well, here it would be even worse. In this country we have not the resources nor many wealthy Catholics. At present the Protestants have their own schools and they fear to send their daughters to a convent lest they be converted to Catholicism. That is the real reason for the small boarding school. Is it prudent to go into debt and pay a high rate of interest to build new additions? As things are now, much good is being done with the orphans and in the crowded free school, and there are others who could pay if you received them as day pupils.

In all the convents good is being done and more is hoped for in the future. With the growth of population and wealth will come increased opportunities for good. The Ursulines of New Orleans and Canada have at times been in conditions much harder than those of your houses here, but now they are as well off as their Sisters in Europe, perhaps even better off. Let us follow, then, the guidance of Divine Providence; it will not fail to uphold us. That is what those newly come from Europe do not know and do not want to know. But we know it after years of experience. Their views must not be placed before those of experienced persons. I pray you to pardon me if I speak so frankly. I sincerely desire the prosperity of your convents. . . .

So Philippine renewed her courage in prayer and purified her motive of love for the Sacred Heart, and continued to carry her burden in St. Louis. Its weight was increased just at this time by anxiety regarding the health of both Mother Regis Hamilton and Mother Octavie Berthold, whose suffering seemed to grow more intense with every hour and who could no longer appear in public because of facial cancer. Jottings in the *Journal* tell the things that weighed on Philippine's heart during this period:

February. Father Cellini, a Roman priest and excellent physician, came from St. Michel des Mines to St. Louis at our request to examine Mother Hamilton and suggest a treatment for paralysis of the nose. The remedies he tried were unsuccessful. An operation may be necessary.

February 26. Departure of Sisters Anne Stegar, novice, and Helen Mayette, aspirant, for Grand Coteau. . . .

March 15. News from Mother Eugenie Audé, who informs us that she has been authorized by our Mother General to close the convent at La Fourche, with the approval, of course, of the bishop of New Orleans. He gave his consent very reluctantly. The two superiors of St. Michael's and Opelousas carried out the instructions. On March 26 the five religious who remained at La Fourche will go to Opelousas; the others went to St. Michael's. The house has been closed and given back to the bishop, to whom the property belongs. The religious of this convent, the pupils, and their parents were greatly grieved by this action.

The objective tone of this entry in the *Journal* contrasts sharply with the emotion expressed by Mother Duchesne in her letter of March 17 to Monseigneur Rosati. A sudden terror had gripped her heart and she bared it to the bishop in all its stark reality:

Letters from Louisiana give me very different versions of the closing of the convent at La Fourche. According to Mother Eugenie, she was about to have another lawsuit on her hands. According to those who were obliged to forsake that convent: 1) she would have had, on the contrary, a house that would have cost her nothing; 2) Monseigneur de Neckere was misinformed; they told him the house at Opelousas would be closed unless it received the help of the religious from La Fourche; 3) the parents were distressed and offered to increase the tuition of their children, only five of whom went to St. Michael's. 4) They say Mother Thiéfry will soon be in charge here in St. Louis. . . . These reports urge me, Monsiegneur, to beg this favor of you: if they try to precipitate matters here in the same manner, please oppose them firmly, requiring that the article of the Constitutions which forbids the closing of a house of the Society without the approval of the Cardinal Protector be held to rigidly. It took just three days to destroy a convent that had cost so much painful effort. . . .

Visiting the St. Louis convent on March 19, Bishop Rosati quieted Philippine's fears and shared her anxiety about Mother Hamilton. Ten days later he returned, bringing

a skillful doctor from Baltimore whom Divine Providence had sent to perform the operation on Mother Hamilton. We had feared [Philippine noted in her *Journal*] there was no doctor in St. Louis who could do it and had been advised to take her to one of the Eastern cities for it. The matter was entrusted to St. Regis, and we recognize in the arrival of this good doctor [Stephen W. Adreon] an answer from our saint.

Heart-suffering of another kind was renewed when on April 6 Mother Duchesne received a letter from the Superior General which dealt with the matter of the supervision of the convents in the Mississippi Valley. From Lyons Mother Barat wrote:

> The time set for the meeting of the General Council is approaching. I feel, dear Mother, that since your houses are so far away from the center of the Society, it is becoming more difficult to govern them from such a distance, at least as to details. So I have decided to have you all name an Assistant General for Louisiana and Missouri. She would have the necessary powers, and all would be bound to obey her. In order to be enlightened on this matter, I want you to carry out this plan for me: in each of the five houses let the Superior have the professed religious vote by secret but signed ballots. These will be sent under seal to you, and you will send them sealed to me—but recommend the use of thin paper. Do not make any of the changes I suggested until after the nomination of your Assistant General. God will give her the light to put all in order.

Mother Duchesne communicated this news to Bishop Rosati, adding:

> I am quite sure that the little progress made by this house is attributed to me. . . . There is no denying the fact that in the academy we are weak for English. It seems to me that Divine Providence is offering us a means to overcome this: if Mr. Taylor would give English lessons several times a week, we would receive his two children as boarding pupils in payment. They are so young, it would be almost impossible for them to come as day pupils. Will you sound him out on this matter?

This move to interest Mr. Francis H. Taylor in the work of the school was wise and successful. He was a convert to Catholicism who had formerly edited the *Catholic Press* in New Haven, Connecticut. Coming to St. Louis in the spring of 1832, he proposed to Bishop Rosati the idea of publishing a Catholic newspaper which would have as its objectives to inform and instruct Catholics in the Mississippi Valley and to combat the vicious, even scurrilous, attacks by which the non-Catholic press strove to "save the valley" from Romanism. The bishop accepted the proposal and assisted Mr. Taylor financially, giving the publication his backing to such an extent that *The Shepherd of the Valley*, as it was titled, became known as "the bishop's paper," and proved a powerful factor in Catholic development during its brief existence.

Bishop Rosati approved of Mother Duchesne's suggestion of

adding Mr. Taylor to the teaching staff of the convent school, but again he firmly opposed her change of residence and she submitted. At the summit of her soul there was total adherence to the divine will, and this gave sovereign peace. But at the lower level she shrank from the suffering that was inherent in her position. She felt that instinctive dread that every human heart feels when faced with pain, humiliation, failure. For years she had realized how untenable was her position as "provincial," when such an office did not yet exist in the Society. But she had clung to the supernatural conviction that she had grace for any circumstance that might arise, and her love was ready to give its full co-operation. She had always the bishop's friendship and support, and her confidence in his judgment was complete. He understood that her shrinking from positions of authority was not a weak evasion of responsibility, not cowardice or dread of failure and criticism. He knew that she was profoundly convinced of her own incapacity, but he also knew that grace was achieving a mastery in her soul that called for an ever fuller gift of self, an acceptance of the whole will of God sincerely, courageously, and without reserve.

Quite unexpectedly, one day early in May, Mother Anne de Coppens arrived from St. Michael's. She had been unhappy in Louisiana, and thinking she was not needed in a community of thirty-five, who seemed quite sufficient to care for the one hundred and fifty boarders in the academy, she had presumed permission to travel north. Mother Duchesne gave her a kind welcome, but could not sanction the step she had taken. As a matter of fact "Madame Anne" became something of a thorn in her superior's side.

But there was more personal heart-suffering in store for Mother Duchesne as distressing news from France told that cholera was carrying off thousands of victims. The *Missouri Republican* was printing the "latest from France," always about six weeks old. An item in the issue of June 19 reported the illness of Casimir Perier. A month later came the news that he was dead. Philippine's heart was heavy with grief for the handsome lad who had taught her arithmetic, the Deputy of the Opposition whom she had seen in Paris just before leaving for America, and with sympathy for Augustin and Josephine, "her first and dearest friends." *The Shepherd of the Valley* gave details of Casimir's last illness and death, but only later on did Philippine learn of the courage, even heroism, with which he had visited the Hotel-Dieu in Paris in company with the King while many cholera patients in the hospital were in their death-agony. Three days later he was stricken and on May 16, 1832, he died.

The dreaded plague was devastating Canada in July, and *The Shepherd of the Valley* was warning St. Louis to look to the condition of its streets and alleys. In early August the danger of another revolution in France was not so vital a news item as the fact that the cholera was gaining headway in the United States. It was in Boston, Philadelphia, Baltimore, Detroit; and a letter from Chicago told that the dreadful epidemic had appeared in that village. It was a time for earnest prayer and sensible precautions. The health situation in St. Louis, however, was still normal, so the school work was continued.

During the first week of August both Bishop Rosati and Mother Duchesne received letters from Mother Barat written from Aix on May 8 in answer to those sent from St. Louis in February. To the bishop the Superior General stated frankly her own views about the administration of the convents in Missouri and gave willing acquiescence to his. To Philippine she wrote:

> Your letter of last February reached me on the 4th of this month, my dear daughter . . . and I want to send you an answer at the same time that I answer the letter of Bishop Rosati, which reached me a few days before yours. I yield to his Lordship all the more readily since it cost me much to make the former decision. I had acceded to your wishes, so perseveringly and energetically expressed. And then, too, so many other seemingly well-informed people agreed with you. I am delighted to know, my dear Philippine, that they are mistaken, and that on your side it is humility alone that urged you to make the request. I trust that God will aid you, as he has done thus far, in the exercise of your difficult charge. Continue, then, to fill it as well as you can. This is the wish of your bishop; it is also mine. I love to find myself in complete accord with him. After this decision we shall change nothing. Do what you think best for the three [Missouri] houses. . . . Consider whether you can build in St. Louis without acting imprudently. I made some suggestion about this in my last letter to you. If you accept these, we shall try to put 10,000 francs at your disposal within a year. You can pay us back later on. . . . *Adieu,* dear daughter. Pray for your Mother and receive, for yourself and for all your religious, the assurance of the tender love I bear you. . . .

Philippine made a laconic entry in her *Journal:* "News from France. Our Mother General wishes us to build here in St. Louis and offers a loan of 10,000 francs." When and how could she ever pay back a loan of 10,000 francs? Bills for food and fuel and clothing kept her constantly pressed for funds, and there was no one to whom she could turn for financial aid. Still she carried on the work and the scholastic year closed on September 6 with a brave little effort at entertainment in the form of "a little pastoral play composed for the occasion by Mother Berthold and addressed to the bishop under the title of *The Shepherd of the Valley*."

Classes were resumed on October 1 with fifteen pupils in the boarding school, but within ten days all but six had gone home, for the cholera had appeared in St. Louis. During this enforced vacation, Mr. Taylor determined to keep the boarding school before the Catholics of St. Louis, at least in print. Under the heading *Education* in the Catholic paper's issue of October 13 he wrote:

> The Female Academy under the direction of the Ladies of the Sacred Heart (St. Louis) is already well known by the accomplished young ladies who have received a finished education in it and who have brought from it to the bosom of their families, and to the world, a greatful [sic] affection for their teachers who, with tender and maternal care, guided them in their advance to virtue and useful knowledge.

So the City House, St. Louis, had formally adopted the title of "academy" and was offering as comprehensive a study program as could be found in any girls' school west of the Alleghenies, along with all the arts and skills required in feminine education of that day. In her planning, at least, Mother Duchesne was not behind the times, but for the moment there was but a handful of children in the school, and these were for the most part the orphan girls. In mid-October the people of St. Louis were advised by the *Missouri Republican* to "Keep cool, remain at home, do not worry, and trust in Divine Providence for exemption from the pestilence," but it was admitted that out of ninety-three cases that week, thirty-three had resulted in death.

St. Louis was in a frightful condition that autumn, for the cholera raged "with very alarming malignity" and there was hardly a person in the town who did not "weep the loss of relative or friend." Early in November, however, the civil authorities felt that the disease was under control.

On November 21 Bishop Rosati brought to the convent a prel-

ate whom Mother Duchesne had desired for many years to meet—
Bishop Benedict Joseph Flaget of Bardstown, Kentucky. She had
heard so much about this great missionary that she felt as if she was
already acquainted with him, yet she was meeting him at perhaps
the most difficult period of his long career. During the previous
year Bishop Flaget, weighed down by responsibilities and suffering
from spiritual depression and a conviction of inability to administer
his vast diocese properly, had written to Rome, tendering his resignation and asking that the burden he had carried for twenty years
be shifted to younger shoulders. During his visit to St. Louis in
November, 1832, he learned that his resignation had been accepted
and that Bishop John David, his co-adjutor and two years older
than he, had been named second Bishop of Bardstown. Along with
this news came the information that the Catholics of Kentucky
were loud in their protests against his retirement and the proposed
changes.

Mother Duchesne could sympathize with Bishop Flaget in this
painful situation when he came to offer Mass at the convent on the
first of December. She was happy to be of service to him when
Bishop Rosati, coming from the convent infirmary where he had
visited Mother Octavie, proposed that she make the ex-Bishop of
Bardstown a new cassock from the piece of purple silk she had on
hand in the sacristy. At once she set to work, taking measurements
while the two great missionary prelates discussed the situation in
Kentucky and the heavy losses sustained by the Church during
the cholera epidemic. Detroit had lost its hero-priest, Gabriel
Richard, and Cincinnati, its first bishop, Edward Dominic Fenwick,
a relative of Mother Regis Hamilton.

Mother Duchesne had been uneasy about the presence of
Mother de Coppens in St. Louis since May and had discussed the
matter with Bishop Rosati, even written to him, asking him to
persuade her to return to Louisiana. When she learned that he was
accompanying Bishop Flaget back to Kentucky, she begged him
to use his influence and authority. Mother de Coppens agreed to
give Louisiana another trial, and Mother Duchesne helped her pack
her satchel and boxes. The *Journal* tells how "Bishop Rosati and
Bishop Flaget started together for Kentucky, Mother de Coppens
traveling on the same steamboat to return to St. Michael's. At Ste.
Genevieve, where the prelates transferred to an Ohio River boat,
Bishop Rosati was obliged to send her back to St. Louis, as she was
ill again."

2. 1833—1834

DURING THE BISHOP'S ABSENCE, Father Borgna, who was acting as chaplain at the convent, took on the duty of confessor also. Sometimes Father John Timon, C.M., came in his place. Then Philippine was more at ease, for in spite of her long friendship with Father Borgna she did not wholly trust him, and she had reason to believe that his influence on some members of the community was not strictly in line with religious spirit and supernatural obedience. The bishop knew the circumstances on which she based her fears and understood what was implied in the questions she asked in a little note she sent him in January, 1833:

> I am very anxious to know whether we may hope to see you this week [for confession]—or is it indiscreet even to expect this? Shall we go on accepting Father Borgna's services? I shall be submissive, but not indifferent, in this matter.

At the convent on February 1 the bishop entertained the community with an account of his trip, dwelling particularly on his stay in Cincinnati. Mother Duchesne was glad to be able to tell him in turn of a letter recently received from Mother Barat approving plans sent from St. Louis and urging her to begin building as soon as she received the money from Paris. She had not the satisfaction of a confidential talk with him, so she wrote on February 4:

> It was not the moment, at your first visit, to renew our demands on your kindness to us. It seemed selfish when I realized how over-burdened you are with pressing affairs. But your silence worried me. I know well that your time is precious and that it must be difficult for you to give us part of it each week. I am greatly torn between the dread that you may decide against coming and the fear of being importunate. I can only abandon myself to your paternal goodness, which calls for our complete submission. . . .

Bishop Rosati yielded to her repeated entreaties and continued to come to the convent for confessions as regularly as his other duties would allow. Only when stricken with illness in the following July did he give up this service which Mother Duchesne appreciated so highly. There was cholera in St. Louis during May, and several serious cases appeared in June, but the convent was again spared this trial. Then came the crushing news that at St. Michael's the plague had carried off five religious in four days, among them Mother Therese Detchemendy. Mother Duchesne recorded this in her *Journal* and added:

> The epidemic has raged with terrific virulence in the river and bayou towns of Louisiana. The Ursulines [of New Orleans] have been attacked by it, and we have learned of the death of holy Father [Benedict] Richard, the constant friend and protector of our convents and our first chaplain at St. Charles.

The feast of the Sacred Heart was celebrated solemnly, with Father Le Clerc preaching "a very touching sermon" on devotion to the Sacred Heart. Within a month he was dead, Bishop Rosati lay dangerously ill, as did Mother Hamilton also, and Mother Octavie Berthold received the Last Sacraments. Yet on June 23, when Mother Duchesne learned of an opportunity to send mail to France by a dependable traveler, she could write far into the night, sending Josephine a long letter in which her personal anxieties found expression only in the closing paragraphs:

> You simply overwhelm me, dearest Cousin, with your friendship and your gifts. I received your interesting letter along with the gift you announced in it. Nothing could have been more acceptable. We have undertaken the construction of an addition to our building, which was so small the school could not grow. We had no infirmary, no assembly room, no private rooms, and this was very hard on the sick—and these make up most of the community. As for myself, I keep my strength and any place is good enough for me. I spend my most restful nights in the most crowded corners, and for several years I have not minded carrying my mattress from one room to another according to circumstance. I would roll it up in the morning and put it somewhere else the following night. I have understood by experience St. Augustine's saying: "It is better not to need much than to have much." So that good thousand francs—for which I thank you a thousand times—will be better employed for the general needs of the convent than for my own personal needs, and that will give me the greatest amount of satisfaction. . . .
>
> I have never been so completely without a moment's peace. My heart is never free from suffering—and this is what attaches me most of all to this house, for how could I leave these poor, suffering nuns? There are 13 in the community, and today 7 are under medical treatment. That has been the condition for a long time. I have been waiting a month for time to answer several letters. For-

give me if I stop abruptly, but very affectionately, in the Heart of Jesus. . . .

The grave illness from which Monseigneur Rosati rallied in late July and slowly recovered put an end to the devotedness he had shown toward Mother Duchesne and her community as their confessor. Her reaction to this decision shows how deeply she felt it personally, for she wrote to the Bishop on August 16:

> I have already told you of my sorrow at the news that we are no longer under your personal direction. You have tried to reassure me, but I am not at peace. I realize only too well that a bishop's time is precious and that frequently he is no longer master of it. Moreover, I have pondered how grievous it would be and how culpable we would feel if we sought our own welfare rather than the general good of this large diocese, especially in your weakened state of health. Your prospective absence, which is announced for next month, weighs me down still more, as well as the fact that we must address ourselves now to a priest who is more suited to persons of the world than to those who should have a piety that is both interior and serene. I must tell you, however, that several members of the community are not of my opinion and are happy enough with the new arrangement, but their reasons seem to me to carry no weight. I am ready to sacrifice my taste and my peace of soul in yielding to the general good, but I shall not be satisfied until I have placed before you what I think would be for the greatest benefit of this convent, and it is to appoint for us, or at least for those who feel the need, a confessor who has the same rules as our own. . . .

Soul-suffering such as this was for Philippine "the secret of the King," and never did she betray to her family the anguish she endured. Bright interesting letters crossed the ocean whenever she knew of a traveler going to Europe. Two days after her heart-cry to Bishop Rosati she was writing to Madame Jouve:

> My dear One,
> I received your letter from Lyons in April after your return from Grâne. I am delighted to know that my letter reached dear Amelie, but believe me, this is not the only one I have written. I recall quite distinctly writing to her several times recently. . . . But it is not surprising that letters from such a distance get lost. . . . Perhaps this letter I am writing will go to Lyons with Father Odin, a missionary priest of this diocese. He is going to make a tour of his homeland on business. He is president of a college in our state and is very successful.

The college of St. Louis has been erected into a university by the legislature of Missouri; it is conducted by the Jesuits. As they have nearly one hundred resident students, they will need some of their confreres to help them. I should love for Henri to be chosen for this work. He would find in the state of Missouri and in the Territory beyond, which is much bigger than the state, plenty of scope for his zeal. Religion is spreading, and not a year passes without the erection of several churches. The Cathedral in St. Louis will not be finished until next year. It will be beautiful, and so will the church at the seminary, thirty leagues from here, but it was planned on too grand a scale for the country and so cannot be completed for lack of funds. . . .

I thank God for having disposed all things by his adorable Providence so that you and your husband can spend your days in peace and happiness, and also Monsieur Lebrument. God will be favorable also, I trust, to Madame Bergasse, who draws blessings on her family, as did our dear Adelaide. *Adieu,* dearest one; my love to all your dear ones and especially to your husband. The love of my heart for you will never grow old. . . .

On Philippine's sixty-fourth birthday Mr. John Mullanphy died at his St. Louis residence on North Main Street. On the following day the girls of the orphanage walked in the funeral cortege, dressed in black and white. Early in September it became evident that Mother Octavie Berthold's suffering life was drawing to a close. More tenderly than ever Mother Duchesne nursed her, and more constantly. There was distressing news from Louisiana, where cholera was raging again. Bishop de Neckere had been for some weeks at St. Michael's, recuperating from illness and overwork. All who knew and loved him prayed that he would remain in comparative safety, but he could not be persuaded to do so, and on September 4 his career was cut short by the plague in New Orleans.

The distribution of prizes was set for September 16 at the academy, but the Sacred Heart had other designs for that day, as Mother Duchesne noted in her *Journal:*

> Our dear Mother Octavie Berthold took a sudden turn for the worse and at ten o'clock in the morning gave back her beautiful soul to God. She was assisted by Father Borgna, the Vicar General. Her agony lasted but a moment, and she had received Holy Communion early in the morning. Her body was laid out in our chapel, where there were people praying continually. The altar was draped in black and the Office for the Dead was recited that evening. Next morning Fathers Borgna, De Smet, and Doutreluingne

offered low Masses for her. At eight o'clock the High Mass was sung by Father Verhaegen with deacon and subdeacon.

At the far southwestern corner of the convent property they buried Octavie Berthold in the little cemetery staked off the previous May. The first grave had been opened for Father Le Clerc, a cholera victim after just six weeks in St. Louis. Another victim, a Sister of Charity, had been laid to rest on September 9. Mother Octavie's burial was the last before the city began to cut streets through the Mullanphy grant and the cemetery was condemned.

It called for faith and courage and high supernatural resolve to carry out the plans that had been made for the closing exercises, but Mother Duchesne faced the duty, erect and self-controlled, and gave a cordial greeting to Father Verhaegen and to the parents of the children, who had been invited to the little gathering. Mr. Taylor, who attended the performance, described it as the "Literary Exhibition held annually at the Female Academy of the Ladies of the Sacred Heart," and reported that "one room in the spacious new brick building recently erected" was "elegantly decorated with specimens of embroidery, needlework, and several other branches of a female education." He was impressed by the "melody of voices," the "soft sounds of the piano," recitations of prose and poetry in both French and English, and the awarding of prize books and crowns for success in studies and deportment. In conclusion he remarked: "This establishment, we are happy to state, is daily growing in public confidence and is undoubtedly entitled to the most extensive patronage."

The October enrollment was fairly good, though the nuns must have been disappointed when there were a few empty beds in the dormitory. Mother Duchesne made no allusion to this, however, in a letter written to the convents in France on October 19. She was preoccupied with the sorrows and losses of the past year, but in the last paragraph one feels that she is pleased with the new building, though it is not yet paid for:

> The distribution of prizes took place on the 18th of September. For this occasion we used the studyhall of the new building, which is fifty feet long by thirty feet wide. On the floor that is partly underground there is a large refectory and a room in which we shall put a coal stove that will give heat from under the house. Above this there is a large studyhall, along the full length of which runs a pretty covered gallery where one can enjoy fresh air in bad weather. This leads into a vestibule giving entrance to the

chapel. Above all this is the dormitory and a small washroom. The attic is well plastered and will provide another dormitory. It adjoins the old one, now used as the children's linen room. . . .

During the autumn of 1833 Mother Duchesne's thoughts and prayers turned constantly toward Paris, where the fifth General Council of the Society was being held. That assembly would be concerned in a special manner with the welfare of the American convents. While the council was in session, she learned of the death of two more religious at St. Michael's. Along with other news items she noted in her *Journal* the providential help that came from several sources, enabling her to pay off almost the entire debt on the new building:

> Bishop Blanc writes that he has on hand the $200 left us by Father Benedict Richard. We also received $450 from Grand Coteau as a gift for the new building and $200 from Madame de Rollin. We have agreed to receive the two Grolet girls, orphans from Grand Coteau, for six years for $1500 in three payments, the first in advance. We marvel at the ways of Divine Providence. With this money we are able to pay almost all we owe on the new building, which cost $4000.

While rejoicing in this good fortune, Mother Duchesne also shared the happiness of Mother Mathevon, who was busy with plans for a brick convent at St. Charles to replace the old Duquette house that was falling in ruins. Father Van Quickenborne, who was pastor there, was taking up a subscription to finance the project and had already collected $1500 when Mother Duchesne went to St. Charles for a visit in November. The plans laid before her were almost identical with those of the Florissant convent, with the addition of a well finished basement a half-story underground. The convent would stand on the first bluff, facing the river and closer to the new church than the Duquette house was. In the near future, it was hoped, it could be extended to the north so as to meet the wall of the sanctuary of the church, giving the religious a cloister chapel like the one at Florissant. Mother Mathevon was proving a competent and much loved superior, and Father Van Quickenborne was mellowing considerably.

Joy and sorrow often came together in Philippine's life. The closing of the old monastery of Sainte-Marie-d'en-Haut was a blow she had endeavored to avert by penance and prayer. Six months earlier St. Madeleine Sophie had written to her: "A piece of news that will pain you, dear Philippine, is the perspective before us of

having soon to evacuate your beloved convent of Sainte Marie."
And in a letter of October 10 she announced the *fait accompli:*
"What a heartbreak it is to be forced to give up your cradle, that
house so dear to you. We were obliged to do so. The city took it
from us." This letter had reached St. Louis during Christmastide,
and Philippine had answered on December 28, 1833: "It must
have been hard for you to decide to abandon that house. It is still
the place to which I am most deeply attached and the greatest
sacrifice I could offer at the crib of the Divine Infant. If God
strikes the green wood thus, what will he do to the dry, worm-
eaten wood we build with here?"

An opportunity to send mail free of charge as far as New
Orleans in January called for a letter to Josephine. At the time
she did not know that the Perier family was in grief again, this
time for her beloved Augustin. He had stood close to Casimir with
advice and support and had been raised to the peerage in gratitude
by Louis Philippe. All unaware of his death, Philippine wrote:

Dearest Cousin,

I have received all your generous gifts—the two thousand francs
which you had the goodness to send me in two payments came
in quick succession. It is a joy to owe you so great a debt of gratitude, though you know my friendship for you has no personal
selfishness in it. I love you tenderly and value you highly just because of what you are in yourself. . . . They write me that there
is no way to save Sainte Marie to the Society, that the convent
must be closed. . . . I never thought I might see that beloved
place again, but it was a joy for me to think of it as a home of
God-fearing virtue, zeal, and innocence. It is very bitter for me to
think that perhaps I am responsible for the closing of that house,
because I did not merit the graces needed to support it. I have no
desire for new endeavors. It seems to me that what we build here
is but a house of cards compared with the massive pile of that noble
monastery, its vast proportions, its charming situation, its silent
church remote from all distractions. . . .

Our new building to which you contributed so generously is
now complete, except for the plastering. It presents such an attractive appearance, the number of boarding pupils has already
doubled. I should not have believed this possible. You will be glad
to know that all the Catholic institutions in the United States are
prospering at present. Congress has as its *chaplain*—that is to say,
its *preacher*—a Catholic priest! The President [Andrew Jackson] is
quite favorable to Catholic priests, and many Protestants prefer to
entrust their children to celibate priests rather than to professors

whose duties are divided between interest in studies and care of a family. New Orleans has at last decided to entrust its hospital to the Sisters of Charity. They have won the admiration of people of all creeds in St. Louis by their work in our hospital. . . .

In almost everything she wrote Philippine revealed herself. At times, however, a character trait is emphasized in an unexpected way. She was accused of being too severe a disciplinarian, too rigid and unyielding toward the parents who consulted her, yet she writes to Bishop Rosati on January 15, 1834:

> I refrained from speaking to you this morning about our doctor, as he said he was going to talk to you himself about his only daughter. Since the death of their son, his wife cannot bring herself to part with the child. She came herself to ask if she might place her with us as a day pupil, and on Mother Regis' refusal she was greatly disappointed. I spoke to her afterwards and told her we would think it over and give the doctor an answer. Mother de Kersaint is quite opposed to receiving this little girl as a day pupil, 1) because others will want the same privilege or complain of preferences being made; 2) because it is against our regulations. I answered that I would not be afraid to say that we are making this one exception for our doctor who has taken care of us so generously, and that it would be difficult ever to repay him for his many visits. I should not have to give the same consideration to our other children whose fathers are doctors. There are exceptions to every rule and I shall do what you advise. I beg you to make the decision. I have avoided seeing the doctor so I would not feel obliged to give him the answer his wife desires.

In a matter of this kind Mother Duchesne might have made the decision without consulting members of the community. But she did not act independently. The burden of her responsibility seemed to grow heavier every day, and early in the New Year this was borne in on her in a way that made her heart cry out to Mother Barat:

> I am entirely behind the times. Here one must now talk of advanced sciences, astronomy, chemistry, philosophy. But I am drawn to know nothing but Jesus as the subject matter of the one science necessary, and to seek him in solitude. My patron for this year is St. Andrew and his cross. That cross, that good cross, I long for in one of two things: either the end of my life or the end of my position as superior.

She was striving hard at this time to restore union and charity in the community, which had been disrupted by Father Borgna's unwise direction and Mother de Coppens's critical spirit. This condition of affairs distressed her, for it seemed beyond her power to check and eradicate it. The matter was still preying on her mind, gnawing at her heart, when she wrote to Mother Barat on March 2:

Our new building is being used in part, and at Easter, when the plastering is finished, we shall have the use of all of it. It has already brought us double the number of boarding pupils we had —there are now thirty-four—and if more come, as seems certain to happen, we shall be no better off for the community than we were before. We still have no infirmary, no community room. . . .

I spend very little time in the boarding school now, for I really feel that I am not liked. I am not offended by this, for I realize that my age [she was in her sixty-fifth year] does not appeal to young people, and it is quite apparent. But I have plenty to occupy me from four o'clock in the morning till eleven o'clock at night: treasury, pantry, sacristy, nuns' linen room, a class with the children of the free school, two hours a day with the orphans, surveillance of the workmen, visits, letters, etc. You may think I want to do everything myself, but I may also have to take charge of the children's linen room, for the three choir religious who speak English have all they can do—not a quarter of an hour free— so they cannot take that employment. The same holds for Mother de Kersaint, because of the music. Mother de Coppens, who was in charge, did the work so poorly, I am told, there were continual complaints. . . . Our infirmarian has been threatened with consumption, and she would be an irreparable loss. Mother Hamilton is very busy, but she continues to act as mistress of health for the children. . . . I beg you earnestly to give us a surveillante for her and also three other religious of tried virtue. . . .

I have no doubt that you have received written complaints against me, for the spiritual director about whom I wrote to you, urged some of the nuns to do this, I am told, and he himself sent off the two letters. Things will turn out as God wills. I hold to nothing and I know they can make complaints about me that are very true. I long to see an end of my embarrassing situation. If I can believe Anne [de Coppens], the four younger choir nuns have formed a clique against me, but these four (more truthful than she) accuse her of falsehood. . . . One would need the power to read hearts in order to get at the truth in all this and form a fair judgment. I cannot write you everything about this religious, but she does disturb the union in our community. . . .

That letter had scarcely left the country when Mother Duchesne wrote in her *Journal:*

> We have learned the results of the General Council that closed in November, 1833. The Assistants General are Reverend Mothers Desmarquest, de Charbonnel, de Gramont, and Eugenie Audé for America. She has received instructions from our Mother General to make a visitation of the American houses and then return to France to give her report.

So preparations for the visitation began. Mother Duchesne was glad the new building would be plastered, finished, and in use by April, glad too that there were thirty-four pupils enrolled in the academy and twenty-two in the orphanage, but she realized that the convent in St. Louis would make a poor showing in comparison with those of Louisiana and that discontented members of the community might have a sympathetic listener in the Mother Visitatrix. But all was in God's hands, in God's will. She could repeat unwaveringly, *"Portavi et portabo,"* as she had in 1829.

Reverend Mother Audé arrived on April 13, having put Mother Bazire in charge at St. Michael's. After three days with Mother Duchesne's community she visited first St. Ferdinand, then St. Charles. Bishop Rosati came to pay his respects to the new Assistant General. Mothers Mathevon and Thiéfry conferred with her again in St. Louis, then she left for France. "She had edified us all and been lavished with gifts," noted Mother Duchesne after her departure. She had, of course, taken advantage of this opportunity to write to the Mother General—a plain, matter-of-fact letter, with here and there a dash of the real Philippine:

> I should have answered your last letter sooner, had I not been daily expecting Mother Eugenie, who can carry our letters to you without postage and in great security. She is here now and awaiting the first steamboat that will take her [up the Ohio] most directly toward her goal. She has visited all the convents and is in a position to give you an account of them better than anyone else could. She will tell you the steps she has taken with regard to the spiritual direction of this house and the success obtained in this matter. In this respect no houses are better off than Florissant and St. Charles. These parishes are directed by the Jesuits and always will be, according to the contract with the bishop. This is a strong motive for supporting them. They in no way hinder the progress of the house in St. Louis, and if they were closed one evening, they would be reopened next morning by the Sisters of Charity, who

are highly esteemed by the clergy and the people, as they conduct hospitals, boarding schools, and orphanages for boys and girls—all equally well. . . . If we do not maintain our schools well, they will put us in the shade.

I was struck by this sentence in your last letter: "When Mother Eugenie returns to America, she will bring precise orders; and I hope they will not meet with opposition." From whom do you expect opposition? Or what gave you cause to fear it? Mother Anne [de Coppens], who so often complained of being stationed here, is expressing no desire to return to France, but she may ask to do so later on, though Mother Eugenie's departure is offering her the best opportunity possible. . . .

When Mother Audé sailed for France, Mother Duchesne was ignorant of some of the facts about her departure. The Mother Visitatrix seemed the very embodiment of success that stemmed from natural ability, religious zeal, and supernatural courage. She had done fine work in Louisiana, endured severe trials in the past two years, suffered physical collapse and long illness, and most of the time had kept her troubles so entirely to herself that Mother Barat had had to demand news before she received it. Then Eugenie's courage faltered; emotion had overwhelmed her; and on December 21, 1833, she had poured out a dramatic account of the past months of epidemic and death. As she brought it to a close she wrote:

My heart is broken; each religious who died took from me part of my life. . . . A little while close to you would strengthen me, revive my poor soul, prepare me for further suffering. Oh, Mother, my dear Mother, will you not grant my request? But—forgive me; such a request is contrary to complete abandonment. Do what you will with your Eugenie.

This appeal to the Mother General—not the first Eugenie had made for a return to France—had crossed a letter from Mother Barat containing the lines:

You have been chosen Assistant General for America. Our Mothers in the Council made their decision in accord with the plurality of votes of the professed religious in that part of the world. . . . We enjoin on you the duty of acccepting this burden, which Jesus will help you to carry. As soon as you receive this letter, begin the visitation of the other four houses, if your health permits, then sail for France to give an account of your mission.

So Mother Audé had assumed her new office, but she would

never see America again, not even when Mother Barat expressed
the need she had of her services. The American houses were now
less unified than before, though in Missouri there was security in
the presence of Mother Duchesne. She had lost all delegated
powers when Reverend Mother Audé superseded her, but the
power of her sanctity remained, as well as the influence she exerted
on the religious who knew and loved her, and there were very
few who did not recognize in her the true religious superior.

The "sickly season" was upon St. Louis early in June. A light
form of cholera prevailed in July, and as several of the religious
were stricken, Bishop Rosati advised advancing the summer holidays and sending most of the community to Florissant to recuperate. Mother Duchesne and Sister Lamarre remained in St. Louis
with the orphans. Reduced to penury, they were obliged to borrow
money from the bank for living expenses. Prayer and toil filled the
long, hot days, and all was offered in a spirit of reparation. The
terrible plague with which God had repeatedly scourged so many
parts of the world, and particularly the Mississippi Valley, seemed
to Philippine and to many holy priests with whom she talked a
punishment for sin, infidelity, blindness born of worldliness, ambition, avarice. A lively sense of responsibility before God, a
pressing sense of guilt that nothing seemed to relieve, kept her
prostrate in spirit, pleading in prayer that there might be an end
to this terrible condition, that souls might turn to God in sincere
repentance. Saints are certainly more sensitive to the malice of
sin than are the rest of people, and Philippine Duchesne was very
close to God.

Realizing the presence of evil and being powerless to prevent
it was terrible suffering for her. So she strove to make reparation
for at least some fraction of it by her own penance and prayer and
by strengthening the religious convictions of the children under
her care—a mere handful of orphan girls. But fervent love could
increase a hundredfold the value of their reparative efforts. So she
strove to share with them the burning thirst of her incessant desire
to bring souls back to Christ and to give Christ to souls. The dominant thought in her soul was always the thought of extending the
reign of the Sacred Heart. In these August days of 1834 that
thought obsessed her.

September brought the reopening of classes with postponed
reviews and examinations. There was news from France—a letter
from her sister Euphrosine told of the death of her husband, Jean-
Joseph Jouve, and Philippine wrote at once, "We have prayed for

him and for you, my beloved Sister, who are so sad and lonely."
An October letter to Mother Barat contained a statement of the
financial condition of her convent: the contractor had been paid;
a Negro couple had been purchased for the service of the house;
a promissory note for 3,000 francs had been signed in favor of
Mother Mathevon, who was hard pressed for money to continue
the work on the new convent at St. Charles; and another thousand
francs was owed at the Bank of St. Louis. In closing Philippine
added:

> Mrs. Mullanphy has turned over to me the 750 francs she received
> for us in France, 500 coming from Madame de Rollin. She also
> brought us, among other things, the new plan of studies, the rule
> for the Children of Mary who have left school, the method of com-
> piling accounts, and the biographies of our religious who have died.
> These touch me very deeply. . . . The change in my health and
> physical strength makes me realize more plainly than ever my in-
> capacity as superior, and I long for a discharge from the office. . . .
> The consecration of the Cathedral is set for the 26th of this month.
> Monseigneur wishes quite positively to have some of our nuns
> assist at the ceremony in a private tribune. We hope Mother
> Eugenie is already en route to America. . . .

The consecration of the St. Louis Cathedral had been announced and Mother Duchesne and her community were looking
forward, not to attending the ceremony, but to the clerical visitors
whom they expected and for whom the pupils would give a little
reception, of which uniforms, gloves, curtsies, music, and an address were the traditional ingredients. The reception would take
place as planned, but Mother Duchesne would not be at the City
House to greet the guests. Unknowingly she had given the Mother
General a last account of her stewardship in St. Louis.

As Mother Barat had stated that no changes were to be made
in Missouri until the return of Mother Audé, Philippine was unprepared for the letter that reached her on October 7, enclosed in
a circular letter from the Superior General to the convents in
Louisiana and Missouri. Mother Barat wrote on July 29, 1834,
after hearing an account of conditions prevailing in the American
houses:

> As I send off the circular letter to our American houses, my dear
> Philippine, I want to write a few lines to explain a sentence in one
> of my letters which you quoted in the last one I had from you. It
> was about the opposition that I encountered in regard to your

change of residence. You recall that I was obliged to give up that plan—at least I was persuaded to do so. It was not you, my dear Mother, that I had in mind when I wrote that I hoped Mother Eugenie would help me overcome that opposition. . . . Now I feel that I know conditions [in America] better, so I have not hesitated in deciding on a change of residence for you. . . . Moreover, dear Philippine, you need a rest and an easier field of administration. So you will call Mother Thiéfry to St. Louis to take your place, and you will take hers at Florissant. Mother Eugenie will write by this same post to your Reverend Bishop to inform him, or I shall do it myself, if I can—that would be better. I have also indicated some other changes, but I leave you free to modify these if you think it necessary. Confer with Mother Thiéfry about the matter. . . . I shall be so happy to have your answer to this letter; give me details about your new place of residence. I recommend myself to your prayers, dear Philippine. Be assured that I pray for you with all my heart. You know how dear you are to me. . . .

Philippine began at once the preparations necessary for her departure, but she took time to write to Josephine on October 8, saying in part:

I have not had direct news from you in a long time, but you speak constantly to me by your benefactions. A letter from Lyons informs me that 500 francs which I received through some ladies of our city who had been in Paris came from you. Really you are too generous, and I simply do not know how to thank you enough. That money came at a time when we were in such great need, I have thanked Divine Providence and my beloved provider-friend a thousand times. Severe fever and dysentery among the nuns had forced us to send home the boarding pupils. As a result, our funds were exhausted. . . .

I am going to move from the convent in St. Louis to that of St. Ferdinand, which I left six years ago to come here. It is just about five leagues from here. This change gives me additional work, so I must be brief. I learned from Madame Jouve of the death of her husband. Not knowing her exact address, I am enclosing my letter to her in this. A thousand loving messages to Mesdames Teisseire, [Augustin] Perier, [Hippolyte] Duchesne, and de Mauduit. The last named should not complain, for I have written to her several times recently. Moreover, she knows my love for her, and that love can never change.

Bishop Rosati came for confessions on Saturday, October 11. When she greeted him in the parlor as he came from the chapel, she gave him the letter Mother Barat had written, asking his approval of the changes. There was no "opposition" on his part, though he was reluctant to have her leave that very afternoon. But she was ready to make her sacrifice, and less than an hour later she was bidding *au revoir*, first to the children, then to her community —some of them her very dearest daughters, Regis Hamilton, Suzanne McKay, Gonzague Boilvin, Judith Shannon, and Catherine Lamarre—all of them so dear to her great, generous heart. Into the hired carriage they put her meager luggage, and she drove off alone, yet not alone, for those mid-day hours spent traversing the autumn-tinted Valley of Florissant were also spent in intimate converse with the Sacred Heart.

eleven

Sharing the Lot
of the Saints

I. 1834—1836

THE CHILL OF AUTUMN was in the air. Sere and brittle leaves scurried and swirled around the Florissant convent as the sharp wind blew from the northwest. The atmosphere inside was damp and cold and penetrating, but Philippine gave little heed to it as she knelt in the cloister chapel, her eyes fixed on the tabernacle. She still seemed deep in retreat, though she had already completed the eighth day. It had been a time of spiritual aridity and trial in spite of the fact that she had used as her guide through the Ignatian Exercises the notes of a retreat given in Paris by Father Varin himself. Struggle as she would, she found it beyond her power to relinquish the hope she had had of being freed from her position of authority. And there were the recommendations made by the last General Council, stressing the use of certain methods of meditation and examen, which troubled her, though she realized their general usefulness.

The silence of the night was broken at times by whispered pleadings and offerings. Spontaneously the words she loved and had used since girlhood formed her colloquies. The prayers of Mother Marie of the Incarnation had inspired her in her youth, and by them she had inspired the children she had taught, whether in France or America, with devotion to the Sacred Heart. They often formed the substance of her holy hours or holy nights of adoration, and she never tired of dwelling with contemplative desire on the simple, all-embracing sentiments of love and reparation they expressed:

> O Eternal Father, I come to you through the Heart of my Jesus, who is the Way, the Truth, and the Life. Through this divine Heart I adore you for those who do not adore you; I love you for those who do not love you; I gratefully acknowledge you to be my God for all who in wilful blindness and contempt refuse this recognition of your goodness. By this Divine Heart I desire to make satisfaction for the neglect of all mankind. In spirit I go through the whole world in search of every soul redeemed by the Precious Blood of my Divine Spouse, in order to make reparation for all through his Sacred Heart. . . .

The retreat left her spiritually disturbed. As she sat writing to Mother Barat on November 9, the lines in her strong, mobile face were deep-set; her friendly eyes were troubled. In all the world there was only one person to whom she could freely unburden her soul, and to her she poured out all the pent-up personal suffering of the past month:

> I have just finished my retreat, which I made by myself shortly after coming here. I wish I could assure you that I shall lead a better life here in solitude and far from the occasions that so often caused me to fall. But it always seems to me that for my own security and for the good of others I should be in a position of lower rank, and I await this second favor from your charity. Besides the experience of my whole past life, these new regulations and directives frighten me. They are so detailed, and my memory is so faulty in regard to new things, much more so than for things of the past. My heart is so dry, I can scarcely think through all these rules and methods, so it will be far worse for me to try to carry them out. . . . I have never been able to reflect on a subject. I see it as a whole, and what I have once seen I shall see for ten years without change or addition. I never see things in detail or in parts. I see a thing, there is the whole thing; I do not see its divisions. . . .
>
> I feel that I am a wornout instrument, a useless walking stick that is fit only to be hidden in a dark corner. God allows everything to deepen this impression in my soul. I have never at any time attracted people's confidence, and the same thing is true here. . . . I came here in great peace of soul as to my assigned post, but the devil did not leave me long in peace. In the letters I received from St. Louis several persons told me the remark was made by some

that they *never* wanted to see me again. From that I concluded that they wanted me to be sent further away, and I have not the courage to accept that. Here I have more spiritual help than anywhere else in the United States. This is all I ask for the rest of my life. I know Mother Xavier Murphy once said she thought I would spend the last years of my life near her, but I dread being sent [to Grand Coteau]. For three months they have had no Mass, not even on Sundays and feast days. My conscience is not tranquil enough to allow me to live in peace without the possibility of receiving the last Sacraments. I dread the river, the traveling, the heat especially, because of an illness from which I have not fully recovered. I beg you, Reverend Mother, let me die here in Missouri. I shall obey anyone you place over me. . . .

Here is a picture of spiritual suffering which was deepened by a feeling of incapacity, a sense of utter failure. She was a spent force; she was puzzled and bruised, and her sensitive nature cringed under the thoughtless blows that rained on her. All natural supports seemed to have crumbled, and she knew not where to turn. To accept the bitterness inside herself and not to add to it by external resentment or by cynicism called for high courage. If she seemed to falter inwardly, she only leaned the more reliantly on God for support, and the trials she suffered served to strengthen her faith immeasurably, while self was being slowly, painfully, ground out of her.

Ten days later she was writing to Mother Barat on the important subject of the religious profession of a young nun who had been one of her own novices:

Mother Thiéfry has written to ask my opinion about the fitness of Mother Stanislaus Shannon for final profession. She has placed the utmost confidence in her. I refused to pass judgment, for I was under the impression that this young religious was not sufficiently dependent on authority. But I did say that she loves her vocation sincerely, that she has just reached her twenty-fifth year, and that she has been very generous and devoted in the hardest kinds of employments. It is unfortunate that while so young she was placed second in authority in the convent, and she has had full charge of all business and financial affairs because of her knowledge of English. She has charge of the studies, and in this matter she has followed faithfully the instructions given her. But the Constitutions require that she be sent to the house designated for probation, and I do not see how she can be replaced here.

During the weeks that followed, Philippine was troubled by

the thought that in her impetuous outburst to Mother Barat she had shown a lack of abandonment and religious spirit. After submitting this scruple to her Jesuit director, peace of soul returned and she followed his advice, as her letter at the close of December shows. She was also ready to express a very favorable opinion of Mother Shannon now and to request from Mother Barat permission for her final vows:

> At this season of the year I always feel obliged to ask pardon for the pain I have caused you for so many years. I hope your great charity grants it to me, along with the favor I have already solicited—of being freed from all official position. Both God and men alike say that I am less fit than ever for them. I pray that in this coming year God will pour out upon you his best blessings, and also on the Society and on our kind Fathers. On the advice of one of them I wish to retract, though very regretfully, the request I made you not to send me away from here. I am ready to obey, no matter what it may cost me, in any change you may be pleased to make and no matter how I may dread that change. . . .
>
> I have now formed a very good opinion of Mother Stanislaus Shannon. The difficulty is that this convent could not get along without her, and there is no one to take her place. I am like a stranger here to the Americans, as I cannot talk to them. . . . I want to ask you to let her remain here for the six months of her last probation. If you think it advisable, you could add the condition that she ask the help of the Father Superior and Master of Novices. She would have better direction here than in St. Louis, and more according to the spirit of our institute. . . .

Of her position at Florissant Philippine had written some weeks before this: "My life here is about the same as in St. Louis. I wake the religious in the morning, make the last rounds at night, clean the outhouses, scrub, sweep—these are my ordinary occupations." Of her solitude she would write six weeks later: "There is no news to give you from this house. The front door is not opened all day long; the parlor, opened once a week, stays closed from Sunday to Sunday. This solitude is entirely to my liking."

A little note written in January to Mother Gonzague Boilvin shows the strong bond that united them in a friendship that was rooted and grounded in love for the Sacred Heart. To the young aspirant, frail in constitution, sensitive in temperament, talented and gifted spiritually, the older religious—more than twice her age —gave strength, courage, and training that would make her an excellent religious. Never afraid to show affection when she knew it would be understood, Philippine wrote on New Year's Day:

> I received your two letters, my beloved Sister, and though you did not tell me you had made what you sent me, I had no trouble in recognizing you in all of it. Thank you so much for all, but especially for that which is the symbol of our union, the object of our dear devotion, the mirror in which we should both perceive our own faults and find the model of the virtues we lack. My great wish for you at the beginning of this year is that you may obtain these virtues, which can be drawn from the study of the Sacred Heart.
>
> I do not need all his charity in order to pardon all your faults toward me, for I cannot recall a single one. As to the faults that have displeased God, they are forgiven seventy times seven times if you detest them. As I have the same hope for myself, I trust that the Heart of Jesus will unite us once more in the same community. In him I am all yours. . . .

Sympathy with sickness and suffering was a natural quality in Mother Duchesne's character. Her *Journal* at this period shows her concern for both the religious whom she had left in St. Louis and those she found at Florissant. At the City House there had been illness all winter, but in January it became alarming. The climate was, of course, partly to blame, for in Missouri, where the first snows, coming in November, melted quickly and were followed by "spells" of bright, mild weather, the real winter usually set in after Christmas. But this year, Mother Duchesne recorded in February, "the cold was something extraordinary, the worst in twenty years, and that throughout both the United States and Canada. . . . Actually our lips froze together, and at night our breath froze on the pillows and sheets."

Mother Boilvin suffered most that winter at the City House. Anxiety about her led Philippine to ask Mother Thiéfry to send her to Florissant where she herself might nurse her back to health. On receiving a refusal, she decided to put the matter before the bishop, who had always taken a fatherly interest in the Boilvin girls. So she sent him a pleading little note, and early in March Mother Boilvin came to Florissant to recuperate. It was a joy for Mother Duchesne to be able to care for her, a relaxation for her to talk with her in the little room adjoining her own, where the aspirant was lodged. French was a bond between them and there were so many things to talk about. *The Shepherd of the Valley* was carrying alarming rumors of war with France over certain indemnities guaranteed in a treaty made during Casimir Perier's ministry. There was good news from Louisiana, where St. Michael's had one hundred and fifty pupils and fifty orphans, and Grand Coteau had eighty girls in the academy. New convents had been opened in France, and Mother Duchesne could point out their location on an old map she had treasured through the years and dwell with loving insistence on the motivating force within the Society—the glory of the Sacred Heart and the love that urged its members on to works of apostolic zeal that would draw souls into the Kingdom of Christ.

Then came word from St. Louis that a fire had endangered the new cathedral. The heat had broken some of the stained glass windows and caused other serious damage. But these were the least effects of the fire in Philippine's estimation. "Monseigneur Rosati nearly died that night," she recorded, "and has been ill ever since." Out of her poverty she made him an offering, after consulting Mother Shannon as to how much they could possibly spare. The brief accompanying note must have touched his heart:

> I have been haunted by the thought of the great danger to which you were exposed. We have assembled together to pray for your recovery and for the cessation of the trials which are enough to overwhelm you. I wish it were in my power to repair all the damage done to the cathedral. I am sending you all I can spare just now, and I hope to double this small amount soon. . . .

In June Mother Duchesne had the joy of presenting to Mother Shannon the Superior General's permission for the young nun's final vows. Arrangements for her probationary training had already been discussed with Father De Theux, S.J., when Philippine wrote to Mother Barat:

> I received a letter from Mother Audé which testified to your kindness in my regard. As to my health, it is good now. All desire is extinct in me except that of enjoying God and of preparing myself for that by withdrawing from all occasions of faults—but I shall always have these. It grieves me to be an obstacle to the advancement of those who are under my care, and I shall be until I am relieved of superiority. . . . Mother Stanislaus Shannon was delighted with the permission to prepare for her final vows. As she cannot be replaced, so necessary is her very name in this house, the Father Superior has consented, with zeal and interest, to direct her himself during the six months, which cannot begin before vacation. Could you not shorten the probation in view of her ten years of assiduous service to the Society? That would give me as much joy

as it would give her. My eye-sight is very poor today, so I cannot write more. . . .

The temporary extinction of all lesser desires in view of the highest good was a spiritual experience that seems to have come frequently to Philippine Duchesne. It was a grace that led to more intimate union with God in the sanctuary of her own soul and to more generous imitation of Christ in the daily contacts of community life. She had no false or complicated notions of perfection. To her perfection lay in giving oneself wholly to God and in going the whole length of opportunity in the service of others. It was the reflex of this charity that made her enter so heartily into the joys and sorrows of her companions.

August was drawing to a close when one hot, humid day Mother Duchesne met Mother Shannon on the stairway—there was only one stairway in the little convent—and made her a sign to follow her. When they reached the doorway of her room, the Superior said to her young treasurer, "Where do you expect to procure a profession cross for yourself?" "From your cupboard, Mother," came the quick reply, and they both laughed heartily. "Yes," said Mother Duchesne, "it is there, and you shall have it soon, for this very day you are going to begin your probation. Are you pleased with that news?" The answer was an explosion of joy, for that was Mother Shannon's way.

During the months of probation the young nun's love and admiration for Mother Duchesne increased daily, and throughout her long life Mother Shannon always spoke of her as "my holy Mother." Years afterwards she used to say:

> My holy Mother thought that a religious of the Sacred Heart was not worthy of her name unless she offered herself with ardent love to the work of reparation and expiation, and therefore led as penitential a life as her strength would allow. Perhaps we had strong constitutions or received special graces in answer to her prayers, but we certainly practiced great austerities and were none the worse for it. We lived as long as other people, and many of us have reached an advanced age.

Another passage from the biography of Mother Shannon gives a deeply moving picture of the superior at Florissant at this time. The young nun was walking in the garden one day, saying her rosary. Ornamental plants and shrubs were not cultivated there; only potatoes, onions, and other common vegetables grew in neat patches. Going noiselessly down a pathway hedged by berry bushes, she came quite unexpectedly on Mother Duchesne, who had been trimming off the rank outer leaves from the cabbages, but was now resting a little, seated on a boulder by the path. The commonplace, prosaic background of the picture was symbolic of the rough ways of humility and self-sacrifice along which Mother Duchesne followed her Divine Master, and Mother Shannon realized, as she stood watching her, that some deep sorrow was crushing her heart. The holy old religious was holding her rosary in one hand and with the other was trying to brush away the tears that were pouring down her cheeks. As she sat there, weeping silently, her whole posture and expression revealed unspeakable suffering patiently borne. The young nun could not hold back her own tears at the sight and longed to console her loved superior, but this sorrow was too personal, too sacred to intrude upon, and she withdrew as noiselessly as she had come, leaving her "holy Mother" alone with God.

Although the convent at Florissant was remote and solitary, it was a place to which many visitors were now drawn by the presence of Mother Duchesne. Old friends brought new ones to see her, and she noted their names faithfully in the *Journal*. Father Brassac came with Father Lutz; Father Timon came with Father Badin, "first missionary in Kentucky"; Bryan Mullanphy brought the noted French scientist and explorer, Monsieur Nicollet; Father Van de Velde came with Father Carrell, a new recruit for the Jesuit novitiate, and returned some days later with another interesting personage, Pierce Connelly, "newly converted Protestant minister, who is going to Rome and will carry our letters and commissions."

But Mother Duchesne had no letters to send, for she soon became desperately ill. August floods had brought the water so high that access to both church and convent was cut off for some time. As the water receded, sickness began to take its toll in the community—first Sister Missé, then Mother Shannon, then Mother Duchesne herself. Her illness was so alarming that Mother Shannon sent for Mother Thiéfry in September, but Philippine would not allow her to remain. She felt that she could manage without her, and she knew the St. Louis community needed its superior. It was, however, "a great consolation," as she wrote to Bishop Rosati, "and a source of peace to know that she was willing to come and stay at Florissant." In November she told Mother Barat:

As I did not lose consciousness during my illness nor the power to read, I could keep an eye on things, though confined to bed. I was not ready to die; I still have need and reason to do penance. . . . Our little boarding school is attended by Americans who speak English all the time. However, I take an hour of surveillance in the studyroom.

Early that same November, Father John Odin returned from Europe, bringing parcels and a packet of mail for Florissant. There were letters from Philippine's family and from the nuns in France, gifts, remembrances, books—all carried in the satchel of this kind Vincentian friend. One letter called for immediate action and an answer by the first opportunity. In it Mother Barat had written:

I often think that your convent at Florissant really ought to be closed. The works are so small. Then St. Louis and St. Charles would get aid and it seems to me these two establishments would be sufficient. Tell me what you think about this; consult your neighbors [the Jesuits]. If they advise this, then I shall write to Monseigneur and you will receive your obedience. I think it is high time we opened convents in sections of the country that would furnish us with vocations. . . . Mother Eugenie cannot leave France yet. Her health is very poor, and the doctors advise against her taking the trip. *Adieu*, dear Mother; I have written enough for this time. Our friends send you affectionate greetings, especially Father Varin and my brother. They, too, are growing old. Soon we shall all disappear. Fortunately we have already left all things. . . . Oh, how I should love to follow your example and make the same request that you address to me. . . .

After consulting Father De Theux, Mother Duchesne answered, after New Year's greetings to the Superior General:

Now I come to the chief topic of your letter—the merging of the Florissant convent with that of St. Louis. I wrote at once to the superior of the Jesuits to ask his advice. Here are the exact words of his reply: "It would grieve me to have your house at Florissant closed. I hope this will never happen. If Mother Barat has made up her mind about it, could you not suggest to her that this convent be used as a central novitiate for all your American houses, with only a free school attached to it? I think this would be an excellent way of forming your novices, and thus your Society would continue its good work among us. But for goodness' sake, do not let them close your house! Offer my humble respects to Mother Barat, please. As for yourself, after having done all in your power to save this very useful convent, do not be discouraged. This is the way God treats his servants."

As for myself—if I may express my opinion—I think, 1) that this house with its little boarding school will give more recruits to the Society than the other two in Missouri. . . . 2) here at Florissant we shall always be assured of the finest spiritual direction because of the Jesuit establishment near by; many fervent apostles are being trained there; 3) none of the children of this academy would transfer to the other boarding schools, and the nuns from here would be a burden to other communities, while here we can live on the produce of our garden. . . . 4) we built this house at a time when prices were very high, so it cost about 40,000 francs. We could not get 10,000 for it now, and I am sure that if it were put up for sale, it would be bought by subscription to make a country house for the Sisters of Charity. . . .

I wrote to Mother Thiéfry to tell her what you suggested in regard to our convent. Though I am better, I am in no condition to drive to St. Louis. The least exposure to cold or dampness brings on fever and a bad cough. She will write directly to you, my beloved Mother. I hasten to finish this so I can send it by a traveler. If you follow the advice of the Jesuit Father, this house could be placed under Mother Thiéfry's guidance again. She has not built up the academy in St. Louis to any great extent. Mother Hamilton would be more pleasing to everyone there. Mother Shannon would help Mother Thiéfry quite effectively where English is needed. . . .

New Year's holidays for the pupils had by this time become the custom in the boarding schools in and near St. Louis. This gave the nuns an opportunity to spend the last day of December in recollection and to take a little relaxation on New Year's Day. Philippine used a few free moments to thank Mother Boilvin for a Christmas gift:

I recognize the goodness of your heart, my dearest Sister, in the charity you have shown me by making these gifts that remind us of the love of the Heart of Jesus and of his Cross. The last emblem you made seems to me more perfect than former ones. I do not know whether or not that was due to the finer material you used to paint on. . . . Your letter gave me joy, for I read in it the unction that the Divine Infant poured into your heart as you knelt at his crib. The crib and Calvary are the two dwelling places dearest to those who love Jesus. Pray to him for me, that I may never leave those dwelling places.

On March 7, 1836, Mother Shannon made her final vows. The bishop's absence was a disappointment to the community, but Father Philip Borgna, as Vicar General, presided at the ceremony and preached with unction and eloquence. Perhaps it was by visitors who came for the day that Mother Duchesne sent the following undated note to Mother Boilvin, for it belongs quite evidently to this period:

> Be assured, my dear Sister, that you have not caused me any pain, but rather consolation, for I see in you a person who can render valuable services to the Society of the Sacred Heart. I fear in a way that you realize this and so may lose the merit which could be gained from your work. That is why I felt I should deal a blow to your self-love in order to make way in your soul for divine love and fraternal charity. The worst evil in the world would be to consider yourself free from faults. Being too greatly saddened by one's faults can come from having one's pride humiliated. Try to be like that Hospitaler Sister who got a chapter of fifty-two faults and just plunged with undiminished confidence into the merciful Heart of Jesus Christ. . . . I am rather put out with you because you did not admit sooner that you were suffering. . . . Whenever you feel the need of medicines, you must say so. Those in charge cannot always discover our ills simply by looking at us. It would be a real pleasure for me to take care of you. . . .

Boxes from France always caused a stir in the convent, and Philippine was quick to thank for all that reached the mission. On March 20 she sent to her sister, Madame Jouve, a letter that seems especially self-revealing:

> Just recently, my dearest Sister, I received your letter of April 3, 1835, dated from Conflans, and put in a case that was coming to us from Paris. In it was also the beautiful present you sent me. It is what I would have desired more than anything else, for the first vestment you sent me in 1819 is worn out and needed to be replaced. I knew from a letter that came more rapidly by mail that you had been to see your daughter Mother Amelie Jouve, and I shared in the pleasure of that visit. As to the income of which you write, I do not recall the conditions, and it is not in my power to change them now because of my vow of poverty. But in any case it is most natural that it should go to Amelie, who is nearer to you and younger than I. In this way we would avoid bank fees and the risk of death, which, I trust, will come to me before it comes to your daughter. She can do much for the cause of religion, but my days are numbered. I am growing weak. In this country where I still do not understand the language well, I shall soon be useless. I almost forget that I am French; that language is studied only as a foreign tongue by the Americans, who are growing more numerous and now occupy all the prominent positions here.
>
> I beg God to enlighten both you and your daughter Josephine as

to the vocation God wills for her. I should grieve to see you alone, yet it would be a consolation to see her sheltered safe from the many dangers that threaten one's faith. Even the most enlightened maternal care has not been able to safeguard several of your children. By the generosity of your sacrifice for them you will increase your own merits and make their true happiness more secure. The world was saved by the Cross. Those who spread the Gospel preached only the Cross. And solid virtue flourishes only in its shadow. The necessity of carrying the cross and of living as a follower of Jesus Christ in toil and tears prevents the return of so many brothers who have wandered from the truth. We do not want a religion that is sad, they say, or one that requires suffering; we want pleasures. They want Paradise without paying the price of suffering, but can they give the lie to the Gospel? . . .

The plan to close the Florissant convent was dropped temporarily. In April Mother Hamilton came for a brief visit, bringing Mother Boilvin to recuperate again. Once more Philippine nursed the delicate aspirant back to health, but this time she decided to ask the Mother General's permission to keep her at Florissant. Although Mother Duchesne did not mention the fact to the Superior General, illness had laid its hand on her, too, during Lent, but under Mother Shannon's care she rallied and was able to be with the community at Easter. Before the close of April, Florissant had quite an unexpected invalid in its infirmary. From Louisiana came Mothers Antonia Potier and Louise Penel, both unannounced and both tubercular, the former from St. Michael's, the latter from Grand Coteau. On their arrival in St. Louis, Mother Thiéfry decided to share with Mother Duchesne the problem of caring for them and so sent Mother Penel to Florissant. This new member of the community found it difficult to accept the conditions and the climate in Missouri, and very soon Mother Duchesne realized that she had not only an invalid but also a mental case to deal with. In a building as small and crowded as the convent at Florissant, this was a severe trial. No hint of this appeared, however, in Philippine's correspondence that spring, but encouragement came to her in May, when a very affectionate letter reached her from Mother Barat:

This very moment, dear Mother and beloved daughter, I received your letter of November 1. It was balm to my afflicted heart. . . . I was dreading what might come of your long illness reported by Mother Shannon and I thanked God when I saw your handwriting. Now we can hope once more to keep you on earth. May Jesus be blessed for this! I am greatly preoccupied about the convents in your country. How I wish I could send you recruits, especially a Mistress of Novices to carry out the plan suggested! . . . Dear Mother, beg the Heart of Jesus to send us subjects according to his Heart. Pray for me, too, and be assured of our loving union.

Philippine's answer, written on Pentecost Sunday, May 22, 1836, reveals the workings of her mind and heart in the midst of very trying circumstances:

I am so relieved and consoled to know that this Florissant convent will remain devoted to the Sacred Heart and forever consecrated by the vow you allowed me to make in honor of our patron, St. Regis. He is no longer honored at Grenoble. I feared this trial would go even further. As to myself, I am growing very old. I have never wanted to be in a position of authority; still less do I want it now, for I realize more and more clearly how unfit I am for the office of superior. To soul-suffering there is added bodily suffering that shows me even more plainly my incapacity. At one time I begged you not to change my place of residence because none of our other convents equals this one in drawing souls to the love and practice of solitude, and here we always have the best spiritual help. This convent is well suited to receive young novices, but the closing of the boarding school would take away the hope of vocations. We now have just fifteen pupils, but I believe this small group will give us more stable vocations than will any one of the other four boarding schools. . . . One must be in this country to appreciate the shades of difference in various localities. . . .

In June Mother Duchesne and her assistant, Mother Shannon, who also retained the office of treasurer, were busy making up the expense accounts of the past six months, which were to be forwarded to the Mother House in July. Had Florissant ever sent in so good a record before? The house was not only out of debt, but also had on hand an almost incredible surplus, after having loaned one hundred and fifty dollars to St. Charles for the digging of a new well and the purchase of furniture. This improvement in financial conditions was due in part to the increase and stability of the enrollment in the boarding school, which Mother Duchesne attributed to Mother Shannon's influence, and Mother Shannon attributed to Mother Duchesne's prayers. The fate of the convent seemed still in the balance when Philippine sent the accounts to the Mother General with a brief letter on July 1:

The changes suggested for this house would come at a time when it is prospering better than ever before. We have more pupils in both schools than they had while Mother Thiéfry was here, and many others have applied. None of them will go elsewhere. I owe you this information . . . but *fiat.* Mother Penel is a very sick person. I am trying to nurse her, as well as our two other invalids, but I have reason to dread the coming winter. Who will care for them? If only I could be completely hidden in a corner, so as not to be tempted to think about things that are really not my business! My recovery at Easter makes me fear I shall again have to face troubles and trials. I really am in no condition to nurse the sick and watch by them, to work in the garden, to give the morning call and make the night visit. But there is no one else to do these things. All are either too delicate or too busy.

The October enrollment was astonishing—twenty-four pupils in the boarding school! But the happiness of the community was overshadowed by a letter from the Mother General telling them not to count any longer on Mother Audé's return to America because of her broken health, and by the news of the death of Mother Xavier Murphy at Grand Coteau. "She was just forty-three years old," Mother Duchesne wrote in her *Journal,* "and a violent fever carried her off in a few days." Within a week it had also claimed as a second victim Mother Rose Elder, who had nursed her with such loving care.

Winter came early to Florissant Valley, and the extreme cold brought Mother Penel so close to death that Extreme Unction was administered. The melancholy she had suffered from for several months now resulted in complete mental unbalance, a condition very depressing in so small a community. Under the pressure of circumstances the nuns were finding it more and more difficult to carry on their classes and housework and the duties of their religious life. The hired man, moreover, had given notice that he was leaving them. After prayer and consultation Mother Duchesne decided to try to purchase a Negro slave. Previous efforts she had made through the Fenwicks at Ste. Geneviève had failed, so in December she turned to Father John Timon at the Vincentian seminary. He advised her to hire a reliable Negro woman rather than go into debt for a slave, and soon Mathilde was installed in the convent kitchen.

In a letter to Bishop Rosati at Christmas, Mother Duchesne expressed deep concern about Mother Penel's condition, and the year closed in depressing sadness. The *Miserere* was chanted on the Office tone after Mass. Benediction followed, at which a few voices tried to sing the *Magnificat,* for there were not enough nuns to attempt the *Te Deum*. A token kiss of peace was given in the evening without a conference, for so many in the household were ill. Short holidays gave a respite from classwork, and the children had just returned, when Philippine experienced once more the strengthening sympathy of Bishop Rosati's friendship. Through the snow and ice of a bitterly cold day he drove to Florissant to offer spiritual help. He visited Mother Penel, praying with her and for her, and consoled Mother Duchesne by his assurance that the devil had no part in the invalid's condition. "God heard the bishop's prayers," wrote Philippine gratefully in her *Journal*. On January 15 lucidity returned and Mother Penel was able to receive absolution and Holy Communion. Just an hour later she expired.

In February Mother Duchesne learned with satisfaction that Mother Aloysia Hardey had been named superior at St. Michael's and Mother Julie Bazire had gone to fill that office at Grand Coteau. On March 10 came news of the death of a very fervent and active religious, Sister Helen Mayette. That was the sixth of her Missouri religious to die in Louisiana and the realization of this fact was depressing, for Philippine had sent of her best religious to the Southern houses. However, a letter from St. Madeleine Sophie just at this time afforded her consolation by the hope it held out of recruits from France and by the tenderness of its closing lines:

> What memories the months of November and December bring to my mind! Those happy days of long ago, gone forever! Now there is only the cross and naked detachment. It must be that way. . . . *Adieu*, dear Mother and beloved daughter. I am losing my hope of ever seeing you again, Philippine. . . . *Adieu* once more.

2. 1837—1840

IN THE BOARDING SCHOOL Philippine had the consolation of seeing the girls respond to Mother Boilvin's training. Although April began with "extraordinary cold and a fall of snow," the convent was aglow with joyous fervor when Jane Pettigrew was baptized and she and Ezelda Musick, another convert, received their First Holy Communion. These were American girls to whom Mother Duchesne could give little more than a smile, a few halting words of encouragement in English, and a festal gouter of pancakes and syrup, but her joy in them was great, for they had learned to know and love the Sacred Heart. Her regret at being unable to help actively in the apostolate with the children is reflected, along with her joy, in a letter of intimate self-revelation written to Josephine the day after the Communion ceremony:

> Not long ago I received your December letter, my dearest Cousin. I am always so grateful for the proofs of your constant friendship, to which I make a very eager and glad return. One thing displeases me in your expressions—they flatter me so much, and I am far from meriting them. Self is always with me, and in a double vocation which should lead me to sanctity, I cling to faults which many people of the world and in the world would have corrected in themselves. God sees to it that I expiate these faults. To be praised from afar and often blamed near at hand is a safeguard against vanity. This recalls to my mind St. Augustine's word about Plato: "What benefit is it to you, Plato, to be praised where you are not, if you burn where you are?"
>
> It seems to me I have outlived myself. I see the time coming when I shall be good for almost nothing. As my health has taken on new vigor, that uselessness will be harder to bear after I have had so much to do. The children here all speak English; very few know French, and I cannot even teach religion to the two Negro women who work for us, nor to the little children in the free school, for although I can read English, as I know the meaning of the printed words, it is quite a different thing to understand it when it is spoken, or to speak it myself, because of the extreme difficulty of the pronunciation, which one can never master at my age. . . . In the meantime I shall have time to plant and tend our truck garden. They say we shall have small success this year, for the ground has been covered with snow three times since the beginning of this month, and nearly all the seed had been sown before that. I find in this quiet work one very great advantage— it brings such peace of soul, and this arises, no doubt, from contact with the beauty of nature, which lifts one up to the Creator.
>
> I have not had answers to the last letters I wrote to my sisters, Mesdames de Mauduit and Jouve. I understand the latter is all alone. Look at the three of us—Amelie, Euphrosine, and me—each in different circumstances of detachment. There is not a single religious from France in the community here. But we meet at the same center—the Heart of God, whose Providence watches over us, whose arms uphold us. May He bless us! I am always your friend.

By this time Philippine had learned that her niece, Josephine Jouve, had entered the Convent of Perpetual Adoration in Lyons. She waited, however, for her sister to tell her of this last great sacrifice—the fifth child she had given to the service of God. Then she wrote in loving sympathy and abounding joy to Madame Jouve. Tender and virile, the letter is a counterpart of its author:

I have just received your letter of March 16, my dearest Sister. The generous sentiments you express in it are very consoling to this sister of yours who loves you in a special way in God. But your loneliness and your sacrifices add to the tender affection which I have always felt for you and which can only increase as your trials are prolonged. If Abraham's oblation has been so highly praised, if God himself rewarded it and praised it so nobly, what will he not do for you, who have offered five beloved children as victims to his grateful Heart? They were not undesirables in the family, led to the altar as good riddance for the household, in order the better to provide for children that were loved more tenderly. They were the loveliest ones, four of them your first fruits, like the offerings of Abel and Solomon. They were truly the chosen ones, the pride of the family, and they would have had a brilliant place in society, shed luster on their parents, married well. In every respect you gave the best to God in sacrifice.

If you are already receiving some part of the hundredfold in this world from the high esteem that people have for these children you gave to God, think what your joy in heaven will be when you see them all crowned in glory, blessing the hand that guided them and paying honor to their mother through the many souls who will accompany them and who shared in her guidance, as it were, and so walked in the way of salvation. Do not fear that I love your daughter Josephine less than the others. God has created all the religious orders; He has privileged souls in all of them. Their paths may be different, but they lead to the same goal, where I trust we shall all meet. It is a joy for me to know that you can visit Josephine often and that you enjoyed Father Henri's stay in Lyons. When you see him again, tell him to pray for his godmother. . . .

You gave me consolation by telling me that Sainte Marie has been put once more to a good, useful, and religious work. . . . It is a joy for me to think that Madame de Rollin is also the originator of that good work. Thank her for me, for all that touches the glory of God is personal to me, and I rejoice in it as a personal gain. Do not forget to give my love to Madame de Mauduit. We are three old sisters. Our lifelong friendship will last forever, for God is the strongest tie that binds us to one another. . . .

This letter had not reached France when Amelie Duchesne de Mauduit was stricken at Grâne and died of a cerebral congestion. Many letters came to tell Philippine the news. Of her answers only the one to Josephine is extant:

I received your letter, dearest Cousin, telling me of the death of my dear sister Amelie. My brother was the first to send me the news, then Madame Jouve and her daughter Amelie. I sent answers to these letters and hope they have received them. I want to thank you very particularly for all the dear and edifying details you gave me about the death of this sister whom I esteemed so highly. I am sure her piety and good works have already gained for her the life of eternal happiness. I weep rather for us who remain "under the tents of Cedar," exposed in a thousand ways to losing the crown that is merited only by perseverance. Since death took our beloved Augustin and Scipion, Camille and Casimir, no loss has pained me so much as this one. So many ties, natural and supernatural, united me to this dear sister, I cannot help thinking her death is a warning for me to prepare, and there is so much for me to do in order to assure a favorable judgment. . . .

Your heart is asking, perhaps, about my health. I am well enough, but Madame de Mauduit's death does not reassure me about living much longer. Madame Jouve thinks she had a cerebral fever. That illness often comes quite suddenly, so it warns me to be ready. . . .

The severe judgments Philippine often passed on herself were in no way shared by those who lived with her at Florissant. It was during these years that they came to call her "the Francis Assisi of the Society," as years before she had been called its "Xavier." In one way she considered herself less poor than in former days, for she could no longer claim the closet under the stairway as her living quarters. Mother Thiéfry had used the small room on the second floor which Philippine had been forced to occupy after several attacks of illness, and now she was obliged to accept this again. The community commented jokingly that she only camped there, for at first she scorned the little bedstead and put her mattress on the floor. Renewed illness, however, brought her to accept the service of the bed.

Her poverty was beautiful in the excess of its love, but her worn-out clothing was at times a sight to behold, and she would never have allowed her religious daughters to appear in the patched habit and veil that were her joy. Both naturally and supernaturally she was a lover of poverty, claiming that it was a matter of personal taste as well as a means of imitating the Poor Man of Nazareth. Perhaps the greatest suffering she endured in virtue of poverty was the bitter winter weather. Her letters and her *Journal* bear witness to the fact that in middle age and later life she was exceedingly sensitive to cold, yet she refused the luxury of a fire in her room, except when illness forced it upon her.

There were times when members of the community remonstrated with her for the severity of her mortification in the refectory. Stale bread and weak coffee for breakfast seemed to make fasting a year-round habit with her. But she had a ready answer: "Now what is that compared with the heroic acts of St. John of the Cross, St. Bruno, St. John Berchmans?" Sanctity was her goal, heroism, her model, and she would reach the heights, no matter what price she had to pay. Yet in her own eyes she was always walking the lower levels of the spiritual way.

Mother Margaret Cornelis described the remarkable activity of Mother Duchesne in this second Florissant period when she was approaching seventy years. She was always at work, and mending was a favorite occupation. When the household was asleep, she went noiselessly through the dormitories of both religious and children, examining shoes, stockings, clothing, carrying off what needed mending, making repairs at once or replacing articles with fresh ones—and all of this in the silence of the night. Only when her needle refused to thread easily would she seek out someone with good eyes who was still awake. The children, who slept soundly, could never understand by what mysterious providence the clothing they had left ripped or torn on their chairs at night was always intact when they put it on next morning.

She had a remarkable gift for nursing the sick, not just by caring intelligently for their physical ailments or disease, but by strengthening their soul through charity. She often brought her sewing and sat by the bedside, enlivening the long hours by her interesting and inspiring stories. Where the illness was grave, she refused to yield her place to anyone; and her services were bestowed not only on the religious and the children of the boarding school, but on Theotiste, the old Creole woman who acted as the convent commissionaire, on Mathilde, the Negro cook, and her frail little girl, on the wife of the hired man and on his children.

There is danger of underestimating the supernatural motive and value in all this charity, of taking it for granted that Philippine's character lent itself easily to this inexhaustible devotedness. As an actual fact her soul was frequently a battleground where human forces contended for the upper hand and grace triumphed only after a hard fight. She was a woman of positive tastes, strong likes and dislikes, intense affections, yet she embraced with her charity every soul that came within the ambit of her influence in her effort to be all things to them all and so lead them all nearer to the Sacred Heart of Christ. She loved Florissant with a kind of vehemence, loved its material poverty and inconvenience and solitude, its spiritual wealth under Jesuit direction. But she was often so weary that she could scarcely drag herself to the chapel for prayer or to the sacristy for work, so weak that she seemed more in need of nursing than those to whom she carried a cup of tea or a bowl of porridge. Only the strength of an indomitable will and the charity of Christ himself urged her, upheld her, in the round of daily work and prayer.

The *Maison de Campagne* at Florissant had, among other advantages in Philippine's eyes, that of offering hospitality to the religious from the "City House" in St. Louis. August and September brought Mothers and Sisters in small groups each year, some for their retreat, others for relaxation and a change of air, though there was really very little change. In this way Mother Duchesne made the acquaintance of some of the novices whom Mother Thiéfry brought for holidays at Florissant. Old friends came too— Mothers Hamilton, de Kersaint, Roche from St. Louis, Mothers Mathevon, O'Connor, McKay, and Guillot from St. Charles, and young Mother Mary Knapp joined Mother Duchesne's community in August, 1837.

In the midst of these happy comings and goings the mail brought a letter from Mother Barat, who wrote from Rome on May 25:

> Your last letter reached me here in Rome, dear Philippine, and in spite of all my occupations I want to answer it at once. I see the cross is accompanying you to the very end of your life. Certainly you cannot do the amount of work you used to accomplish, but I know you do not give in to fatigue and your house gives glory to the Heart of Jesus. Why do you want to relinquish your cross voluntarily? Wait until we tell you to, and until then, do the best you can. I have given up the idea of transferring the novitiate to Florissant. Money would be needed to support that convent, and we have none. The postulants do not bring any with them—nor even the clothes they need.
>
> While awaiting the time when I can send an Assistant General to visit your section of America, this is what I have decided on: leave the novices in St. Louis under Mother de Kersaint. I think she will succeed with them. . . . You, dear Mother, remain at Florissant and sanctify yourself there. . . . We have lost our father and

benefactor, Abbé Perreau. This will sadden you. He was deeply attached to you. Have a Requiem service for him. . . .

The solemn Requiem service was held for Father Perreau on August 25. On the last day of the month the service was repeated for Father Charles Felix Van Quickenborne. He had returned from his Kickapoo mission in very poor health some months before this and had taken up the new duties assigned to him at Portage des Sioux, where he died on August 17, 1837, in his fiftieth year of age and his fourteenth year on the frontier. In his death Missouri lost one of its greatest pioneer missionaries, and Philippine lost a sterling friend in whose missionary ventures she had had a vital share through constant prayer.

New names, along with familiar ones, were being entered in her *Journal* now, as new pastors came to the Church of St. Ferdinand and new missionaries took up their residence at the Florissant novitiate. Father Paillason and Van Assche were old friends, but Fathers Gleizal, Helias, and DeVos were new. More interesting, however, were the visits of Father Christian Hoecken, after whose name Philippine wrote words that thrilled her soul: Indian missionary. An even greater thrill came the day she said *au revoir* to Father Aelen and his companions as they set out for the Potawatomi encampment. And it was more truly *au revoir* than anyone could foresee. But Philippine enjoyed most of all the little visits paid by Father Peter Verhaegen, now superior of the Missouri Mission, who took up residence at the Florissant novitiate in the autumn of 1837, and Father De Smet, who had returned recently from a begging trip in Flanders.

The crowning visit of that year, however, was an unexpected pleasure, when Bishop Rosati brought to Florissant the prelate whom Philippine had so longed to meet in 1834—Bishop Simon Bruté of Vincennes. At last she met the churchman of whom she had heard so much, and particularly that he greatly resembled Father Louis Barat "in learning and spirituality." In her *Journal* she made no comment about him, because she was so concerned about other things, especially the servant problem.

Father Timon had advised against the purchase of a Negro slave, for prices were just then exorbitant. He had, instead, directed her to hire a trusty servant from a Catholic slave-owner in the vicinity of Florissant. That arrangement had worked well for a time, but at the beginning of winter the owner had withdrawn the woman and there was no one to tend the cows and cook the meals but Mother Shannon, who had as a helper "the Lynch girl, an orphan to whom we have given a home." Happily Mathilde, the reliable and efficient Negro woman, soon returned to work at the convent, bringing along her little eight-year-old girl.

A letter from Mother Barat, intended as an encouragement to Philippine, did not lessen her anxiety. The Superior General had written on July 20, 1837:

> I received your last letters, my good, my very dear Mother and daughter, and they grieved me. You have your troubles and I share them with you. My intimate affection for you has never diminished; neither time nor distance can lessen it. On the contrary, it has gone on increasing. Your zeal, your long years of labor for the Society in America have doubled it, for I am always mindful of all you have done and endured. I wish I were able to accede to your wishes and procure for you the rest you have so much right to expect from our affection and also from our gratitude. But please realize the position I am in. I cannot find superiors for the houses in France and other countries. Mother Audé cannot return to America. Who, then, can I find to take your place? You know well that I wanted to close Florissant and so help the other houses, but you yourself gave me good reasons for preserving that establishment whose solitude makes it so suitable for a novitiate. Just as soon as I can send a Mistress of Novices and provide a regular income for that house, you will be free from the office of superior, and what would hinder you from coming back to finish out your life in France? At least we could see each other once more. We shall provide for all that in our next General Council. Meanwhile pray for us. Cholera is at the gates of Rome and we cannot leave here. We trust our Lady to protect the city. *Adieu*, dear Philippine. Be assured of the unchanging love with which I am all yours in C.J.M.

There was joy in the Florissant community at Easter, 1838, when Mother Boilvin received permission from the Superior General for probation and final vows. There was sorrow at the end of May when Mathilde's little girl fell ill and died. The child had been baptized and was being prepared for her First Holy Communion in view, one would suspect, of her delicate health. She was buried from St. Ferdinand's Church, and four of the pupils carried the little coffin to the cemetery.

The feast of the Assumption was celebrated with more than usual pomp that year, for the College Choir from St. Louis University came to sing the solemn High Mass and to furnish the music for the procession planned for the late afternoon. All went well enough at the Mass, and the twenty choir members were having breakfast at the convent when Bishop Rosati and Father Elet arrived unexpectedly. Provisions by this time had run low and the dinner served to the bishop and his companion "suffered sadly, to our great confusion," according to the *Journal*. Fortunately the choir was invited to the novitiate for dinner, so the nuns were spared further embarrassment. Perhaps it was the strain of this unusual hospitality that discouraged Mathilde, the Negro cook. At any rate she left for a second time and there was "no one to take her place," noted Mother Duchesne pathetically.

While taking extra work upon herself, she was determined to give Mother Boilvin a lighter schedule during the weeks that immediately preceded final profession. On the outer, unused page of a letter addressed to herself, Philippine wrote her a little undated note to this effect:

Dearest Sister,
Would that I had the zeal and unction of your good Father to express to you my desires and sentiments at the approach of the holy ceremony at which you will contract your sweet, and I trust your eternal, alliance. Just one month, and the happy day will be here. We shall try to give you more time to yourself, more time for prayer and acts of humility and recollection. It is in the calm of solitude that your Beloved wishes to speak to you of his love, of the conditions of this alliance, of the graces it will draw down upon you, of the ornaments in which you should present yourself to him. We are meditating today on these ornaments: the Cross, the thorns, the binding cords—these are the jewels of Calvary and of the altar that will witness your vows. Have courage. Others have worn them before us and have seen them changed into treasures immortal and incomprehensible in their grandeur.
In C.J.,
Phil.

It was time, in early September, to arrange with the bishop about the profession ceremony. He had been absent from the city for some days, so when Mother Duchesne heard of his return she wrote at once to him. His answer brought disappointment, as he delegated Father Van Assche to represent him at the ceremony, which took place on September 30, six days after Adeline Gonzague Boilvin completed her twenty-fifth year. A short note to her sister Euphrosine shows Philippine as she felt and described herself a few days after the ceremony:

. . . I have not had a letter from you since the one you wrote after Amelie's death, but my brother has given me news of you since then, and so has Madame de Rollin. If you want some news about me I shall tell you that going into my 70th year I feel the infirmities of that age: I cough and totter and fall, and the thought of death is always with me. So many of our family who were younger and stronger than I have died. Join your prayers to mine; ask your dear daughters to pray for me; ask prayers at the shrine of Our Lady of Fourvière. On my side I promise you frequent remembrance before God. Love, family ties, religion, all inspire my prayer. . . .

The tone of depression so evident in this paragraph runs through some entries in the *Journal* as winter came on—a hard winter indeed. Even the children were at times so intractable under the hand of their Mistress General, Mother Boilvin, that there were no ribbons merited at the distribution of prizes before they took their New Year's holiday. Perhaps the most moving entry in the whole *Journal* is the one that opens the account of 1839:

We have no servants at all, so we could scarcely find time to gather in the community for New Year's greetings. The one who could help us refuses to do so. We hired a young Negro girl, but she is just added trouble. She is not honest and has to be watched continually. So we are obliged to have our night recreation in the kitchen in order that she will not be alone with the orphan to whom we give a home. So side by side with them, in the midst of the noise of dishwashing and kitchen arrangements, with the wind sweeping in on all sides, we renewed our sacrifice as we remembered the evenings in France.

In the little group of nuns there was only one who "remembered the evenings in France," but she gave no hint of depression when she wrote to her sister in February. On the contrary, she seems to have been reacting deliberately against such feelings in the hope of cheering her lonely sister, whom she addresses not only as "My dear Sister," but also as "my loving Friend," clinging to the old form she had used with Euphrosine for more than thirty years:

It seems to me that since we have lost so many members of our beloved family who have been taken from us by death, you are becoming doubly dear to me. But another idea comes still more forciby to my mind. It is this: we are united by the same principles, and this makes us one in joy and sorrow. I share with the liveliest interest the consolations you have had in the children whom you have so generously offered to God. I have had the opportunity of hearing high praise given to the two who are in our Society, and the one who went to heaven is our protectress. Your son Henri, my godson, will enrich both his own crown and yours by drawing souls to God, and perhaps he is destined to bring back to his way of thinking the members of his family who have strayed from the right path. Remember me to him, and also to your daughter Josephine, who is your neighbor and your joy.

I received the letter in which you remarked on how long mine was delayed. That always happens when we give them to people who are traveling, so I shall use the mail more frequently, as that is the safest and speediest way. Thank you a thousand times for the very useful gift you are sending me. I have not received it yet, but you put it in very good hands. We hope to receive one or two more religious from France soon. I think they will take charge of everything that is being sent to us.

You are the last member of the family who has given me any news. Madame de Rollin writes from time to time, but in her last letter she complained of ill health, which caused me sorrow, for she is supporting so many good works. What astonishing changes have taken place in her family and ours! What a scattering of dear ones, and how many have died! . . . Pray for all our missions, and especially for me. I do not do much in this world, and I do still less that is of value for the next. Embrace your dear daughter for me and think of Philippine as your most steadfast friend.

The bitter winter continued into March, with biting wind and heavy snowfalls. The convent seemed more remote and solitary than ever, but there was plenty of activity within its walls and Mother Duchesne took a generous share in the labor. There were times, however, when she found time to write long letters and also to make plans for enlarging the convent at Florissant by the addition of a brick refectory and kitchen. The experiences of the past winter had proved that the old wooden building used for this purpose was no longer fit for use. Going to St. Louis in July to consult Mr. Hugh O'Neil about the work, she had an opportunity to inspect the new building erected by Mother Thiéfry for the boarding school. The increased enrollment and the desire for adequate accommodations for the novices had made this addition a necessity. Work on the Florissant project began on September 1. "It will give us a brick refectory and larger living quarters for the hired man," Mother Duchesne noted in the *Journal*. It had called for a good deal of courage on her part to undertake the work, for it meant borrowing some money, a thing she always dreaded, but she had Mother Shannon to rely on and that was a comfort to her. Satisfaction at the outcome of the undertaking is evident in the *Journal* entry three months later: "We are delighted with our new brick refectory, but [she adds ruefully], we have had to build a wooden house for the hired man, who has brought his family from Germany. One room was not enough for them, and we had the children on top of us."

While the Religious of the Sacred Heart in America were carrying on their laborious apostolate, some in prosperity, some in poverty, all in the joy of a life wholly dedicated to God, there was a struggle facing the Society in Europe that had no counterpart in the remote missions of the Mississippi Valley, yet its repercussions were to be felt throughout the entire order. In a circular letter from Paris in December, 1838, the Superior General announced that a general council would be convoked in the following year. The French capital was disturbed and revolution threatened, so Mother Barat chose Rome for the meeting place. Reaching there in April, 1839, she convoked the council to meet on June 1. Nine out of the twelve members composing the deliberative body were able to be present, among them Reverend Mothers Desmarquest, de Charbonnel, and Audé, the Assistants General, and Mothers de Limminghe, d'Olivier, and Maillucheau, old friends of Mother Duchesne. Mother Elizabeth Galitzin's office of secretary allowed her to take part in the deliberations. These religious were truly one heart—but they were not one *mind*, for some of them were too deeply imbued with the idea that there was need for sweeping changes in the organization of the order. Admiration for the Society of Jesus had engendered in them a desire to imitate its manner of life, while the Mother Foundress wished her daughters to be themselves, "to lead their own characteristic life, without the artificiality and constraint of trying to be something which was not their very self." Two subjects were proposed as the principal matter for discussion: the modification of the fourth section of the *Constitutions*, which deals with the mode of government, and the choice of a fixed place of residence for the Superior General. The first motion was to relieve the Superior General of a portion of her burden by dividing the Society into provinces to be governed by Mothers Provincial, whose duty it would be to visit and direct the convents under their authority, but subject to the control of the Superior General. Together with the Assistants General the Provincials were to form the council that would aid the Mother

General by advice and co-operation. Corresponding as it did to similar statutes in the Jesuit rule, this arrangement was unanimously approved. Twenty years before this Mother Barat had delegated the powers of a Provincial to Philippine Duchesne.

This was but the beginning of changes, however. Within a month the "reformers," led by Mothers de Limminghe and Galitzin, had brought about forty-six other changes in the *Constitutions*, all directed toward a closer resemblance to the Ignatian ideal. Most important of all was the decision which removed the seat of government in the Society from Paris to Rome, and it was this point that later excited the most opposition. In the elections which closed the council Mothers de Charbonnel, Desmarquest, de Limminghe, and Galitzin were chosen assistants general, the last named retaining the post of secretary general. Mother Thérèse Maillucheau was named visitatrix of the American convents and prepared at once to set out on the voyage, but for some undisclosed reason this nomination was canceled and she returned to France.

Late in November Mother Duchesne received a letter from Mother Thérèse, telling of the appointment and of her keen sorrow at having to sacrifice the chance to see her loved friend again. The *Journal* entry is terse: "Mother Thérèse was all ready to set out for America, coming to visit the Convents of the Sacred Heart, but destination was changed. She is returning to Nantes to inaugurate there the novitiate for the Province of the west of France. Our Society has been divided into provinces since the council." This seems to have been the first news Mother Duchesne received about the Sixth General Council's activities. Mother Barat informed the Society in November, 1839, of the changes initiated in the meetings and of the three-year trial to which they would be submitted. Her letter showed apprehension with regard to the wisdom and utility of the changes, but also the sincere humility with which she had bowed to her councilors.

In the American houses the new decrees were accepted, in as far as they were understood, and the good will to put them into execution abounded everywhere. The adoption of the Jesuit rule does not seem to have entered into the consideration of the religious in the Mississippi Valley as seriously as was intended by the councilors who drew up the decrees. Strangely enough there is not the least mention of them in Mother Duchesne's *Journal*. She records, however, the transfer of Mother Shannon to the City House in St. Louis early in 1840 and the arrival of Mother Anne Josephine Egan and Sister Catherine Campbell at Florissant. Then came the news that Bishop Rosati was leaving for Rome after the Fourth Provincial Council of Baltimore, which was to convene on May 17. Father Peter Verhaegen, S.J., was appointed Vicar General of the diocese, and Father James Fontbonne, secretary, to replace Father Joseph Lutz, who was accompanying the bishop to Baltimore and to Europe.

There is no estimating the sacrifice which the bishop's departure exacted of Mother Duchesne. For nearly fifteen years he had been, quite literally, her best friend in America, a friend in the highest, finest sense of that beautiful word. She had been at ease with him; she had relied on him; she had turned to him in any need; and he had never failed her trust. He had understood her when so many others had not. Now he was going out of her life, though she did not know how true her premonition of this fact was. He came to pay a farewell visit and she gave him a letter for Mother Barat— of all her American letters the one written in the most careful and beautiful penmanship:

I envy the good fortune of our venerable bishop, Monseigneur Rosati, who hopes to see you in Rome. We are very much afraid his health may oblige him to remain in his native land. In that case our diocese would sustain a great loss. It is simply marvelous to see the remarkable changes brought about through his indefatigable zeal. God has visibly blessed his apostolic labors, and more especially his great piety and the charity that makes him a worthy follower of St. Vincent de Paul.

We are eagerly awaiting the arrival of our Provincial, but if you are very hard pressed to give her some recruits for us, we can get along as we are. Mother Thiéfry was quite upset by your reprimand and sent us an excellent Sister. With her help all can run smoothly in our little convent, even if God should call me from it. I would not leave a vacancy. Mother Gonzague Boilvin, though quite young, has natural talents like Mother Bigeu's for governing a house. . . . She would have as helpers two young choir religious, former pupils of ours, who speak both languages, and so does the religious in charge of the free school. That school can never be very numerous here. Even the free school in St. Louis has diminished. Mother Thiéfry is suggesting changes that would take Sister Catherine Lamarre away from here. That dear old Sister is now quite infirm. She has confided to me that she longs to finish her days here, where she can still find some scope for her zeal by teaching the free school children who speak French. As there is only one professed in this community besides myself, I have neither assistant nor admonitrix.

The City House in St. Louis seems to have a greater financial burden than it can meet. The enrollment in the academy has diminshed; many postulants bring nothing with them when they enter—not even enough clothing; and more than fifty orphans have been accepted. When Mother Thiéfry asked my opinion with regard to postulants, I replied that it was imprudent to accept more than she can conveniently support. . . . The young women who have been our pupils will always make the best teachers and will be the most constant in their vocation. . . .

Before his departure Monseigneur blessed the little cemetery we had marked off. It will serve for the convents of both St. Louis and St. Ferdinand. Mother Thiéfry will have the bodies of our religious who are buried in St. Louis transferred here, as a street is to be cut through the convent cemetery in town. As for ourselves, no one in the community has died except Mother Penel, who was sent here from Louisiana. . . . My dear Mother, my venerated Mother, accept the grateful expressions of a heart that realizes all it owes to you. The thought of death is ever before me, but it will not be as easy a passage as it would be if I had always occupied the lowest place in this holy house.

The thought of death that so frequently finds expression in Philippine's letters was no obsession in her mind, nor did it make any practical difference in her activity. She was as laborious and industrious as her increasing physical infirmities would allow. She still reduced food and rest to the minimum for herself, still tried to do the hardest work, to give the most hidden devotedness. She seems never to have been disappointed with herself in a sensitive and personal way. She gauged her incapacity as she saw it and was not surprised at small success, but she had a constant dread lest God had been known, loved, and served less well because of her. Perhaps the gulf between the ideal and the actual depressed her sorely. Cut off, for the most part, from the apostolate she had envisioned, by the insurmountable language difficulty on the American frontier, she might have grown impatient with the vicissitudes that plagued her missionary career.

Yet the evidence all tends the other way. God had been working so secretly, so subtly in her soul that she had no perception of what his grace was accomplishing. Union with him in prayer and love had developed in her a humility so great that it seemed to hamper her external work. In order that she might reflect in her life the passion of the Sacred Heart of Christ, her achievement had to be as secret, as obscure as his on Calvary. The apostle can never accomplish real good without suffering, and that in proportion to the good he does, to his share in the redemptive work of Christ. So it was with Philippine Duchesne.

Sometimes she steadied her will by rereading letters she had received from France and copied into her thick, heavily bound note-books. One from Father Varin in the early weeks of 1840 was like a handclasp across the sea. He, too, was thinking of death, and like her he was in his seventy-first year when he wrote:

> My dear Mother and always my dear daughter in our Lord:
> It shall not be said of me that I left this world without sending you a reassurance of the sentiments which I feel toward you. Long years ago, almost from your very entrance into the Society, I foresaw that the Divine Master would call you to labor in distant lands beyond the sea, to spread the knowledge and love of his Sacred Heart. Happily his will in your regard has been accomplished, and you have been an instrument of his mercy in those remote lands. *Courage* and *Confidence* to the very end! What a consolation it will be for you, when the Divine Master calls you to himself, to leave behind you a large community which will continue with loving ardor the work for which you sacrificed your liberty, your rest, your life!

As he wrote these lines, Father Varin knew of circumstances that would soon put to the test all the courage and confidence Philippine had stored up through the years. In the spring of 1840 the Superior General announced her choice of Reverend Mother Elizabeth Galitzin to act as provincial and visitatrix of the convents of the Sacred Heart in the Mississippi Valley, and to explain the new decrees and insure their proper application. She knew her secretary well, knew her ardor for foreign missions and her remarkable physical energy. She also knew her autocratic nature, her dogmatic vehemence, her close approach to despotic intransigence which Monsignor Baunard has described as *gouvernement à la Russe*. In a letter to the American convents St. Madeleine Sophie prepared her religious for the arrival of her delegate, and on September 1 the Mother Visitatrix and her companions reached New York after a trans-Atlantic passage of forty-five days. Traveling west over the Cumberland Road by stage-coach and down the Ohio River by steamboat, Mother Galitzin reached St. Louis about three weeks later.

She was a conscientious and thorough visitor, whose vigilance nothing escaped. Wherever she went, she noted the needs of sacristy and infirmary, parlor and pantry, school and community. Efficiency characterized her work, but sympathy was often lacking. Externals were carefully regulated, while sensitive souls quivered under the scrutiny of the Provincial. Perhaps the keenest sufferer was Philippine Duchesne, but the visitation began for her with joy. Going to St. Louis to greet the Mother Provincial on September 24, she knelt to kiss the hand of the representative of highest authority in the Society and to beg with all the old fire and impetuosity for release from her position as superior. Mother Galitzin was prepared for this request and granted it immediately in the name of Mother Barat. But when approached on the subject of an Indian mission, she gave an evasive answer which Philippine knew how to interpret, for on September 30 she wrote to the Superior General:

> My Reverend and beloved Mother,
> We are rejoicing at last in the happiness of seeing your representative in the New World. We owe you a deep debt of gratitude for the sacrifice you have made in our favor of a religious who was so helpful to you. I beg God to bless this sacrifice and pour consolation into your heart by reason of the good a person of such great talent can accomplish in our houses for the glory of the Divine Heart of Jesus.
> On my side I thank you most sincerely for having at last lifted the burden I have carried so inefficiently, a burden that would have been such a trial in my last hours. I desire death and I fear it. But God, who is so good, will give me the means of expiating my faults, for I realize quite clearly that crosses will follow me, though of quite another kind—if only that of changing from a very busy life to one of almost complete inactivity. There is no hope of going to the savages just now. Nothing has been prepared for such a mission. But besides that, I have perceived that whenever I have expressed my desires and my regrets on that subject, I have been judged unfit for the work. And even if there were only my age against me, that would be reason enough for a negative answer. I pray earnestly to God for interior spirit, and I have much to do to acquire it.

Before returning to Florissant to gather together her precious notebooks and old letters, a few books, and some other personal belongings, as well as her scant supply of worn and mended clothing, Philippine wrote to Mother Louise de Vidaud, from whom she had received a letter when Mother Galitzin reached St. Louis. Thoughts of Sainte Marie came crowding in upon her as she began to write on October 1:

> Your six years' silence has not kept me from thinking of you, my

dearest Mother. Memories of France, and above all of Grenoble, are too much with me ever to let me forget you. However, it is less to the land of my birth and of my family that I cling than to memories of God's mercies in my regard, the marked protection of St. Regis, and the excellent religious who were trained on that holy mountain and who now work in all parts of France and in Italy for the glory of the Sacred Heart. I recognize the same love for our holy sanctuary of Ste. Marie in all the religious who lived there and from whom I sometimes receive news.

At present I cannot tell you to what community I belong. A week ago I came here from St. Ferdinand to see Mother Galitzin and her seven companions. They are all well. The foundation in New York will not be made until next spring. Reverend Mother will spend the winter in Louisiana and so avoid the severe cold of Missouri. The Jesuits have opened several Indian missions in this part of the world and are already having some success. . . . I beg the prayers of all my Sisters for my old age.

A few days later Mother Duchesne drove from Florissant to the City House and took her place, without distinction except that of seniority in profession, in the ranks of the community among the Mothers and Sisters who had for so many years looked to her as the representative of the foundress herself in the American convents of the Society. With the entry of this little trip Philippine ended the *Journal* she had kept so faithfully for twenty-two years.

twelve

Among the Potawatomi

1840—1842

IN THE INFIRMARY AT THE CITY HOUSE Mother Duchesne lay critically ill. The malady had been difficult to diagnose. Beginning with anguish of mind and heart and nervous depression which her strong will could not control, it had developed into a high fever accompanied by pain throughout her entire body. Her limbs were swollen; her breathing was labored; her pulse, uneven. The doctors ordered remedies of many kinds, chiefly mustard plasters. They dared not bleed the patient again, lest life itself be drained from her body.

Mother Shannon kept watch in the sickroom, yielding her place at times to her sister Judith or to Mother Regis Hamilton. They had not much faith in the efficacy of plasters to relieve the patient. They knew no amount of medication could draw the pain from her heart. Nor were they able to do so by their loving care and deep compassion. It would take time and the healing balm of grace from the Sacred Heart to supply the resignation, abandonment, and blind acceptance of the ruthless act that had so nearly broken the tenuous thread of health that kept body and soul together.

Sometimes in sleep she murmured, "A vow . . . a promise made in France . . . to God and to St. Regis." At other times

418

her tears flowed silently. No least sob escaped her, just great tears coursing down her sunken cheeks. Those who nursed her wiped them away, scarcely seeing through the mist in their own eyes, but they could not relieve the pain that caused those tears. Never would it be relieved, she had declared, for the shrine of St. Francis Regis had been taken from the chapel at Florissant. The picture she loved had been relegated to the attic, and that in spite of her protests to the Mother Provincial, who had ordered what Philippine considered a desecration. True, she had replaced it by a painting of the Sacred Heart, and that was the Society's dearest devotion, but the shrine had fulfilled the promise made in France to gain the saint's protection over the American mission. Argument and reasoning did not calm the old nun's distress, and the illness consequent on moral anguish and an already broken physical condition lasted many weeks.

But time and prayer and the continued loving care of those who nursed her brought a slow improvement, and by mid-December she was able to make her way, with some help, to the chapel. Once that was possible, she seemed to gain new strength; and by Christmas she was asking to move from the infirmary back to the room she had chosen when she was transferred from Florissant in October.

> You should see her room [wrote Mother Mathevon to the Superior General when she came from St. Charles for a visit]. Her bed is in a cubbyhole under a stairway. She says it is quieter there than anywhere else in the house, and to tell you the truth, there are few places available. She is an Alexis, a wonderful example for the St. Louis convent. . . . Though she is obliged to have mustard plasters on her swollen limbs, she drags herself to her superior's room to ask permissions. . . . Few canonized saints have practiced as much virtue as she does.

Often she spent her hours of convalescence rereading the old letters she treasured or paging through her *Journal*. Work with the Indians was still her goal, and in these old manuscripts she found joy and a stimulation of her desires. She had never given up her hope of someday keeping the vow that she and her four companions had made on leaving France in 1818 to devote themselves to the salvation of the Indians. Thinking of her four companions, she realized that she alone could hope to carry out the vow. Mother Audé was ill in Rome; Mother Berthold had gone to her reward; Sisters Catherine and Marguerite, the one at Florissant, the other at

Grand Coteau, were old and broken in health, while she had only her strong will, braced by faith and love, to rely on now. Circumstances, she knew, had indicated unmistakably the will of God and hindered the fulfilment of the promise, but through toil, privation, sickness, lack of success, and now a chronic state of ill health, the ardor of her desire had not slackened, the term of her ambition had not changed.

She recalled the arrival of the Flathead delegation in St. Louis and the enthusiasm with which she had written about it to Mother Barat in January, 1832. The answer had been only slightly encouraging: "For such a mission you would need religious of tried virtue and mature age who speak English. Where will you find them? . . . Write to me again about this project, if it is really feasible."

Nothing had come of the project, for the difficulties inherent in it staggered both Bishop Rosati and Father Van Quickenborne, but Philippine had not given up hope. By her prayers and by small gifts of money, altar linens, and clothing she had aided the Jesuits who had gone into the Indian country closer to St. Louis. How often their names were on her lips as she prayed in the words of Mother Marie of the Incarnation: "Eternal Father, through the adorable Heart of Jesus I offer you all the priests who are working to spread the Gospel throughout the world. By his merits I beg you to fill them with your holy spirit. On this Sacred Heart, as on a divine altar, I offer you in a very special manner . . ," and other names came slowly, as she implored God's blessing on Fathers Van Quickenborne, Hoecken, De Smet, Verhaegen, and so many other splendid missionaries who were her friends.

One day in the late summer of 1837, just before she learned of Father Van Quickenborne's death, she had received a letter from Father Verhaegen that revived all her missionary zeal. He had been visiting the Kickapoo mission which Van Quickenborne had established so laboriously in the summer of 1836. It lay beyond the western border of Missouri, where the frontier marked the fringe of white settlement and presumably gave the Indians a region all their own forever. So far the harvest gathered by the missionaries had been distressingly meager, but Father Verhaegen gave no hint of that when he wrote:

> On June 20 I reached the Kickapoo encampment and was taken that morning to see the Indian lodges. When the chief of the tribe learned of my arrival, he came to visit me and showed me much

affection. He is a savage in the full extent of that term. He paints his face black, with a little red around the eyes, and he glories in the fact that he has adopted no single article of the white man's dress. The savages come each week for the religious instruction which Father Christian Hoecken gives in their own language. He speaks it so well, the savages call him Father Kickapoo. Eight or ten adults have been baptized, and more than one hundred children. . . . They call God the Great Spirit and every morning pray for his blessing. If they feel sad or guilty, they blacken their faces and fast for an entire day, taking no food at all. When a brave dies, they bury his horse beside him, so that his soul may ride to the palace of the Great Spirit, which they think is far away from their village beyond the western prairie. . . . Pray, Mother, that God may send workers into this vineyard and may bless their labors for his greater glory.

Mother Duchesne knew that, although the Jesuits had endeavored earnestly to Christianize the tribe, these Indians had not responded to the efforts expended on them. Father Verhaegen soon considered the mission "utterly sterile," and in the autumn of 1840 he decided to close it in favor of a more promising field of endeavor for Christ. Mother Duchesne could trace in her *Journal* the beginnings of the Mission at Sugar Creek.

The Potawatomi were of Algonquin stock, closely allied with the Ottawa and the Chippewa. Their name, signifying "firemakers," or "people of the fire-place," originated from the fact that they separated from the nation to which they had belonged and built for themselves a new fire, thus becoming an independent tribe. From their homes along Lakes Huron and Michigan they drifted southward into Illinois and Indiana. They were a warrior race and lovers of the hunt, little given to tilling the soil, even for a scant harvest of maize. Jesuit missionaries had toiled amongst them during the seventeenth and early eighteenth centuries, but without great results. The priests who came amongst them later on realized what the encroachments of white settlers would mean to these forest folk. The Government was pursuing its policy of dispossessing the Indians of their lands by forced treaties and assigning them other homes and hunting grounds beyond the Mississippi. Mother Duchesne had alluded to this policy again and again in her letters.

In 1835 a delegation of Potawatomi selected territory on the Osage River in the present state of Kansas and began moving there at once. Some of them were Catholics. When their chief, Nesfwawke, learned that there were Black Robes in the Kickapoo settlement, he begged them to visit his people and instruct them. Father Hoecken made the trip in January, 1838, and found the Indians in heart-rending poverty and suffering. Though he had nearly lost his life in a blizzard and had done little to alleviate their physical miseries, he considered the journey well worth while, for he had given spiritual help and encouragement to a few faithful braves and squaws and had left them with the promise that missionaries would come to live in their encampment. Father Verhaegen went with him in the following May when he visited the Potawatomi and was so favorably impressed that he consented to the establishment of a permanent mission station among these Indians.

Their number had been increasing by the arrival of groups designated as Wabash and St. Joseph Potawatomi, and with them had come Father Benjamin-Marie Petit, a young missionary from France whom Bishop Bruté had ordained in 1837. His first and only assignment was with these Indians. He had shared the privations of his flock on the journey westward to Sugar Creek and within a year he fell dangerously ill. Father Hoecken cared for him until he recovered enough strength to start for St. Louis, where he was received with great kindness by the Jesuits. On February 10, 1839, Father Petit died.

Mother Duchesne had noted these facts in her *Journal*, and she would refer to them later on when pleading the cause of the Indian mission. She was deeply moved by the heroism of Father Petit; and after the Jesuits took charge of the Potawatomi Christians, she begged both St. Madeleine Sophie and Bishop Rosati to let her share in the work. She was seconded in this by Mother Lucille Mathevon, whose missionary vocation, like her own, had first been directed toward the Indians. When Bishop Rosati called on Mother Barat in Paris in the summer of 1840, the conversation turned quite naturally to this subject, and the Superior General surprised the bishop by telling him that Mother Duchesne was pleading the cause of the Indians with such loving insistence that it seemed impossible to refuse her the permission. Knowing the precarious state of her health, the bishop had some doubts as to the wisdom of her attempting such a mission, but he was delighted at the prospect of the religious at work among the Potawatomi and at once wrote to Mother Duchesne, sending the letter by Mother Galitzin, who was just setting out for America. The bishop journeyed on to Rome, and in an audience with Pope Gregory XVI spoke of the missionary desires of Mother Duchesne and the prospect now opening up for her. By the end of November a letter from Bishop Rosati informed Mother Barat that the Holy Father had expressed a desire to see the Religious of the Sacred Heart at work among the Indians. Had Philippine but known it, the cause was won.

Meanwhile in St. Louis Father De Smet was using his influence to bring about the same result. In an interview with Mother Galitzin during her first visit there, he told her bluntly that the blessing of God on the Society of the Sacred Heart in America depended directly on the foundation of a mission school among the Indians. The Mother Provincial assured him that Mother Barat desired such a foundation with all her heart, but that both recruits and money were lacking just now. She spoke with her usual finality and left for Louisiana before winter set in.

On January 6, 1841, Father De Smet called at the convent in St. Louis. During a visit with Mother Duchesne he urged her to make another appeal for permission to open a school among the Potawatomi, promising on his side to raise the funds necessary for beginning the work. Suddenly she drew from her pocket Bishop Rosati's letter of the previous July. Together they read:

> The example you have given in leaving Europe to make the first foundation of the Sacred Heart in America is still very powerful in influencing others to follow you. God be praised for this! But I am really surprised to learn that you are now pleading to leave Missouri in order to go among the savages. However, when one loves God, one never says "Enough." If I did not know you well, I might say it is too much for you. But knowing you as I do, I say: "Go! Follow your attraction, or rather the voice of God. He will be with you." I beg him to bless you.

Together the vigorous priest just entering his fortieth year and the broken old nun now past seventy discussed the possibilities of a school for Indian girls at Sugar Creek. The urgency of love and zeal smoothed away obstacles to their plans, and the vision of souls gained for Christ made every sacrifice seem paltry in comparison. It was agreed that she would write to Mother Galitzin at once and he would begin a begging tour for funds, not in St. Louis, for the Catholics of that city were neither mission-minded nor generously inclined to such appeals, but in New Orleans, where there was more wealth and more Catholicity.

On January 7 Mother Duchesne composed her letter to the

Mother Provincial, beginning with a little summary of her missionary aspirations and the several times she had tried to carry out the promise made in France to work among the Indians.

> So far [she continued] we have been disappointed in our hopes—at least I have, for all my inclinations and desires urge me to work among these tribes. . . . Yesterday, the feast of the Kings, a visit from Father De Smet, who has come back from the Rocky Mountains, roused my ardor once more, and that to such an extent that I experienced a sort of physical resurrection as a result of the hope I feel that I may be among those chosen for a mission that is now offered to us under very favorable auspices.
>
> Beyond the western boundary of Missouri, this Father tells me, there is a very good tribe that comes from Canada, already partly converted to Christianity. They are called the Potawatomi. A holy Breton priest, Father Petit, consecrated his life and labors to them, and before his death he turned over his beloved flock to a Jesuit, who has since come to see us. . . . He now lives the same hard life as his new charges and finds great consolation in working among them. . . . The Government has contributed to the expense of building a log church and may also help build us a house. The missionary whom I saw yesterday considers it a duty for us to seize this opportunity before others of non-Catholic faith do so. I showed him the letter you brought me from Bishop Rosati, in which he wrote to me so positively: *Follow your attraction.* At the time I received it, I did not pay much attention to it; for my soul was crushed and all my offers were rejected. Now I think it really is the voice of God. Our Mother General has often expressed this desire, and our Lord will so arrange matters that you will lend a hand in this enterprise.

After suggesting the names of the religious whom she considered best suited for the work of the Indian mission, she added: "God is going to cure me. I shall be just an extra member of the group, helping with the housework and other labors."

At St. Michael's Mother Galitzin was astonished, when called to the parlor one day by "a priest from St. Louis," to find herself face to face again with Father De Smet. Her surprise increased when he presented her with a second letter from Mother Duchesne and five hundred dollars in gold, the fruit of his begging tour in New Orleans and among the planters of the Gold Coast of the Mississippi. Father De Smet left on record an account of what happened at St. Michael's:

> I was the bearer of Mother Duchesne's request. . . . At first the

petition met with no success and was rather firmly rejected—"It could not be thought of." I humbly begged Mother Galitzin not to come to so hasty a conclusion on a matter of so great importance, to ponder it quietly and lay it before the Lord at the foot of the tabernacle. A few days after that the approval of Mother Duchesne's request was granted. I still have in my possession the letter of Mother Galitzin in which religious were named to commence the Potawatomi Mission. . . .

Mother Galitzin was not to be hurried from Louisiana in midwinter, but from her answer Father De Smet concluded that his mission was accomplished. A month later she received from the Superior General the letter that was decisive in the matter. The wish of the Sovereign Pontiff, Gregory XVI, was law for the Society of the Sacred Heart; and when Mother Galitzin reached St. Louis in March, she announced the decision that had been reached; two new foundations were to be made this year, one in the East, in New York City, and one in the West, at Sugar Creek. There were volunteers for the mission to the Potawatomi in the three Missouri houses, most vocal among them being Mother Lucille Mathevon and her close associate at St. Charles, Mother Mary Ann O'Connor.

Mother Mathevon's nomination as superior of the Indian mission band was no surprise, for her ardent desire for this work was well known. Mother Regis Hamilton was named to take her place as superior at St. Charles and went there in April. Mother O'Connor accompanied Mother Mathevon to St. Louis, for she, too, had won a place on the mission band, along with Sister Louise Amyot. As yet there was no mention of other names. Mother Eleanor Gray, superior at the City House since February, tried to console her beloved Mother Duchesne, while Mother Galitzin gave her little encouragement because of her ill health and Mother Mathevon wrote to St. Madeleine Sophie on May 10: "Mother Duchesne is growing considerably weaker. I fear she would not be able to go far." "There is scarcely a breath of life in her," she had written two weeks before this, and Mother Duchesne admitted her condition honestly at the close of a letter to Mother Barat on May 18:

> My writing and my scratching out show you the weakness of both my head and my hand. The miracle of my cure has not taken place. I await the will of God. Mother Lucille is to be the head of the mission band. I kneel for your blessing, Reverend Mother, with love in the Sacred Heart of Jesus. . . .

Mother Galitzin left St. Louis for the foundation in New York at the end of April, taking with her Mothers Catherine Thiéfry and Judith Shannon. They were joined in mid-May by Mothers Aloysia Hardey and Ellen Hogan from St. Michael's, and later by Mother Adeline Boilvin and Sisters Gallien and Pratt. It had been a satisfaction for Mother Duchesne to have the talents and virtues of her beloved "Gonzague" recognized, but they both knew that the parting was for life. It was not, however, a breaking of the ties that united them so affectionately, and Mother Boilvin treasured the letters she received from Mother Duchesne during a few short years. The first of these is dated June 4, 1841:

> I have already sent a short note in answer to your letter from Pittsburgh, hoping to write at greater length when there would be an opportunity to send a letter by a traveler. Our music master will take this to you. His place is being filled by Mother Crawford from St. Michael's, a very lovable person. She now has six pupils for either harp or piano. Mother [Evelina] L'Eveque is not very well. I suffer for her when I hear the long hours of music practice. Mother Aloysia [Hardey], to whom I send my regards, knew their delicate health and it was her prudence that inspired the recommendation necessary to save these two religious who are so useful. . . .
>
> They tell me you will not be installed in your new home before August. This time of waiting will be a very profitable period for you to grow in virtue and knowledge. I do not know what good learning has been to me; but when I recall how I enjoyed it, how I esteemed it, and how little use it has been to me, I rejoice in the thought that in heaven *all earthly knowledge will be lost in God.* There we shall say only the eternal *Amen* and "Holy, holy, holy Lord." I have no hope now of finishing my embroidery. Adieu.

Philippine needed the grace to say that *Amen* even as she was writing this letter, for all around her there were bustle and subdued excitement of preparations for the mission venture. No least share could she have in the work; and she found it difficult to understand why she was being spared fatigue that would have been a comfort to her, since there seemed to be no human hope of her going to Sugar Creek. She had almost resigned herself to the fact that, feeble and ill as she was, she could not bear the tiring trip nor the hardships of the life that awaited the missionary nuns. Yet she prayed the more earnestly, even for a miracle, were that the only means of securing the privilege. And miracle it would have

been, judging from Mother Mathevon's description of her condition at this very time:

> The doctor thinks she is in continual danger of death, yet she
> wanted to fast and abstain all during Lent. Since then the swelling
> has increased, and it extends from her feet up to her chest, so that
> she is liable to be smothered at any moment. She feels that she is
> very near to death, yet once our Mother General gives her the
> permission, she will consider it an order and no one will be able to
> hold her back.

The date of departure had not been set when Father Verhaegen
appeared at the convent one morning quite unexpectedly. He had
decided to visit the Sugar Creek mission early in July and thought
it advisable for the religious to travel in safety under his escort. As
he talked with Mothers Gray and Mathevon, Mother Duchesne
sat with them in the parlor, for Father Verhaegen never called at
the City House without asking for her. They were discussing the
business side of the trip—the steamboat, the baggage, the date and
hour of departure, the reservations for the three religious. For
three? Father Verhaegen had expected four. He turned to where
Mother Duchesne sat praying silently, tears falling unheeded on
the darkened, toil-worn hands that held her rosary. "But she must
come, too," he said to Mother Gray, and his strong face lighted
up with reverent affection. *She* was the person he wanted most of
all at Sugar Creek. "Even if she can use only one leg, she will come.
Why, if we have to carry her all the way on our shoulders, she is
coming with us. She may not be able to do much work," he added,
and his kind eyes narrowed to thin slits in a characteristic smile,
"but she will assure success to the mission by praying for us. Her
very presence will draw down all manner of heavenly favors on
the work."

How much of this vehement declaration Philippine understood
is a matter of conjecture, but its outcome was immediately clear
to her as Mother Gray put loving arms about her and said words
so like those she had heard from St. Madeleine Sophie in Paris on
a May day in 1817 when the holy foundress had consented to the
American mission. Mother Mathevon, however, was reluctant to
assume the responsibility of one so loved, so venerated, and so
enfeebled, and Philippine was quick to sense this attitude without
realizing its true cause. So there was heart-suffering in the midst
of joy, but she could repeat the little prayer she had made her
own: "Lord, I lean on you alone for strength. Give me your arm

to support me, your shoulders to carry me, your breast on which to lay my head, your cross to uphold me, your Eucharist to nourish me. In you, Lord, I shall sleep and rest in peace."

The little mission band boarded the Missouri River packet on June 29, 1841. Besides the four nuns there were two Jesuits, Fathers Verhaegen and Smedts, and a diocesan priest, Father Francis J. Renaud. On the levee a crowd of friends had gathered to say good-bye, and Bishop Jean-Marie Chanche of Natchez was there to give them his blessing. The steamboat *Emilie* was booked to sail at noon, but during a two-hour delay the bishop remained with the nuns, telling them of the problems that faced him in Natchez, where there was but one priest for the whole newly created diocese.

The river trip was pleasant; accommodations on the steamboat were good, though not so luxurious as those on the smart packets now plying the Mississippi. Mother Duchesne gathered fresh strength as the boat ascended the muddy stream and was able to walk the deck with a remarkably firm step. She was interested in all she saw and heard and was a center of interest among the passengers. By a spontaneous gesture these people took up a collection amounting to fifty dollars for the nuns, while traders on board contributed provisions to the value of forty dollars. These were confided to the care of Edmund, a young Negro from the convent in St. Louis, who had been brought along to help with the heavy work of installation.

Mother Mathevon's account of the journey is a charming bit of narrative:

> Our trip, as far as Westport, was very pleasant. We made it in four days. I should never have imagined that Missouri was so thickly populated. We passed fifteen towns, at least, containing several thousand inhabitants each. Some of them are really lovely, and there are delightful homes along the river. Yet this large population is entirely without churches or priests and has not a single school. . . . On July 4, the festival of Independence, Father Verhaegen preached to the passengers. When the sermon was over, great applause ensued, with clapping of hands and stamping of feet. Then everybody, ourselves included, drank iced sherry. We are all very well. As for Mother Duchesne, she walked up and down the deck as if she were young again. It took four days after leaving the boat to reach Sugar Creek, our destination. We could have made it in two, but the kind Fathers thought it best to travel by slow stages and so avoid greater fatigue. . . .
>
> The Indians had been warned of our coming, so the entire village

assembled and waited a day. We had stopped about eighteen miles away on the banks of the Osage River at the home of a French settler, where we were most kindly received. The Indians, impatient of our arrival, sent ahead two of their number to find us. These came and knelt before the Father Superior to receive his blessing. We gave them supper; then they started back to announce to their tribesmen that we would be with them the following day. As we advanced next morning, we met, every two miles along the way, two Indians mounted on fine horses. They had come to greet us and show us the safest and best road.

About a mile from the mission house a band of five hundred braves appeared in gala dress—bright blankets, plumes and feathers, and moccasins embroidered with porcupine quills. Their faces were painted black, with red circles around the eyes that gave them a frighteningly grotesque appearance. As the mission wagon advanced, the Indians performed a series of equestrian evolutions, now in semi-circles, now in circles, and always with such precision that never was a horse out of position.

The first letter Mother Duchesne sent to St. Madeleine Sophie was headed: "From the Tribe and Village of the Potawatomi," and covered the sheet so completely, there was not even space at the end for a signature.

> My dearly loved Mother [she began], At last we have reached the country of our desires. We left St. Louis with the Father Superior, who is replacing Monseigneur Rosati in everything that is not exclusively the duty of a bishop, and two other Jesuit Fathers. We traveled first by water, leaving St. Louis on the beautiful feast of St. Peter, after a visit with the Bishop of Natchez, who also gave us his blessing. He is going to have more difficulties than we are. There are no difficulties here except when people worry too much about *tomorrow*.
>
> This tribe, which like many others was driven out of Michigan by the Americans, is now about half Catholic. These people have built their village at a distance from the pagans, who are being converted gradually. Once baptized, they never revert to drunkenness or stealing. Whatever is found is placed at the door of the church to be claimed by the owner. Not a single house has locks on the doors, yet nothing is ever missing. The Indians gather in groups (men and women separate) for morning prayers, Mass, and catechism. In the evening they assemble again for prayers. They eat seven times a day. . . .
>
> Mother Galitzin gave us 250 dollars, which she considered enough for the erection of a wooden house. I thought the money

had already been sent to the pastor, and we were told in St. Louis that our house had been built. But it was the pastor's house, and also the church, for which he obtained money from the Government. On reaching here, we were greatly disappointed to find no house ready for us, and we showed our distress. . . . When the steamboat passage was paid, we had scarcely twenty dollars left. But what pained me most of all was the fact that so many seculars were invited to come to see us before we left. They were a nuisance and ate up our time.

The pastor has given us two fine cows and put at our service a pair of oxen, a good horse, and a charette. It will be easy to plant a nice vegetable garden, so have we anything to complain about? We brought with us the Negro man from St. Louis. He is a carpenter and will help with the manual work. Our baggage has not arrived yet, so I was obliged to use this thick paper. I have been ill again, and I find it difficult to think. This is a weakness I never experienced before. It accounts for the condition of my letter, but the facts are correct. You may, however, receive some exaggerations.

It was hard for Philippine to have to admit that she had been ill again, but it was much harder to realize that her feebleness cut her off from the activities of the other missionaries. The Indians, however, seemed to appreciate her from the moment she set foot in the Sugar Creek encampment. Even though she could not teach their children as Mother O'Connor was doing by mid-July, or cook for them as Sister Louise did, or read their language as Mother Mathevon could after three or four weeks amongst them, they loved her and respected her and brought her all manner of things— fresh corn, newly-laid eggs, chickens, wild plums, sweet, clean straw for her pallet. "Whatever they have, they bring to the *good old lady*, as they call Mother Duchesne," wrote Mother Mathevon in August. And later on:

> She stayed all morning in the church, so Sister Louise would take her a cup of coffee each day, and she drank it at the door of the church. After dinner she went again for three or four hours of prayer. The Indians had the greatest admiration for her, recommended themselves to her prayers, and called her Woman-who-prays-always. Everyone admitted that a great number of baptisms resulted from her prayers. Almost every Sunday afternoon three or four men or women and their families were baptized. Mother Duchesne inscribed all their names in the register.

But in all this there was no sense of achievement, no reassurance.

In her own heart, "last lurking place of self," she had to face the fact that to all appearances she had failed in the dearest hope of her life. She was completely unaware of the graces she was receiving or of those that were coming to others through her prayers, but the results were all the more powerful for this very reason. Her incapacity for active work brought her loneliness of heart which she admitted and accepted with love, but not without pain. The solitude at Sugar Creek was not merely a physical remoteness, but also a spiritual aloneness that grew out of the sensed fact that she was a burden on those who cared for her, an anxiety for them. Borne in close union with the mystery of Christ's loneliness, this suffering only drew her closer to his Sacred Heart, where she buried the pain by renewed and more loving surrender.

News of the venture into the Indian country had reached Philippine's family in France, and soon they were writing her letters and sending her gifts in the generous fashion that had characterized them through the past twenty years and more. One of the few extant letters she wrote from Sugar Creek was addressed to her brother and written from her arm-chair desk in an Indian hut on September 12:

> Just a few days ago, my dearest Brother, I received the letter you wrote for kind Monsieur de Mauduit, at the end of which you assured me once more of your loving sentiments in my regard. As you said in your preceding letter that you would carry out your promise only after my arrival here, I did not fail to write you that I am here. But I was very agreeably surprised soon after reaching this mission to find enclosed in a letter from Madame de Rollin your note for 500 francs ($100) on the Bank of New Orleans. That was the best way to send the money, though bank failures are frequent, both in New Orleans and throughout the United States, even in the case of banks that have the best standing, and this sometimes makes it difficult to cash a letter of exchange. I sent the draft to St. Louis at once to the gentleman to whom we owe the most for the loan of money to pay our traveling expenses, and I am sure it will be readily accepted in partial payment of what he advanced. . . .
>
> To remove from your mind all suspicion that there is folly in our enterprise, let me tell you that this little tribe is very good, professes our religion, and welcomed us cordially. Behind our house we have an excellent plot of ground large enough for a yard and a truck garden. And to add further details, the pastor has put at our disposal a horse, oxen, and a charette for farm work and transportation. He has sent us three fine cows, many chickens, some

geese, and a litter of little pigs. There are calves in a meadow, and every day the cows give them a little nourishment. Then the cowherds milk the cows, take what is needed for the priests and others, and give us the rest. There is almost enough milk to suffice for our whole nourishment, but we have vegetables and can get meat at just five and a half cents a pound. . . .

The language is extremely difficult, and the alphabet, which has four letters less than ours, is sounded just as in French. Our nuns have learned quite readily to read the language and are teaching the children as one teaches little children to read Latin, only here things are reversed: the children—not one of them knowing how to read before—understand the meaning of the words which we do not understand at all. . . .

After giving Duchesne a language lesson in Potawatomi by writing out the *Gloria Patri* and a dozen Indian words which she had mastered at least on paper, such as God, man, woman, sun, moon, salt, fire, finger, in true grammarian style, Philippine continues:

Let me add that some words in this barbaric tongue run to ten, nine, eight syllables, and as yet there is no published dictionary, no grammar, and just one book of prayers. I think I shall never learn such a language.

Tell Madame de Rollin that I shall write to her just as soon as I receive the letter she tells me is on its way to me. Say to that dear cousin and to your wife all the most affectionate things you can think of. After reading this letter, please send it to Madame Jouve. I shall add here a few more lines to her and you both. *Adieu*, my kind brother. I pray to our Lord for you and hope to see you once more in that life that knows no ending and is always happy.

Your grateful sister,
Philippine

In general Mother Mathevon agreed with what Mother Duchesne had written to her brother about the abundance of food and the improvement in the health of the missionary nuns. "On our Indian beds," she wrote, "we sleep better than we would in the palaces of kings. Dairy products, vegetables, rice, cornbread, and bread made of wheaten flour, lard—that is our diet. We have good appetites and our health is much better." But her report to Mother Galitzin in the autumn contained a passage relating to Mother Duchesne that shows her physical condition:

She is here just to suffer, for she has aged much in this short time and is sometimes like a little child. She no longer has the fine mind of other days. She is feeble; her limbs are swollen; her digestion is poor. I fear she will have a stroke. To tell you the truth, we cannot understand how the Father Superior could have insisted on bringing her here. But he said that she would pray for the missions and that she must be given the consolation of dying here. All she can do at present is pray, sometimes lying for a little while on her bed, and knit stockings. That is all. It is a great anxiety for us to have to care for her without being able to give her what she needs, for one has to send twenty leagues for things. We are doing all we can for her. She has done so much for the Society, it is only right that we give her all possible care in her old age.

The religious took possession of their new log cabin on October 9. It was primitive and poorly built, but it was clean. There was not much privacy in it, for the Indians came and went as they pleased during the daytime, but the nuns had grown accustomed to this. A wood stove and some shelves occupied one side of the room. This was designated as the dining room and kitchen; but when winter came on and icy wind swept in from the western prairies, the nuns and the Indian pupils huddled near the fire, even while meals were being prepared. Sensitive as she had become to cold, because of the fever that seldom left her now, Mother Duchesne suffered more than the others. Yet she made her way through the snow to the unheated mission church for Mass each morning. When Mother Mathevon forbade her to return to the icy building during the day, she accepted the prohibition in the spirit in which it was given. She knew Mother Lucille's love for her, though at times she felt that her superior misunderstood her or exaggerated her physical infirmity, which she herself would have liked to ignore.

The Potawatomi, like other Indians, were thoughtless and improvident by nature and had never learned to protect themselves against the bitter cold of winter. As a result there was much illness among them during this season. The nuns visited the sick, cared for them as far as they were able, aided and consoled them, and prayed with the dying. In this, at least, Mother Duchesne could have a share when she was able, and allowed, to drag herself from the cabin-convent to the native huts. The Indians were deeply touched by this kindness, especially when they saw her, feeble and worn by the rigors of the winter, bending over the rough pallet of a dying woman whose life she had failed to save, but whose soul had been won for Christ.

The long winter came on, with now and then a spell of moderate weather. In February, Mother Duchesne told her sister optimistically: "My health has improved very much in this part of the country. I have gained some strength; my eyesight is better; and I retain the use of all my faculties, though I am in my seventy-third year. Wherever I am, my heart goes out to you and I am glad to be able to assure you that I love you." Mother Mathevon, however, wrote the following day: "Mother Duchesne is aging more and more. She is often in a very suffering condition. The life here is much too hard for a person her age." But the valiant missionary was keenly interested in the work at Sugar Creek and alert to all that was going on.

> Congress [she wrote to Madame Jouve] forced the Potawatomi to move into this region and will pay them an annual sum of money which, as long as the arrangement lasts, will save them from dire misery. This year we have seen them making good use of part of their money by buying shoes, shirts, and other articles of clothing such as the white people wear. But the blanket is always an important item in their dress. Christianity changes these unfortunate people so noticeably that a pagan among them can always be identified by his fierce and unkempt appearance. In our school some dear little girls are beginning to read in their own language and some in English also. More than twenty have learned to spin and knit; but even before we came here, many knew how to sew quite well. They are, on the whole, very interesting children, but they find it very difficult to stay at the same work for any length of time. The pastor guides this tribe as a shepherd leads his lambs. . . .

Although Mother Duchesne was, in a sense, crushed by her own helplessness at Sugar Creek, frustration had no part in her reaction to circumstances, for these were for her the manifest will of God. At times her physical weakness may have left her powerless to think clearly, but she was very alert mentally when she wrote to Father De La Croix after seven months at the mission. Knowing his interest in all that concerned the Society of the Sacred Heart in America, she gave him news about people and places and left on record details about Sugar Creek that may not be found in other sources. With remarkable vigor and buoyancy she wrote on February 20, 1842:

> How can I ever express my joy on receiving your letter which is of such value to me? It is easy to see that like an affectionate father you never forget the children on whom you bestowed both tem-

poral and spiritual goods. They will always miss you. I hope I can answer satisfactorily all your kind inquiries by giving you news of each of our religious families, even at the risk of telling you what you already know. I shall begin with the most recent foundation—that of New York, where the superior is a French religious (Mother Bathilde Sallion), but Mother Aloysia Hardey, the Mistress General, is the soul of the boarding school. The people of New York, and especially the clergy, have been kind to our nuns. . . .

Now I come to my own story—the chapter since your departure. If I knew how to profit by suffering, I would be able to say, like you, that I am perfectly content. But I needed to be tried, and God has directed my steps along *vias duras*, even while guiding me to the mission for the savages, so long the goal of my desires. Here I suffer still because I can do nothing at all. First of all, I was transferred from St. Louis to St. Ferdinand, where there were continual threats that the convent would be closed. Then, in answer to prayers and representations, they placed the novitiate there. I was transferred to St. Louis, passing from a very active life to one of complete nullity, and I was ill for a long time. Father De Smet returned from the Flathead mission in the *Rokis*—a three months' journey—and his coming gave me new life. He led me to hope that we would make a foundation there within two years, and he vigorously urged our Mother Provincial to send us here to work among these Indians.

After narrating the story of the migration of the Potawatomi and the death of Father Petit, she continues:

We thought we were going to find a convent ready for us when we arrived, but we had been misinformed. Our first shelter was the hut of an Indian in which we lived from July to October, when our house, nineteen feet square, was ready, but without a fireplace and without a stairway up to the loft, which was to be our dormitory. One climbs a ladder to reach it. The lower room is parlor, classroom, kitchen, refectory, etc. Neither the St. Louis convent nor any of the others were able to give us much help. Our Mother General sent us a gift that is to pay for an addition that will double the house and give space for orphan children and those of other tribes. We have not the means to feed them, however. The Government has done nothing for us, in spite of the efforts of Father Verhaegen, who is himself in great need of financial help to support the novitiate, to complete the college church, and to carry on mission work. Could you not send us some money to buy food for the little Indian girls? So many are ready to come to the school, and there are the missions of the *Roki* mountains, too. Give me only your prayers for a happy death and your fullest blessing. . . .

P.S. Mother Lucille has decided to write to you herself, so I still have room on this sheet to beg prayers more earnestly, especially at the Holy Sacrifice of the Mass, for a happy death. That is a moment to be feared when one has worked with so little fervor. I want to add also a few more lines about our good Potawatomi. The Catholic Indians live in a village quite separate from the pagans, who honor the evil spirit in order to ward off harm. Among the Catholics there is no drunkenness, no dancing, no gambling. Every Sunday one sees at least a hundred at the Holy Table; at Christmas four hundred received the sacraments. On the feast of the Assumption fifty made their First Communion, the greatest number of these being newly baptized adults. Since last July about seventy old people have been baptized, and they are all persevering. In the church the men and women sit on opposite sides and sing hymns in their own language. They do this also at night and they say the family rosary, each one carrying a pair of beads always. More than two hundred received the scapular of our Lady on a single day. Charity is practiced among them as it was among the early Christians.

The log church at Sugar Creek was a neat and spacious structure, situated on a bluff about a hundred feet above the level of the bottom land and blessed on Christmas Day, 1840, under the title of the Immaculate Conception of the Blessed Virgin. As the entire mission was dedicated to our Lady, Philippine found herself once more at *Sainte Marie*, but similarity to the Alpine monastery ended with the name. The convent erected at Sugar Creek stood close to the church on an eminence commanding a fine view of the surrounding country, but the little stream, bordered by sugar maples and called Sugar Creek, bore no resemblance to the swift Isère of Dauphiny, nor could the Indian encampment evoke the memory of Grenoble and the lovely Vale of Grésivaudan. Just half of the convent had been built in the summer of 1841. Material for the second half was being prepared when Mother Duchesne and her companions learned news that distressed them. So she got out her writing materials again, feeling that there were many things she must tell Mother Barat, whether the news was correct or not. On February 28 she wrote:

> We have just learned in our village that you have suddenly recalled our Mother Provincial to France; and she writes to us that, unless she receives a counter order, she will not be able to visit us. We are all distressed at this news. There is not enough time for us

to point out to you the need we have of seeing her and getting everything settled with the Fathers who are guiding our work. But our one consolation is to think of the pleasure you will have in seeing her again and of the great help she will be to you once more in your immense labors. We thank God for your restoration to health, and we continually beg him to preserve it.

We are all in better health since we came to work among the Indians. We are never in want of anything, as far as food goes, having our good cows and just as good meals as those served in our larger convents in the United States. Only the lodging gives us some reason for sacrifice, for we still have only a log house nineteen feet square. The logs have been prepared with which to make it more than twice that size, but builders are lacking. The savages are not workmen. The men who built the church charged ten francs a day, and it cost fifty francs a week to feed them. The church was built at the expense of the Government, which spends a great deal of money for the civilization of these poor tribes, yet makes little headway. None of the schools opened so far have succeeded. This tribe is the farthest advanced, and all the progress has been made in the past year. . . .

Madame de Rollin wanted to send me something (500 francs), but the letter of exchange was not accepted. I have written to my brother about this. If Madame de Rollin has not died in the meantime, I think the money will reach us. Will you please let us use it for just one thing—a little wooden chapel opening into the large new stone church which is to be built soon? This would assure to us a private place. We have a place now beside the confessional, but we are always being chased out of it when anyone of importance comes—and that is usually on Sundays, when many members of this good tribe go to Communion.

They tell us that there are many saints buried in the little cemetery. When I walk out of doors, I always go there, and I kneel and beg of God the favor of being buried beside them. I feel, however, the same longing for the *Rocki Mountain* missions and any others like them, that I experienced in France when I first begged to come to America, the same longing I felt for the Indian missions, once I reached this country. They say that in the *Rocki* people live to be a hundred years old. As my health has improved and I am only seventy-three, I think I shall have at least ten more years to work.

I used to think it more perfect to wait for things to take their course and so decide my fate. But now, Reverend Mother, will you not authorize me to go farther west if they want me to do so? Of course, that is still rather doubtful, but here I am only a burden to others, as I have no real employment, and there is no doubt about it, they would be glad to have me recalled. I knew from the beginning that I was not wanted. One of the missionaries got permission to remain as long as he desired, even though he was wanted at the college. That makes me hope for a similar favor. . . .

The log convent was completed by mid-March. The crevices between the mural logs were packed with mud, while inside the cabins, set side by side about ten feet apart, heavy cotton cloth was stretched over the walls and whitewashed. On windy days this canvas often swelled out like the sails of a vessel, and when a fierce gale swept across the prairie it sometimes ripped the cloth from its fastenings. While the work was at its height, Philippine was begged to remain in safety in the church. Nothing could please her more than this, and there were such vital intentions to lay before her Eucharistic Lord: the mission and her dread of having to leave it, the coming General Council that was so important in Mother Barat's eyes, the novitiate at Florissant. As she knelt motionless before the tabernacle, lost in prayer, the Indians would steal into the church and watch her intently, then noiselessly approach her, kneel, and kiss the hem of her worn habit or the fringe of her old shawl. To them she was *Quah-Kah-Ka-num-ad*—Woman-who-prays-always.

Quite unexpectedly Mother Galitzin arrived at Sugar Creek on the eve of Palm Sunday for a two days' visit. She saw the mission in full activity, received a hearty welcome from the braves and squaws, complete with parade, equestrian demonstration, and hand-shaking, and examined the hand-work of the little girls. By some undisclosed means the nuns procured a bed for her, and she was not permitted to climb the ladder-stairs to their dormitory loft. What she thought of the Sugar Creek mission is not recorded; it certainly had little appeal for her, and she made few suggestions for improved methods or equipment. One change, however, was decided on, though it was kept secret for the present from the one whom it most concerned: Mother Duchesne would have to go back to one of the Missouri convents within a few months.

There seems to have been no suspicion of the impending change in Philippine's mind when on Easter Sunday she stood as a witness with Brother Van der Borget, S.J., to the marriage of Pierre Drayard and Theresa Rose Kusto, Potawatomi Indians, nor even when she wrote to her sister two weeks later on April 24:

> I hope you will not object if I answer your letter and that of your beloved daughter Josephine together. I did not know her in France, but I love her dearly because of all I have heard about her

and because of the joy she gives you. Tell her to pray much for me and for Mother Lucille, whom she loved so much at Sainte-Marie-d'en-Haut. She is here at the Indian mission with me. There are just four of us, but that is enough as we have only day pupils at present.

One really could not find better people than these good savages. Two of them work for us, and as they do not like to stay at any one thing for long, they amuse themselves and laugh like children—always happy, yet looking tall and straight as warriors. When we do our washing, they bring their soiled clothes, too, and their mending. The children who come to school are very skilful, but quite lazy. Of course we receive no remuneration from anyone and are obliged to furnish the materials for their sewing, etc. They have already exhausted our supply of needles for darning and sewing; thimbles, scissors, thread, all disappear quickly. They do nothing unless we furnish all the material. I saw one poor mother of a family whose husband was ill and whose children were in rags, but she could not borrow enough thread among the Indians to mend their clothes. Sometimes poor Indians come to us and show us their torn clothing, making us understand by signs that they have no needles and thread. And they go away very happy if we supply their need. So whenever you want to give me a present, I shall ask for some galloon—medium width, for a vestment, some thread of different colors for cross-stitching, some needles, thimbles, scissors, and some small, light-weight knives. Since German-speaking people have opened stores in St. Louis, we can get everything else we need, but at a high price. But we cannot get church goods there.

You would be deeply moved by the piety of this good tribe, which had already been converted to the faith in large numbers before being moved into this region. . . . There are baptisms of adults almost every week, some even from neighboring tribes. The priest often calls on one of his catechists to give a little sermon for their benefit. The Indian rises quite readily. Wrapt in his blanket, with his eyes lowered, he begins to speak. As he becomes more animated, he stretches his arm from under the blanket, then finishes his discourse with the air of an experienced orator. The same thing happens at the daily catechism lesson. This is held in the Indian language, as are also the night prayers. The church erected with the help of 4000 francs donated by the Government is already too small. When they are able, the Fathers will build a larger church and use the old one as a hospital, for there are many sick people in the tribe who are not cared for properly as they have no homes, no relatives, no means of support. . . .

Do not think, my beloved Euphrosine, that distance from you

dims my memory of you. In prayer I frequently beg God to bless you and yours. In return please have a Mass offered for me at Notre Dame de Fourvière. If you have an opportunity to speak to dear Mother Geoffroy and the community at La Ferrandière, tell them we are very much at home here. We are growing fat on the milk of our fine cows and we are all in good health. *Adieu,* my dearly loved Sister. . . .

That last extant letter from the Indian mission contains dramatic material for a mural: the Jesuit missionary and his neophytes in the log church, the baptismal ceremony, the young brave with lowered eyes standing among them, wrapt in his bright-hued blanket and speaking with dignified gestures to his fellow tribesmen of God, the Great Spirit now made known to them in the light of Christian truth, the intent, motionless figures in the background—men and women still groping in the darkness of paganism, and there in a corner by the confessional the old nun, clasping her rosary, the baptismal register on her knees and the rapture of heaven in her eyes. She had attained her goal. She had, all unconsciously, proved the constancy of her courage, the heroism of her faith, the unfathomable depth of her selfless love.

Yet a trial awaited her that would test, once and for all, the fine steel of her endurance. The bright vision of work among the Indians that had for more than thirty years steadied her faith and hope in the darkest hours at St. Charles, at Florissant, and in St. Louis, was to fade into the shadows of the past, like the momentary glory of a sunset, and she was to know a darker path and an even greater need for ardent faith and supreme confidence.

Springtime and early summer at Sugar Creek were crowded with activity. Mother Duchesne went about the mission with firmer step and more vigorous determination. Sometimes small groups of Indian girls gathered about her as she sat in a shady place, and she helped them with their knitting, or showed them the mysterious thing she still carried in her pocket—the watch she brought from France so long ago, or let them handle reverently the big rosary she wore at her side.

She was looking forward to the visit of Monseigneur Kenrick, Coadjutor Bishop of St. Louis, who was coming in early June to administer confirmation at the mission. She hoped he would be friendly and understanding like her good friend, Bishop Rosati, who was now back in Rome to report to the Holy Father the outcome of his trip to Haiti. She wondered about the new bishop's French. That was always a problem for her. Bishop Kenrick was all that she had anticipated, except on one point—he disapproved of her remaining at Sugar Creek. The prelate who ten years later would call her "the holiest person he had ever known," was not content to let her "lay her bones to rest in the Indian cemetery," as she had so often expressed the wish. He counseled a return to St. Louis. It was not an order, but she knew there was more behind it than counsel. The weekly mail soon brought the dreaded letter from France—Mother Barat was asking of her "eldest daughter" the supreme sacrifice of the Indian mission.

As soon as Father Verhaegen was informed of the order, which was announced by another letter to Mother Gray, he planned a trip to Sugar Creek. He had escorted Mother Duchesne up the Missouri to the Indian Territory; he would bring her back safely, though it was a bitter disappointment for him to have to do so. On June 19 they left the mission, after a demonstration of affection on the part of the Indians that must have moved Philippine to tears. Traveling slowly in a rough, jolting wagon through dust and heat, they stopped to say good-bye to Napoleon Bourassa and his Potawatomi wife, Memetekosikwe, who had so often befriended the nuns during the past year. Four days later they boarded the river packet at Westport and reached St. Louis on June 29, 1842, exactly a year from the day they had set out for Sugar Creek. No sudden spurt of courage and generosity had carried Mother Duchesne through this hardest ordeal of her cross-strewn career, but the habits of a lifetime, above all the habit of simple acceptance of God's will through love.

After a short rest at the City House, Mother Duchesne drove to St. Charles with Mother Eleanor Gray. The cordial and loving welcome given her by Mother Regis Hamilton and her community helped to lessen the sorrow that weighed heavily upon her. In the hurried preparations for leaving Sugar Creek there had been some distraction from grief, but in the quiet routine of life at St. Charles, the realization of *failure* crept over her once more, bringing with it an agony of disappointment that summed itself up in the haunting thought, "All that effort of love in vain!" But she knew in her inmost heart that it had not been in vain, and peace came flooding into her soul as she knelt in the cloister chapel and renewed her complete surrender to God's will, a surrender involving what was most dear to her, the hardest submission God had asked of her. She must have found it bewilderingly hard to accept, yet not a trace of rebellion appears in the letters she wrote shortly after she took her place as the nineteenth member of the St. Charles community. Interest in the welfare of others dictated them, but there was no artificial stifling of her own feelings as she wrote to Mother Boilvin on August 7:

> Two days ago, my dearest Sister, I sent Mother Bathilde two letters for France, and here are two more. I hope this is not ill-advised on my part. My correspondence with all in France will be more and more limited hereafter.
>
> I heard that you were miserable physically, and my loving interest in your health makes me fear you have tried to do more than your strength allows. You have always needed to spare your voice in singing and to have a little more sleep than the rest of the community. So have the humility and the simplicity to admit your needs and accept the proper care.
>
> From my last letter you learned of my departure from Indian Territory. I cannot forget the savages, even though I am surrounded by everything that can edify me and fill me with gratitude. The religious whom I had never met, as well as those whom I had known for a long time, are full of kind thoughtfulness for me. . . .
>
> I left our Sisters at Sugar Creek in good health. . . . A little five-room house had been built for us before I left. Many of the children had learned to read, knit, card wool, and spin. Some already knew how to sew when we went there, and they like this kind of work best of all. They are beginning to settle down; and as they are quite intelligent, we may hope that, with the help of the prayers offered to God and the perseverance of the nuns in caring for them, they will make progress in virtue and knowledge. . . .

One of the letters for France which Philippine mentioned to Mother Boilvin was written to Father De La Croix. In it she repeated her appeal for funds to help the mission at Sugar Creek, supporting her request with some information about economic conditions in the Mississippi Valley, where recovery from the financial crisis of 1837 had been very slow. She closed her letter with a touching little reference to herself:

> I received a letter from you which you had given a long time ago to the Bishop of Detroit. It reached me only when I had gone to the Indian country. I answered from there, begging help from the Society for the Propagation of the Faith for our establishment, which has only one purpose, the instruction of the little savages. My Superior General considers me too old for that work, so she wrote me to return to St. Charles, our first American home. I thought I should write to you and ask you to address any funds

you intend sending for the work among the savages to the Provincial of the Jesuits, who will be best acquainted with the needs and the situation of each mission. Already two have had to be abandoned, for drunkenness was introduced and nothing more could be done. . . .

Economic affairs are in a bad condition in New Orleans. Enrollments in our academies in Louisiana have diminished. . . . The same money shortage exists in St. Louis, so the academy there is reduced from sixty to thirty pupils. The novitiate has been transferred from St. Ferdinand to a place near Philadelphia, and there is only a day school left. At St. Charles, where I am living now, a good brick building was put up some years ago through the efforts of Father Van Quickenborne. As I live a very solitary life, I can employ all my time in making reparation for the past and in preparing for death. But I cannot put out of my mind the thought of the savages, and my ambition carries me even to the *Roki.* I can only adore the designs of God, who has taken from me the thing I had so long desired. . . .

thirteen

The Reality of
God's Will

I. 1842—1847

THE YEAR 1842 WAS CRITICAL in the history of the Society of the Sacred Heart. The period of trial accorded the new decrees formulated by the Sixth General Council was drawing to a close, and the whole Society was in eager anticipation of the coming council. "It will be a very important meeting," Mother Barat had written to Philippine in August, 1841, "and we have great need of God's help. Pray. . . ." During the autumn and winter of 1840–1841 the Superior General had been unable to carry out her plan of visiting all the convents in France before the council took place. In June, 1841, however, she began her visitation of the houses of northern France and Belgium. She was well satisfied with these communities. Returning to Paris for a few days, she set out again in September, visiting houses to the east and south and arriving in Rome before Christmas.

In February, 1842, she received from Pope Gregory XVI the unequivocal statement that she should return to France and make that her ordinary place of residence. Consulting Cardinal Lambruschini, Papal Secretary of State, as to where the coming council should be held, she was told emphatically, "In France and not elsewhere, and this in order to accede to the wishes of the French

444

bishops," and the Cardinal named Lyons as the most suitable place.

Acting on this advice, Mother Barat issued a circular letter to the Society on February 21 to prepare the way for the Seventh General Council. At the same time she told Mother Galitzin of her intention of returning to France in July and holding the assembly there. Accordingly Mother Galitzin sailed for France in May with Mother Hardey, who was to represent the American province at the council. From Paris they went directly to Rome, only to find that Mother Barat was already at the convent of La Ferrandière in Lyons. They had the pleasure, however, of being presented to the Holy Father by Bishop Rosati and of experiencing his personal interest in all that concerned the Society's work in America and, above all, its great pioneer missionary, Philippine Duchesne.

The councilors who assembled at Lyons formed a numerous body—Assistants General, Provincials, several local superiors, and a professed delegate from each province. Of all who had been expected to take part in the deliberation only Mother Eugenie de Gramont was missing. In her stead came a letter from Monseigneur Affre, Archbishop of Paris. Arrogating to himself the title of ecclesiastical superior of the order, an office abolished in 1826, he forbade the Mother General to hold the council anywhere outside his episcopal city. Moreover, his letter carried an ominous threat: he had calculated all the consequences of this prohibition, and the Mothers would have reason to regret it if they disobeyed his orders. He had communicated his opposition to Lyons and his disapproval of the decrees of 1839 to the twenty-two French bishops having convents of the Sacred Heart in their dioceses, and they all joined him in his protest. Mother Barat could only appeal to Rome to enlighten the Archbishop on the matter of ecclesiastical superiority in the Society, but that meant weeks of delay while a commission of eight cardinals investigated the matter and answered the petition.

The Mothers who had assembled for the council went into retreat under the direction of Father Joseph Barelle, S.J. But when the exercises were completed, no answer had come from Rome, so there could be no council. As the Archbishop of Lyons had arbitrarily imposed silence on Mother Barat regarding the cause of the indefinite adjournment she was now obliged to give, the Superior General bore the full responsibility of it in the eyes of the astonished Society and the interested outside world. At the end of August the Mothers Councilor dispersed, each to the house from which she had come. The answer of the commission of cardinals, supported by a papal brief, proved clearly that Monseigneur Affre possessed no special jurisdiction over the Religious of the Sacred Heart, and in November Mother Barat submitted this answer to the Archbishop. The resulting complications necessitated Rome's re-examination of the *Constitutions* of the Society, which happily led to a decree confirming in their entirety the rules approved in 1826.

In the meantime Mother Hardey had returned to America, bringing with her several recruits for the American foundations. They were on the high seas when, on October 24, Mother Duchesne wrote to her sister a letter marked with a personal touch and a flash of the old fire. In it one feels how distressed she is at the poverty of the convent at St. Charles, but she does not beg financial help from her family:

> At the beginning of August, dearest Sister, I wrote to Madame de Rollin and asked her to share the letter with you. I took the liberty of accepting your offer and suggested that you send me some galloon for a chasuble. In my present life of solitude I have the very satisfying occupation of embroidering a cross for the chasuble with the remnants of the silks you sent me, and I use them so economically, I shall even have a good deal left over. I am very fortunate to have saved them so long. You realize, of course, that my work is quite imperfect, but I enjoy it very much. I cannot finish the vestment, however, until I get the galloon. . . .
>
> I hope soon to receive some of the income due me from the royal treasury, in which my father invested a trust fund in my name. I believe they think I have lived too long. At the time of the last payment they declared they would send me no more unless the judge who signed the attestation saying I was alive also stated that he had seen my baptismal record or birth certificate. I asked my brother to send me a copy. I should have received it by this time. Please ask him if he sent it. If he has not done so, tell him to have it copied on thin paper and sent by post from Havre. . . . Affectionate messages to this dear brother. I hope he does not regret his generosity to me at the Indian mission, where he predicted I should not remain two years. He was right, but I had no desire to leave there, and his money was used most beneficially. God will reward him for sending it. Madame de Rollin inquired the best way by which to send things to me. Tell her to send through the procuratrix, Mother de Lemps, at Rue de Varenne, Paris. I have just as much need now as when I was with the Indians. All our houses are in straitened circumstances as a result of the business depression which has been produced, no doubt, by the circulation of

paper money that has met the same fate as our *assignats* in France long ago.

For an authentic picture of the home in which Philippine Duchesne spent the last decade of her life, one has only to read the description written by her niece, Mother Amelie Jouve, who visited her there in 1847:

> The convent at St. Charles is very pleasantly situated on the bluffs overlooking the Missouri River. It is an unpretentious little building, enlarged on one side by a cloister chapel that looks into the sanctuary of the parish church. Here the religious can assist at all services and hear the instruction given by the Jesuit Fathers. At the [south] end of that chapel [beyond a partition wall] there is a small room, about eight feet wide by fifteen or sixteen feet long. These are the two places in which Mother Duchesne spent most of her time—now at prayer, now at manual labor. The furniture of her little room consisted of a low cot, a chair, a wooden box in which she kept her treasures—and what treasures they were! Some instruments of penance, some spiritual notebooks, some letters of our Mother General. There were two or three old pictures of pious subjects on the walls and some well worn prayerbooks on a little table.

As Philippine sat by the window in her little room sewing or reading or looking out at the wide, turbulent river and the rolling country beyond, memories of her first year in America must have come crowding into her mind. She was by disposition reminiscent, and recreating the past was often a delightful distraction for her. From the back porch of the convent she could look up the hillside to the dilapidated old Duquette "mansion," now used as a washhouse. Often in warm weather she saw the children in their pink gingham uniforms and green sunbonnets playing on the gallery of the house or under the big trees on the playground. They were such a small group, it seemed at times a waste of effort and energy to run the boarding school for them, but Mother Hamilton clung to the hope that it would survive the depression years and be built up again. To this intention Philippine applied her most earnest prayers. At a short distance behind the church she could see the little cemetery that had been staked off before Mother Mathevon left St. Charles. One white cross was there when Philippine first visited it in 1842, and that marked the grave of Mother Eulalie Guillot, but soon there were other crosses driven into the little leveled plot at the base of the second bluff.

When winter came and the cold was severe, Mother Duchesne recalled the bitter weather of her first winter in Missouri and refused to have a charcoal brazier lighted in her room. What was the chill of the brick convent in comparison to the icy atmosphere of the log church at Sugar Creek or the unplastered room at Florissant? There were sick nuns in the infirmary who had more need of the little heater, she thought. Sometimes she made her way slowly up the steep stairway to visit them, to cheer them with thoughts of God and stories gathered from missionaries and Catholic chronicles and spiritual books. She often inserted stories in the letters she wrote to her family in France. A letter to her sister Euphrosine opens with a charming picture of Philippine in her little room on May 5, 1843, as happy as a child on Christmas morning:

> Surrounded by the wealth of gifts you have sent me, dearest Sister, I hasten to acknowledge the receipt of them. If I had prepared a list of all the things I wanted, you could not have succeeded better in satisfying all my desires. Accept my most heartfelt thanks. I had sent you word by Madame de Rollin that I knew the package had arrived in America, but it was delayed somewhere on our frozen rivers during the long, severe winter, and I received it only today. . . .
>
> It seems to me that in leaving the Indians I left my real element, and now I can only yearn for that land from which there will be no departure. God knows why I was recalled, and that is enough. My greatest joy now is to hear about the hopes raised by the mission in the Rocky Mountains. The leader of these missionaries, Father De Smet, is obliged to go to Europe to beg help, for he must have money to undertake and carry on this enterprise. At the risk of telling you what you already know from Catholic publications, I am going to relate two incidents that show God's great mercy to this vast country. . . .

And she was off on a story-telling expedition in company with Indian children, Black Robes, and the Blessed Virgin. Then she continues:

> The mission where I was stationed, just beyond the Missouri border, is doing well. The savages are becoming more civilized; many are accepting Catholicism; and many are learning to farm. All this takes time, for they will be happy only when they can overcome their natural laziness. Our nuns write that they no longer have to urge the children to do their work; they love it. The Indian agent who visited that tribe was highly pleased and

gave an order for all the school supplies they needed—pens, paper, books, cotton for spinning—and he promised to recommend the school to Congress. . . .

The work of the Society in New York and Pennsylvania was also of particular interest to Mother Duchesne because it was being done in large part by religious whom she knew personally and whose names occur frequently in her letters. The foundation at McSherrystown near Conewago was made under Mother Galitzin's supervision in the spring of 1842, Mother de Kersaint becoming superior and mistress of novices and Mother Margaret Murphy from St. Louis, Assistant. Mother Mary Ann Roche soon joined the community, which included several novices from New York and Louisiana. The free school quickly enrolled fifty children, but the academy made little progress. Changes, accidents, and an alarming decline in the health of the community make the record of the years at McSherrystown sad history. When Mother de Kersaint was chosen for the foundation of the first Canadian convent of the Sacred Heart in the autumn of 1842, Mothers Caroline Cauche and Catherine Cruice, who had come from France with Mother Hardey, became superior and mistress of novices, respectively. In December, Zoe Mignard, a novice from Louisiana, died of tuberculosis at McSherrystown—the first among many to succumb to the disease.

In March, 1843, while Mother Cauche was inspecting the work being done on the roof by laborers, about whose safety she was worried, a heavy plank fell from the scaffolding and struck her on the head. Her life was saved by prompt medical care, but the mental incapacity that followed called for a new superior at McSherrystown, and Mother Adeline Boilvin was chosen for the position, with the double work of guiding the community and school and directing the novices, as Mother Cruice was called back to New York, where Bishop Rosati's prediction was fulfilled and another novitiate was opened. Mother Boilvin had been but a few weeks at her new post when she wrote to Mother Duchesne, telling her of the changes and begging her prayers. On October 18, Philippine replied with sympathy and encouragement:

> Yesterday, my dear Mother, I received your letter and began at once the novena you asked for; today I received Holy Communion for the same intention. I was completely ignorant of the fact that Mother Cauche was ill and that you had replaced her. I am not at all surprised that you were astonished at this change and distressed

by it. But after all, God willed the blow that has struck you; his will is expressed by the orders of superiors and by the great need there was of replacing these dear Mothers. Your natural inclination is thwarted, and this shows that on your side there was nothing done even to suggest the promotion by which you—and such a little person you are—now find yourself a superior.

You must, then, bend your shoulders under the yoke of two heavy offices, those of superior and mistress of novices. If humility is always desirable, generous humility is still more so now. Obedience has not destined you to be an Alexis or a Benedict Labre, but rather to imitate the courage of St. de Chantal and St. Teresa without the least human respect. . . . These women were great saints. I hope you will become one also by acting in your present position just as if you were engaged in the lowliest employments. I shall pray much for you and your large religious family. The family you gave up for God seems about as usual. Your Grandmother St. Cyr can still go to church and she seems physically stronger than Maria. I shall give them news of you, just in case you have not done so. They say Maria makes use of her infirmities to advance in perfection. . . . Our Mother Provincial has not arrived yet, but she is expected any day now.

Mother Galitzin had returned to America in the spring of 1843. Realizing the harm she had done in pressing too vehemently the acceptance of the Jesuit Rule and the decrees of 1839, she had begged to be allowed to revisit the convents in the United States and restore the original organization of the Society as established there by Mother Duchesne and her companions. She spent the summer in New York, Canada, and Pennsylvania, then turned westward over the route now familiar to her. When Mother Hamilton went to St. Louis to see her and report on conditions in the convent she was directing, the Visitatrix made a swift decision and ordered the closing of the boarding school at St. Charles. It was Mother Hamilton's difficult duty to carry out this order in the midst of very trying circumstances. Within the space of a few days, eight of the religious who had been teaching at St. Charles were transferred to either St. Louis or Florissant, where the boarding school had been reopened for the fourth time, and six of the nine pupils had joined their City House companions.

Mother Galitzin was advised by the doctors in St. Louis to go south as soon as possible in order to avoid the rigor of the Missouri winter. On reaching St. Michael's, she found yellow fever raging. With the rashness that characterized her generosity she insisted on nursing the sick, and on December 1 she herself was stricken.

God had accepted the sacrifice of her life, made the year before at La Ferrandière, when she thought the existence of the Society was threatened, and death came to her on the feast of the Immaculate Conception.

Mother Duchesne's reaction to the upheaval at St. Charles and the death of the visitatrix appears in a letter to Mother Boilvin, answering a New Year's greeting from McSherrystown:

> You took a very tiny piece of paper to write to me, and I am devoting the largest part of this big sheet to answer your letter, and still it seems small in comparison with all I have to tell you. First of all, let us talk about your Grandmother: Father Van Assche told me she is getting along as well as possible and goes to church almost every day. Maria is still very weak. She was in bed the last day the good Father was there. He is confessor of this convent on the Ember Days. You already know that Father Verhaegen fills the position of pastor here now. We are very much afraid this arrangement will not last long. . . .
>
> You have also learned of the great loss the Society sustained in the death of Reverend Mother Galitzin. Mother L'Eveque, who cared for her during her painful illness, is inconsolable. With your sympathetic heart you can easily understand the sorrow felt in Missouri. Before she left St. Louis, she was ill with fever and so could not visit us at St. Charles. She sent for Mother Hamilton, and on hearing how few children we had and how much sickness there had been in the community, she struck us a severe blow—had the children transferred to St. Louis, along with several of the nuns, and sent others to St. Ferdinand. There are just eight of us left in this big house. Only Mother Hamilton and Sister Couture speak French. In just a few days we found ourselves living in solitude, with the last—that is the parish school—having become the first. Our convent was offered to the Visitandine religious at Kaskaskia, who want to leave their present place of residence because of illness. They refused this one, however, wishing to establish their monastery nearer St. Louis. They may be there already.
>
> I still hold on to some hope that our Mother General will not sanction these measures, which are so heart-breaking, especially for me. I saw the work begin here, and perhaps I shall see it destroyed. I wrote to her with all the urgent entreaties I could employ, begging her to renew the life of this house and allow us once more to admit the children who would support it. At present we can take no measure by which to do so. They were counting, perhaps, on Louisiana, but money is as scarce there as here, and the enrollments are low. The Jesuits are suffering a great deal.
>
> I have written enough to show you the state of my poor heart.

Do not fail to get earnest prayers for our resurrection; and when you write to Mother Barat, plead our cause. You ought to tell her also that it would give great satisfaction generally, both outside the convents and inside, if we had a Mother Provincial who was American by birth and language. You know Mother Hardey well. You could tell our Mother General your opinion of her. She is the one I would choose, if my advice were asked. Try to bear up under your burden. God is very good to have eased it by the sincere and affable character that marks all your family. . . . Pray more earnestly than ever to St. Francis Regis for St. Charles and St. Ferdinand. I attribute all our troubles and anxieties to the destruction of his shrine. How I long to erect it again! The latest news from Sugar Creek was good. *Adieu*, my dear Mother. Pray for me that I may have a happy death.

In pleading with Mother Barat for the survival of the convent at St. Charles, Mother Duchesne had voiced not only her own sentiments but also those of many of the religious who loved that convent with special affection. Among them was Mother Regis Hamilton, who sent an earnest plea to the Superior General, representing how unsatisfactory the new arrangement was and how destitute it left the community. Six months passed before a letter from Mother Barat brought the desired answer: the academy was to be reopened the following school year and at least two members of the community would return from St. Louis at once. That the little group of nuns at St. Charles considered this letter as addressed to themselves is revealed in this entry in the *Journal* of the convent on May 2: "We have received a letter from our Mother General containing the joyful news that some of our dear absent Sisters are to return to us and that this house is not to be broken up." The letter was addressed to Mother Hamilton, the superior, and contained no separate answer for Philippine.

This was a great disappointment to her, a shock to her sensitive and affectionate heart, and she interpreted it as a reproof for having written as she did. On her recall from Sugar Creek she had written to Mother Boilvin, "My correspondence with all in France will be more and more limited hereafter." Now she seems to have renewed that determination, though it must have caused her keen suffering to carry it out. But in this matter she was acting in accordance with a recommendaion of the Sixth General Council which Mother Galitzin had emphasized and which would later on be written into a decree to the effect that, although all the religious were at full liberty to write to the Superior General, they should refrain from doing so except in a case of real importance and necessity, and this because of her numerous and important occupations. Mother Galitzin's orders and influence in the Missouri convents remained in force for several years after her death, as evidence will show later on.

The study of conditions facing the Mother General from 1843 to 1846 reveals a continuous need for visits to the many convents that had been opened in France, an increasingly heavy correspondence with superiors and other religious in posts of importance in these convents, and a proportionately lessened correspondence with the close friends to whom Mother Barat had been accustomed to write charming and deeply spiritual letters. No one felt this enforced silence of her beloved friend more than Mother Duchesne. But the knowledge that St. Charles was to continue its apostolate brightened her outlook, and her pen was often busy with letters to her family and to other religious and priests.

News from McSherrystown that summer told that the cross of illness was weighing heavily on the community. Within the space of four months, three deaths occurred from tuberculosis, while a novice returned home to die of the same disease. Mother Margaret Murphy was the last victim at this time but five other religious who had contracted the disease succumbed within five years. Bishop Kenrick visited the convent and sympathized paternally in these losses, but begged the nuns to continue their work. Partly out of compassion for the bishop, who was experiencing the outrages of religious bigotry in Philadelphia, Mother Boilvin encouraged her community to perseverance, though it was evident that she herself was far from well.

When Mother Duchesne heard of all this, she wrote to Mother Boilvin:

> Ever since I learned of the successive blows that have been testing your resignation to God's will, I have been continually occupied about you in prayer, begging God to be your strength and to let these great sacrifices work toward the good of your convent. Already the consolation you have drawn from the virtue shown by your daughters has strengthened your afflicted heart and proved to you that their eternal happiness far surpasses the pain you felt at losing them. I think, too, that the zeal and fervor of our dear Mother Murphy is going to be handed down to all those who saw and admired her virtue, and they in turn will imitate her. I trust

that a sweet calm has followed the storms and that all that has happened will procure the greater glory of the Sacred Heart in your peaceful convent.

Every day we are expecting Mothers Cutts and Sallion. The flooding of the Missouri River prevented them from going to Sugar Creek, so they went down to Louisiana to make their visitation before coming here. All I know is that we are going back to the former Rules and Constitutions of the Society and that our house and that of Florissant are again allowed to receive boarding pupils. But God sends successive trials that slow up everything. We have had the worst flood ever known here, and it has ruined the entire countryside. It was followed by much sickness, and this continues. Families that had already lost their homes, furniture, cattle, crops, and harvest, are now reduced to the utmost misery, and no one here is rich enough to contribute large sums of money for charitable relief. They are doing a great deal in St. Louis, however, and some individuals, not particularly rich people, have taken in as many as seven sick families that came from the flooded districts of Illinois, and they are providing for all their needs over a period of six months. . . . *Adieu*, kind and dear Mother. No one takes a greater interest in all that concerns you than I do.

The community at St. Charles was increased in August by the return of several religious to teach in the academy, which was reopened in September, 1844. The small enrollment might have been discouraging, had it not been for the joy in the hearts of the nuns at this new beginning. The presence of the children enlivened the convent, and Mother Duchesne took particular interest in the little Johnson girls and their cousins, all of whom were related to Mother Boilvin. At the end of October she went to St. Louis on business connected with the cutting of streets through the property still held by the Society under the contract and deed made to her by John Mullanphy in 1827. She told Mother Boilvin about this little trip and much else in a letter that traveled eastward in the pocket of Father Verhaegen. His departure for Maryland in December was a sacrifice keenly felt by all at St. Charles, but particularly by her.

I was greatly astonished one day when Mother Gray arrived out here to take me to the city to revise my will. She had had some difficulty about Mr. Mullanphy's grant to us. . . . The lawyer whom she consulted said I should make my will in legal form, giving approval of the improvements made since I left there. It took three weeks to complete this little bit of business; then Mother Aloysia Jacquet and Mother Prud'hom accompanied me back to

St. Charles. We went by way of St. Ferdinand, which I had not seen since you and I parted there. Pray that that holy house may be reorganized successfully. Fathers Van Assche and Gleizal are eager for this. The latter says he can always recognize in the confessional young people who were our pupils there by the good method they use in approaching this sacrament. You deserve more praise than I for this, for you were the one who instructed them. See to it that your present pupils are as well trained. . . .

Less than two weeks later Philippine was writing again to Mother Boilvin, about whom she was growing anxious, as she had heard that her health had also been undermined and that there was some question of closing the McSherrystown convent:

I wrote to you about two weeks ago, when Reverend Father Verhaegen came to ask what messages and commissions we wanted to send to the East. He was leaving for Georgetown, as the Fathers at that college had requested the Father General to send him there. So he had to go, carrying the burden of both Provincial and Visitor. The latter office will bring him to see you. . . . I have written to Mother Geoffroy at Lyons, asking her to send you the collection of the *Annals of the Faith*, from the establishment of the Society that bears that name in 1822 to 1844. I think there are in all fifteen or eighteen volumes. They are printed in seven languages now. You ought to procure the English version and pay the subscription fee of the associates, which will entitle you to the six booklets published each year. Perhaps the association has been established in Philadelphia or New York. You know the rates: one sou a week. I have never in all my life read anything more interesting nor better calculated to enkindle zeal. . . . This reading is my delight. . . .

Put your trust in Divine Providence, dear Mother, and in the protection of St. Francis Regis, making him some promise, as I suggested in my last letter. But try to make one that you are sure you yourself can carry out. I fear the failure to keep the promises made to the saint for Grenoble and St. Ferdinand may have caused the closing of the house at Grenoble and the wretched condition now prevailing at St. Ferdinand. . . .

Among the treasures lovingly safeguarded at St. Charles for more than a century are the twelve bound volumes of the *Annales de la Propagation de la Foi* in which Mother Duchesne took such delight. Here and there on the printed page one finds corrections in her handwriting and even slips of paper inserted and pasted in, on which she wrote correct versions of stories she had heard or events she had witnessed or taken part in. For her truly apostolic soul it was a satisfaction to share in spirit at least in the sufferings, labors, and achievements of the missionaries who were leading souls out of darkness and error into the light of truth. Often she became so absorbed in these accounts, she would willingly have given her night hours to reading, as in the past she had given them to writing and to prayer, had not the community bell signaled to her that it was time to close the book.

In May, 1845, there was sacrifice again at St. Charles, when Mother Regis Hamilton was relieved of her duties as superior and Mother Emilie St. Cyr was installed in her place. These two former pupils and novices of Mother Duchesne were very different in character and temperament, manner and outlook on life, yet they were both loyal and devoted to the one whom they considered the main channel through which devotion to the Sacred Heart had come into their lives. Where Regis was cordial and demonstrative, Emilie was timorous and reserved under the impact of responsibility. Mother Amelie Jouve attributed her overemphasis on strict observance to the fact that she was young and inexperienced. She was thirty-nine years old in 1845. Never having been placed in authority before, she was inclined to interpret both her rights and her obligations in a somewhat narrow and rigid manner. She had been in Louisiana for twenty years and so had lost contact with the religious in Missouri. Mother Hamilton, on the contrary, had been Mistress General at the City House for ten years before replacing Mother Mathevon at St. Charles.

The change of superiors would have been more costly for Mother Duchesne if Mother Hamilton had not remained another eighteen months at St. Charles as Assistant to the new superior. A few days after Mother St. Cyr's arrival, Philippine wrote to Mother Boilvin:

> Reverend Mother Cutts came here last week, bringing with her your dear aunt Josephine [Emilie] St. Cyr, whom she gave us as superior. Mother Hamilton remains here as her assistant. . . . At first I did nothing about the Masses at La Louvesc until I should hear again from you. I spoke to Father Gleizal, however, but he says he does not know anyone who is stationed at the saint's shrine now, and he would not take the responsibility of writing. So I have done it myself. I wrote to my sister who lives in Lyons. She can attend to it through one of my nieces who is in Mother Geoffroy's community, or through another who is at the Visitation in Romans. They can find frequent occasions through pilgrims who go each year to La Louvesc. But I did not know how many Masses

you promised, so write the number in the place where I put "Number of Masses" between parentheses, then seal the letter, pay the postage and, if you think well of the suggestion, add a little note, but I think it can go as it is. Our kind Mother St. Cyr wants me to give you affectionate greetings. If, by distraction, she sealed the letter to my sister, just put a little note in with another seal.

With the coming of Mother St. Cyr, Philippine had more frequent opportunities to help Mother Hamilton in little ways. But this made her feel more keenly at times the restrictions placed on her zeal and activity. She was physically much better than when she had returned from Sugar Creek. Her mind was clear and active, and she was as eager as ever to advance the Kingdom of Christ. Yet she was obliged to confine the urgency of her love to a little work with a few French-speaking children in the free school. She longed to lend a hand at household work, but she was unable to do this and so found herself alone most of the day. "But her solitude was brightened, sweetened, [wrote a member of the community] by the fact that she could always be close to Jesus in the Blessed Sacrament of his love, Jesus, the Friend who is faithful and near when all other friends disappear. He had not forsaken 'his poor servant,' as she called herself, and more than ever he let her experience the sweetness and joy of his presence."

Besides the long hours she spent in adoration, she had the privilege of giving the Latin responses at all the Masses offered in the church or in the cloister chapel, for acolytes were few and unreliable. Even at the age of eighty years she continued to do this, kneeling upright without support, not only during one Mass, but during several offered in succession. She was also very punctual about the recitation of Office to the very last days of her life, as the private recitation decreed in 1839 continued to be the custom in the houses in Missouri for more than a decade, so slowly was the work of Mother Galitzin undone.

By a happy coincidence in the August of 1845 a letter from Josephine de Savoye-Rollin reached Philippine as she was celebrating in her own heart her seventy-sixth birthday. It contained a gift of money, as usual, and announced the shipment of a package that should reach St. Charles in the near future. But more precious to Philippine was the wealth of family news it contained. Answering on September 14, she commended her letter to St. Anthony of Padua, as had been her custom throughout the quarter-century she had spent in America, and wrote what is her last extant letter to Josephine Perier:

> I am always deeply touched, my dearest Cousin, by your generosity toward me and above all by the loving words that accompany your gifts. I do not know how to thank you, but our Heavenly Father hears, and will hear every day of my life, the voice of my prayers by which I try to pay my debt to you. My prayer has been heard long since, I trust. The interesting details you give me about your dear family, about the piety that reigns there, especially among the young married women who give so much consolation to their mother, all speak to my heart and make me realize that my daily prayers for Marine have been answered by the Sovereign Master, who has made gratitude a duty. I draw from his treasures to pay my own debt. The news that Masses have been offered for me at Fourvière and La Louvesc gave me great joy. The protection of heaven has been very evident and our house near Philadelphia that promised those Masses has been freed from illness and death, which had struck terror into the hearts of the young religious. . . . The founding of several new convent schools in the vicinity of St. Louis will draw many children away from our schools, but we desire only to serve God, and we must be content with the rather mediocre success we have. The generous sum you sent us will remove all fear about the coming winter, for it will buy the provisions we are most in need of.

Other members of her family were showing their love in the same generous way that had marked their attachment to her for nearly half a century in France and in America. From her brother came some precious volumes of the *Annals of the Propagation of the Faith*. From her sister came the sewing materials with which she was still able to make and mend vestments and altar linens. For her personal use she desired nothing. She was the poorest nun in the community and the most mortified. Never was she to be found idle. Even in the last years of her life she allowed herself no retrenchment of her ordinary way of living, no little comforts to ease the pain and weariness inherent in her physical condition. Her food was chiefly milk, vegetables, and fruit. On fast days she ate only one meal, taking a cup of black coffee in the morning and a cup of tea in the evening. She loved to read in the community refectory during meals, but her voice had become so faint that it was difficult for the religious to hear her. Still they did not let her know this, for it would have added to that sense of uselessness that frequently depressed her.

A letter to her sister in March, 1846, shows her as interested and as interesting as ever, and as lovingly grateful for things that enabled her to compensate by a remarkable industry for the inactivity to which she felt "condemned":

Your heart, my beloved Sister and Friend, has found fullest expression in the promptitude and eagerness with which you are supplying my old age with holy and very happy occupations. I have never enjoyed reading and sewing more than I do now, when they fill my days, along with prayer. As soon as I receive the books, I shall let my brother know and shall express my gratitude to him. As for you, my loving Sister, I am always thinking of you; and even if I could forget you, the last two packages of sewing materials you sent me are certainly very dear reminders of you. They have enabled me to make six vestments. I thought at first that I should have scarcely enough for one. . . . This multiplication of material makes me admire more than ever the Providence of God, who takes such care of me. You may imagine what kind of embroidery I can do now and how incapable I am, but I am helping poor churches that are being built on all sides. Not a single Catholic paper I read but has an account of several new churches consecrated—and some of them are very beautiful. In general, all the churches have organs and good singing. . . .

I often picture your home and the young family gathered about you, and it gives me so much pleasure to know what great joy they bring you. Thank you so much for giving me news of the grandchildren and of other members of the family. Greetings to all who know me. *Adieu*, dear Sister. In the Heart of Jesus I am your faithful friend and sister. . . .

Through the spring months of 1846, Mother Duchesne was often to be seen kneeling in the cloister chapel, her gaze fixed on the tabernacle, tears flowing unheeded down her cheeks. She was wrestling in prayer for the existence of the convent at Florissant. For years she had hoped against hope that the Society would never give up what was to her its dearest home in America. She had saved it before when a like fate threatened—saved it by pleading with God and with the Superior General. It was nearly two years and a half since she had written to Mother Barat. The barrier formed in 1844 had remained, though St. Madeleine Sophie, overwhelmed by problems, anxieties, visitations, and successive illnesses of which Philippine had no conception, was quite unaware of the reason for her old friend's pen-silence.

Toward the close of May, Mother Cutts arrived at St. Charles. One reason for her visit was the decision that had been reached regarding Florissant. When it was announced, it took all the courage and fortitude Philippine could muster to accept the blow. And before she did so, she exerted every effort to parry it. From Mother Cutts she turned to Bishop Kenrick, but his answer to her letter brought her small comfort, though she recognized the supernatural truth he was suggesting when he wrote: "This is the cross that Jesus, your Divine Spouse, wishes you to carry for love of him." Even before his letter reached her, she had decided to write just as she would have talked to Mother Barat, explaining her past silence and urging her present petition with all the earnestness of her glowing, if impractical, zeal. Her letter closed with a heart-cry that must have caused anguish to the Mother General: "If you refuse my petition [in regard to Florissant], I shall submit, but I shall never be reconciled. The wound is too deep. I kneel at your feet awaiting the decision, and I retain always my deep respect for you and for the beloved Father who laid the foundation of our holy Society."

The decision regarding Florissant had long since been made and this letter remained unanswered. Months passed. When Philippine spoke with Mother Hamilton about this silence on the part of Mother Barat, they found no solution to the problem, such as there had been in 1844. If Philippine had grieved then, she was desolate now, for she feared that the friend whom she loved more than anyone else on earth was displeased with her. In her humility she attributed this to some serious fault on her part, yet the most searching self-examination failed to reveal any action that could have merited such punishment. There was no querulous resentment in her reaction to this unexpected silence, no least tinge of bitterness in her comments. When she spoke of it to Mother Hamilton, she was always hopeful: mail was slow; letters were often delayed, and many were lost. She had said these very things in her letters recently. Perhaps by New Year's she would receive an answer. Meanwhile the convent at Florissant stood vacant and the picture of St. Francis Regis had been left behind in the attic.

Then came another unexpected sacrifice—Mother Hamilton was transferred to Canada, leaving St. Charles on November 8, 1846. Philippine could not restrain her tears. She had found strong comfort in the sympathy and friendship of this beloved Mother. But now, a long, bleak road seemed to stretch before her, and she must walk its dark way alone, and yet not alone, for she could always put out her hand in the darkness and go forward unseeing, yet guided securely by luminous faith and unswerving trust. The desolation of these months was a dreariness that must be endured, and there seemed to be no way to deal with it except by a simple surrender of herself to the reality of God's will. Free from self-pity, she thought of herself as a creature of no importance, buried away unnoticed in the obscurity of the Society's poorest convent. Yet here was another seed growing silently and destined to bear fruit a hundredfold in her own soul and in the souls of countless members of the Mystical Body.

At New Year's she wrote in loneliness and gratitude to her sister:

> It is a long time since I had any news from you, my dearest Sister. I wonder if you are dead. I would not want to survive you. It is too hard to see all those one loves pass ahead into eternity. I have the same fears with regard to Madame de Rollin, who has so many claims on my heart. Her last letter was so affectionate, it filled me with dread lest it was her last *adieu*. I had that same feeling the last time my Father visited me at Ste. Marie. His parting words, "*Adieu, Philippine*," left me in tears. I thought at once that he would not return to see me, and I was not mistaken. When you answer this letter, do not fail to give me news of my brother, of Madame de Rollin, her sister, and all that is dearest to us.
>
> I never can thank you sufficiently for your gift of the *Annals of the Propagation of the Faith*. Those books are as enjoyable as they are edifying, and they are my delight. I have a great desire to be enrolled in that society, and such a thing is quite impossible here, as there is no branch established in this section of the country. Will you enroll me and pay the penny a week for me? If you cannot do so, please ask the superior of our convent on Rue Boissac to do me this service, presenting to her my respects and the needs of my old age by way of excuse. I do not know her personally, but I count on her charity. Recommend me to the prayers of your dear religious daughter who lives near Our Lady of Fourvière, so that she may pray to that good Mother for me and also ask the prayers of her Sisters in the community. . . .

Although her infirmities kept her most of the time in her own little room or in the chapel, Mother Duchesne went faithfully and gladly to the community recreations. She loved conversation and talked well, for her mind was stored with interesting information and lively stories of the past, of personal experiences, and of people whom she had known in France, in Louisiana, and in Missouri. As the years passed, however, her voice became a mere whisper and only those who sat close to her could hear and enjoy what she said. It often happened that in good weather the community recreations were spent out of doors, where the religious walked for exercise and pleasure in the lanes and groves of elm and oak and maple on the convent grounds. Mother Duchesne spent these hours in the chapel, where she forgot her loneliness in prayer.

One of the pleasures she most enjoyed and was never asked to sacrifice was the visits of Father De Smet. He wrote about her and about his visits to her twenty years after her death:

> I keep the memory of Mère Duchesne in the highest respect and veneration. Her praise has been and is on the lips, not only of her own Sisters in religion, but of all those who had the honor and the happiness of her acquaintance. On every return from my Indian missionary visits, I deemed it a most agreeable duty to pay my respects to good Mother Duchesne, and I never returned from one of these visits but with an increase of edification, with a full conviction that I had conversed with a truly living saint. I always considered Mother Duchesne as the greatest protectress of our Indian missions. For years she offered two Communions a week and daily prayers for the conversion of the Indians. She loved these poor, benighted children dearly and nothing seemed to make her happier than to hear of their conversions, of their fervor and zeal in the practice of their religious duties after having entered the true fold of our Divine Redeemer. I entertain no doubt, many were brought over to the Holy Faith of Christ by the many acts of mortification she performed, and by the constant prayers she offered up for the salvation of these, her dearly beloved Indian children. . . .

In 1847, Father De Smet, on a begging tour in Belgium, visited the Convent of the Sacred Heart at Jette-Saint-Pierre. One of those who listened to him made notes of what he said:

> This holy missionary held us spell-bound for an hour as he told us of his distant missions. He also spoke of Mother Duchesne, whom he had seen a short time before this. He said she had climbed all the rungs of the ladder of sanctity, and never had he seen a soul more ardent in love for our Lord. In his opinion she rivaled St. Teresa. Never had he known a person who was poorer in all that concerned her private life, and in this she imitated St. Francis of Assissi; nor a more apostolic soul, eager for the salvation of souls, and he thought St. Francis Xavier had shared with her his zeal for the conversion of the infidels. As he ended his talk, he said: Now she is on the sorrowful way of Calvary to which old age and infirmities have condemned her; but, no matter how hard that road may seem to her, she is climbing it with all the fervor of youth. She has struck deep roots in American soil and they will one day

bear an abundant harvest. I should not be surprised, the Father said, if some day she were raised to our altars.

While there are no documents to prove the fact, it seems most probable that, from Canada, Mother Hamilton informed St. Madeleine Sophie of the distress which her silence was causing Mother Duchesne. When Mother Adele Cahier, then Secretary General, received a little letter from Philippine, she was surprised at the formal message in its closing lines: "I respect our Mother General's time too much to write to her. I beg you to offer her my regards and devoted affection, and the same to my very dear Father Joseph, the Assistant General, and Mother Thérèse."

For several months the Superior General had been wondering why she had not heard from Philippine again. Puzzled by this silence and by the reports she had received, Mother Barat determined to set all at rights by the most acceptable means in her power. She had granted Mother Amelie Jouve's request for service on the American mission and assigned her to the latest Canadian foundation. She was to sail from France late in July. Disregarding the geography of the route, Mother Barat directed her to make the journey from New York to Montreal by way of St. Charles, Missouri. Mother Jouve has left a brief, impersonal account of her meeting with Tante Philippine in September, 1847:

> That fortunate niece was received by Mother Duchesne as an angel from heaven. After reading the letter sent to her by our Reverend Mother General, who was her dearest friend, she seemed transported with joy. Tears flowed down her cheeks, and she was speechless with emotion. After a little while she exclaimed, "So our Mother General still thinks of me, still loves me? She has been so good as to show me that love by sending you to visit me?" She was radiant with joy.

More personal impressions occur in a letter written by Mother Jouve on September 14:

> I may say with Anthony that I have seen Paul in the desert. Yes, I have seen a great saint and one who is drawing near the end of her earthly pilgrimage. I found her very weak and her voice so feeble that it is hard to hear what she says. She received me like an angel come down from heaven. The cross has ever been her portion, and for some time past she has suffered intensely, believing that she had incurred our Mother General's displeasure. An ecstatic happiness lighted up her face when she read our Very Reverend Mother's letter and heard that she had sent me to St. Charles just

to see her. We had long talks about the past; the names of our Mothers and Sisters in France recurred over and over again, and the recollections of the early days of the Society.

And to St. Madeleine Sophie she wrote:

> You would be deeply touched, Reverend Mother, by the poverty of St. Charles. It could hardly be greater. Mother Duchesne's room is like a veritable sanctuary of this virtue. Certainly in the whole Society there is no one more poorly housed or clad or shod. Blessed Benedict Labre could claim her for his sister. And it is quite useless to argue with her in this matter—it is her *attrait*. I did, however, remove her Office book, which was in tatters, and substitute one that is somewhat less worn out.

To Mother Barat, Philippine herself wrote on September 10, after reading the letter and examining the many presents brought to her by Mother Jouve:

> Your letter and your gifts, my dear Mother, chosen with such exquisite taste, have been a life-giving balm to my soul. Oh, how I thank you and the God of all goodness for them! I was sorrowfully convinced that I had lost my place in your heart; and because I thought it was through some fault of mine, my own heart was the more grief-stricken. . . .
>
> God has favored me here with a room that is next to the chapel. I go from one to the other. My greatest happiness is to pray for the missions, for the Society, for you, my loved and venerated Mother, who hold God's place in my regard. . . .

After commenting on conditions in the Missouri convents and regulations that had been established in 1840, she continued: "All our American houses accepted respectfully the changes inaugurated by Mother Galitzin because they considered them as coming from you. At a word from you now I am sure they would return gladly to the old order of things."

During her visit Mother Jouve did her best to discover what would give pleasure to her dear old aunt, or what had caused her pain. Neither pleasure nor pain seemed of interest to her then. She had the assurance of the unaltered love of her dearest friend, and that was enough. At length, however, she admitted that there were two desires in her heart: the rescue of the picture of St. Regis from the attic at Florissant and the return of Mother Hamilton from Canada. The first desire was not difficult to fulfil. Mother St. Cyr was able to arrange with the Sisters of Loretto, then living in the convent of St. Ferdinand, to return the picture, and it was given a place of honor in the cloister chapel. The second request took longer to accomplish, and four years elapsed before Mother Duchesne had the satisfaction of welcoming Mother Hamilton back to St. Charles.

On a third point Mother Jouve reassured Mother Duchesne: somewhere a letter from St. Madeleine Sophie had certainly gone astray. "Whether lost or intercepted" [to use Mother Jouve's own words], she could not say, nor did she lay the blame for its disappearance on any individual. Letters had been lost before, even so important a letter as the one from Mother Barat recalling Philippine to France twelve or fifteen years before this. "Thinking that America could do without her for at least a few months, Mother Barat wrote, 'Come, my dear Philippine.' That invitation would have been an order for Mother Duchesne, but it never reached her. Pressing affairs supervened and she was directed by Paris not to make the trip if she had not already set out."

In her *Life* of St. Madeleine Sophie, Mother Adele Cahier writes: "It is impossible to say either how or why Mother Duchesne failed to receive Mother Barat's answer to her letters," but she blames no one. Mother Marjorie Erskine, in her beautiful volume on Mother Duchesne, brings out the fact that, after 1843, Philippine "relapsed into a silence which did not inspire Mother Barat to write," and moreover, "the Superior General would naturally write seldom to one whom she loved when that one was no longer in authority." This conclusion is borne out by the fact that in the years following Mother Jouve's visit in 1847 there were very few letters exchanged between them, and each complained that the other wrote so seldom.

One further point needs some elucidation in fairness to the religious, who, after Mother Duchesne herself, suffered most keenly as a result of this whole unhappy affair. The blame for having intercepted Mother Barat's letter, or letters, to Mother Duchesne was laid rashly on Mother Emilie St. Cyr, superior at St. Charles during the years 1845–1851, and this not after her death, but during her lifetime, and the insinuation cast a shadow over the last years of her life. The accusation appeared in Monsignor Louis Baunard's *Histoire de Madame Duchesne*, veiled in so transparent a statement that Mother St. Cyr's name might just as well have been printed on page 513. The book, published in 1878, appeared while Mother St. Cyr was still alive. More than once she declared in private conversation that she had never been guilty of so deceitful, so unthinkable a deed. When toward the close of her life she was asked to speak out in self-defense, she replied, "No, no! That cross was the hardest and the heaviest of my religious life. It has been my sanctification. Let's leave it buried in the Heart of Jesus." An answer worthy of a religious trained in the school of Philippine Duchesne!

Although Mother Jouve's visit to St. Charles lasted but two weeks, one of its most satisfying outcomes was the correspondence it initiated between Mother Duchesne and her niece. The first of Philippine's letters to Mother Jouve was written shortly after their parting:

> I received the letter you wrote to me from St. Louis. It was hard to see you leave me forever, for we can never hope to see each other again this side of heaven. So we must strive to reach there, you and I, but by such different paths—I doing nothing and you accomplishing great things for God through the education of youth. God has given you the necessary talents, and you must use them to produce a hundredfold in his service. But never forget that the road to heaven is the way of the cross. Jesus has called us to follow him, bearing the cross as he did. We have no choice about it—we must take it up and carry it if we are to be saved. . . . I made my retreat shortly after your departure. In it God seemed to give me only the cross, so beg for me the grace to know how to carry it well.

Mother Duchesne's joy in Amelie's visit would be difficult to describe, but it is reflected in her next letter to Madame Jouve, which contains quaint reassurances for the mother who had sacrificed this talented daughter to the cause of the American missions. Writing on December 12 she says:

> It would be very difficult for me to put into words the pleasure your daughter's visit gave. More than thirty years had passed since I had seen her, and during that time she has acquired much virtue. She gave me all the details that delighted me about our big family, most of whom I do not know now, but I often recommend them to God, all together and individually. I marvel at the merit of your sacrifice in consenting to the departure of that Sister and friend whom I had here for a little while. The whole community of St. Charles was delighted to see her and wanted to keep her always. And it was the same in St. Louis, a much larger house than that of St. Charles.
>
> Do not worry about her health. Canada is a very healthy place. All the Canadians I have ever met were quite robust, and our re-

ligious who bore the burden of the foundation there and several who were attacked by consumption and sent there are now in much better health than they were in either Missouri or Louisiana. And they have suffered less from the cold than we do in Missouri because the houses are built more solidly and are better heated. Except when they go out of doors, the boarding pupils wear the same kind of clothing in winter as in summer. Could they say that about Paris, which is at the same latitude?

Our first convent in Canada was situated too far from Montreal and so the boarding school did not prosper. . . . The second one, much larger, now has many pupils. It is called St. Vincent [on *Ile Jesus*]. That is where our dear Amelie is stationed. . . . A thousand affectionate messages to Madame de Rollin and my brother. Ask him to send me the rest of the Annals, from January, 1845, on. I did not know about your daughter's trip to America any sooner than you did.

In a long letter to Mother Amelie, Philippine gave small but telling space to herself when she wrote: "I have carried out your wishes and am well wrapped up day and night in the gifts our Mother General sent me. As to food, I am acting without scruple; and when I can eat my little piece of meat, I do so, making no secret of it. . . . Everyone loves you and prays for you." So Philippine thought she was making great concessions to nature by wearing a warm shawl by day and a woolen camisole by night, by eating a bit of meat prepared especially for her, and by taking a few other mild precautions during the rigorous winter season, but the religious who lived with her saw little change in the austere manner of life she prescribed for herself.

2. 1848—1852

THE YEAR 1848 brought Philippine fresh heart-suffering. News from France told of revolution in that country as well as others in Europe. It was, indeed, a year of revolutions, and the Religious of the Sacred Heart were among the victims of persecution in Italy, Piedmont, Switzerland, and France. As early as April 15, Philippine was asking her sister for news about her loved ones and about the homeland. Her note that day was short: "My eyesight has grown weaker this year," she wrote, "and varies from time to time. Today I can see very little." But her heart was full of the old affection, and she closed her letter with a touching phrase, *"Toute à toi, chère et tendre amie."*

She seems to have been gripped once more by the idea that it would be better for her to refrain from correspondence with friends, even members of her own family, in France. The revolution had cut off mail for a time; and when she heard from her sister in June, she immediately forwarded the letter to Mother Amelie, then confided to Madame Jouve:

> I have not written recently to my brother or to Cousin Josephine, not knowing where they were and fearing my letters might displease them. I have maintained the same reserve with regard to Madame Sophie, my highest Mother Superior, but you would give me pleasure if, being on the spot, you would find out where she is—they will know at Rue Boissac, Lyons—and write to her yourself. Tell her the convent at St. Ferdinand stood vacant a year and then was rented at a low price by the Sisters of Loretto, who are conducting a school there. As the house still belongs to us and a good deal of our furniture and chapel furnishings were left there, as if awaiting our return, we are eager to know whether we may take back that house for our religious who could come from France to live there. They could open an entirely French school. That language is well appreciated now, but it is difficult to learn it at the same time as English, for the children turn back to their native language continually. But no education is complete without a knowledge of French, and people are very eager about it. Try to do as I ask in this matter and get an answer for me. . . .

This renewed effort on the part of Philippine to establish a community of the Sacred Heart once more at Florissant was in line with the movement throughout the Society to offer a refuge to its members whom persecution had driven from their convents. The American religious were stretching out welcoming hands across the sea to their Sisters in Europe, and in Mother Duchesne's eyes no refuge could have been more suitable than the little home she had built more than a quarter-century before this on the frontier. Once more her plans were impractical, her efforts abortive.

A very personal heartache for her that summer was the news that Mother Boilvin's health had broken under the pressure of work and anxiety, and she, too, had been declared tubercular. For a time she tried to carry on her work at Eden Hall, the beautiful convent she had opened near Philadelphia in 1847, but she was obliged to give up at the close of the first scholastic year. Hoping a change in climate might save her, Mother Hardey took her to Canada and entrusted her to the care of Mother Amelie Jouve, who had been named superior at St. Vincent, Ile Jésus, that summer. Learning of these events Mother Duchesne wrote to Mother Jouve on August 30:

> See, my dearest Mother, how God gives joy to some and sorrow to others! I come in between. I do not rejoice to see you in a position of trust, but I bless God, who lets you dread the position of superior so that you may bear this burden with self-diffidence and lean on him for support. He is too good ever to leave you without support. Dear Mother Boilvin, who is with you now, went through the same trial, and the Jesuit Provincial, Father Elet, told me he had known few people more highly esteemed than she. . . . So say your *Fiat* generously.

On October 22 Philippine received the news of Mother Boilvin's death. Her short career of thirty-six years closed in a manner that reflected the courage and holiness of her consecrated life. In the little cemetery on Ile Jésus they laid to rest this "child of Florissant and daughter of Mother Duchesne in pioneer days, Julie Adeline Boilvin, one of America's most distinguished religious of the Sacred Heart." Then Mother Jouve sent a letter off to Tante Philippine, who replied immediately:

> The sad news of Mother Gonzague's death was not a surprise, but just the same it was a great sorrow. For me she was a support and a consolation, for the Society a valuable and edifying member, for God a docile child and a faithful spouse of the Sacred Heart. I am firmly assured of her present happiness after so holy a death, but it is sweet and consoling to think about her and recall her virtues as I fulfill toward her the obligation we have to pray for our deceased members.
>
> I received the letter in which you told me what a burden had been laid upon you, and I answered immediately, encouraging you to carry that burden with resignation. Happily God has smoothed your path by drawing to you the affection of all those with whom you live. That is what has been written to me from all sides. So take heart, since besides accomplishing the unmistakable will of God, you are able to contribute so easily to the prosperity and regularity of an institution that does so much good in a country where religion is still so highly honored and is so vital a force. . . . I greet all your community in the Heart of Jesus, for I love you all in the Sacred Heart and in him I am all yours. . . .

Through the winter of 1848–1849, Mother Duchesne worked

steadily with her needle for poor churches and for the missions. In the spring she sent a large package of her handiwork to Father De Smet, whose note of thanks touched her so deeply that she at once packed up another bundle, writing at the same time:

> It made me so happy to know that you had accepted the poor offerings of my making and had offered two Masses for my intention. I trust you will also accept what I am now sending you for the savages—two quilts, one of them made of little stars, and the other a larger one, and some small altar linens. It is the gift of a poor person, offered to the poor, who are the true friends of Jesus Christ. Your charity will overlook all the defects.

The courageous effort she must have expended on quilts and altar linens and knitted garments may be inferred from a letter to her sister at this time:

> Each time I send you a letter I think it is the last I shall write in this life. Old age tells me this, and today an illness stresses it with more certainty. This illness is a swelling that goes from one side of my body to the other, and when it attacks some vital spot, they say, it will end my life. I have been in this condition, more or less suffering, since the end of November. I am far from trying to escape death; indeed I would long for it, had I not so much reason to fear the Judgment, since even the just man has no assurance of his lot, as *God must judge even the just.* That thought is terrifying, so pray and ask others to pray for me. I do the same for you and your family. I may, however, drag on for a long time. God alone knows when the end will come. . . . *Adieu,* dear Sister. Oh, the happy day when we shall be together once more! Then all sorrows will end and we shall have eternal happiness in the Heart of our Savior, in whom I am your loving sister and friend. . . .

The terrible scourge of cholera that ravaged St. Louis and the great fire that wrought havoc on the waterfront filled Philippine with sorrow and distress and urged her to more insistent, more persistent, prayer. Between January and August, 1849, the epidemic claimed more than six thousand victims out of the sixty thousand inhabitants of the city. In the vicinity of Chouteau's Pond and the newly settled district beyond the Mill Creek the plague was at its worst. The panic of fear that seized upon the people was increased as a flood of refugees streamed in from the South, for the plague had infested almost the entire Lower Mississippi Valley. The City House had escaped the epidemic of former years, but in 1849 six religious and three children died in less than three weeks, while many others were dangerously ill.

When Bishop Kenrick insisted on a change of air for all the household, the majority of the community went with the orphans to St. Charles, where there had been no cases of the disease. "It would be difficult," wrote the chronicler of those days, "to describe the charity lavished on us during our weeks there. Dear and venerable Mother Duchesne could not do enough for us." Charity, self-denial, and prayer were her way, along with an insatiable zeal for souls. In her letter of July 29 to Mother Jouve her spirit shines through the phrases of encouragement she uses and the descriptions she gives, and there is a zest and freshness in her style quite remarkable in an octogenarian:

> In these times of epidemic and political upheaval, my dearest Mother, one really needs to draw consolation from one's friends. Our correspondence is carried on under great difficulties through the mail. It is easier to get an answer from France than from Canada. I expressed to Mother Hardey my anxiety about your discouragement under your difficult burden. She replied from Halifax that she had received a letter from you in which you seemed more resigned. I sympathize sincerely with you in your situation, but I cannot change it. Every day I pray to Divine Providence for you and invoke the loving care of the Sacred Heart of Jesus and of his holy Mother. They are my best assurance that all will turn out well for you. If you suffer, you also acquire merit, and by your resignation you can draw down graces on our Holy Father, on the Church, and on France, which is resting on a volcano. Let us realize that we are sinners and so have much to expiate, and that others less culpable than we are suffer much more than we do.
>
> St. Louis is the city that has suffered most cruelly from the ravages of the cholera. There were more than 100 deaths daily for a while, and some days 150 to 180. In a single week there were 900 deaths. Now the civil authorities are relieved when there are only about thirty deaths a week. But the epidemic has spread through the rural districts and is attacking people who have come recently from Europe. . . . We escaped the cholera, but it has ravaged the country around us. It is believed that the great fire, which destroyed 300 buildings on eight blocks and burned for several days afterwards, helped to increase the contagion. Try to form some idea of the poor who were left helpless and exposed to the weather and without food, etc. Of all the priests who worked day and night among the sick, not one died of the epidemic.

Having passed her eightieth birthday, Philippine wrote to her sister in a brisk and vigorous style, with a breadth of interest that ranged over Europe and America. It is easy to picture her rapt in prayer in the cloister chapel or bending intently over her needle-work, but to fancy her sitting at her window scanning a newspaper might seem far-fetched, did not her own words put the authentic stamp upon this sketch of herself.

I must answer two letters I have received from you, dearest Sister. . . . The second, written in July, gives me details about the June revolution. I knew about it through our newspapers, which are so common in the United States that even the workmen and servants receive their own copies of the papers. They are printed in small towns as well as cities, and the telegraph, which is remarkably widespread in this country now, brings European news quite rapidly. It comes to the East from England and France in a week, and those two countries get it from all parts of Europe. Our city of St. Louis has three gazettes, two being daily papers, printed on large sheets, and the third a weekly, printed on sheets three feet long.

The city of St. Louis has just furnished us with a terrible example of the punishments God sends down on those who break his law by excessive luxury, drinking, disregard for the sacredness of Sunday by manual work and non-attendance at Mass. First there was a great fire that destroyed thirty-six steamboats in all and three hundred buildings on the streets near the river. The fire broke out again and burned five more steamboats. This disaster was followed by cholera and dysentery. These two diseases carried off nearly 10,000 inhabitants of the city. . . . Next to St. Louis, the city most severely attacked by the plague was, I think, Cincinnati.

How earnestly I wish that the misfortunes of this deceitful world would bring my brother and my brother-in-law back to the service of God. Everyday I bring them in prayer to the foot of the altar. Our dear Amelie wrote me from Montreal that she had a visit from her youngest brother Eugene, who has settled in New York. She seems less burdened now by the office of superior, and she is greatly loved by her community. I hope she will be as good a superior as Constance is. . . .

During the cholera epidemic the President of the United States sent a message to every state in the Union, appointing the First Friday of August as a day of prayer, with all public works stopped, so that the people might humble themselves before God and obtain a cessation of the epidemic. This President, who was Zachary Taylor, commanded the American Army during the war with Mexico. He often took his relaxation with a Jesuit Father [Anthony Rey] who was chaplain of the Catholic troops, a very learned and perfect religious. He was killed by the savages whom he was trying to evangelize. . . . Find here, dearest Sister, the expression of my deep affection in the Hearts of Jesus and Mary.

An unexpected joy came to Mother Duchesne as the year 1849 drew to a close. Among the religious who came from France that year was one to whom Mother Barat entrusted a letter—the first, it would seem, that she had written to Philippine since the one sent by Mother Jouve in 1847. It is not difficult to picture the old nun kneeling close to the sanctuary railing in the cloister chapel and reading:

> I am so happy, my dear, good Mother, to think that Mother Guinand may have the consolation of seeing you and giving you our affectionate personal messages. She will tell you, dear Mother and old daughter of mine, that you are always in my prayers and that we often think of you and speak about you, especially to our young religious in order to rouse their zeal for the salvation of souls and their generosity and willingness to sacrifice all for the love of Jesus Christ. But alas, we get little response from them. Strong vocations are becoming rare, and parents raise so many obstacles. . . . The reason is that our life requires so much sacrifice, and health is much weaker now than formerly. Pray then with us, dear Mother, in order to obtain from the Sacred Heart of Jesus strong and generous souls like those our dear Master gave us at the beginning of the Society. . . .
>
> What a long time has passed, dear Mother, without any news from you! My heart is eager to hear from you. When you have an opportunity, give us details about all that is of interest to us. If you are in need of anything, my loved friend, I shall be so happy to send it to you. *Adieu,* dear good Mother. Be assured of my deep affection for you in C.J.M. . . .

Philippine's answer was a cry of gratitude and joy, but she admitted that she was often lonely and depressed, for old age was, she thought, a sad time. Her weakening eyesight cut her off from the reading and sewing with which she loved to fill her days. "But God is good," she added to Mother Barat, "always so good. I have the consolation of spending my time in silence close to the chapel. By the grace of God I am still able to be up and around. Every day I assist at two or three Masses and almost every day our Lord admits me to his holy Table."

Holy Communion often transfigured her. Those who saw her were struck by the glow that radiated from her countenance during her thanksgiving after Communion. As they left the chapel, the children often waited to curtsey to her in reverent silence; then they whispered to one another, "Mother Duchesne is still praying." Sometimes the radiance was noticed by people in the church who saw her kneeling at the altar railing to receive Holy Communion. "I never saw anything like it," said one old man to a member of the community. "Mother Duchesne is a saint," and he described the light he had seen shining from her.

In February, 1850, she was again writing to Father De La Croix at the bidding of Father Van Assche: "He would like a bell for the church at St. Ferdinand, weighing about 1000 pounds, and in spite of my repugnance to begging from you, he insisted that I be his agent in this matter. Please let me know whether you can satisfy his desire." At the close of this long, chatty letter giving news of the Indian missions, the twelve convents of the Sacred Heart now in America, the fire and the cholera, and the failure of St. Louis to reform its morals after such punishments, she adds a few lines about herself:

> I have now reached my eighty-first year, and I have been in America thirty-one years. How little I have accomplished for our good Master! Pray to him for me and please offer a Mass for me that I may have a happy death. I now have as superior, Mother St. Cyr, whom you knew at St. Ferdinand and at Opelousas. Give us both your blessing for the love of the Heart of Jesus.

She had been busy that winter and spring preparing useful articles of clothing and sacristy supplies for missionaries and wrote to offer them to Father De Smet. The month of May was drawing to a close when he paid a visit to St. Charles in company with Father Christian Hoecken, another kind friend of Mother Duchesne and a great missionary. They were still at St. Charles when she wrote on May 30 to Mother Jouve:

> We have just been visited by Mother Cutts. She left us this morning and will leave St. Louis in a week. She begged us to pray for the health of our religious in the South . . . for workers are lacking for the harvest. St. Michael's has 140 pupils, Opelousas 110, Natchitoches 100, including the day pupils in the academy. I do not know the numbers in the other houses. . . .
>
> Here at St. Charles for the past two days visitors at the Jesuit residence have procured for us six Masses each day. One Mass was offered for my intention. I made the responses at another, kneeling between two altars [one in the church, the other in the chapel], where the Holy Sacrifice was being offered by our two greatest missionaries, Father De Smet, who has four times crossed the continent from here to the Pacific and has visited the native tribes in that area, and Father Hoecken, who is so skilled in the native languages he can speak twelve or fifteen, but he longs to undertake

new conquests. Fancy my delight to find myself between these two saints whose charity toward me is so great that they often offer the Holy Sacrifice of the Mass for me. You would do well to procure from Paris the books on the missions by Father De Smet. They are printed in Lille, and also in Flanders, I think. He presented me with two volumes, each a separate work. I rarely get any news from my family; you must certainly have heard more recently than I. . . . Share this letter with Mother Hamilton, if she is still at St. Jacques. . . .

In 1850 the Religious of the Sacred Heart were preparing to celebrate their fiftieth year of corporate existence. But that year of jubilee was marked by sorrow, for in April Father Joseph Varin died. Mother Barat announced this loss to the whole Society in a circular letter of April 19, and the European convents received the news promptly. But mail to America was still slow at times and often uncertain. Mother Barat's letter had been nearly two and a half months on the way and had not reached Missouri when Philippine wrote to her on June 30:

My beloved and venerated Mother,
I answered the letter you sent me by Mother Guinand. I have not had the pleasure of meeting her yet, but she has written to me. I did not know how to contain my joy on reading your letter, nor can I express my gratitude for your gifts. I tried to do so in my letter to you, but I could find no satisfactory words. So I must continually present to God the debt I owe you in order that he may pay it for me. I wrote to you a second time, but the last letter I received from you was that of September, 1849. I am certainly privileged to receive letters from you, as I have become perfectly useless. Charity alone can prompt you to write to me.
When I learned how the health of Reverend Father Varin was failing, I hoped we would receive letters keeping us informed about his condition. But it was in a Kentucky newspaper that I learned of his death. In that paper he was called the author of our *Constitutions*. How many memories his death has awakened! How much gratitude I owe him—a debt I could never repay! How deeply I sympathize with my venerated Mother, who had already been so sadly tried by the loss of a brother who was her support! Only your great soul could bear the weight of so much sorrow, along with all the disasters caused by the revolutions. . . .
We are very eager to have Mother Hamilton back. She has a special talent for handling the parish sodalities. She was loaned only for a year, and she has been gone three years. The two Canadian convents are prospering after the initial trials, and in general so are

those in the United States. Our convent now has as many religious and pupils as it can care for. There is some talk of an addition, and this is badly needed for the sake of health. . . .

It is evident that Mother Duchesne was wide awake to all that was happening at St. Charles and interested in all that concerned the growth of the Society in America. Because her character is so clearly revealed in her letters, a great many of them have been cited in this narrative of her life. Her virtues were graphically sketched by Mother Jouve, who gathered information from the religious who were closest to Mother Duchesne during the years of her pioneering in the face of almost insuperable difficulties. Hence Mother Jouve's pen-portrait of her is of far greater value than any twentieth-century analysis or commentary.

Among the many virtues which were so noticeable in Mother Duchesne, these, she thought, were most promient: her devotion to the Sacred Heart in the Blessed Sacrament, her love of poverty, her deep humility, her self-denial and penance, her zeal for the salvation of souls, and her charity. This brief enumeration shows how "of a piece" was the development of her sanctity. The seeds of these virtues were planted in girlhood; they grew to strong and vigorous maturity under the action of divine grace during her active life in France and America; they yielded a hundredfold of harvest in the last decade of her life at St. Charles.

Describing that development, Mother Jouve stresses the fact that Tante Philippine was of a naturally serious disposition, yet she was always joyous and animated at the community recreations or when the religious came for little visits with her in her room. This attitude was the more meritorious because she was often at grips with spiritual trials, her soul submerged in dryness, bitterness, and an overwhelming sense of worthlessness. By reason of her natural disposition toward self-contempt and an exaggerated notion of personal responsibility for all that went amiss around her, "she was her own heaviest cross." In spite of her constant efforts to learn meekness and humility from the Heart of Christ, God left her with a certain brusqueness of manner that betrayed itself at times in the tone of her voice, the impetuosity of her actions, the roughness that frequently damaged the very things she was using or making. She misplaced the things she needed, forgot the things she had promised to do, spoke hastily at times. But never did she allow such faults to pass without reparation. Her apologies to her Sisters or to the community were but a shadow of the contrition which filled her soul and prostrated her in humblest self-annihilation before God. But long before her life drew to its close she had so conquered self that those who lived with her spoke only of her sweetness, her gentleness, her patience, her humble gratitude for the least service, and above all her spirit of prayer.

Into her sanctity there were welded depths of thought and sacrifice and union with God, self-renunciation and supernatural living of which the world can understand very little, depths, too, of calm and peace and joy which the world can never give. She judged herself severely. At times she was crushed with sorrow for sin, not only her own little faults of frailty that loomed so large in her eyes, but also the sins of the world, especially of that little world of hers on the Missouri frontier. The norms of ordinary life were never hers. Faith—living, active, informed by charity—led her to ever greater purity of intention and delicacy of conscience. In Father Peter Verhaegen she found a spiritual guide who understood and who was prepared to help her in the final stage of her ascent to God.

The ladder by which she continually made that ascent was prayer of adoration and love in the presence of the Blessed Sacrament. Prayer was her life, but she lived that prayer-life in a simple, yet heroic, way. At times she seemed to be struggling through a desert land, yet she had always the living water of grace to quench her thirst, and she drew that living water from its fountain-head, the Blessed Sacrament. In the years of her active life sun and shadow had fallen unpredictably across her days, but the long hours of her nightly vigils before the tabernacle had steadied her course. In the last obscure years, as she looked forward to the day that knows no declining, the privilege she stressed most frequently in her letters was that of living close to the Blessed Sacrament; the occupation she loved best was needlework for the sanctuary. Both her work and her prayer were worship, for that was the paramount purpose of both—not personal perfection or growth in holiness, but the worship and love of the Heart of Jesus tabernacled in the Blessed Sacrament.

> During the last years of her life [wrote Mother Jouve], when she was free to follow the attraction of her soul, she seldom left the chapel on days of Exposition of the Blessed Sacrament. One day a young religious, fearing that Mother Duchesne was exhausting her strength by her long hours of prayer, knelt beside her and asked in a low voice, "Mother, won't you come to your room to rest for just a little while?" The old nun looked at her with a smile and

whispered, "Sister, could one grow tired when she is with our Lord?"

As it was from the tabernacle that she had drawn her strength and her inspiration in the years of heaviest labor, so in the years of utter weakness she found there both courage and the power to endure the physical exhaustion that was so great a trial. From the experienced reality of the Sacramental Presence she had learned to embrace the reality of God's will, expressed in every circumstance and event of life. And as she approached her eighty-first birthday, life was still very interesting to her. She was still writing lengthy letters to old friends like Father De La Croix, filling them with statistics, which she loved, in order to spread a numerical panorama of some sections of Catholic development in America. The pupils of her earliest mission days were remembered, too, and mentioned lovingly.

In August Philippine learned of the death of her last surviving brother-in-law, Constans de Mauduit. He had long been the object of her daily prayers, she told her sister, and she was consoled by the news of his return to God and reception of the sacraments. She was concerned about her nephew Eugene, who seemed to be roving the American continent, and she wrote to his mother on August 4:

> He has gone to Mexico, whence I fear he will proceed to California, where the rage for gold is attracting crowds of people. But I believe what was stated in a letter from that part of the world recently—that for one person who makes a fortune, five hundred are impoverished and have not even enough money to pay their way home, for extravagance, dancing, and entertainments of all kinds are to be found side by side with suffering and extreme misery. . . .
>
> Do not worry about my health; it is as good as could be expected when one is past eighty years old. You and I are closely united, being nearly the same age and having been bound to each other not only by family ties but by the closest friendship. I am all yours in the Sacred Heart.

News of the death of Josephine de Savoye-Rollin reached Philippine on November 8 in a letter from her brother. "Mother of the poor and my closest friend," she called her, when writing next day to Mother Jouve, but there was no further comment, except a wistful sentence: "God, who saw that her soul was ready for heaven, took from her the consciousness of her approaching end, for she had always feared death." She apologized for scribbling so badly that day, and blamed this on her weakened eyesight, but undoubtedly the hot tears had welled up from her loving heart at the mention of her beloved Josephine.

The Society of the Sacred Heart celebrated its golden jubilee on November 21, 1850. Mother Barat was then in Rome on important business that concerned the whole order. It now counted two thousand and fifty-five religious, living in sixty-five convents scattered through France, Italy, Belgium, Austria, England, Ireland, Canada, and the United States. Such an organization could no longer be directed as a whole by the Superior General, even with the aid of Mothers holding the title of visitatrix and reporting on conditions in the houses they inspected. The necessity of dividing the houses into provinces which would be under provincial superiors was patent, but the refusal of the Holy See to allow this in 1842 made the reintroduction of the subject a very delicate matter. However, when a commission of cardinals examined the proposal in the spring of 1851, an affirmative answer was given. Pope Pius IX preferred the title *Mothers Vicar* to that of *Provincials* for the superiors who were to be placed in charge of the divisions of the Society, and these divisions were, therefore, called *vicariates*. Thus the "finishing touches" were given to the Constitutions of the Society during the lifetime of Philippine Duchesne.

Early in 1851 she began to experience sudden attacks of weakness which she feared might so incapacitate her as to make her a burden to the community. Telling Mother Jouve of this, she added: "I should like to write also to Mother Hamilton. Never before has she been silent with me for such a long time. But at the age of eighty-two I experience great fatigue from writing, and I console myself with the thought that she may be en route to join us here." When Easter came and there was no indication of Mother Hamilton's return, Philippine wrote to Mother Barat:

> Last year I heard that you were going to Rome and that we should not write to you except in a case of real necessity. So I kept silence. But I can no longer force myself to keep silence, since I hear that our Reverend Visitatrix, Mother Cutts, has been ill for a long time at St. Michael's, and they think she cannot possibly come for her visit this year.
>
> We have reached the end of Mother St. Cyr's term of superiority. This being so, we had hoped to be governed once more by Mother Hamilton, who was loved by all because of her many virtues. Here, as in St. Louis, we need a superior who can speak English, for

visitors always ask for the superior. True, Mother Hamilton dreads going to the parlor and still more being superior, for she is very scrupulous. But the big obstacle to her return seems to be the need they have of her at St. Jacques in Canada, where only a French person or one who speaks French can govern the house. . . . My beloved Mother, I am growing very old. Be so good as to help me to prepare for death by a little message of the sweet and touching kind you alone can give. I implore you to sustain this house of St. Charles. . . .

In a little letter of June 12 she admitted to her niece that she was not able to write just then to Madame Jouve: "I beg you to explain to her why I do not write. . . . My mind is greatly confused and my body very weak." She suffered severely from the prostrating summer heat, but there was no evidence of mental confusion in the letter which she addressed to Mother Barat on August 18, 1851, and which ended with these paragraphs:

After telling you our problems, I beg you to sustain this house. Do not treat it as Florissant was treated. In spite of all the difficulties, we shall always have day pupils who pay a little, the poor children who have no other chance for education, and some boarding pupils from the vicinity and even from St. Louis, as we have at present, and they pay very well. All the American houses lament their lack of religious to carry on the work. The reason is that the time of aspirantship is too long, and as a result the candidates for religious life go to other orders.

If you could see the pretty place we have here, standing beside the church, as it does, you would not have the courage to take it from us, even if there were only four of us to carry on the work. . . . Mother Bathilde, who came for a visit with us and with whom I had long talks yesterday, told us confidentially that she is leaving us soon. She spoke to me of all the crosses you have carried. I sympathize with you sincerely, but I beseech you, take mine away by safeguarding the existence of this, our first dwelling place in America. . . . Pardon the condition of my letter; so much has been against me—pen, ink, etc.

Philippine's plea for St. Charles was heard, though she did not receive an answer immediately. She had news, however, that brought great joy to her affectionate heart—Mother Hamilton was returning to St. Charles. How soon she did not know, but she told her "dearest Amelie" in October:

I saw in a letter from Mother Regis that she had visited you at St. Vincent, but she has been delayed in New York on account of some business. I am writing to thank you for all your kindness to me. I have not written often recently—old age makes it impossible— and I have been hoping that Madame Jouve and my brother keep you posted with regard to our family. Madame Teisseire is very near death, if she is not already in eternity. She dreaded death, and it is a time in which we need many prayers. I beg you earnestly to procure them for her. I am growing very old, gradually losing my memory and my strength. Perhaps you will not receive another letter from me. I hope I shall always have your prayers and those of your dear community, to whom I recommend myself. . . .

Mother St. Cyr appended a little note to this letter to say:

I hope, dear Mother, that you will excuse me for not writing. Let me assure you that only a lack of time has prevented me from doing so. . . . The weakness of our holy Mother Duchesne keeps us in fear, but her fervor and regularity encourage us in the practice of virtue. Pray for her—pray for us all.

Mother Hamilton reached St. Charles in November and the convent journalist noted: "Our holy and venerated Mother Duchesne's declining days seem to have acquired renewed animation and vigor from the sight of her loved and devoted daughter, Mother Regis Hamilton." Soon Mother Hamilton was happy to be able to tell Mother Jouve:

You know that I am now back at St. Charles with my holy Mother Duchesne, who, instead of saying her Nunc Dimittis, is almost rejuvenated. When I first saw her, the day I arrived, scarcely able to walk or to make herself heard, I was overcome with indescribable sadness. She asked me if I wanted to sleep in her room. Fancy my joy! I prepare her for bed at night; I help her dress in the morning; and I care for her as best I can, but not as I should like to; for she still has the idea that she must do penance, and she considers everything too good for her. The result is that we sometimes have little arguments. Now I win and now I lose. . . .

Through the winter and the spring of 1852 the community at St. Charles was in constant admiration at the change brought about in Mother Duchesne by the tender care given her by her devoted nurse. Those who had lived at the City House in the years when Mother Hamilton had so often been dangerously ill and Philippine had expended on her all the practical skill she had acquired through nursing the sick over more than thirty years, now saw the picture reversed and Regis sparing no effort to bring some strength back into the worn and wasted body that housed the ardent soul of her loved Mother in Christ. They often talked about the happenings in France that winter at La Ferrandière, where the Seventh General Council of the Society was being held. Its special purpose was to insure uniform observance of *Rule* and *Constitutions* as they were interpreted before 1839, to promulgate the modifications in government allowed by the Holy See in May, 1851, and to organize the Society's sixty-five convents into ten vicariates, two of them in America. Reverend Mothers Hardey and Cutts, who had represented the American houses at the council, were appointed to the office of vicar, the former to direct the nine convents in the eastern section of the United States and Canada, the latter the seven in the Mississippi Valley. To Mother Cutts, St. Madeleine Sophie entrusted her letter of February 18, 1852, for her loved "old daughter" Philippine.

> Our Mothers leave tomorrow, dear, good Mother [she wrote], to return to their dear Mission. I am sure Mother Cutts will hasten at once to visit you, to talk to you about the Society and your old friends who treasure such an affectionate memory of you. Above all, she will tell you how consoling our reunion was and, I hope, how profitable for the whole Society. I am sure this will be one of the consolations of your old age.
>
> My dear Philippine, confidence in the Society is increasing; the order is spreading in almost all parts of the world; and from all sides we receive requests which we must refuse. Ah, if we only had Mothers as zealous and selfless as those who first went into the land where you now live, we would not need so many religious for each house, and foundations could be made more easily. Pray, then, dear and loving Mother, pray earnestly that our sweet Master may have mercy on the souls who call for us and may send us apostles according to his own Heart. He will listen to you, I am sure, dear old daughter of mine, for you have always understood so clearly the value of souls and have never recoiled before an obstacle when Jesus summoned you to their aid. . . .

This letter reached St. Charles in mid-April, and Philippine set herself to the congenial, but now very difficult, task of answering it at great length. Her heart was full of joy, her mind alert to all that concerned the community and school, the Indian mission, and the whole Society. She was certainly very much herself as she wrote on April 22, 1852:

> I was astonished and greatly consoled on receiving your letter. Since Easter of last year I have not been expecting to live another twelve months; especially during last summer there were times

when I could not even write my own name. When the weather got cool, that gave me back some strength, but my memory has been failing more and more, and also my eyesight. God gave me a great joy in the return of Mother Hamilton. For a long time hearts and arms had been reaching out to welcome her. The religious who knew her before had often been tempted to beg for her return, and those who had not known her rejoiced in the Lord, and all are very happy after many trials that had resulted from disappointed hopes. The Jesuit Fathers esteem her highly and are delighted; the boarding pupils are more attached to her than to her predecessors, and so are our friends outside the convent. All this is a subject for thanksgiving to God, who lifts us up after casting us down by trials.

The charity of our Mother Superior is a wonderful example for all. She sleeps in the same room with me, and this gives her an opportunity to exercise her charity. She has also had still more opportunities because of the illness and death of one of our Sisters and a pupil; they were buried at the same Requiem service.

We have enrolled a good number of new pupils, but we cannot take more than thirty-five without being overcrowded and risking fresh cases of illness. There is real need for an addition to the building; and since I am so useless, I have begged God to take me to himself, as that would give place for two more people. If the convent in St. Louis could help, the addition could be built quite easily.

My love for the savages urges me to describe to you the progress of the school we have in their midst. It is greatly retarded by a lack of teachers, but there are none to send. All the American houses are begging for religious. Mother Lucille Mathevon wrote me that she has more than sixty pupils in her boarding school. There are four lay teachers (half-breeds) who help the nuns and who have religious vocations. The Government pays for the upkeep of all who are needed at the mission, both priests and religious, and of a certain number of pupils, both boys and girls. Funds for the support of the others come from the sale of surplus produce from the immense property given to the establishment, or from tuitions paid by the Indian parents. The lands are being cultivated, and this past year they had an abundance of corn to sell, more than sixty head of cattle, and plenty of vegetables.

It would be very easy to train, right there, both teachers and religious who would be assigned to that mission and later on to other missions where they are needed. Should such holy people be deprived of religious life just because they have Indian blood? For the most part they have as good minds as the white people, and they are capable of high sanctity. Recently there was a scourge of small pox, which is very terrible when it attacks the savages. The vast majority of those who had it died like saints. Spiritual help is abundant there. The mission is now the residence of the bishop of all that territory [Bishop Miège, S.J.]. Five or six Jesuit priests reside there, and eight Brothers carry on the farming and other work, and they teach and aid the savages. They, too, receive support from the Government. . . .

I know very few people who have the happiness of seeing you now, but I am eager to recommend myself to Mothers Des-maraquest, Thérèse, and Constance Jouve, whom I knew only as a child. My letter is very badly written, but I cannot see to rewrite it. I have strength, however, to kneel in spirit at your feet to receive your blessing with all possible love and respect in the Heart of Jesus. . . .

Summer came on gently that year and June was pleasant. Early in July, Philippine received a letter from her sister which she hastened to answer, not knowing that the Jouve family in Lyons was in great sorrow over the death of Mother Constance Jouve at Chambery on June 15 at the age of forty-five.

Yesterday, my dearest Sister [wrote Philippine on July 7], I received a letter from you that was written in January. This surprised me very much, for letters reach us now without delay. No doubt God willed that I should feel not only the absence of my loved ones, but also that of news from them. One must be resigned. For us there remain only the sufferings of old age, in addition to the events of life that are contrary to our desires. At our age we should like to enjoy peace, tranquility, and the sweet pleasures of friendship, and yet we must bear our burden of years along with the suffering that comes from unhappy events, whether in public affairs or in our personal lives.

I am surprised that you are obliged to complain about silence on the part of your dear daughter Amelie, though everyone accuses her of laziness in the matter of letter-writing. But she is very active in her convent. They sing her praises loudly and all goes well. She rarely writes to me, while formerly I did not need to be urged to write, but I sometimes think it best to stop writing letters lest I appear ridiculous. This was especially true last summer, when I lost both memory and intelligence for a time. But instead of dying during the winter, which was very severe, I found myself stronger when spring came, and now I have stopped calculating when I shall meet death. It will be when God wills. Old age has many sacrifices to make, and it can be a period of great value as one's purgatory. It will certainly be a less rigorous one than that of the next life.

After telling Madame Jouve that the "mission for the savages is doing very well," she gives a long paragraph about it, closing with a sentence about the death of her good friend, Father Christian Hoecken: "Last year the outstanding missionary, who could speak fourteen or fifteen Indian dialects as well as several civilized languages, died of cholera, which he contracted while attending victims of the epidemic. Another [Father Bax] is at the gates of death in the Osage mission. These are great losses." The last sentence of this letter shows the union and charity that made community life so happy under Mother Hamilton's guidance: "There is no one in this community who knows you, but charity makes us all pray for the loved ones of those whom we love in religious life, so you have a share in all our prayers."

With characteristic determination Philippine resolved to make the retreat with the community, though the weather had become very hot and humid and she was oppressed and very restless. "I thought it was my duty to begin my retreat," she told Mother Barat. "I spent most of each day in the chapel, and I grew wearier every day. Our confessor told me I did not need to apply my mind to the meditations, and I felt that myself." As forgetfulness and mental lapses became more frequent, Mother Hamilton grew alarmed and called the doctor.

> The doctor [wrote the patient herself a few days later] discovered that I had very high fever, but I did not mind that so much as having lost my head for a while. In order to be able to face my present condition and the prospect of losing my mental balance, I really must hold firmly to the conviction that God does everything for our good. Everything possible is being done for me. Mother Hamilton sleeps in my room and attends lovingly to my every need. I meet with utmost kindness from all my Sisters, and I ask you to include them all in the prayers I beg for myself, especially from our Mothers whose names I cannot recall, for all names escape me now. I humbly beg pardon for all the suffering I have caused you. I do not think I shall do so again. . . .

On August 16 the dear old invalid was so weak that she asked for the last sacraments. Father Verhaegen came and anointed her. She thanked him with a radiant smile. Next day she was better and penned three little notes with a firm hand. That was a triple *adieu* to all she loved best in this world—the Society and its holy foundress, her family, and the Indian missions. To Mother Barat she wrote:

According to all appearances this is the last time I shall be able to write to you. Yesterday I received the last sacraments, but God may still keep me waiting for the happiness of seeing him. The mental wanderings I was suffering from were caused by a high fever that I was going about with all the time. At present I do not know when the end will be, but I come once more to kneel at your feet, beg your pardon, and assure you of my loving veneration.

To her sister her pen was again the interpreter of her heart:

I have just received a letter from you, my dear, loving Sister, which I must hasten to answer. Yesterday I received the last sacraments. I am leaving you with sorrow because you are so alone. But God has promised the hundredfold to those who leave father and mother for his sake, and you deserve the hundredfold, too, for your sacrifices have been far greater than those your children made. You share in the merit of all the good works they accomplish. Courage, then. One is always richer for having made sacrifices for God. Have your pious children pray for me. I carry into eternity with me the memory of them and of you. *Adieu,* loving and dear Sister.

Philippine

Father De Smet was in St. Louis when he received her little note of August 17:

Your kindness toward me in the past gives me the assurance that I shall see that kindness continue to the end of my life. Yesterday I received the last sacraments, and I hope you will not forget me in your prayers. If you do me the favor of asking prayers for me, that will be a great charity. Will you please write to Reverend Father de Coen for me? He will not forget me, either. If God is merciful to me, you will have a large share in my prayers. I beg your blessing and I am your humble servant,

Philippine Duchesne

From St. Louis University Father De Smet answered, assuring her of his prayers and those of all the Jesuits in the vicinity. When she had regained a little more strength, she wrote again to Father De Smet:

Your touching letter filled me with gratitude. God must be very good indeed to give me an intercessor like you. Thank you a thousand thousand times for the Masses offered to God for my poor soul, which I beg you to protect with your prayers, for if God sees fit to prolong my life in the midst of infirmities of both soul and body, I shall be exposed to many temptations. This is why I have recourse to your charity, that it may not abandon me in the midst of temptations to which a long old age exposes one. If God has mercy on me, I shall not fail in the duty of gratitude which I owe to you on so many counts.

I am with deep respect your humble servant,

Philippine Duchesne
who attained her 83rd year on
August 29.

It was evident to Mother Hamilton and the community that Mother Duchesne was growing weaker every day. Neither the medical attentions of Dr. Behrens nor the mixtures he prescribed could check the gentle ebbing of her life. The convent stock of remedies was replenished: elder flowers, slippery elm bark, powdered Virginia snake root, orange peel and gentian, quinine, cordial, claret and honey, a pint of French brandy—all purchased for the sick. But the invalid preferred a little milk.

Every morning at the hour for Mass she came into the chapel, almost carried by the religious who helped her, and took her seat close to the sanctuary railing. It was the Mass that mattered, and Holy Communion was her "Daily Bread." Feeble, tottering, bent, her gaunt frame clothed in patched garments, her once luminous eyes now dimmed, she might have evoked pity from a stranger who saw her seated there. But her Sisters in religion looked on her with awed love and veneration, knowing the truth of which she was unconscious, reverencing the sanctity of which she was unaware. Her message to them, though unspoken, was a message of lively faith. She had put God first in her life because she had realized with astounding clarity that He *is* first, and also last— Alpha and Omega—and that between Him and all else in the universe there is, there can be, no comparison.

After the Holy Sacrifice she was taken back to her little room, to spend the day in quiet communing with God. She could no longer sew or read; she could only rest in the Heart of Christ and lose herself completely in God's will. Each afternoon she went to the chapel for adoration. Her prayer was a quiet looking and listening, the restless mind stilled, the eager will satisfied, petitions laid before the Master in faith and confidence and at once abandoned to His will. "*Je ne suis rien, je ne puis rien, je ne sais rien,*" was more than a quotation copied into her breviary. It was a conviction lived and loved. Her nothingness was a reality in her own mind, for she had given her all to God and fashioned the offering in a prayer she had written in a spiritual notebook years before, a prayer she had lived through nearly thirty-five years on the American frontier:

> O my God, I desire to live as a victim offered in a spirit of penance and love. Then let me prepare all that is needed for a sacrifice of love whose perfume will rise even to the Heart of Jesus. May my *whole being* be the victim, all that I am and all that I have. May my own *heart* be the *altar*, my *separation* from the world and all earthly pleasures the sacrificial *knife*. May my love be the consuming *fire*, and my yearning *desires* the *breeze* that fans it. Let me pour on it the *incense* and *perfume* of all virtues, and to this mystical sacrifice let me bring *all that I cling to*, that I may offer all, burn all, consume all, keeping back nothing for self. O Divine Love, my very God, accept this sacrifice which I desire to offer You at every instant of my life.

Tuesday, November 16, was a dismal day of torrential rain, biting wind, and penetrating cold. Mother Duchesne wished to rise as usual to assist at Mass, but she was so weak that Mother Hamilton forbade her to do so, and she obeyed. During the course of the morning a carriage drove up to the house, there was an unaccustomed stir, and Mother Hamilton came to tell her that visitors had arrived just to see her—Mother Cutts and Mother Anna Du Rousier, who was representing the Superior General as visitatrix in America. She had come to bring a last message to Philippine from Mother Barat. On learning this the dying nun gripped her visitor's hand and begged a blessing, which Mother Du Rousier gave in the name of St. Madeleine Sophie. In turn she asked a blessing from Mother Duchesne, who raised her thin hand and traced a cross on the forehead of the Mother Visitatrix. "I still seem to feel that cross," Mother Du Rousier often said afterwards, "and I trust it to bring me happiness." When someone suggested that Mother Duchesne should offer her sufferings for the Mother Visitatrix's work, Philippine answered quickly, "But I am not suffering." "Then offer your privations, Mother." "Yes, I will offer them," she said, and her feeble voice was steady and grave.

On the following day she was decidedly weaker, and a dry, persistent cough gave her no rest. Mother Hamilton was constantly at hand to give her a little soothing drink. Toward midnight when she presented the cup, Mother Duchesne refused, fearing to break her Eucharistic fast. "Take it," urged Mother Hamilton, "it is not yet midnight." "Are you very sure?" asked Philippine in a tone that brought tears to her nurse's eyes—for it was the Philippine of younger days checking on her religious daughter.

In the chill hour before the dawn, Father Verhaegen made his way from the rectory to the church and prepared to bring Holy Communion to the invalid. The community had already gathered in the cloister chapel for prayer. When Sister Couture kindled a little fire in the room, Mother Duchesne said reproachfully, "You think only of material things. It would be better to say a *Pater* and an *Ave* for the good of my soul." Mother Hamilton then told her the religious were all praying in the adjoining room. "Oh," she exclaimed, "how fortunate I am to die in a house where such charity reigns!" The tinkle of a little bell announced the coming of the priest to hear her last confession and give her the Viaticum. Then he returned to the altar to offer the Holy Sacrifice. Later in the morning he came to anoint her again, for she was sinking rapidly. Yet when she heard the invocation, "Jesus, Mary, Joseph," she could answer audibly, "I give you my heart, my soul, and my life—oh, yes—my life, generously." As the noonday Angelus ceased ringing, that eighteenth day of November, 1852, the heroic life of Philippine came to an end.

They laid her in a plain deal coffin, made by the village carpenter, and watched beside her in silent joy and grief. They chanted the Office for the Dead in the chapel and left her alone before the tabernacle for her last night of vigil. Father Verhaegen offered the funeral Mass in the Church of St. Charles Borromeo, with many priests in the sanctuary and an unexpected crowd of friends filling the pews. After the requiem service she was laid to rest in the cemetery on the hillside, and the pastor returned to the sacristy to record the burial. He had known the vigor of her early years at Florissant, the suffering and humiliation of the years in St. Louis, and the pathos of her helplessness in the Indian encampment, the obscurity of her last years at St. Charles. He had known the inmost secrets of her soul and could say, "She was a perfect religious, and as far as I can judge, she never lost her baptismal innocence." Now that death had led her into eternal life he wrote:

On the 20th of November, 1852, I, the undersigned, buried the mortal remains of Madame Philippine Duchesne, professed religious of the Society of the Sacred Heart, aged 83 years.

Madame Duchesne was a native of France, and came to the United States of America with a small number of religious of the Society of the Sacred Heart in 1818. She may be considered the foundress of all the houses of the Sacred Heart in the United States. Eminent in all virtues of religious life, but especially in

EPILOGUE | *Sanctity on the Frontier*

CANONIZATION BY ACCLAMATION has long since disappeared from Catholic usage, but the witness of contemporaries forms a vital part of the evidence accepted by the Church in the process of determining the heroicity of the virtues of one whose cause is under consideration by the Sacred Congregation of Rites. A few days after Mother Duchesne's death, Mother Anna Du Rousier wrote from St. Louis:

> Mother Galwey has promised to give the details of the edifying death of our venerated Mother Duchesne. It is the general opinion here that we have lost a saint. The clergy, and the archbishop in particular, speak of her with the greatest admiration. Monseigneur Kenrick declared she was the noblest and most virtuous soul he had ever known. Father De Smet says that while living she was worthy of canonization. Our American houses owe everything to her. She opened the way to us through many fatigues and privations. I feel that I am acting in accordance with the wishes of our Mother General in soliciting for her the suffrages prescribed in the Society for a deceased Superior Vicar. It is a homage of gratitude which we owe to the memory of this venerable Mother. I arrived just in time to receive her blessing and to recommend to her the needs of our missions, and she promised she would treat of them earnestly with our Lord. I count much upon her intercession, for I believe she is all-powerful with the Heart of Jesus.

PHILIPPINE DUCHESNE was beatified by Pope Pius XII on May 12, 1940, and the seventeenth day of November was assigned as her feast day. In the Roman Martyrology we read:

> At St. Charles, in the State of Missouri, in (the United States of) North America, the birthday of Blessed Philippine Duchesne, Virgin, of the Society of the Religious of the Sacred Heart of Jesus, illustrious for the practice of severe mortification and for unflagging zeal in winning souls for Christ. Pope Pius the Twelfth enrolled her among the Blessed.

PRAYER

O God, who loves souls, and have in all ages chosen apostolic hearts and endowed them with your knowledge and your love, hear the prayers which we offer through the intercession of your servant, Blessed Philippine Duchesne. Kindle in us the zeal with which her life was consumed. Grant that after following her example in charity, self-denial, and prayer on earth, we may be admitted one day to the same glory in our heavenly country. Through Christ our Lord. Amen.

APPENDIX I | *Tables 1 and 2*

ANTOINE DUCHESNE, 1711–1783
m. (1737)
MARIE LOUISE ENFANTIN

Marie Louise	Françoise	X*	Marie–?	Pierre–François	X 1748–1760	Claire–Julie
1738–1778	1739–1810		1742–1770	1743–1814	died as a novice	1749–1830
Visitandine	m.		Visitandine	m. (1765)	Visitandine	Visitandine
Sr. Françoise–Melanie	Jean L. Tranchand		Sr. Marie–Fortunée	Rose–Euphrosine Perier		Sr. Claire–Euphrosine

Marie Julie, b. 1768
Visitandine
Sr. Claire–Julie

Marie–Adelaide	Marie–Amelie	Charlotte–Euphrosine	Agathe–Justine	Adelaide	Hippolyte	Augustine–Melanie
1767–1778	1771–1837	1772–1857	1775–1776	1779–1824	1781–1854	1786–1828
ROSE–PHILIPPINE	m. (1786)	m.		m. (1798)	m. (1814)	Visitandine
1769–1852	Constans de Mauduit	Jean–Joseph Jouve		Henri Lebrument	Coralie Durand	Sr. Marie–Xavier
R.S.C.J.	1760–1850					

Children of Marie–Amelie and Constans de Mauduit:
1. Augustine 1787–1847 m. Augustin Jordan
2. Amédée 1790–1875 (Army officer, unmarried)
3. Amelie 1795–1869 m. (1818) Henri Bergasse
4. Adrien 1805–1817

Children of Charlotte–Euphrosine and Jean–Joseph Jouve:
1. Auguste
2. Euphrosine, 1796–1821 R.S.C.J., *Aloysia*
3. Amelie, 1797–1879 R.S.C.J.
4. Henri, 1800–18 ? S.J.
5. Hippolyte, 1802–1877 m. (1) Marie J. Neal (2) Amelie Bergasse
6. Alexandre, 1805–18 ?
7. Constance, 1807–1852
8. Camille, 1809–1897
9. Josephine, 1811–18 ? Religious of Perpetual Adoration (Lyons)
10. Eugene, 1814–1887
(Five other children died in childhood.)

Children of Adelaide and Henri Lebrument:
1. Caroline, 1799–1854 R.S.C.J.
2. Henriette, 1800–1854 m. Dr. Tourret
3. Eugenie, 1802–1857 Visitandine
4. Marine, 1803–1861 m. M. Barras
5. Delphine, 1805–1833 Visitandine
6. Amelie, 1806–1828 m. M. Gauthier
7. Octavie, 1812–1893 m. M. Munaret
(Two other girls and a boy died in infancy.)

*X—according to Msgr. Baunard there was a son older than Pierre–François Duchesne.

JACQUES PERIER, 1702–1782
m. (1741),
MARIE–ELIZABETH DUPUY, d.1799

Claude 1742–1801 m. (1766) Marie–Charlotte Pascal	Jean 1743	Jean–Antoine 1744–1793(?)	Hélène–Elizabeth 1745–1796 m. Pierre Jordan	Jacques–Augustin 1746–1793 m. Charlotte Carrier	Marie–Elizabeth 1748–1796 m. Alexandre Gueymar	Rose–Euphrosine 1748–1797 m. Pierre–François Duchesne

See Table I:
The Duchesne Family

Children of Hélène–Elizabeth & Pierre Jordan:
1. Camille, 1771–1821
2. Noel
3. Augustin

Children of Claude & Marie–Charlotte Pascal:
1. Jacques–Prosper, 1768
2. Elizabeth–Josephine, 1770–1850, m. Jacques–Fortunat de Savoye–Rollin
3. Euphrosine–Marine, 1771
4. Augustin–Charles, 1773–1833, m. Louise de Berckheim ....
5. Alexandre–Jacques, 1774–18 ?
6. Antoine–Scipion, 1776–1821, m. Louise de Dietrick (3 children)
7. Casimir–Pierre, 1777–1832, m. Marie–Cecile Loyer (2 children)
8. Adelaide–Hélène (*dite* Marine), 1779–1851, m. Hyacinth Teisseire ....
9. Camille–Joseph, 1781–1844
10. Alphonse, 1782–1868
11. Amédée–Auguste, 1785–18 ?
12. André–Jean–Joseph, 1786–18 ?

Children of Augustin–Charles (4):
Camille–Josephine, 1800–1826, m. François–Charles, Comte de Rémusat
Alexandrine, 1801–1824, unmarried
Adolph–Scipion, 1802–18 ?, m. Natalie Dumottier de Lafayette
Eugene–Fortunat–Paul, 1809–1849
Marie–Amelie, 1806–1827, unmarried

Children of Adelaide–Hélène (8):
Charles–Joseph, 1797–1858, m. Mathilde de Salcette
Amelie, 1800–18 ?, m. Louis Bergasse
Josephine, 1802–1803
Henriette–Marie, 1803–18 ?, m. Achille Chaper
Marie–Josephine, 1804–182?, unmarried
Camille–Alexandrine, 1803–1823
Emmanuel–Paul, 1809–18 ?
Louise–Philippine, 1814–18 ?, m. (1835) Charles–François Rolland

index

499

A NOTE ON THE TYPE

IN WHICH THIS BOOK IS SET

This book is set in Janson, a Linotype face, created from the early punches of Anton Janson, who settled in Leipzig around 1670. This type is not an historic revival, but rather a letter of fine ancestry, remodelled and brought up to date to satisfy present day taste. It carries a feeling of being quite compact and sturdy. It has good color and displays a pleasing proportion of ascenders and descenders as compared to the height of the lower case letters. The book was composed and printed by The York Composition Company, Inc., of York, Pa., and bound by Moore and Company of Baltimore. The typography and design are by Howard N. King.